ROUTLEDGE HANDBOOK
OF SPORTS COACHING

Over the last three decades sports coaching has evolved from a set of customary practices based largely on tradition and routine into a sophisticated, reflective and multi-disciplinary profession. In parallel with this, coach education and coaching studies within higher education have developed into a coherent and substantial field of scholarly enquiry with a rich and sophisticated research literature.

The *Routledge Handbook of Sports Coaching* is the first book to survey the full depth and breadth of contemporary coaching studies, mapping the existing disciplinary territory and opening up important new areas of research. Bringing together many of the world's leading coaching scholars and practitioners working across the full range of psychological, social and pedagogical perspectives, the book helps to develop an understanding of sports coaching that reflects its complex, dynamic and messy reality.

With more importance than ever before being attached to the role of the coach in developing and shaping the sporting experience for participants at all levels of sport, this book makes an important contribution to the professionalization of coaching and the development of coaching theory. It is important reading for all students, researchers and policy makers with an interest in this young and flourishing area.

Paul Potrac is a Senior Lecturer within the Department of Sport, Health, and Exercise Science at the University of Hull, UK. His research interests focus on exploring the social complexity of sports coaching, with a particular emphasis on the political and emotional nature of coaching practice.

Wade Gilbert is a Professor and Sport Psychology Coordinator in the Department of Kinesiology at California State University, Fresno, USA. He is an active researcher and consultant in the areas of coach education, coaching effectiveness and athlete talent development.

Jim Denison is an Associate Professor in the Faculty of Physical Education and Recreation, University of Alberta, Canada, and Director of the Canadian Athletics Coaching Centre. A sport sociologist and coach educator, his research examines the social construction and historical formation of coaching 'knowledges' and coaches' practices.

ROUTLEDGE HANDBOOK OF SPORTS COACHING

Edited by Paul Potrac, Wade Gilbert and Jim Denison

Routledge
Taylor & Francis Group

LONDON AND NEW YORK

First published 2013
by Routledge
2 Park Square, Milton Park, Abingdon, Oxon OX14 4RN

Simultaneously published in the USA and Canada
by Routledge
711 Third Avenue, New York, NY 10017

Routledge is an imprint of the Taylor & Francis Group, an informa business

British Library Cataloguing in Publication Data
A catalogue record for this book is available from the British Library

Library of Congress Cataloging in Publication Data
Routledge handbook of sports coaching / edited by Paul Potrac, Wade Gilbert,
and Jim Denison.
p. cm.
1. Coaching (Athletics)--Handbooks, manuals, etc. I. Potrac, Paul, 1974-
II. Gilbert, Wade. III. Denison, Jim, 1963-
GV711.R68 2013
796.07'7--dc23
2012024821

ISBN: 978-0-415-78222-7 (hbk)
ISBN: 978-0-203-13262-3 (ebk)

Typeset in Bembo Std by
Saxon Graphics Ltd, Derby

CONTENTS

Contents

ILLUSTRATIONS

Figures

Tables

CONTRIBUTORS

Kenneth Aggerholm is a PhD student at Aarhus University, Denmark. His research is mainly concerned with existential and phenomenological perspectives on coaching, learning and performance within team sports. He was honoured with the 2011 R. Scott Kretchmar Student Essay Award by the International Association for the Philosophy of Sport.

Jake Bailey is a Senior Lecturer in Sports Coaching at the Cardiff School of Sport, Cardiff Metropolitan University, UK. His research interests lie in the sociology of sports coaching. He has been National Coach for Welsh Trampoline-Gymnastics and personal coach to many trampoline-gymnasts who have competed at the national and international level.

Andrea J. Becker is an Assistant Professor in the Department of Kinesiology at California State University, Fullerton, USA where she teaches classes and conducts research in the areas of sport psychology and coaching. She is also a certified sport psychology consultant and active member of the Association for Applied Sport Psychology.

Jed Blanton is a doctoral candidate at Michigan State University, USA and a research assistant at the Institute for the Study of Youth Sports. He specializes in research and outreach efforts geared toward understanding and enhancing youth leadership and the team captaincy position.

Gordon A. Bloom is an Associate Professor of sport psychology at McGill University in Montreal, Canada. His current research focuses on coaching knowledge and behaviours, leadership, team building and post-concussion injury rehabilitation. From a personal perspective, Gordon can often be found coaching his children in ice hockey, baseball or soccer.

Jennifer Bruening is an Associate Professor of Sport Management at the University of Connecticut, USA. Her research interests include the intersection of race and gender in women's sport and mentoring through sport as a developmental tool for youth and their college mentors.

Brendan Burkett joined the University of the Sunshine Coast, Australia in 1998 following an international sporting career and as a professional engineer. Brendan has extensive experience in coaching which spans coach development at the regional level though to elite performance at the Paralympic Games.

Laura Burton is an Associate Professor of Sport Management at the University of Connecticut, USA. Her current research interests include how to increase women's representation in leadership positions in sport management, and how the experience of sport participation influences women's career progression in business management and sport management.

Richard M. Buscombe is a Senior Lecturer in Sport and Exercise Psychology at the University of East London, UK. Richard's PhD dissertation investigated expectancy effects in sport and he has published work in this area.

Ted M. Butryn is an Associate Professor of Sport Sociology and Sport Psychology in the Department of Kinesiology at San José State University, USA. He currently teaches courses in qualitative research, sport sociology and the psychology of coaching. His main areas of research include the application of cyborg theory to sport and cultural sport psychology.

Sarah Carson is an Assistant Professor of Kinesiology and Coordinator of the Coaching Education Minor program at James Madison University, USA. A graduate of Michigan State University, Dr Carson's research interests include positive youth development through sport and coaching strategies for teaching life skills.

Tania Cassidy is a Senior Lecturer in Pedagogy in the School of Physical Education at the University of Otago, Dunedin, New Zealand. She is the lead author of *Understanding Sports Coaching* (Routledge) and is on the editorial board of seven international journals that publish research in sports coaching.

Melissa A. Chase is an Associate Dean in the School of Education, Health and Society and Associate Professor in the Department of Kinesiology and Health at Miami University in Oxford, Ohio, USA. Dr Chase's research interests are self-efficacy beliefs, coaching efficacy and motivation, and she is the current editor for *Journal of Sport Psychology in Action*.

Mette Krogh Christensen is an Associate Professor within the Centre of Medical Education, Aarhus University, Denmark, and external Associate Professor within the Institute of Sports Science at University of Southern Denmark. Her research interests revolve around talent development in elite sport and the development of coaching expertise. She has published in, for example, the *Sociology of Sport Journal* and *Sport, Education and Society*.

Derek Colquhoun is a Professor and Head of the School of Education at the University of Tasmania, Australia. Professor Colquhoun has been involved in researching health-promoting schools over many years with his latest research focusing on the impact of enhancing school food as well as on health-promoting schools and school improvement.

Jean Côté is a Professor and Director in the School of Kinesiology and Health Studies at Queen's University in Kingston, Canada. His research interests are in the areas of sport expertise, children in sport, coaching and positive youth development.

Hamish Crocket is a Lecturer in Socio-Psychological Perspectives on Sport and Leisure at the University of Waikato, New Zealand. His current research draws on sociological and psychological theories to examine athletes' understandings of ethics. Hamish coaches the lifestyle sport, Ultimate Frisbee.

Diane Culver is an Associate Professor in the School of Human Kinetics, University of Ottawa, Canada. Her research on coaching and coach education has been funded by the Social Sciences and Humanities Research Council of Canada and the Coaching Association of Canada. Her research has been published in various international journals.

Christopher Cushion is a Senior Lecturer in the School of Sport, Exercise and Health Sciences at Loughborough University, UK, where he leads the MSc in Coaching. His research and teaching and research interests include the coaching process, coach education and performance analysis. He is also a highly qualified football coach.

Dave Day was a professional swimming coach for some years and he is now a Senior Lecturer in Coaching and Sports History at Manchester Metropolitan University, UK where his research interests focus on the history of coaching practice and training and the biographies of nineteenth- and early twentieth-century coaches.

Jim Denison is an Associate Professor in the Faculty of Physical Education and Recreation and the Director of the Canadian Athletics Coaching Centre at the University of Alberta, Canada. A sport sociologist and coach educator, his research examines the formation of coaches' practices through a Foucauldian lens.

Sue Dickens is an Associate Lecturer in the School of Human Movement Studies at The University of Queensland, Australia. Her role and research interest is the development of effective online learning technologies specific to the requirements of sports coaches.

Kristen Dieffenbach is an Assistant Professor of Athletic Coaching Education at West Virginia University, USA, is an Association of Applied Sport Psychology certified consultant and is a professional endurance coach. She is the NASPE Sport Steering Committee coaching education representative and a National Council for Accreditation of Coaching Education board member.

Marlene Dixon is an Associate Professor and Fellow in the M.G. Seay Centennial Professorship for Education at The University of Texas, USA. Her primary research interests include the multilevel factors that impact the work–family interface and enduring involvement in sport careers. Her work has been published in a variety of journals including the *Journal of Sport Management* and *Sport Management Review*.

Karl Erickson is a PhD candidate in sport psychology in the School of Kinesiology and Health Studies at Queen's University, Canada, under the supervision of Dr Jean Côté. His research interests focus on coaching in youth sport. In particular, Karl's work examines the influence of coach–athlete interactions on athlete development.

Kari Fasting is a Professor at the Department of Social and Cultural Studies at the Norwegian School of Sport Sciences in Oslo, Norway. Her research examines various aspects related to sport and exercise in the lives of women. Her recent focus has been sexual harassment and abuse in sport.

Dean Garratt is Professor of Education in the Faculty of Education and Children's Services at the University of Chester, UK. His principal research interests centre upon the philosophy and practice of qualitative research methodologies, including phenomenology, philosophical hermeneutics and post-structural approaches with a substantive interest in the critique of social and education policy.

Wade Gilbert is a Professor in the Department of Kinesiology at California State University, Fresno, USA. He is a frequent contributor to academic journals, books and popular media reports on sport coaching, and directs applied research and consulting in the areas of coaching effectiveness and coach development.

David Gilbourne is a Professor of Critical Qualitative Research and Director of Research at the Department of Sport, Exercise and Health at the University of Hull, UK. He co-founded *Qualitative Research in Sport, Exercise and Health*. His research interests include critical reflective practice and the practice of critical social science.

Diane L. Gill is a Professor in Kinesiology and the Linda Arnold Carlisle Distinguished Excellence Professor of Women's and Gender Studies at the University of North Carolina at Greensboro, USA. Her scholarly publications include several book chapters, and over 100 journal articles related to social psychology and physical activity.

Daniel Gould is the Director of the Institute for the Study of Youth Sports and Professor in the Department of Kinesiology at Michigan State University, USA. Dr Gould is widely published and is a sought-after speaker, coaching educator and consultant in the area of applied sport psychology.

Ryan Groom is a Senior Lecturer in Sports Coaching at Manchester Metropolitan University, UK. He has previously worked for a number of Premier League and international football teams as a performance analyst. His main research interest is in coaching pedagogy. Ryan also conducts coach education work for the English Football Association.

Kristoffer Henriksen is a Post-Doctoral Researcher within the Institute of Sports Science at University of Southern Denmark and an experienced sport psychologist working together with Danish National Teams. His research interests focus on the ecology of talent development in sport. He has published in, for example, *Psychology of Sport and Exercise*.

Laura Hills is a Senior Lecturer in Youth Sport at Brunel University, UK. Her research and teaching interests centre on the sociology of gender and physical activity. Recent projects include a critical examination of mixed-gender sports policy in the UK and an evaluation of schemes to increase participation in sport among disadvantaged girls.

Ying Jin is a PhD student studying with Dr Nicholas Myers at the University of Miami's Research, Measurement, and Evaluation programme, USA. Her programme of methodological research currently focuses on advanced quantitative methodologies within educational and psychological measurement.

Luke Jones is a PhD student at the University of Alberta, Canada, studying coach education. He is a former elite soccer player and currently Assistant Coach for the University of Alberta women's soccer team.

Robyn L. Jones is a Professor at the Cardiff School of Sport, Cardiff Metropolitan University. His research examines the complexity of coaching and how coaches manage the power-ridden dilemmas that arise. He has published several books and articles on coaching and pedagogy, and is the Editor-in-Chief of *Sports Coaching Review*.

Sophia Jowett is a Reader in Psychology at Loughborough University, UK. Sophia is a widely published researcher and theorist with over 90 articles, chapters and books. She is developer of Closeness, Commitment, Complementarity and Co-orientation (3+1Cs) coach–athlete relationship model. Sophia is a Chartered Psychologist and Associate Fellow of the British Psychological Society.

Cindra S. Kamphoff is an Associate Professor at Minnesota State University, Mankato, USA, where she coordinates the graduate programme in Sport and Exercise Psychology. Her research focuses on gender and culture. She is a certified consultant with the Association for Applied Sport Psychology and currently serves on the Executive Board.

Göran Kenttä earned his doctorate degree in psychology at Stockholm University, Sweden. He currently holds a research position and is director of the Coach Education Programme at The Swedish School of Sport and Health Sciences in Stockholm. His research focuses on elite-level athletes and the training process with a stress–recovery perspective.

Eileen Kennedy is a researcher and lecturer in the sociology of sport and education studies. Current appointments include: Associate Researcher with the School of Sport and Education, Brunel University, UK, and Adjunct Professor in Sociology of Sport with Syracuse University (London). She is the co-author (with Laura Hills) of *Sport, Media and Society* (Berg).

Larry Lauer is the Director of Coaching Education at the Institute for the Study of Youth Sports and Men's Tennis assistant coach at Michigan State University, USA. He is Co-Chair of a USOC task force on coaching education and an educator for USA Hockey, United States Tennis Association and many other organizations.

David Llewellyn is a Principal Lecturer in Drama at Liverpool John Moores University, UK. Throughout his academic career he has continued to maintain a professional profile in drama alongside his teaching and research. David specializes in teaching, acting and playwriting, and is currently researching and writing in the area of ethnodrama.

Ross Lorimer is a Chartered Psychologist at the University of Abertay Dundee, UK. His interest is in intra/interpersonal perception in coaching; how coaches and athletes see the world and how they work together. Ross is also the Sport Science Officer for the Mountaineering Council of Scotland and a climbing instructor.

Todd M. Loughead is an Associate Professor of sport psychology at the University of Windsor, Canada. His current research interests include group dynamics in sport with a specific interest in cohesion, team building, and the influence of coaching and athlete leadership in sport and its impact on team functioning.

John Lyle is an Adjunct Professor of Sports Coaching at the University of Queensland, Australia, and combines academic and consultancy roles. He has published several influential textbooks, and is currently Interim Editor of the *International Journal of Coaching Science*. His primary research interests are conceptual analyses of sports coaching and modelling coaches' practice.

Rachel Madsen is an Assistant Professor of Sport Management at Niagara University, USA. She was previously a collegiate basketball coach and assistant athletic director at Roger Williams University and the California Institute of Technology. In her free time, she participates in multiple outdoor activities and watches college basketball.

Clifford Mallett is an Associate Professor with the School of Human Movement Studies at The University of Queensland, Australia, and a Principal Research Fellow with the Australian Institute of Sport. He coordinates the Master of Sport Coaching program at UQ and his research focuses on high performance coach development, coach and athlete motivation, and mental toughness.

Phil Marshall is a Lecturer in Sports Coaching and Performance at the University of Hull, UK. His research interests focus on the sociological aspects of sports coaching. He is currently undertaking PhD work into the role of emotions, micro–politics, and self-deception in coaching practice.

Eric Martin is a PhD student at Michigan State University, USA, where his research focuses on youth sports, specifically youth specialization, the millennial athlete, passion and burnout. He is an active member and a regional representative for the Association for Applied Sport Psychology.

Joseph Mills is a PhD student in coach education at the University of Alberta, Canada. He is a BASES Accredited Sport and Exercise Scientist and a Body Control Pilates teacher.

Kevin Morgan is a Senior Lecturer in Sport Coaching and Physical Education in the School of Sport at Cardiff Metropolitan University, UK. He is Programme Director for the MSc in Sport Coaching and leads the undergraduate Physical Education modules. His primary research interests are in pedagogy and motivational climate.

Nicholas D. Myers' programme of research at the University of Miami, USA, currently focuses on two related areas. His first research focus is measurement and evaluation of some key psychosocial constructs within coaching effectiveness models. His second research focus concentrates on evaluating advanced quantitative methodologies that he most frequently applies in his first line of research.

Lee Nelson is a Lecturer in Sports Coaching and Performance at the University of Hull, UK. His research principally focuses on the interdisciplinary analysis of coach/athlete learning and the use of video-based technology in elite level sporting contexts.

Julian North is a Senior Research Fellow in Sport and Coaching at Leeds Metropolitan University, UK. He has undertaken and published social and sports research in a variety of policy, practice and academic roles over the last 20 years in Australia and the UK.

Richard Pringle is an Associate Professor in Sport Sociology at the University of Auckland, New Zealand. He is the past Associate Editor for *the Sociology of Sport Journal*, the co-author (with Pirkko Markula) of *Foucault, Sport and Exercise*, and co-editor (with Murray Phillips) of *Critical Sport Histories: Paradigms, Politics and the Postmodern Turn*.

Paul Potrac is a Senior Lecturer in Coaching and Performance at the University of Hull, UK. He is an Associate Editor for the *Sports Coaching Review*, and the co-author of *Sports Coaching Cultures: From Practice to Theory, Understanding Sports Coaching* and *The Sociology of Coaching*.

Laura Purdy lectures in Sports Coaching Science at the University of Worcester, UK. Her research and teaching principally address the sociological and pedagogical aspects of coaching practice. Her publications have focused on the experiences of coaches and athletes in relation to the concepts of identity, power and interaction.

Thomas D. Raedeke is an Associate Professor in Kinesiology at East Carolina University, USA. Given his interest in motivation, stress and well-being, one of his research specialities focuses on burnout. Prior to university employment, he served as a research assistant at the American Coaching Effectiveness Program/Human Kinetics and United States Olympic Training Center.

Ian Reade is the Director of Athletics at the University of Alberta, Canada. His teaching area includes sport management and coaching. Reade's research examines the relationship between coaches' work environments and the satisfaction and retention of coaches.

Steven Rynne is a Lecturer in the School of Human Movement Studies at The University of Queensland, Australia. Steven has worked and conducted research with a number of national and international sport organizations in the areas of high performance coach learning and Indigenous sport.

Lars Tore Ronglan is Associate Professor and Head of Department of Coaching and Psychology at Norwegian School of Sport Sciences. He has published books and articles on leadership and coaching in sport; e.g. co-edited *The Sociology of Sports Coaching* (Routledge 2011) and *Nordic Elite Sport: Same Ambitions – Different Tracks* (Norwegian University Press 2012).

Jane M. Stangl is a Class Dean and Lecturer of Exercise and Sport Studies at Smith College, USA. Her research examines women in coaching, team naming practices and the intersection of Buddhism with sport. She teaches occasional golf day-clinics for the LPGA.

Gloria B. Solomon is a Professor in the Department of Kinesiology at Texas Christian University, USA, where she teaches and advises graduate and undergraduate students in sport psychology. As Director of the Sport Psychology Lab she is involved in conducting research on expectancy effects in competitive sport.

William G. Taylor is a Senior Lecturer in Coaching Studies at the Department of Exercise and Sport Science of Manchester Metropolitan University, UK. His research interests are varied, and include: the conceptualization and critical deconstruction of professionalism in sports coaching, coaching in the 'risk society', and the use of critical sociology to examine coaching practice.

Andrew Thompson, a former top-level athlete and graduate of the Cardiff School of Sport at the University of Wales Institute Cardiff, UK, is an independent researcher. His investigative interests lie within the micro-sociology of sports coaching, exploring the everyday tactical and manipulatory actions of coaches and other contextual stakeholders.

Pierre Trudel is a Professor in the School of Human Kinetics, University of Ottawa, Canada. He has published over 100 articles, and has been a consultant for many sport organizations, developing programmes and supervising coaches. He is the current Chair of the Coaching Association of Canada's coaching research committee.

Ineke Vergeer, originally from the Netherlands, completed a PhD in Sport Psychology at the University of Alberta, Canada in 1994 with a research focus on coaches' decision-making using a mixed methodology. Following a post-doc in Hong Kong, she has been lecturing in the UK since 1997, most recently at Durham University.

Marvin Washington is an Associate Professor of Management at the University of Alberta, School of Business, Canada. His research examines institutional and organizational change. Most recently, he has examined issues in sport settings that range from women's professional volleyball, youth hockey and Canadian Olympic Governance Structures.

Penny Werthner is a Director and Associate Dean in the School of Human Kinetics, University of Ottawa, Canada. Her research on coaching and coach education has been funded by the Social Sciences and Humanities Research Council of Canada and the Coaching Association of Canada and has been published in various journals.

Bradley W. Young is an Associate Professor in Sport Psychology and Pedagogy in the School of Human Kinetics at the University of Ottawa, Canada. A former high school and inter-university coach in athletics, his research on long-term developmental pathways of coaches has been funded by the Coaching Association of Canada.

INTRODUCTION

Paul Potrac

UNIVERSITY OF HULL, UK

Jim Denison

UNIVERSITY OF ALBERTA, CANADA

Wade Gilbert

CALIFORNIA STATE UNIVERSITY, FRESNO, USA

The last three decades have witnessed a substantial proliferation in the amount of, and the importance attached to, coach education and sports coaching research in higher education, most notably in the UK, USA, Canada, Australia and New Zealand. With regard to the former, in British universities there are 217 specific sports coaching undergraduate degree programmes and 11 postgraduate courses (Bush 2008). This trend can in part be attributed to the increasing importance attached to coaching in the sporting and social policy arenas, where policy makers have recognised the importance of coaches as 'significant others' in developing and shaping the sporting experience for participants at all levels. This is particularly true in the UK, where £25 million has been invested in the development of a network of community coaches in an attempt to improve the efficiency and the outcomes of sports coaching.

The growth in the importance attached to coach education and the professional preparation of sports coaches in the higher education sector has also been matched by scholarly research. Indeed, while sports coaching is not an established sports science in the same vein as sports psychology, sports sociology, physiology and biomechanics, it is rapidly making up for lost time. In fact, it would be fair to say that coaching, as it relates to improving others' sporting experiences and/or performances, is now recognised as a bona fide area of scholarly inquiry (Gilbert 2002; Gilbert and Trudel 2004). We suspect this development is at least in part directly influenced by global efforts to situate sports coaching as a legitimate and formal profession (Duffy *et al.* 2011). For example, in May 2011 the International Council for Coach Education (ICCE) announced the formation of a project group, comprising representatives from around the world, to develop a plan to guide the development and recognition of coaching qualifications on a global basis (ICCE 2011). The plan, referred to as the International Sport Coaching Framework, specifically identifies a 'robust model of coach development' as the foundation for accomplishing their strategic plan. Although the comprehensive portraits of coaching research provided in this *Routledge Handbook of Sports Coaching* shows there is no consensus on a 'single' model of coach development, or coaching, sports coaching has most certainly become a robust field of study.

Of particular relevance to this book is the significant growth in the research literature examining coaching from psychological, sociological and pedagogical perspectives. Such work is contributing towards the development of an understanding of coaching that reflects its complex, dynamic and messy reality. However, we would argue that the research that has been undertaken towards these aims has principally been driven by a number of small groups and individuals working on topics from their own disciplinary perspectives (e.g. sociology, psychology or pedagogy) without a great deal of collaboration and sharing of ideas (Rangeon *et al.* 2012). Indeed, it could be argued that while such work has produced some valuable and fascinating insights into the realities, problems and everyday nature of coaching and coach education, because the research and researchers in this area remain somewhat disconnected the impact this work has had on the development of more effective coaching practices has been limited.

Accordingly, when we set out to put this book together we wanted its contribution to advance the field of coach education by taking stock of the research into sports coaching from the social sciences that has flourished in the last three decades. Equally important to us was to bring scholars from different disciplinary backgrounds together to discuss how we can further our research endeavours around sports coaching in a meaningful and productive fashion. In this respect, we believe the *Routledge Handbook of Sports Coaching* serves a valuable purpose in terms of mapping the territory and nature of sports coaching research. Indeed, while coaching scholarship is certainly growing, it is perhaps doing so in a somewhat erratic and haphazard manner. Therefore, we believe this book provides a valuable resource for researchers, policy makers, graduate- and undergraduate students wishing to undertake and use research on sports coaching, by pointing out potential areas for future inquiry and summarising key findings from the collective body of research. Significantly, the ethos of this book is not just simply about providing reviews of what research has been done, but also outlining how we can continue to evolve our understandings of particular aspects of sports coaching through the production of new, cutting edge, and inter-disciplinary research endeavours. In this regard, we believe the *Routledge Handbook of Sports Coaching* is an important step in the evolution of research on sports coaching that will contribute to the development of coach education as a legitimate academic field and the practice of sports coaching as a respected profession. Indeed, as editors, we take this opportunity to thank Routledge for not only supporting this book project, but also for their wider sponsorship of coaching research and scholarship.

References

Bush, A. (2008) 'Doing coaching justice: Promoting critical consciousness in sports coaching research', unpublished PhD thesis, University of Bath, Bath, UK.

Duffy, P., Hartley, H., Bales, J., Crespo, M., Dick, F., Vardham, D., Nordmann, L. and Curado, J. (2011) 'Sport coaching as a "profession": Challenges and future directions', *International Journal of Coaching Science*, 5(2): 93–123.

Gilbert, W.D. (2002, June). *An Annotated Bibliography and Analysis of Coaching Science: 1970-2001*, Washington, DC: American Alliance for Health, Physical Education, Recreation, online, available at: www.aahperd.org/rc/programs/upload/grantees_coaching_science.pdf.

Gilbert, W.D. and Trudel, P. (2004) 'Analysis of coaching science research published from 1970–2001', *Research Quarterly for Exercise and Sport*, 75: 388–399.

ICCE (International Council for Coach Education) (2011, May) *International Sport Coaching Framework*, online, available at: www.icce.ws/documents/ICCE-ASOIF_Joint_Communication_18May2011.pdf.

Rangeon, S., Gilbert, W. and Bruner, M. (2012) 'Mapping the world of coaching science: A citation network analysis', *Journal of Coaching Education*, 5(1): 83–108.

PART I

Historical and conceptual overview of sports coaching

What do we know about the field of sports coaching and how to study it?

A

Foundations of sports coaching

1

HISTORICAL PERSPECTIVES ON COACHING

Dave Day

MANCHESTER METROPOLITAN UNIVERSITY, UK

Introduction

Contemporary coaching practice has become the subject of considerable academic analysis during the last decade. This research has fuelled debates both about the way coaches operate and the best means of educating them effectively. However, such work has largely occurred in an historical vacuum, with little reference to the long-established patterns of coaching practice which emanated from oral traditions and replicated the craft practices of other skilled artisans. Coaching scholars have not been helped by the general lack of interest shown in coaching history by sports historians and, although Park (1992, 2011), Mewett (1995, 2002) and Radford (1985) have specifically investigated training methods, historical studies chronicling coaching lives or detailing coaching practice have been limited (Phillips 2000; Semotiuk 1982; Carter 2006, 2011). However, recent work aimed at deconstructing the biographies and working patterns of nineteenth and twentieth century English coaches (Day 2008, 2011) has begun to uncover some of the processes involved and this chapter draws on some of that material to explore the current state of knowledge in this field and to suggest the means and direction for future research. In particular, the author emphasises the need for researchers to expose more thoroughly the life courses and social networks established by previous generations of coaches and trainers to help illuminate how the traditional precepts of sports coaching were transmitted and sustained prior to the widespread introduction of coach certification.

It has to be recognised of course that words like 'coaching' have modern connotations from which they cannot be divorced and the use of current sports terminology in an historical context can be misleading even if the behaviours, practices and values of relevant individuals have some congruence with those of their modern counterparts. The term 'coach' first appeared in English as referring to a carriage but it had also become a colloquial expression for a private tutor by the early nineteenth century. The transfer of the term from education to competition preparation was initiated by public school and university sportsmen and it is significant that when 'coaching' became associated with sports it should be in those activities most closely associated with this social class (e.g. rowing and cricket), while the nomenclature 'trainer' survived almost intact in working-class sports like pedestrianism and boxing. Although there was a class component to this differentiation, there was also a more practical distinction in that rowing in a crew or batting in cricket required the subtle refinement of skills while plebeian sports focused more on physical attributes. However, since the terms have never been mutually exclusive, 'coach' will be used interchangeably with 'trainer' within this chapter.

Methods and sources

Like historians in general, sports historians, including those exploring the life courses of trainers and coaches or the evolution of coaching practice, rely on a range of primary and secondary sources to inform their work. Important secondary sources, which help provide context, include historiography, the term most often applied to the collections of previously published work about a particular topic, such as the development of coaching in Britain. Key primary sources for the sports historian include organisational archives and minutes, pictures and photographs, diaries, films, autobiographies and biographies, and private family papers. Newspaper and periodical archives have featured heavily within this kind of work, especially sporting papers such as *Bell's Life in London and Sporting Chronicle* and the *Athletic News*, and the way in which this information has been recorded and reported can also say a lot about the wider aspects and traditions within any historical period although the tendency for sports historians to become over-reliant on the press has come under some criticism (Polley 2007). The digital age has made accessing newspaper archives much easier and has also encouraged more historians to incorporate other online material such as census returns into academic research, the use of which has proved vital in the construction of biographical dossiers by supplying, and verifying, personal information about trainers as well as tracking them over time (Day 2010a). Other critical primary sources for coaching historians are the instructional and biographical texts written by prominent athletes, coaches and administrators because they tell much about the attitudes of the period they were written in and about the coaching and training practices of the time.

Irrespective of the sources utilised, historical research is not an uncontested arena and when historians examine and discuss issues, such as the differences between American and British attitudes to coaching, each researcher brings their own perspective to bear on the topic which, in turn, engenders further debate. It is more appropriate, therefore, to refer to 'histories of coaching' rather than 'a history of coaching' and to see history as more about interpretations and the construction of meanings rather than recreating the past as it actually was. Sports historians have traditionally adopted an empiricist approach, interrogating surviving sources of the past and piecing them together systematically to form a supposedly definitive explanation of a topic such as coaching, but this methodology has been increasingly challenged by those who believe that the writing of history is informed much more by interpretation than facts. The way in which archives have been utilised, for example, has provoked some debate about their efficacy in informing sporting narratives (Booth 2006; Johnes 2007). These differences have led to the development of a more pragmatic attitude to writing history which recognises that imagination and inventiveness are integral to creating an historical narrative (Elton 2002) and accepts that historical discourses are essentially subjective because even researchers able to access unlimited sources would still have to interpret their collection of facts. The result is a 'narrative truth' (Carroll 2001), within which historical facts are marshalled to construct an accurate representation of the past while creating a story which remains open to interpretation (Marwick 2001).

Coaching origins

The limited empirical research previously conducted into the origins of modern coaching practices (e.g. Day 2008) has produced a 'narrative truth' which suggests that sports coaching did not develop spontaneously, since practitioners invariably drew from, and elaborated on, existing practices and knowledge. From the twelfth century onwards, all social groups engaged in activities that involved competition, the outcome of which was determined by physical skill, strategy, or chance, and the preparation for which required appropriate training from expert fencing and riding professors, falconers, wrestling trainers and masters at arms, who gathered information and then employed verbal and visual methods to pass on their experience. Their accumulated knowledge, combined with increased entrepreneurial opportunities and regulation, provided a platform for individuals to further develop coaching and training in the eighteenth century and this was reflected in the competitive preparation of a rising number of professionals. The gambling culture that funded professional livelihoods was evident in both rowing and pedestrianism, where aristocrats placed running footmen with professional trainers to prepare for wagers, and in boxing, where the gradual refinement of regulations, techniques and training practices were recorded in a number of boxing manuals published during the latter stages of the century. By the 1820s, training usually involved participants preparing for around two months under the guidance of a professional. The coach familiarised himself with the specific characteristics of the athlete before serious training began so that he could assess how best to organise the training elements while progress was monitored by analysing training components, separately and in combination, to ensure the athlete was improving, physically and psychologically, and to rectify any training errors (Walker 1837). As in all eras coaches did not work without some constraints on their behaviour and trainers were required to follow the rules laid down by their employers who would check their credentials before engaging them and then monitor them closely throughout the training period. For his part, the trainer had to be intelligent and firm in his manner, lead by example and report progress truthfully to his man's backers (Dowling 1841).

The expertise of these men was publically acknowledged. Sinclair (1807) noted the 'incredible perfection' which coaches had brought to the art of training, and Dr Thomas Graham (1827) thought their art had provided new information about physical changes that could be made to the human body. Robert Barclay's training regime, developed from his own experiences and the knowledge passed down to him by his trainer Jacky Smith, was regarded at the time as the most effective and Egan (1823: 9–22) described Barclay as an intuitive trainer whose detailed planning and scientific approach in researching and experimenting with training factors would have brought credit to 'any anatomist'. However, reflecting the ongoing nature of coaching practices as contested terrain, Barclay's ideas were not accepted uncritically with others recommending different types and amounts of liquids and diet, as well as variations in daily scheduling and programme content (Maret 1818).

Coaching as craft

In interpreting this evidence, drawn mostly from texts and newspapers of the period, it appears that succeeding cadres of coaches never found it necessary to reinvent core coaching practices which were transmitted and subsequently sustained through traditional mechanisms. Coaches generally emerged from within the activity as retired performers and often used the knowledge and practical skills developed during their competitive lifetime to formulate their own training methods, understanding of skills, and approaches to contests. From their ongoing experiences as coaches, and the continuing mores of oral tradition, individuals further developed their coaching toolbox, an assortment of coaching techniques and sport-specific practices related to skill development and physical preparation. Since no generation can be exempt from contemporary influences, skilled coaches also experimented in applying emerging knowledge, intuitively accepting or rejecting appropriate material, especially during times of significant educational and scientific advances. Tradition notwithstanding, each coach thereby added something to the training process, predominantly in periods when sport provided commercial opportunities when the incentive to innovate was strong, particularly for those who relied financially on their coaching ability.

These practices imply that the operation of coaching practice replicated that of a craft or skilled trade, which had long been the basic unit of the labour process. In each craft, the worker was presumed to be the master of a body of traditional expertise, which encompassed both knowledge and skill and the master-apprentice relationship at the heart of craft training engaged individuals from both inside and outside of the family. The tacit nature of craft transmission involved the master modelling and the apprentice continually observing, a process described as 'stealing with the eyes' (Gamble 2001). Oral memory was especially important in the passing on of traditional skills and customs since tradition is not self-perpetuating and each new generation had to be indoctrinated into patterns of coaching behaviour. It has been argued that this inhibited innovation, since an apprentice was taught only to copy, but coaching craft requires flexible adaptation to constraints and craftsmen have always been stimulated to experiment by external forces such as potential competitors, commercialisation and emerging technologies (Clegg 1977).

Use of the word 'craft' does not imply incorporation into formalised guilds since 'craft' knowledge was embedded within informal structures, communities of practice, created by coaches engaging in a process of collective learning which, in contrast to the vertical transmission implicit in teacher/pupil and mentoring relationships, occurred between individuals in a horizontal and mainly non-cognitive fashion. Every community regenerated itself, as new members gradually moved closer to the coaching practitioners who served as exemplars of expert practice. As such, skills and knowledge were reproduced across generations not through instruction, but through the granting of access to shared understandings (Wenger 1998). These features can be clearly identified in the close-knit groups surrounding many prominent Victorian and Edwardian coaches. For sports where finesse and skill were paramount, many coaching communities reproduced the long-term family involvement observed in traditional 'crafts'. Fencing professor William McTurk saw sons William and David both become fencing masters and golf professional James Paxton's son Peter also became a golf professional. Edmund Tompkins was a professor of tennis by 1851 and his sons, grandsons and in-laws were involved as professional tennis players, proprietors of tennis courts and tennis instructors, for over sixty years (Census Returns 1841–1911). In sports like pedestrianism, the transfer of coaching knowledge often occurred through the coach-athlete relationship. James Parker had a well-established training headquarters in Preston by 1851 when he had nine pedestrians in his stable (*Bell's Life* 1851), a number of them living with their trainer (Census Returns 1841–1911). Analysis of newspaper reports from the 1840s to the 1860s suggests that he trained at least eighty pedestrians over the course of his career, many of whom went on to become trainers themselves, an integral feature of coaching communities. At the beginning of the twentieth century, Scipio Augustus Mussabini drew up training and racing schedules for double Olympic champion Albert Hill and when Mussabini retired, Hill took over his coaching role and used his methods with Sydney Wooderson (Moon 1992). In 1918, Alfred Shrubb was appointed as the first professional athletics coach at Oxford University where he employed training ideas developed by his own coach, Harry Andrews (Hadgraft 2004).

Theory and practice

While the passing on of coaching expertise through communities of practice was critical, it was by no means the only information source for nineteenth-century coaches. An increasing volume of literature, general, sports related and scientific, was becoming available and, by the end of the century, more coaches were producing their own instructional manuals. These are excellent sources for the coaching historian because they discuss the explicit knowledge expected of coaches, such as training methods, psychology, ergogenic aids and diet, although there was little attempt to address the more implicit aspect of the trainers' work, the practice of coaching itself, because it was assumed that such knowledge could only be achieved practically through experience, observation, and trial and error. Andrews (1903) noted, for example, that trainers would have a range of experiential methods with which to assess an athlete's potential, although some men were especially gifted in this respect.

These coaching texts highlight that professional coaches prioritised dealing with the athlete rather than applying universal laws of nature and that their practical understanding was rarely directly related to theoretical underpinning. Despite the increasing institutionalisation of science, coaching practice continued to use traditional knowledge at all stages of the training process and, although systematic in their approach, coaches consistently described themselves as practical men. While this has been interpreted by some as meaning uneducated, it really represents the constant friction between theory and practice that affects almost every area of human endeavour and, in part, it reflects the tension between empirical 'scientific' knowledge and tacit 'craft' knowledge. Andrews (1903) noted that, if his ideas ran counter to emerging theory, it was because he had presented tried and tested methods which had proved successful. Similarly, for Mussabini (1913), the experienced, intelligent coach combined his skills with a common sense that came with years of practice in his craft.

It is likely that the nature of coaching was altered during the late nineteenth century by the formation of governing bodies of sport, dominated by a professional middle class who outwardly rejected coaching and training and who attacked working-class coaches for their lack of theoretical underpinning. Wilkinson (1868: 71–79) advised sportsmen to avoid professional coaches and their 'stereotyped code of rules' while professional training lore developed from experience was condemned as being 'diluted with ignorance and absurdity' (Albermarle and Hillier 1896: 172–181). The most prominent critics were medical men like Dr Henry Hoole (1888) who observed that while some coaching practitioners had recorded their training methods, a lack of scientific accuracy made their contributions worthless. Because these 'shallow, uneducated and often dissolute' trainers had been allowed to determine the physiological content of training it was no surprise that the path of the professional coach was 'strewn with the shattered constitutions' of their athletes (Hoole 1888: 7). This antipathy to professional coaches was reflected in the regulatory mechanisms amateur administrators employed to exclude them from their activities or to keep them in their place. When the Amateur Swimming Association (ASA) decided in 1899 that professional teachers were essential for increasing participation they tried to ensure that they remained under control by instituting a Professional Certificate, although certificates were only granted if officials were 'satisfied as to the character and antecedents of an applicant as well as to his ability as a professional teacher' (Keil and Wix 1996: 25).

Although this is the accepted view of English sport during this period there are alternative interpretations emerging concerning the relationship between British athletes and coaches, which suggests that the late nineteenth-century amateur hegemony in sport did not eliminate professional coaching cultures. Critics ignored the realities of rational sport in which ethical and philosophical considerations were often overridden by the desire for attainment. Indeed, for many amateurs the symbolic capital and feelings of personal satisfaction they received from winning were sufficient motivation for them to engage professional coaches. For those concerned with elite performance there were always tensions between the rhetoric of amateurism and the desire to be competitive and by 1911 it was recognised that a gentleman amateur could not expect to be a champion unless he was 'prepared to devote the whole of his leisure time to training' (Wade 1911: 98). Inevitably, this desire for success meant adopting professional help, especially since it was generally accepted that the employment of a trainer markedly improved a man's performance.

As a result, there was considerable leakage around the margins of amateur hegemony with respect to the employment of professional coaches although the important point for many British amateurs was the type of man the coach was and the nature of the relationship established between athlete and trainer. Just as some English working men could be considered worthy and respectable, so some professional sportsmen with teaching or coaching responsibilities could become icons of hard work and prudence, thereby reinforcing amateur-like qualities (Light 2005). Pedestrian Jack White, who trained amateurs from the 1870s onwards, became trainer to the London Athletic Club (LAC) in 1889 before subsequently securing employment as a coach with Cambridge University in 1893. Andrews coached amateur athletes, swimmers and cyclists while Mussabini was employed by Polytechnic Harriers as their senior coach and his athletes won medals at the Olympic Games from 1912 to 1924. It was Olympic rivalry that proved to be a significant catalyst for increasing flexibility concerning serious coaching among some governing bodies. The Amateur Athletic Association (AAA) appointed F.W. Parker, supported by additional trainers, to advise potential Olympians prior to Stockholm in 1912 when the British team was accompanied by eleven professionals, including Walter Brickett, attending his second Games as swimming trainer (Day 2010b). Men like Brickett experienced a different relationship with their athletes from that of their counterparts in America, where coaching had emerged as a specialised, technical profession, and ideological clashes between English and American sportsmen revolved partly around their diametrically opposed perceptions of coaching, more particularly about the amount of control that was to be given to the professional coach.

Contemporary researchers have emphasised that coaches only realise their ambitions through the success of their athletes so coaching reputations depend on what athletes learn and on how their increased capability translates into improved athletic performance. As a result, although coaches can never gain absolute predictive control, they are inclined to tightly manage the coaching process and the coaching environment (Jones and Wallace 2005). These tensions were clearly recognised during the Victorian period even by amateur coaches like Woodgate (1890: 119–120), who noted that 'autocracy is the first requisite for a trainer, and implicit subordination for a crew', but it was the manner in which this was applied that was important. In 1901, it was observed that American trainers were 'more autocratic than the German Emperor' (*Observer* 1901: 6). The 'ludicrous' admiration accorded some of these coaches led to teams being referred to as 'Mr. So-and-so's men', which implied a 'certain lack of dignity' (ibid.). Following failures in Stockholm in 1912, the AAA established training sites in major cities and appointed official trainers while the ASA proposed the appointment of six professional instructors; initiatives that led to concerns that a horde of Americanised trainers, employing their purely empiric craft, 'based upon a smattering of physiology and a vast self-assurance' (*Daily Mirror* 1912: 7) would become an integral part of the sporting landscape. Many Englishmen remained wary of professionalised sport controlled by specialised trainers and, from the current evidence available, it seems that when elite athletes turned to trainers for advice they adopted a peculiarly British compromise. The important thing was that professionals recognised their place within the greater scheme of amateur-controlled sport and as long as coaches adopted their allotted role as servants then suitable men might prove to be acceptable. Stockholm Olympic athletic trainers Alec Nelson and Bill Thomas both went on to have long careers at Cambridge and Oxford respectively, but the limited archival material available always highlights the influence of patronage and the ongoing master-servant relationship that existed between university athletes and their coaches. Their appointments as official trainers in 1912 highlights the increasing opportunities afforded to British professional coaches by the creation and expansion of formal international competitions but the final decision about whether or not their skills were to be employed remained firmly within amateur control.

Future research directions

Partly because of the paucity of evidence available, sports historians have tended to downplay the significance of agency and concentrated instead on the impact of predominantly middle-class interests (Booth 2000). For the majority of trainers and coaches connected with individual sports, who made all or part of their living by teaching and instructing, references to their life courses normally only appear as an occasional adjunct to a discussion of a particular athlete's past performances. It is no surprise, therefore, that it has been professionals associated with football and cricket, or those who had connections to Oxbridge athletics and rowing, who have left a significant mark on the historical record. The contrasting examples of two men intimately concerned with the 1908 Olympics highlight this dilemma for the coaching historian. President of the Games, Lord Desborough, who had a long career as a Member of Parliament, has a well-documented life course, including an entry in the *Oxford Dictionary of National Biography*. As the professional for LAC, Charles Perry became the leading world expert on running tracks and he was in charge of the construction of the tracks for all the Olympics up to 1920, including 1908. References to Perry occur only as an aside, if at all, and the exploits of most trainers remain largely unrecorded because these working-class individuals lacked the public profile and access to resources of a man like Desborough. The end result is that little trace remains of the majority of professional coaches. This, in turn, has led to historians adopting a 'top-down' approach to sport, and other aspects of social life, by relying almost exclusively on the well-documented accounts of prominent individuals. There is a pressing need for further work in this area to uncover the narratives of individuals who worked within the constraints established by those who articulated the amateur ethos. It is by teasing out and examining the lives of those engaged in making a living from sport that a better understanding can be achieved of aspects of sporting life that have only been dealt with previously in terms of the generalities of class. For example, the tendency has been to view the 1912 Games as an important turning point in attitudes to coaching and training in Britain. The subsequent coaching initiatives, and the middle-class debate about coaching that appeared concurrently in the national press, have been used as evidence of a significant change in attitudes to both training and trainers but the limited work detailing the experiences of Edwardian trainers suggests that the 1912 Games may have been less of a watershed in attitudes to British coaching and more of an acceleration in an already existing trend.

In order to inform these kinds of debates a few researchers (e.g. Oldfield 2012) are turning to prosopography, the investigation of the common background characteristics of a group of actors in history by means of a collective study of their lives (Stone 1971). The method involves establishing a universe to be studied, such as Victorian trainers, and then asking a set of uniform questions, about birth and death, marriage and family, social origins and inherited economic position, place of residence, education, amount and source of wealth, working lives, religion and so on in an attempt to uncover the social context of groups and the networks of which each individual forms a part (Keats-Rohan 2007). This type of prosopography, which examines social ties and connections between people, helps to explain ideological or cultural change by examining surviving evidence and documentation relating to persons of lower social status, such as trainers. The method is not adverse to a small-scale approach and Cunningham (2001) argues that even a small selection of biographies can be used to understand individuals on a collective scale. Biographies of coaches and trainers need to be constructed from a broad spectrum of key primary sources such as newspaper and periodical archives, photographs, trade directories, census material, contemporary maps, and local and family histories (Barber and Peniston-Bird 2009), highlighting the continuities and changes in the roles adopted by these individuals and exposing their origins and economic class, together with their social networks and daily practice. Prosopography benefits from the computer age, especially access to online archives and, as a result, prosopographers have been able to increasingly interrogate some nineteenth-century constituencies (Erben 1996; Kennedy 2003; Poulsen 2004) but this is in its early stages and there is a pressing need for many more studies in subject-specific areas such as sports coaching. Although the subsequent narratives may lack evidence in parts, this does not invalidate the research as, according to Bale (2004: 26), these narratives do not need to be 'stuffed with truth' since extreme detail does not necessarily reveal 'the essence of the real man'.

This kind of research would help both in developing a better understanding of coaching developments and in explaining some of the variations observed in amateur approaches to sport. While the amateur impact on sport at the end of the nineteenth century was interpreted by some early researchers as leading to the exclusion of the sports professional, Holt (2006: 353) has described amateurism in all its guises as a 'complex phenomenon with complex causes' and it seems that the application of the amateur ethos may have been interpreted differently at various levels of sport. Amateurism never implied that winning was unimportant but simply that it needed to be kept in perspective, which was part of the problem with the Americans whose system of specialisation was condemned as 'a *reductio ad absurdum*' of the meaning of sport (*Manchester Guardian* 1912: 16). More work is required in order to explain similarities and differences in British and American approaches to coaching at elite levels of sport during the early twentieth century since it is still not clear whether these kinds of statements would have been supported by British Olympians of the period.

Research into the development of coaching practices and the life courses of the men involved is still in its infancy, and while previous work has focused on Victorian and Edwardian periods there is a need for this to be extended into the latter stages of the twentieth century. In particular, the impact of the Soviet and American models of the 1950s and the coaching 'arms race' that developed during the Cold War period would benefit from investigation since this probably had a significant impact on the evolution of an industrialised model of coaching practice. In the British context, studies are required into developments in coaching following the Second World War and the Wolfenden Report (1960), and into the relationship between amateurism and the more widespread acceptance of professional coaching. Another historical tool, the use of oral histories, will prove invaluable to those researchers wishing to explore the changes and continuities experienced in the working lives of coaches of a more recent vintage than Andrews or Mussabini. A deeper understanding of these and similar historical discourses will help inform scholars in their debates about the nature and direction of coaching practice.

Historical coaching practices and contemporary debates

The limited research already completed into the origins of coaching practice suggests that nineteenth-century professional coaching cultures, acting through tightly connected communities of practice, grew out of a form of cottage industry led by local experts, whose knowledge was transmitted orally or through demonstrated practice, and whose methods were perpetuated, in turn, by their close confidants. Coaching was never a sociable club in the way that amateur sport was envisaged since sharing knowledge effectively deskilled the practitioner. Sinclair (1807) experienced difficulty in extracting information from trainers because their methods were a valued commodity and it made sense to retain this material within their own communities, a practice contemporary authors refer to as 'regimes of appropriation' which recognises that financial incentives prevent those who have competitive knowledge from sharing it with outsiders. Many groups may simply not want to share, or they may want to hide what they know (Teece 1986; Duguid 2005). The very nature of Victorian coaching communities, being small, non-regulated and self-contained, could lead to traditionalism, and certainly led to criticism for perpetuating 'fads' and secret training methods, but they also gave considerable scope for innovation and for the use of deductive and intuitive elements in applying and evaluating training.

Bloomfield argued that international level coaching was 'no longer a matter of techniques which are passed down from the coach to the player, who in turn becomes a coach' (Woodman 1989: 206). While this 'apprentice-type education' had worked well in the past, so much science was now involved in elite performance that a more formal education of coaches was required. However, recent studies suggest that communities of practice which prioritise experience over explicit knowledge have retained their potency and that expert coaches still learn through sharing with other coaches. When soccer players graduate into coaching roles, their own methods remain heavily influenced by their playing experiences, irrespective of their levels of formal qualification (Potrac *et al.* 2007) while better-qualified elite swimming coaches do not necessarily produce the best swimmers (Stewart and Hopkins 2000: 880–881). The processes coaches engage in remain highly dependent on a combination of experience and knowledge, and practitioners have been found to possess a largely implicit form of knowledge which shares similar characteristics with craft knowledge (Jones *et al.* 2003). Effective coaching is a skill to be learnt and Sage (1989) refers to the notion of 'organizational socialization', where aspiring coaches, in addition to learning the technical, tactical and physical aspects of the job, are inculcated with shared understandings regarding the coaching role. As a result, individuals usually enter coaching already socialised into ways of acting and provided with comprehensive 'maps of meaning' from previous experiences as athletes (Sage 1989). Contemporary coaches consistently identify other coaches as their most important resource in terms of developing the skill of coaching, with trial and error or experimentation, and their own past experiences, as other key reference points (Irwin *et al.* 2004). In all these respects, despite social changes, and scientific and technological advances, it appears that professional coaches of the Victorian and Edwardian periods have clear and recognisable links to twenty-first century coaching practice.

References

Albermarle, E. and Hillier, G.L. (1896) *Cycling*, London: Green and Co.

Andrews, H. (1903) *Training for Athletics and General Health*, London: C. Arthur Pearson.

Bale, J. (2004) 'The mysterious Professor Jokl', in J. Bale, M.K. Christensen and G. Pfister (eds) *Writing Lives in Sport: Biographies, Life-Histories and Methods*, Oxford: Aarhus University Press.

Barber, S. and Peniston-Bird, C.M. (2009) *A Student's Guide to Approaching Alternative Sources*, London: Routledge.

Bell's Life in London and Sporting Chronicle, 7 September 1851.

Booth, D. (2000) 'From allusion to causal explanation: The comparative method in sports history', *International Sports Studies*, 22(2): 5–25.

Booth, D. (2006) 'Sites of truth or metaphors of power? Refiguring the archive', *Sport in History*, 26(1): 91–109.

Carroll, N. (2001) 'Interpretation, history and narrative', in G. Roberts (ed.) *The History and Narrative Reader*, London: Routledge.

Carter, N. (2006) *The Football Manager: A History*, London: Routledge.

Carter, N. (2011) *Coaching Cultures*, London: Routledge.

Census Returns, 1841–1911.

Clegg, A. (1977) 'Craftsmen and the rise of capitalism', *History Workshop*, 4(1): 243–246.

Cunningham, P. (2001) 'Innovators, networks and structures: Towards a prosopography of progressivism', *History of Education*, 30(5): 436–451

Daily Mirror, 1 August 1912.

Day, D. (2008) 'From Barclay to Brickett: Coaching practices and coaching lives in nineteenth and early twentieth century England', unpublished doctoral thesis, De Montfort University, UK.

Day, D. (2010a) 'London swimming professors: Victorian craftsmen and aquatic entrepreneurs', *Sport in History*, 30(1): 32–54.

Day, D. (2010b) 'Walter Brickett: A respectable professor', in B. Snape and H. Pussard (eds) *Recording Leisure Lives: Sports, Games and Pastimes in 20th Century Britain*, London: LSA.

Day, D. (2011) 'Craft coaching and the "discerning eye" of the coach', *International Journal of Sport Science and Coaching*, 6(1): 179–195.

Dowling, F.L. (1841) *Fistiana*, London: Wm. Clemen.

Duguid, P. (2005) 'The art of knowing: Social and tacit dimensions of knowledge and the limits of the community of practice', *The Information Society*, 21(2): 109–118.

Egan, P. (1823) *Sporting Anecdotes: Original and Selected*, New York: Johnstone and Van.

Elton, G.R. (2002) *The Practice of History*, Oxford: Blackwell Publishers.

Erben, M. (1996) 'A preliminary prosopography of the Victorian street', *Auto/Biography*, 4(2/3): 53–68.

Gamble, J. (2001) 'Modelling the invisible: The pedagogy of craft apprenticeship', *Studies in Continuing Education*, 23(2): 190–196.

Graham, T. (1827) *Sure Methods of Improving Health and Prolonging Life*, second edition, London: the author.

Hadgraft, R. (2004) *The Little Wonder: The Untold Story of Alfred Shrubb, World Champion Runner*, Westcliff-on-Sea: Desert Island Books.

Hoole, H. (1888) *The Science and Art of Training: A Handbook for Athletes*, London: Trübner and Co.

Holt, R. (2006) 'The amateur body and the middle-class man: Work, health and style in Victorian Britain', *Sport in History*, 26(3): 352–369.

Irwin, G., Hanton, S. and Kerwin, D. (2004) 'Reflective practice and the origins of elite coaching knowledge', *Reflective Practice*, 5(3): 425–442.

Johnes, M. (2007) 'Archives, truths and the historian at work: A reply to Douglas Booth's "Refiguring the Archive"', *Sport in History*, 27(1): 127–135.

Jones, R.L. and Wallace, M. (2005) 'Another bad day at the training ground: Coping with ambiguity in the coaching context', *Sport, Education and Society*, 10(1): 119–134.

Jones, R.L., Armour, K.M. and Potrac, P. (2003) 'Constructing expert knowledge: A case study of a top-level professional soccer coach', *Sport, Education and Society*, 8(2): 220–224.

Keats-Rohan, K.S.B. (2007) *Prosopography Approaches and Applications: A Handbook*, Oxford: Linacre College.

Keil, I. and Wix, D. (1996) *In the Swim: The Amateur Swimming Association from 1869 to 1994*, Loughborough: Swimming Times.

Kennedy, D. (2003) 'The division of Everton Football Club into hostile factions: The development of professional football organisations on Merseyside, 1878–1914', unpublished doctoral thesis, Leeds University, UK.

Light, R. (2005) 'Ten drunks and a parson? The Victorian professional cricketer reconsidered', *Sport in History*, 25(1): 71–73.

Manchester Guardian, 23 July, 1912

Maret, G. (1818) 'Remarks on training', *Blackwood's Edinburgh Magazine*, IV(XXI): 317–318.

Marwick, A. (2001) *The New Nature of History: Knowledge, Evidence and Language*, Basingstoke: Palgrave.

Mewett, P. (1995) ' "Nothing is better for dinner than a pint of good dry champagne": The "gentleman" amateur and sports training in the second half of the nineteenth century', in C. Simpson and R. Gidlow (eds) *Proceedings of the Second Australian and New Zealand Leisure Studies Association Conference*, Canterbury: ANZALS.

Mewett, P.G. (2002) 'From horses to humans: Species crossovers in the origin of modern sports training', *Sport History Review*, 33(2): 95–120.

Moon, G. (1992) *Albert Hill: A Proper Perspective*, Cheltenham: Greg Moon.

Mussabini, S.A. (1913) *The Complete Athletic Trainer*, London: Methuen and Co.

Observer, 4 August 1901.

Oldfield, S. (2012) 'Narrative, Biography, Prosopography and the Sport Historian: Historical Method and its Implications', in D. Day (ed) *Sports and Coaching: Pasts and Futures*, Manchester: MMU IPR Publication.

Park, R.J. (1992) 'Athletes and their training in Britain and America, 1800–1914', in J. Berryman and R. Park (eds) *Sport and Exercise Science: Essays in the History of Sports Medicine*, Champaign, IL: Illinois University Press.

Park, R.J. (2011) 'Physicians, scientists, exercise and athletics in Britain and America from the 1867 boat race to the four-minute mile', *Sport in History*, 31(1): 1–31.

Phillips, M. (2000) *From Sidelines to Centre Field: A History of Sports Coaching in Australia*, Sydney: University of New South Wales Press.

Polley, M. (2007) *Sports History: A Practical Guide*, Basingstoke: Palgrave Macmillan.

Potrac, P., Jones, R.L. and Cushion, C.J. (2007) 'Understanding power and the coach's role in professional English soccer: A preliminary investigation of coach behaviour', *Soccer and Society*, 8(1): 33–49.

Poulsen, A. (2004) 'Female physical education teachers in Copenhagen, 1900–1940: A collective biography', *The International Journal of the History of Sport*, 21: 16–33.

Radford, P. (1985) 'The art and science of training and coaching athletes in late eighteenth and early nineteenth century Britain', in J.A. Mangan (ed.) *Proceedings of the 1985 HISPA Congress*, Glasgow: HISPA.

Sage, G. (1989) 'Becoming a high school coach: From playing sport to coaching', *Research Quarterly for Exercise and Sport*, 60(1): 81–92.

Semotiuk, D. (1982) 'Human energy in sport coaching: Historical perspectives from ancient Greece', *Canadian Journal of History of Sport*, XIII(2): 18–29.

Sinclair, J. (1807) *The Code of Health and Longevity*, Edinburgh: Arch. Constable and Co.

Stewart, A.M. and Hopkins, W.G. (2000) 'Seasonal training and performance of competitive swimmers', *Journal of Sport Sciences*, 18(11): 873–884.

Stone, L. (1971) 'Prosopography', *Daedalus*, 100(1): 46–79.

Teece, D.J. (1986) 'Profiting from technological innovation: Implications for integration, collaboration, licensing, and public policy', *Research Policy*, 15(6): 285–305.

Wade, H. (1911) 'Cross-country running', in *The Encyclopaedia of Sports and Games*, New York: J.B. Lippincott Co.

Walker, D. (1837) *British Manly Exercises*, Philadelphia, PA: Thomas Wardle.

Wenger, E. (1998) *Communities of Practice: Learning, Meaning, and Identity*, Cambridge: Cambridge University Press.

Wilkinson, H.F. (1868) *Modern Athletics*, London: Warne.

Woodgate, W.B. (1890) 'Rowing and sculling', in E. Bell (ed.) *Handbook of Athletic Sports*, London: George Bell and Son.

Woodman, L. (1989) 'The development of coach education in Australia', *Sporting Traditions* 5(2): 204–224.

2

COACHING WITH FOUCAULT

An examination of applied sport ethics

Richard Pringle

UNIVERSITY OF AUCKLAND, NEW ZEALAND

Hamish Crocket

UNIVERSITY OF WAIKATO, NEW ZEALAND

Introduction

Sporting stories of sexual abuse, violence, drunkenness, cheating, corruption and doping are now routinely circulated in the global media. Indeed, the notion that ethical problems exist in sport has become so ingrained in the public sphere that many now speculate, for example, that certain elite athletes must have taken performance-enhancing drugs. The quixotic notion that 'sport builds character' through the inculcation of virtues such as honesty, fair play and humility, correspondingly, appears increasingly dubious. Consequently, the concept of the 'trustworthy coach' has also taken a hit. Although we may mourn for a nostalgic sporting past that was seemingly more innocent, the gradual erosion of the assumption that sport builds character (e.g. Miracle and Rees 1994; Carr 1998) in connection with increased coverage of sporting scandals, has contributed to sport ethics becoming 'a "hot" topic' (Fraleigh 1997: vii).

The increased interest in sport ethics has directed attention to coaching: not simply in relation to *apparently* obvious ethical dilemmas, such as how to deal with sexual or verbal abuse, but in relation to applied problems and broader understandings of ethical concerns. As Morgan (2007) expressed, the moral horizons of the art of coaching have expanded. Coaches are now encouraged to employ select pedagogical practices to produce athletes as 'moral' citizens (Shields and Bredemeier 1995; Arnold 1997). Deeper critical questions have also begun to be examined. Shogan (1999; 2007), for instance, asked whether there is a case to re-examine seemingly 'normal' coaching practices and consider them as unethical. Researchers are questioning, for example, whether it is ethical for a coach to demand that athletes follow rigid, but nutritionally approved, diets (e.g. Chapman 1997; Johns and Johns 2000).

We will argue in this chapter that there are no universally accepted or objective ways of determining answers to ethical dilemmas. Such a position may disappoint coaches or athletes who are hoping to find clear-cut answers to specific problems. This does not mean, however, that we believe that ethical issues are subject to extreme forms of relativism. In contrast, we argue that resolutions to moral quandaries depend on how one conceptualises morality, the community to which one belongs, and to which moral and/or social theories one subscribes. In this respect, we concur with Morgan (2007) who stresses that the field and thus the analysis of sport ethics is enormously complex.

In this chapter, to develop a deeper understanding of the ethical complexities associated with coaching, we begin by providing a historic overview of how the field of sport ethics has developed. This is followed by an examination of the three major ethical paradigms that have been employed to analyse issues within sport: *deontological*, *contractarian* and *virtue* theories. In providing this overview, we develop the argument that the analysis of sport ethics is in the process of shifting from modernist to postmodernist conceptualisations. By this we mean that individuals' understandings of moral behaviour are shifting away from a faith in universal codes of conduct towards localised solutions in local contexts. In recognition of this shift we conclude by illustrating how Michel Foucault's postmodern theorising can provide a framework for negotiating ethical dilemmas in coaching.

An overview of the field of coach ethics

The terms 'ethics' and 'morality' are often used interchangeably within sport coaching literature to refer to issues concerned with how people should behave and the distinctions between 'good' and 'bad' behaviour (Cassidy *et al.* 2009). Examinations into coaching ethics have, however, typically focused on coaches' actions deemed to be inappropriate and the various factors that are assumed to encourage these behaviours (Lyle 2002). This negative focus has developed in relation to a growing acknowledgement that the coaching context is a 'fruitful context within which unethical behaviour can occur' (Cassidy *et al.* 2009: 152).

Two key reasons have been offered to explain this ethical predicament. First, as Arnold indicated, the 'syndrome of "winning at all costs"' (1997: xv) has pervaded the sporting domain and encouraged some coaches to develop dubious values and practices. The desire to be a winning coach, as an example, has been linked with rule infractions, such as doping and deliberate acts of violence (Arnold 1997). Other researchers have further argued that an excessive focus on winning is linked with inappropriate behaviour off the field and the development of problematic athletic 'identities' (Messner 1992; Shields and Bredemeier 1995; Robinson 1998). Second, Lyle (2002) has argued that coaching contexts can be prone to ethical problems given the somewhat unique characteristics of coach-athlete relationships which can involve elements of close contact, psychological dependency, emotional passion and various 'power differentials' (p. 237) related to maturity, age, experience, gender and knowledge.

Ethical concerns about coaching have encouraged the relatively recent development of various codes of conduct or 'fair play' doctrines for coaches (e.g. the 1996 British National Coaching Foundation code). In addition, many Western countries have developed qualifications and/or training programmes to encourage the development of professional coaches. These various coaching courses, such as the *New Zealand Coach Approach* (SPARC 2010), are now emphasising an athlete-centred coaching style (e.g. see Kidman *et al.* 2005). In an associated manner there has been a shift to viewing coaches as educators and as having a moral duty to care for their athletes' long-term wellbeing and moral conduct (e.g. see McNamee 1998; Jones *et al.* 2004; Jones 2006).

The development of coaching codes of conduct and the institutionalisation of coach-education programmes which emphasise how a coach, in principle, 'ought to act', is reflective of a deontological approach to ethics. This approach, which emphasises the duties of athletes or coaches, provided the dominant theoretical lens for understanding sport ethics throughout the 1980s and early 1990s. Fraleigh's (1984) *Right Actions for Athletes* was an influential text in promoting such an approach. The deontological approach has similarities to contractarian ethical theory which has also been widely discussed within sport literature (e.g. Simon 2004). However, in more recent years, many sport ethicists have been influenced by MacIntyre's (1981) *After Virtue: A Study in Moral Theory*. Subsequently, the field of ethics known as 'virtue ethics' has become influential. In the following section, we discuss these three significant ethical theories and detail their respective strengths and weaknesses in relation to coaching.

Ethical sporting theories: deontology, contractarian and virtue

Coaches face many ethical dilemmas: for example, is it ethical for a coach to encourage players to feign injury in order to draw a penalty? What level of rehabilitation should an injured athlete achieve before being selected to play again? Can coaches ethically not select a player for a representative team because they assume that the player's sexuality or ethnicity will create disharmony in a team? In attempting to answer such questions sport ethicists have drawn on various ethical theories. The first two we discuss, deontology and contractarian ethical theory, are based on notions of duty and rules, respectively. They share common origins in Western modernist philosophy, such as in the work of Kant and Mill, and the desire to develop categorical imperatives or rules of moral behaviour. The third approach, virtue ethics, replaces concerns with duties and rules with the issue of how to develop moral character within specific communities of practice.

Deontology, in a simplistic manner, is based on the assumption that sport participants have a moral duty to follow the rules of sport. Deontology is split into two camps: those following Huizinga (1970), who define sport as a type of play (e.g. Feezell 2004), and those following Suits (1988), who define sport as a type of game (e.g. Hurka 2007). While these two approaches are distinct from each other in terms of content, the structure of their arguments is similar. We, accordingly, focus only on the game-playing approach.

Suits (1988) argued that participation in sport requires athletes to adopt a 'lusory' goal and attitude. The lusory goal is simply the goal of the game, for example, to score more points than your opponents. The lusory attitude is the acceptance that the lusory goal can be achieved only by following the rules of the game. Following Suits (1988), a number of sports ethicists (e.g. Delattre 1988; Fraleigh 1988; Keating 2001; Boxill 2003; Pearson 2003) have argued in favour of deontology: all offering some formulation of the proposition that 'a player who deliberately breaks the rules of the game is no longer playing the game' (Pearson 2003: 82). In this manner, we could conclude – somewhat paradoxically – that Ben Johnson was *not* competing in the final of the men's 100 m sprint in Seoul (1988) as he was no longer following the rules of sprinting. Although the deontological focus has encouraged many to explore the complexities associated with moral duty, this ethical theory has been problematised in recent years with recognition that athletes are often encouraged to break or bend the rules of their sport (Leaman 1988; Lehman 1988). Many basketball coaches, for example, encourage their players to deliberately draw the foul as a strategy to regain possession in the closing stages of a game. This awareness highlights three prime weaknesses of deontological theory.

First, McFee (2004) argued that deontologists are only able to argue that every athlete must follow the rules of the game because they *assume* that athletes have developed a lusory attitude or a commitment to follow the rules. In other words, deontologists do not *establish* that athletes are obliged to follow rules, rather they *begin* with this assumption. Second, McFee argued that rules always require interpretation. For example, many sports have an 'advantage' rule, whereby the referee may allow play to continue after a rule infringement if he/she thinks that the non-infringing team may benefit from play continuing. The application of this rule requires active interpretation of the rule every time it is applied. Consequently, rules, by themselves, cannot be sufficient in guiding player conduct – ethically or tactically – because the rules themselves cannot be applied without interpretation. Third, a deontological approach requires individuals to make ethical decisions from a seemingly impartial standpoint, as detached from the 'real world' or the values that circulate in their sporting communities (Morgan 2006). Yet, as Morgan argued, associating ethics with impartiality, 'forces us into a rather simple dichotomy between moral objectivity and non-moral subjectivity' (2006: 86). Instead, we should ground our ethical decision making in the values of the communities to which we belong.

The second approach to sport ethics is *social contract theory*. This theory is based on the assumption that all athletes have made a tacit agreement as to the manner in which they should play the game (Eassom 1998). Players are accordingly deemed to have agreed to both the written and *unwritten* rules of the game. The deliberate foul in basketball can, in this manner, be understood as tacitly agreed upon. The most widely cited proponent of this theory is Simon (2004), who argued we should understand sport as a mutual quest for athletic excellence, as opposed to victory. Because excellence is the aim, he suggested that a challenging but co-operative opposition is preferable to an opponent that is easily dominated. Clearly, such a view is debatable.

Certainly some level of tacit agreement is necessary for a sport to be recognisable, as beyond a certain level of cheating, a particular sport would cease to exist (Lehman 1988). However, as Eassom (1998) points out, the grounds for assuming that athletes can be considered to have tacitly agreed to a social contract are weak. He argues that in order for sport to be governed by a social contract, it would need to be: removed from the context of people's wider lives; freely chosen from a number of alternatives; played with a single purpose by all athletes; and, finally, for the rules to be designed with that single purpose for playing in mind. None of these requirements seems to be plausible in the context of contemporary sport. Moreover, Morgan (2007) argued that the process of undertaking ethical work may be sidestepped by those who subscribe to this theory. For example, in rugby union, unwritten rules suggest that a player may take some form of physical retaliation against an opponent if that opponent deliberately fouled them. In this manner, players have agreed that a certain level of rule bending (e.g. shirt pulling, pushing, elbowing and even punching) has been agreed to. Morgan would suggest, however, that in accepting this social contract, players and coaches avoid doing any ethical work as critical reflection on player behaviour is avoided.

Since the 1990s there has been a perceptible swing away from the modernist philosophies of deontological and contractarian theories in favour of virtue ethics (e.g. Jones 2008; McNamee 1998, 2008; Sheridan 2003). Virtue ethicists shift the focus from rules and principles to issues associated with examining how can individuals live a 'good' or moral life (McNamee 1998). They argue that rule/contract-based ethics cannot account for the social and cultural contexts in which ethical decision-making takes place (Sheridan 2003). As such, they advocate for greater ethical flexibility (Shields and Bredemeier 1995).

Virtue ethics focus on *practices*, which are social groupings or communities that are concerned with a particular pursuit and have a shared understanding of their practice's history, values and traditions. Any given sport, in this manner, may be thought of as a practice insofar as it has its own community that defines standards of excellence based on shared knowledge. Within particular practices, virtues become important as they are understood not as 'mere social constructions but presuppositions of the very idea of a community or society' (McNamee 2008: 5). In other words, virtues are qualities of character that allow those within certain practices to live communally (e.g. honesty, responsibility, courage). Virtues, correspondingly, are used to guide moral behaviour but are not viewed as duties or rules to dictate behaviour, as practical wisdom is also deemed important in the process of making ethical decisions (Morgan 2007). A coach facing an ethical dilemma, for example, would ask, 'What would a virtuous person do in this situation?' and then apply practical wisdom to further reflect on the situation.

Although virtue ethics acknowledges the complexities associated with moral dilemmas and affords more flexibility in managing such problems, it has also been subject to critique. Primarily, applications of virtue ethics in sport rarely elaborate on what the virtues are beyond a brief list. Sheridan (2003), for example, simply stated that 'we prefer the trustworthy to the untrustworthy, the just to the unjust and so on' (2003: 174) without considering that we may not always be able to draw such sharp distinctions in every situation. Morgan (2007) further questioned: how should we 'handle situations in which the virtues clash, and in which, therefore, it is not at all clear which virtues should be acted on and which silenced or even rejected' (2007: xxxiv). He concluded that it is bordering on naïve, if not duplicitous, to hold that virtues will always act in concert with one another, that the moral instructions they convey will always point us in the same direction (ibid.).

While we see virtue ethics as an important step towards acknowledging the social and cultural basis of our experiences and actions, we feel that it is limited in its potential to question the nature and application of concepts such as justice, truth, fairness and so on.

Towards a sport ethic based on postmodern social theory

In our review of the three dominant sport ethics theories it becomes apparent that ethical dilemmas in coaching are complex. Each ethical theory provides a different lens for understanding how to solve a coaching issue and each has particular strengths and weaknesses. A coach, correspondingly, could select a different theory and construct a differing strategy of action. Moral 'solutions', accordingly, are subjective constructions open to various interpretations. This understanding problematises modernist approaches for solving moral dilemmas in coaching, as the process of solving ethical dilemmas is not a purely rational or linear, objective process. As such, we argue that coaches cannot, with impunity, depend upon abstract sets of moral principles, codes of conduct, processes of 'rational' disengagement or a belief that there exists a coherent set of virtues that can be relied upon as a moral compass. We are not, however, suggesting that broad sets of moral principles or codes of conduct should be jettisoned as they are clearly useful for helping think through coaching issues. In contrast, we are encouraging coaches to approach any strategy for negotiating moral dilemmas with a critical eye or a degree of scepticism. Our position, as such, resonates with a postmodern approach to managing ethical dilemmas.

Postmodernism can simply be understood as a scepticism of metanarratives (Lyotard 1984) or a 'doubt that any method or theory, discourse or genre, tradition or novelty, has a universal and general claim as the "right" or the privileged form of authoritative knowledge' (Richardson 2000: 8). For some, the rejection of a search for universal social truths, certainty or the ability to claim that knowledge has been constructed objectively, is undoubtedly troubling. Yet Lyotard (1984) argued that the loss of universal meanings or certainty should not be mourned, as we can now celebrate difference and diversity which can reinforce 'our ability to tolerate the incommensurable' (2000: xxv). We suggest that a postmodern ethical approach could be beneficial for coaches as they are, at times, faced with seemingly incommensurable problems.

Given the complex array of intersecting 'social' factors that both produce and complicate moral dilemmas for coaches, we support the various calls for coaches to engage with social theory (e.g. Denison 2007; Lyle 1999; Potrac and Jones 1999). Jones *et al.* (2003), for example, argued that the coaching process is primarily a social activity and coaches are 'social beings operating in an environment, so their activities ought to be examined and explained as such' (2003: 35). Social theory is one of the prime tools that sociologists use to examine how humans construct, make sense of, interact within and attempt to change our social world (Coakley 2007). Social theory, accordingly, can provide a useful lens for understanding the complex social context within which ethical dilemmas are constructed and subsequently negotiated. In comparison with modernist ethical theories, social theories offer a broader-based approach for understanding how power operates, identities are (trans)formed, ideas constructed, knowledge circulated and associated strategies for critical thinking devised. Moreover, given the now common observation that 'moral dilemmas in coaching ... are often better viewed as "shades of grey"' (Cassidy *et al.* 2009: 150), we advocate the use of postmodern social theory for interrogating sport ethics. More specifically, we support Shogan and Ford's (2000) promotion of Michel Foucault's theorising and his postmodern, but pragmatic, approach to examining ethics.

Foucauldian sport ethics

Foucault has been variously described as a postmodern or poststructural social theorist, yet his prominence within social theory has meant that many now simply call his theorising 'Foucauldian'. Although best known for his writings concerned with knowledge/power, sexuality and governmentality, his later and less well-examined work focused on ethical modes of existence (Foucault 1987, 1988a, 1988b). Paul Rabinow (1997) was so impressed with this later work that he suggested: 'Ultimately ... Foucault may well be remembered as one of the major ethical thinkers of modernity' (1997: xxvi). Indeed, Foucault's ability 'to ask new questions, think differently and allow for the creation of new understandings and possibilities' (1997a: 273), has played a role in the transformation of the understandings of ethics. Bernauer (1988), for example, stated that Foucault's approach to ethics works to:

> denature or historicize Kant's great questions ... Not 'what can I know?,' but rather, 'How have my questions been produced? How has the path of my knowing been determined?' Not 'what I ought to do?,' but rather, 'How have I been situated to experience the real? How have exclusions operated in delineating the realm of obligation for me?'
>
> *(1988: 46–7)*

Foucault's impetus to study ethics stemmed from his examination of the workings of power and his concerns with freedom and subjectivity. Although Foucault (1988b) conceptualised multiple forms of power he also suggested, in simplistic terms, that power can be understood as a relation between humans and, more specifically, as an attempt by an individual 'to direct the behaviour of another' (1988b: 11). Foucault further clarified that there cannot be 'relations of power unless the subjects are free' (1998b: 12). In other words, when individuals are coerced or exist in a state of domination (e.g. slavery) they are not 'free' and a power relation does not exist. Moreover, this liberty – even if the power relationship is imbalanced, as it is in many coach/athlete relationships – ensures that 'there is necessarily the possibility of resistance, for if there were no possibility of resistance – of violent resistance, of escape, of ruse, of strategies that reverse the situation – there would be no relations of power' (1998b: 12). The following sport example helps illustrate Foucault's notions of the omnipresence of power relations:

> A coach and an athlete, for example, exist within a specific power relation, in that the coach typically attempts to guide the athlete's conduct or performance. Although the coach can develop strategies to direct the actions of the athlete, such as by keeping an athlete on the bench, the athlete is still relatively 'free' to decide his/her response and ultimately whether he/she will continue to be coached. The actions of the athlete can also reciprocally influence the actions of the coach. If the athlete, for example, was to tell the coach that he/she was thinking of quitting this might induce a change in the coach's future actions. Thus, although the coach and athlete's relationship of power may be unbalanced, they can still be thought of as existing within a specific power relation.
>
> *(Markula and Pringle 2006: 35)*

Through connecting freedom to relations of power, Foucault (1988b) suggested that we are continually faced with the ethical issue: 'How can one practice freedom?' (1998b: 4). The problem for Foucault was not that power relations were necessarily bad, but rather that we inevitably are engaged in attempts to control others' behaviour and be controlled by others. Thus, we should consider the question, 'How do I understand myself as someone actively engaged in power relations?' Foucault suggested that it would be advantageous for individuals to develop 'the techniques of management, and also the ethics, the *ethos*, the practice of self, which would allow these games of power to be played with a minimum of domination' (1998b: 18). He subsequently turned his attention to examining the techniques of ethical self formation used by free men in Ancient Greece. His interest in studying these particular techniques of self stemmed from his recognition that the Greeks were not governed by stringent sets of laws or ethical guidelines. In this manner, he speculated that a similarity existed with respect to how contemporary individuals negotiate ethics, as in contemporary times many 'no longer believe that ethics is founded in religion, nor do we want a legal system to intervene in our moral, personal, private life' (Foucault 1997b: 225).

In examining the techniques of self, Foucault (1992) differentiated between morality and ethics. He stated that morality refers to a set of rules of conduct that are promoted by various regulatory agencies, such as the church, governments or international sporting bodies (Pringle and Hickey 2010). Although these rules or values are, at times, transparent they can also be conveyed diffusely 'so that, far from constituting a systematic ensemble, they form a complex interplay of elements that counterbalance and correct one another, and cancel each other out on certain points, thus providing for compromises or loopholes' (Foucault 1992: 25). Indeed, official sporting rules may forbid acts of cheating but the unwritten rules in some codes may allow for the rules to be bent. Foucault, in this manner, argued that compliance with a moral code is not necessarily *ethical*. Ethics, in contrast, can be understood as 'the manner in which one ought to "conduct one self" – that is, the manner in which one ought to form oneself as an ethical subject acting in reference to the prescriptive elements that make up the code' (Foucault 1992: 26). Ethical performances, therefore, revolve around 'the relationship of the self to the code and on the methods and techniques through which this relationship is worked out' (Shogan and Ford 2000: 51).

Foucault, in drawing from the ancient Greeks, developed a framework involving four questions that could be used to determine whether an individual might 'ethically' accept or reject a moral code and in the process form themselves as an ethical subject (Pringle and Hickey 2010). The first question, concerned with the *ethical substance*, asks 'Which is the aspect or part of myself or my behaviour which is concerned with moral conduct?' (Foucault 1997a: 263). The second question, the *mode of subjection*, is concerned with how an individual reflects on one's relationship to the code of conduct associated with the ethical substance, with particular respect to why he/she either respects or disregards this code. The third, *ethical work or practices of self*, questions what an individual can modify about their self to become ethical. Finally, the *telos* asks what kind of being do we aspire to be '[W]hen we behave in a moral way?' (Foucault 1997a: 265). This last question has similarities to virtue ethics (which also has lineage back to the Greeks) given its concern with the formation of good character. Yet the Foucauldian framework does *not* rest on an assumption that pre-existing virtues – such as courage, honesty, reliability – cohere in a complementary manner. Moreover, the Foucauldian framework encourages individuals to initially problematise or critically reflect on the code of conduct: in this manner, certain virtues that might be embedded in the code could be critiqued given the specifics of the context. Shogan and Ford (2000) suggest:

> If Foucault's approach to ethics was taken as a model for sport ethics, sport ethics would be more concerned with how each participant understands how [the] rules and demands of sport shape them as people. Sport ethics would also be concerned with how each person makes decisions to comply with or refuse certain rules and demands of sport. This approach has pedagogical, political, and scholarly implications for a new sport ethics.
>
> *(2000: 51)*

In the last section we provide an example to illustrate how Foucault's ethical framework has been used by one of the authors to manage ethical dilemmas in coaching.

Applying a Foucauldian framework: Hamish's experiences

I coach Ultimate Frisbee (Ultimate) and have played to an international level. I have found that many males who play on mixed (co-ed) teams assume that the presence of women on their team means they are somehow progressive or non-sexist. However, over a period of time, I came to question this assumption. I noted, *pace* Thornton (1998), that gender roles were remarkably fixed. On defence, marks were assigned by gender without questioning if this was tactically sound given the abilities of the players on each team. On offence, women were rarely entrusted with making critical plays, while many men had substantial freedom regardless of their success rate.

Eventually, I realised I was uncomfortable with how males were dominating females in Ultimate and decided that I needed to address this, as an equity issue, in how I coached my team. This ethical dilemma (sexism) formed my *ethical substance*. My *mode of subjection* was the process through which I reflected on my coaching in relation to feminist codes of conduct and my understanding of the Spirit of the Game – an Ultimate-specific doctrine of fair play, written into the rules of Ultimate. More specifically, I considered how my coaching might have reinforced gendered roles. On reflection I realised that my game plan emphasised the team's strongest throwers and fastest runners, all of whom were male. Correspondingly, I recognised that the game plan disadvantaged our female players.

For my *ethical work*, I considered how I could change my coaching to remove this gendered bias. I subsequently implemented two coaching strategies. First, I changed the way I coached throwing. Previously, I had coached throwing as a series of progressions – with shorter throws needing to be perfected before medium, and then long throws were taught. I now have all players practice all types of throws. I encourage every player to develop their throwing to the point where they can throw to as many parts of the field as possible, whereas I suspect that before I inadvertently encouraged some women to restrict their learning of throws to those less than 20 metres. However, I balanced this change of approach with the request that players select throws within their own limitations for tournament play.

Second, I emphasised individual match-ups for both cutting and throwing. I emphasised that what mattered most was whether any given player could beat their defender. This meant that who could run the fastest or throw the furthest on my team was no longer as relevant. For throwing, this required a change in strategy, to emphasise breaking the mark – throwing around or past your marker to the side of the field they are trying to stop you throwing into. Breaking the mark is a throw based on effective pivoting and faking, not power. Thus my *ethical work* consisted of enacting two specific changes in my coaching in the hope of encouraging my team to be less gender-restricted in terms of its playing style.

My *telos* was to coach a mixed Ultimate team according to the *Spirit of the Game*. As a coach I needed to offer all my players a range of playing roles which allowed them access to a game in which 'highly competitive play is encouraged, but [which] should never sacrifice the mutual respect between players, adherence to the agreed-upon rules of the game, or the basic joy of play' (WFDF 2009: 2).

I believe these changes worked to minimise harmful relations of power within my club but I also recognise that my potential to effect significant changes to discourses of gender was constrained. Nevertheless, the Foucauldian framework provided me with a way to think through the ethical challenges posed by gendered roles within mixed Ultimate and to find a solution based on my own locally situated context.

Summary

This completes our overview of the field of sport ethics, its development as a field of study, the complex issues it faces and the prime theories used by sport ethicists. We have suggested that a shift has occurred within sport ethics, away from rule- or duty-based theories, towards a gradual adoption of a postmodern approach. In line with this shift we have endorsed the call made by many prominent scholars (e.g. Denison 2007; Lyle 1999; Potrac and Jones 1999) that coaches could benefit through engagement with recent developments in social theory. In recognising the importance of social theory for examining the complexities of the coaching context and the shift away from modernist ethics, we have advocated the utility of Foucauldian theorising and, more specifically, his framework for managing ethical dilemmas. A Foucauldian approach will not provide universal solutions to ethical sport dilemmas yet it can help coaches work through their specific problems. In this manner, we encourage coaching with Foucault.

References

Arnold, P.J. (1997) *Sport, Ethics and Education*, London: Cassell.

Bernauer, J. (1988) 'Michel Foucault's ecstatic thinking', in J. Bernauer and D. Rasmussen (eds) *The Final Foucault*, Cambridge, MA: The MIT Press.

Boxill, J. (2003) 'The ethics of competition', in J. Boxill (ed.) *Sports Ethics: An Anthology*, Oxford: Blackwell.

Carr, D. (1998) 'What moral educational significance has physical education? A question in need of disambiguation', in M. McNamee and J. Parry (eds) *Ethics and Sport*, London: E. & F.N. Spon.

Cassidy, T., Jones, R. and Potrac, P. (2009) *Understanding Sport Coaching: The Social, Cultural and Pedagogical Foundations of Coaching Practice*, 2nd edn, New York: Routledge.

Chapman, G.E. (1997) 'Making weight: Lightweight rowing, technologies of power, and technologies of the self', *Sociology of Sport Journal*, 14(3): 205–23.

Coakley, J. (2007) *Sports in Society: Issues and Controversies*, 9th edn, New York: McGraw-Hill.

Delattre, E.J. (1988) 'Some reflections on success and failure in competitive athletics', in W.J. Morgan and K.V. Meier (eds) *Philosophic Inquiry in Sport*, Champaign, IL: Human Kinetics.

Denison, J. (2007) 'Social theory for coaches: A Foucauldian reading of one athlete's poor performance', *International Journal of Sports Science and Coaching*, 2(4): 369–83.

Eassom, S. (1998) 'Games, rules, and contracts', in M. McNamee and J. Parry (eds) *Ethics and Sport*, London: E. & F.N. Spon.

Feezell, R. (2004) *Sport, Play, and Ethical Reflection*, Urbana, IL: University of Illinois Press.

Foucault, M. (1987) *The Care of the Self: History of Sexuality, Vol. 3* (trans. R. Hurley), New York: Pantheon (Original work published in 1984).

Foucault, M. (1988a) 'Technologies of the self', in L.H. Martin, H. Gutman and P.H. Hutton (eds) *Technologies of the Self: A Seminar with Michel Foucault*, Amherst, MA: University of Massachusetts Press.

Foucault, M. (1988b) 'The ethic of care for the self as a practice of freedom: An interview with Michel Foucault on January 20, 1984', in J. Bernauer and D. Rasmussen (eds) *The Final Foucault*, Cambridge, MA: The MIT Press.

Foucault, M. (1992) *The Use of Pleasure: History of Sexuality, Vol. 2* (trans. R. Hurley), New York: Pantheon.

Foucault, M. (1997a) 'On the genealogy of ethics: An overview of work in progress', in P. Rabinow (ed.) *Michel Foucault: Ethics, Subjectivity and Truth*, New York: The New Press.

Foucault, M. (1997b) 'Preface to the *History of Sexuality*, Volume Two', in P. Rabinow (ed.) *Michel Foucault: Ethics, Subjectivity and Truth*, New York: The New Press.

Fraleigh, W. (1984) *Right Actions for Athletes: Ethics for Contestants*, Champaign, IL: Human Kinetics.

Fraleigh, W. (1988) 'Why the good foul is not good', in W.J. Morgan and K.V. Meier (eds) *Philosophic Inquiry in Sport*, Champaign, IL: Human Kinetics.

Fraleigh, W. (1997) 'Foreword', in P.J. Arnold (ed.) *Sport, Ethics and Education*, London: Cassell.

Huizinga, J. (1970) *Homo Ludens: A Study of the Play-Element in Culture*, London: Maurice Temple Smith.

Hurka, T. (2007) 'Games and the good', in W.J. Morgan (ed.) *Ethics in Sport*, Champaign, IL: Human Kinetics.

Johns, D.P. and Johns, J.S. (2000) 'Surveillance, subjectivism, and technologies of power: An analysis of the discursive practice of high-performance sport', *International Review for the Sociology of Sport*, 35(2): 219–34.

Jones, C. (2008) 'Teaching virtue through physical education: Some comments and reflections', *Sport, Education and Society*, 13(3): 337–49.

Jones, R. (2006) *The Sports Coach as Educator: Re-conceptualising Sports Coaching*, London: Routledge.

Jones, R., Armour, K. and Potrac, P. (2003) 'Constructing expert knowledge: A case study of a top-level professional soccer coach', *Sport, Education and Society*, 8(2): 213–29.

Jones, R., Armour, K. and Potrac, P. (2004) *Sport Coaching Cultures: From Practice to Theory*, London: Routledge.

Keating, J.W. (2001) 'Sportsmanship as a moral category', in W.J. Morgan, K.V. Meier and A. Schneider (eds) *Ethics in Sport*, Champaign, IL: Human Kinetics.

Kidman, L., Hadfield, D. and Thorpe, R. (2005) *Athlete-Centred Coaching: Developing Inspired and Inspiring people*, Christchurch, NZ: Innovative Print Communications.

Leaman, O. (1988) 'Cheating and fair play in sport', in W.J. Morgan and K.V. Meier (eds) *Philosophic Inquiry in Sport*, Champaign, IL: Human Kinetics.

Lehman, C.K. (1988) 'Can cheaters play the game?', in W.J. Morgan and K.V. Meier (eds) *Philosophic Inquiry in Sport*, Champaign, IL: Human Kinetics.

Lyle, J. (1999) 'Coaching philosophy and coaching behaviour', in N. Cross and J. Lyle (eds) *The Coaching Process: Principles and Practice for Sport*, Oxford: Butterworth-Heinemann.

Lyle, J. (2002) *Sports Coaching Concepts: A Framework for Coaches' Behaviour*, London: Routledge.

Lyotard, J.F. (1984) *The Postmodern Condition: A Report on Knowledge*, Manchester: Manchester University Press (original work published in French in 1979).

MacIntyre, A. (1981) *After Virtue: A Study in Moral Theory*, Notre Dame, IN: Notre Dame Press.

Markula, P. and Pringle, R. (2006) *Foucault, Sport and Exercise: Power, Knowledge and Transforming the Self*, London: Routledge.

McFee, G. (2004) *Sport, Rules, and Values: Philosophical Investigations into the Nature of Sport*, London: Routledge.

McNamee, M. (1998) 'Celebrating trust: Virtues and rules in the ethical conduct of sports coaches', in M. McNamee and J. Parry (eds) *Ethics and Sport*, London: E. & F.N. Spon.

McNamee, M. (2008) *Sports, Virtues and Vices: Morality Plays*, Abingdon/New York: Routledge.

Messner, M.A. (1992) *Power at Play: Sports and the Problem of Masculinity*, Boston, MA: Beacon Press.

Miracle, A. and Rees, R. (1994) *Lessons of the Locker Room: The Myth of School Sport*, Amherst, NY: Prometheus Books.

Morgan, W.J. (2006) *Why Sports Morally Matter*, Abingdon/New York: Routledge.

Morgan, W.J. (2007) 'Ethics, ethical inquiry, and sport: An introduction', in W.J. Morgan (ed.) *Ethics in Sport*, 2nd edn, Champaign, IL: Human Kinetics.

Pearson, K.M. (2003) 'Deception, sportsmansip, and ethics', in J. Boxill (ed.) *Sports Ethics: An Anthology*, Oxford: Blackwell.

Potrac, P. and Jones, R. (1999) 'The invisible ingredient in coaching knowledge: A case for recognising and researching the social component', *Sociology of Sport On Line*, 2(1), online, available at: http://physed.otago.ac.nz/sosol/v2i1/v2i1a5.htm.

Pringle, R. and Hickey, C. (2010) 'Negotiating masculinities via the moral problematisation of sport', *Sociology of Sport Journal*, 27(2): 115–38.

Rabinow, P. (1997) 'Introduction', in P. Rabinow (ed.) *Michel Foucault: Ethics, Subjectivity and Truth*, New York: The New Press.

Richardson, L. (2000) 'Writing: A method of inquiry', in N.K. Denzin and Y.S. Lincoln (eds) *Handbook of Qualitative Research*, 2nd edn, Thousand Oaks, CA: Sage.

Robinson, L. (1998) *Crossing the Line: Violence and Sexual Assault in Canada's National Sport*, Toronto: McClelland and Stewart.

Sheridan, H. (2003) 'Conceptualizing "fair play": A review of the literature, *European Physical Education Review*, 9(2): 163–84.

Shields, D. and Bredemeier, B. (1995) *Character Development in Physical Activity*, Champaign, IL: Human Kinetics.

Shogan, D. (1999) *The Making of High Performance Athletes: Discipline, Diversity, and Ethics*, Toronto: University of Toronto Press.

Shogan, D. (2007) *Sport Ethics in Context*, Toronto: Canadian Scholars' Press.

Shogan, D. and Ford, M. (2000) 'A new sport ethics: Taking Köning seriously', *International Review for the Sociology of Sport*, 35(1): 49–58.

Simon, R.L. (2004) *Fair Play: The Ethics of Sport*, 2nd edn, Boulder, CO: Westview Press.

SPARC (2010) *NZ CoachApproach*, online, available at: www.sportnz.org.nz/Documents/Communities%20and%20Clubs/Coaching/nz-coachapproach-supporting-notes.pdf (accessed 20 October 2010).

Suits, B. (1988) 'The elements of sport', in W.J. Morgan and K.V. Meier (eds) *Philosophic Inquiry in Sport*, Champaign, IL: Human Kinetics.

Thornton, A. (1998) 'Ultimate masculinities: An ethnography of power and social difference in sport', unpublished thesis, University of Toronto.

WFDF (2009) *Rules of Ultimate*, online, available at: www.ukultimate.com/system/files/WFDF%20Rules%20of%20Ultimate%202009.pdf (accessed 13 September 2010).

3

COACHING AND PROFESSIONALISATION

William G. Taylor

MANCHESTER METROPOLITAN UNIVERSITY, UK

Dean Garratt

UNIVERSITY OF CHESTER, UK

Introduction

This chapter is concerned with the professionalisation of sports coaching. It seeks to meet three main objectives: (1) locating professionalisation as it relates to sports coaching and the sports coach in a historical and policy context; (2) reviewing existing and emerging research contributions that consider wider notions of professionalism, professionalisation and the professions; and (3) proposing a number of explicit research areas and questions which remain as yet unanswered, but are inherent in the continuing professionalisation of sports coaching and the coach. In conclusion, we argue that this process is neither benign nor innocent, and, as it gathers pace, will recast both those who acquire professional status into 'new agents of sport' as well as those who have been educated procedurally and thus bound by regulation and governance. In doing so, we suggest it may realign the existing volunteer leaving them uncertain, marginalised and vulnerable to the increasing influence of state-defined policy.

The professionalisation of coaching in a historical and policy context

Like many academic considerations of coaching, the history of the activity has, until recently, been given scant regard (Day 2010; Phillips 2000). One exception to this lack of attention has been the special issue of the journal *Sport in History* (2010), which devoted its entire contents to the history of coaching cultures.

In the United Kingdom (UK), it was the emergence of the professional athlete in sports such as pedestrianism, pugilism and swimming which, in turn, helped establish and legitimise a systematic form of coaching engagement (Day 2010). Those individuals who were involved in the deliberate training and instruction of others went under a variety of names; the term 'professor' was commonly adopted by those who had once competed as a professional and now trained others for competition. The transfer of this coaching knowledge was often kept as part of an oral tradition within the family or passed onto athletes in the immediate geographical location, who in turn themselves became professors. One aspect that is evident from the limited amount of research conducted in the area is that there was a growing sense of craft knowledge about these athlete/coach engagements in which there was little separation between 'the knowledge of' and 'the ability to do' coaching. Cataloguing of the methods, tactics, practices and philosophies employed were kept to a minimum, were isolated and received limited public scrutiny. This culture of knowledge is often referred to as tacit knowledge, where 'we can know more than we can tell' (Polanyi 2009: x).

It was with the emergence of the middle classes in the late nineteenth century that the regulation and codification of sporting activities and, by implication, modern coaching, began. Born from the public school system from which the new breed of sports administrators came, the philosophy of the virtuous amateur saw the slow demise of the professional coach. This change in occupational make-up was not uniform across all sports and, as Foucault (1972) argues, while individuals may be subject to a shared history, it is their relationships to the structures of power and subordination which determine their trajectories from any epoch or historical moment.

The status of coaching as an occupation has recently been the focus for a number of inquiries in different countries (e.g. UK: Lyle 2002; Taylor and Garratt 2007, 2008, 2010a, 2010b; Canada: CAC 2010; China: Li *et al.* 2007; He *et al.* 2009), reflecting the significant global growth in the vocation of coaching. Recently, the International Council for Coach Education (ICCE) has also considered this issue (Duffy *et al.* 2010), while national lead organisations have begun to consider how the term 'profession' relates to their coaching systems and coaches (Sports Coach UK 2008; South African Sport Confederation and Olympic Committee 2010).

Up until the late 1960s and early 1970s, within the UK successive governments had what can be described as a 'distance approach' to sport, its National Governing Bodies (NGBs) and the coaching practices found therein (Houlihan 1997; Roche 1993). Individual NGBs and their coaches were seen as the 'experts in the field', and their autonomy and sovereignty was recognised and valued by both sides (Green and Houlihan 2005). The 1970s saw a number of government reports and policy documents which began to draw tighter links between sport and the state (e.g. Cobham Report 1973). Few of these documents made any explicit reference to the occupation of coaching; however, they had aspirations to alter the relationship between sport and government at a fundamental level. This structured an agenda to employ sport (and by implication its coaches) as a social and welfare tool thereby bringing it to the attention of a wider body of policy makers concerned with the welfare state (Brown and Butterfield 1992; Roche 1993). The following decade thus saw a more explicit focus on coaching. The Great Britain Sports Council strategy, *Sport in the Community: The Next Ten Years* (Sports Council 1982), provided grants to NGBs for elite coaching and its development. Both *Coaching, Sports Science and Sports Medicine* (Sports Council for Wales 1987) and *A National Strategy for Coach Education and Coach Development* (Scottish Sports Council 1988) followed suit and produced their own documents with the intention of enabling coaching to develop. *Coaching Matters: A Review of Coaching and Coach Education* (Sports Council 1991) and later, the UK Sports Council's *The Development of Coaching in the United Kingdom: A Consultative Document* (1991) formalised this call for a more integrated approach and focused direction. In *Coaching Matters: A Review of Coaching and Coach Education* it was suggested that:

> the dogged manner in which a number of our governing bodies have hung onto outdated attitudes, some of which have their roots in the 19th century amateurism [and that] governing body administrators and the national coaches appear to work in parallel universes ... lip-service was paid to early coach education programmes.
>
> *(Sports Council 1991:14)*

The criticisms gained little affection or tolerance within the realm of NGBs whose collective representative in the shape of the Central Council for Physical Recreation (CCPR) maintained the position of defence:

> the increasing influence that Government manifestly sought to exert on sport and sport's governing bodies at local, regional, and international levels, for reasons which are sometimes unclear, necessitated constant vigilance if sport was to retain the uniquely British tradition of independent management.
>
> *(Sports Council 1991:10)*

More recently, there has been a proliferation of debate concerning the professionalisation of coaching and the establishment of a framework for a coaching profession (DCMS 2002; Sports Council 1991; Sports Coach UK 2009; UK Sport 2001). For example, in their *UK Vision for Coaching*, UK Sport (2001: 5) strongly recommended that the standards of coaching be elevated to those of 'a profession acknowledged as central to the development of sport and the fulfilment of individual potential'. Following the publication of the *Government's Plan for Sport* (DCMS 2001), came the establishment of a Coaching Task Force set up to review the role of coaching and to tackle:

> the shortage of coaches, both professional and voluntary, and recognise coaching as a profession, with accredited qualifications and a real career development structure.
>
> *(DCMS 2001:5)*

This ambition was developed in response to earlier concerns regarding the lack of standards for coaching and strategies for training and employment, which have tended to evolve informally in concert with the many and diverse traditions of sports coaching UK-wide (Sports Council 1991). The catalogue of public policy and state documentation relating to the professionalisation of coaching offers us a useful barometer of the shifting discourses and their associated language. It would be simply too crude to suggest that there has been a 'single moment' where government became interested in sport and, by implication, its coaches and the activity of coaching. However, from the Wolfenden Report: Sport and the Community of 1960 (CCPR 1960) to the *UK Coaching Framework* of 2008 (Sports Coach UK 2008), there has been a perceptive, yet fractured and discontinuous call for the organisation and regulation of coaches, coaching systems and coach education (Houlihan and Green 2009). Few, however, have gone as far as offering details on the actual workings of the professionalisation process. This was so until the publication of the *UK Coaching Framework*. This framework fleshed out the details of the commitment to professionalise the act of sports coaching and also provided a six point strategic action plan.

Research contributions that consider notions of professionalism, professionalisation and the professions

For a number of authors (e.g. Freidson 2001; Lawson 2004), professionalisation and the professions were seen in a positive light. They suggested that this 'third logic of modernity' (Freidson 2001) protected both the public and acted as a buffer to the prevalence of over-zealous state intervention. It was also argued that it provided a legitimate occupational outlet for those individuals who with education, service ideals and particular skills wished to establish themselves in a professional setting that offered status and reward. Overall, while these treatments have been beneficial in as much as they outlined the characteristics of existing professions, established the key elements of a distinct knowledge base, and prolonged engagement with education and membership of a professional body, they have failed to treat the professionalisation process in a more critical manner. This critical dialogue with the discourses of professionalism is significant and necessary as the emergence of new professions becomes a key feature of modernity and its concomitant occupational developments (McEwan and Taylor 2010).

In the latter half of the twentieth century, the archetypal professional groups came under increasing scrutiny and attack from a number of sources. Governments of Western Europe, North America and Australasia began to treat the professions with a degree of suspicion, aligned with a political shift to a regime of neo-liberal policy making and market economics. These professional groups (a) were seen as representing protected market advantage through membership status and restricted education; and (b) their influence in the public sector (health, education and social services) was seen as a hurdle in the re-evaluation of government funding for these sectors and related manner of their working practices. In concert with this, the public's trust in the professions began to wane. A number of high profile scandals ranging from the treatment of Rodney King in the United States (policing), the inappropriate behaviour of medical staff (Alder Hey Hospital in the UK) and the reluctance of the Catholic Church to take responsibility for the actions of some of their clergy (allegations of child abuse), all added to a breakdown in the social contract, cited at the heart of traditional practice and professionalism. Various governments took this as an opportunity to argue for re-regulation of existing professionals and their organisations. For those emerging groups who were seeking professionalisation, government subjected them to a series of managerially inspired conditions, which had their roots in the mechanisms of the audit culture and a raft of procedural constraints (McEwan and Taylor 2010).

Freidson (1973) suggests that the professionalisation pathway of any occupation is neither linear nor uniform. Nor is it without problems, for each occupation has its own nuanced history and educational culture, which serve to establish new professional relationships and boundaries. While we might draw some parallels with other groups and emerging occupations, when considering sports coaching we must be mindful of the historical and situational nuances of sport and its coaching activity. Indeed, one of the central criticisms we offer against the state's notion of professionalism as manifested in discourses articulated by the state and its central sports bodies (in the UK), is that it is totalising in effect. That is, it offers, and presumes to deal with, all sports and all coaches in a unified and somewhat prescriptive manner (Taylor and Garratt 2010a, 2010b). In doing so, it has mirrored, as best it can, the experiences of other 'new' professional occupations. This conceptual massification, while offering simplified solutions to a perceived common problem, has few sympathies with the fragmented nature and individual cultural histories that have moulded both the belief and culture of sport and practice of coaching.

Adopting a rationalistic and functionalist perspective, much of the literature has tried, with varying degrees of success, to benchmark where coaching as an occupation was within the professionalisation process, and has made further suggestions to enable the coaching community to move forward. Yet, at no time was any critical, conceptual understanding shown of the cultural, historical and situational complexities engendered within the individual sports systems of different countries (Houlihan and Green 2008). Nor was any level of awareness demonstrated towards the individual and unique position of coaches in terms of their professional development. This dual preoccupation with 'policy borrowing' (where policy is imported from other countries on the assumption of a natural cultural 'fit')

(Phillips and Ochs 2003) and benchmarking (particular grades of coaching in a predetermined march towards professional status), disregarded both the complexity and nuanced nature of NGBs, and the culturally rich heritage of British coaching as a whole. Ironically, in fact, these assumptions served to divert attention away from a form of organic development that would have allowed coaches and their sports the opportunity to move beyond limiting structures of volunteerism. In doing so, they could have moved towards something of an emerging profession, one that was mindful of its own history and location(s), yet which intended to bring the ambitions of practising coaches to the forefront in its own efforts to fashion professional definitions, understandings and occupational boundaries.

Lyle (2002) considers the professionalisation process in his book *Sports Coaching Concepts: A Framework for Coaches' Behaviour*. He suggests that achieved status for coaches could be gained by the acquisition of certified qualifications and its position could be enhanced by the 'increasing scientification of practice and the value placed on sport itself' (Lyle 2002: 200). Within this, he alludes to the lack of theoretical analysis of sports coaching and the inclusion of the professional status of coaching by suggesting much of the critical commentary and empirical research has been 'issues focused'. Other authors, namely Nichols (2003, 2005, 2006; Nichols *et al.* 2004; Nichols *et al.* 2005) (working within a British and European context), have addressed the changing perspective of the role of NGBs under the guise of state-inspired moderation policies. These bodies have been central players in the development of new structures to support the education and promotion of coaches and coaching in the UK. Thus, to discuss the professionalisation of sports coaching and its individual practice without paying due attention to these organisations is, in fact, failing to give appropriate consideration to their importance in the future development of the professionalisation movement.

Gaps in the market

There is a notable scarcity of research and writings explicitly dealing with the professionalisation of sports coaching. In fact, rather than referring to gaps in the research literature, it might be more accurate to identify the limited nature of documented offerings to date. The available research has dealt with the professionalisation of sports coaching in a conceptual manner, placing the act as a political one that is best studied as an expression of the state's extension of neo-liberal managerialism into occupations that had once been the preserve of the volunteer sector (Taylor and Garratt 2008, 2010a, 2010b). While we would like to argue this work had some merit in as much as it located the subject as one of concern, there is much that we do not understand and is necessary if we are to move the debate forward. Lyle (2002) and Lyle and Cushion (2010) have argued that achieving understanding and clarity about what the nature of coaching actually is can only be achieved when a clear demarcation exists between the acts of the sports leader (basic introductory role), the sports coach instructor (mainly developing skills), and the sports coach (working within competition focus). This boundary clarification process, if achieved, would certainly aid research into professionalisation, for then we can consider particular groups and stages of the process without the shortcomings of treating all activity and engagement relating to sports coaching as being one and the same. In treating sport and its organisational bodies as a single collective entity and presenting its struggles with the amateur/professional, volunteer/full-timer binaries as the sole foci of epistemological concern, we risk underplaying nuances, the various and subtle shifts in individual sport locations, spaces and emplotments. In addition, there are a number of contested and contradictory movements within coaching and sports administration that require further expression. One historical characteristic of a 'professional' is that they are often asked to make decisions that are located within a framework of implied autonomy. The trust between coach and athlete that allows coaches to act on their behalf, can only work if central to coach education is the concept of self-governance. This is where decision making operates within a context of ethical engagement, and where there is appropriate resistance of central regulation that serves to inhibit professionalism through various prescribed forms of behaviour.

Professionalisation, professionalism and professional practice are not end points; their definitions and characteristics are under continuous tension while responding to levels of expectation from government, other professions and changes in public and sporting demand (Taylor and Garratt 2008, 2010a, 2010b). The developing profession of sports coaching will have to respond to athletes, participants, employers, international structures and shifting market demands. The catalogue of public policy and state documentation relating to the professionalisation of coaching have matured in status from general statements of intent to timetables of practice and policy implementation. The increasing centrality and governance articulated in such recent formal documents is both an example of, and central to the notion of new managerialism and the development of the new professions as envisaged by the politics of neo-liberalism.

A research agenda for professionalisation and the sports coach

In this section, we would like tentatively to set a proposed agenda for those who wish to conduct research in and around the professionalisation of sports coaching. In doing so we foreground four research topics. These are ones which we believe are worthy of detailed consideration and are also areas where little or no research has been conducted. We do not present these as an exhaustive list, but more a representation of the questions we have asked ourselves in the process of our own work born from our enquiries and critical perspectives. We would also contend that not only do these topics have academic value, but they should also be a central concern to the wider sports' coaching community; those sporting bodies whose remit is the development of coaching policy; and those individuals who are charged with the development of coach education syllabi and research programmes.

The perspective of the traditional volunteer and the professionalisation

There is little doubt that a version of professionalisation, one that represents the aspirations of coaches themselves, could bring forth many advantages for a range of individuals and groups. This requires a model that has at its core the strong sense of community that many sports organisations, clubs and coaches espouse. Indeed, it is this sense of service and duty, similar in nature and ethos to that found in existing established professions that must be built upon. This is crucial if, in time, coaching is to re-evaluate itself as having the same status as other professional groups found elsewhere in the service and commercial sectors. There are few, if any, professions that have seen this degree of transformation, especially given the distinct historical influences of sports coaching's volunteer and 'mutual aid' foundations. Although there may have been some calls from within coaching communities for coaching to develop its own professional practices and to raise its own status, it has never been politically or occupationally strong enough to enact such change. With a state-imposed professionalisation agenda, any mechanisms of change must take account of the fragmented nature of coaching in the UK and thus be sympathetic to the insecurities this transformation is likely to engender.

Once at the heart of sports coaching, the traditional volunteer is now perceived to be recast, debarred and excluded from the very activity that previously defined their existence. Thus, not only has there been a change in the relationship between what is and what is not valued, but the multiple and diverse relationships that once served to support coaching emplotments are now also subject to radical redefinition. At one time, the key relationship of the sports coach was defined in conjunction with the athlete(s) and clubs; at the level of community volunteer, it was the athlete and sports community who operated as the main arbiters of value and currency. Clearly, in some cases, these important relationships will continue to define practice and success within contexts of performance and engagement. The present movements towards certification and qualifications, we argue, have fundamentally changed the relationship between coach and athlete, and coach and club. Once the arbiters of local currency, this role has now been adopted by the state through their requirements to gain certification in a culture of performativity and credentialism. What remains is to ask what model of professionalism do the majority of coaches aspire to? Can we really talk of a professionalisation of practice while it remains fundamentally voluntary in nature? Is there room for professionalism without a coaching profession? Is the professionalisation of the volunteers' practice enough to satisfy these calls? If a university degree education is seen as a prerequisite before claiming the status of professional coach, where does that leave the willing parent and/or ex-player?

The commodification of knowledge

We now offer our perspective on the commodification of experience, knowledge and practice. One central facet of the growth of a new managerialism approach to the professionalisation of coaching is the manner in which it has altered the way knowledge is valued through the commodification of experience. This notion of professionalisation is concurrently aligned with the importance awarded to gaining new knowledge(s) and undertaking ongoing professional development. The premise is that modern professionals should be informed, accountable for their own knowledge base, and regulated in their achievement. Experience is often required to be documented, detailed, recorded and offered externally for comment, examination and evaluation. Applying a Foucauldian lens to the issue (Foucault 1994), it can be seen as a mechanism of the 'conduct of one's conduct', where the virtuous self, the newly professionalised coach, judges the value of practice by reference to the ascription of internalized criteria rather than by their own authentic value systems. The subject is now held accountable for their own currency, the responsibility for experience and documentation is theirs alone, but the value given to that experience is not. The self-disciplined coach self-regulates their own ongoing training through the appeasement of prescribed formulae answering to the calls to be current and up to date. Foucault (1991) goes on to state:

> The power of normalisation imposes homogeneity; but it is individualized by making it possible to measure gaps, to determine levels, to fix specialities and to render the difference useful by fitting them against one another ... the norm introduces, as a useful imperative and as a result of measurement, all the shading of individual differences.
>
> *(Foucault 1991:184)*

Therefore, the normalisation of knowledge becomes a disciplining act in itself, with some individuals requiring more discipline than others (Foucault 1982, 1991). Those coaches who are no longer current, who have yet to convert from old systems (pre-professionalised) to the new (professionalised), and those who need to update in order to maintain their 'right' to practice, are systematically identified by degrees of compliance.

Not only has the act of acquiring of knowledge become subject to standardisation, but so has knowledge itself. Knowledge is now valued by its instrumental efficiency, for its usefulness and utility. Experience is to be consumed as an isolated, siloed exercise, as a weekend or two-day module where knowledge and practice is sanitised, episodically packaged and sold as a regime of corrective technical training (see Jones *et al.* 2004 for an interesting account of elite rugby coach Ian McGeechan). Rarely is the training located in the sporting space of the individual's practice, where contextualisation is more readily available and local conditions mediate the learning. Evidence from education research strongly indicates that this type of de-contextualised Continuing Professional Development (CPD) often fails to render long-term improvements in practice (Askew *et al.* 1997; Bennett *et al.* 2010; Cordingley *et al.* 2003).

This form of orthodoxy, where experience is automatically conflated with knowledge acquisition, removes the role of subjective learning and reflection from the individual and, in turn, embeds the process, albeit falsely, within the content of the programme itself. The syllabus is often aligned directly to so-called practice competences, ones that can be copied, repeated, measured and recorded. The conclusion of this bringing together of experience with the consumption of knowledge as a purely instrumental endeavour, devalues reflective consideration and nullifies the potency for experience to be part of a developmental and practice-based notion of learning. Reflection on, with, and for learning is no longer required as the learning objectives of these blocks of experience are clearly stated and benchmarked against external criteria. This criticism is not to relegate the notion of further coach education and training to be valueless, but rather to argue that the removal of the individual's power to determine their own educational needs resonates with the move toward a technocratic model of knowledge consumption, its application and usage. Where knowledge acquisition, development and application becomes an instrumental experience, the emergence of counter and novel ways of practice become problematic, if not actively discouraged by the agents of legitimisation. Organic practice that is born from habitus (Bourdieu 1990), inspired experience is relegated and forgotten because it is seen as local, restricted, individualised and pertinent only to particular sporting spaces and demands.

What remains is to ask what model of professional education can be utilised in order to allow a more holistic notion of knowledge-based practice? How can professional currency be valued and ascertained through a value placed on organic delivery and practice? To what degree will coaches be allowed to value and consider their own non-mediated learning opportunities? And can these sit alongside more formulaic notions of professional education?

Working outside of convention

The identification and regulation of a knowledge base has commonly been cited as a precursor to the legitimisation of any group gaining professional status. Unfortunately, by definition, this movement to claim ownership to the educational processes by which knowledge is acquired and defined will include and exclude certain ways of knowing and exhibiting knowledge. We would argue that this process is both a political act inasmuch as vested interests and discourses will be served, and sets to define not just what is valued, but also who is valued. Any coach who is seen as a practitioner of 'alternative delivery' could be viewed as nonconformist and cast aside as 'non-professional', lying outside agreed convention.

The maverick, often valued and accommodated in the past for bringing forth novel and radical practices of coaching, is effectively ostracised, remaining non-valued in both an ideological and certificated sense. Advancements in coaching and sporting practices have often been found outside the conventions of so-called perceived wisdom. Those whose education, influences and environments sit apart from the constraining forces of institutional and institutionalised processes may, in fact, be in the best place to find alternative and novel ways of delivery and thinking about the practices of coaching. Without access to the various avenues of legitimation by which such novel thinkers can gain an audience and tolerance for their 'heresy', are we in danger of strangling innovation through the sanitisation of the process of recognising, reproducing and certificating those who are deemed professional? If, in the scramble to ring-fence what is and is not professional knowledge, do we exclude novel, contradictory and counter-hegemonic thoughts and prevent such notions from contesting the status quo? Moreover, do we risk the chance of stagnating the knowledge base, as vested interests serve to protect and preserve existing bodies of thought?

What we wish to consider is where does tacit, innovative or marginalised knowledge feature in the new model of the professionalised coach? For tacit knowledge, where 'we know more of than we can speak', is embedded in the craft-based histories and non-mediated learning that characterise much coaching practice. If, by the nature of it being only exhibited within practice, where does tacit knowledge fit in the professionalisation process? Its resistance to be regulated and measured casts it outside the domain of traditional knowledge accumulation, a procedure espoused by many professions (Nettleton *et al.* 2008). For some, being the 'knowledgeable other', the knowing professional, requires a display of knowledge that is underpinned by evidence-based practice, research and higher forms of training. Without the ability to support and justify practice, to create opportunities for tacit knowledge to be made more genetically explicit, is the tacit dimension then to be cast aside and demoted? If this form of knowledge and 'knowing' can be displayed and witnessed only by the actions of the coach, then it may be lost to more traditional forms of professional education as it is based on instinctive practice and not necessarily cognitive understanding. This model of a coach who is encouraged to see knowledge as something to be displayed, observed and recorded, and not something intuitively personalised, organic and directly related to the individual's sporting disposition, devalues much of the craft-based knowledge which historically coaches have possessed. By building up the professional status of those who seek to privilege particular forms of propositional knowledge, behaviour and practice, will we retard the organic development of difference, diversity and individuality?

The new professional landscape

Sport and, by implication, the majority of coaches are required to be part of the health and welfare intervention movement. These new roles, implicit in wider health discourses, have yet to be articulated in the fields and domains of coaching where they remain unspoken, but nevertheless powerful in as much as they fashion the future. This multiplicity of roles and identities widens the remit of coaching but, at the same time, brings additional issues of confusion and tension, with critics suggesting that coaches of the new profession have been reduced to mere technicians through a loss of autonomy and increasing accountability (Hursh 2005).

Alongside notions of elite performance, sports coaching can also be regarded as a vehicle through which issues of community involvement and corporate social responsibility may be addressed (Harris 1998; Jarvie 2003). The role of 'sports leaders' and coaches have, thus, been conflated to involve developing the quality of guidance on habitual 'life health practices' and physical activity levels (Lawlor *et al.* 1999; Parsons *et al.* 1999). Rhetorically at least, the new 'professional coach' can be seen to encapsulate both an 'official identity' (an embodiment of the new professional orthodoxy through the implementation of a UK-wide system of certification) and a moral identity, in which core moral purposes are combined with objectives towards widening participation, ambitions to promote social inclusion and the development of social capital. This redefinition of the coach as an agent of the welfare state brings an accompanying demand for coaching to enter into new fields and professional relationships. Not only is there pressure to redefine existing modes of practice, but also an identified need to develop new alliances with other professional groups, whose imposed inclusion may or may not be welcomed as part of a wider social agenda.

Introductions of multi-professional and trans-professional ways of working have led to the formation of new identities that force the acquisition of new forms of professional knowledge. Potentially, these bring positive and negative outcomes (Headrick *et al.* 1998; Kvarnström 2008). On the one hand, new practices may serve to secure the activity of sports coaching within the supportive frame of the welfare state, whereas on the other, coaches are ostensibly subjected to a new and onerous regime of challenging responsibilities; that is, a regime that complicates existing practices while simultaneously conflating professional roles and identities.

Accordingly, the contemporary coach needs to be 'professional' in terms of the acquisition of new forms of knowledge and training, 'capable' in terms of forging new professional networks and relationships, and morally 'compliant' with the imperative towards community responsibility bestowed by the state. These novel vistas and newly conceived roles for coaches demand new relationships, new forms of accountability and, consequently, new credentialised coaches. The danger is that the newly cast coach will remain unprepared and uneducated for the emerging and implicit roles that will be asked of him/her, in two important senses. In one sense, tentative in terms of habitus and how new fields are likely to emerge. In another, in terms of where and how ontological security can be found within newly imposed identities, identities that are likely to remain in a state of flux for some time to come. For some, these changes will represent new opportunities and an ability to earn a living from their coaching. They have been welcomed by those who feel that the emergence of the market and economic capital will cast forth new relationships within coaching that will benefit their own practice and personal security. In addition, the growth of the market within coaching will allow the participant to select opportunities on price and value (where knowledge exists) and to withdraw patronage where practice remains unsatisfactory. While coaching craft knowledge will continue to find relevant expression within the confines of the coach-athlete relationship, its extant value (capital) is likely to become a form of devalued symbolic capital, as newly defined forms of economic and cultural capital come to the fore and coaching becomes increasingly institutionalised in the name of 'professionalisation'.

Conclusion and ways forward

The process of the professionalisation of coaching and the coach is not innocent. We have argued that the promoted model of professionalism and the professionalising process has, at its core, a new managerial commitment; one that echoes with the primacy of market economics, certification and individual accountability. This is a model where traditional notions of professional autonomy have been replaced by systems, collective 'best practice' and compliance, and which resonates with the audit culture and its various manifestations and proposed solutions (Beck and Young 2005). Whether this movement serves both the aspirations of the state as well the desire of sporting communities is yet to be decided. Our intention in this chapter has been to move 'beyond the taken for granted' treatment which has been previously applied to questions of professionalisation, and offer a more thoughtful and problematic consideration of a movement that will fundamentally shape the nature of the act of coaching and practice of the coach for years to come.

These research questions will necessitate methodologies and sympathetic approaches that have at their heart an ability to understand more discernibly the nature of the volunteer and professional sports coach, the particular nuances of practice, and shifting demands from athletes, participants, employers and deployers within the field. If these approaches are adopted it is likely that ethnographic and interactionist methodologies would provide the most effective manner by which to examine the feelings, needs and wishes of these groups. Just as one of the many shortcomings of the models of professionalism is the treatment of coaching as a homogenous practice, we would similarly suggest that research approaches need to be sympathetic and germane to context. Not all sports have the same occupational make-up, history of professional coaches or level of engagement with the market place. Provision and expectation varies between each country, and indeed within countries. Research approaches need to be judged not only on their ability to seek answers to key questions, but also to be mindful of difference and diversity in provision across multiple sporting boundaries.

References

Askew, M., Brown, M., Rhodes, V., William, D. and Johnson, D. (1997) 'Effective teachers of numeracy: Report of a study carried out for the Teacher Training Agency (TTA)', London: King's College.

Beck, J. and Young, M.F.D. (2005) 'The assault on the professions and the restructuring of academic and professional identities: A Bernsteinian analysis', *British Journal of Sociology of Education*, 26(2): 183–197.

Bennett, J., Braund, M. and Lubben, F. (2010) 'The impact of targeted Continuing Professional Development (CPD) on teachers' professional practice in science', National Science Learning Centre, York: University of York.

Bourdieu, P. (1990) *The Logic of Practice*, Cambridge: Polity Press.

Brown, B. and Butterfield, S.A. (1992) 'Coaches: A missing link in the health care system', *American Journal of Diseases of Children*, 146(2): 211–217.

CAC (Coaching Association of Canada) (2010) 'Coaching Association of Canada 2010–2014 Strategic Plan', online, available at www.coach.ca/who-we-are-s13411 (accessed 31 October 2011).

CCPR (1960) *Sport and the Community: The Report of the Wolfenden Committee on* Sport, London: CCPR.

Cobham Report (1973) *Second Report of the Select Committee of the House of Lords on Sport and Leisure*, London: HMSO Publications.

Cordingley, P., Bell, M. and Rundell, B. (2003) 'How does CPD affect teaching and learning? Issues in systematic reviewing from a practitioner perspective', paper presented at the Annual British Educational Research Association (BERA) conference, 4–6 September, Edinburgh, UK.

Day, D. (2010) 'London swimming professors: Victorian craftsmen and aquatic entrepreneurs', *Sport in History*, 30(1): 32–54.

DCMS (Department for Culture, Media and Sport) (2001) *A Sporting Future for All: The Government's Plan for Sport: Annual Report*, London: DCMS.

DCMS (Department for Culture, Media and Sport) (2002) 'The Coaching Task Force: Final Report', online, available at: www.apexslm.com/wp-content/upLoads/2011/07/coaching_report.pdf (accessed 18 May 2006).

Duffy, P., Hartley, H., Bales, J. and Crespo, M. (2010) 'The development of sport coaching as a profession: Challenges and future directions in a global context', keynote lecture presented at the Canadian Sport Leadership conference, 18–21 November, Ottawa, Canada.

Foucault, M. (1972) *The Archaeology of Knowledge and Discourse on Language*, New York: Pantheon Books.

Foucault, M. (1982) 'How is power exercised?', in H.L. Dreyfus and P. Rabinow (eds) *Michel Foucault: Beyond Structuralism and Hermeneutics*, Brighton: Harvester Press.

Foucault, M. (1991) *Discipline and Punishment: The Birth of the Prison*, London: Penguin Books.

Foucault, M. (1994) 'Structuralism and poststructuralism', in J.D. Faubion (ed.) *Michel Foucault Aesthetics, Method, and Epistemology: Essential Works of Foucault 1954–1984*, New York: Penguin Books.

Freidson, E. (1973) 'Professionalism and the occupational principle', in E. Freidson, (ed.) *The Professions and their Prospects*, Beverly Hills, CA: Sage.

Freidson, E. (2001) *Professionalism: The Third Logic*, Cambridge: Polity Press

Green, M. and Houlihan, B. (2005) *Elite Sport Development: Policy Learning and Political Priorities*, London: Routledge.

Harris, J. (1998) 'Civil society, physical activity and the involvement of sports sociologists in the preparation of physical activity professionals', *Sociology of Sport*, 15(2): 138–153.

He, Z-L., Dong, Z-M. and Gong, B. (2009) 'Status quo and developmental strategy of competitive sport in China's institutions of higher learning under new situation', *Journal of Shanghai Physical Education Institute/Shanghai*, 33(5): 73–76.

Headrick, L.A., Wilcock, P.M. and Batalden, P.B. (1998) 'Interprofessional working and continuing medical education', *British Medical Journal*, 316: 771–774.

Houlihan, B. (1997) *Sport, Policy and Politics: A Comparative Analysis*, London: Routledge.

Houlihan, B. and Green, M. (2008) *Comparative Elite Sports Development: System, Structures and Public Policy*, Oxford: Butterworth- Heinemann.

Houlihan, B. and Green, M. (2009) *Modernization and Sport: The Reform of Sport England and UK Sport*, Loughborough: PSA.

Hursh, D. (2005) 'The growth of high-stakes testing in the USA: Accountability, markets and the decline in education equality', *British Education Research Journal*, 31(5): 605–622.

Jarvie, G. (2003) 'Communitarianism, sport and social capital: Neighbourly insights into Scottish Sport', *International Review for the Sociology of Sport*, 38(2): 139–153.

Jones, R.L., Armour, K.M. and Potrac, P. (2004) *Sports Coaching Cultures: From Theory to Practice*, London: Routledge.

Kvarnström, S. (2008) 'Difficulties in collaboration: A critical incident study of interprofessional healthcare teamwork', *Journal of Interprofessional Care*, 22(2): 191–203.

Lawlor, A., Keen, A. and Neal, R.D. (1999) 'Increasing population levels of physical activity through primary care: GPs' knowledge, attitudes and self-reported practice', *Family Practice*, 16(3): 250–254.

Lawson, W. (2004) 'Professionalism: The golden years', *Journal of Professional Issues in Engineering Education and Practice*, 130(1): 26–36.

Li, R.-X., Si, H.-K. and He, L.-L. (2007) 'Occupational professionalization of sports coaches', *Chinese Journal of Physical Education*, 14(8): 121–124.

Lyle, J. (2002) *Sport Coaching Concepts: A Framework for Coaches' Behaviour*, London: Routledge.

Lyle, J. and Cushion, C.J. (2010) *Sports Coaching: Professionalism and Practice*, London: Elsevier.

McEwan, I.M. and Taylor, W.G. (2010) 'When do I get to run on with the magic sponge? The twin illusions of meritocracy and democracy in the professions of sports medicine and physiotherapy', *Qualitative Research in Sport and Exercise*, 2(1): 77–91.

Nettleton, S., Burrows, R. and Whatt, I. (2008) 'Regulation medical bodies? The consequences of the "modernisation" and disembodiment of medical knowledge', *Sociology of Health and Illness*, 30(3): 333–348.

Nichols, G. (2003) 'The tension between professionals and volunteers in English national governing bodies of sport', paper presented at the 6th Australian and New Zealand Association for Leisure Studies Conference, 16–19 May, Sydney, Australia.

Nichols, G. (2005) 'Stalwarts in sport', *World Leisure Journal*, 47(2): 31–37.

Nichols, G. (2006) 'Research into sports volunteers: Reviewing the questions', *Voluntary Action*, 8(1): 55–65.

Nichols, G., Taylor, P., James, M., Garrett, R., Holmes, K., King, L., Gratton, C. and Kokolakakis, T. (2004) 'Voluntary activity in UK sport', *Voluntary Action*, 6(2): 31–54.

Nichols, G., Taylor, P., James, M., Holmes, K., King, L. and Garret, R. (2005) 'Pressures on the UK Voluntary Sport Sector', *International Journal of Voluntary and Nonprofit Organizations*, 16(1): 33–50.

Parsons, T.J., Power, C., Logan, S. and Summerbell, C.D. (1999) 'Childhood predictors of adult obesity: A systematic review', *International Journal of Obesity Related Metabolic Disorders*, 23(8): 1–10.

Phillips, M.G. (2000) *From Sidelines to Centre Field: A History of Sports Coaching in Australia*, Sydney: UNSW Press.

Phillips, D. and Ochs, K. (2003) 'Processes of policy borrowing in education: Some explanatory and analytical devices', *Comparative Education*, 39(4): 451–461.

Polanyi, M. (2009) *The Tacit Dimension*, Chicago, IL: The University of Chicago Press.

Roche, M. (1993) 'Sport and community: Rhetoric and reality in the development of British Sports Policy', in J.C. Binfield and J. Stevenson (eds) *Sports, Culture and Politics*, Sheffield: Sheffield Academic Press.

Scottish Sports Council (1988) *A National Strategy for Coach Education and Coach Development*, Edinburgh: Scottish Sports Council.

South African Sport Confederation and Olympic Committee (2010) *South African Coaching Framework Consultant Document: Building Pathways and Transformation through Sport Coaching in South Africa October 2010*, online, available at http://hp.sascoc.co.za/the-south-african-coaching-framework (accessed 31 October 2011).

Sport in History (2010) Special Issue: Coaching Cultures, *Sport in History*, 30(1), 1–187.

Sports Coach UK (2008) *The UK Coaching Framework*, Leeds: Sports Coach UK.

Sports Coach UK (2009) *The UK Coaching Framework: The Coaching Workforce 2009–2016*, Leeds: Sports Coach UK.

Sports Council (1982) *Sport in the Community: The Next Ten Years*, London: Sports Council.

Sports Council (1991) *Coaching Matters: A Review of Coaching and Coach Education in the United Kingdom*, London: Sports Council.

Sports Council for Wales (1987) *Coaching, Sports Science and Sports Medicine*, Cardiff: Sports Council for Wales.

Taylor, W.G. and Garratt, D. (2007) 'Notions of professionalism: Conversations with coaches', paper presented at the Leisure Studies Association Conference, 3–4 July, University of Brighton, Eastbourne.

Taylor, W.G. and Garratt, D. (2008) *The Professionalisation of Sports Coaching in the UK: Issues and Conceptualisation*, Leeds: Sport Coach UK.

Taylor, W.G. and Garratt, D. (2010a) 'The professionalisation of sports coaching: Relations of power, resistance and compliance', *Sport, Education and Society*, 15(1): 121–139

Taylor, W.G. and Garratt, D. (2010b) 'The professionalisation of sports coaching: Definitions, challenges and critique', in J. Lyle and C.J. Cushion (eds) *Sports Coaching: Professionalism and Practice*, London: Elsevier.

UK Sport (2001) *The UK Vision for Coaching*, London: UK Sport.

UK Sports Council (1991) *The Development of Coaching in the United Kingdom: A Consultative Document*, London: Sports Council.

4

READY, SET, ACTION

Representations of coaching through film

Laura Hills

BRUNEL UNIVERSITY, UK

Eileen Kennedy

BRUNEL UNIVERSITY, UK

When Timo Cruz begins his recitation "Our deepest fear is not that we are inadequate. Our deepest fear is that we are powerful beyond measure", to the street-wise basketball team who have, on their own initiative, set up desks to study in the school gym, the cinema audience knows that Coach Carter has done his job. A basketball coach can be a miracle worker who changes the lives of young people. Representations of coaching in films construct images with enormous and enduring appeal. The majority feature a male protagonist in the role of coach, who performs masculinely in accordance with the demands of filmic heroes. Beynon argued that the carefully crafted, idealised constructions of masculinity in Hollywood movies "often have a more powerful impact than the flesh-and-blood men around the young and with whom they are in daily contact" (2002: 64). Young people's expectations of their sports coach may be influenced by their interpretation of popular representations of the coach-athlete relationship and associated codes of masculinity. Acknowledging the importance of the media, and understanding the cinematic codes that construct the coach-athlete relationship, can provide coaches with ways of exploring, evaluating and challenging popular representations of coaching.

In order to support coaches in this endeavour, the chapter will draw on methods and approaches from film and media studies to explore the ways that films invoke and ignore bodies of knowledge surrounding coaching practice and masculinities to construct the Hollywood coach-as-hero in three films: *Coach Carter* (2005), *Hoosiers* (aka *Best Shot* 1986) and *Remember the Titans* (2000). Each of the three films construct narratives around male coaches of male high school teams. The coaches are all involved in struggles to reach young people through their coaching practice in ways that transcend sport (for example, building community, addressing social and educational exclusion, combating racism). The chapter will assess the extent to which the styles of coaching represented in the movies are, in fact, styles of (Hollywood) masculinity by asking the questions: how far do the coaching styles exhibited in the movies correspond with established techniques associated with the effective coaching of young people and how far do they accord with codes of the Hollywood hero?

Recommendations for coaches wishing to engage athletes in a reflexive discussion about these and other cinematic representations of coaching masculinities will follow this analysis.

Coaching, media and masculinity

Contemporary studies of men and gender have begun to question many of the assumptions that have sustained inequality between the sexes and restricted the myriad of ways that men can culturally embody masculinity. By casting a critical lens on masculinity, it is possible to undermine its semblance of inevitability and power. The implications of so doing have liberatory potential for both women and men, whose identities have been constrained by its narrow, monolithic definition. Masculinity is far from being a stable entity. Despite the constraints of culture, masculinity has the potential to manifest itself in multiple ways. So important is this theoretical observation, that within masculinity research, the term 'masculinity' has become replaced by its plural, 'masculinities'. However, as Connell (1998: 5) observed, these plural masculinities "exist in definite social relations, often relations of hierarchy and exclusion". In most contexts, including sport, a hegemonic form of masculinity exists. Nevertheless, many men may live "in a state of some tension with, or distance from, hegemonic masculinity" (ibid.), and the hegemonic form of masculinity may not even be the most common form of masculinity to be found in a given culture. Masculinities are patterns of gender practice that "are sustained and enacted not only by individuals but also by groups and institutions' including sport" (ibid.).

Different sporting contexts construct a range of masculinities as well as the hierarchies between them. There are plural masculinities embodied by players on a team, their coaches, doctors, managers and supporters and the culture of sport orders them in a shifting hierarchical arrangement. Not everyone involved in sport experiences masculinity in the same way. The body is central to the relationship between sport and masculinity. Through sports, the male body is "addressed, defined and disciplined … and given outlets and pleasures" (Connell 1998: 5). Sports bodies are actively produced through an engagement with the demands of the institution of sport. The results of this process, however, are not always coherent. Sporting masculinities are complex, often contradictory, always in process and never finished.

Sports films not only provide an opportunity to study the range of masculinities constructed in a specific sporting context, but also to understand the ways that, as an audience, we are being asked to make sense of the relationships between them. By critically analysing masculinities on film, it is possible to de-naturalise what is constructed as given and obvious, revealing the fluidity and multiplicity of gender. This can be seen as part of a political project to destabilise the categories of gender, and in order to facilitate such a project, it may be helpful to borrow from the analytical approach termed by Saco (1992) "masculinity-as-signs".

At the heart of Saco's (1992) approach is an understanding that the media do not simply reflect or represent gender difference, but help construct that difference. Rather than analysing the media as offering representations of *real* gender differences (that is, that exist separate from the text), Saco suggests a move towards the analysis of gender differences as (re) presentations, using the parentheses to call into question the possibility of any direct knowledge of masculinity outside of representation. Saco's (1992: 26, original emphasis) theoretical position is to shift "from the *signs of masculinity* to *masculinity as signs*".

In Saco's terms a sport film can be considered a system of signs that the film audience needs to decode. The audience of a sport film is, therefore, involved in a kind of conversation with it. In order to make sense of the text, audience members must adopt an appropriate relation to the text, to put themselves in the right place. Because of the complexity of the sign combinations films will only make sense from particular perspectives. When cinematic masculinity makes sense to the audience, the audience members have stepped into the film's address and have actively helped to construct that meaning. In this way, the portrayals of masculinity in sports films help construct the gender identities for their audience, since they ask the audience to consider themselves in relation to what is represented on the screen.

Easthope (1990) considered sport to be one of the central forms through which masculine action is represented. It was also necessary, he maintained, to look closely at the style of that action. This "masculine style" (1990: 79) explained how certain popular cultural texts effectively appealed to men. To consider Hollywood films depicting the coach–athlete relationship in these terms, then, is to draw attention to the way that representations of styles of coaching might also correspond to styles of masculinity. The way the coach–athlete relationship is constructed in a movie may owe more to conventions surrounding the effective cinematic action hero than to accumulated wisdom derived from coaching practice and scholarship. Far from portraying the plurality of possible masculinities, encouraging coaches and athletes among the audience to construct flexible gender identities to meet the complex demands of sport, movies draw on established and restrictive styles of masculinity. The next section considers how these carefully constructed representations of masculinity entice audiences through their idealisation of particular codes of masculinity.

Beynon (2002) suggests that the body is central to screen images of masculinity, celebrated for its power and strength. Boyle (2010: 48) summarised research around the theme by pointing to the way that muscles "have long been a leitmotif of national and racial supremacy in the cultural imagination of the United States". How a male body appears, however, is less important, according to Beynon (2002) than what it does in the all-action film, where violence is sexualised and skill, toughness and endurance are revered. In the external world, the screen male demonstrates qualities of leadership through his actions: "'proper' men exercise authority and behave courageously in adversity and sport" (Beynon 2002: 65). On the other side of this, Neale (1983: 7) pointed to the way that filmic masculinity is "marked not only by emotional reticence, but also by silence, a reticence with language".

However, there are a great many contradictions within the outward depiction of masculinity and the capacity that men have to live up to the image. Furthermore, contradictions exist in the power implications of making the masculine hero into a cinematic spectacle. As a result, film theorists such as Neale (1983) and Dyer (1982) have drawn attention to the "array of conventions are used to negate the feminising (and homoerotic) implications of any prolonged look at the male body" (Brown 2002: 128). There is no one definition, no singular formulation of the cinematic hero, therefore. The hero can be omnipotent or vulnerable, a figure with which the viewer can identify or gaze upon with desire. As Sparks (1996: 352) observed, heroes "can occupy a variety of positions in relation to social institutions: they may be integral or marginal figures, upholders or opponents of secular authority and so on". Mulvey (1975) explored the way that the violent hero of the Western film genre may be reintegrated into society through marriage at its closure, or may prove unassimilable and reject it in favour of lawlessness. Sparks (1996: 353) concluded that the "main business of many movies is just the evocation of an heroic masculinity whose principles of absolute individuation, solitude, probity, and personal resourcefulness themselves demand the social marginality of the principal figure, much as their Western antecedents did".

The cinematic hero is made even more complex by considering his relationship to femininity. Critics have argued that during the Reagan/Bush era, the backlash against feminism resulted in an increase of images of "hard bodies", muscular masculinities which compensated for a perceived loss of power. There is a racial dimension to this construction of cinematic heroism. The "tough guise" has been regularly aligned with black masculinity and defined by "urban life, rampant materialism, fatalistic attitudes, physical strength, and the acquisition of respect through violence or the implicit threat of violence" (Henry 2004: 121). The contradictions and lack of stability within the hero role has resulted in a new genre, the "double-protagonist" movie (Greven 2009: 22). In the double-protagonist movie, two male leads are depicted as complementary halves of one masculine consciousness, each character struggling to achieve narrative dominance. Using this device, "Hollywood films suggest that manhood's centre cannot hold, that manhood is split, that the warring elements of manhood spill out beyond the individual subjectivity of the star-protagonist" (Greven 2009: 25). The effective Hollywood hero, therefore, may be contradictory and unstable, resulting in the adoption of a "tough guise", and may even be portrayed by two characters rather than one.

If the cinematic coach were to be coded according to the conventions that surround the Hollywood hero, therefore, it might be expected that he would appear physically powerful, authoritative and emotionally reticent. He would adopt a "tough guise" and possess a hard body. His heroism might mark him as an outsider, with only the possibility of assimilation into society. The coach-as-hero may even be represented by more than one character, as two halves of a warring whole. The end result of such coding may be highly seductive to an audience, who may be encouraged to understand their own relationship to masculinity and sport in the terms offered by films. Nevertheless, the coach-as-hero may not coincide with their own needs as athletes, and may stand in marked contrast to effective coaching practices espoused in the research literature. Many sport films featuring coaches, including the three analysed here, depict coaches of youth teams. Scholarship on coaching young people is well developed and the following section explores some of this research in order to highlight the approaches that could inform the ways that coaching is portrayed in sport films.

Coaching young people

Sport experiences have often been assumed to contribute to the psycho-social development of young people by nurturing sport skills, encouraging motivation and enhancing personal characteristics and values such as self-esteem, discipline, perceived competence, teamwork and sportspersonship. Debates exist within the research, however, as to the precise qualities that might constitute positive, transferable life skills, challenging common-sense assumptions that sports participation automatically benefits young people (Ewing *et al.* 2002) and identifying the characteristics of youth sport programmes that can facilitate young people's development (Danish 2002; Fraser-Thomas *et al.* 2005). For example, the development of a task or mastery-oriented climate may enhance young people's intrinsic motivation, persistence, commitment and work ethic (Petitpas *et al.* 2005). The coach has been shown to be central to any attempt to promote young people's positive sport experiences (Smith and Smoll 1997; Ewing *et al.* 2002; Petitpas *et al.* 2005).

Smith and Smoll's (1997) Coach Effectiveness Training programme (CET) has been lauded as one of the most methodologically sound approaches to understanding the characteristics of quality youth sport coaching (Hedstrom and Gould 2004; Conroy and Coatsworth 2006). They found that leadership style influenced young people's experience and that training coaches to be more effective leaders resulted in young people's increased enjoyment, improved self-esteem, decreased anxiety and reduced withdrawal. The five principles that underpin their programme can be summarised as: focusing on effort and enjoyment rather than winning; emphasising positive reinforcement, encouragement and task-focused instruction rather than punitive or hostile feedback; developing positive social relationships and team-building skills; engaging young people in decision-making processes; and encouraging coaches to be reflexive about their coaching practice.

Effective coaching within a youth sport context means creating enjoyable, motivating and developmentally valuable experiences for young people rather than emphasising the team's win-loss record (Smith *et al.* 1995). From this perspective, young people benefit from a team climate that emphasises personal development, effort and mastery with reduced attention to performance goals (Horn 2008). Cumming *et al.* (2007) found that the motivational climate of the team was more important than winning in predicting youth enjoyment and that young people preferred the coach to engage in mastery-oriented behaviours. This type of mastery-based motivational climate has also been shown to facilitate perceptions of competence, enjoyment and reduced anxiety in young people and is supported by coaching styles that emphasise instruction, support and positive feedback (Smith *et al.* 1995; Horn 2008). Punitive and hostile feedback has been linked to reductions in intrinsic motivation, decreased enjoyment in young people, and even withdrawal from the team. An early study by Smith *et al.* (1979) found that young people preferred coaches who they perceived as providing instructional and task contingent feedback. Further research using CET indicated that young people preferred coaches who provided positive reinforcement, support and technical instruction and engaged in limited punishment (Smith and Smoll 1997).

Autocratic and democratic approaches to decision-making in leadership have also been shown to impact young people's enjoyment (Chelladurai and Saleh 1980). Autocratic coaching styles are associated with an emphasis on performance, coach-centred decision-making, limited input from athletes, strict discipline and control. Martin *et al.* (1999) found that young people and their parents preferred more democratic styles of coaching where young people were involved in decision-making. They were less likely to prefer autocratic coaching, desiring directive behaviour only in relation to instructional feedback and broader team decisions. Democratic styles are more consistent with Smith and Smoll's (1997) principles of coaching and have been shown to foster self-determination, encourage young people's participation in decision-making, de-emphasise outcomes and increase perceived competence. Intrinsic motivation and persistence may be increased when the coach is flexible and provides a context where players perceive autonomy support and opportunities for self-determination rather than control (Amorose and Horn 2000; Horn 2008).

Smith and Smoll's (2007) final principle focuses on the need for coaches to reflect on their practice and seek opportunities for self-awareness since coaches are not always aware of their coaching styles and behaviours. Training programmes for coaches have been shown to have a positive impact on player satisfaction, indicating the potential for coaches to learn to implement new and potentially more effective styles and strategies for enhancing youth development.

Representations of the coach-athlete relationship could be a valuable part of the coach education process for both athletes and coaches, were these images to reflect the principles that Smith and Smoll (1997) delineated such as portraying coaches emphasising effort and enjoyment over winning, providing positive feedback rather than punishment, involving athletes in decision-making, and reflecting on practice. However, the construction of the cinematic coach is also and possibly more influenced by the cinematic requirements of the

Hollywood film male. The next section will analyse scenes from three movies (*Hoosiers, Coach Carter* and *Remember the Titans*) that depict coaches' first encounters with the players in order to explore how far the cinematic portrayal of the coach-athlete relationship corresponds to coaching scholarship or to conventions of cinematic masculinity.

The Hollywood coach

Films use signifying systems to construct meaning involving the camera, lighting, editing, sound and the arrangement of people and objects within a shot (Kennedy and Hills 2009). The analysis that follows will consider the way each of these elements operate in combination with each other to advance the narrative within the film sequences. The analysis will focus on the scene in each film where the coach first meets the team and articulates and enacts his coaching style. This approach will elicit the ways that the scenes construct the film's protagonists in terms of both masculinity and coaching qualities.

Hoosiers (Best Shot)

Hoosiers (aka *Best Shot*) centres on the coach of an Indiana high school (Norman Dale played by Gene Hackman). Coach Dale was formerly a highly successful college basketball coach who was banned for striking a player. He joins the school after serving 12 years in the Navy. Dale's chequered past, his lack of recent experience and unconventional ways positions him as an outsider, at the margins of the small town community.

On Dale's first meeting with the team, he enters the gym to the sound of a male voice shouting "Move it!" and pauses with the appearance of consternation. The players are shown on the basketball court with the former assistant coach, George, running practice. Dale stands silently before decisively walking to the centre of the gym. Immediately Dale is constructed as the outsider, with a need to establish himself quickly as the leader, quelling forces of opposition (represented in this scene by George, a member of the local community). George says: "Oh, there you are. I thought we'd go twenty minutes on, ten off, twenty on". Dale replies, "I had a different schedule in mind", only briefly looking at the coach, but turning his body towards the players, with a forced smile. George tries to assert control of the training, but Dale cuts him off by turning towards him and speaking mechanically but with the semblance of affability: "First of all, let's be real friendly here, my name's Norm. Second of all, your coaching days are over".

Dale establishes his position as dominant by humiliating his contender. His communication style (periods of silence, forced smiles, sarcastic dialogue) is closed and subdued. He is constructed in the mould of the taciturn, tough and emotionally withdrawn hero (Neale 1983). Nevertheless, Dale reveals inconsistencies in this image as he opens himself up to the players.

Dale calls to the players to "Huddle up!" and they exchange remarks revealing vulnerability on both sides. There are few players, including one who says he counts as only half a player "too short, no good". Dale reveals that he has coached college ball for ten years, but it has been 12 years since he has "blown this" (holding his whistle aloft), saying: "I am going to be learning from you just like you learn from me". This admission causes a small group of players to begin whispering and joking. Dale confronts the ringleader, who replies that he is "curious to know when we start". Pointing a finger at him, Dale tells him that they start when he says so. When the player responds with more backchat, Dale kicks him off the team: "Don't come back until you learn to keep your mouth shut and listen". The player leaves the gym shouting: "Have fun, Coach, trying to win with five, well make that four and a half, players" and slamming his hand against the door jam in frustration.

The coach-athlete relationship is quickly constructed in hierarchical, autocratic terms. Dale is shown to favour coach-centred decision-making, responding to input from athletes with excessive censure – banning players who talk back. The possibility of him learning from the players remains underexplored as he continues to impose his style of discipline, strategy, training and values on the team. When a player complains that his training is like being in the army, Dale replies, "You are in the army, my army," further reinforcing the masculine hierarchy and the need for unquestioning subservience to his punishing regimen. Complaints from the players about the lack of scrimmaging in practice results in a "My practices are not meant to be fun." While Dale does not embody many of the characteristics seen to be effective in coaching young people, he does embody the characteristics of a cinematic hero. The violence in his past that may be least associated with good coaching, is effective in confirming his Hollywood masculinity.

Coach Carter

There are remarkable similarities in the scenes portraying the initial meeting of coach and athletes in the film *Coach Carter* (2005) despite the differences in setting (black, urban California school versus rural white Indiana). The film also tells the story of an outsider, a successful businessman, entering a school to coach a basketball team at the behest of the retiring coach Ray White. Carter formerly attended the high school but his success in business, his dress, his style of speaking, and his educational aspirations for the student-athletes mark him as different. White accompanies Coach Carter during his first meeting with the players. In contrast to White's relaxed body language, Carter maintains a controlled, upright posture and adopts an expressionless stare, eyes fixed on a spot in the distance, indicating toughness, resilience and immovability. When White leaves, Carter addresses the players in a scene shot from below, making them appear confident and powerful in the space of the gym. Each player is tinged with light from the window. Immediately, Carter is constructed as uncommunicative emotionally and lacking the sentimentality of his predecessor. Carter's autocratic leadership style and his propensity to violence as a means of gaining respect – thus completing his cinematic "tough guise" (Henry 2004: 121) – is demonstrated in the following scenes.

Carter raises his voice to gain the attention of the noisy players. As in *Hoosiers*, the players are initially rebellious, challenging the coaches' authority. One player, Worm, engages Carter in resistant banter saying "Oh we hear you dog, but we can't see you. The glare from your big, black-assed head is hell of shiny, man … do you buff it?" In retort, Carter remarks "Oh, you got jokes to go along with that ugly jump shot of yours, huh?" causing the player to become the object of the others' laughter. Carter directs the players' attention to his record of distinction as a former player, and lays down rules "if basketball practice starts at three, you are late as of two fifty-five". Carter picks on a young white player and asks "what's your name, sir?" In close shot, he replies "Jason Lyle, but I ain't no sir". The camera cuts to a shot from behind Lyle's shoulder, framing Carter who begins to move towards him "You ain't a sir. Well, are you a madam?" The image shows Lyle flanked by black players and Carter in front of him, "As of now, you are a sir". The word "bitch" can be heard in a humorous, stylised voice from some of the players. Carter explains how the players will gain his respect, draws their record of poor results from Lyle, and distributes contracts promising them that to sign will mean that "the losing stops now".

Worm says under his breath that Carter is a "country-assed nigger" and his team-mate repeats the insult. The camera cuts from Carter's face to the player who tells the Coach that he is "Timo Cruz ... sir!" Carter is shown in sharp focus against a blurred background, explaining that "we treat ourselves with respect – we don't use the word nigger." The camera cuts back and forth between Cruz and Carter, emphasising their opposition, as Cruz challenges Carter and Carter responds. Eventually, the camera is positioned behind Cruz's head, looking up at Carter as he says with an expression of utmost seriousness "Okay, Mr. Cruz, leave the gym right now." Cruz asks, "For what?" and Carter repeats the command: "I'll ask you for one last time to leave the gym before I help you leave." With the camera looking down on him, Cruz moves forward, responding emotionally to Carter's suggestion that he is a "scared young man": "Scared of who? I'm supposed to be scared of you? I ain't scared of nobody. I would lay your ass out." Carter says in a fierce voice, "I don't think so." Cruz feigns acquiescence before launching himself at Carter in attack. In a scene shown in wide shot reminiscent of a police arrest, Carter is shown blocking the boy's punch and pinning his arm behind his back, as the assembled players look on. Carter physically propels Cruz across the basketball court, shoving him up against a wall, one hand grabbing the hair on the back of his head, the other still twisting his arm behind his back. Shocked players look and look away. Cruz complains with his face squashed against the wall: "Teachers ain't supposed to touch students." Carter replies "I'm not a teacher," his mouth very close to Cruz's ear. Carter tugs Cruz's head further back and says: "I'm the new basketball coach."

Carter, like Dale, fulfils few of the characteristics associated with effective coaching of young people in these scenes. Instead, he demonstrates his superior physical strength, even resorting to physical violence, to silence and punish players who resist his authority. The closeness of similarity in detail (the coach coming from outside to enter the gym already occupied by players, thus requiring him to assert his dominance through verbal and physical violence and the physical banishment of opposition) indicates that the shared codes correspond to Hollywood conventions of masculinity borrowed from other genres such as action-adventure or the Western. The film's lead actor is Samuel L. Jackson as Ken Carter, who is well known for his previous film roles as a no-nonsense, hypermasculine hero including that of a contract killer in *Pulp Fiction* (1994). Coach Carter can even be said to evoke the characteristics of this former role, particularly in his iron resolve, violence and proclivity for sermonising.

Remember the Titans

Remember the Titans (2000) may be considered to differ in certain respects from the representations of coaching in *Coach Carter* and *Hoosiers*. *Remember the Titans* features two coaches, not one: the displaced white Coach Yoast and the black Coach Boone. The film is set in 1971 as two Virginian high schools experience the tensions of racial integration under federal mandate. Despite the successful record of the coach of the former white school (Yoast), a black coach (Boone) is appointed as head coach at the newly integrated high school. The appointment conflicts with both men's sense of justice, but Yoast decides not to leave because of his students, while Boone makes connections with the black community, who construct him (in spite of his protestations) as a leader ("I'm not an answer to your prayers. I'm not a saviour, Jesus Christ, Martin Luther King or the Easter Bunny. I'm a football coach, that's all – just a football coach"). Boone is, nevertheless, depicted as very much the outsider in relation to the newly integrated team. His initial meetings with first the black, then the white, players share a great deal with the representations discussed earlier.

Boone first meets the black players in the school gym. The team are shown acting playfully, singing and joking about their rosy prospects with a black coach and no white players who "won't play for no brother". Boone's arrival is announced by the sound of a whistle. A wide shot then frames a gym bathed in sunlight, making the players indistinct and casting Boone and his assistant into silhouette. Boone strides across the floor and up to the players with an angry expression on his face. Boone commands that one of the players, Petey, puts down his raised arm. The player's expression of joy quavers as he draws down his arm, his fist appearing to be shaped into a soft version of a black power salute. Boone's face is shown in startling proximity to Petey's as he says "You're smiling?" and begins to bark at him, military style, demanding that he be called "Sir" and asking again "Why are you smiling?" Petey's face is shown from the front, his twinkling eyes searching out those of Boone in eager communication, as he explains that it is because he loves football, football's fun. Boone corrects him: "Fun, sir". A quick interchange between them takes place, as the camera cuts back and forth, confusing Petey:

> It's fun, you're sure? … [I think so…] Now you're thinking, first you smile, then you think. You think football is still fun? [er…yes!] Sir! [Yes, no, sir] No? [It was fun…] Not anymore, though, is it? Is it? [no, no …] No, it's not anymore, not even a little bit [a little … no] Make up your mind [No, no] Think, since you're thinking, now go on … [No] Is it fun? [no] No? Absolutely not? [Zero fun, sir].

Boone marches along the length of the assembled players in a scene reminiscent of an army parade ground. The eyes of the players follow him as he moves. The scene ends as Boone asserts "This is no democracy. It is a dictatorship. I am the law. If you survive camp, you will be on the team … if you survive."

Boone is depicted as autocratic, ruling with strict discipline. Ultimately the white players join the team and Boone establishes his position with them as well. His willingness to humiliate players who resist his authority is illustrated in the scene depicting his confrontation with two players as they board the bus for camp.

Against a soundtrack of "Express Yourself", two of Boone's white players confront him with demands that half of all positions be reserved for their former school as the camera switches between the players' faces and Boone's. Boone deliberately mistakes one of the students' names (Garry) for Jerry, making a connection between the pair and the comedy duo, Jerry Lewis and Dean Martin. Boone turns to address the assembled crowd of parents sending off their children to camp: "Ladies and gentlemen, I've got an announcement to make. We've got Jerry Lewis and Dean Martin going to camp with us here this year". Boone asks Garry to point out his mother and tells him in a hushed tone, "Take a good look at her, because when you get back on that bus, you ain't got no mama anymore. You got your brothers on the team, and you got your daddy. You know who your daddy is, don't you?" The camera shows Boone's face inches from Garry's: "Garry, if you want to play on this football team, you'll answer me when I ask you – who's your daddy?" Boone lowers his head and peers up into Garry's eyes, which are cast down: "Who's your daddy, Garry? Who's your daddy?" Eventually, Garry replies quietly, his lips seeming to have difficulty forming the word, "You". Boone pushes him further, "And whose team is this, your team or your daddy's team?" An image of a concerned Yoast is interjected before Garry answers "Yours." This scene of public humiliation, presents Boone's coaching style as once more reminiscent of military techniques of subordinating new recruits or prisoners.

Coach Yoast, however, is represented differently. Yoast's style is depicted as calm and encouraging, routinely juxtaposed with the uncontrolled emotions and passion of his young daughter Sheryl. Yoast appears modest about his outstanding record, bowing his head while a member of his staff informs Boone that he has been nominated to the Virginia High School Hall of Fame. In contrast, Boone is depicted as highly ambitious and aggressive in pursuit of his goals ("I can guarantee you this, Coach – I come to win").

Remember the Titans corresponds to the "double-protagonist" movie discussed by Greven (2009: 22). The two sides of the hero are represented by Boone and Yoast, each struggling for narrative dominance. The film depicts both Yoast and Boone's coaching styles as lacking. While Yoast is presented as kind, fair and innately authoritative, he lacks passion in his approach to competition, which is often supplemented by the character of his daughter. The competitive fervour of Boone, on the other hand, is depicted as near psychotic which can conflict with his ability to give care to his charges. The film's resolution, however, brings the two styles together, fusing their characteristics into a model of aggressive, paternalistic, disciplinarian masculinity. Far from following a model for effective coaching that emphasises personal development, effort and mastery over performance goals (Horn 2008), Yoast's lack of passion for victory is seen as a failing, and Boone's will to win as a positive corrective.

Each of the films portrays coaches in the style of Hollywood masculinity. The characteristics associated with this style of masculinity construct the coach as narrative hero but conflict with the principles of effective coaching practice with young people. A good movie coach is not necessarily a good flesh-and-blood coach. These coaches disdain 'fun' in favour of discipline and military style training, they require unquestioning obedience even when their demands verge on athlete abuse (1,000 suicides, no water breaks, physical confrontation), resistance can result in banishment and punishments occur regularly. Ultimately the coach is accepted when the team wins, eschewing any real criticism of his approach (apart from the evaluative eye of Coach Yoast). Nevertheless, the movie coach is likely to be a highly attractive figure, precisely because of the qualities he possesses that deviate from the principles of good coaching. For audiences of movies that instantly recognise the characteristics of the Hollywood hero, the coaches that are depicted in these films may appear extremely effective. It is important, therefore, to unpack what qualities are being represented and the reasons for their appeal.

Conclusion and recommendations

The forms of heroic masculinity that are repeatedly embodied by cinematic youth sport coaches may form part of our cultural landscape but they are not consonant with much of the research-based conceptualisations of what constitutes quality coaching. By paying attention to the codes that are used to construct the Hollywood coach-as-hero, it is possible to observe the process by which we are entranced and seduced by the cinematic image. In this way, we can consider the coaching styles represented within the films as styles of Hollywood masculinity and, by interrogating these constructions, begin to question some of our common-sense understandings of what coaches are – or should be – like. We can see that the Hollywood coach has a limited script which needs to accord with the conventions of the hypermasculine hero role. This leaves little room for alternative constructions of the coach-athlete relationship that are more reflective of good coaching practice than of Hollywood masculinity.

Coaching literature suggests that coaches' coaching strategies are similar to the styles in which they were coached. Coaching styles may also be influenced by representations of coaches that permeate media forms. As Smith and Smoll (2007) suggest, a key characteristic of developing effective youth coaches is implementing opportunities for reflection and self-awareness. Critical analysis of the heroic construction of coaches in film and the associated styles of masculinity could form part of a coach training programme serving as a catalyst for discussion or a basis for reflexivity. If we explore how Hollywood coaching movies construct their allure, we can make more sense of their usefulness for understanding coaching practice. Such movies often dramatise inspirational "true stories", appearing to portray idealised coaching practice. Yet, narrative is inevitably involved in a recomposition of events, such that the "truth" of the story may be sacrificed for drama. The desire to make a difference and be an inspiration may be shared among many involved in coaching but the reality may involve much more mundane caring work. A coach-athlete relationship built on trust, support, reciprocity and reflexivity does not fit well within existing codes of Hollywood masculinity. Unless the characteristics of cinematic coach-as-hero expand to incorporate different masculinities, good coaching practice may remain off-screen.

Unpacking Hollywood coaching styles could help young people differentiate between the allure of movie masculinity and coaching best practice. Activities such as asking young people to list or describe the preferred qualities of youth sport coaches and comparing their list to the qualities of coaches in film can help them to become aware of the ways that Hollywood heroics may be incongruent with quality coaching. We tried this with university students who were amazed at the discrepancy between their list of attributes (e.g. supportive, good listener, approachable) and the qualities that emerged through a close analysis of scenes from the films used in this chapter. Again, these practices form a basis for discussing coach-athlete relationships, preferred coaching styles, shared expectations, and approaches to decision-making. For coaches employing more democratic and participatory styles of coaching, the analysis of coaching in films provides an additional opportunity to encourage reflection and critical awareness of values and beliefs and the influence and impact of mediated sport.

References

Amorose, A.J. and Horn, T.S. (2000) 'Intrinsic motivation: relationships with collegiate athletes' gender, scholarship status, and perceptions of their coaches behaviour', *Journal of Sport Exercise Psychology*, 22(1): 63–84.

Beynon, J. (2002) *Masculinities and Culture*, Buckingham: Open University Press.

Boyle, E. (2010) 'The intertextual terminator: The role of film in branding "Arnold Schwarzenegger"', *Journal of Communication Inquiry*, 34(1): 42–60.

Brown, J.A. (2002) 'The tortures of Mel Gibson: Masochism and the sexy male body', *Men and Masculinities*, 5(2): 123–143.

Chelladurai, P. and Saleh, S.D. (1980) 'Dimensions of leader behaviour in sports: Development of a leadership scale', *Journal of Sport Psychology*, 2: 34–45.

Connell, R. (1998) 'Masculinities and globalisation', *Men and Masculinities*, 1: 3–23.

Conroy, D.E. and Coatsworth, J.D. (2006) 'Coach training as a strategy for promoting youth social development', *The Sport Psychologist*, 20(2): 128–144.

Cumming, S.P., Smoll, F.L., Smith, R.E. and Grossbard, J.R. (2007) 'Is winning everything? The relative contributions of motivational climate and won-lost percentage in youth sport', *Journal of Applied Sport Psychology*, 19(3): 322–336.

Danish, S.J. (2002) 'Teaching life skills through sport', in M. Gatz, M.A. Messner and S.J. Ball-Rokeach (eds) *Paradoxes of Youth and Sport*, Albany, NY: State University of New York Press.

Dyer, R. (1982) 'Don't look now: The male pin up', *Screen*, 23(3/4): 61–73.

Easthope, A. (1990) *What a Man's Gotta Do: The Masculine Myth in Popular Culture*, London: Unwin Hyman.

Ewing, M.E., Gano-Overway, L.A., Branta, C.F. and Seefeldt, V.D. (2002) 'The role of sports in youth development', in M. Gatz, M.A. Messner and S.J. Ball-Rokeach (eds) *Paradoxes of Youth and Sport*, Albany, NY: State University of New York Press.

Fraser-Thomas, J.L., Cote, J. and Deakin, J. (2005) 'Youth sport programs: an avenue to foster positive youth development', *Physical Education and Sport Pedagogy*, 10(1): 19–40.

Greven, D. (2009) 'Contemporary Hollywood masculinity and the double-protagonist film', *Cinema Journal*, 48(4): 22–43.

Hedstrom, R. and Gould, D. (2004) *Research in Youth Sports: Critical Issues Status, White Paper Summaries of the Existing Literature*, Institute for Youth Sports MSU, East Lansing, MI: Michigan State University.

Henry, M. (2004) 'He is a "Bad Mother*$%@!#": *Shaft* and contemporary black masculinity', *African American Review*, 38(1): 119–126.

Horn, T.S. (2008) 'Coaching effectiveness in the sport domain', in T.S. Horn (ed.) *Advances in Sport Psychology*, Champaign, IL: Human Kinetics, pp. 239–268.

Kennedy, E. and Hills, L. (2009) *Sport, Media and Society*, Oxford: Berg.

Martin, S.B., Jackson, A.W., Richardson, P.A. and Weiller, K.H. (1999) 'Coaching preferences of adolescent youths and their parents', *Journal of Applied Sport Psychology*, 11(2): 247–262.

Mulvey, L. (1975) 'Visual pleasure and narrative cinema', *Screen*, 16(3): 6–18.

Neale, S. (1983) 'Masculinity as spectacle: Reflections on men and mainstream cinema', *Screen*, 24(6): 2–17.

Petitpas, A.J., Cornelius, A.E., Van Raalte, J.L. and Jones, T. (2005) 'A framework for planning youth sport programs that foster psychosocial development', *The Sport Psychologist*, 19(1): 63–80.

Saco, D. (1992) 'Masculinity as signs: Poststructuralist feminist approaches to the study of gender', in S. Craig (ed.) *Men, Masculinity and the Media*, London: Sage, pp. 23–39.

Smith, R.E. and Smoll, F.L. (1997) 'Coach-mediated team building in youth sports', *Journal of Applied Sport Psychology*, 9(1): 114–132.

Smith, R.E. and Smoll, F.L. (2007) 'Social-cognitive approach to coaching behaviours', in S. Jowett and D. Lavellee (eds) *Social Psychology in Sport*, Champaign, IL: Human Kinetics.

Smith, R.E., Smoll F.L. and Barnett, N.P. (1995) 'Reduction of children's sport performance anxiety through social support and stress-reduction training for coaches', *Journal of Applied Developmental Psychology*, 16(1): 125–142.

Smith, R.E., Smoll, F.L. and Curtis, B. (1979) 'Coach effectiveness training: A cognitive-behavioural approach to enhancing relationship skills in youth sport coaches', *Journal of Sport Psychology*, 1(1): 59–75.

Sparks, R. (1996) 'Masculinity and heroism in the Hollywood blockbuster: The culture industry and contemporary images of crime and law enforcement', *British Journal of Criminology*, 36(3): 348–360.

5

ISSUES OF EXCLUSION AND DISCRIMINATION IN THE COACHING PROFESSION

Cindra S. Kamphoff

MINNESOTA STATE UNIVERSITY, U.S.A.

Diane L. Gill

UNIVERSITY OF NORTH CAROLINA AT GREENSBORO, U.S.A.

Introduction

This chapter reviews the evidence and explores issues of exclusion and discrimination in the coaching profession, specifically focusing on issues related to gender, race, and sexuality within coaching. Although a growing number of athletes are women and racial minorities, the coaching profession remains largely a White, male domain (Acosta and Carpenter 2012; Lapchick *et al.* 2009). As reviewed in the following sections, research suggests that the coaching profession can be non-welcoming for women, racial minorities, and sexual minorities (e.g. Abney 2007; Kamphoff 2010; Kamphoff *et al.* 2010; Krane and Barber 2005; Thomae and Kamphoff 2012). Notably, most of the research to date has explored gender rather than race and sexuality issues. It is also important to note that this chapter reflects our perspective. Specifically, our perspective is informed by feminist scholarship (e.g. Hall 1996), by our review of the largely U.S. research, and by our own cultural identities and experiences.

Sport as a cultural practice

Before proceeding to a more in-depth discussion about issues of gender, sexuality, and race in coaching, it is important to take a step back and consider the culture of sport. Sport is an important part of social life with enormous influence on culture; without examining sport as a social institution we lose an understanding of the context in which coaches coach. As Coakley (2009) clearly argues, sport is more than just scores and performance statistics; instead sport remains one of the few arenas in our society where gender and racial differences are embraced. Phrases in our language such as "sports make boys into men," "don't throw like a girl," or "white men can't jump" demonstrate our gender and racial ideologies – ideas that justify and explain social life as natural and common sense (Coakley 2009; Sage 1998). Furthermore, women and racial minorities have historically been excluded from organized sport (Bray 2004; National Federation of State High School Associations 2010) and coaches (Lapchick *et al.* 2009). Sport has traditionally been defined as a male activity, with athleticism and traditional femininity seen as "mutually exclusive" (Hall 1996: 147). Research has also demonstrated the historically persistent homophobic nature of sport (Anderson 2005; Griffin 1998); gay and lesbian coaches do not feel supported, leave coaching (Kamphoff 2010), or are fired when they come out of the closet (Griffin 1998). In other words, sport is a location in which inequalities and power struggles regarding gender, race, and sexuality are reproduced; we cannot understand sport without reference to these power relations. This culture of sport has a tremendous impact on female, racial minority, and gay and lesbian coaches as shown in the following sections.

Gender issues in coaching

Gender bias in coaching

A good deal of research has documented the lack of female coaches and gender bias in coaching throughout the world. Acosta and Carpenter's (2012) longitudinal report clearly demonstrated this dramatic decline of women coaches and administrators in the U.S. (see Chapter 33 by Bruening *et al.* in this Handbook for a more in-depth discussion on the lack of female coaches). In sum, women made up over 90 percent of coaches and administrators in women's collegiate athletics in 1972, but only 42.9 percent of coaches and 20.3 percent of administrators in 2012. In fact, women only coached one out of five teams (men and women) in 2012, and less than 3 percent of men's teams are coached by a woman (Acosta and Carpenter 2012). The lack of women coaches has been documented at other levels (e.g. elite, youth, high school), and the limited data available suggest that there are fewer women coaches at the youth level than at the collegiate level (LaVoi 2009; Messner 2007).

The under-representation of women coaches at the elite level has been well documented in many countries. Data on the United States Olympic Committee's (USOC) website indicated that only 8 of 40 (20 percent) head coaches of women's teams were women in the 2008 Summer Olympics in Beijing, and no women coached a men's Olympic team. Similarly, Norman (2010) indicated that only 9 of 43 (20.9 percent) coaches at the senior national teams of both men and women's major teams sports in the U.K. were women, and Leberman reported that only 26 percent of female teams and only 1 percent of men's teams in New Zealand during the last Olympics were coached by a woman (Kamphoff *et al.* 2008). Additional data from the U.K. (Women's Sport Foundation UK 2007) and Canada (Marshall 2010) confirm that the lack of women coaches is a worldwide issue.

Certainly, women are underrepresented at all levels of coaching. At best, we find about one in five coaches is a woman, but often this percentage is much lower. Beyond the data summarized here – which includes few countries and only some levels of sport – a more systematic analysis is needed with data more representative of countries throughout the world. More information is needed on the actual number of women coaches beyond the college level, and particularly in youth sports, which has far more numbers and more diverse participants.

The explanation for the lack of female coaches is multifaceted with many overlapping reasons. I (Kamphoff 2010) interviewed and surveyed women who had left U.S. collegiate coaching and found that the gendered and patriarchal nature of coaching presented challenges and influenced women's decisions to leave coaching. Women reported receiving few resources, older facilities, lower salaries, more responsibilities, and less administrative support

– all of which contributed to their decision to leave coaching. Other authors report similar findings in the U.K. and Canada (Norman 2010; S. Robertson 2010; Theberge 1993).

Women tend to drop out of the coaching profession within the first five years of coaching (Kerr 2010), and gender bias may explain this drop out. One reason that women leave coaching is because the profession is seen as "men's work"; a "good coach" is typically thought of as a "male coach" and women have a difficult time establishing credibility and working in the system (Kamphoff 2010; Knoppers 1992; Norman 2010). Women coaches also report being excluded from social networks such as conversations with other coaches or late night trips to the bar (Marshall 2010), and describe this as being excluded from the "good old boys' network." Although socializing may appear to be a non-essential part of coaching, it is one way to build social capital and relationships (Eagly and Carli 2007).

Not only can gender bias lead to drop outs, but research also suggests that women are less interested in the coaching profession compared to men because of perceived gender bias (Kamphoff and Gill 2008). Difficulties attracting and retaining female coaches have also been attributed to conflicts with motherhood, homophobia and a homonegative environment, homogeneous reproduction (i.e. male athletic directors hire male coaches), harassment and bullying, a lower salary, a higher rate of burnout, a lack of recruitment and mentoring programs, and a lack of female role models (Demers 2010; Humphreys 2000; Kamphoff 2010; Kelley *et al.* 1999; Kerr 2010; Krane and Barber 2005; Marshall 2010; Stangl and Kane 1991).

Future research is needed to more clearly identify types and sources of gender bias in the coaching profession, its effects on women coaches and future women coaches. If gender bias is indeed a key source of the low numbers of women coaches, then strategies to eliminate gender bias and ensure that the coaching profession attracts and retains women must be developed and examined.

Coaching and motherhood

Marshall (2010) suggests that one reason that it is difficult to attract and retain female coaches is the perceived conflicts in balancing work and family. The coaching profession is seen as a "24 hour job" which can be difficult for women with family obligations, including caring for children or elderly parents. In fact, all of the women interviewed as part of Kamphoff's (2010) study struggled with balancing work and family and this difficulty ultimately led several of the women to leave coaching. Furthermore, in 2005, Drago and colleagues described the extreme workload of the coaching profession in The Coaching and Gender Equity Project (CAGE) as "family-unfriendly." More specifically, the long hours, the unpredictability of the coaching job, the family-unfriendly hours required for games, practice, and recruiting trips, and the administration and culture of sport not welcoming family commitments were cited by coaches and administrators as characteristics of sport.

As Hochschild's (1989) language of the "second shift" implies, "work" is also done related to family. She argued that most women work for pay as well as work a "second shift" at home (e.g. cooking, cleaning, laundry, taking care of children, etc.). This "double burden" (Marshall 2010) is prominent regardless of whether or not women have children (Hochschild 1989: 4). Women, as a whole, are primarily responsible for more household labor or family responsibilities, even though there has been a substantial increase in men's household activities since the 1960s (Sayer 2005). Many women perceive the difficulty of balancing work and family, and decide not to have children (Hewlett 2003). Research specifically within coaching suggests that some successful collegiate coaches have decided not to have children because of the difficulty they perceived in having a successful coaching career and children (Kamphoff *et al.* 2010).

Mercier (2000), in her study with Canadian coaches, argued that women see a disconnect between work and family because work and family are seen as separate domains and "work" for pay has traditionally been seen as a male domain, whereas "family" has been viewed as the woman's primary domain. Ranson (2005), who interviewed women working in engineering, stated that women enter engineering not as women, but conceptually as "men," making it difficult for women to find a balance between the status of "mother" and "engineer." This conceptual "cover" is blown when they become mothers. Ranson (2005) argued that mother and engineer are two potentially incongruous identities. A similar argument could be made that mother and coach are incompatible. Male coaches, for example, are assumed to have a partner (i.e. "wife") who is more accountable for family responsibilities; hence "father" and "engineer" (or "father" and "coach") rarely conflict. Successful women coaches with children have indicated that it is important for their spouses to have flexible schedules to support their time-consuming job, and that their athletic director was particularly supportive of coaches with families (Kamphoff *et al.* 2010).

Future research should further examine the struggle with work-family balance and the unique pressures that women experience when coaching and having children. An in-depth examination of successful coaches who are mothers would provide valuable insights for other mothers who coach and strategies for improving the environment and support for coaches who are mothers at all levels of coaching. For example, coaches in youth programs are often parents, yet there is no research on differential pressures, perceptions, and experiences of mothers and fathers. Researchers could examine how working conditions within an athletic department or sporting organization accommodate coaches who are mothers, with the goal of retaining more women coaches.

Women coaching men

Little research has been conducted on the experiences of the few women coaching male athletes but a few studies exist. Two early studies focused at the high school level (Kane and Stangl 1991; Staurowsky 1990), and more recent work has focused on the collegiate level (Kamphoff *et al.* 2010; Yiamouyiannis 2007). Most recently, my colleagues and I (Kamphoff *et al.* 2010) interviewed 15 of the 39 women who coached men at the most competitive level within collegiate athletics. Interestingly, two-thirds of the 39 women coached a combined men and women's cross country/track and field program and all 39 women coached a men's minor sport including cross country, golf, swimming and diving, tennis, and track and field. Kanter (1977) argued that segregation may take place through the marginalization of women into less desirable occupational positions. Marginalization was clearly evident as no women coached a male "major" collegiate sport (i.e. football, basketball, soccer, baseball, hockey). This marginalization keeps women from moving into athletic leadership roles and "contains" women in less powerful or prestigious sports. Furthermore, these findings are similar to Kane and Stangl's research, which is over 20 years old.

We also found that women who coach men at the highest level of collegiate sport must have a decorated background either as an elite athlete (i.e. Olympic or professional level) or extremely successful coach. This is not the case for male coaches. Although it may help, men do not need to be highly decorated athletes or coaches to coach. In fact, many men who coach a Division I collegiate women's or men's team have never played the sport in which they coach. We found that some women who coach men had difficulty recruiting male athletes, particularly before they established themselves as good coaches. In addition, many of the women in the study had never considered the possibility that women could coach men at this high level. Norman similarly found that two highly qualified women coaches in the U.K. reached their positions "as a consequence of chance" rather than a clear structure in place to assist women coaches. Hence, it appears that most women do not even consider that coaching men is a possibility, eliminating half of the opportunities to coach!

Given our results, as well as the Yiamouyiannis (2007) study, we need to get the word out that coaching men is possible. Additionally, Thomae *et al.*'s (2012) study on male athletes' perceptions of women coaching men found that male athletes' willingness to play on a team with a female head coach was significantly predicted by: (1) attitudes toward a hypothetical female coach; (2) the perceived masculinity of the sport of the athlete; (3) experience with female coaching in the past; and (4) a strong identification with masculine descriptors.

More research is needed in order to better understand women's experiences coaching men and male athletes' perceptions of female coaches. Much of the research available on women coaching men has been conducted in the U.S. collegiate sport – further research is needed in other countries and at other levels. Also, as seen in recent media stories, highlighting a woman coaching a male team may show other women coaches or future coaches that the door is open to them (e.g. Associated Press 2010; Gunderson 2009; Halley 2010).

Race issues in coaching

A history of racism in U.S. sports

Racial discrimination is deeply rooted in U.S. society and this discrimination can be seen through sports. In fact, Coakley (2009) argues that sports have a long history of racial and ethnic exclusion in the U.S., and racial minorities have been underrepresented in all levels of sport. Segregation and slavery has specifically impacted African Americans in the U.S. African Americans are the only racial group to be intentionally segregated by law in the U.S. and endure an extended period of slavery – both of which have drastically impacted African Americans' experiences in sport as athletes, coaches, and sport administrators. In fact, it was only roughly 60 years ago that racial minorities were allowed to participate in mainstream sport. In 1945, Branch Rickey, the general manager of the Brooklyn Dodgers, signed Jackie Robinson to a contract in which he broke the "gentleman's agreement" and signed the first African American in Major League Baseball. Lapchick *et al.* (2009) argues that this act changed America forever.

Racial minorities now participate in several sports in large numbers, yet some sports remain almost exclusively White (Coakley 2009; Lapchick *et al.* 2009; Sage 2007). More specifically, there are a large number of African American athletes in men's and women's basketball, track and field, and football, but few other racial minority athletes in any sports. In Division I football the percentage of African American and White athletes are relatively equal with African Americans accounting for 46.4 percent and Whites holding 46.6 percent (Lapchick *et al.* 2009), but few other racial minorities (roughly 7 percent) participate in Division I football. Similarly, African American women make up 50.1 percent of all Division I female basketball athletes, whereas White women are 42.6 percent with all other racial and ethnic minorities at very low numbers (Lapchick *et al.* 2009). Softball has the highest percentage of Latina athletes (7.2 percent), an increase from 2001, but still 78.5 percent of female softball athletes are White.

Myths and stereotypes have been advanced to explain African American athletes' dominance in some sports. Some claim, for example, that African Americans possess a biological "gene" that makes them faster and stronger than White athletes. Most social scientists (e.g. Harris 2007) agree that the socio-cultural conditions cannot be ignored in explaining the dominance of African Americans in these high-publicity sports. Sage (2007), for example, argues that many African American youth spend hours honing their sports skills because they desire to escape from their environment and therefore are motivated to excel in sports. Furthermore, there is no scientific evidence to suggest that any specific genes relate to sport performance (Coakley 2009).

The lack of racial minority coaches

Research led by Richard Lapchick at The Institute for Diversity and Ethics in Sport tracks and provides detailed reports that highlight the lack of racial minority coaches. Lapchick and colleagues' latest "Racial and Gender Report Card" (2009) suggested that although we have seen an increase in participation of racial minority athletes in certain sports, there are very few racial minorities as coaches and even fewer in administrative positions. Whites dominate collegiate coaching holding approximately 89 percent of the head coaching positions of both men's and women's teams at all divisions. In fact, African Americans hold only 7.0 percent of Division I women's coaching positions, followed by 5.1 percent of Division II, and 4.4 percent of Division III coaching positions. These percentages are similar in the men's head coaching positions across all three divisions.

Looking closer, African American men held 22.9 percent of head coaching positions in Division I basketball and African American coaches (largely men) are at 13.6 percent for women's basketball, but those numbers are far below the proportion of African American basketball athletes. Other racial minority coaches (e.g. Asian, Latino, Native Americans) are almost completely absent from the collegiate coaching profession. Women minority coaches are at particularly low numbers. The percentage of African American women coaches is roughly the same percentage of women coaching men (2 percent) which is "simply appalling" (Abney 2007: 51). Furthermore, collegiate administration remains solidly White male. Whites held 90 percent of the Division I athletic director positions, for example, and males held 92.2 percent of those positions (Lapchick *et al.* 2009). Clearly racial minorities and particularly women minorities are not moving into power positions in U.S. collegiate sport.

Racial minority coaches hold more coaching positions at the professional level than in U.S. collegiate sport. For example, at the start of the 2009 Major League Baseball (MLB) season, 32 percent of the coaching positions were held by racial minorities: African Americans held 14 percent, Latinos held 17 percent, and Asians held 0.4 percent (Lapchick *et al.* 2010b). Although the percentage of racial minority athletes (40.2 percent) was still higher than the percentage of racial minority coaches, Lapchick and colleagues (2010b) argued that Bud Selig, the MLB Commissioner and his executive team, have positively impacted racial minority hiring practices and developed programs to "make MLB's central and team front offices look like America" (1). Similarly, Lapchick *et al.* (2010d) have praised the National Football League (NFL) for the Rooney Rule, which helped to triple the number of African American head coaches from two in 2001 to six in 2005. The Rooney Rule requires that people of color be interviewed as part of hiring and search process for a head coach.

In separate reports, Lapchick and his colleagues (2010c) also report on the National Basketball Association (NBA) and the Women's National Basketball Association (WNBA).

They reported that the percentage of racial minority head coaches in the NBA actually dropped from 40 percent to 30 percent at the beginning of the 2009–10 season. The percentage of assistant coaches was 41 percent, dropping from 42 percent a year earlier, and almost all of those racial minority coaches were African Americans with less than 1 percent of Latino coaches and no Asian assistants. Similarly, in the WNBA, there were four African American head coaches at the start of the 2010 season, and 41 percent of African American assistant coaches but no Latino or Asian assistant coaches (Lapchick *et al.* 2010a).

A number of explanations have been offered to explain the dearth of racial minority coaches, and the almost non-existence of female racial minority coaches. These reasons include discrimination and racism (Abney 2007; Cunningham and Sagas 2005; Sartone and Cunningham 2006), a lack of racial minority athletic directors or administrators (Lapchick 2007), the intent of racial minority coaches to leave coaching sooner (Cunningham *et al.* 2001), the glass-ceiling effect (Abney 2007; Cunningham 2003), the clustering of racial minority athletes into certain sports and positions (Abney 2007; Cunningham 2003; Smith 1992; Suggs 2001), a lack of role models (Abney 1988; Abney and Richey 1991), a lack of access to career resources and networks (Abney 2007), and both gender and racial discrimination, or "double jeopardy," for racial minority women (Abney 2000, 2007).

Fink *et al.* (2001) argue that coaches and other sport professionals that are different from the majority (i.e. White, heterosexual male) frequently face difficult work environments. In fact, Sagas and Cunningham (2005) demonstrated that the lack of career mobility of African American collegiate football coaches is a result of discriminatory practices and stereotypical beliefs that African Americans lack characteristics necessary to be successful in a managerial role. In addition, Cunningham and Sagas (2005) found evidence of "access discrimination," defined as limitations not related to their actual or potential performance, that minority group members encounter when the coaching position is filled, such as limited advertising of the position. They also noted that the proportion of African American assistant coaches (33 percent) was significantly less than the potential African American coaching pool and that African Americans assistant coaches were significantly underrepresented on the coaching staffs of White head coaches (30 percent), but not African American head coaches (45 percent), suggesting that race impacts the coaching network and, therefore, the likelihood of being hired for a head coaching position.

The clustering of minority athletes into certain sports also directly affects the hiring. Suggs (2001), for example, reported that the majority of African American female athletes compete in basketball and track and field. Suggs (2001) suggested the percentage of minority women coaches remains low because the growth of women's sport has been in White, upper-class suburban sports such as soccer, lacrosse, rowing, and golf. The resources and opportunities including equipment, green space, and available coaches to play these sports may not be available to racial minority athletes. If racial minority athletes are limited to a few sports, this also limits the "potential pool" of racial minority coaches and the growth of racial minority coaches in sports other than football, basketball, and track and field will remain limited.

Furthermore, scholars have also documented that African American women face both gender and racial discrimination (Abney 1988, 2007; Abney and Richey 1991; Smith 1992). This "double jeopardy" adds to the difficulty that African American women face in seeking positions within coaching (Abney 1988: 123). In their interviews with African American female athletic administrators and coaches, Abney and Richey (1991) found a lack of support and stated "there is a desperate need for support groups, career mentors, and role models for Black women in athletics" (Abney and Richey 1991: 20).

In sum, across the U.S. collegiate and professional sports, there are few racial minority coaches. Those few racial minority coaches are typically African American, and more often assistant coaches than head coaches. Coaches that are both women and racial minorities are almost completely absent. Research from a wider range of sports and levels outside of the U.S. is needed to gain a more complete picture of the number and experiences of racial minority coaches. Racial issues are historically and culturally based and the impact on coaches varies. We have provided a limited snapshot of the racial issues in U.S. sport; more wide-reaching research is needed.

Gay/lesbian issues in coaching

The limited advances in attitudes toward gay and lesbian people in the larger society have not been seen in sport. At best, sport offers a "don't ask, don't tell" policy towards sexual minority coaches and athletes (Krane and Barber 2005; Wolf-Wendel *et al.* 2001). That is, people in sport avoid discussing lesbian, gay, bisexual and transsexual (LGBT) issues with the hopes that "it will go away". LGBT athletes and coaches are involved in sport and will not go away. In fact, most authors agree that the percentage of gay and lesbians in sport is similar to the proportion in society, about one in ten people (Demers 2010).

Homophobia, or the generalized fear or intolerance of gays or lesbians, is pervasive in sport at all levels. Most of the research on sexual minority issues in coaching is focused on lesbian women's experiences (Demers 2010; Griffin 1998; Kamphoff 2010; Krane and Barber 2005) and to date only one study has described gay men's experiences in coaching (Thomae and Kamphoff 2012).

Lesbian women coaches

Pat Griffin's book, *Strong Women, Deep Closets*, is arguably the most influential work related to our understanding of homophobia in women's sports. Griffin argued that one of the most effective means of controlling women in sport is to challenge a woman's femininity and heterosexuality by calling her a lesbian. The threat of being called a lesbian affects *all* women, regardless of one's sexual orientation, and particularly in sport when women who do not act "normal" (i.e. heterosexual) are ostracized. Because many women fear being called a lesbian, their sporting experiences are controlled and they avoid masculine sports such as hockey or football, or they engage in activities to "prove" their heterosexuality such as wearing makeup and feminine clothing, or dating a man (Hargreaves 2000). Male athletes and coaches do not have to "prove" their heterosexuality, however, they are assumed to be heterosexual – which is one of the major differences in how men and women experience homophobia in sport. As Krane and Barber (2005) contend, sport is a location where women are perceived to be lesbian, and the athletic environment is perceived to be a hostile environment for lesbian coaches and athletes. In fact, many of the lesbian coaches Krane and Barber interviewed described a culture in sport of "overt and covert homonegativism" (i.e. a negative attitude towards homosexuality or homosexual people) and they reported that homonegative behaviors were accepted as part of the sport culture.

Krane and Barber (2005) report that lesbian coaches feel "silenced"; that is, they conceal their lesbian identity and do not have an open conversation with their team about how they identify. For example, all but one of the coaches Krane and Barber interviewed kept their lesbian identity silent, and none of the lesbian women Kamphoff (2010) interviewed were open about their lesbian identity with their team. One reason lesbian coaches conceal their identity is for fear that they will lose their job. Coaches can be let go for any reason and athletic directors may fire women coaches if they suspect they are lesbians (Griffin 1998). Many times athletic directors count on the coach's fear of being called a lesbian to prevent her from challenging harassment or discrimination. A few recent situations demonstrate that lesbian coaches may be fired or let go if they are open about their lesbian identity (cf. Olson 2010; C. Robertson 2010).

Lesbian coaches also avoid being open about their sexual orientation in concern over how it would impact recruiting. Research has demonstrated that negative recruiting is rampant, which occurs when a coach uses negative information about a coach from another college to "persuade" an athlete to attend their college (Demers 2010; Griffin 1998; Krane and Barber 2005; Kamphoff 2010). Negative recruiting may occur in relation to a lesbian coach's "perceived" or actual sexual orientation. Other coaches may make the assumption that a female coach is a lesbian if she does not have a male partner or spouse. Some lesbian coaches are also concerned that parents will have difficulties with their daughter playing for a lesbian coach, and some coaches believe that being out about your lesbian identity while coaching can "destroy you" in the recruiting process (Kamphoff 2010).

Lesbian coaches may attempt to gain power and status in sport through the use of other social mobility techniques including passing, distancing, and covering their lesbian identity (Krane and Barber 2005). Lesbian women may act in a heterosexual way to "pass" as heterosexual such as dress in a feminine way or wear makeup. For instance, one lesbian coach in Krane and Barber's study discussed how she never corrected people when they assume that she is straight. The women in their study also used distancing to avoid situations where their lesbian identity might be disclosed and intentionally did not socialize or discuss their personal life with their athletes or colleagues.

The experiences of lesbian coaches may be unique compared to other working women given new research that suggests when lesbian coaches left coaching, they were less likely to experience homophobia in their new positions outside of coaching (Kamphoff 2010). Sport for men is closely linked with masculinity and heterosexuality, but sport for women disrupts gender constructions. As Messner (1996) argued, the 'dualities of *lesbian versus heterosexual* and *gay versus heterosexual*' have been differently constructed for women and men in sport (225, italics in the original). Messner (1996) further argues that sport participation offers a normalizing equation for men as "athleticism=masculinity=heterosexuality," yet the same is not true for women in sport. For women, the equation has been more paradoxical and is represented by "athleticism? femininity? heterosexuality?" (225). This equation is certainly not held for *all* working women. Even if a woman works in predominately male-dominated professions (e.g. law or medicine), her sexuality is seldom questioned just because she works in that profession.

As demonstrated, lesbians face dramatically limited opportunities to be successful (Kamphoff 2010), and limited opportunities for coaching positions (Demers 2010). Some women choose to leave coaching to escape the homonegative environment of sport; many are able to be out about their lesbian identity once they are no longer coaching. Few studies have been conducted on the experiences of lesbian coaches. Researchers could examine the factors that contribute to the success of lesbian coaches such as the sport they coach, their support system, or the atmosphere of the athletic department or sport organization.

Gay male coaches

As mentioned, male and female athletes and coaches experience homophobia differently. Male athletes and coaches, for example, do not need to "prove" their heterosexuality. In fact, sport is uniquely powerful in society because it provides a location for men to reaffirm their masculinity, and males are assumed to be heterosexual if they are involved in sport. Yet even among men, a hierarchy exists that privileges some forms of masculinity and subordinates other forms (Anderson 2005; Coakley 2009; Messner and Solomon 2007). Hegemonic masculinity, or the most dominant form of masculinity, is accepted as the status quo and privileged in our society. This dominant form of masculinity includes attributes that we see as "standard" for men including being aggressive, non-emotional, competitive, muscular, powerful, and heterosexual. This dominant form of masculinity is so pervasive that even those that are marginalized (i.e. women or gay men, for example) accept it as standard practice.

Eric Anderson's book *In the Game* provides insight into hegemonic masculinity and the experiences of gay males in sport. He argues that to be a man in a hegemonic culture includes "not to *be*, *act*, or *behave* in ways attributed to gay men" (2005: 22, italics in the original). He also suggested that the term "gay athlete" is an oxymoron because sport is so homophobic that many athletes maintain that there is no possibility of gay males involved in sport, and that "homosexuality is synonymous with physical weakness and emotional frailty" (13). Anderson describes the homophobic language that occurs in sport including the use of terms like "fag," "queer," "faggot," and "wuss." The use of these terms are used to maintain the masculine environment of sport, police gendered behaviors, and motivate males (i.e. a coach saying, "You run like a faggot").

Hence, the use of these terms contributes to gay male athletes and coaches distancing themselves from the slightest possibility that they are gay and in many ways "acting" like they are heterosexual (Messner 1999). As Messner contends, gay athletes "do heterosexuality" when they date a women or act in a heterosexual (i.e. masculine) way to cover they are gay. According to Messner, doing heterosexuality allows gay athletes: (1) to avoid stigma, embarrassment, or ostracism that they may experience if they are suspected to be gay; and (2) to allow themselves to align with systems of power and privilege that "real men" experience.

Some scholars suggest that gay athletes self-select out of coaching and do not even enter the coaching ranks because of the marginalization they expect to experience (Anderson 2005; Thomae and Kamphoff 2012). Woog's (1997, 2002) stories of a few gay coaches suggest that gay coaches experience difficulties in the coming-out process including being threatened, insulted, and experiencing vandalism to their property. When they do come out to their team, their team can experience taunts, intimidation, and even fistfights. Some athletes want to quit the team, and some do quit after their coach comes out of the closet. The athletes, however, also talked about how they learned more about homosexuality and about the importance of being honest in their lives. Woog's story of coming out to his team and the community provided an inspirational story of athletes that supported his decision and accepted him as a gay coach.

Until recently there has been no research to systematically examine the experiences of gay coaches. The only study we know of is the Thomae and Kamphoff (2012) study of collegiate gay coaches' experiences negotiating their multiple identities as homosexuals, men, coaches, and members of the college staff. Surprisingly, the majority of the gay coaches interviewed were out about their sexuality to their team, and most felt supported by their athletes, collegiate department, and university. A few of the gay coaches talked about harassment and bullying they experienced – some by head coaches when they were assistant coaches. A few of the coaches were out about their sexuality as athletes and then were hired at their university; hence, they were out before being hired. The majority of gay coaches, however, dismissed the significance of being gay as a collegiate coach and downplayed the importance or the impact that it may have on their male athletes. For example, the coaches indicated that they are "coaches first" and "it shouldn't or doesn't matter" that they are gay. The gay coaches stated that they did not want to be treated differently, but to be treated equally.

Clearly, more research is needed on the experiences of gay coaches. Advances could have a drastic change in our understanding of diversity issues in sport. Additional research on gay coaches' experiences will not only allow us to better understand the experiences of gay coaches, but to change sport for the better. Future research should be expanded to include a more diverse sample of gay coaches including more traditional sports (i.e. football, basketball, etc.) and at the high school or youth levels.

Power lines crossing

As we discuss issues of gender, race, and sexuality, we want to add a note of caution in that to better understand the experiences of coaches we cannot simply add up these multiple identities. If we want to understand the experiences of Black women coaches, we cannot simply "add" their experiences as racial minority coaches to their experiences as a woman coach. We must, therefore, consider how multiple identities intersect.

Scholars have argued that additive models (Black + woman, for example) do not offer a comprehensive analysis to understand the complexity of racial and gender issues, or allow us to understand the complexity of people's lives. As Hall (1996) argues, "Race does not merely make the experience of women's oppression greater; rather, it qualitatively changes the nature of that subordination" (44). Black, Latina, Asian, and Native American women do not simply experience increased oppression; their disadvantaged status in sport and more specifically coaching, is qualitatively different from their White counterpart and different from each other (Birrell 1990; Jamieson 2000; Smith 1992).

Birrell and McDonald (2000) argue that discussion of discrimination issues often privileges one identity (e.g. race, class, gender) while ignoring the others. In fact, a person's identities do not work independently and cannot be understood in isolation of each other. To move beyond binaries is to understand the "space in the middle" or the "third space" (McDonald and Birrell 1999; Jamieson 2003). This "third space" is outside the binaries and a space without labels in which the most powerful work can be done. In focusing on only one identity, we produce an 'incomplete and dangerously simple analysis' (Birrell and McDonald 2000: 7). Hence, we suggest this should be considered when attempting to understand the mix of race, gender, and sexuality issues in the profession of coaching.

Summary and implications for practice

The issues women, racial minorities, and sexual minorities face in coaching are likely to remain until there is widespread institutional change within sport. Instead, most of the focus has been on how women, racial minorities, or gay/lesbian coaches must change to "fit into" the system of sport with little analysis on how sporting organizations must change to make sport a more inclusive place. By only focusing on an individual approach instead of an organizational approach, we assume that women, racial minority, or gay/lesbian coaches do not have the proper training, interest, motivation, or skills to succeed in coaching. We know this is not the case! We must move beyond the thinking that women, racial minorities, or gay/lesbian coaches are the "problem" and recognize that sport is not neutral. In fact, as demonstrated, the culture and organization of sport leads to many of the issues experienced by women, racial minority, and gay/lesbian coaches. In other words, we must look hard at the sport and the structural organizations of sport within the U.S. If we only focus on individual solutions, we will not experience sustainable changes.

The sport coaching profession is almost solidly White male; research has documented the exclusionary nature of coaching in terms of race, gender, and sexual orientation. It is clear that women, racial minorities, and sexual minorities face challenging issues as they work to be successful and remain in the coaching profession. We close this chapter with some suggestions to address discrimination issues that women, racial minority, and gay/lesbian coaches experience. These suggestions are based on our research as well as the suggestions of Abney (2007), Eagly and Carli (2007), Marshall (2010) and Werthner *et al.* (2010).

- Each sport organization should take a critical review of the policies, or lack of policies, regarding discrimination within the organization.
- Every coaches association and sport organization should have a standing committee that creates agenda for change – and one of those agenda items could be to increase the percentage of women, racial minority, and sexual minority coaches.
- Establish a mentoring program to help women, racial minority or gay/lesbian coaches. Consider pairing beginning coaches with senior coaches to provide support.
- Colleges and sport organizations should adopt statements of non-discrimination and inclusion of minorities for their players, coaches, and administrative staff.
- Organizations should look at how they recruit candidates for the coaching positions. Consider expanding traditional recruitment networks to seek candidates that are different from the majority (e.g. "The Rooney Rule" in the National Football League).
- Take steps to ensure that women and racial minorities hold leadership roles in the sport organization in enough numbers that their voices can be heard.
- Take a look at the sport organization's media guides, web pages, and newsletters and ensure that "different" people are present in terms of gender and racial diversity.
- Ensure that day-care is available. Consider allowing children to attend practices, camps, and competitions with appropriate child care to make it easier for female (or male) coaches who are parents of young children.
- Provide women, racial minorities, and gay/lesbian coaches an opportunity to represent the sport organization at conferences or workshops.
- Encourage women, racial minorities, and sexual minorities to enter the coaching profession. Be their mentor, but also be up front about the issues they may face.
- Ensure that women, racial minorities, and gay/lesbian staff and coaches experience challenging job responsibilities and are given the tools to advance in their positions. Support coaches in "becoming good to great." See Mercier's (2010) chapter on how women coaches get the most out of their professional lives, and encourage all your coaches to read her chapter.
- Respect athletes', coaches', and administrators' multiple identities. Do not tolerate rude or disparaging comments about women, racial minorities, or sexual minorities.
- Recognize your own biases and address the biases of others. Do not assume a woman coach who is not married, for example, is a lesbian.

References

Abney, R. (1988) 'The effects of role models and mentors on career patterns of Black women coaches and athletic administrators in historically Black and historically White institutions of higher education,' unpublished doctoral dissertation, University of Iowa.

Abney, R. (2000) 'The glass-ceiling effect and African American women coaches and athletic administrators,' in D. Brooks and R. Althouse (eds) *Racism in College Athletics: The African American Athlete's Experience* (2nd ed.). Morgantown, WV: Fitness Information Technology.

Abney, R. (2007) 'African American women in intercollegiate coaching and athletic administration: Unequal access,' in D. Brooks and R. Althouse (eds) *Diversity and Social Justice in College Sports: Sport Management and the Student Athlete*. Morgantown, WV: Fitness Information Technology.

Abney, R. and Richey, D. (1991) 'Barriers encountered by black female athletic administrators and coaches,' *Journal of Physical Education, Recreation and Dance*, 62(6): 19–21.

Acosta, V.R. and Carpenter, L.J. (2012) 'Women in intercollegiate sport: A longitudinal, national study thirty-five year update 1977–2012,' online, available at: www.acostacarpenter.org.

Anderson, E. (2005) *In the Game: Gay Athletes and the Cult of Masculinity*, Albany, NY: SUNY Press.

Associated Press (2010, February 12) 'Alaskan boys hockey team rare female coach,' online, available at: http://highschool.rivals.com/content.asp?CID=1051468.

Birrell, S. (1990) 'Women of color, critical autobiography, and sport,' in M.A. Messner and D.F. Sabo (eds) *Sport, Men and the Gender Order*, Champaign, IL: Human Kinetics.

Birrell, S. and McDonald, M.G. (2000) 'Reading sport, articulating power lines: An introduction,' in S. Birrell and M.G. McDonald (eds) *Reading Sport: Critical Essays on Power and Representation*, Boston, MA: Northeastern University Press.

Bray, C. (2004) '2002–03 NCAA gender equity report,' *National Collegiate Athletic Association*, available at: www.ncaapublications.com/p-3827-2002-03-gender-equity-report.aspx.

Coakley, J.J. (2009) *Sports in Society: Issues and Controversies* (10th edition), New York: McGraw-Hill.

Cunningham, G.B. (2003) 'Already aware of the glass ceiling: Race-related effects of perceived opportunity on the career choices of college athletes,' *Journal of African American Studies*, 7(1): 57–71.

Cunningham, G.B. and Sagas, M. (2005) 'Access discrimination in intercollegiate athletics,' *Journal of Sport and Social Issues*, 29(2): 148–163.

Cunningham, G.B., Sagas, M. and Ashley, F.B. (2001) 'Occupational commitment and intent to leave the coaching profession: Differences according to race,' *International Review for the Sociology of Sport*, 36(2): 131–148.

Demers, G. (2010) 'Homophobia in sport: Fact of life, taboo subject,' in S. Robertson (ed.) *Taking the Lead: Strategies and Solutions from Female Coaches*, Edmonton: The University of Alberta Press.

Drago, R., Hennighausen, L., Rogers, J., Vescio, T. and Stauffer, K.D. (2005) 'CAGE: The Coaching and Gender Equity Project,' online, available at: www.epi.soe.vt.edu/perspectives/policy_news/docs/CAGE.doc

Eagly A. and Carli, L. (2007) 'Women in the labyrinth of leadership,' *Harvard Business Review*, September: 62–71.

Fink, J.S., Pastore, D.L. and Riemer, H.A. (2001) 'Do differences make a difference? Managing diversity in Division IA intercollegiate athletes,' *Journal of Sport Management*, 15(1): 10–50.

Griffin, P. (1998) *Strong Women, Deep Closets: Lesbians and Homophobia in Sport*, Champaign, IL: Human Kinetics.

Gunderson, D. (2009, December 29) 'Female coach a rare sight for boys' high school teams,' *Minnesota Public Radio*, online, available at: http://minnesota.publicradio.org/display/web/2009/12/28/women-coaches.

Hall, M.A. (1996) *Feminism and Sporting Bodies: Essays on Theory and Practice*, Champaign, IL: Human Kinetics.

Halley, J. (2010, March 11) 'Washington D.C. woman lands prep football head coaching gig,' *USA Today*, online, available at: www.usatoday.com/sports/preps/football/2010-03-11-washington-dc-woman-lands-prep-football-coaching-job_N.htm.

Hargreaves, J. (2000) *Heroines of Sport: The Politics of Difference and Identity*, London: Routledge.

Harris, O. (2007) 'Taboo's explanation of black athletes dominance: More fiction than fact,' in D.D. Brooks and R.C. Althouse (eds) *Diversity and Social Justice in College Sports: Sport Management and the Student Athlete*, Morgantown, WV: Fitness Information Technology.

Hewlett, S. (2003) *Creating a Life*, New York: Miramax Publishers.

Hochschild, A. (1989) *The Second Shift*, New York: Penguin.

Humphreys, B.R. (2000) 'Equal pay on the hardwood: The earnings gap between male and female NCAA Division I basketball coaches,' *Journal of Sport Economics*, 1(3): 299–307.

Jamieson, K.M. (2000) 'Reading Nancy Lopez: Decoding representations of race, class, sexuality,' in S. Birrell and M.G. McDonald (eds) *Reading Sport: Critical Essays on Power and Representation*. Boston, MA: Northeastern University Press.

Jamieson, K.M. (2003) 'Occupying a middle space: Toward a mestiza sport studies,' *Sociology of Sport Journal*, 20(1): 1–16.

Kamphoff, C.S. (2010) 'Bargaining with patriarchy: Former women coaches' experiences and their decision to leave collegiate coaching,' *Research Quarterly for Exercise and Sport*, 81(3): 367–379.

Kamphoff, C.S. and Gill, D.L. (2008) 'Collegiate athletes' perception of the coaching profession,' *International Journal of Sports Science and Coaching*, 3(1): 55–72.

Kamphoff, C.S., Armentrout, S. and Driska, A. (2010) 'The token female: Women's experiences coaching men at the Division I level,' *Journal of Intercollegiate Sport*, 3: 297–315.

Kamphoff, C.S., Armentrout, S.M. and Leberman S. (2008, May) 'Women as elite coaches: Strategies for sport and social change,' *Sport and Social Change Conference*, Toronto, Canada.

Kane, M.J. and Stangl, J.M. (1991) 'Employment patterns of female coaches in men's athletics: Tokenism and marginalization as reflections of occupation sex-segregation,' *Journal of Sport and Social Issues*, 15(1): 21–41.

Kanter, R.M. (1977) *Men and Women of the Corporation*, New York: Basic Books.

Kerr, G. (2010) 'Female coaches' experiences of harassment and bullying,' in S. Robertson (ed.) *Taking the Lead: Strategies and Solutions from Female Coaches*, Edmonton: The University of Alberta Press.

Kelley, B.C., Eklund, R.C. and Ritter-Taylor, M. (1999) 'Stress and burnout among collegiate tennis coaches,' *Journal of Sport and Exercise Psychology*, 21(2): 113–130.

Krane, V. and Barber, H. (2005) 'Identify tensions in lesbian intercollegiate coaches,' *Research Quarterly for Exercise and Sport*, 76(1): 67–81.

Knoppers, A. (1992) 'Explaining male dominance and sex segregation in coaching: Three approaches,' *Quest*, 44(2): 210–227.

Lapchick, R.E. (2007) 'The buck stops here: Assessing diversity among campus and conference leaders for Division IA schools,' online, available at: www.tidesport.org/Grad%20Rates/2008-09_FBS_Demographics_Study.pdf.

Lapchick, R.E., Bartter, J., Diaz-Calderon, A., Hanson, J., Harless, C., Johnson, W., Kamke, C., Lopresti, C., McMechan, D., Reshard, N. and Turner, A. (2009) '2009 Racial and Gender Report Card,' online, available at: http://web.bus.ucf.edu/sportbusiness/?page=1445.

Lapchick, R.E., Caudy, D. and Russell, C. (2010a) 'The 2010 Women's National Basketball Association Racial and Gender Report Card,' online, available at: http://web.bus.ucf.edu/sportbusiness/?page=1445

Lapchick, R., Kaiser, C., Caudy, D. and Wang, W. (2010b) 'The 2010 Racial and Gender Report Card: Major League Baseball,' online, available at: http://web.bus.ucf.edu/sportbusiness/?page=1445

Lapchick, R.E., Kaiser, C., Russell, C. and Welch, N. (2010c) 'The 2010 Racial and Gender Report Card: National Basketball Association,' online, available at: http://web.bus.ucf.edu/sportbusiness/?page=1445

Lapchick, R.E., Kitnurse, J.M. and Moss, A. (2010d) 'The 2010 Racial and Gender Report Card: National Football League,' online, available at: http://web.bus.ucf.edu/sportbusiness/?page=1445

LaVoi, N. (2009) 'Occupational sex segregation in a youth soccer organization: Females in positions of power,' *Women in Sport and Physical Activity Journal*, 18(2): 25–37.

Marshall, D. (2010) 'Introduction,' in S. Robertson (ed.) *Taking the Lead: Strategies and Solutions from Female Coaches*, Edmonton: The University of Alberta Press.

McDonald, M. and Birrell, S. (1999) 'Reading sport critically: A methodology for interrogating power,' *Sociology of Sport Journal*, 16(4): 283–300.

Mercier, R. (2000) 'Supporting women who coach *and* have families,' *Canadian Journal for Women in Coaching*, 1(2), online, available at: http://23361.vws.magma.ca/WOMEN/e/journal/nov2000/support_eng.PDF.

Mercier, R. (2010) 'The business of greatness,' in S. Robertson (ed.) *Taking the Lead: Strategies and Solutions from Female Coaches*, Edmonton: The University of Alberta Press.

Messner, M.A. (1996) 'Studying up on sex,' *Sociology of Sport Journal*, 13(3): 221–237.

Messner, M.A. (1999) 'Becoming 100 percent straight,' in J. Coakley and P. Donnelly (eds) *Inside Sports*, New York: Routledge.

Messner, M.A. (2007) *It's All for the Kids: Gender, Families, and Youth Sports*, Berkeley, CA: University of California Press.

Messner, M.A. and Solomon, N.M. (2007) 'Social justice and men's interests: The case of Title IX,' *Journal of Sport and Social Issues*, 31(2): 162–178.

National Federation of State High School Associations (2010) '2011–12 High School Athletics Participation Survey Results,' online, available at: www.nfhs.org/content.aspx?id=3282.

Norman, L. (2010) 'The UK coaching system is failing women coaches,' *International Journal of Sports Science and Coaching*, 3(4): 447–467.

Olson, R. (2010, December 10) 'Coach says U demoted her because she's a lesbian,' *Star Tribune*, online, available at: www.startribune.com/local/south/111645094.html.

Ranson, G. (2005) 'No longer "one of the boys": Negotiations with motherhood, as prospect or reality, among women in engineering,' *Canadian Review of Sociology and Anthropology*, 42(2): 145–166.

Robertson, C. (2010, December 17) 'Lesbian coach's exit from Belmont U. has Nashville talking,' *New York Times*, online, available at: www.nytimes.com/2010/12/18/education/18belmont.html?src=twrhp.

Robertson, S. (ed.) (2010) *Taking the Lead: Strategies and Solutions from Female Coaches*, Edmonton: The University of Alberta Press.

Sagas, M. and Cunningham, G.B. (2005) 'Racial differences in the career success of assistant football coaches: The role of discrimination, human capital and social capital,' *Journal of Applied Social Psychology*, 35(4): 773–797.

Sage, G.H. (1998) *Power and Ideology in American Sport: A Critical Perspective* (2nd ed.), Champaign, IL: Human Kinetics.

Sage, G.H. (2007) 'Introduction,' in D.D. Brooks and R.C. Althouse (eds) *Diversity and Social Justice in College Sports: Sport Management and the Student Athlete*, Morgantown, WV: Fitness Information Technology.

Sartone, M.L. and Cunningham, G.B. (2006) 'Stereotypes, race and coaching,' *Journal of African American Studies*, 10(2): 69–83.

Sayer, L.C. (2005) 'Gender, time, and inequality: Trends in women's and men's paid work, unpaid work, and free time,' *Social Forces*, 84(1): 285–303.

Smith, Y.R. (1992) 'Women of color in society and sport,' *Quest*, 44(2): 228–250.

Stangl, J.M. and Kane, M.J. (1991) 'Structural variables that offer explanatory power for the underrepresentation of women coaches since Title IX: The case of homologous reproduction,' *Sociology of Sport Journal*, 8(1): 47–60.

Staurowsky, E.J. (1990) 'Women coaching male athletes,' in M.A. Messner and D.F. Sabo (eds) *Sport, Men, and the Gender Order: Critical Feminist Perspectives*, Champaign, IL: Human Kinetics.

Suggs. W. (2001) 'Left behind,' *The Chronicle of Higher Education*, 48(14): A35.

Theberge, N. (1993) 'The construction of gender in sport: Women, coaching, and the naturalization of difference,' *Social Problems*, 40(3): 301–313.

Thomae, J. and Kamphoff, C. (2012) 'Emerging from silence: Experiences of gay male coaches in the NCAA,' under review.

Thomae, J., Kamphoff, C., Devine, J., Makepeace, A., Long, A., Dennis, J. and Sandstrom, K. (2012) 'Experience matters: Predictors of male Division-I athletes' attitudes toward female coaches,' under review.

Werthner, P., Culver, D. and Mercier, R. (2010) 'Changing the androcentric world of sport – Is it possible?' in S. Robertson (ed.) *Taking the Lead: Strategies and Solutions from Female Coaches*, Edmonton: The University of Alberta Press.

Wolf-Wendel, L.E., Toma, J.D. and Morphew, C.C. (2001) 'How much difference is too much difference? Perceptions of gay men and lesbians in intercollegiate athletics,' *Journal of College Student Development*, 42(5): 465–479.

Women's Sport Foundation UK (2007) 'The issues surrounding women and coaching,' online, available at: http://documentsearch.org/pdf/the-issues-surrounding-women-and-coaching.html.

Woog, D. (1997) *Jocks: True Stories of America's Gay Male Athletes*, Los Angeles, CA: Alyson.

Woog, D. (2002) *Jocks 2: Coming Out to Play*, Los Angeles, CA: Alyson.

Yiamouyiannis, A. (2007) 'Occupational closure in intercollegiate athletics female head coaches of men's sport teams at NCAA colleges,' unpublished doctoral dissertation, George Washington University.

B

Analysing sports coaching

6

COACHING EFFICACY BELIEFS

Melissa A. Chase

MIAMI UNIVERSITY, USA

Eric Martin

MICHIGAN STATE UNIVERSITY, USA

Introduction

Effective coaches teach their athletes new skills and tactics and prepare them to perform at their highest potential. Some would argue, depending upon the age or developmental level of the athlete, coaches are also responsible for the athlete's enjoyment, motivation to play, character development, and advancement of a strong work ethic. Achievement in all of these areas is asking a lot of the coach. Those coaches who believe they can affect the learning and performance of their athletes are thought to have coaching efficacy (Feltz *et al.* 1999). Coaches with high coaching efficacy tend to be more effective in providing tactical skills, motivational skills, contingent feedback techniques, and show more commitment to coaching (Feltz *et al.* 2008). In turn, their athletes and teams tend to be more satisfied, efficacious, motivated, and perform better. Therefore, coaching efficacy beliefs and the outcomes associated with these beliefs are important to understanding effective coaching behavior. This chapter provides an overview of the coaching efficacy research, suggestions for future areas of inquiry, and practical ideas for coaching practice.

Overview of coaching efficacy

A conceptual model for coaching efficacy was first proposed in 1999 by Feltz, Chase, Moritz and Sullivan. They defined coaching efficacy as "the extent to which coaches believe they have the capacity to affect the learning and performance of their athletes" (Feltz *et al.* 1999: 765). Performance was defined as the psychological, attitudinal, and teamwork skills of athletes as well as their physical behavior. Their model provided a structure for examining the relationship between coaching efficacy, effective coaching behavior, and the outcomes associated with the performance of athletes and teams. Prior to the conceptualization of a model for coaching efficacy, some researchers borrowed from frameworks for teacher efficacy (Gibson and Dembo 1984), a multidimensional model of sport leadership (Chelladurai 1990), or a mediational model of leadership in youth sport coaches (Smoll and Smith 1989) to study similar aspects of coaching behaviors and beliefs. With the development of a conceptual framework for coaching efficacy (e.g. proposed sources of coaching efficacy, dimensions of coaching efficacy, and outcomes for coaches and athletes) and an instrument to measure coaching efficacy beliefs (e.g. Coaching Efficacy Scale, Feltz *et al.* 1999), a new line of coaching efficacy research emerged. The next section explains the conceptual model for coaching efficacy, describes the Coaching Efficacy Scale, and reviews previous research in coaching efficacy.

Conceptual model for coaching efficacy

The conceptual model for coaching efficacy is a sport-oriented model that takes into account the uniqueness of sport and specific sport-oriented goals for athlete and team performance (see Figure 6.1). Based upon Bandura's work in self-efficacy (1977, 1986) and Woolfolk's, Denham's and colleagues' work in teacher efficacy (Denham and Michael 1981; Woolfolk *et al.* 1990), the conceptual framework for coaching efficacy went beyond describing a positive effect the teacher has on student learning to include other sport-specific dimensions that are concerned with performance of athletes and teams in athletic competition. Coaching efficacy as described by Feltz and colleagues (1999) proposed there were four sources of coaching efficacy: extent of coaching experience/preparation; prior success or win/loss record; perceived skill of athletes; and social support from school, parents, community or administrators. Coaching efficacy was composed of four dimensions from the original model in 1999 (motivation, game strategy, teaching technique, and character building), and one new dimension, physical conditioning, suggested in 2008 (Myers *et al.* 2008).

Motivation efficacy was defined as the confidence coaches have in their ability to affect the psychological mood and psychological skills of their athletes. Game strategy efficacy was defined as the confidence coaches have in their abilities to lead during competition. Technique efficacy was defined as the confidence coaches have in their ability to use their instructional and diagnostic skills during practice. Character building efficacy was defined

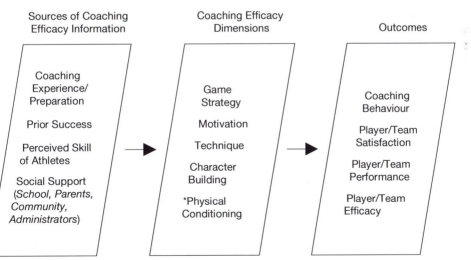

Note: *Physical conditioning proposed in 2008.

Figure 6.1: Conceptual model for coaching efficacy (adapted with permission from Feltz *et al.* 1999: 766).

as the confidence coaches have in their ability to positively influence the character development of their athletes through sport. Physical conditioning efficacy was defined as the confidence coaches have in their ability to prepare their athletes physically for participation in their sport. The five dimensions are described as the key components of coaching efficacy that are developed from sources of efficacy information and influence coach, player, and team outcomes in unique ways. For example, technique efficacy may be formed by a coach's preparation (e.g. coaching education workshops) and her prior success (e.g. five winning seasons in a row) and this positively relates to her coaching behavior, such as the positive reinforcement she uses when teaching fundamental skills. Her character-building efficacy stems from the social support she receives from the community and positively relates to her team's performance, such as lack of penalties for personal fouls. Each efficacy dimension can be developed from a combination and individual weighting of the various coaching efficacy information sources. The coaching efficacy dimensions can influence coach, player, and team outcomes, such as coaching behavior (e.g. feedback, management styles, organizational skills), player and team satisfaction with the coach and sport experience, player and team performance (e.g. player/ team statistics, win-loss record, teamwork, penalties), and player and team efficacy.

Coaching Efficacy Scale

At the same time that Feltz and colleagues (1999) conceptualized the model of coaching efficacy, they developed the Coaching Efficacy Scale (CES) to measure coaches' overall perception of their coaching efficacy and the multidimensional components of coaching efficacy beliefs (e.g. motivation, game strategy, teaching technique, and character building). The CES used the stem "*How confident are you in your ability to ...*", followed by 24 items meant to reflect each of the four dimensions, on a ten-point Likert scale ranging from zero (*not at all confident*) to nine (*extremely confident*). The CES was developed with a sample of high school varsity boys' basketball coaches and deemed appropriate for high school and lower-division collegiate coaches in the United States or similar contexts. Development of the CES as a valid and reliable scale to measure coaching efficacy was critical to the advancement of research in this area. Feltz, her graduate students, and other colleagues began to explore the relationships proposed in the coaching efficacy model, which lead to confirmation of some aspects of the model, extensions to other aspects of the model, and revisions to the CES.

In 2008, Myers *et al.* published a revised version of the CES called the Coaching Efficacy Scale II for High School Teams (CES II-HST). The new scale added a fifth dimension of coaching efficacy, physical conditioning efficacy, changed the stem to read "*in relation to the team that you are currently coaching, how confident are you in your ability to*", changed a few individual items, and reduced the Likert scale from ten-point to four-point. The CES II-HST is appropriate for use with head coaches of high school teams, primarily in team sports where coaches have the opportunity to intervene during competition. For example, the CES II-HST might not be as appropriate for swimming coaches who cannot always coach their athletes in a meaningful way during competition. In 2011, Myers and Chase felt it was important to develop a coaching efficacy scale for youth sport coaches. The CES-HST was modified by changing nine of the 18 items to address the uniqueness of youth sport coaching. The Coaching Efficacy Scale for Youth Sport Teams (CES-YST) is an appropriate measure for youth sport coaches, with athletes between the ages of 8 and 13 years (Myers *et al.* 2011). The authors recommend that research with other types of sports (team and individual), higher-division collegiate or professional coaches should use the CES until other level and sport-specific versions are available (Myers *et al.* 2008).

Research in coaching efficacy

Based upon Feltz and colleagues' (1999) initial work and the development of the Coaching Efficacy Scale, many lines of research have emerged. Most of the research has been conducted with North American samples of high school and collegiate athletes and coaches, so consider that the context may be unique to this constituency. The first section examines research that has focused on identifying specific sources of information that lead to the development of coaching efficacy. Research in the second section examines the relationship between the dimensions of coaching efficacy and coach, player, and team outcomes.

Sources of coaching efficacy research

Feltz and colleagues (1999) found initial support for perceived team ability, amount of coaching experience, past winning percentage, and social support as sources of coaching efficacy, with their study of male varsity high school coaches. Since 1999, additional research has examined other potential sources of coaching efficacy, with male and female coaches at the high school and collegiate ranks. Several studies have found that coaching education programs and programs leading to certification can influence the development of coaching efficacy. Malete and Feltz (2000) found coaches who participated in a coaching education program showed significantly higher coaching efficacy than coaches who did not participate in a coaching education program. Game strategy and technique efficacy dimensions showed the greatest differences between the two groups. Lee *et al.* (2002) found that after controlling for years of experience, certified coaches in Singapore were higher than non-certified Singapore coaches in both game strategy and technique dimensions of coaching efficacy. Campbell and Sullivan (2005) examined the effect of a coaching course from the National Coaching Certification Program (National Coaching Certification Program 2002) on the coaching efficacy levels of novice coaches. They found all dimensions of coaching efficacy had significant increases from pre-test to post-test after completing the course. Malete and Sullivan (2009) found that Botswana coaches in coaching education programs and those coaches who gained certification had significantly higher scores on the technique dimension of coaching efficacy than coaches not in the coaching education program. Malete and Sullivan also examined the coaches' playing experience and coaching experience as sources for all of the dimensions of coaching efficacy, which are described in the next section.

Previous playing experience in sport seems to be common among coaches. If someone enjoyed the sport experience as an athlete, he or she may be more likely to continue involvement in the sport as a coach. Recent research across a wide range of coaching contexts support the importance of hours of athletic participation and the developmental profiles of successful coaches (Becker 2009; Côté and Gilbert 2009; Gilbert *et al.* 2006; Gilbert *et al.* 2009). Interestingly, not all good athletes are good coaches and some very good coaches never played the sport they coach. In terms of coaching efficacy, it seemed possible that some coaches may transfer the efficacy beliefs they had as an athlete to their beliefs about their ability to coach. Sullivan and colleagues (Sullivan *et al.* 2006) investigated playing experience of the coach as a source of coaching efficacy in curling coaches. They found that after controlling for coaching experience, game strategy efficacy was significantly predicted by playing experience. Malete and Sullivan (2009), in their research with coaches from Botswana, found that playing experience and coaching experience were significant sources for all of the dimensions of coaching efficacy except character building.

Fung (2002, 2003) conducted two studies with coaches from Hong Kong that investigated coaching experience (e.g. the time spent coaching) as a source of coaching efficacy. In the first study, Fung (2002) found that the more years spent coaching, the higher the coaching efficacy. However, the number of hours spent coaching in the previous year was not significantly related to coaching efficacy. In the second study, Fung (2003) found no relationship between coaching efficacy and coaching experience or hours spent coaching. In addition, Marback and colleagues (Marback *et al.* 2005) suggested that previous coaching experience has the strongest influence on game strategy efficacy, motivation efficacy, and character building efficacy. Kavussanu *et al.* (2008) found that years of coaching experience predicted technique coaching efficacy.

Using a qualitative approach, Chase and colleagues (Chase *et al.* 2005) extended the previous research by means of structured interviews, with 12 male high school varsity basketball coaches. Six distinct sources of coaching efficacy emerged from their deductive content analysis of the data: player development; coaches' development; knowledge/preparation; leadership skills; player support; and past experience. Player and coach development were unique sources as coaches described the importance of developing or improving as a player/coach and person. The authors concluded that their findings supported and extended the original model of sources of coaching efficacy (Feltz *et al.* 1999) and encouraged further research to investigate other sources of information.

Myers *et al.* (2005) added to the literature by examining sources of coaching efficacy in collegiate coaches. Results from their study confirmed that perceived team ability, social support from athletes' parents and the community, career winning percentage, and head coaching experience were important sources of efficacy information. The most important of those sources for college coaches was the perceived team ability. Female coaches perceived social support from the community influenced their character-building efficacy and support from athletes' parents influenced their character-building efficacy, technique efficacy and motivation efficacy.

Short and colleagues (Short *et al.* 2005) studied imagery use as a source of coaching efficacy. They predicted that different imagery techniques would correspond to the different dimensions of coaching efficacy. They found that Motivation General Mastery imagery was a significant predictor of total coaching efficacy, after controlling for career win/loss record and total years coaching. Cognitive General imagery was the only significant predictor of the technique efficacy dimension and Motivation General Mastery imagery was the sole predictor of motivation efficacy. Imagery use as a source of information to help prepare coaches for competition and increase their coaching efficacy beliefs is the only mental training skill examined so far in the literature. Perhaps other mental training skills, such as self-talk, arousal control, or energy management could influence the development of coaching efficacy and will need further study.

In summary, research confirms coaching experience/preparation, prior success or win/loss record, perceived skill of athletes, and social support – all sources proposed in the model of coaching efficacy – do serve as sources of coaching efficacy. Several new sources of coaching efficacy have also emerged. Coaching education programs, certification programs, previous playing experience, player/coach development, imagery, and possibly other mental skills training techniques might also influence the coaches' development of coaching efficacy. Some gender differences in sources of coaching efficacy information were found, primarily in social support of the coach, but more research is needed before conclusions can be drawn. Overall, more research is needed that examines coaching efficacy sources related to each specific coaching efficacy dimension. This is especially true where differences in the level of sport competition (e.g. recreational versus elite) and age of the athletes (e.g. youth, high school, collegiate) seem to influence the relationship between sources and coaching efficacy (Feltz *et al.* 2008).

Coaching efficacy and coach/player outcomes research

The relationship between coaching efficacy and outcomes of coaching behavior (e.g. commitment, burnout, leadership style), player/team satisfaction, player/team performance, and player/team efficacy has been examined in several studies. In the initial study by Feltz and colleagues (1999), they found that higher efficacy coaches did display different coaching behaviors as measured by the Coaching Behavior Assessment System (CBAS; Smith *et al.* 1977). High efficacy coaches used more praise and encouragement than lower efficacy coaches. Lower efficacy coaches seemed to spend more time, with less efficiency, in organizing practice drills and therefore used more instructional and organizational behaviors than higher efficacy coaches. Coaching efficacy did not predict coaching commitment or perceived effort as expected. The authors explained this finding was likely due to their sample of part-time high school coaches who were all committed to coaching or they would not be coaching in addition to their full-time employment.

Kent and Sullivan (2003) explored the relationship between organizational commitment and coaching efficacy with international and collegiate coaches. The authors concluded that highly efficacious coaches are more committed to their current situation than those coaches who are less efficacious. They suggested future research should examine coaching turnover. Haugen *et al.* (2004) investigated the relationship between burnout and coaching efficacy over the course of a season in high school basketball coaches. Findings indicated that coaches had higher burnout scores and lower coaching efficacy scores at the post-season, when compared to pre-season scores. Additionally, coaching efficacy scores and burnout scores were negatively related at both time periods, with lower efficacy coaches having higher burnout scores than higher efficacy coaches. This is the only published study that examined coaching efficacy and burnout in coaches, suggesting much more research in this area is needed.

Sullivan and Kent (2003) investigated the coaching efficacy and coaches' leadership style of collegiate coaches in Canada and the United States. They found that motivation efficacy and technique efficacy positively influenced leadership behavior in coaches, such as teaching and instruction, and positive feedback. This suggests that coaches with higher coaching efficacy, specifically technique efficacy, perceived that they displayed better teaching or instructional leadership styles.

Coaching efficacy can also influence several player and team outcomes, directly or indirectly, through athlete's perceptions of the coaches' behavior. Players who play for coaches with high efficacy were more satisfied with their experience on high school teams (Feltz *et al.* 1999) and college teams (Myers *et al.* 2005) than players who play for coaches with low efficacy. The same relationship was found for player/team performance when measured by wins and losses. Teams with high efficacy coaches had better win-loss records than teams with low efficacy coaches. Myers and colleagues (2005) found high motivation efficacy and character-building efficacy in collegiate coaches also correlated with better winning records for their teams.

The relationship between coaching efficacy and team/players' efficacy was examined in a sample of female high school varsity volleyball players and their coaches (Vargas-Tonsing *et al.* 2003). Self-efficacy and team efficacy was measured for each athlete and then scores were compared to their coach's level of coaching efficacy. Results showed that coaching efficacy was a significant predictor of team efficacy but not of player efficacy. In particular, motivation efficacy and character-building efficacy were effective in predicting team efficacy. This suggests that high efficacy coaches can positively influence their teams' efficacy beliefs. The authors suggested that team success is easier to observe than individual player success in team sports, which may explain why coaching efficacy did not predict individual player's self-efficacy.

In summary, coaching efficacy has been examined as a predictor of coaching behavior (e.g. commitment, burnout, leadership style), player/team satisfaction, player/team performance, and player/team efficacy. The evidence so far supports the predicted relationships in the model of coaching efficacy (Feltz *et al.* 1999), although more research is needed. Motivation efficacy, character-building efficacy, and technique efficacy seem to be the most important predictors of coach, player, and team outcomes (Feltz *et al.* 2008). Surprisingly, perceptions of game strategy efficacy have not been a significant predictor of many outcomes. New research is needed that includes physical condition efficacy as a dimension of coaching efficacy and a possible predictor of coach, player, and team outcomes. Most of the research, with the exception of the Feltz and colleagues' (1999) study, has measured perceptions of coaching behavior and not actual observed behavior. Research with behavioral measures would be beneficial in understanding how each efficacy dimension, as well as overall coaching efficacy, influences coach, player, and team outcomes. Other studies, while they have not directly tested the proposed coaching efficacy model, have contributed to understanding the relationship between coaching efficacy and a variety of other variables. Those studies are summarized in Table 6.1.

Future research

Since the conceptual model for coaching efficacy was first proposed (Feltz *et al.* 1999), we have learned a lot about coaching efficacy. Nevertheless, much more work remains. Two areas for future research are outlined below. Specifically, we suggest that coaching efficacy with athletes competing in individual sports or those teams where coaches do not have the opportunity to intervene during competition and coaching efficacy with coaches of different developmental levels of sport be examined.

The coaching efficacy scales established (CES, CES II-HST) and under development (CES-YST) were intended for team sports where coaches have the opportunity to intervene during competition. Examples of these types of sports include football, American soccer, basketball, baseball, or field hockey. In other sports, such as track and field, swimming, tennis, or cross-country, coaches have little or no access to athletes during competition. This suggests that the game strategy dimension of coaching efficacy would need to be reconceptualized and specific items that address changes a coach makes during competition altered. Future research might examine a better method to conceptualize coaching efficacy for these more individual sports.

Future coaching efficacy research with coaches of different developmental levels of sport can be examined from two viewpoints. The first viewpoint defines developmental level of sport by the level of competitiveness and participant's goals with their specific context. Lyle (2002) proposed that coaching contexts could be described as participation coaching or performance coaching. Participation coaching is defined as having a low emphasis on competition and participants are less engaged with the sport. Their reasons for participating might be focused more on enjoyment and health-related outcomes. Performance coaching is

Table 6.1: Studies that contribute to coaching efficacy literature

Authors	Year	Variables	Findings
Chase, Lirgg and Feltz	1997	Coaches' team efficacy Performance	A coach's efficacy beliefs in her team can predict team performance.
Vargas-Tonsing, Myers and Feltz	2004	Efficacy-enhancing techniques Athlete perceptions Coach perceptions	Athletes perceived the coach's use of instruction drilling, acting confident themselves, and encouraging positive talk most effective to enhance efficacy.
Short and Short	2004	Coaching efficacy Athlete perceptions	Athletes tend to rate their coach's efficacy higher than their coach rated his coaching efficacy.
Kowalski, Edginton, Lankford, Waldron, Roberts-Dobie and Nielsen	2007	Coaching efficacy Age Gender Previous Experience Coaching Education Playing Experience	A combination of the personality variables did not significantly predict the overall level of coaching efficacy.
Cheung and Fung	2007	Coaching efficacy Developmental demands	Less efficacious coaches were more concerned about their own performance in coaching and did not think they needed development in coaching related activities.
Harwood	2008	Consulting intervention to increase coaching efficacy	Hardwood's 5Cs: commitment, communication, concentration, control and confidence influenced players' concentration levels, self-control and self-confidence.
Kavussanu, Boardley, Jutkiewicz, Vincent and Ring	2008	Predictors of coaching efficacy Athletes' perceptions of coaching effectiveness	Athlete sport experience negatively predicted coaching effectiveness; athletes' rating of coaching effectiveness significantly lower than coaches' rating of coaching efficacy.
Boardley, Kavussanu and Ring	2008	Coaching efficacy Athletes' perceptions of coaching effectiveness Athlete outcomes	Athlete evaluation of coach's ability to motivate, instruct, and instill attitude of fair play, influenced athlete effort, commitment, enjoyment, and pro-social behavior.
Thelwell, Lane, Weston and Greenlees	2008	Emotional intelligence Coaching efficacy	Coaching efficacy and optimism and social skills were related. Coaches' appraisal of their emotions, and appraisals of others' emotions were related to coaching efficacy.
Vargas-Tonsing	2009	Coaches' pre-game speech Athlete self-efficacy	A coach's pre-game speech can impact athletes' self-efficacy and emotion prior to competition.
Vargas-Tonsing and Oswalt	2009	Coaches' confidence Gay, lesbian and bisexual athletes	Coaches reported high efficacy in most aspects of coaching GLB athletes, female coaches had significantly higher efficacy scores than male coaches.

defined as a more engaged commitment to performance and competition. A coach would be much more involved with higher levels of preparation. Trudel and Gilbert (2006) classified three coaching contexts as recreational sport, developmental sport, or elite sport. Recreational sport coaching is defined as the context in which participation and skill development is emphasized over competition. Participation is not limited to the most skilled and there is a low level of commitment and intensity. Developmental sport coaching is defined as the context in which participation is restricted and based on the skill level of the athlete. There is a more formal competitive structure that often requires travel and a higher commitment from athletes and coaches. Elite sport coaching is defined as the context that includes university teams, national and Olympic teams, and professional sport teams, with the highest level of athlete skill and commitment. With both of these examples of how the coaching context is defined, we would see differences in the type of skills, knowledge, and coaching efficacy needed to be effective coaches. Future research might examine coaches at the various developmental levels and investigate their sources, dimensions, and outcomes of coaching efficacy specific to their coaching context.

The second viewpoint might conceptualize developmental level of competition by the age level of the athletes typically found in North America (youth, high school, collegiate, professional). In this context, coaching efficacy has almost exclusively been studied in high school and lower-division collegiate coaches. One study by Feltz and colleagues (Feltz *et al.* 2006) studied volunteer youth sport coaches from a variety of sports to assess their sources of coaching efficacy information. Results indicated that youth coaches considered themselves highly efficacious on all four dimensions of coaching efficacy, regardless of the number of years of coaching experience. Youth sport coaches in this sample relied on their playing and coaching experience, athlete improvement, and social support as sources of information. Current work by Chase, Myers, and colleagues (Chase *et al.* 2011; Myers *et al.* 2011) focuses on learning more about youth sport parent-coaches and development of the Coaching Efficacy Scale for Youth Sport Teams (CES-YST). Their work examines sources of coaching efficacy and the similarities and differences between coaches and parent-coaches in coaching efficacy, motivation to coach, and qualifications to coach at the youth sport level. Clearly, more research is needed with youth sport coaches given the vast number of youth sport teams and the impact that coaching behavior can have on young athletes.

The coaching efficacy research should also be expanded to higher competitive levels, such as collegiate and professional sports. This would include tests of the structural validity of the CES or CES II–HST with this population and consideration of whether there are sources, dimensions, and outcomes that should be added to or deleted from the coaching efficacy model according to the context of this level of play. For example, Feltz *et al.* (2008) suggest that recruitment efficacy (Bandura 1997) (e.g. the ability to recognize talent and recruit them to your team) and managerial efficacy (e.g. ability to work with behaviorally difficult athletes) might be considered relevant for upper-level coaches. Whether coaches can recruit a highly talented athlete might be just as important to their coaching efficacy as compared to whether they can teach their athletes sport skills (e.g. technique efficacy). Upper-level coaches have a lot of support staff and assistant coaches who take on some of the roles those coaches at lower levels of play might traditionally be responsible for implementing. For example, collegiate and professional sport coaches have access to strength and conditioning coaches who work with their team year round. Does this mean that physical conditioning efficacy is not important to those coaches? Future research might examine the role of character-building efficacy. With several recent off-the-field personal conduct issues among high profile athletes being discussed in the popular press, it would be interesting to know if coaches believe they can have an impact on the character of their athletes (e.g. character-building efficacy). Perhaps some dimensions of coaching efficacy in the coaching efficacy model are not salient for professional coaches. For example, is motivation efficacy defined in the same way for professional athletes who play their sport for millions of dollars? We also do not know which sources of information are important to coaches or how their coaching efficacy impacts related outcomes for athletes, teams, and coaches at higher levels of sport. These are a few suggestions for future research in selected areas.

Implications for coaching practice

Interventions with coaches have to maintain a balance between theory and practice, where theory informs practice but practice also informs theory. We now have enough knowledge from the research in coaching efficacy to be able to provide best practice advice to coaches. The obvious implication for coaching practice is to help coaches improve or maintain their coaching efficacy so that athletes and teams can experience the positive outcomes associated with high coaching efficacy. Coaches have an overall perception of their coaching efficacy and dimension specific coaching efficacy beliefs (e.g. game strategy efficacy, technique efficacy, motivation efficacy, character-building efficacy, physical conditioning efficacy). It is important to remember that coaches can perceive themselves to be high in one dimension and low in another. Therefore, efforts to enhance coaching efficacy should target a specific dimension. For example, a coach may be low in physical conditioning efficacy because he lacks any educational experiences in kinesiology and never learned the basic principles of fitness and conditioning. At the same time, his game strategy efficacy is very high because his mother was a coach and he learned game rules and tactics at a very early age. He spent a lot of time discussing strategy with his parents so he believes in his ability to coach during competition. This particular coach should focus on improving his physical conditioning efficacy, while maintaining his game strategy efficacy. Table 6.2 provides some suggestions unique to each dimension, with all focused on improving the knowledge coaches have and the behavior they exhibit. This needs-based approach to improving coaching efficacy is consistent with current suggestions for effective coach education (Trudel *et al.* 2010).

We conclude this chapter with suggestions for how coaches can learn these efficacy-enhancing techniques. Many of these suggestions relate to sources of coaching efficacy information, and have been previously discussed in the coach education literature (e.g. Trudel and Gilbert 2006). Coaching education programs, workshops, conferences, or courses have a positive influence on coaching efficacy. Coaches should select a mentor coach to help with their development and provide feedback about their coaching. Working on communication skills with athletes, parents, and community members can help coaches gain efficacy information. Some coaches might benefit from video-taping themselves at practices and games to listen and observe their coaching behavior from a new perspective. Reflection on their coaching behavior is also a good way to gain insight and assess their abilities. Coaches who set achievable goals are more likely to attain success and mastery experiences, which can lead to enhanced efficacy (Feltz *et al.* 2008). All coaches should have a support system in place (e.g. family or friends) to provide a sounding board and safe environment to talk through tough times that are bound to occur during a competitive season. In closing, putting in the time and effort to gain experience and knowledge can help coaches feel prepared to succeed. Without proper preparation, coaches will have a difficult time feeling efficacious.

Table 6.2: Efficacy-enhancing techniques for specific coaching efficacy dimensions

Character-Building Efficacy

- Know your community values.
- Set clear behavioral expectations for athletes.
- Build relationships with athletes and parents.
- Be consistent with enforcement of team rules.
- Model good sportsmanship.
- Inspire an attitude of respect for others.

Game Strategy Efficacy

- Learn to recognize your team's strengths and weaknesses during competition.
- Learn to recognize your opponent's strengths and weaknesses during competition.
- Understand how to handle stress.
- Communicate well with players and assistant coaches.
- Know the rules and tactics of the game.
- Be consistent and confident in your decision-making.

Motivation Efficacy

- Understand how to build confidence in your athletes.
- Build trust with your athletes and team.
- Learn how to motivate all the athletes on your team.
- Invite your mentor to evaluate your coaching behavior and communication skills with athletes.
- Read and learn more about mental skills training for your team.

Physical Conditioning Efficacy

- Learn methods to assess athletes' conditioning levels.
- Prepare in-season and out-of-season physical conditioning plans for athletes.
- Understand principals of fitness and conditioning.
- Model good physical conditioning to your athletes.

Technique Efficacy

- Understand the technical skills of your sport.
- Practice recognizing skill errors and correcting them.
- Know correct techniques for all positions in your sport.
- Understand how to teach basic skills during practice.
- Understand how to effectively demonstrate skills and tactics.
- Be able to provide athletes informational feedback about their performance.

References

Bandura, A. (1977) 'Self-efficacy: Toward a unifying theory of behavioral change,' *Psychological Review*, 84(2): 191–215.

Bandura, A. (1986) *Social Foundations of Thought and Action: A Social Cognitive Theory*, Englewood Cliffs, NJ: Prentice-Hall.

Bandura, A. (1997) *Self-Efficacy: The Exercise of Control*, New York: W.H. Freeman.

Becker, A. (2009) 'It's not what they do, it's how they do it: Athlete experiences of great coaching,' *International Journal of Sports Science and Coaching*, 4(1): 93–119.

Boardley, I., Kavussanu, M. and Ring, C. (2008) 'Athletes' perceptions of coaching effectiveness and athlete-related outcomes in rugby union: An investigation based on the coaching efficacy model,' *The Sport Psychologist*, 22(3): 269–287.

Campbell, T. and Sullivan, P.J. (2005) 'The effect of a standardized coaching education program on the efficacy of novice coaches,' *AVANTE*, 11(1): 38–45.

Chase, M.A., Lirgg, C.D. and Feltz, D.L. (1997) 'Do coaches' efficacy expectations for their teams predict team performance?' *The Sport Psychologist*, 11(1): 8–23.

Chase, M.A., Feltz, D.L., Hayashi, S. and Hepler, T. (2005) 'Sources of coaching efficacy: The coaches' perspective,' *International Journal of Sport and Exercise Psychology*, 3(1): 27–40.

Chase, M.A., Pierce, S.W., Martin, E., Bergman, C. and Markwart, L. (2011) 'Coaching efficacy and motives to coach for parent and non-parent youth sport coaches: Why are they coaching?' paper presented at the Association of Applied Sport Psychology Conference, Honolulu, Hawaii, September 2011.

Chelladurai, P. (1990) 'Leadership in sports: A review,' *International Journal of Sport Psychology*, 21(4): 328–354.

Cheung, S. and Fung, L. (2007) 'Concerns and developmental needs of highly confident and less confident elementary coaches in Hong Kong,' *African Journal for Physical, Health Education, Recreation and Dance*, 13(2): 119–126.

Côté, J. and Gilbert, W. (2009) 'An integrative definition of coaching effectiveness and expertise,' *International Journal of Sports Science and Coaching*, 4(3): 307–323.

Denham, C.H. and Michael, J.J. (1981) 'Teacher sense of efficacy: A definition of the construct and a model for further research,' *Educational Research Quarterly*, 5: 39–63.

Feltz, D.L., Chase, M.A., Moritz, S.E. and Sullivan, P.J. (1999) 'A conceptual model of coaching efficacy: Preliminary investigation and instrument development,' *Journal of Educational Psychology*, 91(4): 765–776.

Feltz, D.L., Hepler, T., Roman, N. and Paiement, C. (2006) 'Coaching efficacy and volunteer youth sport coaches,' *The Sport Psychologist*, 23(1): 24–41.

Feltz, D.L., Short, S.E. and Sullivan, P. J. (2008) *Self-Efficacy in Sport*, Champaign, IL: Human Kinetics.

Fung, L. (2002) 'Task familiarity and task efficacy: A study of sports coaches,' *Perceptual and Motor Skills*, 95(2): 367–372.

Fung, L. (2003) 'Assessment: Coaching efficacy as indicators of coach education program needs,' *Athletic Insight*, 5(1): 12–18.

Gibson, S. and Dembo, M.H. (1984) 'Teacher efficacy: A construct validation,' *Journal of Educational Psychology*, 76(4): 569–582.

Gilbert, W., Côté, J. and Mallett, C. (2006) 'Developmental pathways and activities of successful sport coaches,' *International Journal of Sports Science and Coaching*, 1(1): 69–76.

Gilbert, W., Lichtenwaldt, L., Gilbert, J., Zelezny, L. and Côté, J. (2009) 'Developmental profiles of successful high school coaches,' *International Journal of Sports Science and Coaching*, 1(1): 415–431.

Harwood, C. (2008) 'Developmental consulting in a professional football academy: The 5Cs coaching efficacy program,' *The Sport Psychologist*, 22(1): 109–133.

Haugen, C., Short, S.E., Brinkert, R. and Short, M. (2004) 'The relationship between coaching efficacy and coaching burnout,' poster session, *Journal of Sport and Exercise Psychology*, 26(1 Suppl): S89.

Kavussanu, M., Boardley, I., Jutkiewicz, N., Vincent, S. and Ring, C. (2008) 'Coaching efficacy and coaching effectiveness: Examining their predictors and comparing coaches' and athletes' reports,' *The Sport Psychologist*, 22(4): 383–404.

Kent, A. and Sullivan, P.J. (2003) 'Coaching efficacy as a predictor of university coaches' commitment,' *International Sports Journal*, 7(1): 78–87.

Kowalski, C., Edginton, C., Lankford, S., Waldron, J., Roberts-Dobie, S. and Nielsen, L. (2007) 'Coaching efficacy and volunteer youth soccer coaches,' *Asian Journal of Exercise and Sports Science*, 4(1): 9–13.

Lee, K.S., Malete, L. and Feltz, D.L. (2002) 'The strength of coaching efficacy between certified and noncertified Singapore coaches,' *International Journal of Applied Sports Sciences*, 14(1): 55–67.

Lyle, J. (2002) *Sports Coaching Concepts: A Framework for Coaches' Behaviour*, London: Routledge.

Malete, L. and Feltz, D.L. (2000) 'The effect of a coaching education program on coaching efficacy,' *The Sport Psychologist*, 14(4): 410–417.

Malete, L. and Sullivan, P.J. (2009) 'Sources of coaching efficacy in coaches in Botswana,' *International Journal of Coaching Science*, 3(1): 17–27.

Marback, T., Short, S.E., Short, M. and Sullivan, P.J. (2005) 'Coaching confidence: An exploratory investigation of sources and gender differences,' *Journal of Sport Behavior*, 28(1): 18–34.

Myers, N., Chase, M.A., Pierce, S.W. and Martin, E. (2011) 'Coaching efficacy and exploratory structural equation modeling: A substantive-methodological synergy,' *Journal of Sport and Exercise Psychology*, 33(6): 779–806.

Myers, N., Feltz, D.L., Chase, M.A., Reckase, M. and Hancock, G. (2008) 'The Coaching Efficacy Scale II – high school teams,' *Educational and Psychological Measurement*, 68(6): 1059–1076.

Myers, N., Vargas-Tonsing, T. and Feltz, D.L. (2005) 'Coaching efficacy in intercollegiate coaches: Sources, coaching behavior, and team variables,' *Psychology of Sport and Exercise*, 6(1): 129–143.

National Coaching Certification Program (2002) *3M National Coaching Certification Program*, online, available at: www.skatecanada.ca/GetInvolved/BecomeaCoachorOfficial/ CoachesTraining/ NationalCoachingCertificationProgram/tabid/8496/language/en-US/ Default.aspx (accessed 2 August 2012).

Short, S.E. and Short, M. (2004) 'Coaches' assessment of their coaching efficacy compared to athletes' perceptions,' *Perceptual and Motor Skills*, 99(2): 729–736.

Short, S.E., Smiley, M. and Ross-Stewart, L. (2005) 'Relationship between efficacy beliefs and imagery use in coaches,' *The Sport Psychologist*, 19(4): 380–394.

Smith, R.E, Smoll, F.L. and Hunt, E. (1977) 'A system for behavioral assessments of athletic coaches,' *Research Quarterly*, 48: 401–407.

Smoll, F.L. and Smith, R.E. (1989) 'Leadership behaviors in sport: A theoretical model and research paradigm,' *Journal of Applied Social Psychology*, 19(18): 1522–1551.

Sullivan, P.J. and Kent, A. (2003) 'Coaching efficacy as a predictor of leadership style in intercollegiate athletics,' *Journal of Applied Sport Psychology*, 15(1): 1–11.

Sullivan, P.J., Gee, C.J. and Feltz, D.L. (2006) 'Playing experience: The content knowledge source of coaching efficacy beliefs,' in A.V. Mitel (ed.) *Trends in Educational Psychology Research*, New York: Nova Science Publishers.

Thelwell, R., Lane, A., Weston, N. and Greenlees, L. (2008) 'Examining relationships between emotional intelligence and coaching efficacy,' *International Journal of Sport and Exercise Psychology*, 6(2): 224–235.

Trudel, P. and Gilbert, W.D. (2006) 'Coaching and coach education,' in D. Kirk, M. O'Sullivan and D. McDonald (eds) *Handbook of Physical Education*, London: Sage.

Trudel, P., Gilbert, W. and Werthner, P. (2010) 'Coach education effectiveness,' in J. Lyle and C. Cushion (eds) *Sport Coaching: Professionalisation and Practice*, London: Elsevier.

Vargas-Tonsing, T. (2009) 'An exploratory examination of the effects of coaches' pre-game speeches on athletes' perceptions of self-efficacy and emotion,' *Journal of Sport Behavior*, 32(1): 92–111.

Vargas-Tonsing, T. and Oswalt, S. (2009) 'Coaches' efficacy beliefs towards working with gay, lesbian, and bisexual athletes,' *International Journal of Coaching Science*, 3(2): 29–42.

Vargas-Tonsing, T., Myers, N. and Feltz, D.L. (2004) 'Coaches' and athletes' perceptions of efficacy-enhancing techniques,' *Sport Psychologist*, 18(4): 397–414.

Vargas-Tonsing, T., Warners, A. and Feltz, D.L. (2003) 'The predictability of coaching efficacy on team efficacy and player efficacy in volleyball,' *Journal of Sport Behavior*, 26(4): 396–407.

Woolfolk, A.E., Rossoff, B. and Hoy, W.K. (1990) 'Teachers' sense of efficacy and their beliefs about managing students,' *Teaching and Teacher Education*, 6: 137–148.

7

COACHING COMPETENCY AND EXPLORATORY STRUCTURAL EQUATION MODELLING

Nicholas D. Myers

UNIVERSITY OF MIAMI, USA

Ying Jin

UNIVERSITY OF MIAMI, USA[1]

Introduction

The purpose of this chapter is to provide a brief substantive-methodological synergy (Marsh and Hau 2007) of potential importance to future effective sport coaching research. The methodological focus is exploratory structural equation modelling (ESEM; Asparouhov and Muthén 2009), a methodology that integrates the advantages of exploratory factor analysis and confirmatory factor analysis within the general structural equation model. The substantive focus is the emerging role for, and particularly the measurement of, athletes' evaluations of their coach's competency (Myers *et al.* 2006a) within conceptual models of effective coaching (Horn 2008).

Overview of research on coaching competency: the substance

Models of coaching effectiveness

Much of the research in sport leadership has been directed toward identifying particular coaching styles that elicit successful performance and/or positive psychological responses from athletes (Horn 2008). The two most prominent models of leadership effectiveness in sport, the Multidimensional Model of Leadership (Chelladurai 1978) and the Mediational Model of Leadership (Smoll and Smith 1989), have served as frameworks for much of the related research. Horn (2008) combined elements of both models to form a model of coaching effectiveness.

Horn's (2008) model of coaching effectiveness is founded on at least three assumptions. First, both antecedent factors (e.g. coach's personal characteristics, organizational climate) and personal characteristics of athletes influence a coach's behaviour indirectly through a coach's expectancies, beliefs and goals. Second, a coach's behaviour directly affects athletes' perceptions and evaluations of a coach's behaviour. Third, athletes' perceptions and evaluations of a coach's behaviour mediate the influence that a coach's behaviour has on athletes' self-perceptions (e.g. self-efficacy) and attitudes (e.g. satisfaction with a coach), which in turn directly affects athletes' motivation and performance. Because athletes' perceptions and evaluations of a coach's behaviour are believed to play a critical role in coaching effectiveness, improving the measurement of athletes' evaluations of key coaching competencies is important to the continued improvement of coaching.

Coaches' behaviour

There are many instruments designed to measure a coach's behaviour. The Coaching Behavior Assessment System (CBAS; Smith *et al.* 1977), the Leadership Scale for Sports (LSS; Chelladurai and Saleh 1980) and the Decision Style Questionnaire (DSQ; Chelladurai and Arnott 1985) are the most prominent of such instruments. As reviewed by Horn (2008), these instruments have also been used to assess athletes' perceptions of their coach's behaviour (e.g. how often does your coach use positive reinforcement with athletes?) and/or decision styles (e.g. what type of decision style would your coach employ in order to select a team captain?). However, none of these instruments measure athletes' evaluations of their coach's behaviour (e.g. how competent do you believe your coach is in teaching the skills of your sport?). While each of these instruments has contributed mightily to the understanding of coaching behaviour over the last few decades, Smoll and Smith (1989: 1527) themselves note that, 'the ultimate effects that coaching behaviour exerts are mediated by the meaning that players attribute to them' – effects these instruments were not designed to measure.

Athletes' evaluations of a coach's behaviour

Unlike the CBAS, the LSS and the DSQ, the Coaching Evaluation Questionnaire (CEQ; Rushall and Wiznuk 1985), the Coaching Behavior Questionnaire (CBQ; Kenow and Williams 1992) and the Coaching Behaviour Scale for Sport (CBS-S; Côté *et al.* 1999) were designed at least to some extent to assess athletes' evaluative reactions to specific aspects of their coach's behaviour. Rushall and Wiznuk suggest that the CEQ allows athletes to evaluate a coach on his or her personal qualities, personal and professional relationships, organizational skills, and performance as a teacher and a coach. The stated purpose for these measures is to provide immediate feedback to coaches in order to enhance their ability to relate more effectively to athletes. Although the items are intended to measure separate constructs, scores are to be totalled across items or formed at the item-level. Psychometric evidence for measures derived from the CEQ appears to be limited to item-level test-retest reliability.

The CBQ allows athletes to evaluate what they perceive to be their coach's typical behaviour, specifically his or her negative activation and supportiveness/emotional composure during competition against a top opponent. The purpose of collecting these measures appears to be to provide coaches with information on how a coach's negative activation/supportiveness and emotional composure affects their athletes' performance and relevant psychological states during competition against a top opponent. Psychometric work for measures derived from the CBQ provided evidence for the proposed two-factor structure, internal consistency reliability, and the external aspect of the validity of measures from the instrument (Williams *et al.* 2003). Evidence for the use of the CBQ for the intended purposes is accumulating. The CBQ provides a valuable tool to measure athletes' evaluative reactions to aspects of their coach's behaviour, but it measures a fairly specific and narrow subset of coaching behaviour (negative activation and supportiveness, and emotional composure) and in a targeted scenario (competition against a top opponent).

As described by Mallett and Côté (2006: 214), the CBS-S 'attempts to provide a comprehensive assessment of high-performance coaches' behaviours that are exhibited in training, competition, and organizational settings'. The instrument asks an athlete to rate how *frequently* he/she experiences the following coaching behaviours. The intended factors measured by the 47 items that comprise the CBS-S include: physical training and planning, goal setting, mental preparation, technical skills, personal rapport, negative personal rapport and competition strategies. The frequency measures produced by the CBS-S have demonstrated evidence of predictive validity (e.g. Baker *et al.* 2000; Baker *et al.* 2003; Côté *et al.* 1999). Thus, there is clear evidence that the CBS-S provides reasonably accurate measures of the perceived frequency of important coaching behaviours.

An athlete's perception of the frequency of a coach's behaviour (e.g. how frequently a coach provides instructional and diagnostic feedback) likely only partially informs an athlete's evaluation of a coach's behaviour (e.g. how competently a coach provides instructional and diagnostic feedback). Three competency domains stipulated in the *National Standards for Athletic Coaches* (NASPE 2006) that are not fully covered by existing instruments are (a) growth, development and learning of athletes; (b) psychological aspects of coaching; and (c) skills, tactics and strategies. Within the growth, development and learning of athletes, an expected competency is that a coach provides instruction to develop specific motor skills. Within the psychological aspects of coaching domain, expected competencies include that a coach demonstrate effective motivational skills and that a coach conduct practices and competitions to enhance social/emotional growth and promote good sportsmanship in athletes. Within the skills, tactics and strategies domain, an expected competency is that a coach applies appropriate competitive strategies. The Coaching Competency Scale (CCS; Myers *et al.* 2006a) was designed to measure athletes' evaluations of their head coach in these areas.

Coaching competency and coaching efficacy: the first iteration

The CCS was derived via minor changes to the Coaching Efficacy Scale (CES; Feltz *et al.* 1999). The CES was developed to measure a *coach's belief* in his or her ability to influence the learning and performance of his or her athletes. The specific factors measured – instructional technique, motivation, character building and game strategy – purposely overlap with the expected competency domains articulated in the previous paragraph and are congruent with self-efficacy theory (Bandura 1997). According to models of coaching effectiveness, however, *why* a coach's beliefs (e.g. coaching efficacy) are related to athletes' self-perceptions and performance is due to the influence that these beliefs exert on a coach's behaviour. But the influence that a coach's behaviour exerts on athletes' self-perceptions, motivation and performances is mediated, at least in part, by athletes' evaluations of their coach's behaviour. The purpose of the CCS, therefore, was to measure *athletes' evaluations* of their head coach's ability to affect the learning and performance of athletes. There is evidence that measures derived from both the CES and the CCS relate to theoretically relevant variables (Feltz *et al.* 2008; Myers *et al.* 2006c).

Both the CES and the CCS posited that four latent variables co-vary and influence responses to 24 items. From this point forward the terms competency and efficacy were generally not included alongside any particular dimension of coaching competency. The latent variables purportedly measured by the CCS were defined as follows. *Motivation* was defined as athletes' evaluations of their head coach's ability to affect the psychological mood and skills of athletes. *Game strategy* was defined as athletes' evaluations of their head coach's ability to lead during competition. *Technique* was defined as athletes' evaluations of their head coach's instructional and diagnostic abilities. *Character building* was defined as athletes' evaluations of their head coach's ability to influence the personal development and positive attitude toward sport in their athletes. Myers *et al.* (2006a) referred to this multidimensional construct as *coaching competency*; a convention frequently adopted in this chapter. High school and lower division collegiate athletes of team sports comprise populations for which the CCS was intended.

Model-data fit within the confirmatory factor analytic framework for both the CES and CCS has generally not met heuristic values for close fit (e.g. Hu and Bentler 1999). The history of model-data fit for the CES is more extensive than the relevant history for the CCS. Feltz *et al.* (1999) reported the following model-data fit for high school coaches: $\chi^2(246, N=291)=790$, comparative fit index (CFI) $=0.89$, and root mean square error of approximation (RMSEA) $=0.08$. Subsequent studies with youth coaches (Lee *et al.* 2002) and collegiate coaches (Sullivan and Kent 2003) reported similar levels of model-data fit. All of these studies imposed a single-group confirmatory factor analysis (CFA) that assumed factorial invariance by coach gender. Evidence against this assumption has since been provided (Myers *et al.* 2006b).

Model-data fit for the CCS closely paralleled the relevant history of the CES. Myers *et al.* (2006a) reported the following model-data fit for non-Division I collegiate athletes ($N=585$) clustered within men's ($g=8$) and women's ($g=24$) teams: $\chi^2(246)=1266$, CFI $=0.91$, Tucker-Lewis Index (TLI) $=0.90$, and RMSEA $=0.09$. Differences between the CCS study and the CES studies included: post hoc modifications; the range and magnitude of interfactor correlations; and the data matrix analysed. Post hoc modifications by Myers and colleagues included allowing a motivation item to also indicate game strategy and freeing the covariance between two pairs of residual variances (see Figure 7.1). Interfactor correlations in the Myers *et al.* study ranged from $r_{\text{technique, character building}}=0.80$ to $r_{\text{game strategy, technique}}=0.92$, which suggested both a narrower range and generally greater values than typically observed in data derived from the CES (e.g. Myers *et al.* 2005; range: $r_{\text{technique, character building}}=0.54$ to $r_{\text{game strategy, technique}}=0.86$). Given the high interfactor correlations, Myers *et al.* explored models with fewer latent variables, all of which yielded statistically significant worse fit.

Data derived from the CCS have a history of dependence. Myers *et al.* (2006a) reported item-level intraclass correlation coefficients (ICC; ratio of variance attributable to team versus total variance) ranging from 0.22 to 0.44, $M=0.32$, $SD=0.05$. Multilevel confirmatory factor analysis is an appropriate methodology when data violate the assumption of independence (Muthén 1994). Simulation research has indicated, however, that a relatively large number of groups (~100) may be necessary for optimal estimation, particularly at the between-groups level (Hox and Maas 2001). When group-level sample size is not large, imposing a single-level model on the within-groups covariance matrix, $\mathbf{S_W}$, as opposed to the total covariance matrix, $\mathbf{S_T}$, controls for probable biases in fitting single-level models to multilevel data (Julian 2001). Myers *et al.* modelled the $\mathbf{S_W}$. Limitations of the approach taken by Myers *et al.* included the between-teams factor structure was not investigated and factorial invariance by athlete gender was assumed but not tested.

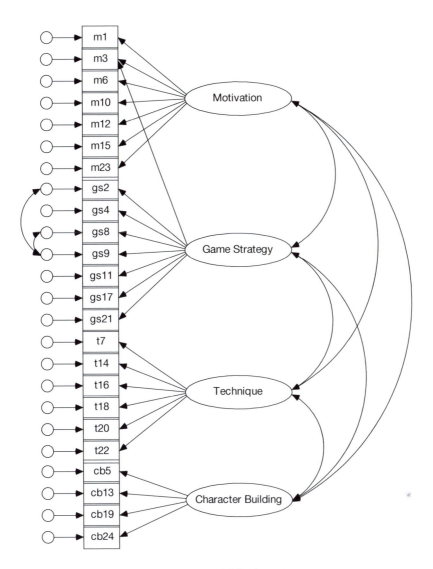

Figure 7.1: Athlete-level a priori measurement model for the CCS.

Coaching competency and coaching efficacy: the second iteration

The Coaching Efficacy Scale II–HST (CES II–HST; Myers *et al.* 2008) was derived via major changes to the CES. The Athletes' Perceptions of Coaching Competency Scale II – High School Teams (APCCS II–HST; Myers *et al.* 2010) was derived via minor changes to the CES II–HST. There is evidence that measures derived from the CES II–HST and the APCCS II–HST relate to theoretically relevant variables (Myers *et al.* 2011b; Myers *et al.* 2011a).

Myers *et al.* (2008) implemented recommendations for revision to the CES put forth by Myers *et al.* (2005) in a six-step process that resulted in the CES II–HST. The first two steps served to make substantive revision to the CES. The entire validity framework for the CES was reconsidered in collaboration with external content experts. Resultant changes included a narrowing of the intended population and multiple changes to the instrument itself. Step 3 and Step 4 consisted of data collection and item selection, respectively. Specifically, data ($N = 799$) were collected from head coaches of 14 relevant sports. A sub-sample of this data ($n = 250$) provided evidence, via exploratory factor analysis, for the expected five-factor oblique structure. Step 5 imposed a single-group CFA and provided evidence for close fit: $\chi^2(70, n = 549)$ ranged from 103, $p = 0.006$ to 114, $p < 0.001$, RMSEA $= 0.03$, SRMR $= 0.03$, CFI $= 0.99$, and TLI $= 1.00$ (SRMR is the standardized root mean square residual). Step 6 provided evidence for factorial invariance by coach gender. Evidence also was provided for both the stability of all latent variables and for the reliability of composite scores.

Two substantive revisions implemented in the CES II–HST were pertinent to this chapter. First, the intended population was delimited to head coaches of *high school team sports* where a head coach has the opportunity to meaningfully intervene during competition. This sharpened focus was consistent with empirical evidence for non-invariance by level coached (Myers *et al.* 2006b), type of sport implied by some CES items, *Standards for Educational and Psychological Testing* (American Educational Research Association *et al.* 1999) and previous research: 'This is the level at which we believe coaching efficacy has its greatest influence' (Feltz *et al.* 1999: 767).

The second substantive revision in the CES II–HST pertinent to this chapter was a set of changes to the CES itself. These changes included the addition of a new dimension of coaching efficacy, revised operational definitions for two of the previous dimensions, and a majority of new or revised items. *Physical conditioning* was the new dimension in CES II–HST. Ability to physically condition athletes is a key coaching competency (NASPE 2006). The operational definitions for character building and technique were revised to improve the clarity of the definition and to decrease the likelihood for empirical redundancy with game strategy, respectively. In accordance with the previous changes, all but one of the 18 items that constituted the CES II–HST either were revised (nine items) or were new (eight items) as compared to the CES.

The internal model for the APCCS II–HST occurred at two-levels in Myers *et al.* (2010) because there was strong evidence for dependence due to the clustering of athletes ($N = 748$) within teams ($G = 74$). Specifically, ICCs ranged from 0.18 to 0.35, $M = 0.29$, $SD = 0.05$. There was evidence for close fit for the multilevel internal model: $\chi_R^2(201)$ ranged from 375, $p < 0.001$, to 405, $p < 0.001$, RMSEA $= 0.04$, CFI $= 0.99$, TLI $= 0.99$, SRMR$_{within} = 0.03$, and SRMR$_{between} = 0.04$. Evidence also was provided for both the stability of all latent variables and for the reliability of composite scores. There is evidence that the measurement model underlying responses to the APCCS II–HST may be better understood than the measurement model underlying responses to the CCS. While Myers *et al.* took a multilevel approach, the focus of this chapter was on the athlete-level (Level 1) model only.

The internal model for the APCCS II–HST specified that five dimensions of coaching competency co-vary and influence responses to 17 indicators. *Motivation* (M) is measured by four items and was defined as athletes' perceptions of their head coach's ability to affect the psychological mood and psychological skills of her/his athletes. *Game strategy* (GS) is measured by five items and was defined as athletes' perceptions of their head coach's ability to lead his/her athletes during competition. *Technique* (T) is measured by four items and was defined as athletes' perceptions of their head coach's ability to utilize her/his instructional and diagnostic skills during practices. *Character building* (CB) is measured by three items and was defined as athletes' perceptions of their head coach's ability to positively influence the character development of his/her athletes through sport. *Physical conditioning* (PC) is measured with two items and was defined as athletes' perceptions of their head coach's ability to prepare her/his athletes physically for participation in her/his sport. Figure 7.2 depicts the athlete-level measurement model (less the bolded arrow). Myers *et al.* (2010) provided evidence for factorial invariance, except for one residual variance, by athlete gender.

Deriving measures of coaching competency: future iterations

There is growing evidence for the importance of coaching competency in coaching effectiveness models. An important foundational question for this emerging line of research going forward is: how best to derive measures from responses to the CCS and APCCS II–HST? In cases where the population of interest is high school team sports the APCCS II–HST, and its proposed measurement model, seems appropriate. In cases where the population of interest is not high school team sports the CCS, and its less well understood measurement model, may be appropriate. While the measurement model for CCS appears to be understood at a level below typical close-fitting confirmatory factor analytic standards, it also seems to be understood better than imposition of a mechanical exploratory factor analytic model would imply. Perhaps a framework situated between traditional exploratory factor analytic and traditional confirmatory factor analytic would be appropriate for deriving measures from responses to the CCS.

Interdisciplinary research considerations: the methodology

Exploratory structural equation modelling (ESEM; Asparouhov and Muthén 2009), is a new methodology that integrates the relative advantages of both exploratory factor analysis (EFA) and confirmatory factor analysis (CFA) within the general structural equation model (SEM). A technical paper (Asparouhov and Muthén 2009) and a substantive-methodological synergy (Marsh *et al.* 2009) introduced ESEM to the methodological community. The focus of this section of this chapter is to briefly introduce ESEM to the coaching community. Facets of the extant literature key to the purpose of this chapter are summarized and ESEM is put forth as a new methodological framework for the next generation of coaching research to consider.

From EFA to CFA to ESEM

Over a century ago Spearman (1904) articulated what has come to be known as EFA. Several decades after this articulation, EFA became a widely used multivariate analytic framework in many disciplines, including sport coaching. Over the past few decades, however, some limitations in the way EFA is typically implemented in software has probably impeded the use of the technique in favour of CFA – even when the available a priori measurement theory was insufficient to warrant a confirmatory approach. Examples of limitations in the way that EFA is typically implemented in software include the absence of standard errors for parameter estimates; restrictions on the ability to incorporate a priori content knowledge into the measurement model; an inability to fully test factorial invariance; and an inability to simultaneously estimate the measurement model within a fuller structural model.

The most common measurement model within SEM is Jöreskog's (1969) CFA model (Asparouhov and Muthén 2009). CFA provides standard errors for parameter estimates, allows a priori content knowledge to guide model specification; provides a rigorous framework to test factorial invariance; and allows the measurement model to be a part of a

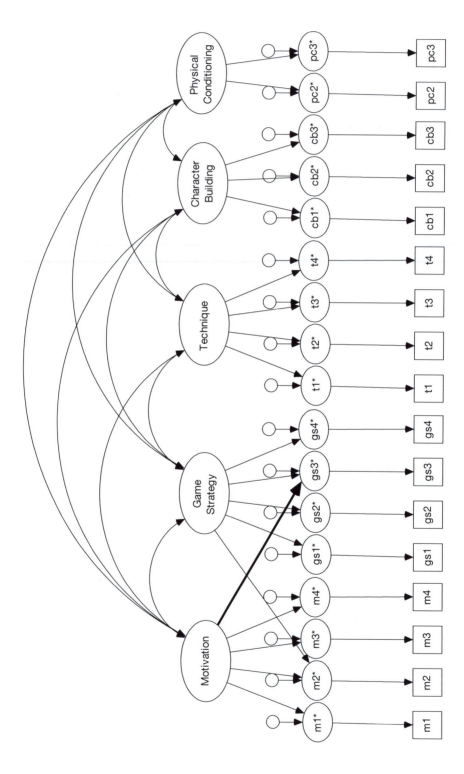

Figure 7.2: Athlete-level a priori measurement model for the APCCS II-HST. Thick (bolded) arrow denotes a post hoc modification proposed in this chapter.

fuller structural equation model. An often overlooked but necessary condition for appropriate use of CFA, however, is sufficient a priori measurement theory. Absence of such theory often results in an extensive post hoc exploratory approach guided by modification indexes. Such an approach is susceptible to producing an accepted model that is inconsistent with the true model – despite possible consistency with a particular dataset (MacCallum *et al.* 1992). EFA, not CFA, may often be the better framework for post hoc explorations in search of a well-fitting measurement model (Browne 2001).

A common misspecification in CFA is when non-zero paths from latent variables to measurement indicators are fixed to zero. This type of misspecification often results in upwardly biased covariances between the latent variables and biased estimates in the non-measurement part of the structural equation (Asparouhov and Muthén 2009). Both of these problems can, and probably have, impeded sport coaching research and practice. An example of upwardly biased covariances between latent variables may have occurred in Myers *et al.* (2006a).

In M*plus* (Muthén and Muthén 1998–2010), the ESEM approach integrates the relative advantages of EFA and CFA within SEM. Like EFA, ESEM imposes fewer restrictions on the measurement model than common implementations of CFA and integrates advances in possible direct rotations of the pattern matrix (Jennrich 2007). Like CFA, ESEM can be part of a general SEM which affords much greater modelling flexibility than observed in the traditional EFA framework. In fact, within a single SEM specification, both CFA and ESEM can be imposed simultaneously. This latter point is of special interest because when sufficient a priori measurement theory exists, the more parsimonious CFA is preferred (Asparouhov and Muthén 2009). An important methodological question within effective coaching research going forward is: how can ESEM be applied within models of effective coaching?

The general ESEM

The general ESEM is summarized for the continuous outcomes case consistent with Asparouhov and Muthén (2009). The statistical model is presented as a broad methodological framework within which the next generation of effective coaching research may evaluate fuller models of effective coaching. Note that the full range of parameter estimates typically available in SEM is available in ESEM. The first equation often is conceptualized as the measurement model (Bollen 1989):

$$\mathbf{Y}_{pxl} = \mathbf{v}_{pxl} + \mathbf{\Lambda}_{pxm}\mathbf{\eta}_{mxl} + \mathbf{K}_{pxq}\mathbf{X}_{qxl} + \mathbf{\varepsilon}_{pxl}, \text{ where} \tag{7.1}$$

p is the number of continuous observed dependent variables
m is the number of continuous latent variables
q is the number of observed independent variables
and
$\mathbf{Y}$ is a vector of continuous observed dependent variables
$\mathbf{v}$ is a vector of intercepts or means
$\mathbf{\Lambda}$ is a matrix of pattern coefficients
$\mathbf{\eta}$ is a vector of continuous latent variables
$\mathbf{K}$ is a matrix of regression coefficients: $\mathbf{Y}$ on $\mathbf{X}$
$\mathbf{X}$ is a vector of observed independent variables
$\mathbf{\varepsilon}$ is a vector of residuals for $\mathbf{Y}$
$\mathbf{\Theta}$ is a pxp covariance matrix for $\mathbf{\varepsilon}$

The second equation is often conceptualized as the latent variable model (Bollen):

$$\boldsymbol{\eta}_{mxl} = \boldsymbol{\alpha}_{mxl} + \boldsymbol{\beta}_{mxm}\boldsymbol{\eta}_{mxl} + \boldsymbol{\Gamma}_{mxq}\mathbf{X}_{qxl} + \boldsymbol{\zeta}_{mxl}, \text{ where} \tag{7.2}$$

$\boldsymbol{\eta}$ is a vector of continuous latent variables
$\boldsymbol{\alpha}$ is a vector of intercepts or means
$\boldsymbol{\beta}$ is a matrix of regression coefficients: $\boldsymbol{\eta}$ on $\boldsymbol{\eta}$
$\boldsymbol{\Gamma}$ is a matrix of regression coefficients: $\boldsymbol{\eta}$ on $\mathbf{X}$
$\mathbf{X}$ is a vector of observed independent variables
$\boldsymbol{\zeta}$ is a vector of residuals for $\boldsymbol{\eta}$
$\boldsymbol{\Psi}$ is a *mxm* covariance matrix for $\boldsymbol{\zeta}$

Readers are referred to Asparouhov and Muthén for a thorough accounting of technical details omitted in this review. Readers are referred to Marsh *et al.* (2009) for examples of modelling possibilities within the general ESEM framework that are beyond the scope of this chapter.

EFA only in ESEM

EFA (with means) only within the more general ESEM framework is presented here. Note that some arrays in the eq. (7.1) and eq. (7.2) drop out in eq. (7.3) and eq. (7.4). The first equation can still be conceptualized as the measurement model:

$$\mathbf{Y}_{pxl} = \boldsymbol{v}_{pxl} + \boldsymbol{\Lambda}_{pxm}\boldsymbol{\eta}_{mxl} + \boldsymbol{\varepsilon}_{pxl}, \text{ where} \tag{7.3}$$

$\mathbf{Y}$ is a vector of continuous observed dependent variables
$\boldsymbol{v}$ is a vector of intercepts or means
$\boldsymbol{\Lambda}$ is a matrix of pattern coefficients
$\boldsymbol{\eta}$ is a vector of continuous latent variables
$\boldsymbol{\varepsilon}$ is a vector of residuals for $\mathbf{Y}$
$\boldsymbol{\Theta}$ is a *pxp* covariance matrix for $\boldsymbol{\varepsilon}$

The second equation can still be conceptualized as the latent variable model:

$$\boldsymbol{\eta}_{mxl} = \boldsymbol{\alpha}_{mxl} + \boldsymbol{\zeta}_{mxl}, \text{ where} \tag{7.4}$$

$\boldsymbol{\eta}$ is a vector of continuous latent variables
$\boldsymbol{\alpha}$ is a vector of intercepts or means
$\boldsymbol{\zeta}$ is a vector of residuals for $\boldsymbol{\eta}$
$\boldsymbol{\Psi}$ is a *mxm* covariance matrix for $\boldsymbol{\zeta}$

Rotation

Direct analytic rotations of the pattern matrix implemented in ESEM are based on several decades of related research in the EFA framework (Asparouhov and Muthén 2009). Rotation of the pattern matrix is accomplished via post-multiplication of the pattern matrix by the inverse of an optimal transformation matrix:

$$\boldsymbol{\Lambda}^{*}_{pxm} = \boldsymbol{\Lambda}_{pxm}(\mathbf{H}^{*}_{mxm})^{-1} \tag{7.5}$$

An optimal transformation matrix, $\mathbf{H}^*$, is determined by minimizing a continuous complexity function of the elements in the pattern matrix, $f(\mathbf{\Lambda})$. Various rotation techniques define the $f(\mathbf{\Lambda})$ criterion differently but each was typically designed for the purpose of providing the simplest solution. Readers are referred to Browne (2001) for a thorough review.

Two particular direct rotation options, geomin (Yates 1987) and target (Browne 2001), were the focus of this chapter. Oblique rotation was chosen over orthogonal rotation to reflect the belief that a majority of factors in effective coaching will be correlated with each another. Geomin was selected because Asparouhov and Muthén (2009) provided evidence that it performs well when little is known a priori about the true pattern matrix and variable complexity (i.e. number of factors where an item has a non-zero pattern coefficient) is moderate (i.e. $m \leq 3$). There will probably be many instances in sport coaching research where oblique geomin rotation will be an appropriate choice.

Target rotation was selected because it was designed to rotate the pattern matrix toward a partially specified (i.e. targeted) pattern matrix, which can take advantage of a priori content knowledge without fixing parameters to specific values as in CFA. Target rotation, orthogonal and oblique, has been developed over decades (Browne 2001) and can be thought of as 'a non-mechanical exploratory process, guided by human judgment' (125). A given model will be mathematically equivalent under either target or geomin rotation, but the factors may be defined more consistent with a well-developed a priori theory under target rotation. There will likely be many instances in sport coaching research where a level of a priori measurement theory is available that is below what is required for common specifications of CFA but above what is often assumed in a typical (i.e. not targeted) EFA approach.

Rotation identification

Understanding rotation identification, while complex, can be an important condition for successfully specifying an exploratory model. Under oblique rotation $\mathbf{H}^*$ is a non-symmetric square matrix that results in m^2 indeterminacies (Asparouhov and Muthén 2009). Imposing m^2 constraints on $\mathbf{\Lambda}$ and $\mathbf{\Psi}$ is a necessary condition for rotation identification. Setting the scale for each latent variable to unity provides m constraints. A set of sufficient conditions for imposing the remaining $m(m-1)$ constraints include: (a) each column of $\mathbf{\Lambda}$ has $m-1$ elements specified as zeros, and (b) each submatrix $\mathbf{\Lambda}_s$, where $s = 1,\ldots,m$, of $\mathbf{\Lambda}$ composed of the rows of $\mathbf{\Lambda}$ that have fixed zeros in the sth column must have rank $m-1$. Allow the rank of a matrix to be defined as the maximum number of independent rows or columns in that matrix.

An example

Target rotation can meet condition (a) and condition (b) by strategic specification of the target matrix ($\mathbf{B}_{pxm}$). Note that the dimensions of $\mathbf{B}_{pxm}$ match the dimensions of $\mathbf{\Lambda}_{pxm}$. Allow the targeted elements within $\mathbf{B}$ to be those pattern coefficients that were expected to be zero (i.e. an item was expected to have a trivial loading on a particular factor) and the non-targeted elements to be denoted by a 1. The athlete-level measurement model for the APCCS II-HST was selected for demonstration because it appears to be better understood than the athlete-level measurement model for the CCS (see Figure 7.3). Note that condition (a) was met in that each column had four zeros. Figure 7.4 displays how condition (b) was met. The logic embedded in this worked example can be extended to other applications in coaching research.

Item	GS	PC	M	T	CB
GS1	1	1	1	1	1
GS2	1	0	0	0	0
GS3	1	1	1	1	1
GS4	1	1	1	1	1
PC2	1	1	1	1	1
PC3	0	1	0	0	0
M1	1	1	1	1	1
M2	1	1	1	1	1
M3	1	1	1	1	1
M4	0	0	1	0	0
T1	0	0	0	1	0
T2	1	1	1	1	1
T3	1	1	1	1	1
T4	1	1	1	1	1
CB1	1	1	1	1	1
CB2	1	1	1	1	1
CB3	0	0	0	0	1

Figure 7.3: A possible target matrix for the APCCS II–HST.

$$\mathbf{B}_1 = \begin{bmatrix} \beta_{62} & \beta_{63} & \beta_{64} & \beta_{65} \\ \beta_{10,2} & \beta_{10,3} & \beta_{10,4} & \beta_{10,5} \\ \beta_{11,2} & \beta_{11,3} & \beta_{11,4} & \beta_{11,5} \\ \beta_{17,2} & \beta_{17,3} & \beta_{17,4} & \beta_{17,5} \end{bmatrix} = \begin{bmatrix} 1 & 0 & 0 & 0 \\ 0 & 1 & 0 & 0 \\ 0 & 0 & 1 & 0 \\ 0 & 0 & 0 & 1 \end{bmatrix}, \text{rank}(\mathbf{B}_1) = 4$$

$$\mathbf{B}_2 = \begin{bmatrix} \beta_{21} & \beta_{23} & \beta_{24} & \beta_{25} \\ \beta_{10,1} & \beta_{10,3} & \beta_{10,4} & \beta_{10,5} \\ \beta_{11,1} & \beta_{11,3} & \beta_{11,4} & \beta_{11,5} \\ \beta_{17,1} & \beta_{17,3} & \beta_{17,4} & \beta_{17,5} \end{bmatrix} = \begin{bmatrix} 1 & 0 & 0 & 0 \\ 0 & 1 & 0 & 0 \\ 0 & 0 & 1 & 0 \\ 0 & 0 & 0 & 1 \end{bmatrix}, \text{rank}(\mathbf{B}_2) = 4$$

$$\mathbf{B}_3 = \begin{bmatrix} \beta_{21} & \beta_{22} & \beta_{24} & \beta_{25} \\ \beta_{6,1} & \beta_{62} & \beta_{64} & \beta_{65} \\ \beta_{11,1} & \beta_{11,2} & \beta_{11,4} & \beta_{11,5} \\ \beta_{17,1} & \beta_{17,2} & \beta_{17,4} & \beta_{17,5} \end{bmatrix} = \begin{bmatrix} 1 & 0 & 0 & 0 \\ 0 & 1 & 0 & 0 \\ 0 & 0 & 1 & 0 \\ 0 & 0 & 0 & 1 \end{bmatrix}, \text{rank}(\mathbf{B}_3) = 4$$

$$\mathbf{B}_4 = \begin{bmatrix} \beta_{21} & \beta_{22} & \beta_{23} & \beta_{25} \\ \beta_{6,1} & \beta_{62} & \beta_{63} & \beta_{65} \\ \beta_{10,1} & \beta_{10,2} & \beta_{10,3} & \beta_{10,5} \\ \beta_{17,1} & \beta_{17,2} & \beta_{17,3} & \beta_{17,5} \end{bmatrix} = \begin{bmatrix} 1 & 0 & 0 & 0 \\ 0 & 1 & 0 & 0 \\ 0 & 0 & 1 & 0 \\ 0 & 0 & 0 & 1 \end{bmatrix}, \text{rank}(\mathbf{B}_4) = 4$$

$$\mathbf{B}_5 = \begin{bmatrix} \beta_{21} & \beta_{22} & \beta_{23} & \beta_{24} \\ \beta_{6,1} & \beta_{62} & \beta_{63} & \beta_{64} \\ \beta_{10,1} & \beta_{10,2} & \beta_{10,3} & \beta_{10,4} \\ \beta_{11,1} & \beta_{11,2} & \beta_{11,3} & \beta_{11,4} \end{bmatrix} = \begin{bmatrix} 1 & 0 & 0 & 0 \\ 0 & 1 & 0 & 0 \\ 0 & 0 & 1 & 0 \\ 0 & 0 & 0 & 1 \end{bmatrix}, \text{rank}(\mathbf{B}_5) = 4$$

Figure 7.4: Rank for each submatrix within the specified target matrix.

Targets within **B** were selected based on both content knowledge and previous empirical information. From a content perspective, gs2, *make effective strategic decisions in pressure situations during competition*, was expected to have trivially sized pattern coefficients on all factors except game strategy within the measurement model. Each of the other items that were involved in the targets (pc3, m4, t1, cb3) could be interpreted in a similar form. Note that unlike in CFA, the pattern targets were not *fixed* to zero. Rather, **B** simply informed the rotation criterion as to the structure that **Λ** should be rotated towards.

Summary

This substantive-methodological synergy attempted to merge an extant conceptual model (Horn 2008, coaching effectiveness model) and a new methodological framework (ESEM, Asparouhov and Muthén 2009). The synergy was a demonstration of how ESEM may be used, guided by content knowledge, to develop better (or confirm existing) measurement models for coaching competency. The fuller ESEM was presented as a broad methodological framework within which the next generation of effective coaching research may evaluate fuller models (beyond just measurement) of effective coaching.

Coaching competency occupies a central role in models of coaching effectiveness, which makes measurement of this construct an important area of research. The CCS and the APCCS II–HST were designed to measure coaching competency. The initial athlete-level measurement model for responses to the CCS and the APCCS II–HST both were put forth prior to the emergence of ESEM (i.e. fitted to CFA). The authors of this chapter recommend that the ESEM framework should be strongly considered (as opposed to just EFA or CFA) in subsequent validity studies within coaching effectiveness research – for new and/or existing instruments.

While the substantive part and the methodological part of this chapter both were focused primarily on measurement, the fuller ESEM was presented as a broad methodological framework within which the next generation of effective coaching research may evaluate fuller models of effective coaching. Almost any latent variable model that could be imposed within the SEM framework could also be imposed within ESEM framework (Asparouhov and Muthén 2009). An advantage of the ESEM framework, in instances of insufficient a priori measurement model(s), is reduced likelihood of biased estimates wrought by misspecification of the measurement model(s). Simply, coaching effectiveness studies not focused on measurement can still be adversely affected by misspecification of the measurement model(s) because misspecification of the measurement model(s) can produce biased path coefficients (Kaplan 1988).

There is much important work yet to be done to investigate the utility of coaching competency within broader models of coaching effectiveness. Close model-data fit for a measurement model implies nothing about the ability of resultant measures to relate to theoretically relevant external variables. While a few studies have explored the ability of coaching competency to predict satisfaction with the head coach (Myers *et al.* 2006c; Myers *et al.* 2011a), many other key relations implied within Horn's model await empirical research. For example, coaching competency is specified to at least partially mediate the effect of coaching behaviour on three sets of variables: (a) athletes' self-perceptions, beliefs and attitudes; (b) athletes' level and type of motivation; and (c) athletes' performance and behaviour. Future research that explores these (or other) important implied relations is encouraged. More broadly, the authors of this chapter believe that it is time for research on coaching competency to evolve beyond such a strong focus on measurement alone because it has long been suspected that 'the ultimate effects that coaching behavior exerts are mediated by the meaning that players attribute to them' (Smoll and Smith 1989:1527) – effects measurement models do not test.

Note

1   We would like to thank Tihomir Asparouhov for his review of a draft of this chapter.

References

American Educational Research Association, American Psychological Association and National Council on Measurement in Education (1999) *Standards for Educational and Psychological Testing*, Washington, DC: American Educational Research Association.

Asparouhov, T. and Muthén, B.O. (2009) 'Exploratory structural equation modeling', *Structural Equation Modeling*, 16: 397–38.

Baker, J., Côté, J. and Hawes, R. (2000) 'The relationship between coaching behaviours and sport anxiety in athletes', *Journal of Science and Medicine in Sport*, 3: 110–19.

Baker, J., Yardley, J. and Côté, J. (2003) 'Coach behaviours and athlete satisfaction in team and individual sports', *International Journal of Sport Psychology*, 21: 226–239.

Bandura, A. (ed.) (1997) *Self-efficacy: The Exercise of Control*, New York: Freeman.

Bollen, K.A. (ed.) (1989) *Structural Equations with Latent Variables*, New York: Wiley.

Browne, M.W. (2001) 'An overview of analytic rotation in exploratory factor analysis', *Multivariate Behavioral Research*, 36: 111–50.

Chelladurai, P. (1978) 'A contingency model of leadership in athletics', unpublished doctoral dissertation, University of Waterloo, Canada.

Chelladurai, P. and Arnott, M. (1985) 'Decision styles in coaching: Preferences of basketball Players', *Research Quarterly for Exercise and Sport*, 56: 15–24.

Chelladurai, P. and Saleh, S.D. (1980) 'Dimensions of leader behavior in sports: Development of a leadership scale', *Journal of Sport Psychology*, 2: 34–45.

Côté, J., Yardley, J., Hay, J., Sedgwick, W. and Baker, J. (1999) 'An exploratory examination of the Coaching Behaviour Scale for Sport', *Avante*, 5: 82–92.

Feltz, D.L., Chase, M.A., Moritz, S.E. and Sullivan, P.J. (1999) 'A conceptual model of coaching efficacy: Preliminary investigation and instrument development', *Journal of Educational Psychology*, 91: 765–76.

Feltz, D.L., Short, S.E. and Sullivan, P.J. (2008) *Self-efficacy in Sport*, Champaign, IL: Human Kinetics.

Horn, T.S. (2008) 'Coaching effectiveness in the sports domain', in T.S. Horn (ed.) *Advances in Sport Psychology*, 3rd edn, Champaign, IL: Human Kinetics.

Hox, J.J. and Maas, C.J.M. (2001) 'The accuracy of multilevel structural equation modeling with pseudobalanced groups and small samples', *Structural Equation Modeling*, 8: 157–74.

Hu, L. and Bentler, P.M. (1999) 'Cutoff criteria for fit indexes in covariance structure analysis: Conventional criteria versus new alternatives', *Structural Equation Modeling*, 6: 1–55.

Jennrich, R.I. (2007) 'Rotation methods, algorithms, and standard errors' in R.C. MacCallum and R. Cudek (eds) *Factor Analysis at 100: Historical Developments and Future Directions*, Mahwah, NJ: Lawrence Erlbaum.

Jöreskog, K.G. (1969) 'A general approach to confirmatory maximum-likelihood factor analysis', *Psychometrika*, 34: 183–202.

Julian, M.W. (2001) 'The consequences of ignoring multilevel data structures in nonhierarchical covariance modeling', *Structural Equation Modeling*, 8: 325–52.

Kaplan, D. (1988) 'The impact of specification error on the estimation, testing, and improvement of structural equation models', *Multivariate Behavioral Research*, 23: 467–82.

Kenow, L.J. and Williams, J.M. (1992) 'Relationship between anxiety, self-confidence, and evaluation of coaching behaviors', *The Sport Psychologist*, 6: 344–57.

Lee, K.S., Malete, L. and Feltz, D.L. (2002) 'The effect of a coaching education program on coaching efficacy', *International Journal of Applied Sport Sciences*, 14: 55–67.

MacCallum, R.C., Roznowski, M. and Necowitz, L.B. (1992) 'Model modifications in covariance structure analysis: the problem of capitalization on chance', *Psychological Bulletin*, 111: 490–504.

Mallett, C. and Côté, J. (2006) 'Beyond winning and losing: Guidelines for evaluating high performance coaches', *The Sport Psychologist*, 20: 213–221.

Marsh, H.W. and Hau, K.-T. (2007) 'Application of latent variable models in educational psychology: The need for methodological-substantive synergies', *Contemporary Educational Psychology*, 32: 151–71.

Marsh, H.W., Muthén, B.O., Asparouhov, T., Lüdtke, O., Robitzsch, A., Morin, A.J. and Trautwein, U. (2009) 'Exploratory structural equation modeling, integrating CFA and EFA: Application to students' evaluations of university teaching', *Structural Equation Modeling*, 16: 439–76.

Muthén, B.O. (1994) 'Multilevel covariance structure analysis', *Sociological Methods and Research*, 22: 376–98.

Muthén, L.K. and Muthén, B.O. (1998–2010) *Mplus User's Guide*, 6th edn, Los Angeles, CA: Muthén and Muthén.

Myers, N.D., Beauchamp, M.R. and Chase, M.A. (2011a) 'Coaching competency and satisfaction with the coach: A multilevel structural equation model', *Journal of Sports Sciences*, 29: 411–22.

Myers, N.D., Chase, M.A., Beauchamp, M.R. and Jackson, B. (2010) 'The Coaching Competency Scale II – High School Teams', *Educational and Psychological Measurement*, 70: 477–94.

Myers, N.D., Feltz, D.L. and Chase, M.A. (2011b) 'Additional validity evidence for the Coaching Efficacy Scale II – High School Teams via a multiple-group approach', *Research Quarterly for Exercise and Sport*, 82: 79–88.

Myers, N.D., Feltz, D.L., Chase, M.A., Reckase, M.D. and Hancock, G.R. (2008) 'The Coaching Efficacy Scale II – High School Teams', *Educational and Psychological Measurement*, 68: 1059–76.

Myers, N.D., Feltz, D.L., Maier, K.S., Wolfe, E.W. and Reckase, M.D. (2006a) 'Athletes' evaluations of their head coach's coaching competency', *Research Quarterly for Exercise and Sport*, 77: 111–21.

Myers, N.D., Wolfe, E.W. and Feltz, D.L. (2005) 'An evaluation of the psychometric properties of the coaching efficacy scale for American coaches', *Measurement in Physical Education and Exercise Science*, 9: 135–60.

Myers, N.D., Wolfe, E.W., Feltz, D.L. and Penfield, R.D. (2006b) 'Identifying differential item functioning of rating scale items with the Rasch model: An introduction and an application', *Measurement in Physical Education and Exercise Science*, 10: 215–40.

Myers, N.D., Wolfe, E.W., Maier, K.S., Feltz, D.L. and Reckase, M.D. (2006c) 'Extending validity evidence for multidimensional measures of coaching competency', *Research Quarterly for Exercise and Sport*, 77: 451–463.

NASPE (National Association for Sport and Physical Education) (2006) *Quality Coaches, Quality Sports: National Standards for Athletic Coaches*, 2nd edn, Reston, VA: Author.

Rushall, B.S. and Wiznuk, K. (1985) 'Athletes' assessment of the coach: The coach evaluation questionnaire' *Canadian Journal of Applied Sport Sciences*, 10: 157–61.

Smith, R.E., Smoll, F.L. and Hunt, E.B. (1977) 'A system for the behavioral assessment of athletic coaches', *Research Quarterly*, 48: 401–7.

Smoll F.L. and Smith, R.E. (1989) 'Leadership behaviors in sport: A theoretical model and research paradigm', *Journal of Applied Social Psychology*, 19: 1522–51.

Spearman, C. (1904) 'General intelligence, objectively determined and measured', *American Journal of Psychology*, 15: 201–93.

Sullivan, P.J. and Kent, A. (2003) 'Coaching efficacy as a predictor of leadership style in intercollegiate athletics', *Journal of Applied Sport Psychology*, 15: 1–11.

Williams, J.M., Jerome, G.J., Kenow, L.J., Rogers, T., Sartain, T.A. and Darland, G. (2003) 'Factor structure of the coaching behavior questionnaire and its relationship to athlete variables', *The Sport Psychologist*, 17: 16–34.

Yates, A. (ed.) (1987) *Multivariate Exploratory Data Analysis: A Perspective on Exploratory Factor Analysis*, Albany, NY: State University of New York Press.

8

THE APPLICATION OF VIDEO-BASED PERFORMANCE ANALYSIS IN THE COACHING PROCESS[1]

The coach supporting athlete learning

Ryan Groom

MANCHESTER METROPOLITAN UNIVERSITY, UK

Lee Nelson

UNIVERSITY OF HULL, UK

Introduction

Over recent years there has been an increased academic interest in the use of video-based technology in sport (Groom and Cushion 2004; James 2006; Liebermann *et al.* 2002; O'Donoghue 2006; Wilson 2008). Textbooks within this area have tended to provide an overview of the technology currently available, practical guidelines outlining how to construct analysis systems, and discuss the importance of generating accurate and reliable data, amongst other useful topics (e.g. Carling *et al.* 2004; Hughes and Franks 1997, 2004a, 2008). Research investigations utilising such methods have often focused on the identification of movement and performance patterns within competition (e.g. Hughes and Franks 2004b), the identification and use of key performance indicators in sport (e.g. James *et al.* 2005) and the role of motion analysis techniques to gather information relating to work rate data (e.g. Carling *et al.* 2008).

Although considerable thought has been given towards the analysis of athletic performance, to date, there remains a paucity of work which examines how coaches use video-based feedback in an attempt to enhance athlete learning and performance. Early work in this area has tended to provide visual representations of the use of performance analysis in the coaching process (e.g. Franks *et al.* 1983; Hughes 2008; Robertson 1999). Although this work has provided a useful first step, it could be argued that these 'models' have tended to depict performance analysis as simplistic, unproblematic, and a given series of pre-defined events. Such representations are arguably idealistic models *for* the analysis of performance, rather than being empirically grounded models *of* performance analysis use 'in action' (Cushion *et al.* 2006). Recognising this difference would seem important because, 'the current set of models result in a representation of the coaching process that is often reduced in complexity and scale, and the essential social cultural elements of the process are often underplayed' (Cushion *et al.* 2006: 83). In this regard, Stratton *et al.* (2004: 132) suggest that 'it is not yet clear how to best integrate this technology into coaching practice'. Therefore, the aim of this chapter is two-fold. First, it builds upon the early simplistic depiction of the use of video-based performance analysis within the coaching process, by considering the findings of contemporary scholarly inquiry into coaching. The second, and principal significance of this chapter, is to further suggest ways in which the use of video-based performance analysis within the coaching process may be examined to better understand the implications for athlete learning.

Research gap

Within coaching the importance of providing athletes with feedback to correct or reinforce performance is well established (Côté and Sedgwick 1993; Cushion 2010; Franks 2004; Greenleaf *et al.* 2001). Here, Franks and Maile (1991) have suggested that video can be a useful tool for providing athlete feedback as it offers the ability to record and replay past performances, slow down actions and pause images. While the need to provide athletes with accurate and reliable performance feedback is well accepted (Franks and Miller 1986, 1991), it would seem important to acknowledge that the introduction of video-based technology in sport is a 'positive, although not always essential, step towards achieving this goal' (Liebermann *et al.* 2002: 767).

To date there has been a paucity of research into the use of video-based feedback to enhance athlete learning (Bertram *et al.* 2007). Existing studies have tended to utilise experimental designs to consider whether video feedback is more effective than more traditional methods of learning. For example, Guadagnoli *et al.* (2002) randomly assigned 30 golfers to one of three groups: video instruction, verbal instruction or self-guided. Statistical analysis of the participants' pre, post[1] and post[2] intervention (i.e. distance and accuracy) test scores suggested that after the two-week interval between post[1] and post[2] the video instruction group significantly outperformed the verbal instruction and self-guided groups. Similarly, Bertram *et al.* (2007) randomly assigned 48 golfers (24 novice and 24 skilled) to one of three groups: verbal coaching, verbal and video coaching, and self-guided. Analysis of the pre-intervention and post-intervention tests (i.e. of club head speed, club face angle at impact, and tempo) scores indicated that the positive effects of video feedback were limited in scope and observed to a greater extent in the skilled performers.

While such investigations have usefully contributed towards developing a greater understanding of video-based feedback and its potential for enhancing athlete learning and performance, Franks (2002: 4) has suggested that 'experimental studies used to develop practice guidelines may not be grounded in the realities of "real world" coaching'. In this respect, recent empirical research has depicted coaching as a socially complex and power dominated activity (Cushion and Jones 2006; d'Arripe-Longueville *et al.* 2001; Poczwardowski *et al.* 2002; Potrac and Jones 2009; Saury and Durand 1998). Central to this process is the coach's ability to obtain and maintain the 'trust' and 'respect' afforded to them by the key stakeholders in their coaching context (Nelson *et al.* in press). In light of such findings, Jones and Wallace (2005) have argued that 'knowledge-for-understanding' (i.e. to gain an understand of the phenomenon from a relativity impartial standpoint) projects, using a 'bottom-up' approach, are required if a more realistic and complete appreciation of coaching is to evolve. That is, Jones and Wallace (2005) contend that insights gained through 'knowledge-for-understanding' projects could provide a more secure foundation on which 'knowledge-for-action' (i.e. to bring about improvements in practice from a positive standpoint) could be built and from which more realistic guidelines for coach education could evolve.

Here, we argue that understanding the pedagogical use of video-based performance analysis technology within coaching practice could equally benefit from investigations specifically focusing on the development of 'knowledge-for-understanding'. Indeed, we are of the opinion that such projects could help to develop understanding about what 'knowledge, values, beliefs and expectations' underpins coaches' current video-based practices. Moreover, we believe that research of this nature could help to provide insight into how the opportunities and constraints of human interaction impact on the pedagogical use of such technology and its impact on athlete learning and development (Saury and Durand 1998). In light of the presented arguments, we believe that inquiry into the practical use of video-based technology within coaching practice needs to capture and be sensitive to the ambiguity and complexity inherent in the coaching process. As such, we (Groom *et al.* 2011a) recently initiated a grounded theory project, in collaboration with a colleague, in an attempt to gain a more in-depth understanding of 'how' and 'why' video is used within practical coaching contexts. Data were collected from in-depth interviews conducted with 14 England youth soccer coaches that utilised video-based performance analysis technology within their professional coaching practice.

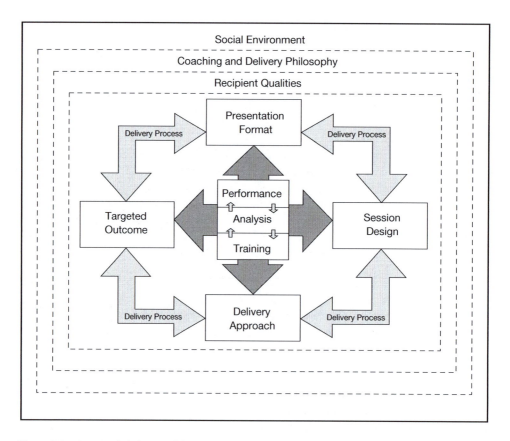

Figure 8.1:   A grounded theory of the delivery of video-based performance analysis by England youth soccer coaches.

At the centre of the grounded theory is the relationship between performance, analysis and training, which were found to be cyclical in nature (see Figure 8.1). In an attempt to assist the learning and development of their athletes, the participant coaches utilised video-based technology where they perceived that a coaching intervention was required (Figure 8.1). When planning their video-based interventions, the participant coaches considered how the targeted outcomes, session design, presentation format and delivery approach utilised might achieve their desired objectives (Figure 8.1). While the participant coaches' pedagogical reasoning was depicted in a simplistic cyclical fashion, the influence of contextual factors was also found to be an inherent feature of the coaches' delivery of video-based performance analysis in their respective coaching contexts (Figure 8.1). In keeping with contemporary understanding about the complex realities of coaching practice, the delivery process was found to be influenced by the social environment, the coaches' philosophy and the qualities of those athletes they had worked with (Figure 8.1). In this respect, it was evident that the coaches' delivery of video-based performance analysis was far from a simplistic, straightforward and unproblematic linear process.

Examining the use of video-based performance analysis in coaching: a future research agenda

In addition to traditional experimental research designs, we believe that scholarly activity into the use of video-based performance analysis technology would benefit from engaging in a socio-pedagogical analysis of contextual factors and how these impact upon coaching practice and athlete learning. That is, to date within the performance analysis literature a similar bio-scientific performance discourse has dominated, to that which has been evident within sports coaching more broadly (Jones 2000; Kirk 2010). In this regard, Kirk (2010) highlights how terms such as 'training', 'conditioning', 'drills' and 'practices' have dominated the sports coaching literature at the expense of 'learning'. In relation to understanding coaching practice, Armour (2011) suggests that pedagogy is composed of three dimensions: (1) knowledge in context; (2) learners and learning; and (3) coaches/coaching. Similarly, Kirk (2010: 167) highlights 'the need for coaches to understand the relations among learning, coaching subject matter and context' to better understand the coaching role. We believe that it is important that future research considers the interrelated elements of pedagogy when attempting to understand how coaches use video technology to facilitate athlete learning. To support this argument we presented some initial findings of a socio-pedagogically based piece of research into how a group of coaches utilised video within their coaching practices. While the presented grounded theory described a host of interlinking processes, perhaps the key finding of this research project was that the interviewed coaches' use of video-based technology fundamentally involved a human interaction between coach and athlete which was situated within a specific social context. In light of this finding, we contend that the field might usefully consider the concept of pedagogy, as this term not only accounts for the key elements of coaching through video, but how they interact as part of an educational endeavour.

Re-conceptualising the use of video as a pedagogical tool is in keeping with the suggestion that coaching, like teaching, is an educational endeavour (Jones 2006, 2007). Here, we argue that the field could usefully consider investigations that have studied classroom interactions and teachers' use of technology within educational settings. In this respect, the field of coaching might learn from the work of Mercer *et al.* (2004: 195) who conclude from reviewing the methods for studying interactions in educational activities that 'the choice of methods in any particular study should take into account the range of well-founded methods that are available, rather than being guided only by researchers' established affinities for particular methods and paradigms'. Therefore, having argued the need to consider the socio-pedagogical interactions occurring between coach and athlete when engaging in video-based performance analysis, we will now outline three methods that researchers might use to initially investigate this area. While we recognise a number of additional methodological approaches exist (i.e. ethnographic observations, narrative analysis, interpretive phenomenological analysis, action research, discourse analysis etc), a description of the full range of methods available is beyond the scope of the present chapter. However, we hope that other scholars will add to these initial suggestions and discussions.

Systematic observation

Systematic observation is a well-established and widely used research method within the education and coaching literature (Cushion 2010; Kahan 1999; Mercer *et al.* 2004). Typically, pre-defined categories of behaviour are identified and recorded when observing teacher-student or coach-athlete interactions (Cushion 2010; McKenzie and Carlson 1989). Through applying this method researchers can record variables such as behavioural frequencies, patterns and durations. Indeed, it has been argued that the systematic observation of coaching behaviour is a useful means of gathering base-line information on a much under-researched activity (Potrac *et al.* 2007). To date, the investigation of coaching behaviour has largely focused on the practices of coaches in training environments (Cushion 2010). We contend that systematic observation could usefully be extended to situations in which coaches and athletes engage in video-based performance analysis. When acknowledging that these situations often mirror more traditional classroom educational settings (Groom *et al.* 2011a), researchers might consider utilising established tools within the educational literature. Arguably, the most widely employed method in this regard is Flander's Interactive Analysis Categories (FIAC) system (Flanders 1970). Utilising established systematic observational instruments might provide insight into the behaviours that both coaches and athletes engage in during these pedagogical encounters (More and Franks 2004). Specifically, these tools could provide descriptive statistics about ratios of coach-to-athlete talk and key patterns of coach-athlete interaction. This would allow coaching scholars to generate greater understanding about the balance of dialogical communication. While using a single quantitative approach to assess behaviours is arguably limited to the generation of base-line behavioural data, such information may provide a useful starting point to further explore the use of video-based performance analysis within the coaching process.

Conversation analysis

Whereas systematic observation attempts to group interactional behaviours into pre-defined categories, conversation analysis (CA) is a functional-linguistic approach that examines 'talk' through detailed verbatim accounts that are mindful of the subtleties of communication 'in action' (e.g. interruptions, overlapping talk, pauses, emphasis, repair, raising and falling intonation etc.). Mercer (2010) highlights that a particular strength of CA is that transcribed talk remains throughout the analysis rather than being reduced to categories at an early stage. Therefore, researchers do not need to make initial judgments about the meaning of the data which cannot be revised (Mercer 2010). CA was historically developed within ethnomethodology (Garfinkel 1967), principally by the sociologists Harvey Sacks, Emanuel Schegloff and Gail Jefferson with the purpose of studying 'talk in action' (Sacks *et al.* 1974).

CA helps to develop understanding about how participants organise their speaking turns by describing the sequential development of conversation and control of topics in an interactive situation (Kumpulainen and Wray 2002). Epistemologically, ethnomethodology is located within a phenomenological paradigm, with the aim of examining 'common-sense thinking' (Seedhouse 2005). Ontologically, ethnomethodology's position is associated with constructionism, in that social phenomena and meanings are constantly being accomplished by social actors (Seedhouse 2005). In this regard, the examples of talk and interaction can be used to show concrete illustrations of data analysis (Mercer 2010). Indeed, Richards (2005) outlines three reasons as to the use of CA in applied research, which we believe are particularly relevant to better understand coaching behaviour:

1   CA is empirically grounded and therefore well placed to generate the sort of discoveries that can inform practice.
2   The focus upon practical accomplishment through interaction establishes a natural link with professional practice.
3   Because raw materials are observable phenomena, these resources are available for subsequent training interventions.

While CA was originally used to analyse 'everyday talk' (pure CA), more recently CA has been used to examine 'institutional talk' (applied CA) within a broader theoretical framework (Ten Have 2000). Ten Have (2000: 189) further explains that

> in 'pure CA', the focus is on the local practices of turn-taking, sequential organisation, etc., in and for themselves, while in 'applied CA' attention shifts to the tensions between those local practices and any 'larger structures' in which these are embedded, such as institutional rules, instructions, accounting obligations, etc.

As such, it has been suggested that CA is able to provide 'a "holistic" portrayal of language use that reveals the reflexive relationship between form, function, sequence and social identity and social/institutional context' (Seedhouse 2005: 263). Indeed, Heritage and Clayman (2010) highlighted how CA has been applied to analyse such institutional contexts as calls to emergency services, doctor-patient interactions, courtroom trials, and political and news interviews. An example of the use of CA to explore coach-athlete interactions within video-based performance analysis feedback sessions can be seen in the work of Groom *et al.* (2012). Using CA as an analytical tool, analysis of the interactions revealed that the coach attempted to exercise control over the sequential organisation of the sessions, via asymmetrical turn-taking allocations, an unequal opportunity to talk, control over the topic of discussion within the interactions and the use of questioning to select speakers to take turns to talk (Groom, Cushion and Nelson 2012). Furthermore, this work emphasised the importance of coaches becoming more aware of the likely impact of such interactional practices upon athlete learning (Groom *et al.* 2012).

Interviews

While systematic observation and conversational analysis may provide a potentially fruitful account of the interactions that occur between coach and athlete during video-based feedback sessions, these approaches are unable to provide insight into 'why' the coach employed certain practices and 'how' athletes experience these pedagogical events (Potrac *et al.* 2000). In this respect, Patton (2002) suggested that interviews allow us to enter other people's perspective, to find out what is in someone else's mind. Moreover, Creswell and Garrett (2008: 322) suggest that qualitative approaches such as interviews are capable of 'yielding detailed information reported in the voices of participants and contextualized in settings in which they provide experiences and the meaning of their experiences'. Interviews have been frequently utilised within the coaching literature and found to provide valuable introspective insight into how understanding and situational factors influence coaching behaviour and decision-making processes (Côté *et al.* 1995; Jones *et al.* 2003). Therefore, we believe that interviews provided an effective means of gaining insight into experiences, thoughts, and perceptions regarding the use of video-based feedback.

Mixed method approach

Although it remains possible to utilise research methods in isolation, Tashakkori and Teddlie (2010) have recently argued that the combining of quantitative and qualitative methods within a project often creates a more coherent, rational and rigorous understanding of the phenomena under investigation. This argument is echoed by Creswell and Garrett (2008), who contend that the bringing together of quantitative and qualitative research methods often leads to a greater understanding than either approach can achieve alone. Creswell and Garrett (2008: 321) further suggest that 'the educational researcher needs a large toolkit of methods and designs to address complex, interdisciplinary research problems'. Such an appreciation would seem to reflect a growing realisation that 'the integrity of the research enterprise need not involve making an ideological commitment to one or the other' (Mercer 2010: 8).

Both quantitative and qualitative methods could be usefully combined to further understand the pedagogical delivery of video-based performance analysis (Nelson and Groom 2012). Indeed, within the coaching literature there are some examples of how these methods have been combined to produce a more in-depth understanding about coaching practices, underpinning understanding and decision-making (e.g. Smith and Cushion 2006; Potrac *et al.* 2002; Vergeer and Lyle 2007). However, we urge scholars to give greater consideration toward mixed-methods research design, by acknowledging and engaging with the various procedures, typologies, and underlying philosophical debates within this area (e.g. Creswell 2009; Morgan 1998, 2007; Morse 1991; Nelson and Groom 2012). Here, thought should be given towards the timing (i.e. sequential or concurrent), weighting (i.e. equal or dominant), mixing (i.e. integrated, connected or embedded), and theorising (i.e. explicit or implicit) of mixed method research design (Creswell 2009).

In the future, coaching scholars might usefully record and analyse the behaviours, experiences and perceptions of coaches and athletes engaging in video-based sessions within a given coaching context. For example, the three methods outlined above could be used concurrently in order to identify macro-level patterns of interaction (i.e. systematic observation), micro-level sequential organisation of talk in action (i.e. conversation analysis), and 'how' and 'why' coaches and athletes responded in the way that they do (i.e. interviews). It is by combining these methods that we believe that the field will start to develop a more in-depth and complete understanding of the socio-pedagogical complexities of video-based coaching practice.

Suggested theoretical frameworks

It is hoped that by using these, and other methods, a greater understanding will develop about 'how' and 'why' coaches use video-based performance analysis technology and what impact these practices have upon athlete learning. Indeed, drawing upon the field of education may offer a valuable insight into new ways of studying the use of technology in pedagogical interactions between coach and athlete. For example, educational researchers have started to explore how teachers might utilise technology to 'orchestrate' interactive learning (Beauchamp *et al.* 2010; Mercer *et al.* 2010). In this regard, there would appear to be a drive towards the promotion of 'dialogic' communication between teachers and students, in recognition that this can enhance student learning (Alexander 2008; Mercer *et al.* 2010). Researchers in education often draw on Mortimer and Scott's (2003) *communicative approach* concept, which provides a perspective on how a teacher will work with students to develop ideas in the classroom (Scott 2008). According to Mortimer and Scott (2003) 'talk' between the teacher and student can be defined along two dimensions: *interactive-non-interactive* and *dialogical-authoritative* (Scott 2008). *Interactive* communication is characterised as allowing for the verbal participation of both teacher and student, alternatively *non-interactive* teaching involves teacher 'talk' through a predominantly 'lecturing' format (Mortimer and Scott 2003). Whereas a *dialogical* communicative approach to teaching is concerned with asking students for their points of view, an *authoritative* approach focuses on transmitting knowledge and has little interest in exploring the views and ideas of students.

Mortimer and Scott's (2003) *communicative approach* concept would appear similar to the distinction that Freire (1970) made in his classic text *Pedagogy of the Oppressed*. Freire contrasted what he termed the *banking* concept of education against *problem-posing* education. Here, Freire argued that a careful analysis of the teacher-student relationship often reveals a fundamentally narrative character, with the teacher lecturing information to students who are expected to passively receive and memorise the content that is delivered to them. Freire attached the *banking* label to this form of education as he considered it to be an act of information depositing. Such an approach is in contrast with Freire's concept of *problem-posing* education, which emphasises the importance of dialogue through open communication. Freire argued that *problem-posing* education transforms the teacher-student relationship as students are no longer docile listeners, but rather critical co-investigators.

It is hoped that the use of both educational and social theory may act as a 'thinking tool' to guide researchers exploring coach-athlete interactions within video-based feedback sessions. Using theory in this way might assist scholars with 'making sense' of the pedagogical practices that coaches employ when delivering video-based sessions and the impact of such practices on athletes. In this respect, we believe that these concepts could help to further develop understanding acquired through initial investigations into how athletes respond to their coaches' delivery of video-based feedback. For example, in a study of an elite ice-hockey player's experiences of receiving video-based coaching, Nelson *et al.* (in press) discovered that the participant's respect for his coaches appeared to influence whether learning was likely to occur. Here, the authors principally drew on theories of respect (e.g. Darwall 1977, 2006; Hudson 1980) and learning (e.g. Piaget 1950; Vygotsky 1962, 1978) to explain their findings. Similarly, using a case study of an international standard female hockey player, Groom *et al.* (2011b) drew upon interview data that indicated that the presence of a video camera, even when operating remotely, mediates the players' practice and imposed a critical gaze of surveillance, discipline and corrective practice upon the individual (Foucault 1991). Moreover, reviewing the video-based feedback within a team environment transformed the coaches' gaze into one which was collectively consumed (Groom *et al.* 2011b). That is, within such team feedback sessions, in addition to the coaches' corrective feedback, other players' perceptions of the athletic performance under review acted as a collective critical gaze and at the same time one of normative correction (Foucault 1991). In this work, Mathiesen's (1997) concept of the synopticon, was theoretically applied to the video-feedback sessions, thereby developing Foucault's concept of Panoptican (based upon Jeremy Bentham's design for a prison watch tower), where the few watch the many, to a situation where many (i.e. coaching staff and team) watch the few (i.e. the selected players in the video example).

Conclusion

In this chapter we have attempted to present the need to consider coaching practitioners' pedagogical delivery of video-based performance analysis. This argument was grounded in the observation that the performance analysis literature has, to date, largely focused on the application of methods for analysing athletic performance, which has left practitioners speculating about how they should incorporate these technologies and techniques into their pedagogical coaching practices. Within this chapter we outlined the findings of an initial study that presented a data-driven grounded theory. While we acknowledge the substantive nature of the grounded theory; this work should not be viewed as either an end-point or a project in isolation. Rather, the grounded theory presented should be considered a starting point for a wider research project. As Strauss and Corbin (1998: 22–23) have suggested, developing such a theory is often a long and complex activity which 'necessitates that ideas be explored fully and considered from many different angles or perspectives'. Therefore, to build upon our earlier work, it is necessary to consider both the *variability* and *modifiability* of the theory within different sports and contexts (Strauss and Corbin 1998). Here, we hope that scholars within the field of coaching will contribute to understanding in this area by conducting research into the pedagogical use of video-based performance analysis technology in coaching practice. Through such a collaborative research endeavour, we are hopeful that findings from other investigations will assist with the transition from a *substantive* to a more *formal* theory (Glaser and Strauss 1967). Consequently, in order to develop a more *formal* theory, we have suggested a number of different methods that may be used either in isolation or combination.

Our future aim, then, is to develop a coaching specific theory in relation to the delivery of video-based performance analysis. However, in so doing, we believe that it would be somewhat naïve to think that theories identified from other disciplines are unable to assist the development of understanding within coaching. In this respect, we find ourselves in agreement with Cushion's (2007) argument that coaching remains ill-defined and under-theorised and that theory from other disciplines can therefore act as valuable 'thinking tools' that can extend existing understanding. Like Cushion (2007), we are mindful that the field needs to avoid being colonised, and, in this respect, coaching needs to develop its own conceptual understandings. Within this chapter, we have briefly introduced a number of potential frameworks that could help make sense of how coaches use video-based performance analysis in their coaching practice. The principle significance of this work lies in its ability to inform the education and ongoing development of coaching practitioners. Indeed, the grounded theory may act as a tool to generate thought, discussion and reflection on the pedagogical use of video-based performance analysis technology within coaching practice. While in its present *substantive* format the theory is specific to the participants studied, as other sports and contexts are investigated the theory will evolve into a more generalisable *formal* theory (Glaser and Strauss 1967). Once a formal theory has been established, we envisage that this may assist in guiding coaches' use of video-based performance analysis, but in a way that is 'grounded in the messy realities of everyday practice' (Jones *et al.* 2010: 23).

Note

1   For the purposes of the present chapter, the use of video-based performance analysis feedback in the coaching process is conceptualised as those situations where an athlete/s performance has been video recorded and analysed (either quantitatively or qualitatively) and a coaching intervention is initiated to change and/or reinforce performance.

References

Alexander, R.J. (2008) *Towards Dialogic Teaching: Rethinking Classroom Talk*, 4th edn, Cambridge: Dialogos.

Armour, K.M. (2011) 'What is sport pedagogy and why study it?' in K.M. Armour (ed.) *Sports Pedagogy: An Introduction for Teaching and Coaching*, London: Prentice Hall.

Beauchamp, G., Kennewell, S., Tanner, H. and Jones, S. (2010) 'Interactive whiteboards and all that jazz: The contribution of musical metaphors to the analysis of classroom activity with interactive technologies', *Technology, Pedagogy and Education*, 19(2): 143–157.

Bertram, C.P., Marteniuk, R.G. and Guadagnoli, M.A. (2007) 'On the use and misuse of video analysis', *International Journal of Sports Science and Coaching*, 2(S1): 37–46.

Carling, C., Bloomfield, J., Nelson, L.J. and Reilly, T. (2008) 'The role of motion analysis in elite soccer: Contemporary performance measurement techniques and work rate data', *Sports Medicine*, 38(10): 839–862.

Carling, C., Williams, A.M. and Reilly, T. (2004) *Handbook of Soccer Match Analysis: A Systematic Approach to Improving Performance*, London: Routledge.

Côté, J., Salmela, J., Trudel, P., Baria, A. and Russell, S. (1995) 'The coaching model: A grounded assessment of expert gymnastic coaches' knowledge', *Journal of Sport and Exercise Psychology*, 17: 1–17.

Côté, J. and Sedgwick, W.A. (1993) 'Effective behaviours of expert rowing coaches: A qualitative investigation of Canadian athletes and coaches', *International Sports Journal*, 7(1): 62–77.

Creswell, J.W. (2009) *Research Design: Qualitative, Quantitative, and Mixed Method Approaches*, 3rd edn, Thousand Oaks, CA: Sage.

Creswell, J.W. and. Garrett, A.L. (2008) 'The "movement" of mixed methods research and the role of educators', *South African Journal of Education*, 28(3): 321–333.

Cushion, C.J. (2007) 'Modelling the complexity of the coaching process: A response to commentaries', *International Journal of Sports Science and Coaching*, 2(4): 427–433.

Cushion, C.J. (2010) 'Coach behaviour', in J. Lyle and C.J. Cushion (eds) *Sports Coaching: Professionalisation and Practice*, London: Elsevier.

Cushion, C.J., Amour, K.M. and Jones, R.L. (2006) 'Locating the coaching process in practice: Models "for" and "of" coaching', *Physical Education and Sport Pedagogy*, 11(1): 83–99.

Cushion, C.J. and Jones, R.L. (2006) 'Power, discourse, and symbolic violence in professional youth soccer: The case of Albion F.C.', *Sociology of Sport Journal*, 23(2): 142–161.

d'Arripe-Longueville, F., Saury, J., Fournier, J. and Durand, M. (2001) 'Coach-athlete interaction during elite archery competitions: and application of methodological framework used in ergonomics research to sport psychology', *Journal of Applied Sport Psychology*, 13(3): 275–299.

Darwall, S. (1977) 'Two kinds of respect', *Ethics*, 88(1): 36–49.

Darwall, S. (2006) *The Second-Person Standpoint*, Cambridge, MA: Harvard University Press.

Flanders, N. (1970) *Analyzing Teaching Behavior*, London: Addison-Wesley Publishing Company.

Foucault, M. (1991) *Discipline and Punishment: The Birth of the Prison*, London: Penguin.

Franks, I.M. (2002) 'Evidence-based practice and the coaching process', *International Journal of Performance Analysis in Sport*, 2(1): 1–5.

Franks, I.M. (2004) 'The need for feedback', in M. Hughes and I.M. Franks (eds) *Notational Analysis of Sport: Improving Coaching and Performance in Sport*, 2nd edn, London: E. and F.N. Spon.

Franks, I.M. and Maile, L.J. (1991) 'The use of video in sport skill acquisition', in P.W. Dowrick (ed.) *Practical Guide to Using Video in the Behavioural Sciences*, New York: John Wiley.

Franks, I.M. and Miller, G. (1986) 'Eyewitness testimony in sport', *Journal of Sport Behavior*, 9(1): 39–45.

Franks, I.M. and Miller, G. (1991) 'Training coaches to observe and remember', *Journal of Sports Sciences*, 9(3): 285–297.

Franks, I.M., Goodman, D. and Miller, M. (1983) 'Analysis of performance: Qualitative or quantitative', *Sports*, March.

Freire, P. (1970) *Pedagogy of the Oppressed*, London: Penguin Books (first published in Portuguese in 1968).

Garfinkel, H. (1967) *Studies in Ethnomethodology*, Englewood Cliffs, NJ: Prentice Hall.

Glaser, B. and Strauss, A. (1967) *Discovery of Grounded Theory*, Chicago, IL: Aldine.

Greenleaf, C., Gould, D. and Dieffenbach, K. (2001) 'Factors influencing Olympic performance: Atlanta and Nagano US Olympians', *Journal of Applied Sport Psychology*, 13(2): 154–184.

Groom, R. and Cushion, C.J. (2004) 'Coaches perceptions of the use of video analysis: A case study', *Insight*, 7(3): 56–58.

Groom, R., Cushion, C.J. and Nelson, L.J. (2011a) 'The delivery of video-based performance analysis by England youth soccer coaches: Towards a grounded theory', *Journal of Applied Sport Psychology*, 23(1): 16–34.

Groom, R., Cushion, C.J. and Nelson, L.N. (2012). Analysing coach-athlete 'talk in interaction' within the delivery of video-based performance feedback in elite youth soccer. *Qualitative Research in Sport, Health and Exercise*, 4(3): 439-458.

Groom, R., Taylor, W.G., Nelson, L.J. and Potrac, P. (2011b) 'Problematising the use of video: Foucaultian notions of corrective training and athlete discipline', paper presented at Sports and Coaching: Past and Futures, 26 June, Crewe, UK.

Guadagnoli, M., Holcomb, W. and Davis, M. (2002) 'The efficacy of video feedback for learning the golf swing', *Journal of Sports Science*, 20(8): 615–622.

Heritage, J. and Clayman, S. (2010) *Talk in Action: Interactions, Identities, and Institutions*, New York: Wiley-Blackwell.

Hudson, S.D. (1980) 'The nature of respect', *Social Theory and Practice*, 6(1): 69–90.

Hughes, M. (2008) 'Notational analysis for coaches', in R.L. Jones, M. Hughes and K. Kingston (eds) *An Introduction to Sports Coaching: From Science and Theory to Practice*, London: Routledge.

Hughes, M.D. and Franks, I.D. (1997) *Notational Analysis of Sport*, London: E. and F.N. Spon.

Hughes, M.D. and Franks, I.M. (2004a) *Notational Analysis of Sport: Improving Coaching and Performance in Sport*, 2nd edn, London: E. and F.N. Spon.

Hughes, M.D. and Franks, I.M. (2004b) 'Analysis of passing sequences, shots and goal scored in soccer', *Journal of Sports Sciences*, 23(5): 509–514.

Hughes, M.D. and Franks, I.D. (2008) *The Essentials of Performance Analysis: An Introduction*, London: Routledge.

James, N. (2006) 'Notational analysis in soccer: Past, present, future', *International Journal of Performance Analysis in Sport*, 6(2): 67–81.

James, N., Mellalieu, S.D. and Jones, N.M.D. (2005) 'The development of position-specific performance indicators in professional rugby union', *Journal of Sports Sciences*, 23(1): 63–72.

Jones, R.L. (2000) 'Towards a sociology of coaching', in R.L. Jones and K.M. Armour (eds) *The Sociology of Sport: Theory and Practice*, London: Addison-Wesley Longman.

Jones, R.L. (2006) *The Sports Coach as Educator: Re-conceptualising Sports Coaching*, London: Routledge.

Jones, R.L. (2007) 'Coaching redefined: An everyday pedagogical endeavour', *Sport, Education and Society*, 12(2): 159–173.

Jones, R.L. and Wallace, M. (2005) 'Another bad day at the training ground: Coping with ambiguity in the coaching context', *Sport, Education and Society*, 10(1): 119–134.

Jones, R.L., Armour, K.M. and Potrac, P. (2003) 'Constructing expert knowledge: A case study of a top-level professional soccer coach', *Sport, Education and Society*, 8(2): 213–229.

Jones, R.L., Bowes, I. and Kingston, K. (2010) 'Complex practice in coaching: Studying the chaotic nature of coach-athlete interaction', in J. Lyle and C.J. Cushion (eds) *Sports Coaching: Professionalisation and Practice*, London: Elsevier.

Kahan, D. (1999) 'Coach behaviour: A review of the systematic observation research literature', *Applied Research in Coaching and Athletics Annual*, 14: 17–58.

Kirk, D. (2010) 'Towards a socio-pedagogy of sports coaching', in J. Lyle and C.J. Cushion (eds) *Sports Coaching: Professionalisation and Practice*, London: Elsevier.

Kumpulainen, K. and Wray, D. (2002) *Classroom Interaction and Social Learning: From Theory to Practice*, London: Routledge.

Liebermann, D.G., Katz, L., Hughes, M.D., Bartlett, R.M., McClements, J. and Franks, I.M. (2002) 'Advances in the application of information technology to sport performance', *Journal of Sports Sciences*, 20(10): 755–769.

Mathiesen, T. (1997) 'The viewer society: Michel Foucault's Panopticon revisited', *Theoretical Criminology*, 1(2): 215–234.

McKenzie, T.L. and Carlson, B.R. (1989) 'Systematic observation and computer technology', in P.W. Darst, D.B. Zakrajsek and V.H. Mancini (eds) *Analysing Physical Education and Sport Instruction*, 2nd edn, Champaign, IL: Human Kinetics.

Mercer, N. (2010) 'The analysis of classroom talk: Methods and methodologies', *British Journal of Educational Psychology*, 80: 1–14.

Mercer, N., Hennessy, S. and Warwick, P. (2010) 'Using interactive whiteboards to orchestrate classroom dialogue', *Technology, Pedagogy and Education*, 19(2): 195–209.

Mercer, N., Littleton, K. and Wegerif, K. (2004) 'Methods for studying the processes of interaction and collaborative activity in computer-based educational activities', *Technology, Pedagogy and Education*, 13(2): 195–212.

More, K. and Franks, I.M. (2004) 'Measuring coaching effectiveness', in M. Hughes and I.M. Franks (eds) *Notational Analysis of Sport: Systems for Better Coaching and Performance in Sport*, 2nd edn, London: Routledge.

Morgan, D. (1998) 'Practical strategies for combining qualitative and quantitative methods: Applications to health research', *Qualitative Health Research*, 8(3): 362–376.

Morgan, D. (2007) 'Paradigms lost and pragmatism regained: Methodological implications of combining qualitative and quantitative methods', *Journal of Mixed Methods Research*, 1(1): 48–76.

Morse, J.M. (1991) 'Approaches to qualitative-quantitative methodological triangulation', *Nursing Research*, 40: 120–123.

Mortimer E.F. and Scott, P.H. (2003) *Meaning Making in Science Classrooms*, Buckingham: Open University Press.

Nelson, L.J. and Groom, R. (2012) 'The analysis of athletic performance: Some practical and philosophic considerations', *Sport, Education and Society*, 17(5): 687–701.

Nelson, L.J., Potrac, P. and Groom, R. (in press) 'Receiving video-based feedback in elite ice-hockey: A player's perspective', *Sport, Education and Society*, DOI: 10.1080/13573322.2011.613925.

O'Donoghue, P. (2006) 'The use of feedback videos in sport', *International Journal of Performance Analysis in Sport*, 6(2): 1–14.

Patton, M.Q. (2002) *Qualitative Research and Evaluation Methods*, 3rd edn, Thousand Oaks, CA: Sage.

Piaget, J. (1950) *The Psychology of Intelligence*, London: Routledge.

Poczwardowski, A., Barott, J.E. and Henschen, K.P. (2002) 'The athlete and coach: Their relationship and its meaning. Results of an interpretive study', *International Journal of Sport Psychology*, 33(1): 116–140.

Potrac, P. and Jones, R.L. (2009) 'Micro-political workings in semi-professional football coaching', *Sociology of Sport Journal*, 26(4): 557–577.

Potrac, P., Brewer, C., Jones, R.L., Armour, K.M. and Hoff, J. (2000) 'Towards an holistic understanding of the coaching process', *Quest*, 52(2): 186–199.

Potrac, P., Jones, R.L. and Amour, K.M. (2002) 'It's all about getting respect: The coaching behaviours of an expert English soccer coach', *Sport, Education and Society*, 7(2): 182–202.

Potrac, P., Jones, R.L. and Cushion, C.J. (2007) 'Understanding power and the coach's role in professional English soccer: A preliminary investigation of coach behaviour', *Soccer and Society*, 8(1): 33–29.

Richards, K. (2005) 'Introduction', in K. Richards and P. Seedhouse (eds) *Applying Conversation Analysis*, London: Palgrave Macmillan.

Robertson, K. (1999) *Observation, Analysis and Video*, Leeds: The National Coaching Foundation.

Sacks, H., Schegloff, E.A. and Jefferson, G. (1974) 'A simplest systematic for the organization of turn-taking for conversation', *Language*, 50(4): 696–735.

Saury, J. and Durand, M. (1998) 'Practical knowledge in expert coaches: On-site study of coaching in sailing', *Research Quarterly for Exercise and Sport*, 69(3): 254–266.

Scott, P. (2008) 'Talking a way to understanding in science classrooms', in N. Mercer and S. Hodgkinson (eds) *Exploring Talk in School*, London: Sage.

Seedhouse, P. (2005) 'Conversation analysis as research methodology', in K. Richards and P. Seedhouse (eds) *Applying Conversation Analysis*, London: Palgrave Macmillan.

Smith, M. and Cushion, C.J. (2006) 'An investigation of the in-game behaviours of professional, top-level youth soccer coaches', *Journal of Sports Science*, 24(4): 355–366.

Stratton, G., Reilly, T., Williams, A.M. and Richardson, D. (2004) *Youth Soccer: From Science to Performance*, London: Routledge.

Strauss, A. and Corbin, J. (1998) *Basics of Qualitative Research: Techniques and Procedure for Developing Grounded Theory*, 2nd edn, Thousand Oaks, CA: Sage.

Tashakkori, A. and Teddlie, C. (2010) *Sage Handbook of Mixed Methods in Social and Behavioral Research*, 2nd edn, London: Sage.

Ten Have, P. (2000) *Doing Conversation Analysis: A Practical Guide*, Thousand Oaks, CA: Sage

Vergeer, I. and Lyle, J. (2007) 'Mixing methods in assessing coaches' decision making', *Research Quarterly for Exercise and Sport*, 78(3): 225–235.

Vygotsky, L.S. (1962) *Thought and Language*, Cambridge, MA: MIT Press.

Vygotsky, L.S. (1978) *Mind and Society*, Cambridge, MA: MIT Press.

Wilson, B.W. (2008) 'Development in video technology for coaching', *Sports Technology*, 1(1): 34–40.

9

OBSERVING THE DYNAMICS OF COACH–ATHLETE INTERACTIONS IN REAL TIME

The state space grid method

Karl Erickson

QUEEN'S UNIVERSITY, CANADA

Jean Côté

QUEEN'S UNIVERSITY, CANADA

Introduction

Côté and Gilbert (2009) recently proposed a definition of coaching effectiveness that includes the coaching knowledge that can potentially characterize effective coaching. However, we still have very little understanding of how coaches' knowledge is translated into effective behaviours (Cushion and Lyle 2010). There is a general consensus that there are a great many things that we do not yet understand about how it is that effective coaches do what they do. In striving to rectify these gaps in understanding, it might be argued that we have been hampered by a methodological inability to collect and analyse data that would offer true insight into what has been previously referred to as the 'art' of coaching (Nash and Collins 2006). To that end, the purpose of this chapter is to provide an initial framework for the application of state space grid methodology (SSG: Hollenstein 2007; Lewis *et al.* 1999), based on dynamic systems concepts, in sport coaching research.

The primary focus of this chapter is a description of the theoretical grounding and logistical underpinnings for putting the SSG method into practice in the study of sport coaching. In the first section of this chapter we present a brief discussion of previous coach behaviour research and relatively recent conceptualizations of the coaching process in order to highlight areas in need of illumination. The second section of this chapter outlines the SSG method as a way to deepen our understanding of the dynamic behavioural relationships that effective coaches entertain with their athletes. Finally we conclude with thoughts on potential implications for coaching research, practice, and education to be derived from SSG-based study.

Previous coaching behaviour research

As noted by Horn (2008) in her comprehensive review of coaching effectiveness, research on coaching has taken a number of different methodological approaches (e.g. qualitative, quantitative questionnaire, observation). Observational methods have been a central component in the study of coach behaviour, in particular the use of systematic observation instruments (see reviews by Erickson and Gilbert in press; Gilbert and Trudel 2004; Kahan 1999). The accumulated body of literature, based primarily on implementation of the Coaching Behavior Assessment System (CBAS: Smith *et al.* 1977) and the Arizona State University Observation Instrument (ASUOI: Lacy and Darst 1984), has had a profound impact on our understanding of the behaviours coaches use, and the relationship between these behaviours and their antecedents and various athlete outcomes (Horn 2008).

This work represents a tremendously important contribution to the study of sport coaching and the practical value of these findings cannot be ignored. However, it is also important to recognize that a number of behavioural components of the coaching process are not fully captured and reflected through these traditional modes of observation and analysis (Horn 2008). As such, our ability to fully comprehend the intricacies of coaching and most effectively promote coach development through education remains limited. These limitations are manifest in one of the central reasons why the existing body of literature on coach behaviour does not tell the whole story (Cushion 2010): while we have a relatively solid grounding in 'what' coaches do, we know next to nothing about 'how' they do it, particularly from an explicitly behavioural perspective. This point – how coaches' behaviour is patterned, structured, and enacted over time – is the primary focus of this chapter.

Part of the reason we have yet to fully examine these qualities of coach behaviour may lie in the conceptualization of the coaching process used to guide research. Most previous observational work has conceptualized coaching as a one-way flow of influence from coach to athlete; the coach behaves in a certain way, which the athlete passively interprets or internalizes and experiences an outcome. This fact is exemplified in Horn's (2008) working model of coaching effectiveness, which was formulated to summarize the existing literature on coach behaviour. Recent theoretical work has suggested that this unidirectional conceptualization, with the coach as the only active agent, may be an oversimplification (Jones and Wallace 2005) with limited relevance to the reality of coaching practice. It is argued that the act of coaching is not such a straightforward enterprise but is instead a complex, 'messy' process where the coach works 'at the edge of chaos' (Bowes and Jones 2006: 240). This complexity or messiness is reflected in a number of dimensions. First, its interactive nature; coaching is inherently a relational activity, occurring not as the actions of one actor alone but rather the reciprocal interactions of both parties – coach and athlete(s). Indeed, the most recent version of the meditational model of coaching proposed by Smith and Smoll (2007) incorporates the reciprocal influence of athletes' responses on subsequent coach behaviour, though this link has yet to be fully explored. Second, coaching is enacted over time. This temporality functions on many time scales, from the course of a single practice to more developmental spans (e.g. the course of a season). Finally, while the coach's aim is to engineer the training and competition environment to produce consistent performance and development outcomes, this environment is composed of many elements that are constantly changing and over which the coach often has little to no direct control.

Such a view of coaching necessitates a more nuanced conceptualization of the coaching process, one that captures the non-linear, unpredictable 'messiness' of coaching reality. With regard to coaching research, Poczwardowski *et al.* (2006) operationalized this conceptualization by advocating for a shift in the unit of analysis from the coach as an independent actor to the coach–athlete dyad, where the interaction between the coach and athlete is the central focus. Similarly dyadic perspectives have guided qualitative research using course-of-action theory (see Jones *et al.* 2010). For example, d'Arripe-Longueville *et al.* (2001) analysed the collective courses-of-action for coach–athlete dyads in elite archery competitions, demonstrating the reactive and constructive course of these interactions built on shared perception and negotiation. This course-of-action based work is particularly noteworthy for its emphasis on the temporal sequencing of coaches' and athletes' shared actions and cognitions (Jones *et al.* 2010). Not only do these actions change and evolve to fit the dynamic requirements of the specific context, but they also unfold over time as preceding events influence subsequent events.

The collected research adopting a more interactive, complex view of coaching represents a step forward in terms of addressing the reality of coaching, rather than trying to force it into traditional linear models of analysis. However, the focus of this work has thus far been primarily on the perceptions and cognitions of coaches and athletes. While a dynamic picture of coach cognition is now emerging, we know comparatively little about the behavioural manifestations of these dynamic perceptions and cognitions. To date, traditional methodologies used to examine coach behaviour have not been able to capture an accurate picture of the dynamic and interactive structures of behaviour in a similar fashion.

To address this discrepancy and move beyond the limitations of traditional methods, we argue that a shift in coach behaviour research focus is necessary, in line with the suggestions of Poczwardowski and colleagues (2006). This shift would move from a focus on strictly coach behaviour – the actions of the coach in isolation, without regard for the reciprocal actions of the intended recipients – to the study of coach–athlete interaction, with specific emphasis on the behaviours of interaction. As noted by Poczwardowski and colleagues, such a shift necessitates a diversification of methodological approaches targeted at the dyadic interactive unit.

SSG methodology

In this chapter, state space grids (SSGs: Hollenstein 2007; Lewis *et al.* 1999) are put forward as a novel dynamic systems methodology explicitly designed to capture the interactive elements of social processes like coach–athlete interaction. We present SSGs as a quantitative observation middle ground between the more cognition-based qualitative methods used thus far to capture the complexity of the coaching process and the behavioural detail offered by traditional systematic observation coaching research unable to fully account for interactive complexity through time. Incorporating aspects of both approaches, we argue that observational research on coach–athlete interaction using SSGs can offer new and previously unavailable insight into the dynamic, interactive, and time-based nature of these behavioural processes. By viewing the interaction between coach and athlete as a dynamic co-acting system rather than simply the sum of independent actors, this interaction can be analysed with regard to its evolving, mutually reciprocal processes over time. We now turn to a discussion of the underlying theoretical basis upon which the SSG method was developed (dynamic systems), followed by detailed description of the mechanics of the methodology using examples from two initial studies using SSGs in coaching research (Erickson *et al.* 2011; Murphy-Mills *et al.* 2010). These same studies are then used to illustrate the nature of insight made available through application of the method. As a relatively new methodology, SSGs have thus far been used only within certain branches of developmental and family psychology (see Hollenstein 2007), with the exception of the two coaching studies used as exemplars throughout this chapter.

Borrowed from the natural and physical sciences, concepts of dynamic (or dynamical) systems explain the development and functioning of open systems with multiple components. The following section provides a brief overview of some of the main dynamic systems concepts relevant to the SSG method and the study of coach–athlete interactions.

A dynamic system is composed of the reciprocal interaction of individual components of the system which influence and are subsequently influenced by each other to produce the functioning of the entire system (Lewis 2000). In this instance, the dynamic system in question is the coach–athlete dyad, with coach and athlete as individual components. Through direct lower order interactions between components, dynamic systems self-organize over time into stable higher order patterns of functioning (Granic and Hollenstein 2003). This emergent self-organization, the idea that a system creates its own structure rather than being predetermined by external principles, is a central principle of dynamic systems theory (Thelen and Smith 1998). In developmental psychology, researchers have productively examined reciprocal dyadic interaction between children and parents (e.g. Hollenstein *et al.* 2004) and between peers (e.g. Dishion *et al.* 2004) by conceptualizing them as dynamic systems.

While any system has a large range of potential patterns in which it may theoretically function (the total 'state space'), systems tend to stabilize within a limited range of these possibilities. Known as attractors, these limited ranges represent states to which the system is drawn and returns to frequently. For example, a dysfunctional coach–athlete dyad might often function in a mutually negative or hostile state and have trouble maintaining interaction outside of this range (i.e. mutually positive or supportive behaviour) for any length of time. As primary characteristics of the functioning of the system, identifying attractors is often a central focus of dynamic systems-oriented research. However, a system is not limited to a single attractor state. Multiple attractors may exist for any system and it is possible to measure the variability (or multi-stability) of the system at any point in time; its tendency to function in more than one state. This variability and related measures are qualities of a system's dynamic structure.

As an example to illustrate structural interaction characteristics, consider Hollenstein and colleagues (2004) who utilized a dynamic systems approach to observe parent and child affect during a series of interactive tasks. Prior to this study, it was generally accepted that parent-child interactions consistently characterized by harsh or hostile content contribute to maladaptive externalizing and internalizing coping behaviours in children. Through the application of observational measures targeted at interaction structures from a dynamic systems perspective, Hollenstein and colleagues were able to go beyond content analysis and revealed that such behaviours were associated with the structural rigidity (or lack of variability) of parent-child interactions, regardless of content. That is, children in parent-child dyads whose interactions tended to get 'stuck' in a dyadic state (positive or negative) were more likely to develop and exhibit these problem behaviours.

While a system's attractors and pattern of movement between them reflect its real-time functioning (e.g. the course of a training session), dynamic systems also function and change in what might be called developmental-time (e.g. the course of a season). In particular, stable real-time patterns of interaction change to new, different stable real-time patterns through what is referred to as a phase transition (Hollenstein 2007). In a phase transition, the stability of the patterned system breaks down as the variability of real-time interaction increases before settling into a different stable pattern. Thus changes in real-time behaviour influence the developmental-time structure of a system's functioning, which in turn influences future real-time behaviour.

Conventional methods for the analysis of dynamic systems have tended to focus on the mathematical modelling of dynamic system parameters with differential equations, often using computer simulations, with the goal of predicting the trajectory of the system (Puddifoot 2000). For the study of coach–athlete interaction, however, given its applied nature and need for relatively immediate practical transfer, these strategies are so complicated and mathematically intensive as to be functionally unusable for the majority of coaching researchers and their outcome of little immediate practical value. The SSG method addresses these concerns while still capturing the qualities and characteristics defining the functioning of dynamic systems. To do so, SSGs provide a graphical representation of the total state space and the coach–athlete system's trajectory within it in real time. This graphical representation then provides the basis for quantification of the systems' functioning and subsequent analysis of its defining characteristics.

The total state space for SSGs is a grid defined by the complete range of possible behaviours for each individual component of the system (in this case, a coach and an athlete), with the behaviour categories for one component (i.e. the coach) making up the x-axis and the behaviour categories for the other component (i.e. the athlete) making up the y-axis. Thus, each cell in the grid represents a pairing of a specific coach behaviour with a specific athlete behaviour – an x and y location coordinate. See Figure 9.1 for a very simplified example of an SSG for a short hypothetical coach–athlete interaction.

The functioning of the system is then located on the grid by coding which specific behaviours the coach and athlete are concurrently exhibiting at any given point in time (as a very general hypothetical example, the coach yelling criticism while the athlete pouts). This corresponds to a specific cell within the state space grid. This is represented graphically by a point in that particular cell, with the diameter of the point corresponding to the duration that the system stays in that cell (e.g. coach keeps yelling and athlete keeps pouting – see point A in Figure 9.1). Since the location of the system is defined by both coach and athlete

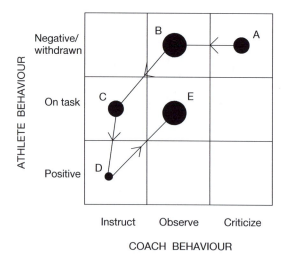

Figure 9.1: Simplified state space grid for hypothetical coach–athlete interaction.

behaviour, the moment either the coach or the athlete (or both) changes their behaviour (e.g. coach stops yelling to observe the athlete, athlete keeps pouting – see point B in Figure 9.1), the system has shifted to a new location. This new mutually defined location corresponds to a different cell in the grid, with the system represented by a point in that cell, and a line is drawn connecting the two points in the two different cells. This process continues every time there is a change in either coach or athlete behaviour for the course of the observation. Continuing with the hypothetical example from Figure 9.1, the coach might then offer some technical instruction, to which the athlete responds by re-engaging in practice activities (see point C). If the instruction is helpful, the athlete might acknowledge agreement with what the coach is saying (see point D) before returning to effortful training while the coach observes (see point E).

Thus, the real-time trajectory of the system – the coach–athlete interaction – is mapped within the total possible state space as a series of dots (representing behaviour content and duration) connected in a sequential order. See Figure 9.2 for a slightly more complex SSG created using real coach and athlete data from the Murphy-Mills *et al.* (2010) study, displaying a short duration (several minutes) interaction trajectory. The trajectory can then be analysed with regard to the areas of the grid within which it functions or to which it is 'drawn', how much of the total state space the system makes use of, the patterning of that use, and the sequences of grid locations through which the system (the coach–athlete interaction) moves. At the simplest level, the trajectory is quantified through either the duration spent in particular cells or areas of the grid or by the number of discrete 'visits' to those cells or areas (or a combination of the two). These two measures provide the basis for more detailed analysis, which will be outlined in a section to follow.

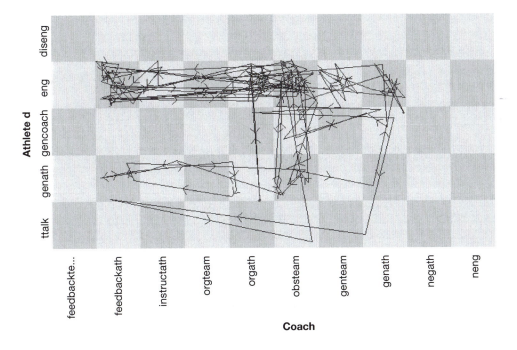

Figure 9.2: State space grid of short duration (several minutes) coach–athlete interaction.

In terms of the creation of the SSGs, while it can done using standard graphing software (e.g. Microsoft Excel) and indeed this was the method used for the first SSG study conducted (Lewis *et al.* 1999), software specifically for the creation and analysis of SSGs was designed by several of the developers of the method. This software, GridWare (Version 1.1: Lamey *et al.* 2004), vastly simplifies the process of creating the grids and deriving quantitative measures from them and is freely available for download by researchers.

In summary, the dynamic systems framework represents a shift in thinking about social processes like coach–athlete interaction. Such a shift encourages us to consider the more complex, interactive, and temporal aspects of coaching and to study it accordingly, using methods such as SSGs. It should be noted, though, that while dynamic systems concepts and properties provided the basis for the development of SSG methodology, SSGs as a method are not limited to the analysis of typical dynamic systems concepts and could be used to examine anything about coaching that involves the interaction of multiple factors or elements in time. However, we limit our focus in this chapter to the study of coach–athlete interactive behaviour.

Research questions

While we are certainly not arguing that it is the only useful technique for research on sport coaching, the SSG method based on dynamic systems concepts allows us to examine a range of new and previously unavailable research questions related to how coaches deal with the messiness of real-world coaching situations. By openly recognizing the dynamic, interactive complexity of coach–athlete interaction, we can then ask questions related to this dynamism and interaction, rather than simply 'controlling for' it (which would essentially sweep these elements under the carpet and out of consideration). The messiness and complexity becomes data, rather than noise. For example, how much behavioural variability do effective coaches exhibit? How do they adapt to changing and uncontrollable circumstances (such as athletes' behaviour)? Do coaches interact similarly with all athletes or do the interactions vary according to the needs of the specific individual? Do coach–athlete dyads get 'stuck' in problematic interaction patterns or do they adapt and adjust to each other? How are these interactions typically sequenced in terms of both micro (e.g. specific feedback interaction) and macro (e.g. over the course of a training session) patterns? Through the use of SSGs we are able to generate quantitative data relating not only to behaviour content but also incorporating time and interaction dimensions, allowing the analysis of structural patterns. Thus we can begin to ask 'how' coaches do what they do in their interactions with their athletes.

Data types

At the simplest level, the SSG method requires two complete sets of sequential behavioural data – in this case, one for the coach and one for the athlete. These two data sets must represent the same event (e.g. the same training session or competition) and be synchronized in time. Behavioural data for SSG analysis is typically categorical, with the set of categories being both exhaustive and exclusive: exhaustive in that all possible behaviours exhibited by a coach or athlete would fall into a category, exclusive in that any given behaviour can belong to only one category (i.e. cannot be classified in two or more categories at once). As well, this categorical data can be most insightfully analysed when continuous and duration-based in nature. Behavioural data is continuous when a behaviour is coded for any and all time points (even when not actively interactive) and the onset (start) and offset (end) time points for each behaviour are recorded (thus indicating the duration) such that the offset of one behaviour is necessarily the onset for the next behaviour. The data for an observation session then takes the form of a continuous string or sequence of behaviours of varying durations, whereby the durations of the coded behaviours sum to the total duration of the observed session. It is possible to conduct event-based (sequential, but without regard for behaviour duration) SSG analyses, but these are limited in their utility and represent a significant reduction in information.

Traditional systematic observation instruments for both coaches (e.g. CBAS, Smith *et al.* 1977; ASUOI, Lacy and Darst 1984) and athletes (see Darst *et al.* 1989) typically provide this event-based frequency data but can be modified to incorporate continuous, duration-based elements of behaviour. For example, for the initial study of coach–athlete interaction using SSGs (Erickson *et al.* 2011), the 12 original CBAS categories were modified to include observation and disengagement from the training context to account for all coach behaviours during the total duration of observed time, rather than only active behaviour events. These modifications allowed coach behaviour to be coded continuously in that they made the category list exhaustive such that there was no time during which the coach could not be coded as exhibiting one of the listed behaviours.

Data collection

There are two primary steps involved with collecting data for SSG analysis (or, for that matter, for any quantitative systematic observation research): (1) observing the target situation; and (2) recording or coding behaviour occurring within it. In order to satisfy the criteria for acceptable data for SSG analysis (exhaustive, exclusive, and sequential categorical data for both coach and athlete coded continuously and representing the same observation session), there are several data collection options for both steps. We will attempt to outline some commonalities shared by strategies that have been used effectively in past SSG studies.

Beginning with the first step, the observation of target situations – in this case training sessions or competitions – can be conducted live or video recorded. Given the vastly increased level of detail involved with continuous coding and the need to observe both the coach and athlete simultaneously, video recording of the session to be observed is highly recommended. By video recording the session, coders can watch any behaviour multiple times to ensure accuracy and reliability of classification and are afforded the luxury of only having to code one actor (i.e. coach or athlete) at a time as they can re-view the entire session to code behaviour for the other actor. These features have proved to be especially valuable, with time for accurate coding often far exceeding the simple duration of the observed session. With the goal of accurate and reliable coding in mind, care should be taken during video recording to get the best possible recording quality and to make sure that coders can clearly see and hear the level of behavioural detail they are expected to code. Both Erickson and colleagues (2011) and Murphy-Mills and colleagues (2010) accomplished this through use of HD camcorders and wireless microphones worn by the coaches which were sensitive enough to capture athlete verbalizations as well.

With regard to the behavioural coding itself, any method can be used that produces appropriate data for SSG analysis. The basis for the production of these data is shared with traditional systematic observation. Indeed these instruments, with their emphasis on reliable and accurate coding of clearly defined behavioural categories, provide an excellent starting point from which to modify to fit the requirements of a particular SSG study. Brewer and

Jones (2002) highlighted the need for any systematic coding system to be tailored to the specific sporting context in which behaviour is to be observed. Both SSG coaching studies used a similar process to develop their coding instruments for coaching behaviour using the CBAS as an initial base, with additional modification to allow for continuous rather than event-based coding. A further consideration for SSG analysis not present for previous systematic coach behaviour observation research is the need to observe and code athlete behaviour. Since few established athlete observation instruments exist within the coaching literature, given the unidirectional conceptualization of coaching mentioned earlier, a number of observation instruments in the physical education literature (see Darst *et al.* 1989) were used as a base for the initial SSG coaching studies.

Following development of the observation instrument and coding manual and extensive coder training to standards of reliability, both the Erickson and colleagues (2011) and Murphy-Mills and colleagues (2010) studies coded the video recorded sessions using Noldus Observer software (Noldus *et al.* 2000). The Observer software is designed to allow continuous coding of multiple actors from digital media files using a categorical coding scheme, such that the behavioural categories correspond to keys on the keyboard. Coders simply press specified keys to identify the actor in question and the onset of a behaviour as they watch the video. The Observer software tracks the coded behaviours as they are coded in relation to the elapsed video playback time, thereby creating a duration-based continuous stream of data for both coach and athlete(s). It is not necessary to use the Observer software, but it is an effective option for producing the necessary data.

Data analysis

The analysis of SSGs is open to many possible options, including but certainly not limited to typical dynamic systems concepts such as attractors, variability, and phase transitions. As presented here, the dynamic systems framework is not intended as overarching explanatory theory, just a perspective that can guide our data analysis toward more complex (i.e. interactive and time-based) processes, providing a few useful concepts from which to start. Potential analyses can be divided into two main strategies: whole grid measures – illustrating qualities of the system's functioning relative to the entire state space, and region measures – illustrating the system's degree of functioning within specific regions or cells of the state space.

Both previous coaching SSG studies began by examining the degree of variability across the entire grid, measured by the number of distinct cells visited and the number of transitions between cells. These measures provide related but distinct information about the coach–athlete dyad's interactive variability, as the interaction could visit many different cells of the grid (reflecting a relatively unpredictable interaction) or simply transition many times between a smaller range of cells (reflecting a moving, but more patterned interaction). These whole grid variability measures revealed the degree of patterning in the observed coach–athlete interactions. Once these whole grid measures were calculated, measures of duration and number of distinct visits (i.e. the interaction trajectory entering a specific cell or area from another area) were used to elucidate where in the state space the interaction was drawn or attracted (the content of the patterning) and to compare regions of theoretical interest (e.g. athletes responding to negative versus positive feedback). Most of these described measures could then be compared between grids, both between multiple dyads (e.g. a coach with different athletes on the same team) or between the same dyad at multiple points in time (i.e. longitudinal analysis). All measures described above can be calculated within the free GridWare software and exported to common statistical analysis programs (e.g. Microsoft Excel, SPSS).

This section was intended to provide a brief glimpse into the possibilities of SSG analysis rather than an exhaustive list of options; for a more thorough review of analysis strategies used in previous SSG research, see Hollenstein (2007). On that note, it is important to remember that SSGs are open to limitless analytical creativity and exploration. They simply provide a way of representing coach–athlete dyadic behaviour in a more complex, dynamic, and interactive manner and allow us to measure these qualities quantitatively. Researchers are by no means limited to the measures and analytical strategies currently in use.

Examples of SSG research on coach–athlete interaction

In this section, we outline how the SSG method as presented above has been successfully applied to the study of coach–athlete interactions. While these studies are limited by their low numbers (i.e. only two studies so far), we draw attention to some of their findings to emphasize the nature of insight revealed by application of the SSG methodology.

In comparing the coach–athlete interactions of more versus less successful youth synchronized swimming teams, Erickson and colleagues (2011) utilized SSGs to show that the more successful team was characterized by highly patterned interactions, consistent across varying situations (i.e. different drills, different training sessions). This patterning was characterized by a deliberate, respectful focus on the individual. The coach typically spent long periods silently observing before offering technical feedback paired with positive reinforcement targeted to individuals rather than the entire team, to which the athletes actively communicated a response and often offered input. The less successful team was characterized by much less predictable, often flurried, interactions, with coach behaviour more often targeted to the entire team rather than individuals and limited athlete response or interaction with the coach. These differences were found despite no differences between the teams on total amount of technical instruction/feedback or positive reinforcement offered by the coach, previously posited as key differentiators of more versus less effective coaching.

Similarly, Murphy-Mills and colleagues' (2010) examination of the coach–athlete interactions in an esteemed swimming program for athletes with disabilities used SSG analyses to identify unique qualities of this program. Interactions between athletes and the lone coach were again highly patterned and predictable, similarly targeted to individuals rather than the group. This individualized interaction pattern incorporated high amounts of humour and positive reinforcement with mutual discussion related to technical performance and, interestingly, was almost equally likely to be initiated by the athlete as by the coach. The finding of highly patterned and predictable interaction styles for effective coaches across both studies resonates with Gallimore and Tharp's (2004) re-analysis of their earlier examination of legendary UCLA basketball coach John Wooden. They noted a very clear and predictable pattern in Wooden's teaching behaviours as one the strongest findings of the study. Further, this finding is also reflected in Smith and Smoll's (2007) notion of behavioural signatures, where coaches' behaviours in different game situations (i.e. winning, tied, losing) is used to generate a context-linked 'signature' for individual coaches. In presenting coaches' behavioural signatures, Smith and Smoll included the calculation of a stability coefficient – a measure of how consistent (or patterned) a coach is in their behaviour in the different game situations (i.e. exhibiting the same behaviours in the same game situation). Though this data was not linked to any athlete outcomes, they did note significant variability across coaches in the stability of their behaviour. The SSG studies allow us to build on these findings and examine them in more depth by incorporating athletes' contributions to the interactions and allowing continuous moment-to-moment tracking through time.

Though to date there have only been two studies completed using this methodology, their combined findings highlight the utility of the method and point to the nature of potentially fruitful future directions for both research and coaching practice/education. In addition, these studies represent only the initial forays into the use of SSGs in coaching research and have only begun to tap the surface of the potential of the method.

Future directions and potential implications for coaching research, practice, and education

Based on the findings of the two coaching studies that have used SSGs and the concepts of dynamic systems outlined earlier, several concrete future research directions present themselves. Notably, Gloria Solomon and colleagues' extensive line of research on coach expectancy effects (see Solomon and Buscombe, Chapter 20 in this volume) has demonstrated the significant effect of coaches' differing expectancies of athletes on coaches' behaviour toward those athletes. The consistency to which the identified coach–athlete interaction patterns are maintained between a coach and different athletes on the same team is not yet known. We also do not know if these patterns hold across coaching contexts (Côté and Gilbert 2009), other than the competitive youth sport settings examined so far (i.e. in recreational or elite level sport). Further, the development of these patterns and structures, perhaps in the form of phase transitions, has not been examined and so longitudinal analysis would also seem a prudent next step. However, we wish to again point to the significant potential for creativity and novel exploration provided by the SSG method. Dynamic systems concepts and previously accepted notions of coach behaviour provide a useful starting point but the needs of coaches and the particularities of coaching contexts must be the primary driver of analytical strategies, rather than unquestioning devotion to theoretical structures and a priori-defined acceptable avenues of inspection. Rather than delimiting specific avenues of research, we propose that the SSG method is simply a valuable new tool to help fill in our understanding of the coaching process by opening doors to a host of new and different questions about coaching and coach–athlete interactions.

If we are able to elucidate the answers to these types of questions through application of the SSG method, we will be better able to explain how specific coaching practices produce specific outcomes. By better understanding how effective coaches do what they do in real-world coaching situations to produce the outcomes they produce, we can better educate future coaches to produce their desired outcomes. While it is often argued that coaching is sufficiently diverse as to negate the usefulness of prescriptions regarding 'what' coaches should do (Cushion 2010), by finding commonalities across this diversity with respect to 'how' coaching objectives are met, we may be better positioned to truly move towards promotion of effective practice.

References

Bowes, I. and Jones, R.L. (2006) 'Working at the edge of chaos: understanding coaching as a complex, interpersonal system', *The Sport Psychologist*, 20: 235–45.

Brewer, C.J. and Jones, R.L. (2002) 'A five-stage process for establishing contextually valid systematic observation instruments: the case of rugby union', *The Sport Psychologist*, 16: 138–59.

Côté, J. and Gilbert, W. (2009) 'An integrative definition of coaching effectiveness and expertise', *International Journal of Sport Science and Coaching*, 4: 307–23.

Cushion, C. (2010) 'Coach behaviour', in J. Lyle and C. Cushion (eds) *Sport Coaching: Professionalization and Practice*, Oxford, UK: Elsevier.

Cushion, C. and Lyle, J. (2010) 'Conceptual development in sports coaching', in J. Lyle and C. Cushion (eds) *Sport Coaching: Professionalization and Practice*, Oxford, UK: Elsevier.

d'Arripe-Longueville, F., Saury, J., Fournier, J.F. and Durand, M. (2001) 'Coach–athlete interaction during elite archery competitions: An application of methodological frameworks used in ergonomics research to sport psychology', *Journal of Applied Sport Psychology*, 13: 275–99.

Darst, P.W., Zakrajsek, D.B. and Mancini, V.H. (1989) *Analyzing Physical Education and Sport Instruction*, 2nd edn, Champaign, IL: Human Kinetics.

Dishion, T.J., Nelson, S.E., Winter, C. and Bullock, B. (2004) 'Adolescent friendship as a dynamic system: Entropy and deviance in the etiology and course of male antisocial behaviour', *Journal of Abnormal Child Psychology*, 32: 651–63.

Erickson, K. and Gilbert, W. (in press) 'Coach–athlete interactions', in J. Côté and R. Lidor (eds) *Conditions of Children's Talent Development in Sport*, Morgantown, WV: Fitness Information Technology.

Erickson, K., Côté, J., Hollenstein, T. and Deakin, J. (2011) 'Examining coach–athlete interactions using state space grids: an observational analysis in competitive youth sport', *Psychology of Sport and Exercise*, 12: 645–54.

Gallimore, R. and Tharp, R. (2004) 'What a coach can teach a teacher, 1975–2004: Reflections and reanalysis of John Wooden's teaching practices', *The Sport Psychologist*, 18: 119–37.

Gilbert, W. and Trudel, P. (2004) 'Analysis of coaching science research published from 1970–2001', *Research Quarterly for Exercise and Sport*, 75: 388–99.

Granic, I. and Hollenstein, T. (2003) 'Dynamic systems methods for models of developmental psychopathology', *Development and Psychopathology*, 15: 641–69.

Hollenstein, T. (2007) 'State space grids: Analyzing dynamics across development', *International Journal of Behavioral Development*, 31: 384–96.

Hollenstein, T., Granic, I., Stoolmiller, M. and Snyder, J. (2004) 'Rigidity in parent-child interactions and the development of externalizing and internalizing behavior in early childhood', *Journal of Abnormal Child Psychology*, 32: 595–607.

Horn, T.S. (2008) 'Coaching effectiveness in the sport domain', in T.S. Horn (ed.) *Advances in Sport Psychology*, 3rd edn, Champaign, IL: Human Kinetics.

Jones, R.L., Bowes, I. and Kingston, K. (2010) 'Complex practice in coaching: Studying the chaotic nature of coach–athlete interactions' in J. Lyle and C. Cushion (eds) *Sport Coaching: Professionalization and Practice*, Oxford, UK: Elsevier.

Jones, R.L. and Wallace, M. (2005) 'Another bad day at the training ground: coping with ambiguity in the coaching context', *Sport, Education, and Society*, 10: 119–34.

Kahan, D. (1999) 'Coaching behaviour: a review of the systematic observation research literature', *Applied Research in Coaching and Athletics Annual*, 14: 17–58.

Lacy, A.C. and Darst, P.W. (1984) 'The evolution of a systematic observation instrument', *Journal of Teaching in Physical Education*, 3: 59–66.

Lamey, A., Hollenstein, T., Lewis, M.D. and Granic, I. (2004) 'GridWare (Version 1.1)' [computer software], online, available at: www.statespacegrids.org.

Lewis, M.D. (2000) 'The promise of dynamic systems approaches for an integrated account of human development', *Child Development*, 71: 36–43.

Lewis, M.D., Lamey, A.V. and Douglas, L. (1999) 'A new dynamic system method for the analysis of early socioemotional development', *Developmental Science*, 2: 457–75.

Murphy-Mills, J., Vierimaa, M., Côté, J. and Deakin, J. (2010) 'An examination of coach–athlete interactions in a highly successful youth sport program for athletes with disabilities', paper presented at Coaching Association of Canada's Sport Leadership Sportif conference. Ottawa, ON, Canada.

Nash, C. and Collins, D. (2006) 'Tacit knowledge in expert coaching: science or art?', *Quest*, 58: 465–77.

Noldus, L.P.J.J., Trienes, R.J.H., Hendricksen, A.H.M., Jansen, H. and Jansen, R.G. (2000) 'The Observer Video-Pro: New software for the collection, management, and presentation of time-structured data from videotapes and digital media files', *Behavior Research Methods, Instruments and Computers*, 32: 197–206.

Poczwardowski, A., Barott, J.E. and Jowett, S. (2006) 'Diversifying approaches to research on athlete-coach relationships', *Psychology of Sport and Exercise*, 7: 125–42.

Puddifoot, J.E. (2000) 'Some problems and possibilities in the study of dynamical social processes', *Journal for the Theory of Social Behaviour*, 30: 79–97.

Smith, R.E. and Smoll, F.L. (2007) 'Social-cognitive approach to coaching behaviors', in S. Jowett and D. Lavallee (eds) *Social Psychology in Sport*, Champaign, IL: Human Kinetics.

Smith, R.E., Smoll, F.L. and Hunt, E.B. (1977) 'A system for the behavioural assessment of athletic coaches', *Research Quarterly*, 48: 401–7.

Thelen, E. and Smith, L.B. (1998) 'Dynamic systems theories', in W. Damon (series ed.) and R.M. Lerner (vol. ed.) *Handbook of Child Psychology: Vol.1 Theoretical Models of Human Development*, 5th edn, New York: Wiley.

10

RECOMMENDATIONS ON THE METHODS USED TO INVESTIGATE COACHES' DECISION MAKING

John Lyle

UNIVERSITY OF QUEENSLAND, AUSTRALIA

Ineke Vergeer

DURHAM UNIVERSITY, UK

Introduction

There is no doubt that coaches' cognitions have become a prevalent theme in the academic coaching literature, although we will argue and demonstrate that this is more evident in conceptual development and rhetoric (Abraham and Collins 1998; Abraham *et al.* 2006; Lyle 2002, 2010) than in a significant corpus of coherent empirical research practice (cf. the diverse contributions of d'Arripe-Longueville *et al.* 2001; Gilbert *et al.* 1999; Jowett and Clark-Carter 2006; Vergeer and Lyle 2009). Nevertheless, there is now a discourse about coping with uncertainty, judgement and decision making, reasoning, problem solving, and mental models and the influence they have on coaching practice. Greater attention is also being paid to coaches' knowledge structures (Abraham *et al.* 2006; Côté and Gilbert 2009; Nash and Collins 2006), although the cognitive processes for building, storing and accessing these structures are much less well understood.

We begin from a position that asserts that, despite the considerable rhetoric about decision making, the empirical research base that informs our understanding of coaches' expertise and practice, and, subsequently, coach education and development, is relatively modest. In this particular chapter, our intention is to focus on the methods that have been employed to investigate coaches' decision making. We consider whether the research paradigms that characterise such work reflect particular discipline epistemologies; whether these have limited the research questions that can be addressed and thereby limited our understanding of coaches' decision making; and whether a greater range of research methods is required to generate the necessary insights.

We are inclined to a definition of sports coaching that stresses its social reality and occupational practice; viewing coaching as an intention to improve and manage sports

121

performance, but composed of such a range of behaviours and processes that generalised definitions become implausible. We take a similar view about decision making, believing that it is such an all-pervading process and subject to such a variety of approaches that any treatment of it must necessarily be selective. Within these caveats, the chapter has two principal objectives. The first is to create a conceptual framework for decision making within coaching, one that will serve to situate coaching research on decision making. The second is to generate a research agenda, based on a review of existing research and a consideration of the potential methods available.

Decision making may be thought to be self-evidently important in sport coaching but the arguments bear repetition. First, there are very obvious examples of 'choice decisions' in relation to matters such as the selection of players and managing tactics in competition, but perhaps most obviously in relation to planning. We will argue that it is in the micro-management of coaching interventions and athlete relationships that the coach's decision making is less evident but crucial. This apparently intuitive management of coaching activity, based on tacit knowledge and rarely-conceptualised principles, has clearly been a challenge to researchers. There will be methodological challenges in coping with the distinctions between deliberative decision making between alternatives, even if based on fuzzy decision policies, and the continuous, serial and complex decision milieux that characterises the coach's delivery practice. Second, coaching belongs to that class of professional activity (similar to teaching and medical practice) in which there is an element of expert 'treatment' that varies both in conception and delivery depending on the context and the 'recipient', resulting in a complexity of practice in which human variability, multiple goals, and ill-defined solutions bedevil decision outcomes.

Dealing as it does with mental processes, much of the writing on decision making falls into the rubric of cognitive psychology. Cognitive psychology, like other disciplines, has characteristic epistemology (the type of knowledge that is adduced by its proponents) and ontology (assumptions about how we 'see' or experience the world). These assumptions about appropriate knowledge lead to particular research methodologies or paradigms being considered acceptable or more likely to generate the kind of research evidence that is considered 'convincing'. For this reason, we include a review of recent research on coaches' decision making in order to establish the balance of approaches to research designs. Gilbert and Trudel (2004) in their extensive review of coaching research had demonstrated that research into cognitive themes had increased appreciably. There had been a significant rise in qualitative methodologies; interview and observation had made significant inroads into the dominant questionnaire-based methods. Before examining the findings of a survey of decision-making research in coaching, we sketch out a conceptual framework for coaches' decision making that will allow us to situate our discussion and recommendations.

Building a conceptual framework for coaches' decision making

Decision making is a cognitive process leading to an action outcome (behavioural option). This may involve a choice between alternatives (including to act or not) or an emerging decision or course of action. The individual is responding to sensory information and acts in the context of purpose/objective, personal bias, and 'frames of reference' about the coaching domain, social context and the other actors involved. Decisions can therefore be examined from a variety of perspectives: rationality, affect, values/ethics, outcomes/effectiveness, accuracy and so on. In order to build our framework, we need to aggregate a number of distinguishing features of decision making.

Decisions can be characterised (Goldstein and Weber 1995; Svenson 1996) as automatic and subconscious, encompassing both routinised activity and intuitive decisions. This latter category is also termed 'associative', and applies to social activity or 'streams of consciousness' decision contexts. Further categories distinguish between decisions with an obvious, uncontested solution and those in which there is a choice of alternatives but with implications for achieving objectives satisfactorily. A final category is sometimes termed real-life, in which only one alternative is considered. Experience, stored as mental models and scripts (stories about how events unfold), enables the individual to 'conjure up' an effective solution. Throughout, there is an implied distinction between decisions for which there is no time pressure (deliberative) and those for which there is some time pressure or uncertainty (non- or semi-deliberative) (Boreham 1994). Overall, a distinction emerges between decisions with clearly articulated alternatives and well-defined objectives, and less-well-structured decisions or series of decisions. The former are characteristic of traditional cognitive psychology, with a controlled, experimental approach to judgement decision making; the latter describes 'naturalistic', 'untidy', and real-life decision making (Klein 2008; Teigen 1996). The latter form of decision making deals with how experts make decisions rather than with mechanisms for achieving the 'correct' solution.

Klein and Weick (2000) offer a simplistic but useful categorisation of decisions into rational, intuitive and experiential. Rational choice decisions involve weighing up various options in the light of a careful analysis of the problem. This form of decision making requires both time and information, and a clear set of objectives, and is subject to personal bias in interpreting the information and the choice of solution. Nevertheless, there will be situations, for example, planning and selection of competition strategy, for which this approach is appropriate. The intuitive category depends on experience and knowledge and is a 'speeded up' way of making decisions. (We should be careful of attributing the term intuitive to coaches' decision making simply because we do not have an adequate explanation of how it happens.) Experiential decision making encompasses the Naturalistic Decision Making (NDM) paradigm (Lyle 2010) for which Klein is the chief proponent (Klein 1998, 2008; Lipshitz *et al.* 2001a). This form of decision making relies on recognising the issue and using associative links to memory and knowledge stores from which a decision emerges. This is not an instinct-type decision; there is an element of pre-recognition (narrowing the likely options), re-consideration or amendment of options, and anticipation or 'playing forward' the consequences. We believe that the experiential or NDM paradigm has much to offer in understanding how coaches make decisions.

The efforts of coaching researchers to illuminate coaches' cognitions are illustrated in the work of researchers such as Abraham *et al.* (2006), Côté and Gilbert (2009), Bowes and Jones (2006), Lyle and Cushion (2010) and Vergeer and Lyle (2009). A criticism applied to research and writing more generally on coaches' cognitions (Cushion 2007) is that it ignores other stakeholders, power relationships and socio-cultural context. However, decision making is a cognitive exercise; it centres on 'how' the actor makes the decision and 'how' the wider context is incorporated into decision making. Any claim that coaches take decisions without reference to context or purpose is a parody of coaching practice. The expertise element of decision making is about how the coach learns to deal with the decision complexity that is implied. Simply saying that the processes are tacit and intuitive does not address the issue of developing this expertise.

Although we do not wish to enter into a debate about a definition of coaching (Cushion and Lyle 2010), it is necessary to offer a short reprise of the academic treatment of sports coaching. This may be portrayed as a tension between the more recent social-constructivist perspective (see Jones *et al.* 2010), which lays particular stress on the complex, messy, unpredictable nature of coaching, and those who conceive of coaching as a more 'controlled' and systematic practice. The search by researchers from the latter camp for regularities and structure in coaching practice are often criticised from an anti-positivist stance, although their methodologies in truth are rather more varied and often pragmatic (Vergeer and Lyle 2007). We suggest that this is less of a true polemic and more of a justification of disciplinary lens. We suspect that both 'camps' would recognise and discuss sports coaching in practice and find common ground. Lyle (2007) suggested that the degree of chaos in the coaching environment was overstated. The dynamic, complex, emotionally charged and untidy coaching milieu certainly seems to characterise many coaching practices but this understates the extent to which expert coaches are able to operate within this environment. They bring a measure of control by employing coping strategies, routines, allowing degrees of freedom in expectations and targets, by the use of thresholds and key markers to decide what to attend to, and by using a set of performance plans to maintain a focus on the main goals. In decision-making terms, this picture of coaching activity places the emphasis on NDM skills (Lyle 2010) such as situational awareness, pattern recognition and building repertoires of solutions (although clearly acknowledging that these are based on knowledge of the constituent parts of sport performance development).

These arguments were presaged in an earlier paper (Lyle 1992) in which data from 30 experienced coaches suggested that a rational, systematic, planned intention was implemented in a more intuitive and subjective manner that made use of knowledge-in-action (Schön 1987). Decision making was conceptualised as an experiential process, triggered by crisis thresholds that threatened progress towards goals. The capacity for making apparently intuitive decisions is based on more deliberative and relatively rational processes. A study into non-deliberative decision making by expert volleyball coaches (reported in Lyle 1999, 2003) identified a 'slow interactive script' model as the predominant cognitive mechanism. Coaches used anticipatory modelling and conservative decision strategies to attempt to control uncertainty and the contested nature of the competition. It was suggested that NDM offered the most plausible explanation for coaches' decision making in such a context. The semi-deliberative 'slow script' (gradual unfolding of a course of action) serial decision making by the coach might be termed the 'micro-management of intervention'. Our experience and the literature confirm that this is a learned expertise but the academic community has had limited success in describing or 'capturing' it, far less designing research that can investigate it.

We conclude, therefore, that decision making is not 'about' something; it is a constant process, decisions-in-action, that is at the heart of coaches' expertise and practice. Yes, there are obvious yes/no decisions and 'choice decisions' that may be deliberative and have a principled rationality. However, the everyday manifestation of coaching expertise is evident in the management of momentum, feedback and progression as the coach works towards the realisation of performance plans. Decisions are negotiated, have ethical and value parameters, are influenced by personal bias, and have historicity and domain specificity. Decision making must be a developed expertise because expert-novice studies demonstrate that experts make different (and better) decisions (Tenenbaum 2003). However, we point to the conversion of knowledge and experience, in response to environmental exigencies, into the management of intervention as a crucial feature of coaching practice. This demonstrates the range of potential research questions about coaches' decision making that might be generated.

Current research

In order to give a rounded picture of current research into coaches' decision making, with a particular emphasis on the methodologies employed, we carried out a survey of published research papers from 1990 to 2010. We did not intend this to be a systematic review, nor to claim that the search was exhaustive. The purpose was to illustrate the range of methodologies and, if appropriate, to identify any obvious trends. Using the SPORTDiscus database we entered the keywords: decision making, coaches and coaching. This elicited over 400 'hits'. Nevertheless, the outcome was disappointing. The majority of papers were concerned with strategies for improving athletes' decision making, and were a mixture of empirical studies and prescriptions for good practice. Although these papers highlighted implications for structuring and delivering coaching interventions, the research evidence did not focus on the decisions taken by the coaches, and did not therefore serve our purpose.

Having eliminated athlete studies, theses and papers derived from the same data source, we were able to identify fewer than 30 empirical studies in the period 1990–2010. A brief overview of this field was given in Vergeer and Lyle (2007). Resisting the temptation to dwell on the findings of the studies and the implications for the development of coaches' expertise, we were able to categorise the studies by the methodologies employed.

The most numerous approach was decision making policy capture by questionnaire. In these studies, coaches typically responded to a series of options or scenarios, from which their decision preferences were inferred. The decision preferences were assessed in relation to variables such as first-aid knowledge (Ransone and Dunn-Bennett 1999) experience (Vergeer and Lyle 2009), situational factors (Vergeer and Hogg 1999), gender (Duke and Corlett 1992), game location (Dennis and Carron 1999), winning/losing (Flint and Weiss 1992) and nationality (Cheng *et al.* 2003). There was a very evident emphasis on injury/return to participation and 'time out' decision contexts. These studies are characterised by very sound (peer-reviewed) research designs but, of course, the responses of the coaches are not given in accountable, real-practice contexts. There is generally an evident or implied novice–expert dimension, although there is no homogeneity in the coaching domains within which the coaches practise. The dates of the studies suggest that this is not a current approach (the Vergeer and Lyle 2009 paper was a reworking of earlier data).

One solution to the problem of accessing real-practice decisions is to use stimulated recall of video footage of the coaches' practice (Lyle 2003). This is generally accompanied by interviews with the coaches. Examples of the approach are Gilbert *et al.* (1999), Demers and Tousignant (1998), Debanne and Fontayne (2009) and Lyle (2002, 2003). Although such studies are limited by the constraints of the various stimulated-recall methodologies, they have the advantage of locating the coaches' decisions in an *in situ*, accountable context of either competition or training. It is important to note that the recall explanation or reflection is invariably accompanied by an interview or interrogation of the decisions taken.

Another approach to increasing the authenticity of the coaches' decisions is to ask them to respond to simulated scenarios (usually by video). This is evident in the work of Schorer *et al.* (2007) and Austin *et al.* (2007). The advantage of this approach is that it is susceptible of controlled manipulation within the research design. The limiting factor is the extent to which the simulation can display context, meaningfulness and relevance to the coach, without losing complexity. An example of this 'reduction' is the simulation of a practice environment by Jones *et al.* (1997), although the researchers' judgements were further limited by a 'systematic observation' research paradigm.

Interviews with coaches are a complementary part of the methods already described (stimulated recall, simulation). However, extended or in-depth interviews may be a principal methodology for interrogating the coach's practice (for example, Saury and Durand 1998). Inevitably these research designs are confined to small numbers of coaches, but the qualitative approach generates a rich illustration of the decision-making process. The approach adopted in such papers (Saury and Durand 1998; Sévé and Durand 1999; d'Arripe-Longueville *et al.* 2001) is interesting for two reasons. First, they work from the premise that cognitions should not be divorced from real-practice, and second, although not directly about choice options, the 'course of action' perspective is redolent of the interactive or serial decision making described earlier (see Bourbousson *et al.* 2010 for an example of this methodology). In the d'Arripe-Longueville *et al.* (2001) study, the authors use a form of stimulated recall to initiate interviews about real-practice decisions.

There is another category of empirical work that is based on the assumption that the myriad decisions taken by the coach can be aggregated into a decision 'style' (typically termed autocratic or person-centred). This approach owes much to the earlier work of Chelladurai (for example 1990) on leadership styles, and decision styles inferred from questionnaires. Examples of these are the relationship between motivation styles and decision styles (Frederick and Morrison 1999) and winning and losing coaches (Quek 1995). There are many examples in the list we reviewed in which the coach's decision style was measured by athlete perceptions of behaviour (for example, Loughead and Hardy 2005). While this category of work contributes to a version of aggregated decision policies, the emphasis on observable behaviours and the lack of attention to the process of decision making rendered this approach less relevant to our purpose.

There were some examples of relevant studies on coaches' decision making that did not fit neatly into the categories just described. Gould *et al.* (2002) demonstrated that athlete performance and coaching effectiveness were influenced by factors attributable to coaches' decision making (also Harville 2005). Abraham *et al.* (2006) and Nash and Collins (2006) used coach surveys to establish the knowledge framework relevant to decision making. Two further forms of research were evident. The first involved the modelling of decisions (Mehrez *et al.* 2006; Jordan *et al.* 2009). The second form does not fall under the rubric of peer-reviewed publications. These take the form of analyses of decisions taken by high-profile professional-sport coaches (for example, Iannantuono and Sgargetta 2008; Jenkins 2010). This is a useful source of insights into decision policies and situational factors, and the identification of potential research hypotheses. Finally, we ourselves used a re-examination of data from a previous study to discuss the virtues of mixed-method research designs (Vergeer and Lyle 2007).

The most immediate reaction to this brief review is a concern for the paucity of empirical studies into coaches' decision making (particularly in the previous ten years). Without wishing to pre-empt the summary discussion at the end of the chapter, it is disappointing to note the relatively small number of studies that involve the real-practice decisions taken by coaches. We will return to this in a discussion of the feasibility of research designs in relation to the complexity of the coaching process. Before that we turn briefly to consideration of the more generic mechanisms for investigating decision making and, in particular, the methods used within the Naturalistic Decision Making paradigm.

The context for research methods

There is some value in putting the methods unearthed in the review of current research in the context of research methods more generally used in cognitive psychology. The characteristic method may be summarised as 'conducting experiments to test hypotheses derived from statistical and mathematical models of ideal choice strategies' (Klein 2008: 3). However, if we cast the net more widely, methods can be classified as introspective, experimental and observational. Experimentation is the most common methodology in judgement decision-making research; independent variables are manipulated and dependent variables measured. This 'control' enables researchers to focus on specific aspects of decision making but limits ecological validity (transfer to other contexts). Self-reporting of one's own cognitions is also common. This may be elicited by an interviewer, stimulated by recall of identified incidents, or 'captured' by process tracing, such as 'think aloud' techniques (Lundgren-Laine and Salantera 2010). These self-report procedures are limiting because they are indirect mechanisms for accessing cognitions (perceiving, learning, remembering, deciding, thinking) but they can be applied to real-life decision making. Observation of decision makers in action may confer an element of realism but accessing the decision-making process remains problematical. Nevertheless this may be an important stage in understanding the decision-making context.

Decision tasks range from hypothetical, domain-specific cases or scenarios to actual real-life decisions. The former can be represented in a number of ways, and have become increasingly more complex and sophisticated; software 'microworlds' attempt to simulate the dynamic and complex nature of decision situations (Elliott *et al.* 2007). On the other hand, questionnaires are a traditional mechanism for accessing opinion and, indirectly, knowledge structures. They are also used to access or represent an individual's likely behaviour. Not surprisingly perhaps, this reduction of knowledge structures or active cognitions to (more or less) standardised questionnaires is acknowledged to serve the needs of survey-based research designs rather than accurately represent decision behaviour. Case studies have the potential to provide rich detail but do not resolve the issue of accessing cognitions. There were no examples of computer modelling, psychobiological or neuropsychological research methods. The options described are not value-free in the sense that they conform to the epistemological expectations of a particular research paradigm. This may be portrayed, rather simplistically, as a tension between the rigour of experimental method versus the contextuality of qualitative-methods-based research designs.

We also made it clear in the previous section that a priority for understanding coaches' decision making was a focus on decisions-in-action, as opposed to discrete choice decision making. This tilted the balance in favour of naturalistic enquiry and experience-based decision making. For this reason, we elaborate on the methods favoured by Naturalistic Decision Making. In overview, these involve observation/orientation by the researcher when possible and a balance between interviews and task simulations (Klein 2008).

The proponents of the NDM paradigm are sensitive to challenges about rigour and generalisability, in addition to the limitations of verbal reports (Lipshitz *et al.* 2001b), and defend their position while acknowledging that 'scientists use different methods depending on their subject matter and research interests' (2001b: 387). In contrast to what they characterise as top-down deductive processes, they 'prefer bottom up approaches, constructing and testing our models by observing decision making and interviewing decision makers' (ibid.). NDM research is carried out on experts because 'experts can benefit from empirically-based prescriptive models because these integrate elements from the decision processes of many experts, and spell out the (often tacit) rationale that accounts for their success' (ibid.). An interesting insight into perspectives is illustrated in research into heuristics (short cuts to decision making); judgement decision sciences emphasise the weakness of heuristics against completely rational choices, whereas naturalists emphasise the strength of heuristics in everyday decision making (Bryant 2002). Similarly, judgement decision scientists view affect as a barrier to decision making, whereas naturalists stress the need to understand its impact on decision making (in the context of winning and losing, a condition that may be very relevant to coaches' decision making) (Blanchette and Richards 2010).

Specific methods favoured by NDM include Critical Decision Method (analysing tough cases), analysis of familiar tasks, constrained processing (amending the context), simulations (Bruce and Gray 2004) and Cognitive Task Analysis (Crandall 2008; Crandall *et al.* 2006; Fackler *et al.* 2009; Hoffman *et al.* 1995, 1998). We should acknowledge that NDM research, although we believe it to have considerable potential for investigating coaches' decision making, has largely been carried out in situations of 'risk-associated' decision making rather than extended 'courses of action'.

Summary

Whether or not you are convinced of the primacy of decision making in coaching research, there is no doubt that it is important and not currently well served by the academic literature. Situational factors such as accessing real-time accountable decisions, contextual dependency, variable objectives, limitations of investigative procedures, and tacit knowledge structures have not yet been overcome by researchers. It would appear that coaches use knowledge structures (schemata, mental models) in an efficient, contingent fashion to maintain a variable flow of decisions-in-action that can accommodate performance planning, athletes' active agency, environmental factors and both a historical and future (anticipatory) perspective. Our review shows that coaching research has yet to make a significant contribution to confirming this hypothesis.

In terms of research output, there were some examples of mathematical models of weighing of cues or attributes, and some comparison between groups, but these tended to be focused on quite narrow decision policies. There were also qualitative descriptive accounts of decision content. However, in the context of the development of coaching-specific models of decision processes, computer simulations of information processing, or building and integrating mental models, there has been very limited progress.

Let us begin with the question of disciplinary lens. The positivist paradigm may be criticised for reducing complexity and for very population-specific generalisation. It does seem unlikely that the experimental approach will capture real-time decision making, but we should examine research using simulated practice as a useful step in that direction. The interpretivist approach embraces the complexity and context but has, thus far, become more of a critical, paradigmatic high ground than an established research field. Nevertheless, there is no doubt that research into decision making must attempt to capture the structure and human agency involved in creating the decision field. Concepts such as 'course of action' research (Bourbousson *et al.* 2010; Jones *et al.* 2010) may assist us. Inevitably we have to recognise that disciplinary acceptance (with its attendant pressure on peer-reviewed publications) will favour the 'pure' approach, but, initially, our understanding is likely to be enhanced by more pragmatic designs and mixed methods.

There would be little disagreement that the methods employed are likely to reflect the questions to be addressed. A good start would be to establish two principles; first, replace 'what would you do', with 'what did you do and why did you do it'; second, research into coaches' real decisions in accountable situations should be a priority. In the context of existing research, we are therefore in danger of making exhortations to better practice rather than exemplifying sound practice. It would also be remiss of us not to acknowledge that in any field of professional activity it is a significant 'practical' challenge to generate research designs into cognitions that adhere to epistemological niceties but contribute directly to practitioner understanding.

There is no doubt that coaches make 'choice of alternatives' decisions, although even these appear to have 'emergent' qualities (Benecki 2010) and there is merit in investigating the basis on which these choices are made. However, we continue to lay stress on the 'continuous course of action' in the coaches' intervention behaviour and practice, and we have made much of the experiential decision maker in a naturalistic context as a metaphor for the coach. We have also shown that the NDM paradigm is often criticised because it does not conform to the traditional methodological assumptions of cognitive psychology research, and its priorities have not been placed on this continuous and aggregative decision making. Nevertheless, we believe that researchers into coaching practice should embrace its associated methods.

For example, it should be possible to design more complex simulations of practice, and to make these interactive. These research designs should not only focus on 'what would you do next', but also 'what information do you need to make a decision', 'give an example of a similar situation', 'what are you seeing as the discriminating markers', and 'what would make you change your mind'. Process tracing has its limitations and these can be acknowledged. However, we could find no 'verbalisation-type' research designs, and we believe that it would be possible to make use of this method, not least to stimulate recall of decisions. Stimulated recall procedures may have limitations of delayed reflection and introspection but it enables researchers (by video capture or critical incidents) to make use of real decisions. In all of these cases, interviews will form part of the research design.

In particular we stress the need for observation as a key element in understanding naturalistic decision fields (see Fackler *et al.* 2009). However, there remains room for experimentation, particularly using simulation. This might focus on issues such as the impact of affect, situational awareness, pattern recognition and framing problems, and some of the tactics used by coaches (for example, delay, conservatism, satisficing) to attempt to retain a measure of control in pressured, complex or contested situations. Although the literature makes assumptions about the use of mental models, there has been very limited attention to how these are constructed or deployed (Dowens 2010).

References

Abraham, A. and Collins, D. (1998) 'Examining and extending research in coach development', *Quest*, 50(1): 55–79.

Abraham, A., Collins, D. and Martindale, R. (2006) 'The coaching schematic: Validation through expert coach consensus', *Journal of Sports Sciences*, 24(6): 549–564.

Austin, N.C., Sparrow, W.A. and Sherman, C.A. (2007) 'Skills of expert basketball coaches: An investigative study', *Applied Research in Coaching and Athletics Annual*, 22: 149–173.

Benecki, R. (2010) 'Lessons learned in the year leading up to Kate's Olympic programme', *ASCA Newsletter*, 3: 14–26, online, available at: www.swimmingcoach.org/Members/index.asp (accessed 31 January 2011).

Blanchette, I. and Richards, A. (2010) 'The influence of affect on higher level cognition: A review of research on interpretation, judgement, decision making and reasoning', *Cognition and Emotion*, 24(4): 561–595.

Boreham, N.C. (1994) 'The dangerous practice of thinking', *Medical Education*, 28(3): 172–179.

Bourbousson, J., Poizat, G., Saury, J. and Seve, C. (2010) 'Team coordination in basketball: Description of the cognitive connections among teammates', *Journal of Applied Sport Psychology*, 22(2): 150–166.

Bowes, I. and Jones, R.L. (2006) 'Working at the edge of chaos: Understanding coaching as a complex interpersonal system', *The Sport Psychologist*, 20(2): 235–245.

Bruce, P.J. and Gray, J.H. (2004) 'Using simulations to investigate decision making in airline operations', online, available at: http://arrow.monash.edu.au/hdl/1959.1/2571 (accessed 31 January 2011).

Bryant, D.J. (2002) 'Making Naturalistic Decision Making "fast and frugal"', online, available at: www.dodccrp.org/events/7th_ICCRTS/Tracks/pdf/066.PDF (accessed 31 January 2011).

Chelladurai, P. (1990) 'Leadership in sports: A review', *Journal of Sport Psychology*, 32(4): 328–354.

Cheng, W.W.M., Carre, A.F., Kim, K. and Carr, R. (2003) 'International comparative analysis of timeout decision making strategies employed by male university basketball coaches' *Journal of Physical Education and Recreation*, 9(2): 66–70.

Côté, J. and Gilbert, W.D. (2009) 'An integrative definition of coaching effectiveness and expertise', *International Journal of Sports Science and Coaching*, 4(3): 307–323.

Crandall, B. (2008) 'What can we learn from Cognitive Task Analysis', *ARA Technology Review*, 4(1): 11–16.

Crandall, B., Klein, G. and Hoffman, R.R. (2006) *Working Minds: A Practitioner's Guide to Cognitive Task Analysis*, Cambridge, MA: MIT Press.

Cushion, C. (2007) 'Modelling the complexity of the coaching process', *International Journal of Sports Science and Coaching*, 2(4): 395–401.

Cushion, C. and Lyle, J. (2010) 'Conceptual development in sports coaching', in J. Lyle and C. Cushion (eds) *Sports Coaching: Professionalisation and Practice*, Edinburgh: Churchill Livingstone.

d'Arripe-Longueville, F., Saury, J., Fournier, J. and Durand, M. (2001) 'Coach-athlete interaction during elite archery competitions: An application of methodological frameworks used in ergonomics research to sport psychology', *Journal of Applied Sport Psychology*, 13(3): 275–299.

Debanne, T. and Fontayne, P. (2009) 'A study of a successful experienced elite handball coach's cognitive processes in competition situations', *International Journal of Sports Science and Coaching*, 4(1): 1–16.

Demers, G. and Tousignant, M. (1998) 'Planifier l'imprévisible: comment les plans de séances se transforment en action' [Unpredictable planning: How practice plans are modified in action], *AVANTE*, 4(3): 67–83.

Dennis, P.W. and Carron, A.V. (1999) 'Strategic decisions of ice hockey coaches as a function of game location', *Journal of Sports Sciences*, 17(4): 263–268.

Dowens, T. (2010) 'Models of coaching and performance: an examination of the influences that have helped form the performance and coaching models of a group of volleyball coaches', unpublished MSc thesis. Leeds Metropolitan University.

Duke, A. and Corlett, J. (1992) 'Factors affecting university women's basketball coaches' timeout decisions', *Canadian Journal of Sport Sciences*, 17(4): 333–337.

Elliott, T., Welsh, M., Nettelbeck, T. and Mills, V. (2007) 'Investigating naturalistic decision making in a simulated microworld: what questions should we ask?' *Behavioural Research Methods*, 39(4): 901–910.

Fackler, J.C., Watts, C., Grome, A., Miller, T., Crandall, B. and Pronovast, P. (2009) 'Critical care physician cognitive task analysis: an exploratory study', *Critical Care*, 13(2): R33.

Flint, F.A. and Weiss, M.R. (1992) 'Returning injured athletes to competition: a role and ethical dilemma', *Canadian Journal of Sport Sciences*, 17(1): 34–40.

Frederick, C.M. and Morrison, C.S. (1999) 'Collegiate coaches: An examination of motivational style and its relationship to decision making and personality', *Journal of Sport Behavior*, 22(2): 221–233.

Gilbert, W.D. and Trudel, P. (2004) 'Analysis of coaching science research published from 1970–2001', *Research Quarterly for Exercise and Sport*, 75(4): 388–389.

Gilbert, W.D., Trudel, P. and Haighian, L.P. (1999) 'Interactive decision making factors considered by coaches of youth ice hockey during games', *Journal of Teaching in Physical Education*, 18(3): 290–311.

Goldstein, W.M. and Weber, E.U. (1995) 'Content and discontent: indications and implications of domain specificity in preferential decision making', in J.R. Busemeyer, R. Hastie and D.L. Medin (eds) *The Psychology of Learning and Motivation, Volume 32, Decision Making from a Cognitive Perspective*, New York: Academic Press.

Gould, D., Guinan, D., Greenleaf, C. and Chung, Y. (2002) 'A survey of U.S. Olympic coaches: Variables perceived to have influenced athlete performances and coach effectiveness', *Sport Psychologist*, 16(3): 229–250.

Harville, J. (2005) 'Decision making: Gather information, analyse options, and choose the best course of action', in C. Reynaud (ed.) *She Can Coach!*, Champaign, IL: Human Kinetics.

Hoffman, R.R., Crandall, B. and Shadbolt, N.R. (1998) 'Use of the critical decision method to elicit expert knowledge: A case study in cognitive task analysis methodology', *Human Factors*, 40(2): 254–276.

Hoffman, R.R., Shadbolt, N.R., Burton, A.M. and Klein, G. (1995) 'Eliciting knowledge from experts: A methodological analysis', *Organizational Behavior and Human Decision Processes*, 62(2): 129–158.

Iannantuono, J. and Sgargetta, D. (2008) 'Puppetry of the coach', *Inside Sport*, 202: 36–37.

Jenkins, L. (2010) 'Last minute timeouts provide glimpse into post-season fervor', *Sports Illustrated*, 22 April.

Jones, R.L., Bowes, I. and Kingston, K. (2010) 'Complex practice in coaching: Studying the chaotic nature of coach-athlete interactions', in J. Lyle and C. Cushion (eds) *Sports Coaching: Professionalisation and Practice*, Edinburgh: Churchill Livingstone.

Jones, D.F., Housner, L.D. and Kornspan, A.S. (1997) 'Interactive decision making and behavior of experienced and inexperienced basketball coaches during practice', *Journal of Teaching in Physical Education*, 16(4): 454–468.

Jordan, J., Melouk, S. and Perry, M. (2009) 'Optimising football game play calling', *Journal of Quantitative Analysis in Sports*, 5(2): 1176.

Jowett, S. and Clark-Carter, D. (2006) 'Perceptions of empathic accuracy and assumed similarity in the coach-athlete relationship', *British Journal of Social Psychology*, 45(3): 617–637.

Klein, G.A. (1998) *Sources of Power: How People Make Decisions*, Cambridge, MA: MIT Press.

Klein, G.A. (2008) 'Naturalistic Decision Making', *ARA Technology Review*, 4(1): 3–9.

Klein, G.A. and Weick, K.E. (2000) 'Decisions: Making the right ones, learning from the wrong ones', *Across the Board*, 37(6): 16–22.

Lipshitz, R., Klein, G., Orasanu, J. and Salas, E. (2001a) 'Taking stock of Naturalistic Decision Making', *Journal of Behavioral Decision Making*, 14(5): 331–352.

Lipshitz, R., Klein, G., Orasanu, J. and Salas, E. (2001b) 'Rejoinder: A welcome dialogue – and the need to continue', *Journal of Behavioral Decision Making*, 14(5): 385–389.

Loughead, T.M. and Hardy, J. (2005) 'A comparison of coach and peer leader behaviours in sport', *Psychology of Sport and Exercise*, 6(3): 303–312.

Lundgren-Laine, H. and Salantera, S. (2010) 'Think-aloud technique and protocol analysis in clinical decision-making research', *Qualitative Health Research*, 20(4): 565–574.

Lyle, J. (1992) 'Systematic coaching behaviour: An investigation into the coaching process and the implications of the findings for coach education', in T. Williams, L. Almond and A. Sparkes (eds) *Sport and Physical Activity: Moving Towards Excellence*, London: E. & F.N. Spon.

Lyle, J. (1999) 'Coaches' decision making', in N. Cross and J. Lyle (eds) *The Coaching Process: Principles and Practice for Sport*, Oxford: Butterworth-Heinemann.

Lyle, J. (2002) 'Coaches' decision making: An investigation into Naturalistic Decision Making characteristics in dynamic decisions', paper presented at 12th Commonwealth International Sport conference, Manchester, 19–23 July 2002.

Lyle, J. (2003) 'Stimulated recall: A report on its use in naturalistic research', *British Educational Research Journal*, 29(6): 861–878.

Lyle, J. (2007) 'Modelling the complexity of the coaching process: a commentary', *International Journal of Sports Science and Coaching*, 2(4): 407–409.

Lyle, J. (2010) 'Coaches' decision making: a Naturalistic Decision Making analysis', in J. Lyle and C. Cushion (eds) *Sports Coaching: Professionalisation and Practice*, Edinburgh: Churchill Livingstone.

Lyle, J. and Cushion, C. (2010) 'Narrowing the field: Some key questions about sports coaching', in J. Lyle and C. Cushion (eds) *Sports Coaching: Professionalisation and Practice*, Edinburgh: Churchill Livingstone.

Mehrez, A., Friedman, L., Sinuany-Stern, Z. and Bar-Eli, M. (2006) 'Optimal threshold in multi-stage competitions', *International Journal of Sport Management and Marketing*, 1(3): 215–238.

Nash, C. and Collins, D. (2006) 'Tacit knowledge in expert coaching: Science or art?', *Quest*, 58(4): 465–477.

Quek, C.B. (1995) 'Decision style choices of high school basketball coaches: The effects of situational and coach characteristics', *Journal of Sport Behavior*, 18(2): 91–108.

Ransone, J. and Dunn-Bennett, L.R. (1999) 'Assessment of first-aid knowledge and decision making of high school athletic coaches', *Journal of Athletic Training*, 34(3): 267–271.

Saury, J. and Durand, M. (1998) 'Practical knowledge in expert coaches: On-site study of coaching in sailing', *Research Quarterly for Exercise and Sport*, 69(3): 254–266.

Schön, D.A. (1987) *Educating the Reflective Practitioner*, San Francisco, CA: Jossey-Bass.

Schorer, J., Baker, J. and Strauss, B.G. (2007) 'An exploratory study on the role of experience for perceptual-cognitive skill in soccer coaches', *Journal of Sport and Exercise Psychology*, 29(July supplement): S21.

Sévé, C. and Durand, M. (1999) 'L'action de l'entraineur de tennis de table comme action située' [The action of the table tennis coach as situated action], *AVANTE*, 5(1): 69–86.

Svenson, O. (1996) 'Decision making and the search for fundamental psychological regularities: what can be learned from a process perspective?', *Organisational Behaviour and Human Decision Processes*, 65(3): 252–267.

Teigen, K.H. (1996) 'Decision making in two worlds', *Organisational Behaviour and Human Decision Processes*, 65(3): 249–251.

Tenenbaum, G. (2003) 'Expert athletes: An integrated approach to decision making', in J.L. Starkes and K. Anders Ericsson (eds) *Expert Performance in Sports: Advances in Research on Sport Expertise*, Champaign, IL: Human Kinetics.

Vergeer, I. and Hogg, J.M. (1999) 'Coaches' decision policies about the participation of injured athletes in competition', *Sport Psychologist*, 13(1): 42–56.

Vergeer, I. and Lyle, J. (2007) 'Mixing methods in assessing coaches' decision making', *Research Quarterly for Exercise and Sport*, 78(3): 225–235.

Vergeer, I. and Lyle, J. (2009) 'Coaching experience: Examining its role in coaches' decision making', *International Journal of Sport and Exercise Psychology*, 7(4): 431–450.

11

A CRITICAL REALIST APPROACH TO THEORISING COACHING PRACTICE

Julian North

LEEDS METROPOLITAN UNIVERSITY, UK

Introduction

Coaching research has provided specific disciplinary, notably psychological and sociological, knowledge of specific layers of coaching and coaching practice. For example, researchers have investigated topics such as coaches' cognitions, behaviours, athlete-coach interactions, and institutional and cultural influences (e.g. Abraham *et al.* 2006; Cushion 2001; Jowett and Cockerill 2003; Lacy and Darst 1985; Potrac *et al.* 2002). These disciplinary perspectives are associated with specific meta-theoretical assumptions – notably scientism and interpretivism – which influence discussions about what coaching is, how knowledge is generated, and how we should use this knowledge to build interventions to support coaches (North in press). This chapter establishes the basis for an alternative approach for understanding, evaluating and developing coaching practice based on the philosophy and social theory of critical realism.

Critical realism is most commonly associated with Roy Bhaskar's analysis of the natural (Bhaskar 1975) and social sciences (Bhaskar 1998), but has been adopted and developed by a number of prominent UK thinkers (e.g. Archer 1995; Collier 1994; Pawson 1989; Sayer 1984). It suggests that the social world has an underlying material and emergent causal structure that is not easily identified through events and our experiences of them. Researchers use theory to speculate about these underlying causal forces and how they relate to each other in specific contexts to produce outcomes/events including those involving coaching.

The chapter highlights three key features of critical realism: (1) ontological depth; (2) layering and emergence in social practice; and (3) open systems and complexity. Within each theme, the assumptions and approaches underpinning existing coaching research are described and critiqued and an alternative position developed. The result is the tentative beginnings of a multi-layered and relational conception of coaching practice, which seeks to identify how a range of causal influences contribute to coaching outcomes. This is captured through an interdisciplinary approach which neither prioritises specific layers of coaching (e.g. the cognitive or social), nor presents coaching practice a priori as simple and stable or complex and dynamic. The configuration of these different causal influences and their resultant outcome patterns are likely to vary considerably between context (Pawson 1989).

Ontological depth

All social scientific research, including coaching research, necessarily makes assumptions about the nature of the social world (ontology) and how we develop knowledge claims about it (epistemology). These assumptions shape the description of the objects under study (e.g. coaches, athletes etc.), their relationship with each other, and the research method chosen. Coaching researchers very rarely make their assumptions explicit, and may often be unaware of their implicit influence on research practice and outputs (North in press).

Existing coaching practice research makes ontological assumptions about coaching on epistemological foundations. For example, it is common for coaching researchers using psychology as a parent discipline to root their work in a scientism epistemology and quantitative methodology (North in press). This presents a view of, or approach to understanding, coaching which has been variously described as atomistic, mechanistic, systematic, controllable and predictable (e.g. Jones and Wallace 2005). These descriptions are an inevitable result of the epistemology and methodology chosen. Coaching is described in this way because the objects of research enquiry are often captured and analysed through reductionist approaches, using simple observation or self-report research strategies, and quantitative analysis. More sophisticated psychological approaches which utilise qualitative methods still result in simplified and generalised accounts of coaching practice because of their residual link with scientism, and the broader aim of providing abstracted 'models' to inform coach development (Cushion 2007; North in press).

Similarly, coaching research using sociology as a parent discipline makes ontological assumptions about coaching practice based on an interpretive epistemology and qualitative methodology. This approach, which can be seen as a reaction to the scientism outlined above, emphasises the human, relational, situational and dynamic characteristics of coaching (e.g. Potrac *et al.* 2000). Again, however, these descriptions can be traced to underpinning meta-theoretical assumptions (North in press). Interpretivism emphasises the 'problem' of meanings and languages used by individuals and groups to describe their actions and relations (Archer 2003; Sayer 2000). This provides the social world with a plurality, complexity and contextuality, which can only be understood by using idiographic qualitative methodologies.

Psychological scientism and sociological interpretivism produce 'flat' ontologies i.e. ontologies which are shaped by their epistemologies, that is, empirical regularities or language concerns (Sayer 2000). Critical realists argue against the conflation of ontology and epistemology by suggesting that the social world has ontological 'depth' – with a stratified threefold distinction between the 'deep', 'events' and the 'empirical' (Bhaskar 1975) (see Figure 11.1). The 'deep' is what exists. It is the material, psychological and social objects and structures, with associated causal powers and liabilities, which underlie and govern events. In a coaching context objects will include, rather obviously, the coaches, athletes and other relevant stakeholders. They will include the physical spaces where sport takes place (e.g. the training ground) and the artefacts involved in the sporting activity (e.g. athletes' equipment). The structures will include, for example, the micro-level interactions between coaches and athletes, the norms, rules and practices associated with coaching groups and particular sports, and the broader social forces playing out beyond this.

Critical realists are particularly interested in how objects and structures possess causal powers and liabilities expressed through the concept of 'mechanisms'. For example, coaching practice is often conceptualised as an intentional activity which focuses on the achievement of specific coaching goals (e.g. Abraham and Collins 2011; Gilbert and Trudel 2004; Lyle 2007). Coaches, athletes and other stakeholders have particular physical, cognitive and

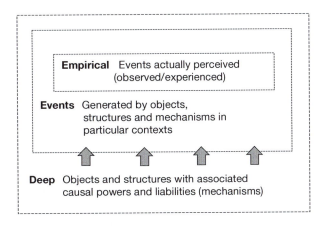

Figure 11.1: Ontological stratification.

affective resources (mechanisms) which enable them to, and constrain them from, pursuing these goals in particular contexts. In this regard, Abraham *et al.* (2006) describe the knowledge bases and decision making apparatus which 'expert' coaches utilise to bring about desirable coaching outcomes. From this resource base, coaches and athletes employ cognitive and behavioural strategies (more mechanisms) such as silence, instruction, observation, facilitation and cooperation (Cushion and Jones 2001; Poczwardowski *et al.* 2002) to intervene actively in the coaching context in line with the goals established. The success of these strategies will be enabled and constrained (even more mechanisms) by the environmental and social structures and forces in these contexts (d'Arripe-Longueville *et al.* 1998; Saury and Durand 1998).

Although objects and structures are associated with particular causal powers and liabilities, these powers may or may not be activated, and this will determine what happens at the level of the second domain – 'events' (Bhaskar 1975). A coach may have the cognitive resources and strategies to bring about specific coaching outcomes but whether these resources and strategies work (are actualised at the level of events) will depend upon other contextual factors. For example, a coach may employ a strategy that works well for the athlete and the coaching goal is achieved. The same strategy may also positively counteract a negative approach by an athlete, and the coaching goal is still achieved. However, at another time and place, the coaching strategy might be weak or inappropriate, but is mitigated by increased effort on the part of athlete; again, the goal is achieved. In all instances, the coaching goal is achieved but the active mechanisms, and the relationship between them, are very different.

The multiplicity of objects, structures and mechanisms, the potentially complex relationships between them, and the difficulty in determining whether or not specific causal powers are activated in relation to specific outcomes/events, is referred to as 'openness' by critical realists (Bhaskar 1998). The openness of social systems introduces problems for researchers working exclusively with the third domain – the 'empirical' (i.e. the events which researchers experience). Empirical observation data of events, for example, is not sufficient for the identification of underpinning mechanisms because they are often hidden from view (Sayer 1984). In a coaching context, it is difficult to determine (without speaking to the coach and the athlete) how observed behaviours relate to the goal, other contextual factors (Potrac *et al.* 2000) and, ultimately, what worked and what did not. Empirical narrative data do not take into account the fact that many important mechanisms operate below the level of consciousness (Sayer 2000), that respondents can 'impression manage' (Goffman 1959), or be mistaken. These approaches (that is, the use of observation and narrative) are common in coaching research but, in isolation, they are insufficient to understand and explain coaching practice.

A critical realist ontology of objects, structures and mechanisms operating in open social system with much that is important hidden from observation and narrative, requires an epistemological and methodological position that reflects (or remedies) this. Critical realists emphasise the use of theory to 'penetrate below the surface to identify underlying social mechanisms or generative processes' (Ackroyd 2009: 524), an analytical procedure known as 'retroduction' (Bhaskar 1975, 1998). In practice, the research process typically begins by examining existing general theory, other relevant theoretical and empirical research, and substantive resources, to build up an initial picture of the area of enquiry (Sayer 1984). This is then used to 'theoretically orientate' new empirical data collection (Layder 1998). Critical realists are relatively relaxed about the methodological strategy adopted and exhibit no specific preference for quantitative or qualitative data (Pawson 2006). That said, intensive research designs (e.g. a small number of cases using qualitative methods), might be more appropriate in areas where there is limited theoretical and empirical evidence from which to explore causal structures. Extensive research designs (e.g. larger data sets using quantitative methods) are more appropriate when descriptive categories are formally established (Sayer 1984). When the data are collected, critical realists use the existing theory and new empirical research to produce new 'adaptive' theory about the phenomenon under consideration (Layder 1998).

In a coaching context, a critical realist researcher would undertake a period of theoretical reflection and immersion, guided by the relevant psychological/social theory, coaching research and other relevant resources (e.g. coaching curricula/texts), again, to build up an initial picture of causal structures and mechanisms. This would then be used to inform an appropriate multiple method/stakeholder research design. The latter might include contextualising background interviews with coaches, athletes and other important stakeholders to understand their goals and strategies, the video/audio capture of sessions, and pre and post session interviews with coaches and athletes. This represents an extension of the multi-method/stakeholder research designs recommended by Cushion (2001), d'Arripe-Longueville *et al.* (2001) and Potrac *et al.* (2000), but with a focus on identifying and developing theory around causal structures in particular coaching contexts. The result will undoubtedly produce a great deal of data. Therefore, a key part of the research process is identifying and 'abstracting' (Lawson 1997) the main mechanisms that influence outcomes (Pawson and Tilley 1997). Finally, the initial theoretical position would then be tested against the new empirical data to develop new adaptive theory about the coaching practice context under consideration.

Layering and emergence

Most coaching research, driven by disciplinary considerations or researcher interest, has focused on specific layers of coaching (Cushion and Lyle 2010). Saury and Durand (1998) illustrate how physical processes (e.g. the weather and sea conditions) impact on coaching goals and practice in sailing. Coaching scholars have focused on the cognitive dimensions of coaching practice and, in particular, knowledge bases (e.g. Abraham *et al.* 2006; Côté and

Gilbert 2009), mental representations/models/relational schemas (e.g. Bowes and Jones 2006; Côté *et al.* 1995; Vergeer and Lyle 2009), and decision making (e.g. Abraham and Collins 2011; Abraham *et al.* 2006; Lyle 2010). Another strand of research considers coaches' behaviours (e.g. Cushion and Jones 2001; Feltz *et al.* 1999). Another stresses how coaches' agential influence is enabled and constrained by local and broader social and historical influences (e.g. Jones 2006; Jones *et al.* 2002, 2004). Furthermore, the relationships within the coaching context (e.g. Jowett and Timson-Katchis 2005), and the macro-social and cultural forces which impact upon them (e.g. Cushion 2001; d'Arripe-Longueville *et al.* 1998; Poczwardowski *et al.* 2002) have also been studied.

Despite producing very useful knowledge about these specific layers (and often for specific purposes) (North in press), the net result is that coaching practice is depicted through a number of narrow/partial frames that ultimately constrain a holistic, contextualised understanding of coaching practice, with particular regard to how coaching goals are translated (or otherwise) into coaching outcomes. Coaching practice, for example, is not just about coaches because this ignores athlete and stakeholder goals, capabilities and strategies in contributing to events (Cushion 2007; Jones and Wallace 2006). Though a number of recent cognitive-based approaches have acknowledged the social nature of coaching and the complexity of 'other people', coaching practice is still viewed rather unproblematically through the lens of the coach (e.g. Abraham and Collins 2011). Equally, coaching practice cannot be reduced to coaching agents' actions and relations in a wider set of social and cultural contexts. There is a need to understand coaching stakeholders' specific reasoning, resources and strategies in producing coaching outcomes and how they are shaped by, and respond to, broader structural conditions and forces.

From a methodological perspective, capturing the breadth of potential influences on coaching practice is a significant undertaking. Critical realists debate the extent to which it is necessary to account for the contributions and combinations of mechanisms at lower levels (e.g. physical, biological), when higher level mechanisms (e.g. cognitive, behavioural, social, cultural) may be sufficient. Some critical realists suggest that our understanding of the social world cannot escape the complex web of biological, chemical and physical interactions (Benton 1991; Carolan 2005). Researchers studying human development clearly attribute a role to biological as well as environmental factors in their explanations (Bronfenbrenner 1994). Other critical realists, however, suggest it is sufficient to understand cognitive, behavioural, institutional and macro-social mechanisms (Carter and New 2004; Manicas 2006; Sayer 2000). This is based on the concept of 'emergence' – layers combine in a manner that is non-additive, non-linear and complex, and give rise to new original phenomena that are irreducible to their constituent parts, even though the latter are necessary for their existence (Archer 1995; Elder-Vass 2010). For example, Sayer (2000) suggests that although talking is dependent on an individual's physiological state, including the signals sent and received around our brain cells, it is not reducible to those physiological processes. Emergence not only provides a process for describing how higher level practices such as coaching evolve and develop, but also the potential for explaining the causal influence of these 'higher level' structures and forces in their own right (Elder-Vass 2010).

The approach endorsed in this chapter, however, is an inclusive view proposed by Sawyer (2005: 7) in which the need to account for the causal influence of particular layers depends on the context being studied, and as such becomes an empirical question: 'Whether or not a social system can be understood solely in terms of its component individuals and their interactions ... [should be] ... resolved anew with respect to each social system'. Both lower level and emergent properties can be casually active in the same context (Noble 2008). The approach approached offered here, therefore, conceives of coaching practice as a multi-layered phenomenon, with the possibility that it is influenced by physical, chemical, biological, neurological, cognitive, behavioural, institutional and macro-social objects, structures and mechanisms (Carolan 2005; Fleetwood 2008; Greenwood 1994; Manicas 2006; Williams 2000) in producing coaching outcomes/events.

An important dimension of the above debate concerns agency and structure. Although coaching research has increasingly used the agency/structure concept (e.g. Bowes and Jones 2006; Jones *et al.* 2002, 2004; Jones and Wallace 2005; Mallet 2007), there has been a particular focus on coaches' agency, often subject to, rather than influencing and changing, pervasive structural conditions. This is understandable. Coaching researchers' are in the business of understanding and helping coaches thus the main focus of attention has been on the coach. Others have sought to counter notions of coaches as 'exclusive controllers' of the coaching environment (e.g. Jones and Wallace 2005) – and, as a result, they have emphasised the importance of recognising and understanding the influence of structural forces. Some have attempted to occupy a more central position. For example, Cushion (2001) explores coach and player experiences in his research on professional youth football (see d'Arripe-Longueville *et al.* 1998, for a similar approach in French judo). Furthermore, Cushion (2001) suggests that coaching practice is the relationship between coach, player and club, between mental and social structures. But even within this more balanced and nuanced analysis there may be issues. Cushion (2001), for example, uses Bourdieu's (1977) concepts of habitus, field and capital to explore coaching practice. Archer (2007), in particular, has been critical of Bourdieu's (1977) treatment of agential reflexivity, suggesting that it underplays the role of agency and leads to the unconscious/uncritical adoption of structural dispositions.

Critical realists suggest agency and structure have distinct causal powers in contributing to outcomes/events (Archer 1995; Elder-Vass 2010). They reject the 'upward conflation' of agential accounts which suggest that social activity can be explained entirely in terms of the aggregation of individual human activity. They also reject the 'downward conflation' of structural accounts, which suggests that social activity can be explained entirely by structural and macro level forces. Some critical realists, for example Archer (2007), also reject the centrally conflated 'elisionist' accounts of agency and structure (e.g. Bourdieu 1977; Giddens 1984).

Human agency, characterised by self-consciousness, cognition, knowledge, intentionality, reflexivity and emotionality, is influenced, although not determined, by the resources and cultural and structural forces at hand. Thus, coaches and athletes, through their resources and reasoning, have interests, exercise choices and pursue projects, but these interests, choices and projects are enabled and constrained by structural and cultural conditions that are not of their making (Archer 1995, 2003). These resources and structures are themselves the product of agency. As Sayer (2000: 18) suggests, 'no structure without actions', but this does not mean that they can be collapsed into one another. Structures are the material resources, practices, norms, rules, power relationships and shared meanings produced, reproduced or transformed by agency at a previous time. These structures then enable or constrain, and are, in turn, reproduced and transformed by agency in the present and into the future (Archer 1995). Compared to the objects and structures studied through the natural sciences, therefore, social structures are only 'relatively enduring', but nevertheless they are sufficiently enduring to have a causal influence on agency. It is the distinct properties and powers of agency and structure, and the timelines over which they act, that entail their irreducibility to each other (Archer 1995; Elder-Vass 2010).

A critical realist approach, therefore, explicitly recognises the agency of all stakeholders (coaches, athletes, others) and how their individual or collective goals, capabilities and strategies are enabled, as well as constrained, by environment and structure in contributing to coaching outcomes and events. Although the contributions of agency and structure are clearly of fundamental importance to understanding coaching practice, it must also be recognised that there are physical dimensions, and that both agency and structure have different layers (e.g. cognitions, behaviours, dyad, group, society) that have to be taken into account. This multi-layered relational approach establishes the basis for, and prescribes, an interdisciplinary approach to knowledge generation (Bhaskar 2005; Carolan 2005; Fleetwood 2008). Manicas (2006: 3) illustrates the point:

> Once we notice that a host of causal mechanisms, biological, psychological and social, are epigenetically implicated in the constitution of a human being – and of their concrete actions – we can see that 'nature' and 'nurture' are inextricably involved and that, in consequence, there is no reason to believe that any one science, psychological or social, could improve on the way we ordinarily explain … behaviour.

This approach allows considerable scope to draw on existing research resources across the disciplines when developing new theory of coaching practice in particular contexts. It also means that coaches, athletes and other relevant stakeholders are an explicit part of its definition and, therefore, research designs.

Open systems and complexity

A notable feature of existing research has been the emphasis on either the simplicity and stability, or the complexity and dynamism, of coaching and coaching practice depending on disciplinary and meta-theoretical assumptions (North in press). As noted earlier, those who tend to work within the discipline of psychology are more inclined to work within a scientism framework. Though there are different strands of coaching research situated within this discipline (e.g. Feltz *et al.* 1999; Smith *et al.* 1978), and the ideas have evolved considerably (e.g. Abraham *et al.* 2006; Côté *et al.* 1995), the resultant models remain focused on general descriptions of coaching components – coaching goals, knowledge bases, behaviours and decision making processes which simplify or ignore the environmental and social dimensions of coaching practice and their influence on coaching outcomes (Cushion 2007; Saury and Durand 1998), mainly to model coaching for the purposes of coach development (North in press). Lyle (2002) presents another multi-dimensional model, which, while recognising the interpersonal and externally constrained nature of coaching, has been interpreted as overly systematic, sequential and mechanistic to represent fully its contingencies (Bowes and Jones 2006; Cushion *et al.* 2006; Jones and Wallace 2005).

Coaching researchers working within the discipline of sociology with interpretivist leanings are more critical about the likelihood of creating representative knowledge, and focus on the differences, pluralities, complexities and disorder of coaching and coaching practice (Brewer 2007; Lyle 2007). Significant warnings are expressed about the value of planning, sequence and control in coaching, and greater play is made of localised meanings, interpretations, relationships, power games and the 'swampy lowlands of practice'. Some coaching researchers go a stage further suggesting coaching could be characterised as having moments of extreme ambiguity, uncertainty, pathos and indeed, chaos (e.g. Bowes and Jones 2006; Jones 2006; Jones and Wallace 2005).

Of course, there is no suggestion that the main strands of coaching research do not recognise a broad continuum of coaching possibilities. Coaching research informed by psychological scientism has noted the complexity and dynamism of coaching (e.g. Abraham and Collins 2011; Côté *et al.* 1995); while sociological interpretive informed research has made reference to its simple and routine elements (e.g. Cushion *et al.* 2006; Jones and Wallace 2005). Rather, it is suggested that each strand's disciplinary and philosophical assumptions and methods lead them to focus a priori on one over the other (North in press). For example, the psychologically orientated work of Abraham and Collins (2011) acknowledges the complexity of coaching but focuses on its more stable and universal elements in the task of providing tools for coach development. The sociologically orientated work of Cushion (2007: 397) suggests coaching practice can be understood as 'structured/regulated improvisation' (following Bourdieu 1977), but ultimately appears to emphasise coaching's more complex and contextualised features in a broader critique of existing conceptualisations and coach education (North in press).

Critical realists support a position which recognises a greater level of complexity and dynamism in practice than positivistic approaches allow, but do not accept a position that suggests a priori complexity and disorder as a normal state of affairs. The objects and causal forces which create complexity and disorder can also have a stabilising influence. For example, Popper (1972) argues that humans are biologically disposed to impose regularities on their environment. Giddens (1984) suggests that because agents seek 'ontological security' they are disposed to act in institutionalised and routine ways. Bourdieu (1977) uses the concept of habitus to describe the 'structured and structuring' tendencies in agents, groups and institutions. Sayer (2000: 13) argues that stability is an 'intentional achievement, a product of making continual changes in order to stay the same, or at least to maintain continuities through change, rather than a result of doing nothing'. Downward *et al.* (2002) suggest that agents counter 'ontological complexity' by developing an appropriate decision making apparatus. Elder-Vass (2010) contends that social institutions have a significant stabilising influence on the social world.

Critical realists, in other words, argue that the complexity and contingency inherent in open social systems may (or may not) be pacified by mechanisms that make order, or something close to order, possible. Thus, for critical realists the social world is neither defined, necessarily, by simplicity or complexity, order or randomness, stability or instability (Archer 1995; Manicas 2006; Stones 1996). Commenting on accounts which prioritise order (modernism) and disorder (post-modernism), Stones (1996: 24) suggested that: 'I do not see why we should choose, a priori, one or the other'. Reflecting on the mechanisms which combine to produce social order/disorder, Sayer (2000: 16) noted that: 'Just how much difference context makes cannot be specified at the level of ontology, for it depends on the nature of the processes of interest … the latter range from the chameleon-like to the relatively context-independent or indifferent'. Thus, for Sayer (2000) the relative simplicity/complexity and/or order/stability of social systems is a context specific and empirical matter. A critical realist approach, therefore, suggests that coaching practice can be simple and complex, stable and dynamic, consensual and have moments of conflict. The line between these polar positions is dependent on context, such as the sport, participants' sporting objectives, age/ stage of development, gender relations and little moments that go right or wrong!

Like the history of the social sciences, only 20–30 years later, coaching research has followed a trajectory that has produced relatively simplistic over-confident positions (psychology scientism) followed by relatively complex pessimistic positions (sociological interpretivism), with the complexities of the latter being an inevitable over-reaction to the simplicities of former (Layder 1998). However, more recently, coaching researchers have started to confront their disciplinary, methodological and (implicit/explicit) philosophical inclinations, with reference to the 'realities' of coaching. For example, Lyle (2007) recognises both the simple and routine, and the complex and innovative in coaching, suggesting that variation may relate to the sport and type of athlete the coach works with (e.g. participation, development and performance). Abraham and Collins (2011: 210) contended that '(good) coaching is and indeed must be systematic. We just had/have to get better at identifying and developing the systems that can and do cope with the "swampy lowlands" '. Cushion *et al.* (2010: 2) suggest

> coaching practitioners do in fact use standardised strategies and routines in an attempt to cope with the many and varied constraining factors of the coaching process; these routines and strategies are purposely flexible by design, so permitting improvised adaptation to the arising contextual demands.

The increasing recognition of both the simple and complex, and stable and dynamic, elements of coaching is likely to reflect a pragmatic and experiential response rather than one based on explicit philosophical assumptions. Outhwaite (1987: 28) suggests that researchers often work with a 'nocturnal philosophy', that is, despite their adopted frameworks suggesting particular approaches and answers, they subconsciously work with other approaches. Other philosophers and methodologists (Miles and Huberman 1994; Outhwaite 1987; Pawson 1989) contend that although researchers may explicitly adhere to, or be labelled as supporting, scientism or interpretivism their practices are often critical realist in nature – although they seldom employ these approaches as far as they should (Sayer 2000). The explicit adoption of a critical realist philosophical framework that identifies and describes the objects, structures and mechanisms and their inter-relations in particular contexts, it is argued, provides a valuable alternative framework to situate these emerging ideas.

Conclusions

In conceiving coaching practice as the inter-relationship between objects (e.g. physical spaces, artefacts, coaching stakeholders), structures (e.g. norms and rules of coaching groups and particular sports) and mechanisms (e.g. the physical and cognitive resources and strategies of coaching stakeholders) in open multi-layered social systems, with routine and non-routine elements, a critical realist approach moves beyond existing psychological-sociological, quantitative-qualitative, agency-structure, coach-athlete, simple-complex and stable-dynamic dichotomies. A critical realist approach provides a broad canvas, an orientating structure, to analyse the causal relationships and connections between coaching goals, coaching stakeholders' cognitions and behaviours, and wider social and environmental influences that can draw on existing research. This allows both the simplicity and stability of coaching practice to be understood, as well as its moments of complexity and dynamism. In addition, it provides a framework for understanding, 'what works, for whom, in what context and why', and through conducting new theoretical and empirical work will help to bring formalised coaching knowledge closer to actual practice.

This approach suggests the need for relatively complex research designs to investigate coaching practice in context. This will undoubtedly produce large quantities of data that would help us to identify and explain the important mechanisms that lead to coaching outcomes in particular contexts. In this way, we give ourselves a chance to break down coaching practice into its fundamental properties and processes, and to understand how these elements relate back to the whole. The result of this work will be a knowledge base that not only reflects on the underlying structures of coaching in particular contexts, but also provides coaches with knowledge for action (Jones and Wallace 2005). This will take many forms but an obvious example is the identification of coaching strategies that have been shown to work in particular contexts, but with a very clear identification of the conditions under which they work, and how their application may vary as conditions change.

References

Abraham, A. and Collins, D. (2011) 'Effective skill development: How should athletes' skills be developed?' in D. Collins, A. Button and H. Richards (eds) *Performance Psychology: A Practitioner's Guide*, Edinburgh: Churchill Livingstone.

Abraham, A., Collins, D. and Martindale, R. (2006) 'The coaching schematic: Validation through expert coach consensus', *Journal of Sports Science*, 24(6): 549–564.

Ackroyd, S. (2009) 'Research designs for realist researchers', in D.A. Buchanan and A. Bryman (eds) *The Sage Handbook of Organizational Research*, London: Sage.

Archer, M. (1995) *Realist Social Theory: The Morphogenetic Approach*, Cambridge: Cambridge University Press.

Archer, M. (2003) *Structure, Agency and the Internal Conversation*, Cambridge: Cambridge University Press.

Archer, M. (2007) *Making our Way Through the World*, Cambridge: Cambridge University Press.

Benton, T. (1991) 'Biology and social science: Why the return of the repressed should be given a (cautious) welcome', *Sociology*, 25(1): 1–29.

Bhaskar, R. (1975) *A Realist Theory of Science*, Leeds: Leeds Books.

Bhaskar, R. (1998) *The Possibility of Naturalism*, 3rd edn, London: Routledge.

Bhaskar, R. (2005) 'Critical realism and the theory and practice of interdisciplinarity', paper presented at the 37th World Congress of the International Institute of Sociology, 5–9 July, Stockholm, Sweden.

Bourdieu, P. (1977) *Outline of a Theory of Practice*, Cambridge: Cambridge University Press.

Bowes, I. and Jones, R.L. (2006) 'Working at the edge of chaos: Understanding coaching as a complex interpersonal system', *The Sport Psychologist*, 20(2): 235–245.

Brewer, B. (2007) 'Modelling the complexities of the coaching process: A commentary', *International Journal of Sports Science and Coaching*, 2(4): 411–413.

Bronfenbrenner, U. (1994) 'Ecological models of human development', in T. Husen and T.N. Postlewaite (eds) *The International Encyclopaedia of Education*, New York: Elsevier Science.

Carolan, M.S. (2005) 'Society, biology, and ecology: Bringing nature back into sociology's disciplinary narrative through critical realism', *Organization Environment*, 18(4): 393–421.

Carter, B. and New, C. (2004) *Making Realism Work: Realist Social Theory and Empirical Research*, Abingdon: Routledge.

Collier, A. (1994) *Critical Realism*, London: Verso.

Côté, J. and Gilbert, W.D. (2009) 'An integrative definition of coaching effectiveness and expertise', *International Journal of Sports Science and Coaching*, 4(3): 307–323.

Côté, J., Salmela, J., Trudel, P. and Russel, S. (1995) 'The coaching model: A grounded assessment of expert gymnastics coaches' knowledge', *Journal of Sport and Exercise Psychology*, 17(1): 1–17.

Cushion, C.J. (2001) 'The coaching process in professional youth football: An ethnography of practice', unpublished doctoral thesis, Brunel University, London.

Cushion, C.J. (2007) 'Modelling the complexities of the coaching process', *International Journal of Sports Science and Coaching*, 2(4): 395–401.

Cushion, C.J. and Jones, R.L. (2001) 'A systematic observation of professional top-level youth soccer coaches', *Journal of Sport Behavior*, 24(4): 354–376.

Cushion, C.J. and Lyle, J. (2010) 'Conceptual development in sports coaching', in J. Lyle and C. Cushion (eds) *Sports Coaching: Professionalisation and Practice*, London: Elsevier.

Cushion, C.J., Armour, K.M. and Jones, R.L. (2006) 'Locating the coaching process in practice: Models "for" and "of" coaching', *Physical Education and Sport Pedagogy*, 11(1): 83–99.

Cushion, C.J., Nelson, L.J., Armour, K.M., Lyle, J., Jones, R.L., Sandford, R. and O'Callaghan, C. (2010) *Coach Learning and Development: A Review of the Literature*, Leeds: Sports Coach UK.

d'Arripe-Longueville, F., Fournier, J.F. and Dubois, A. (1998) 'The perceived effectiveness of interactions between expert French judo coaches and elite female athletes', *The Sport Psychologist*, 12(3): 317–332.

d'Arripe-Longueville, F., Saury, J. and Fournier, J.F. (2001) 'Coach-athlete interaction during elite archery competitions: An application of methodoligical frameworks used in ergonomics to sport psychology', *Journal of Applied Sport Psychology*, 13(3): 275–299.

Downward, P., Finch, J.H. and Ramsay, J. (2002) 'Critical realism, empirical method and inference: A critical discussion', *Journal of Economics*, 26(4): 481–500.

Elder-Vass, D. (2010) *The Causal Power of Social Structures: Emergence, Structure and Agency*, Cambridge: Cambridge University Press.

Feltz, D.L., Chase, M.A., Moritz, S.E. and Sullivan, P.J. (1999) 'A conceptual model of coaching efficacy: Preliminary investigation and instrument development', *Journal of Educational Psychology*, 91(4): 765–776.

Fleetwood, S. (2008) 'Structure, institution, agency, habit and reflexive deliberation', *Journal of Institutional Economics*, 4(2): 183–203.

Giddens, A. (1984) *The Constitution of Society: Outline of the Theory of Structuration*, Cambridge: Polity.

Gilbert, W.D. and Trudel, P. (2004) 'Role of the coach: How model youth team sport coaches frame their roles', *The Sport Psychologist*, 18(1): 21–42.

Goffman, E. (1959) *The Presentation of Self in Everyday Life*, Grantham: Anchor Books.

Greenwood, J.D. (1994) *Realism, Identity and Emotion: Reclaiming Social Psychology*, London: Sage.

Jones, R.L. (2006) 'How can education concepts inform sports coaching?', in R.L. Jones (ed.) *The Sports Coach as Educator: Re-conceptualising Sports Coaching*, London: Routledge.

Jones, R.L. and Wallace, M. (2005) 'Another bad day at the training ground: Coping with ambiguity in the coaching context', *Sport, Education and Society*, 8(2): 213–229.

Jones, R.L. and Wallace, M. (2006) 'The coach as "orchestrator": More realistically managing the complex coaching context', in R.L. Jones (ed.) *The Sports Coach as Educator: Re-conceptualising Sports Coaching*, London: Routledge.

Jones, R.L., Armour, K.M. and Potrac, P. (2002) 'Understanding the coaching process: A framework for social analysis', *Quest*, 54(1): 34–48.

Jones, R.L., Armour, K.M. and Potrac, P. (2004) *Sports Coaching Cultures: From Practice to Theory*, London: Longman.

Jowett, S. and Cockerill, I.M. (2003) 'Olympic medallists' perspective of the athlete-coach relationship', *Psychology of Sport and Exercise*, 4(4): 313–331.

Jowett, S. and Timson-Katchis, M. (2005) 'Social networks in sport: Parental influence on the coach-athlete relationship', *The Sport Psychologist*, 19(3): 267–287.

Lacy, A.C. and Darst, P.W. (1985) 'Systematic observation of behaviors of winning high school head football coaches', *Journal of Teaching in Physical Education*, 4(4): 256–270.

Lawson, T. (1997) *Economics and Reality*, London: Routledge.

Layder, D. (1998) *Sociological Practice: Linking Theory and Social Research*, London: Sage Publications.

Lyle, J. (2002). *Sports Coaching Concepts: A Framework for Coaches' Behaviour*, London: Routledge.

Lyle, J. (2007) 'Modelling the complexities of the coaching process: A commentary', *International Journal of Sports Science and Coaching*, 2(4): 407–409.

Lyle, J. (2010) 'Coaches' decision making: A naturalistic decision making analysis', in J. Lyle and C.J. Cushion (eds) *Sports Coaching: Professionalisation and Practice*, Edinburgh: Churchill Livingstone.

Mallet, C. (2007) 'Modelling the complexity of the coaching process: A commentary', *International Journal of Sports Science and Coaching*, 2(4): 419–421.

Manicas, P.T. (2006) *A Realistic Philosophy of Social Science*, Cambridge: Cambridge University Press.

Miles, H.B. and Huberman, A.M. (1994) *Qualitative Data Analysis: An Expanded Sourcebook*, London: Sage.

Noble, D. (2008) *The Music of Life: Biology Beyond Genes*, Oxford: Oxford University Press.

North, J. (in press) 'Philosophical underpinnings of coaching practice research', *Quest*.

Outhwaite, W. (1987) *New Philosophies of Social Science: Realism, Hermeneutics and Critical Theory*, London: Macmillan.

Pawson, R. (1989) *A Measure for Measures: A Manifesto for Empirical Sociology*, London: Routledge.

Pawson, R. (2006) *Evidence Based Policy: A Realist Perspective*, London: Sage.

Pawson, R. and Tilley, N. (1997) *Realistic Evaluation*, London: Sage.

Poczwardowski, A., Barott, J.E. and Henschen, K.P. (2002) 'The athlete and coach: Their relationship and its meaning: Results of an interpretive study', *International Journal of Sport Psychology*, 33(1): 116–140.

Popper, K. (1972) *Objective Knowledge: An Evolutionary Approach*, Oxford: Oxford University Press.

Potrac, P., Jones, R.L. and Armour, K. (2002) '"It's all about getting respect": The coaching behaviors of an expert English soccer coach', *Sport, Education and Society*, 7(2): 183–202.

Potrac, P., Jones, R.L., Brewer, C., Armour, K. and Hoff, J. (2000) 'Towards a holistic understanding of the coaching process', *Quest*, 52(2): 186–199.

Saury, J. and Durand, M. (1998) 'Practical knowledge in expert coaches: On-site study of coaching in sailing', *Research Quarterly for Exercise and Sport*, 69(3): 254–266.

Sawyer, R.K. (2005) *Social Emergence: Societies as Complex Systems*, Cambridge: Cambridge University Press.

Sayer, A. (1984) *Method in Social Science*, London: Routledge.

Sayer, A. (2000) *Realism and Social Science*, London: Sage.

Smith, R.E., Smoll, F.L. and Curtis, B. (1978) 'Coaching behaviors in little league baseball', in F.L. Smoll and R.E. Smith (eds) *Psychological Perspectives in Youth Sports*, Washington, DC: Hempshere.

Stones, R. (1996) *Sociological Reasoning: Towards a Past-modern Sociology*, London: Macmillan.

Vergeer, I. and Lyle, J. (2009) 'Coaching expertise: Examining its role in coaches' decision making', *International Journal of Sport and Exercise Psychology*, 78(3): 225–235.

Williams, M. (2000) *Science and Social Science*, London: Routledge.

PART II

Perspectives on sports coaching in action

What do we know about the act of sports coaching?

A

Perspectives on Quality Coaching

12

DEFINING COACHING EFFECTIVENESS

A focus on coaches' knowledge

Wade Gilbert

CALIFORNIA STATE UNIVERSITY, FRESNO, USA

Jean Côté

QUEEN'S UNIVERSITY, CANADA

Introduction

Côté and Gilbert (2009) recently proposed an integrative definition of coaching effectiveness that focuses on coaches' knowledge, athletes' outcomes, and the different contexts that coaches typically work in. The definition, based on a thorough review of coaching, teaching, athlete development, and positive psychology literature, is:

> The consistent application of integrated professional, interpersonal, and intrapersonal knowledge to improve athletes' competence, confidence, connection, and character in specific coaching contexts.
>
> *(Côté and Gilbert 2009: 316)*

In-depth discussions about athletes' outcomes (Côté *et al.* 2010; Côté and Gilbert 2009) and coaching contexts (Lyle and Cushion 2010; Trudel and Gilbert 2006) are available in the literature. A similar discussion on the coaches' knowledge component has not been presented, thereby limiting the application of the integrated definition of coaching effectiveness and expertise. The purpose of this chapter is to define in more detail the three forms of coaches' knowledge that underpin coaching effectiveness and expertise. Various ways of classifying the type of knowledge required in coaching have been proposed (Abraham *et al.* 2006; Cassidy *et al.* 2009; Nash and Collins 2006). Although a major component of coaching expertise resides in one's ability to teach sport specific skills (professional knowledge; Jones 2007), coaching expertise also requires the ability to create and maintain relationships (interpersonal knowledge; Becker 2009; Jowett 2007) and the ability to learn from one's own practice (intrapersonal knowledge; Gilbert and Trudel 2001). For the purpose of our discussion specific to sport coaching, we view professional knowledge as content knowledge and how to teach it; hence, it also includes pedagogical content knowledge related to

147

teaching sport skills. Interpersonal knowledge in a sport coaching context might best be framed as emotional intelligence. It is knowledge of how to connect with others (players, coaches, media, administrators, officials, etc.). Lastly, we suggest that the third type of knowledge – intrapersonal knowledge – is most aligned with the concepts of self-awareness and reflection.

Coaches' professional knowledge

Abraham and colleagues (2006) proposed that expert knowledge for coaches includes declarative knowledge in the sport sciences (i.e. ologies), sport specific knowledge, and pedagogical knowledge with accompanying procedural knowledge. These different categories of knowledge can be regrouped under a more general 'professional knowledge' category that defines the large body of specialized knowledge required to coach. The conceptual foundation, then, for professional knowledge in sport coaching is declarative (what) and procedural (how) knowledge. We will avoid elaborating on declarative knowledge for sport coaching because although there is some overlap among sports and settings (e.g. principles of strength and conditioning), declarative knowledge will vary widely among sport settings. The second component of professional knowledge is procedural knowledge – the ability to transform and use declarative knowledge in specific sporting contexts. Although the study of procedural knowledge in sports coaching is limited, it appears that two dominant conceptual frameworks have guided this work – coaching skill and coach decision making.

Examination of procedural knowledge from a coaching skill perspective has been driven by the work of Schempp and colleagues (see Schempp and McCullick 2010 for a review of this line of work). Based on nearly two decades of research – influenced mostly by a series of studies with golf instructors – Schempp and colleagues have identified nine distinct coaching skills that appear to differentiate expert from novice sport coaches. These skills are planning, prediction, intuitive decision making, communication, automaticity, observational analysis, problem solving, self-monitoring and perception. From a skill perspective, then, these nine skills comprise the procedural knowledge for sports coaching. Although these nine skills provide an appealing organizational framework for the study and development of procedural knowledge in sports coaching, this framework does not appear to have been widely adopted in the literature. Clearly much more research is needed before a determination can be made on the efficacy of the coaching skill perspective for understanding procedural knowledge in sport coaching. However, at its core the coaching skill perspective clearly aligns with a more widely adopted perspective on procedural knowledge in sport coaching. The common theme across the nine coaching skills is that 'expert' coaching (transformation and application of declarative knowledge) rests on effective decision making. In fact, Schempp and colleagues refer to effective decision making as 'strategic knowledge' – under which all nine coaching skills may be subsumed.

Unlike the coaching skill perspective, approaching procedural knowledge from a decision-making perspective has been widely adopted in the sports coaching literature. Based on our review of the literature we hold the position that procedural knowledge is inextricably linked with decision making ability (Lyle 2010; Lyle and Vergeer, Chapter 10 in this volume). Isolated studies on coach decision making have been published since the early 1990s. In perhaps the first published research on this topic Duke and Corlett (1992) examined the factors university women's basketball coaches used when calling timeouts during games. The first published study of coach decision making during practice settings appears to be the one on high school basketball coaches' practice planning decisions conducted by Jones *et al.* (1995). These two landmark studies collectively represent two divergent conceptual approaches to coach decision making. Whereas the Jones *et al.* study examined coaches' decision making in a contrived lab-based setting (coaches were instructed to plan and teach a 30-minute practice on a specific play), the Duke and Corlett study examined coaches' decision making in actual games. The Jones *et al.* study could be considered a Judgment/ Decision Making (J/DM) approach as opposed to the Naturalistic Decision Making (NDM) approach used by Duke and Corlett. Since the time of these early studies, the NDM approach has become the dominant and advocated approach for research on coach decision making (Lyle 2010).

Comprehensive summaries of the NDM approach applied to sport coaching research are now available (Lyle 2010; Lyle and Vergeer, this volume). The central theme of NDM is that procedural knowledge rests on a coach's ability to 'make sense' of a situation and formulate a response (decision). These decisions are influenced not only by a reading of the situation, but also by the coach's experience and awareness of athlete profiles. For example, Gilbert and colleagues (1999) found that youth ice hockey coaches cited approximately three unique factors that influenced each interactive decision during games. Furthermore, 21 separate factors in all were identified by the coaches that were separated into two categories (Field Information and Coach Knowledge).

In a deeper analysis of the complexity of coach decision making, this time in the context of training sessions with elite sailing coaches, Saury and Durand (1998) found three constraints that heavily influenced coach decision making:

1   principles of training efficiency;
2   temporal situation of the actions; and
3   uncertainty inherent in athletes' actions and the weather conditions.

Within these constraints, coaches used what were referred to as 'operating modes' – which in our view is simply another way to describe procedural knowledge. Five operating modes were identified:

1   use of organizational routines;
2   cognitive anticipation based on flexible plans;
3   flexible adaptation of plans to unforeseen circumstances;
4   joint control of training; and
5   involvement in the training situation based on reference to past experiences.

Further support for the NDM as a conceptual framework for understanding coaches' procedural knowledge is evident in Debanne and Fontayne's (2009) case study of an elite handball coach's cognitive processes during competition. Whereas Saury and Durand use the term 'operating modes' to describe procedural knowledge, Debanne and Fontayne use 'adjustment routines'. Adjustment routines varied depending on the game conditions (offense or defense) and were influenced by the coach's deep knowledge of the game and athlete profiles. Regardless of the terminology used, both studies provide strong evidence for the validity of the NDM perspective.

Although there are relatively few published studies that could be considered examples of NDM in sports coaching, the evidence clearly shows support for NDM as a valid conceptual framework for understanding coach procedural knowledge. Furthermore, although developing somewhat independently there is considerable thematic overlap both within studies conducted from the NDM perspective and between the decision making and coaching skill perspectives.

For example, from a decision making perspective expert coaches' procedural knowledge rests on their ability to 'forward reason' and anticipate potential outcomes of decision options (Lyle 2010). From a coaching skill perspective, expert coaches' procedural knowledge also rests on this same ability to 'predict outcomes' based on recognition of similarities across situations (Schempp and McCullick 2010). So although one common unifying conceptual framework remains elusive, the common themes for understanding coach procedural knowledge are clearly evident.

Coaches' behaviors in competition and training can be seen as the concrete manifestation of their knowledge base. Accordingly naturalistic behavior research (see Erickson and Côté, Chapter 9 in this volume) should continue to inform and be integral to our understanding of coaches' professional knowledge. The seminal work of Smith and Smoll (2007) is a prime example of behavioral research that has been used to shed light on aspects of coaches' professional knowledge, specifically youth sport coaches' procedural knowledge during teaching sessions. The practical significance, however, of a common framework for understanding coaches' knowledge is not a standardized set of effective coaching behaviors. Rather, the real value of a coaches' knowledge framework is that it increases our ability to help coaches and coach educators develop the knowledge 'competencies' required in order to effectively translate knowledge into action. One might consider the decision-making skills identified in our review of the literature as a starting point for creating a common list of coaches' knowledge 'competencies'. The challenge then is to design formal coach education systems that provide regular and systematic opportunities for coaches to develop these knowledge 'competencies'. Among the many suggestions found in the coaching literature, 'situated learning' coach education opportunities appears to be the most widely supported (Lyle 2010). Examples of 'situated learning' approaches include problem-based learning (Jones and Turner 2006), communities of practice (Culver and Trudel 2008), and learning communities (Gilbert *et al.* 2009). In closing this section, we believe fruitful courses of action at this point are to further refine definitions and terminology, and expand our database of naturalistic coaching behavioral research, to facilitate the generation of an evidenced-based conceptual framework for studying and developing coaches' professional knowledge.

Coaches' interpersonal knowledge

Coaches do not work in isolation; their effectiveness depends on individual and group interactions. To be successful, coaches have to interact regularly with their athletes, as well as assistant coaches, parents, and other professionals. Recent theoretical work (Bowes and Jones 2006; Cushion *et al.* 2006; Jones *et al.* 2010; Jones and Wallace 2006) advocates for a multidirectional conceptualization of coach-athlete interactions which suggests that coaching is a complex, reciprocally influential process based on systems of social interactions. The interpersonal and social skills involved in leading individuals can also be referred to as the 'human' aspect of coaching. Although this has been acknowledged as being a crucial element of effective leaders, teachers and coaches (Becker 2009; Jones *et al.* 2010; Rieke *et al.* 2008), this concept has not been operationalized enough to be measured and studied.

In an attempt to conceptualize the interpersonal aspect of coaching, Lorimer and Jowett in Chapter 26 of this volume highlight the notion of 'understanding' as a way to shed light on coach-athlete relationships. They advocate that understanding and communication are the heart of the relationships between coaches and athletes. Because emotion plays a fundamental role in interpersonal relationships (Caruso *et al.* 2002; Greenockle 2010), the field of emotional intelligence provides us with a concrete model to frame the interpersonal knowledge of effective coaches and their ability to understand their athletes and communicate with others. Emotional intelligence can be seen as a subset of Lorimer and Jowett's concept of understanding and communication that focuses on the coaches' ability to recognize and use emotions to manage their relationships with others and regulate behaviors.

In a review of different emotional intelligence frameworks in sport research, Meyer and Fletcher (2007) reiterate the fact that two broad approaches exist in the general field of emotional intelligence research: a mixed approach and an ability approach. The mixed approach conceptualizes emotional intelligence as including emotional competencies and personality traits such as self-awareness and self-motivation. This approach has been widely popularized by authors such as Goleman (1998). However, the overlapping constructs of emotional intelligence and personality traits inherent in the mixed approach have led authors from a mixed approach perspective to define a field that has little scientific validity (Davies *et al.* 1998). Two drawbacks of the mixed model approach are the difficulty in measuring emotional intelligence traits with self-report inventories and the fact that the model does not appear to exist as a construct separable from other aspects of personality (Meyer and Fletcher 2007).

On the other hand, the ability approach (Mayer and Salovey 1997) conceives emotional intelligence as an ability that can be developed and measured using objective instruments such as the Mayer-Salovey-Caruso Emotional Intelligence Test (MSCEIT). Most importantly, the ability model has been useful in providing guidelines in areas such as group research (Latimer *et al.* 2007) and leadership (Caruso *et al.* 2002). Recently Chan and Mallett (2011) initiated a comprehensive discussion on the value of the emotional intelligence framework for high performance coaching effectiveness. Specifically, in their lead article they illustrated the importance of perceiving, using, understanding, and managing emotions as an important set of abilities for high performance coaches. For the purpose of this chapter and in line with Chan and Mallett's recent recommendations, the Mayer and Salovey (1997) ability approach to emotional intelligence will be used to offer insight into our understanding of how effective coaches interact with others. According to Mayer and Salovey emotional intelligence can be defined according to a four branch model of (1) identifying, (2) using, (3) understanding, and (4) managing emotions. These abilities are essential components of interpersonal skills and the capacity that a coach has for instance, to motivate athletes, plan and make decisions, and to interact with others and build a team.

The first branch is identifying emotions. This branch includes a number of skills, such as the ability to identify feelings in others and express emotions in a constructive manner. Coaches' ability to perceive their athletes' emotions accurately will facilitate communication, prevent conflict, and help deal with athletes who are anxious or lack confidence. Additionally, coaches' ability to perceive emotions in opponents may provide a performance advantage.

The second branch is using emotions. This includes the ability to use emotions to focus attention on relevant cues and to generate emotions that facilitate decision making and problem solving. Coaches' ability to use emotions such as enjoyment with young athletes will likely create a positive and nurturing sporting environment. Furthermore, coaches that are effective at using their own emotions can generate effort, enthusiasm, and concentration in their athletes and eventually develop more confident and competent athletes.

The third branch is understanding emotions. This relates to the ability to recognize the causes of emotions and to understand relationships among emotions. Coaches that are effective at understanding emotions have a good sense of what makes their athletes react one way or another. Coaches' understanding of their athletes' emotions becomes essential for creating a cohesive group and connections with others. The ability to understand emotions provides a coach with the power to recognize other's point of view and ultimately influence behaviors or skills in others.

The fourth branch is managing emotions. This includes the ability to be aware of one's emotion, determine the nature of an emotion, and solve emotional situations effectively. Coaches play a critical role in teaching athletes strategies to achieve an emotional state that will lead to optimal performance. For example, coaches are known to manage emotions in order to arouse their athletes before a competition; conversely, coaches that are effective at managing emotions are also able to use calming emotional strategies to help certain athletes relax before an important competition. Furthermore, many sporting situations create an array of emotions that need to be managed by the athletes and the coaches. Effective coaches possess the ability to teach athletes to respond appropriately to emotionally charged situations in sport (i.e. character building) and will themselves regulate their own emotions when faced with adverse or frustrating situations.

The following hypothetical scenario illustrates how Mayer and Salovey's (1997) ability model provides a useful framework to operationalize the interpersonal knowledge of effective coaches.

Bob is a high school basketball coach in the United States. He has been coaching for ten years for the same school and won a State Championship in his second year of coaching. Bob started his high school career as a physical education teacher and was appointed as a coach when the job became available. He believes that sport offers adolescents opportunities to learn important life skills and develop character, but his main concern is to put a winning team on the floor. Bob is a performance coach for young adolescents.

As a coach, Bob is very effective at teaching skills to his players and designs practices that prepare his players effectively for games. Bob is capable of accurately identifying and expressing emotions, as he often makes insightful observations about his players. The recognition of his own emotions is sometimes inaccurate as, he often claims to be feeling calm when it is obvious to his assistant coaches and players that he is angry and upset at the performance of some of his players. Bob appears to be skilled in some areas of perceiving emotions in his players but sometimes fails to recognize his own emotional state.

Bob is very innovative and is able to use his own emotions to generate excitement in his players and coaching staff. He is able to think creatively and is always positive about his team and program with journalists, parents, and other school staff. Bob's ability to use his own emotion to harness certain moods in his players and the people around him is high.

Bob's ability to understand emotions is not as high as his ability to perceive or use emotions. Bob appears to sometimes not understand the true character of some teachers in the school who believe that the basketball program uses too many resources in the school and creates inequities. He sometimes gets impatient with parents who pull their sons from basketball practices so they have more time to prepare for important exams. Although Bob understands the basics of emotions, he often misunderstands other people's motives.

Bob is fairly effective at managing emotions. He is able to integrate his emotions into his actions and assist his players in responding constructively to upsetting situations such as a losing streak. Although Bob is effective at handling situations that are upsetting to his players, he sometimes avoids confrontations with his coaching staff when they don't agree on certain strategies. Similarly, Bob will try to avoid confrontations with parents who are not happy about their son's playing time or utilization on the team.

Table 12.1 was adapted from Caruso *et al.* (2002) and presents an analysis of how the four branches of the Mayer and Salovey (1997) model can be applied to coaching and more specifically defines the competencies of coaches' interpersonal knowledge. Columns 2 and 3 of the table summarize Bob's ability on four different levels of his relationships with others. An in-depth discussion of the Mayer and Salovey model as a determining factor of leadership and interpersonal qualities in coaching can be found in the recent article by Chan and Mallett (2011).

Table 12.1: Application of emotional intelligence abilities to sport coaching

Ability	Level	Analysis of Bob the Coach
Perceiving: • Identify own emotions. • Identify emotions in others.	Average	Skilled at attending to his players' emotions but sometimes misreads his own emotions.
Using: • Use emotion to facilitate own effective thinking. • Generate emotions to assist own problem solving.	High	Effective at harnessing his own emotions to solve problems and think about creative solutions.
Understanding: • Understand relationships and transitions among emotions. • Understand complex feelings and contradictory states.	Average	Understands well the basic of emotions but often misunderstands other peoples' motives.
Managing: • Ability to manage emotions in oneself and in others.	High/ Average	Effective at managing his own and his players' emotions but avoids confrontations with certain people.

Coaches' intrapersonal knowledge

Intrapersonal knowledge is formally defined as 'the understanding of oneself and the ability for introspection and reflection' (Côté and Gilbert 2009: 311). Sport coaches, and those who have studied them, have long acknowledged the central role of self-awareness in becoming an effective coach. This recognition of self-awareness as the foundation for developing coaching effectiveness transcends time and coaching contexts (Vickers and

Hale 2010). However, there is much less clarity on the underlying conceptual framework that is used to inform our understanding of coaches' intrapersonal knowledge. Although it has been shown that effective coaches have a keen sense of self-awareness (e.g. Gallimore and Tharp 2004), being aware of one's strengths and limitations will not lead to coach development unless this awareness is accompanied by action – either to maintain strengths or address weaknesses (Schempp *et al.* 2007). The term most widely used to describe the act of using self-awareness to improve coaching effectiveness is reflection. In the remainder of this section we discuss coach reflection in order to provide a detailed description of intrapersonal knowledge and the role it plays in the development of coaching effectiveness and expertise.

Coach reflection

One of the earliest examinations of reflection with sport coaches is the multiple-case study of experiential learning with model youth sport coaches conducted by Gilbert and Trudel (2001, 2004, 2005). Since their original work, many others have studied and written about reflection in sport coaching. For example, reflection applied to sports coaching has since been described as a type of 'internal learning situation,' 'where there is a reconsideration of existing ideas in the coach's cognitive structure' (Werthner and Trudel 2006: 201). Others have framed coach reflection as a type of informal coach learning situation (Mallett *et al.* 2009; Nelson *et al.* 2006). Actual studies of coach reflection, however, are still somewhat rare (Irwin *et al.* 2004: Jones and Turner 2006; Knowles *et al.* 2006).

Schön's (1983, 1987) theory of reflection specific to the development of knowledge for professional practice in the context of professional activity underlies much of the literature on coach reflection. For Schön, knowledge creation through experience is accomplished by reflecting-in and -on practice dilemmas, referred to as a reflective conversation. These reflective conversations include repeating spirals of appreciation (problem setting), action (experimenting), and re-appreciation (problem setting). Problems of practice are the triggers for these reflective conversations. The problems themselves are bound by the way practitioners view their roles, referred to as a role frame. Role frames, then, are important to understanding reflection because they act as filters through which problems are constructed and strategies are developed.

Support has been found for all aspects of Schön's theory of reflection and evidence-based definitions for three different types of coach reflection are now available. The first type of reflection is referred to as reflection-in-action. When coaches consciously engage in all or some of the components of a reflective conversation while in the midst of the act of coaching (i.e. while an event is occurring during a competition or training session), we refer to this as reflection-in-action. Using the example of a basketball coach, a coach may observe during a competition that the opponent has changed their offensive strategy, and his team has not adjusted to this move resulting in several easy scores by the opponent. While the play continues on the floor, the coach quickly cycles through the reflective conversation experimenting virtually in his mind with one or more potential adjustments (solutions to a newly observed problem). The coach may even test his proposed solution with members of his coaching staff or players on the bench before moving forward in the reflective conversation to actual (real-world) experimentation. Once a strategy has been selected – and vetted through the reflective conversation – the coach calls out to his players on the court to make a defensive adjustment, or the coach may call a time-out to explain the adjustment in more detail. The reflective conversation then continues as the coach observes the results of his experiment. During reflection-in-action the coach may quickly cycle through multiple rounds of this reflective conversation.

The second type of reflection – reflection-on-action – is defined as engaging in a reflective conversation after an event has occurred but while there still is an opportunity for applying potential solutions to resolve the event. Returning to our basketball example, the coach may decide to wait until the following competition to experiment with a different defensive strategy. Depending on a myriad of factors that influence each and every coaching decision (opponent, time left in the game, time of season, team attributes, score, etc.) the coach may postpone the reflective conversation until there is more time to formally engage in the reflective process.

Building off of Schön's work, we would refer to this as waiting until the 'direct action-present' has passed – that is, the time during which a strategy can be applied to resolve the current problem (this particular opponent scoring during this particular competition). However, if the basketball season has not been completed, the 'action-present' is still open because an adjustment to the defensive system made after the game can be applied (and tested) in subsequent games and therefore impact the team success in that present season. The key distinction, then, between reflection-in-action and reflection-on-action is the action-present in which the reflective conversation occurs. Reflection-in-action occurs in the direct action-present whereas reflection-on-action occurs in the indirect action-present.

Lastly, the third type of reflection found with sport coaches is labeled retrospective reflection-on-action. In this type of reflection a reflective conversation is still triggered by a coaching problem, but the conversation occurs long after the event has happened. Suppose our basketball coach does not make any formal adjustments to his defensive system during the season, or even pause to formally reflect on the need to make an adjustment (i.e. does not set the defensive system as a problem). However, in the off-season the coach engages in a post-season review and at that point it is determined that an adjustment is needed in the team's defensive system. The reflective conversation that occurs at this point – long after the direct and indirect action-present have passed – is an example of retrospective reflection-on-action.

Regardless of the outcome of the defensive adjustment (success or failure), and the time at which the reflective conversation occurs (inside or outside the action-present), changes to coaches' procedural knowledge are dependent upon a coach's ability to effectively engage in a reflective conversation. Clearly reflection-in-action will be constrained by time and attentional capacities, and in many situations may simply be impractical. Perhaps reflection-on-action and retrospective reflection-on-action are more practical means for teaching coaches how to develop and improve their intrapersonal knowledge competency. Regardless of the type of reflection, the more 'situated' (Lyle 2010) the reflective conversation is the more likely that the coaching knowledge that is generated will be meaningful for the coach. In other words, using reflection as a conceptual framework for coaches' intrapersonal knowledge reinforces the importance of using real (situated) coaching situations as the source for reflective conversations.

When studying coach reflection, it would be beneficial to clearly identify the type of reflection that is being investigated while also exploring direct links between this reflection and changes in coaches' procedural knowledge and behaviors. It should also be noted here that there is an emerging body of literature related to coaches' intrapersonal knowledge that is using self-monitoring – as opposed to reflection – as a conceptual framework (Cushion 2010; Schempp *et al.* 2007; Schempp *et al.* 2006). As this body of literature develops it will be important to consider how the two conceptual frameworks may be integrated into a single coherent framework for understanding coaches' intrapersonal knowledge. In terms of application to coach education, efforts designed to stimulate growth in coaches' intrapersonal knowledge clearly would benefit from an emphasis on reflection-in- and on-action. Ongoing situated learning experiences (e.g. learning communities, communities of practice) currently being advocated in the coach education literature provide direction for creating a formal infrastructure to support coach reflection and the development of intrapersonal knowledge (Bertram and Gilbert 2011; Culver and Trudel 2008; Gilbert *et al.* 2009).

Summary and future directions

In this chapter we provided descriptions of the conceptual frameworks that underpin the three types of coaches' knowledge: professional knowledge, interpersonal knowledge, and intrapersonal knowledge (Côté and Gilbert 2009). Decision-making frameworks and coaching behaviors research are used to frame our understanding of coaches' professional knowledge. When examining interpersonal knowledge, emotional intelligence is offered as a guiding framework. Lastly, coach reflection – and its relation to growth in coaches' knowledge – is the conceptual framework used to examine intrapersonal knowledge. Although much progress has been made in the quest to understand coaching effectiveness and expertise, we close this chapter with some thoughts on our ability to measure coaches' knowledge, which may serve as productive areas for future research.

We have argued that professional knowledge is exemplified in coach decision-making competencies. Therefore, assessment of coaches' professional knowledge may best be accomplished by having coaches articulate – either in writing or orally – the rationale behind their decisions. These 'decision narratives' can then be used as a platform for self-reflection and/or peer mentoring (Jones *et al.* 2009). When combined with naturalistic behavior observation tools, these decision narratives will provide robust insight into the content and organization of coaches' professional knowledge. Another potential method for measuring coaches' professional knowledge is concept mapping (Novak and Cañas 2008). Although this method may provide accurate and comprehensive portraits of coaches' knowledge, we acknowledge that it may not be practical for widespread use in organizations and countries that oversee thousands of coaches annually.

Suggestions for measuring coaches' interpersonal knowledge include the Coach-Athlete Relationship Questionnaire (CART-Q; Jowett and Ntoumanis 2004), the Mayer-Salovey-Caruso Emotional Intelligence Test (MSCEIT; Mayer *et al.* 2003) and the observation of coach-athlete interactions using state space grid method (Erickson *et al.* 2011). The CART-Q is a brief (11-item) questionnaire that measures the nature of the coach–athlete relationship from the perspectives of both the coach and athlete. The questionnaire is composed of three subscales that break down the coach–athlete relationship into closeness (emotions), commitment (cognitions), and complementarity (behaviors). The MSCEIT is a 141-item test that measures how well people perform tasks and solve emotional problems. The test is consistent with Mayer and Salovey's (1997) definition of emotional intelligence and measures individual abilities to (1) perceive emotions; (2) use emotions; (3) understand emotions; and (4) manage emotions. Finally, an observation method recently introduced into coaching research – the state space grid (SSG) – holds potential to further our understanding of coach–athlete interactions (Erickson *et al.* 2011). The SSG allows researchers to examine the structural, temporal, and sequential elements of coach–athlete interaction patterns and the influence of these interactions on various psychosocial outcomes.

Short of conducting individual interviews with coaches, there appear to be few practical and valid methods for assessing changes in coaches' intrapersonal knowledge. While some have experimented with having coaches keep reflective journals (Knowles *et al.* 2006), adherence to this procedure appears to be problematic once coaches are in the field. One instrument that seems promising and has been used at least once in coaching research (Bertram and Gilbert 2011) is the Self-Reflection and Insight Scale (SRIS; Grant *et al.* 2002). The SRIS is a 20-item self-reporting scale with two subscales: the self-reflection scale and the insight scale. Self-reflection is defined as 'the inspection and evaluation of one's thoughts, feelings, and behavior' (821) and insight is defined as 'the clarity of understanding of one's thoughts, feelings, and behavior' (821). These definitions align well with our conceptualization of coaches' intrapersonal knowledge.

In closing, our understanding of how coaching effectiveness is defined and developed continues to evolve, and the conceptual frameworks presented herein provide direct links from the literature on effectiveness and expertise across domains to sport coaching. Indeed the future of coaching as a legitimate profession, with a well-defined and coherent body of research-based knowledge, is dependent upon this very type of cross-discipline pollination (Duffy *et al.* 2011). We look forward to continued testing and refinement of the integrated definition of coaching effectiveness and its underlying conceptual frameworks.

References

Abraham, A., Collins, D. and Martindale, R. (2006) 'The coaching schematic: Validation through expert coach consensus,' *Journal of Sports Sciences*, 24(6): 549–564.

Becker, A.J. (2009) 'It's not what they do, it's how they do it: Athlete experiences of great coaching,' *International Journal of Sport Science and Coaching*, 4(1): 93–119.

Bertram, R. and Gilbert, W. (2011) 'Learning communities as continuing professional development for sport coaches,' *Journal of Coaching Education*, 4: 40–61.

Bowes, I. and Jones, R.L. (2006) 'Working at the edge of chaos: Understanding coaching as a complex interpersonal system,' *The Sport Psychologist*, 20(2): 235–245.

Caruso, D.R., Mayer, J.D. and Salovey, P. (2002) 'Emotional intelligence and emotional leadership,' in R.E. Riggio and S.E. Murphy (eds) *Multiple Intelligences and Leadership*, Mahway, NJ: Erlbaum.

Cassidy, T., Jones, R. and Potrac, P. (2009) *Understanding Sports Coaching: The Social, Cultural and Pedagogical Foundations of Coaching Practice* (2nd ed.), Abingdon: Routledge.

Chan, J.T. and Mallett, C.J. (2011) 'The value of emotional intelligence for high performance coaching,' *International Journal of Sport Science and Coaching*, 6(3): 315–328.

Côté, J. and Gilbert, W. (2009) 'An integrative definition of coaching effectiveness and expertise,' *International Journal of Sports Science and Coaching*, 4(3): 307–323.

Côté, J., Bruner, M., Erickson, K., Strachan, L. and Fraser-Thomas, J. (2010) 'Athlete development and coaching,' in J. Lyle and C. Cushion (eds) *Sports Coaching: Professionalisation and Practice*, Edinburgh: Churchill Livingstone Elsevier.

Culver, D. and Trudel, P. (2008) 'Clarifying the concept of communities of practice in sport,' *International Journal of Sports Science and Coaching*, 3(1): 1–10

Cushion, C. (2010) 'Coach behaviour,' in J. Lyle and C. Cushion (eds) *Sports Coaching: Professionalisation and Practice*, Edinburgh: Churchill Livingstone Elsevier.

Cushion, C.J., Armour, K. and Jones, R. (2006) 'Locating the coaching process in practice: Models "for" and "of" coaching,' *Physical Education and Sport Pedagogy*, 11(1): 83–99.

Davies, M., Stankov, L. and Roberts, R.D. (1998) 'Emotional intelligence: In search of an elusive construct,' *Journal of Personality and Social Psychology*, 75(4): 989–1015.

Debanne, T. and Fontayne, P. (2009) 'A study of a successful experienced elite handball coach's cognitive processes in competition situations,' *International Journal of Sport Science and Coaching*, 4(1): 1–16.

Duffy, P., Hartley, H., Bales, J., Crespo, M., Dick, F., Vardhan, D., Nordmann, L. and Curado, J. (2011) 'Sport coaching as a "profession": Challenges and future directions,' *International Journal of Coaching Science*, 5(2): 93–123.

Duke, A. and Corlett, J. (1992) 'Factors affecting university women's basketball coaches' timeout decisions,' *Canadian Journal of Sport Sciences*, 17(4): 333–337.

Erickson, K., Côté, J., Hollenstein, T. and Deakin, J. (2011) 'Examining coach-athlete interactions using state space grids: An observational analysis in competitive youth sport,' *Psychology of Sport and Exercise*, 12(6): 645–654.

Gallimore, R. and Tharp, R. (2004) 'What a coach can teach a teacher, 1975–2004: Reflections and reanalysis of John Wooden's teaching practice,' *The Sport Psychologist*, 18(2): 119–137.

Gilbert, W. and Trudel, P. (2006) 'The coach as a reflective practitioner,' in R.L. Jones (ed.) *The Sports Coach as Educator: Re-conceptualising Sports Coaching*, London: Routledge.

Gilbert, W., Gallimore, R. and Trudel, P. (2009) 'A learning community approach to coach development in youth sport,' *Journal of Coaching Education*, 2(2): 1–21.

Gilbert, W.D. and Trudel, P. (2001) 'Learning to coach through experience: Reflection in model youth sport coaches,' *Journal of Teaching in Physical Education*, 21(1): 16–34.

Gilbert, W.D. and Trudel, P. (2004) 'Role of the coach: How model youth team sport coaches frame their roles,' *The Sport Psychologist*, 18(1): 21–43.

Gilbert, W.D. and Trudel, P. (2005) 'Learning to coach through experience: Conditions that influence reflection,' *The Physical Educator*, 62(1): 32–43.

Gilbert, W.D., Trudel, P. and Haughian, L.P. (1999) 'Interactive decision making factors considered by coaches of youth ice hockey during games,' *Journal of Teaching in Physical Education*, 18(3): 290–311.

Grant, A.M., Franklin, J. and Langford, P. (2002) 'The self-reflection and insight scale: A new measure of private self-consciousness,' *Social Behavior and Personality*, 30(8): 821–836.

Goleman, D. (1998) *Working with Emotional Intelligence*, New York: Bantam.

Greenockle, K.M. (2010) 'The new face of leadership: Emotional intelligence,' *Quest*, 62(3): 260–267.

Irwin, G., Hanton, S. and Kerwin, D.G. (2004) 'Reflective practice and the origins of the elite coaching knowledge,' *Reflective Practice*, 5(3): 425–442.

Jones, D.F., Housner, L.D. and Kornspan, A.S. (1995) 'A comparative analysis of expert and novice basketball coaches' practice planning,' *Applied Research in Coaching and Athletics Annual*, 10: 201–227.

Jones, R. (2007) 'Coaching redefined: An everyday pedagogical endeavour,' *Sport, Education and Society*, 12(2): 159–173.

Jones, R.L. and Turner, P. (2006) 'Teaching coaches to coach holistically: can problem-based learning (PBL) help?' *Physical Education and Sport Pedagogy*, 11(2):181–202.

Jones, R.L. and Wallace, M. (2006) 'The coach as "orchestrator": More realistically managing the complex coaching context,' in R.L. Jones (ed.) *The Sports Coach as Educator: Re-conceptualising Sports Coaching*, Abingdon: Routledge.

Jones, R., Bowes, I. and Kingston, K. (2010) 'Complex practice in coaching: Studying the chaotic nature of coach-athlete interactions,' in J. Lyle and C. Cushion (eds) *Sports Coaching: Professionalisation and Practice*, London: Elsevier.

Jones, R.L., Harris, R. and Miles, A. (2009) 'Mentoring in sports coaching: A review of the literature,' *Physical Education and Sport Pedagogy*, 14(3): 267–284.

Jowett, S. (2007) 'Interdependence analysis and the 3+1 C's in the coach-athlete relationship,' in S. Jowett and D. Lavallee (eds) *Social Psychology in Sport*, Champaign, IL: Human Kinetics.

Jowett, S. and Ntoumanis, N. (2004) 'The Coach-Athlete Relationship Questionnaire (CART-Q): Development and initial validation,' *Scandinavian Journal of Medicine and Science in Sports*, 14(4): 245–257.

Knowles, Z., Tyler, G., Gilbourne, D. and Eubank, M. (2006) 'Reflecting on reflection: Exploring the practice of sports coaching graduates,' *Reflective Practice*, 7(2):163–179.

Latimer, A.E., Rench, T.A. and Brackett, M.A. (2007) 'Emotional intelligence: A framework for examining emotions in sport and exercise groups,' in M. Beauchamp and M. Eys (eds) *Group Dynamics in Sport and Exercise Psychology: Contemporary Themes*, New York: Routledge.

Lyle, J. (2010) 'Coaches' decision making: A naturalistic decision making analysis,' in J. Lyle and C. Cushion (eds) *Sports Coaching: Professionalisation and Practice*, Edinburgh: Churchill Livingstone Elsevier.

Lyle, J. and Cushion, C. (2010) 'Narrowing the field: Some key questions about sports coaching,' in J. Lyle and C. Cushion (eds) *Sports Coaching: Professionalisation and Practice*, Edinburgh: Churchill Livingstone Elsevier.

Mallett, C.J., Trudel, P., Lyle, J. and Rynne, S.B. (2009) 'Formal vs. informal coach education,' *International Journal of Sports Science and Coaching*, 4(3): 325–364.

Mayer, J.D. and Salovey, P. (1997) 'What is emotional intelligence?' in P. Salovey and D. Sluyter (eds) *Emotional Development and Emotional Intelligence: Implications for Educators*, New York: Basic Books.

Mayer, J.D., Salovey, P., Caruso, D.R. and Sitarenios, G. (2003) 'Measuring emotional intelligence as a standard intelligence with the MSCEIT V2.0,' *Emotion*, 3(1): 97–105.

Meyer, B.B. and Fletcher, T.B. (2007) 'Emotional intelligence: A theoretical overview and implications for research and professional practice in sport psychology,' *Journal of Applied Sport Psychology*, 19(1): 1–15.

Nash, C. and Collins, D. (2006) 'Tacit knowledge in expert coaching: Science or art?' *Quest*, 58(4): 465–477.

Nelson, L.J., Cushion, C.J. and Potrac, P. (2006) 'Formal, nonformal and informal coach learning: A holistic conceptualisation,' *International Journal of Sports Science and Coaching*, 1(3): 247–259.

Novak, J.D. and Cañas, A.J. (2008) 'The theory underlying concept maps and how to construct and use them, Technical Report IHMC CmapTools 2006-01 Rev 01-2008,' *Florida Institute for Human and Machine Cognition*, available at: http://cmap.ihmc.us/Publications/ResearchPapers/TheoryUnderlyingConceptMaps.pdf.

Rieke, M., Hammermeister, J. and Chase, M. (2008) 'Servant leadership in sport: A new paradigm for effective coach behavior,' *International Journal of Sports Science and Coaching*, 3(2): 226–239.

Saury, J. and Durand, M. (1998) 'Practical knowledge in expert coaches: On-site study of coaching in sailing,' *Research Quarterly for Exercise and Sport*, 69(3): 254–266.

Schempp, P.G. and McCullick, B. (2010) 'Coaches' expertise,' in J. Lyle and C. Cushion (eds) *Sports Coaching: Professionalisation and Practice*, Edinburgh: Churchill Livingstone Elsevier.

Schempp, P.G., McCullick, B., Busch, C., Webster, C. and Mason, I.S. (2006) 'The self-monitoring of expert sport instructors,' *International Journal of Sports Science and Coaching*, 1(1): 25–35.

Schempp, P.G., Webster, C., McCullick, B., Busch, C. and Mason, I.S. (2007) 'How the best get better: An analysis of the self-monitoring strategies used by expert golf instructor,' *Sport, Education and Society*, 12(2): 175–192.

Schön, D.A. (1983) *The Reflective Practitioner: How Professionals Think in Action*, New York: Basic Books.

Schön, D.A. (1987) *Educating the Reflective Practitioner*, San Francisco, CA: Jossey-Bass.

Smith, R.E. and Smoll, F.L. (2007) 'Social-cognitive approach to coaching behaviors,' in S. Jowett and D. Lavallee (eds) *Social Psychology in Sport*, Champaign, IL: Human Kinetics.

Trudel, P. and Gilbert, W.D. (2006) 'Coaching and coach education,' in D. Kirk, M. O'Sullivan and D. McDonald (eds) *Handbook of Physical Education*, London: Sage.

Vickers, B. and Hale, B. (2010) 'Perceptions of self-development throughout the spectrum of football coaching expertise,' *Journal of Coaching Education*, 3: 117–139.

Werthner, P. and Trudel, P. (2006) 'A new theoretical perspective for understanding how coaches learn to coach,' *The Sport Psychologist*, 20(2): 198–212.

13

COACHES AND TALENT IDENTIFICATION

Mette Krogh Christensen

AARHUS UNIVERSITY

Kristoffer Henriksen

UNIVERSITY OF SOUTHERN DENMARK

Introduction

The topic for this chapter is the formation and social construction of the coaches' role in relation to talent identification in sport. When coaches identify talent, they engage in 'the process of recognizing current participants with the potential to excel in a particular sport' (Vaeyens *et al.* 2008, p. 703). This means that talent identification takes place at almost all levels of sport once it is practiced with the aim of development of specific skills, attaining excellence in sport and winning the game. Because sport (in contrast to physical education in schools) essentially is based on competitive values, hierarchical structures and the code of winning and losing (Møller 2003), even eight- to ten-year-old children playing football in the local club can hardly escape the monitoring eye of the coach when they gambol around on the pitch. The coach's way of recognizing, encouraging and praising specific skills in the children is the preliminary part of the talent identification process, because the coach in his/her feedback pays attention to and points out some skills and not others as worth pursuing. In youth elite sport in particular, the role of the coach in the talent identification process is even more imperative. The coach's power to include and exclude athletes by way of exerting talent identification is a deep-seated way of structuring the field of sport. However, in modern sports, and more than ever in high-performance sports, the coach does not identify talents single-handedly. Instead, many coaches seem to measure his/her own holistic and subjective assessments up against the more detailed and objective data generated by sports scientists. This trend raises important questions concerning the 'subjective' coach's trustworthiness, reliability and expert knowledge in talent identification. In this chapter we will present key issues pertaining to coaches' roles in talent identification. The following section will take a closer look at the historical development from craft coaching to scientific measurements in talent identification. The subsequent sections of the chapter will address the interconnection between on the one hand talent identification and on the other hand talent development. Then we consider the ways in which the coach's expertise and practical sense is brought into play when the coach pinpoints the so-called *talents*. This aspect of the coaches' role in talent identification is illustrated by a sociological study on the social construction of talent in football. Finally, we address interdisciplinary research considerations and suggestions for further explorations.

Talent identification: from craftsmanship to science?

From the early days of competitive sports and the Olympic Games, talent identification has been a key area in the craft of coaching (Day 2011). According to Day (2011), Victorian and Edwardian coaches 'identified talent through a form of natural selection with an athlete chosen for further training as a result of competition performance or through subjective assessment by the coach' (p. 180). But appreciation of the 'discerning eye' of the coach and the craft of 'natural' talent identification is vanishing, Day argues, and the fast-growing sector of sports science in the twenty-first century appears to have marginalized the coach's craft skills for the benefit of systematic anthropometrical, physiological and psychological test batteries to determine an athlete's potential strengths and talents. In this process, talent identification has become detached from the actual coaching craft and is now regarded as a 'scientific' decision preceding talent development in order to ensure inclusion of the 'true' talents in talent development programmes. For example, many elite sport coaches and also national sports federations and professional sports clubs (Houlihan and Green 2008) distribute specific elements of their field of work, including the identification of athletes' strengths and talents, to sports science *experts* (e.g. physiologists and psychologists). Similarly, the scouting system is based on a division of labour between an *external talent scout* in a talent identification programme, that is a person or a group of experts who identify talented athletes but is not taking part in the actual coaching of the athletes, and an *internal coach*, that is the person who provides the most appropriate learning environment to realize the potential of the talented athlete and thus develops the athlete.

The intensified division of labour in elite sport seems to mirror another trend, namely the ongoing rivalry between a traditional idea about early recruitment based on time-economic motives and novel insights in mature-age talent identification (Vaeyens *et al.* 2008). On the one hand, some practitioners and researchers argue for identifying ability and traits of talented players at an early stage in order to develop them over a longer period (Ericsson *et al.* 1993). The traditional idea about talent identification is based on a time-economic motive that originates from the assumptions that: (1) international success in senior elite sport is the result of long-term 'linear' careers in one sport discipline; (2) success increases with extended duration of training and competition practice in this sport; and (3) early training onset, early success, early participation and continuation on promotions programmes will stimulate the development process and subsequently correlate positively with long-term success in senior elite sport (Vaeyens *et al.* 2009). In this tradition, the coach would play the role of a 'fortune-teller', that is the predictor of an eight- to nine-year-old child's performance outcome ten to fifteen years from now, and a manager of target-oriented purposeful training of very young athletes. On the other hand, research also points to the fact that precise and objective criteria for talent identification in the very early years of an athlete's career are remarkably difficult to isolate (Morris 2000; Simonton 1999; Durand-Bush and Salmela 1996). Indeed, novel insights in mature-age talent identification (see for example Vaeyens *et al.* 2008, 2009) argue that current studies do not support the underlying assumptions in the traditional idea about talent identification, and that coaches and sport organizations should consider the dynamic and multidimensional nature of sport talent and specialization pathways (Tranckle and Cushion 2006; Côté *et al.* 2009; Storm *et al.* 2012). This line of research shows that objective criteria for talent identification are hard to determine and that the prediction accuracy to identify talent in open-skill sports with a high number of essential performance components is much lower than in closed-skill sports with a low number of essential performance components (Vaeyens *et al.* 2008). For example, a Swedish study on the effectiveness of the strategic talent identification and development system in football showed that the system identified and developed less than 50 per cent of the senior top-level football players in the Swedish league (Peterson 2011). Nevertheless, many national federations and club teams continue to allocate substantial resources to so-called scientific talent identification programmes, and researchers in the field of sports science and medicine still develop new scientific methods to test physiological capacity and cognitive, perceptual and motor skills in the athletes (Ali 2011; Burgess and Naughton 2010; Gee *et al.* 2010).

In this paradoxical scenery of rivalling ideas and labour division in coaching, the coach is confronted with the questions of 'Who takes care of the move from talent identification to talent development?' And 'What is my role?' Consequently, the swing from craft coaching to rationalized and quantitative measurements of 'talent' leaves the coach in a dilemma: Can I trust the sports scientists or should I rely on my gut feeling and experience as a coach? How do I balance explicit information and implicit knowledge? The core of this dilemma is a dwindling belief in the equal credibility of the coach and the sports scientist – occasionally resulting in the coach depicted as the second-best alternative and as an intuitive, emotional and highly subjective person who really ought to rely on scientific and evidence-based knowledge to be trustworthy as a talent identifier (Day 2011). However, more recent research stresses that talent identification and talent development goes (or ought to go) hand in hand, because talent identification is a dynamic process and should provide the opportunity for development in the long term. This movement seem to re-actualize the important role of craft coaching in talent identification. The next section of the chapter will elaborate on this point.

Identification and development – two sides of the same coin?

In practice, many coaches do not distinguish between talent identification and talent development. They are 'just' coaching and this enterprise includes more or less deliberate actions of selecting and de-selecting athletes. Talent identification is interwoven in the daily practices, such as training and competitions. From a holistic and ecological point of view, athletes and coaches are embedded in a particular environment with a particular organizational culture, and this culture largely dictates the selection and socialization of new members (Henriksen *et al.* 2011; Henriksen *et al.* 2010). Based on his investigation of successful athletic talent development environments in Scandinavia, Henriksen (2010, p. 161) suggested a definition of athletic talent as:

> A set of competences and skills developed on the basis of innate potential and of multiyear interactions with the environment – for example training and competitions – as well as the ability to exploit the strengths and compensate for the weaknesses of the environment and to contribute to its development.

This definition stresses the interaction between athlete and environment, and suggests that an important part of talent is the athlete's ability to use the benefits that the environment provides and to compensate for any lack of resources in the environments as well as to contribute positively to the continuing development of the environment. We may add here that these abilities are recognized in the environment as constituting talent (at least partly) and thus become part of a selection. Put plainly, if you do not fit into a specific sport environment's culture, you are slowly marginalized. In order to qualify the rather disjointed theoretical framework in the talent identification research, the French Canadian psychologist Francoys Gagné developed 'The Differentiated Model of Giftedness and Talent' (DMGT) (Gagné 2004), which seem to bridge the gap between talent identification and talent development. The DMGT is a conceptual framework that acknowledges the complexity of the interactions between five components in what we call 'talent': natural abilities (also called giftedness), the developmental process of learning and practising, and the three catalysts: chance, intrapersonal and environmental factors that influence the developmental process. On this background, Vaeyens and colleagues (2008) recommend that talent identification should be carried out as an integrated part of talent development and in careful consideration of (1) biological maturation and its impact on talent evaluation; (2) the athlete's long-term development instead of early (de-)selection; (3) the use of representative 'real-world' tasks in a multidimensional design; and (4) measuring progression instead of performance.

The important contribution of the DMGT model to the appreciation of talent identification is the multifaceted and yet stringent conception of the talent identification process, in which we believe the coach plays a pivotal role in especially the environmental component. However, the DMGT is a very broad theoretical framework and it does not afford an in-depth understanding of the coach–athlete relation – or other important relations for that matter – and developmental processes. In order to shed light on the coach's role in talent identification and development, the general DMGT model does not give any specific guidelines, but it points at the need for the coach to be aware of his/her pivotal role as both identifier and developer in the learning process of the athlete in his/her sport-specific environment. Vaeyens and colleagues implicitly support this assumption by stating that

> the perceived inefficiency and ineffectiveness of current TID [talent identification] models suggest that scientifically based observations should complement intuitive coaches' judgements. In line with this observation, we suggest that objective TID may be best utilized in reinforcing the subjective opinion of coaches.
>
> *(Vaeyens et al. 2008, p. 710)*

These insights seem to imply a straightforward but nevertheless vital point, namely the importance of sport-specific rather than general talent identification models. This also means that craft coaching may experience a renaissance for the reason that the holistic judgement of talent carried out by an experienced sport-specific coach working every day and year by year with talent development presumably is just as reliable as general talent identification models.

The expertise of the coach

Recently, researchers have devoted their attention to contextual factors surrounding talent identification, and these include the community of practice in which the coach is building his/her experience and knowledge. Tranckle and Cushion (2006) summarize the core premise in this line of research when they maintained that 'talent can only be talent and recognized as such where it is valued' (p. 266). For example, Nash and Collins (2006) concluded that the activities of expert coaches (including talent identification) are based on a complex interaction of knowledge and memory of similar situations, honed by years of experience and reflection. Cushion and Jones (2006) showed that the hierarchical relation between coach and player constructs the categorization of ability and traits of players, and they explained that 'good players' displayed 'a habitus similar to that established by the coaches' (p. 152), whereas the 'rejects' (the 'bad' players) deviated from the expectations with regard to football ability and 'attitude' determined by the coach. Following these lines of research, Christensen (2009) suggested that elite football coaches use their 'practical sense' to recognize patterns of movement among the players, and that talent, of which the coaches act as arbiters of taste, is socially configured in elite football. Two weighty reasons point at the importance to develop more insights in the social construction of coaches' expertise in talent identification: (1) the ability of top-level coaches to be able to identify 'true' talent is a highly sought-after quality that ensures clubs or national teams do not lose time, money and prestige by investing in the 'wrong' players, and (2) nowadays talent identification seem to occur at almost all levels of sport when coaches assess athletes and assign value in training and competitions, and this means that the process of identifying qualities in the athletes becomes an integrated part of the coaching culture and the social configuration of the coach-athlete relationship. Insights into the coaches' role in talent identification help us to understand the ways in which coaching practice (Jones *et al.* 2011) is a matter of managing hierarchical positions in the coach-athlete relationship and a pedagogical endeavour (Jones 2007) which includes the coach's more or less deliberate assessment and identification of qualities in the athletes. Coach education programmes may benefit from these insights in order to prepare novice coaches and expert coaches alike for their role in talent identification in different levels of sport.

Talent identification and the practical sense of the coach

The next section of the chapter presents a sociological study illustrating the social construction of the talent identification in football (Christensen 2009). The study serves as a contemporary example of the way 'the discerning eye' (Day 2011) or 'the practical sense' (Bourdieu 1998) of the coach informs as well as constrains the social construction of talent. Hopefully this example will enlighten the to a certain extent disparaging view on the so-called 'intuitive coaches' judgements [and] the subjective opinion of coaches (Vaeyens *et al.* 2008, p. 710) and underpin the growing interest in the coach's role in the social construction of talented athletes. The study took its point of departure in the sociological assumption that the logic of sport (Bourdieu 1990; Møller 2003) is dominated by struggles over partly institutionalized cultural capital in terms of rankings, medals and records, partly embodied cultural capital in terms of sports specific technical, tactical, mental and social skills. The theoretical framework was based on the French sociologist Pierre Bourdieu's concepts of practical sense, taste and classificatory schemes (see Bourdieu 1984, 1990, 1998) applied in analysis of in-depth interviews with eight Danish coaches of national youth football teams. Below we describe the main structures in these coaches' way of identifying football talent.

Practical sense and visual experience

The coaches described their knack for identifying talents as something that originates from intuition – an inner yardstick described by the coaches as 'my gut feeling', 'something I see with my minds' eye', 'my inner self', 'a visual experience'. In other words, they described a *practical sense* that feels right. According to Bourdieu, practical sense is an acquired system of preferences, of principles of vision and division (what is usually called taste), and also a system of durable cognitive structures (which are essentially the product of the internalization of objective structures) and of schemes of action which orient the perception of the situation and the appropriate response.

(Bourdieu 1998, p. 25)

This 'gut feeling' and 'visual experience' did not fit into declarative knowledge. Rather, it was a practical sense reduced to the name of the player. Like the Victorian and Edwardian coaches, for the coaches in this study talent was something that *looked right*. According to Lakoff and Johnson (1999), *seeing* is a primary metaphor for knowledge. Generally, Lakoff and Johnson argued, individuals receive the greatest amount of knowledge through vision and therefore often use the metaphor of 'seeing' as being synonymous with knowledge, understanding or insight. The logic of sight is transferred to the logic of knowledge. Seeing is knowing. Accordingly, when coaches say talent is something they 'got a glimpse of', something experienced 'as a quick flash' and resembling 'a familiar pattern', they have made a subjective judgement of a visual impression and acquired a personal 'visual experience'. The main source of knowledge of these coaches comes from their constant observation of many types of both national and international players. Being able to see talent, however, is not the same as being able to describe it. Yet, the coaches' certainty about their assessment of the qualities they observed in the athletes should be understood as an evaluation that derived from an intuitive response toward the complete picture that is judged by principles of vision and division (Bourdieu 1998). Bourdieu writes in *The Logic of Practice* (1990, p. 160) that the earliest learning experiences, reinforced by all subsequent social experience, tend to shape schemes of perception and appreciation, in a word, *tastes*, which is applied to potential social relations. In the light of this understanding of practice Christensen (2009) concluded that coaches' perception and appreciation of talent, their taste for talent, is applied to the social relations in which they engage. Consequently, the identification of talents is not based on precise evaluations of isolated elements (for example tests or measurements), but builds on a practical sense of visual impressions as a whole. This means that talent identification in this case rests on a multifaceted intuitive knowledge composed of socially constructed images of the perfect player.

The intuitive knowledge was also a source of frustration among these coaches because they felt a lack of an accepted common language in performing their job, which indicates a characteristic and somewhat problematical quality of the coaches' practical sense, namely that this implicit type of knowledge is not necessarily transformed into an acknowledged explicit language accessible to people who do not occupy the privileged position of coach. More likely, practical sense is passed on in apprenticeship-like relations from coach to coach as symbolic capital in terms of images and pattern recognition rather than in words and explicit theoretical categories, and this raises a twofold concern: On the one hand, the coaches consider existing football language blurred and somewhat irrelevant to the core issue in their craft. On the other hand, they are concerned that their practical sense and implicit knowledge are devalued and ignored as being inferior to explicit and what Bourdieu called 'scholastic' (1998, p. 127) knowledge when they have to justify the selection of young talents to players, to colleagues and to management in football.

The twofold concern – practical sense versus theoretical categories, or craft coaching versus science – seems to characterize a central struggle in the field of top-level football, in which the power to identify talent and 'make distinctions between what is good and what is bad' (Bourdieu 1998, p. 8) is imperative to the 'doxa' (Bourdieu 1990) of the field. Cushion and Jones (2006) argued that 'an examination of the discourse surrounding this space of "good player" reveals how doxa, or assumptions, about occupying the space were legitimated and complied with' (p. 152). In other words, the indisputable positions of the coaches as definers and categorizers of talent and consequently as controllers of the construction of symbolic capital in the field sustain the current logic of talent identification. In summary, both the lack of an accepted, shared terminology and the primacy of visual experience and pattern recognition is a part of the doxa in the field of top-level football, and therefore perceived as legitimate by these coaches. In this way, these coaches reproduce and produce 'orthodoxy', that is, the powerful and dominant structures, ways of doing and ways of knowing in this particular field.

A taste for hardworking, dedicated and teachable players

In stressing visual experience as a matter of pattern recognition – the glimpse that is recognized as an entirety – each coach gives expression to an incorporated *classificatory scheme* (Bourdieu 1984) of principles, preferences and cognitive structures that seem to give the coach confidence in the evaluation of what he or she sees and, therefore, in what he or she knows. According to Bourdieu, the classificatory schemes permit agents to 'make distinctions between what is good and what is bad, between what is right and what is wrong, between what is distinguished and what is vulgar' (Bourdieu 1998, p. 8). In this study, the eight coaches were asked the seemingly simple question: 'Taking a concrete example, how would you describe the qualities of a young talented football player?' In this way, Christensen (2009) challenged the coaches' classificatory schemes and thus their image of talent as something that was observable yet considered beyond definition in precise words. However, in their stories and anecdotes, the coaches actually formulated specific principles and preferences with regard to football talent. In this way the coaches' stories revealed a whole range of interrelated categories that the coaches applied in the identification of 'good' and 'bad' players. Not surprisingly, the 'football skills' and the 'personal qualities' of young players comprise the two overall categories in the classificatory schemes of the coaches.

The classification of football skills relates to identification of the observable, immediate performance of skills among different footballers. The coaches differentiated between two categories of football skills: game intelligence and peak competences. The coaches presented these categories of football skills in widely different ways usually in relation to a certain context or with the use of concrete examples. Their construction of categories for skills identification varied widely and were often described using illustrations of specific players closely connected to a concrete context. Moreover, most of the coaches doubted that football skills could be described thoroughly with either the use of words or numbers. The 'true' identification of talent was, according to the coaches, closely related to contextualized practice and thus to more complex and situated football skills. In this way, these coaches echo the notion of the craft coaching (Day 2011) and talent identification based on the coaches' observation of athletes in 'real-world' tasks in a multidimensional design (Vaeyens *et al.* 2008).

Although research (Morris 2000; Williams and Reilly 2000) examining the connection between personality and talent identification indicated essential problems in the use of traits as predictors in talent identification among young athletes, the study showed a very strong link between the coaches' taste for particular psychological qualities and their identification of football talents. According to the coaches, a talented footballer has a 'drive to succeed' and an attitude signalling 'will and perseverance'. The coaches especially like an attitude that reflects the players' 'willingness to learn, to work hard, and to dedicate themselves' to their sport – not just at the regular training sessions but also in their own time. The classificatory schemes of the coaches concerned not only the present make-up of a player but also the player's presumed potential to learn, to practice, and to improve. Bourdieu argued that, 'when the embodied structures and the objective structures are in agreement ... everything seems obvious and goes without saying' (Bourdieu 1998, p. 81). The same logic seem to apply to talent identification in top-level football: when a coach literally sees a player perform the embodied and the objective structures of top-level football in which that coach is socialized, it seems self-evident that the player is talented – and words seem redundant.

The coach as an arbiter of taste

The coaches described the personal qualities of talented football players as attributes that would not necessarily be fully evident in Saturday games. All the coaches emphasized the importance of confirming or denying the first impression of football skills in face-to-face meetings during training and dialogues with the 'athlete behind the skills'. A pivotal outcome of the use of these classificatory schemes is that talent is socially configured to legitimize the coaches as arbiters of taste. The fact that each coach has his or her own style or philosophy seems to be widely accepted not only in top-level football but also in other parts of the sports field (Christensen 2011; Bennie and O'Connor 2010; Côté and Gilbert 2009). This means that these arbiters of taste are assigned the power and the expertise to judge and label observable skills and perhaps less observable personal qualities. The subjective variation in taste among coaches is further confirmation of their power as the ultimate arbiters in top-level football. Consequently, selection and rejection in the process of talent identification seems to be completely random to outsiders. This conclusion, however, ignores the forces and struggles that are present in the field of football and that construct the coaches' taste and their selection and rejection of players. Moreover, coaches who are inscribed in the field of football, and who are assigned the authority to identify talent by the very field they themselves are both constructing and being constructed by, are able to make the distinction.

If this is the case, then talent identification is a self-perpetuating cycle of construction and reconstruction, which means that the sport-specific field might exclude players, coaches and other agents who are regarded as a threat to the orthodox, or dominant, logic and who might challenge the power of the established coaches. A 'closed' field is characterized by an unwillingness to include different viewpoints and, as such, increases the possibility of mistakes. In contrast, a broadly based scouting system, the distribution of specific elements of the coaching craft to other experts and – perhaps even more importantly – an increased influence by sports science could prevent a 'closing' of the field because scouts and coaches would have to exchange views on talented football players in more 'scholastic' (Bourdieu 1998, p. 127) ways and, in so doing, develop explicit categories that arise from their classificatory schemes.

Interdisciplinary research considerations

Talent identification occurs not only in competitive sport but also in educational contexts (Hay and Macdonald 2010; Bailey and Morley 2006; Gagné 2007) where teachers and educators identify and value students' skills and abilities. The emerging lines of research in coaches' roles in talent identification may gain from including insights from research in teachers' and educators' roles in talent identification. For example, in a study investigating the social construction of ability in physical education, Hay and Macdonald (2010) showed that high-ability students were privileged in terms of achievement possibilities while low-ability students were marginalized in terms of access to contexts in which capital may be acquired and/or displayed, resulting in their enduring low-ability identification. The authors concluded that

> The resources a person possesses, and the way they are employed, invested and acquired in and through the embodied dispositions of habitus, are valued in field-specific ways (depending on the constitution of the field), and configure what it means to be able in that field [...] Ability construction was a dynamic process through and of pedagogic relations that had consequences for students' sense of self, potential achievement and learning opportunities.
>
> *(Hay and Macdonald 2010, p. 15–16)*

Considering the detail that the coach's practice is embedded in the field of (competitive) sport whereas the teacher's practice is embedded in the field of education, these conclusions are not unfamiliar to scholars investigating the social construction of talent in sport (Christensen 2009; Potrac *et al.* 2007; Tranckle and Cushion 2006; Cushion and Jones 2006).

Studies on criteria for talent identification in academia may be an eye-opener for sports coaches. On the background of his DMGT model Francoys Gagné (2007) described ten commandments for academic talent development designed to guide professionals responsible for the academic talent development of K-12 students. The first four commandments regards talent identification: (Gagné 2007, pp. 94–102): 'Thou Shalt Distinguish Horizontally' and acknowledge the large diversity of gifts and talents and relate them to specific domains and fields. 'Thou Shalt Discriminate Vertically' and be aware of differences between mildly and exceptionally gifted and talented students. 'Thou Shalt Identify Multicomponently' and include a multitude of criteria in the identification. 'Thou Shalt Select Armsopenly' and expand the selection ration by broadening the definition of relevant target population. In other words, are we about to identify the excellent 0.1 per cent of year group or are we striving to identify a broader group of young prospects, equalling for example 10 per cent of a year group? These questions concern not only sports coaches but all fields of practice dealing with human development and management of talent.

Gagné's work may be inspiring to sports coaches and their sports organizations given that it highlights the many-sided aspects of talent identification and suggests four specific fields of attention (the first four commandments) that are directly applicable to a sports coaching context. Moreover, the work of Gagné underlines the importance of anchoring and explicating the process of talent identification in the specific environment, be it school, sport or other contexts, in which giftedness and talentedness is judged by educators, coaches, talent programme coordinators, parents and others in the 'business' of talent identification.

Major gaps in understanding of talent identification

Team sports (football in particular) seem to dominate the empirical data in this area of research, consequently we still need more insight in the way in which coaches in different sports develop the practical sense they use in talent identification. The growing professionalization of the football field (Roderick 2006) encourages children of ages ten to fourteen years to choose (or more likely, to be chosen) to devote more time and effort to develop their football skills. This means that coaches in the field of senior football figuratively speaking 'inherit' already chosen football players from the field of junior football. Consequently, research is needed that investigates the taste and classificatory schemes of club team coaches who coach these young players. Possibly coaches responsible for younger football players may not have the same classificatory schemes as the coaches in senior top-level football. As arbiters of taste, coaches have significant influence on the future of young players, not only in the field of top-level football but also at lower levels. The globalization of professional football also requires comparative studies of the formation and social construction of the practical sense among coaches from different cultures and nationalities (Holt 2002), as well as what we have called their eye for talent. We need to know more about coach socialization (Erickson *et al.* 2007; Ramos *et al.* 2011; Lemyre *et al.* 2007; Steinfeldt *et al.* 2011) in order to know more about the way in which informal and non-formal sources of development and formal coach education (Nelson *et al.* 2006) prepare the coaches for identifying different qualities in the athletes, for instance gendered qualities (see Steinfeldt *et al.* 2011).

Summary

The historical swings from coaching as craftsmanship to coaching as sports science and back again question the coach's role in talent identification. Emerging lines of research in talent identification in sport provide insights in (1) ways in which talent identification is interwoven in the daily practices of talent development, training and competitions, (2) the coaches' roles as 'arbiters of taste' and (3) the coaches' development and employment of socially constructed categories of 'good' athletes and 'true' talent. We have illustrated the use of a theoretical framework based on the work of Pierre Bourdieu and shown that it might offer insight into the construction of cognitive structures used by coaches and into the ways they exercise their power in identifying talented footballers. In a 'bodily' field such as sport, the Bourdieuian framework seems an appropriate point of departure in the search for new understandings, because it provides a suitable theoretical basis for the exploration of the interrelation between, on the one hand, the pre-eminence of implicit classificatory schemes as tools for distinctions and actions in top-level sport and, on the other hand, the prioritizing of explicit and apparently quantifiable scientific expertise that is to be found in the surrounding society.

References

Ali, A. (2011) Measuring soccer skill performance: A review. *Scandinavian Journal of Medicine and Science in Sports*, 21, 170–183.

Bailey, R. and Morley, D. (2006) Towards a model of talent development in physical education. *Sport, Education and Society*, 11, 211–230.

Bennie, A. and O'Connor, D. (2010) Coaching philosophies: Perceptions from professional cricket, rugby league and rugby union players and coaches in Australia. *International Journal of Sports Science and Coaching*, 5, 309–320.

Bourdieu, P. (1984) *Distinction: A Social Critique of the Judgement of Taste*. London, Melbourne and Henley: Routledge and Kegan Paul.

Bourdieu, P. (1990) *The Logic of Practice*. Cambridge: Polity Press.

Bourdieu, P. (1998) *Practical Reason: On the Theory of Action*. Cambridge: Polity Press.

Burgess, D.J. and Naughton, G.A. (2010) Talent development in adolescent team sports: A review. *International Journal of Sports Physiology and Performance*, 5, 103–116.

Christensen, M.K. (2009) 'An eye for talent': Talent identification and the 'practical sense' of top-level soccer coaches. *Sociology of Sport Journal*, 26, 365–382.

Christensen, M.K. (2011) Exploring biographical learning in elite soccer coaching. *Sport, Education and Society*, DOI:10.1080/13573322.2011.637550.

Côté, J. and Gilbert, W. (2009) An integrative definition of coaching effectiveness and expertise. *International Journal of Sports Science and Coaching*, 4, 307–323.

Côté, J., Lidor, R. and Hackfort, D. (2009) ISSP position stand: To sample or to specialize: Seven postulates about youth sport activities that lead to continued participation and elite performance. *International Journal of Sport and Exercise Psychology*, 9: 9–17

Cushion, C.J. and Jones, R.L. (2006) Power, discourse, and symbolic violence in professional youth soccer: The case of Albion Football Club. *Sociology of Sport Journal*, 23, 142–161.

Day, D. (2011) Craft Coaching and the 'Discerning Eye' of the Coach. *International Journal of Sports Science and Coaching*, 6, 179–196.

Durand-Bush, N. and Salmela, J.H. (1996) Nurture over nature: A new twist to the development of expertise. *AVANTE*, 2, 87–109.

Erickson, K., Côté, J. and Fraser-Thomas, J. (2007) Sport experiences, milestones, and educational activities associated with high-performance coaches' development. *Sport Psychologist*, 21, 302–316.

Ericsson, K.A., Krampe, R.T. and Tesch-Römer, C. (1993) The role of deliberate practice in the acquisition of expert performance. *Psychological Review*, 3, 363–406.

Gagné, F. (2004) Transforming gifts into talents: The DMGT as a developmental theory 1. *High Ability Studies*, 15, 119–147.

Gagné, F. (2007) Ten commandments for academic talent development. *Gifted Child Quarterly*, 51, 93–118.

Gee, C.J., John, C.M. and King, J.F. (2010) Should coaches use personality assessments in the talent identification process? A 15 year predictive study on professional hockey players. *International Journal of Coaching Science*, 4, 25–34.

Hay, P.J. and Macdonald, D. (2010) Evidence for the social construction of ability in physical education. *Sport Education and Society*, 15, 1–18.

Henriksen, K., Stambulova, N. and Roessler, K.K. (2011) Riding the wave of an expert: A successful talent development environment in kayaking. *Sport Psychologist*, 25, 341–362.

Henriksen, K. (2010) *The Ecology of Talent Development in Sport: A Multiple Case Study of Successful Athletic Talent Development Environments in Scandinavia*. Odense: Syddansk Universitet/University of Southern Denmark.

Henriksen, K., Stambulova, N. and Roessler, K.K. (2010) Holistic approach to athletic talent development environments: A successful sailing milieu. *Psychology of Sport and Exercise*, 11, 212–222.

Holt, N.L. (2002) A comparison of the soccer talent development systems in England and Canada. *European Physical Education Review*, 8, 270–285.

Houlihan, B. and Green, M. (2008) *Comparative Elite Sport Development: Systems, Structures and Public Policy*. Oxford: Butterworth-Heinemann.

Jones, R. (2007) Coaching redefined: An everyday pedagogical endeavour. *Sport Education and Society*, 12, 159–173.

Jones, R.L., Potrac, P., Cushion, C.J. and Ronglan, L.T. (2011) *The Sociology of Sports Coaching*. Abingdon and New York: Routledge.

Lakoff, G. and Johnson, M. (1999) *Philosophy in the Flesh: The Embodied Mind and its Challenge to Western Thought*. New York: Basic Books.

Lemyre, F., Trudel, P. and Durand-Bush, N. (2007). How youth-sport coaches learn to coach. *Sport Psychologist*, 21, 191–209.

Møller, V. (2003) What is sport: Outline to a redefinition. In V. Møller and J. Nauright (eds) *The Essence of Sport* (pp. 11–34). Odense: University Press of Southern Denmark.

Morris, T. (2000). Psychological characteristics and talent identification in soccer. *Journal of Sports Sciences*, 18, 715–726.

Nash, C. and Collins, D. (2006) Tacit knowledge in expert coaching: Science or art? *Quest*, 58, 465–477.

Nelson, L.J., Cushion, C.J. and Potrac, P. (2006) Formal, nonformal and informal coach learning: A holistic conceptualisation. *The Coach*, 35, 59–69.

Peterson, T. (2011) *Talangutveckling eller talangavveckling?* SISU Idrottsböcker.

Potrac, P., Jones, R. and Cushion, C.J. (2007) Understanding power and the coach's role in professional English soccer: A preliminary investigation of coach behavior. *Soccer and Society*, 8, 33–49.

Ramos, V., Graca, A.B.D., do Nascimento, J.V. and da Silva, R. (2011) Professional Learning: Representation of youth sports coaches. Four case studies. *Motriz-Revista de Educacao Fisica, 17,* 280–291.

Roderick, M. (2006) *The Work of Professional Football. A Labour of Love?* Abingdon: Routledge.

Simonton, D.K. (1999) Talent and its development: An emergenic and epigenetic model. *Psychological Review, 106,* 435–457.

Steinfeldt, J.A., Foltz, B.D., Mungro, J., Speight, Q.L., Wong, Y.J. and Blumberg, J. (2011) Masculinity socialization in sports: Influence of college football coaches. *Psychology of Men and Masculinity, 12,* 247–259.

Storm, L.K., Henriksen, K. and Christensen, M.K. (2012) Specialization pathways among elite Danish athletes: A look at the developmental model of sport participation from a cultural perspective. *International Journal of Sport Psychology, 43,* 199–222.

Tranckle, P. and Cushion, C.J. (2006) Rethinking giftedness and talent in sport. *Quest, 58,* 265–282.

Vaeyens, R., Lenoir, M., Williams, A.M. and Philippaerts, R.M. (2008) Talent identification and development programmes in sport: Current models and future directions. *Sports Medicine, 38,* 703–714.

Vaeyens, R., Gullich, A., Warr, C.R. and Philippaerts, R. (2009) Talent identification and promotion programmes of Olympic athletes. *Journal of Sports Sciences, 27,* 1367–1380.

Williams, A.M. and Reilly, T. (2000) Talent identification and development in soccer. *Journal of Sports Sciences, 18,* 657–667.

14

HOLISTIC SPORTS COACHING
A critical essay

Tania Cassidy

UNIVERSITY OF OTAGO, DUNEDIN, NEW ZEALAND

Introduction

It has been suggested that claims regarding the 'need to coach holistically' are increasingly being recognized (Jones and Turner 2006: 181). Yet others have claimed that the so-called movement towards a holistic approach to coach education, coaching practice and coaching research is overstated (Lyle 2010). While there is a lack of consensus on this situation, there appears to be some agreement that, in an effort to recognize the complexities of the coaching process, much has been claimed in the name of holistic sports coaching. Recently, I accepted an invitation from the editor of the *International Journal of Sports Science and Coaching* (*IJSSC*) to write a target article on the state of holistic sports coaching (Cassidy 2010a). The 'Coaching Insights' section of the journal, with its target-commentaries-response configuration, provided an opportunity to explore the relationship between holism and sports coaching with colleagues before reworking the ideas and responding to their commentaries. I am indebted to the 18 commentators, as well as the editor of the journal, for their insights and questions, which can be used to further inform the discussions and practices that occur in the name of holistic sports coaching.

A primary objective of this chapter is to stimulate further discussion and reflection on what is meant by holistic sports coaching and coach education. Unlike many other chapters in this handbook this chapter is not a comprehensive research review, rather it is more akin to a critical essay exploring holistic sports coaching by drawing on research and literature. Consequently, this is not a 'one-stop' chapter that prescribes how to create more, or better, holistic coaches or design holistic coach education programmes. The diverse opinions reflected by the commentators in *IJSSC* (2010, volume 5, number 4) illustrates the folly of thinking that we could all have a common interpretation of holistic sports coaching and therefore common needs and desires. Moreover, the commentaries highlighted how interpretations of holism is context and culturally specific.

The chapter is organized into three sections, with the first two sections focusing on some of the discussions that occur around holistic coaching and coach education in the socio-cultural and psycho-social domains respectively. It has been suggested that domains are a useful mechanism for illustrating the set of assumptions and expectations that inform concepts (Lyle and Cushion 2010). Previously Cushion *et al.* (2006) organized their discussion on the models of coaching using the psycho-social and socio-cultural domains and it is these same two domains that are used in this chapter. By organizing the chapter around domains, readers are able to gain insight into the assumptions and expectations that particular research cultures have of holistic sports coaching. The discussion within each of the domains is divided into sub-sections on sports coaching *and* coach education. This organizational structure does not reflect Lyle and Cushion's (2010) description that sports coaching is 'a term for a family of roles and activities' (248) nor the various typologies of coaching which have been produced by Lyle (2002), Trudel and Gilbert (2006) or Trudel *et al.* (2010) that acknowledge the context specificity of the coaching process. While the above work has merit, the rationale for the organizational structure used here is the lack of explicit discussion on holistic coaching generally makes it difficult to discuss holistic coaching specifically in relation to the various typologies. The focus of the third and final section is a discussion of some possible implications humanism and social research has for research and practice of holistic sports coaching and coach education.

Socio-cultural domain: holistic sports coaching and coach education

The study of sports coaching and coach education within the social-cultural domain has emerged, in part, as a response to a desire to understand and explain the complexities of sports coaching and coach education. In broad terms a socio-cultural perspective can be viewed as the '*ways of life that people create as they participate in a group or society*' and 'encompasses all the socially invented ways of thinking, feeling, and acting that emerge as people try to survive, meet their needs, and achieve a sense of meaning and significance in the process' (Coakley *et al.* 2009: 4 italics in the original). Additionally, culture when viewed as 'a way of life', can be interpreted as including the 'manners, dress, language, rituals, norms of behaviour and systems of belief' of a particular group (Jary and Jary 1991: 138). When culture is viewed this way it can help to explain how: different, albeit similar, sporting codes have different cultures (e.g. rugby union and rugby league); cultural differences can exist between apparently similar countries (e.g. Australia and New Zealand); and sports coaching is context as well as domain specific, with the latter possibly also being culturally specific (Lyle and Cushion 2010).

If we accept that an interpretation and enactment of holism is influenced by cultural norms (Tao and Brennan 2003) then it can be assumed that an understanding of what constitutes holistic sports coaching and coach education is also culturally specific, and any discussion of holistic sports coaching and coach education in the research literature is informed by the cultural norms of associated research cultures.

Sports coaching

In the socio-cultural domain two articles are often cited as focusing on holistic sports coaching (Potrac *et al.* 2000; Potrac *et al.* 2002). Despite them being commonly cited, the discussion of holistic sports coaching in these articles is superficial. For example, Potrac *et al.* (2000) only mention holistic once outside of the title, despite the title of the article being 'Towards a holistic understanding of the coaching process'. When holistic is mentioned it is done so in the context of describing the objective of the paper. There was no discussion on how holism was conceptualized in relation to the coaching process. In the latter article, Potrac *et al.* (2002) argued for a fuller understanding of the research being conducted on the 'holistic nature of the coaching practice' (184). They go on to suggest that adopting a mixed-method approach, which they called a 'holistic mode of inquiry', could 'provide a more holistic understanding of the coaching behaviours', which in their case was of an elite English football coach (185).

Other research that has recognized holistic sports coaching has a similarly limited conceptualization of holistic sports coaching. For example, when Poczwardowski *et al.* (2002) explored the athlete–coach relationship and coaching practice they stated that 'a holistic perspective served as an analytical goal' (98), yet there was no clarification as to what was meant by a 'holistic perspective'. Cushion's doctoral study focused on a practice that was described as 'a holistic, interactive and interrelated coaching process' but in the description of the studies (in Cushion *et al.* 2006: 92) there was no clarification as to how holism was conceptualized. A possible consequence of this earlier work not strongly conceptualizing holistic sports coaching is that later work in the area (e.g. Abraham *et al.* 2006; Hughes *et al.* 2009; Malloy and Rossow-Kimball 2007) has done little to further our understanding.

While Lyle (2002) did not describe the conceptualization of the coaching process as holistic, he did describe sports coaching as a 'process, the effect of which is dependent on the integration of the whole being greater than the sum of its parts' (97). This assumption reflects a principle of Aristotelian holism, which has become familiar through the phrase; 'the whole is *more than* the sum of its parts' (Mallett and Rynne 2010: 453, italics added) and has encouraged others to describe his conceptualization of the coaching process as 'a holistic, interdependent and interrelated enterprise' (Cushion *et al.* 2006: 87).

Coach education

Not surprisingly, given the situation described above, the research reported on holistic coach education in the socio-cultural domain also does little to further our understanding of what is meant by holistic coach education. When reporting on an account of a coach education initiative, Jones and Turner (2006) suggested that problem-based learning is a useful approach to adopt when teaching coach education students about coaching holistically. It is difficult to judge the merit of the claim because, despite the authors stating that the students were introduced to the principles of holistic coaching, the principles were not explicitly stated. What is more, the authors claimed that problem-based learning can be used to assist coaches achieve qualities that 'recent research suggest comprise effective, holistic coaching practice' (199). The description of what constitutes holistic practice initially came from a dictionary before being expanded by using Cassidy *et al.* (2004). Yet Cassidy *et al.*'s description of holistic sports coach education was limited due to it being based on little empirical evidence or philosophical arguments. Similarly, the case Jones *et al.* (2009) made for mentoring to be viewed a useful practice to advance holistic pedagogical strategies in coach education was compromised by drawing on Cassidy *et al.*'s narrow interpretation of holistic coach education. So despite much being claimed in the name of holistic sports coaching, it appears that within the socio-cultural domain there are plenty of gaps in our understanding and conceptualization of what is meant by holistic sports coaching and coach education.

Psycho-social domain: holistic sports coaching and coach education

Psychology has been the dominant discipline for exploring human behaviour, with the social aspects of human behaviour being acknowledged from the early twentieth century. In 1950 Erickson proposed an eight-stage model of human development, which acknowledged the importance of biological maturation as well as social environment and subsequently popularized the term psycho-social. Erikson's eight stages of development, one of which is autonomy, continues to inform psychological research as illustrated by Self Determination Theory (SDT), which focuses on social factors that influence motivation (Mallett 2005). More recently, Mallett and Rynne (2010) described the 'organismic social-cognitive theory of SDT' as being 'consistent with assumptions of the holistic approach to coaching' (454). Over time the term psycho-social has also become associated with numerous perspectives, for example humanism, which at times have been described as reflecting a holistic perspective.

Sport coaching

Within the psycho-social domain a range of interpretations exist as to what constitutes holistic coaching. Some interpretations are not explicitly described as holistic which may explain the claim that those working in the psycho-social domain of sports coaching 'rarely use the term "holistic coaching"' (Kamphoff 2010: 481). But as Hamel and Gilbert (2010) pointed out that 'there is considerable amount of literature related to "holistic" coaching here in North America' (485).

Yet some researchers conducting coaching research within the psycho-social domain do explicitly state how they interpret holism. For example, Mallett and Rynne (2010) state '[h]olistic coaching is concerned with the role of the coach in facilitating athlete growth and development (e.g., physical and psycho-social aspects) and SDT research has reported the benefits of such a humanistic approach to coaching beyond performance outcomes' (454–455). While less specific, and more individually orientated, Duchesne *et al.* (2011) declared that their findings illustrated how coaches 'espoused the importance of advancing their players' individual (holistic) growth, in addition to their athletic attributes'. In addition, when Vallee and Bloom (2005) explored how expert coaches of university teams developed successful programmes, they proposed a conceptual model that identified four variables as being key in the holistic development of athletes.

The focus in psychology is on human behaviour, and in social psychology on the importance of the social environment on human behaviour, so it should come as no surprise that the focus is on individual behaviours, variables or attributes of an individual. Given this focus, and the dominance of the psycho-social domain in sports coaching, it is also not surprising that Hamel and Gilbert (2010: 487) claim that 'most coaches in North America are educated from a "parts" perspective' and why Nelson *et al.* 2010: (465) suggested that 'holistic coaching has tended to be presented as an unproblematic and straightforward activity'. Yet the cultural norms in the psycho-social domain may be shifting. For example, Mallett and Rynne (2010) have suggested that the position that the sum of the parts equals the whole contradicts the Aristotelian phrase, 'the whole is *more than* the sum of its parts' which has been described as the 'general principle of holism' (453, italics added). Lyle (2010) went further by saying 'that the whole may not be divisible into its parts' (450). Over a decade ago a colleague and I suggested that a limitation of educating coaches from a 'parts' perspective is that it raises the question as to whether the 'big picture' will be recognized (Rossi and Cassidy 1999). Heke (2005) adapted the life skill development work conducted by Gould and Danish to fit the cultural context of Aotearoa/ New Zealand. He adapted the GOAL and SUPER life skills programmes by utilizing *Kaupapa Māori*, which is an indigenous research approach. Similarly, Hodge *et al.* (1999) adapted life skill programmes by incorporating elements of Hellison's 'Teaching Responsibility through Physical Activity'. As Robinson (2010) pointed out, responsibility is key to the concept of integrity, a concept that has potential for integrating the cognitive, affective and physical domains and therefore potentially contributing to our understanding of what it means to coach holistically.

Some sports coaching literature that is informed by humanism and humanistic psychology is related to holism as a consequence of the humanistic vision being holistic (Aanstoos 2003). Mallett and Rynne (2010) observed that 'SDT research has reported the benefits of such a humanistic approach to coaching beyond performance outcomes' (454–455). Influential in the discussion of humanistic sports coaching has been Lombardo's (1999) description of a 'Humanistic Model of Coaching'. He described the model as being:

> an educational model devoted to the total development of the individual. It is *athlete-centred*, and focused on enhancing the self-awareness, and growth and development (across three domains of learning) of the participant … Athletes are expected to analyse, think and make important decisions. To facilitate the attainment of these outcomes, humanistic coaches ask many questions, require athletes to figure out strategies and the underlying reasons for both motor and team performances.
>
> *(Lombardo 1999: 4–5, italics added)*

The literature that discusses holistic sports coaching, either explicitly or in a related fashion, within the psycho-social domain has limited impact on coach education in the psycho-social domain literature as illustrated below.

Coach education

In the past decade many countries have heavily invested in coach education and although there has been an increase *in* coach education (see Trudel *et al.* 2010 for an overview) there is limited research conducted *on* coach education. The research that has been conducted, and published in English language journals, is primarily located within the psycho-social domain. Trudel *et al.* (2010) identified and reviewed the literature on coach education programmes between 1998–2007. They organized the literature into three categories; small-scale coach education training programmes (n = 4); university-based coach education programmes (n = 4) and; large-scale coach education programmes (n = 6) and attempted to judge the effectiveness of the programmes. A consequence of the limited discussions on coach education and holism, claims are often made that sports coaching programmes and practices need to be more 'interrelated' and 'integrated'. Often this has resulted in coach education policies and programmes identifying an increasing list of 'variables for coaches to address in a sequential and prescribed manner' (Nelson *et al.* 2010: 465). Given the focus on variables it is not surprising that Trudel *et al.* (2010) set out to analyse the effectiveness of the coach education programmes reported in the literature. While there are various interpretations as to what constitutes effective, they concluded that there was no evidence to suggest that any of the published coach education programmes were effective. Not only were none of the programmes deemed effective, none could be considered holistic even though some of the programmes may have had a holistic intent as a consequence of them being implicitly informed by constructivist perspectives, which recognize coaches as active participants in the learning process. This situation was possibly one of the reasons why Trudel *et al.* (2010) suggested it could be generative to look at developing coach education programmes from a human learning approach. They advocated for the work of Jarvis, who they described as adopting a 'holistic and existentialist perspective', which supports looking at the 'whole person learning in life-wide contexts' (145).

While limited work has been published on holistic coach education, even less has explicitly focused on holistic coach education curriculum. Nonetheless, one example of the latter does exist. Cassidy and Kidman (2010) focused on the New Zealand Coach Development Framework (CDF), a policy document that could be viewed as a coach education curriculum. The CDF reflects a humanist orientation with its focus on an ongoing professional development process, being informed by an applied athlete-centred philosophy and emphasizing 'coach learning and development (formally and informally) rather than focusing on coaches gaining qualifications' (320). The CDF was able to develop the way it did because of the context in which it was developed. For example, in New Zealand, unlike countries within the European Union, a coach education curriculum does not have to align with the 'Bologna Process' and the European Credit Systems for Vocational Education and Training (Crespo 2008).

Implications for research and practice of holistic sports coaching and coach education

This section is not designed to be a prescription for how to research or practice holistic sports coaching and coach education. As stated above, the purpose of this chapter is to stimulate discussion and reflection on what is meant by holistic sports coaching and coach education. As I have said elsewhere, while 'certainty may be desirable for some, aiming for such a state has the potential to close down discussion and experimentation' (Cassidy 2010b: 146). Research articles, not book chapters, are the places for claims to be made for or against holistic sports coaching and coach education, drawing on empirical evidence or philosophical argument. Nonetheless, book chapters do provide an opportunity to make observations based on previously published research and literature as well as to make suggestions for future research and practice. In the spirit of opening up the opportunities to cross the domain borders, and encouraging discussion across the domains and contexts, this section is not organized along domain lines, rather it is organized around two perspectives that can be considered as having holistic intent, specifically humanism and social theories and the implications these have for research and practice.

Humanism and social theories: implications for research

When considering the implications for research on holistic sports coaching and coach education it is useful to remember that, even within domains or contexts, there is no one philosophy, and therefore no one interpretation, of holism. Therefore I would question the merits of maintaining strict adherence to domain borders when researching holistic sports coaching and coach education.

It is widely recognized that Carl Rogers and Abraham Maslow are pioneers of contemporary humanistic psychology (Aanstoos 2003) and that a relationship exists between humanism and holism (Cassidy 2010a). Yet, in his later years Maslow began to recognize the limits of his theory of motivational hierarchy, critiquing it as lacking 'empirical support' and lamenting it having become 'grossly simplified and decontextualised' (Jenkins 2009: 9). At that point, Maslow called humanistic psychology a third force psychology and viewed it as 'transitional, a preparation for a still "higher" Fourth Psychology, transpersonal, transhuman, centred in the cosmos, rather than in human needs and interest, going beyond humanness, identity, self-actualization, and the like' (in Jenkins 2009:10).

Maslow's reflective observation has had, and will continue to have, implications for the research of holistic sports coaching and coach education. For example, transpersonal psychology has already received some attention in the sports coaching literature as evidenced by Jenkins' analysis of Timothy Gallwey's 'Inner Game' series (Jenkins 2008) and John Whitmore (Jenkins 2009). Yet, Kretchmar (2010) questions 'why is it so important to transcend psychological humanism'; what values would transpersonal psychology 'generate that are not available from a humanistic approach' and; how would transpersonal psychology 'provide a clearer and less ambiguous notion of holistic coaching' (446).

Others who have reflected on humanist-informed sports coaching have observed that much of the research that occurs in its name lacks substance and verification. To overcome this limitation Lyle (2010) recommends the humanistic model be 'apprised critically in a rather more context-specific and coaching process-specific way' (451). Mallett and Rynne (2010) observed that much of the humanistic informed research has independently examined the voices of the athletes and coaches thereby understating the complexity of the coaching milieu. In the future, they suggest it may be valuable for researchers to conduct research that provides insight into

> the interdependent voices of coaches, athletes and other actors, in a specific coaching context. Examining the subjective experience of all actors within a specific coaching environment, time and place, will provide a more holistic and qualitative account of the context.
>
> *(Mallett and Rynne 2010: 456)*

The suggestions of Mallett and Rynne (2010) provide opportunities for researchers to conduct research that crosses domain borders. Some researchers are already making links with humanism and social theory, work that has potential implications for future research for holistic sports coaching and coach education (Nelson *et al.* 2010). These researchers, some who have previously critiqued the psycho-social theories for not considering 'the complexity, subtlety, and sophistication that this body of literature may be able to offer the field of coaching' (466), are now beginning to critically explore and engage with humanistic theories (Potrac and Marshall 2010). This latter group of authors contend that 'the work of Carl Rogers deserves greater scrutiny than has been evidenced in the coaching literature thus far' (Nelson *et al.* 2010: 466).

Links have also been made between self-actualisation, a concept attributed to Maslow and Rogers (human psychologists), and life politics as described by Giddens (a social theorist) (Cassidy 2010b). Robinson (2010) further highlighted possible connections between self-actualisation and life politics by explaining that life politics may have connections with the virtue of integrity, which may assist in the difficult and problematic work of integrating the cognitive, affective and physical domains of the person. Moreover, Leidl (2010), drawing on the work of Frankl, suggested that life politics, which focuses on an 'ethics of the personal' (Giddens 1990), can benefit coaches by providing them with opportunities to 'address their personal situations in ways that not only advance themselves, but also impact on the players they lead' (461). Yet Denison (2010) cautions us to remember that '[w]hen individuals are conceived of as free agents, "their psychology" is a matter of personal choice, not a social production generated from a range of historical and cultural processes' (490).

Over the past decade researchers, predominantly with backgrounds in sociology and pedagogy, have made cases for using social theories to understand the coaching process (see Jones *et al.* 2004; Jones *et al.* 2010; Cassidy *et al.* 2004; Denison 2007). Despite recognizing the importance of social and cultural practices the work either engages superficially with the concept of holism, as suggested above, or challenges the humanistic assumptions that inform many interpretations of holistic sports coaching and coach education. Denison and colleagues (2007, 2011) have drawn on the work of Foucault, a well-known critic of humanism, to inform their discussion of issues pertinent to coach education, while Shogan (1999, 2006), Johns and Johns (2000), Jones *et al.* (2005) and Lang (2010) have similarly drawn on the work of Foucault to discuss issues that are related to sports coaching and therefore potentially to coach education. However, by drawing on the theories of Foucault theses researchers challenge the assumptions that inform the research conducted in the sports coaching and coach education context in the name of humanism. Markula and Pringle (2006: 27–28) explained that

> Foucault was critical of how humanism acted to position the 'individual' at the centre of [the] research focus and as free, authentic, rational, unitary and fully coherent… He was concerned … with humanism's promotion of the idea of an inner or essential human condition that, irrespective of social context, could seemingly be relied upon for developing further understandings about humans. Yet his greatest concern related to the manner in which humanism had not necessarily acted to free or liberate humans, but had served as a conceptual tool of domination that resulted in more constrained modes of human behaviour

While calls have been loud as to the value of utilizing social theories to understand the complexity of the coaching process, there is limited discussion and research conducted that explicitly link social theories with the concept of holistic sports coaching and coach education. In part this may be as a consequence of the researchers drawing on Foucault's work not agreeing with the mainly humanistic orientation of holism that is adopted in the sports coaching field. However, researchers utilizing other social theories need to be explicit about how the social theories they utilize can inform our understanding of holistic sports coaching and coach education.

Humanism and social theories: implications for practice

Some have contended that a lack of discussion of holistic sports coaching and coach education has implications for what practice would look like. Lyle (2002) specifically looked at the implications humanism could have on coaching practice and in doing so identified a number of associated coaching behaviours. Yet as Mallett and Rynne (2010) pointed out, more often than not, terms and concepts such as holisms are represented as 'being largely philosophical and aspirational' therefore it is 'difficult (if not impossible) to develop more precise definitions' (454) and arguably more precise practices. Often when policies and practices are designed with holistic intent, coaches and coach educators are urged to better integrate the social, cognitive and physical domains and incorporate an increasing list of 'variables for coaches to address in a sequential and prescribed manner' (Nelson *et al.* 2010: 465). Despite the recognized problems and difficulties of these and associated practices, suggestions continue to be made as to how to utilize humanism and social theories to develop holistic sports coaching and coach education.

A decade ago, Lyle (2002) described a humanistic approach to coaching as 'a benchmark for behaviour in participation coaching, and as a comparator for coaching practice in performance sport' (174). In more recent times, he has suggested that while 'a humanism-based belief system has much to offer coaching practice', and many acknowledge that at an intuitive level there is some appeal in coaches being athlete- or player-centred, it 'has become a mantra that no "official" document can be without' (Lyle 2010: 451). Similarly, Nelson *et al.* (2010) called 'athlete-centred' 'a "buzz-word" used by academics, coach educators, and coaching practitioners' (467). Nonetheless, one who has been influential in the discussion of the humanistic coaching practice is Lombardo (1987, 1995, 1999) and Kidman and Lombardo (2010). Yet he has lamented the limited influence holism, as a philosophy, has had on practices conducted in the performance domain and suggested the prevalence of the professional model also restricts the adoption of a holistic/humanistic agenda in the participation domain. Similarly, Kamphoff (2010) suggested that the focus on winning hampers the adoption of a holistic approach in all the domains.

When a humanistic approach informs the understanding of sports coaching, a prevailing view is that individuals should have 'increased personal responsibility for one's personal life' and if they are provided with a 'rational set of values to guide one's choosing' they will 'begin to actively change the society in which they [live]' (Leidl 2010: 460). When such a view is held in a coach education context, the emphasis is on designing learning opportunities that engage the participants in activities 'relevant to their individual circumstances' (Leidl 2010: 460). This is reflected in the suggestion made by Reinboth and Duda (2006) that coaches may satisfy their athletes' basic needs by applying what is referred as the TARGET dimensions to create a task motivational climate, specifically focusing on the Authority, Evaluation and Grouping dimensions. A focus on the individual, in conjunction with the World Health Organization's multi-dimensional definition of health and well-being, which has been used to describe a holistic approach to health, is reflected in suggested practices.

Some have attempted to link social theories with practice (Jones *et al.* 2004) by integrating coaches' discussions of their work with social theory. Even though this work utilizes social theories, it also reflects a limitation identified earlier by Mallett and Rynne (2010) that the voices of the coaches and athletes are often heard independently. Others have used social theories to explore the interdependence of coach, players and administrators with the aim of gaining an understanding of practice, specifically 'what it means to be a professional AFL [Australian Football League] player and how this identity is currently developed and managed' (Kelly and Hickey 2008: 15). They based their study on the assumption

> that what it means to be a *professional footballer* is a product of the negotiations between different individuals and groups about why players should adopt this identity and the forms of work necessary to produce this identity. We assume that identity is multifaceted.
>
> *(ibid., italics in the original)*

Denison (2010) is another who has drawn on social theories when making suggestions as to how to advance the idea of holistic coach education. In doing so he acknowledged the interdependence of coaches and coach educators. Denison suggested that when coach educators encourage coaches 'to re-examine how they coach and what it is they already do', the coach educators could illustrate how the coaches could 'unpack their practices and beliefs', thereby showing how practices have also been 'influenced by dominant discourses – such as humanism and the sport sciences' (490). These suggestions have implications for the practice of holistic sports coaching and coach education because

> until coaches and coach educators acknowledge how power relations have influenced their taken-for-granted assumptions about how to coach and how to educate coaches, respectively, it will be difficult to identify alternatives to challenge

the many dominant discourses that surround sport and coaching and subsequently advance the practice of coaching

(Denison 2010: 490–491)

Summary

It is difficult to summarize a critical essay, particularly one that does not claim to be a 'one-stop shop', in this case on holistic sports coaching and coach education. The purpose of this chapter was to stimulate discussion and reflection on what is meant by holistic sports coaching and coach education. In an effort to do so I proposed that our understanding of holism and therefore holistic sports coaching and coach education is context and culturally specific. To illustrate this, albeit partially, the first half of the chapter was organized along domain lines, specifically socio-cultural and psycho-social domains. But the domain borders are becoming increasingly porous and this also has implications for how we discuss and reflect on what is meant by holistic sports coaching and coach education. Therefore the second half of the chapter was organized around two perspectives, namely humanism and social theories and the implications these have for the research and practice of holistic sports coaching and coach education. While much has been claimed in the name of holistic sports coaching it is my desire that this chapter tempers these claims, but not the holistic intent of coaches and coach educators. If we are going to realize a holistic intent then we as coaches and coach educators have to become more knowledgeable about what it is that we are attempting to do rather than superficially following the latest trend.

References

Aanstoos, C. (2003) 'The relevance of humanistic psychology', *Journal of Humanistic Psychology*, 43(3): 121–132.

Abraham, A., Collins, D. and Martindale, R. (2006) 'The coaching schematic: Validation through expert coach consensus', *Journal of Sports Sciences*, 24(6): 549–564.

Cassidy, T. (2010a) 'Holism in sports coaching: beyond humanistic psychology', *International Journal of Sports Science and Coaching*, 5(4): 439–443.

Cassidy, T. (2010b) 'Understanding the change process: Valuing what it is that coaches do', *International Journal of Sports Science and Coaching*, 5(2): 143–147.

Cassidy, T. and Kidman, L. (2010) 'Initiating a national coaching curriculum: A paradigmatic shift?', *Physical Education and Sport Pedagogy*, 15(3): 307–322.

Cassidy, T., Jones, R. and Potrac, P. (2004) *Understanding Sports Coaching: The Social, Cultural and Pedagogical Foundations of Coaching Practice*, London: Routledge.

Coakley, J., Hallinan, C., Jackson, S. and Mewett, P. (2009) *Sports in Society: Issues and Controversies in Australia and New Zealand*, Sydney: McGraw-Hill.

Crespo, M. (2008) 'The European framework for the recognition of coaching competence and qualifications', paper presented at the International Coaching Conference, Twickenham, 18–20 November.

Cushion, C., Armour, K. and Jones, R.L. (2006) 'Locating the coaching process in practice: models "for" and "of" coaching', *Physical Education Sport Pedagogy*, 11(1): 83–99.

Denison, J. (2007) 'Social theory for coaches: A Foucauldian reading of one athlete's poor performance', *International Journal of Sport Science and Coaching*, 2(4): 369–383.

Denison, J. (2010) 'Holism in sports coaching: beyond humanistic psychology. A commentary', *International Journal of Sports Science and Coaching*, 5(4): 489–491.

Denison, J. and Avner, Z. (2011) 'Positive coaching: Ethical practices for athlete development', *Quest*, 63(2): 209–227.

Duchesne, C., Bloom, G. and Sabiston, C. (2011) 'Intercollegiate coaches' experiences with elite international athletes in an American sport context', *International Journal of Coaching Science*, 5(2): 49–68.

Giddens, A. (1990) *The Consequences of Modernity*, Cambridge: Polity Press.

Hamel, T. and Gilbert, W. (2010) 'Holism in sports coaching: Beyond humanistic psychology – a commentary', *International Journal of Sports Science and Coaching*, 5(4): 485–488.

Heke, J. (2005) 'Hokowhitu: A sport-based programme to improve academic, career, and drug and alcohol awareness in adolescent Mäori', unpublished PhD thesis, University of Otago.

Hodge, K., Cresswell, S., Sherburn, D. and Dugdale, J. (1999) 'Physical activity-based life skills programmes: Part II – example programmes', *Physical Education New Zealand Journal*, 32(2): 12–15.

Hughes, C., Lee, S. and Chesterfield, G. (2009) 'Innovation in sports coaching: The implementation of reflective cards', *Reflective Practice*, 10(3): 367–384.

Jary, D. and Jary, J. (1991) *Collins Dictionary of Sociology*, London: HarperCollins.

Jenkins, S. (2008) 'Zen Buddhism, sport psychology and golf', *Annual Review of Golf Coaching*, 2008: 215–236.

Jenkins, S. (2009) 'The impact of the Inner Game and Sir John Whitmore on coaching', *Annual Review of High Performance Coaching and Consulting*, 2009: 1–21.

Johns, D. and Johns, J. (2000) 'Surveillance, subjectivism and technologies of power: An analysis of the discursive practice of high-performance sport', *International Review for the Sociology of Sport*, 35(2): 219–234.

Jones, R. and Turner, P. (2006) 'Teaching coaches to coach holistically: Can problem-based learning (PBL) help?' *Physical Education and Sport Pedagogy*, 11(2): 181–202.

Jones, R., Armour, K. and Potrac, P. (2004) *Sports Coaching Cultures: From Practice to Theory*, London: Routledge.

Jones, R., Glintmeyer, N. and McKenzie, A. (2005) 'Slim bodies, eating disorders and the coach-athlete relationship: A tale of identity creation and disruption', *International Review for the Sociology of Sport*, 40(3): 377–391.

Jones, R., Harris, R. and Miles, A. (2009) 'Mentoring in sports coaching: A review of the literature', *Physical Education and Sport Pedagogy*, 14(3): 267–284.

Jones, R., Potrac, P., Cushion, C. and Ronglan, L. (eds) (2010) *The Sociology of Sports Coaching*, Abingdon: Routledge.

Kamphoff, C. (2010) 'Holism in sports coaching: Beyond humanistic psychology – a commentary', *International Journal of Sports Science and Coaching*, 5(4): 481–483.

Kelly, P. and Hickey, C. (2008) *The Struggle for the Body, Mind and Soul of AFL Footballers*, Melbourne: Australian Scholarly Publishing.

Kidman, L. and Lombardo, B.J. (2010) *Athlete-centred Coaching: Developing Decision Makers*, 2nd edn, Worcester: IPC Print Resources.

Kretchmar, S. (2010) 'Holism in sports coaching: Beyond humanistic psychology – a commentary', *International Journal of Sports Science and Coaching*, 5(4): 445–447.

Lang, M. (2010) 'Surveillance and conformity in competitive youth swimming', *Sport, Education and Society*, 15(1): 19–37.

Leidl, D. (2010) 'Holism in sports coaching: Beyond humanistic psychology – a commentary', *International Journal of Sports Science and Coaching*, 5(4): 459–462.

Lombardo, B.J. (1987) *The Humanistic Coach: From Theory to Practice*, Springfield, IL: Charles C. Thomas.

Lombardo, B.J. (1995) *The Humanistic Sport Experience: Visions and Realities*, New York: McGraw-Hill.

Lombardo, B.J. (1999) 'Coaching in the 21st century: Issues, concerns and solutions', online, available at: http://physed.otago.ac.nz/sosol/v2i1/v2i1a4.htm (accessed 30 August 2010).

Lyle, J. (2002) *Sports Coaching Concepts. A Framework for Coaches' Behaviour*, London: Routledge.

Lyle, J. (2010) 'Holism in sports coaching: Beyond humanistic psychology – a commentary', *International Journal of Sports Science and Coaching*, 5(4): 449–452.

Lyle, J. and Cushion, C. (2010) 'Conceptual development in sports coaching', in J. Lyle and C. Cushion (eds) *Sports Coaching: Professionalisation and Practice*, London: Elsevier.

Mallett, C. (2005) 'Self-determination theory: A case study of evidence-based coaching', *The Sport Psychologist*, 19(4): 417–429.

Mallett, C. and Rynne, S. (2010) 'Holism in sports coaching: Beyond humanistic psychology – a commentary', *International Journal of Sports Science and Coaching*, 5(4): 453–457.

Malloy, D. and Rossow-Kimball, B. (2007) 'The philosopher-as-therapist: The noble coach and self-awareness', *Quest*, 59(3): 311–322.

Markula, P. and Pringle, R. (2006) *Foucault, Sport and Exercise: Power, Knowledge and Transforming the Self*, Abingdon: Routledge.

Nelson, L., Potrac, P. and Marshall, P. (2010) 'Holism in sports coaching: Beyond humanistic psychology – a commentary', *International Journal of Sports Science and Coaching*, 5(4): 465–468.

Poczwardowski, A., Barott, J. and Peregoy, J. (2002) 'The athlete and coach: Their relationships and its meaning – methodological concerns and research process', *International Journal of Sport Psychology*, 33(1): 98–115.

Potrac, P. and Marshall, P. (2010) 'Arlie Russell Hochschild: The managed heart, feeling rules, and emotional labour – coaching as an emotional endeavour', in R. Jones, P. Potrac, C. Cushion and L.T Ronglan (eds) *The Sociology of Sports Coaching*, Abingdon: Routledge.

Potrac, P., Brewer, C., Jones, R., Armour, K. and Hoff. J. (2000) 'Toward a holistic understanding of the coaching process', *Quest*, 52(2): 186–199.

Potrac, P., Jones, R. and Armour, K. (2002) 'It's about getting respect: The coaching behaviours of a top-level English football coach', *Sport, Education and Society*, 7(2): 183–202.

Reinboth, M. and Duda, J. (2006) 'Perceived motivational climate, need satisfaction and indices of well-being in team sports: A longitudinal perspective', *Psychology of Sport and Exercise*, 7(3): 269–286.

Robinson, S. (2010) 'Holism in sports coaching: Beyond humanistic psychology – a commentary', *International Journal of Sports Science and Coaching*, 5(4): 489–491.

Rossi, T. and Cassidy, T. (1999) 'Knowledgeable teachers in physical education: a view of teachers' knowledge', in C. Hardy and M. Mawer (eds) Learning and Teaching in Physical Education, London: Falmer Press, pp. 188–202.

Shogan, D. (1999) *The Making of High-Performance Athletes: Discipline, Diversity and Ethics*, Toronto: University of Toronto Press.

Shogan, D. (2006) *Sport Ethics in Context*, Toronto: Canadian Scholars' Press Inc.

Tao, J. and Brennan, A. (2003) 'Confucian and liberal ethics for public policy: Holistic or atomistic', *Journal of Social Philosophy*, 34(4): 572–589.

Trudel, P. and Gilbert, W. (2006) 'Coaching and coach education', in D. Kirk, D. Macdonald and M. O'Sullivan (eds) *The Handbook of Physical Education*, London: Sage.

Trudel, P., Gilbert, W. and Werthner, P. (2010) 'Coach education effectiveness', in J. Lyle and C. Cushion (eds) *Sports Coaching: Professionalisation and Practice*, London: Elsevier.

Vallee, C. and Bloom, G. (2005) 'Building a successful university program: key and common elements of expert coaches', *Journal of Applied Sport Psychology*, 17(3): 179–196.

15

QUALITY COACHING BEHAVIOURS

Andrea J. Becker

CALIFORNIA STATE UNIVERSITY, FULLERTON, USA

Introduction

In an attempt to better understand the factors that underlie great coaching, researchers have studied many aspects of the dynamic coaching process (e.g. Gilbert and Trudel 2004). A central theme throughout this body of literature is the focus on coaching behaviours. This is not surprising considering the direct impact that a coach's actions, reactions and interactions can have on athletes' development, performance and life outside of sport (e.g. Becker 2009; Côté *et al.* 1995b; Horn 2008). As a result, coaching behaviours represent one of the most critical components of great coaching.

According to Becker (2009), the impact of any given coaching behaviour is mediated by the content of information being conveyed, the method of delivery and the overall quality of the behaviour. While a number of research studies and book chapters have devoted efforts toward understanding the content of coaches' behaviours (e.g. instruction or praise) and the methods they use to convey that content (e.g. verbal feedback or visual demonstration), the primary goal of this chapter is to shed light on the qualities that appear to make certain behaviours more effective than others. To achieve this goal, over 300 articles were reviewed to identify the qualities that appear to enhance the impact of coaching behaviours on athletes' development and performance. A total of 148 of these articles contained findings that were extracted and categorized. Based on this analysis, seven qualities were identified including: positive, supportive, individualized, fair, appropriate, clear and consistent. A review of the research supporting these seven qualities is provided in the remainder of this chapter.

Quality #1: Positive

The quality of a coaching behaviour is considered to be positive when it provokes desired changes in athletes' behaviours while also protecting or enhancing their psychological states. This is particularly important considering the relationship between athletes' psychological states and performance. More successful athletes, for example, consistently demonstrate higher levels of confidence, mental toughness, concentration and emotional control (e.g. Bois *et al.* 2009; Crust 2007; Moritz *et al.* 2000). A number of studies have explored the impact of coaching behaviours on athletes' psychological states. Some findings suggest that athletes experience positive psychological outcomes such as increased competence and motivation when coaches exhibit behaviours that are instructive, encouraging and supportive (e.g. Amorose and Horn 2000; Côté *et al.* 1995a; Mouratidis *et al.* 2008). The following sub-headings highlight some of the characteristics that appear to be associated with positive coaching behaviours.

Positive coaching behaviours are instructive

While some coaches are naturally inclined to exhibit positive coaching behaviours, others may philosophically disagree or even feel resentment toward those who continually advocate the importance of being positive. Many coaches get tired of hearing the same old message (i.e. you need to be positive) in coaching education forums, and may even adopt the view that positive behaviours are ineffective – particularly when dealing with athletes who are not improving or performing on a level that meets their expectations. They may also perceive positive coaching behaviours as a form of 'babying' athletes rather than developing mental toughness. Unfortunately, these forms of resistance are likely to be due to the misperception that, in order to be positive, coaches must praise their athletes. While praise may serve to enhance athletes' psychological states, coaches do not need to stroke their athletes' egos with compliments such as 'good job' or 'nice play' in order to be positive. This was first emphasized by highly successful collegiate basketball coach, John Wooden, who suggested that being positive meant being instructive (Gallimore and Tharp 2004). Throughout the coaching literature, instructional behaviours are linked to higher levels of athlete satisfaction, competence, motivation and overall performance (e.g. Amorose and Horn 2000; Mouratidis *et al.* 2008).

Positive coaching behaviours focus on strengths and capabilities rather than weaknesses

Athletes may not always realize what they are capable of achieving and as a result, they may be satisfied with levels of effort or performance outcomes that do not exploit their maximum abilities. To avoid mediocrity, however, great coaches provide their athletes with a vision of what they are capable of doing and becoming (Becker 2009; Voight and Carroll 2006). After giving their athletes something to strive for, great coaches then focus their attention on what their athletes *can* do rather than on what they *cannot* do (Wang and Goldfine 2007). Great coaching is not about changing athletes to fit into a mould, but rather moulding athletes to achieve their highest potential. This, in turn, fuels the athletes' confidence and desire to turn their coaches' initial vision for success into a reality (Becker 2009; Jackson *et al.* 2009).

Positive coaching behaviours convey optimism and confidence

Regardless of whether it is focusing on athletes' strengths and capabilities, encouraging them to think positively, or keeping them in the starting line-up after they have made a mistake, great coaches exhibit behaviours that demonstrate confidence in their athletes (e.g. Becker 2009; Jackson *et al.* 2009). This is important because confidence plays a large role in success and, as an athlete, it is easier to believe in yourself when you think and feel that your coach believes in you (e.g. Jackson *et al.* 2009). Great coaches also exude confidence themselves, and express optimism when communicating with their athletes about the possibility of future success (Voight and Carroll 2006). It is evident in their body language, their tone of voice and their choice of words. In the last few seconds of a close basketball game, for example, a great coach is more likely to use sentences that begin with terms such as '*When we...*' and '*We will...*' rather than '*If we...*' and '*Try to...*'. Essentially, they focus on what their athletes can do and how they will do it correctly rather than on what they should try to do (or avoid doing) and what will happen if they do not execute correctly. When coaches look and talk to their athletes in a manner that communicates confidence, the athletes are less likely to question their own abilities or get distracted by doubts about what their coach may or may not be thinking (e.g. Becker 2009; Jackson *et al.* 2009). This makes it easier for athletes to focus their attention on what is most important in the moment – their own play and performance.

Positive coaching behaviours focus on attitude and effort rather than performance results

When participating in sport, most athletes will experience some form of pressure. The pressure that an athlete might feel during a critical moment in a competition could be considered 'natural pressure' because it is inherent to the sport situation. Unfortunately, however, coaches who focus on performance outcomes often place added or unnecessary pressure on their athletes to perform flawlessly or to achieve a specific outcome (e.g. Smith *et al.* 2005). This type of pressure would be considered 'unnatural pressure', and may serve as a mental distraction that inhibits rather than enhances athlete performance. Coaches can avoid placing unnatural pressure on athletes by focusing on their attitude and effort rather than the potential outcome of their performance.

Positive coaching behaviours focus on performance execution rather than results

In addition to promoting pressure, over-emphasizing performance results may also affect how athletes feel about themselves after competitions. With a strong desire to meet their coaches' expectations, athletes are likely to experience more positive emotions after successful outcomes (e.g. pride, sense of accomplishment, worthiness) and more negative emotions after failures (e.g. disappointment, frustration, blame) (Sagar and Stoeber 2009). While emotional reactions are common in sport, they can be particularly problematic when athletes' solely base their perceptions of competence and self-worth on the results they attain. Due to the nature of sport, a flawless execution may not always translate into the desired result. Therefore, it is important for coaches to emphasize the quality of their athletes' performance. This allows athletes, at the very least, to feel good about their effort in times of failure, and may also increase the likelihood that they will evaluate themselves according to aspects of their performance that are within rather than outside their control.

Quality #2: Supportive

In addition to being positive, great coaches exhibit behaviours that show support for their athletes. Supportive behaviours are those that demonstrate encouragement, caring, empathy and understanding (e.g. Bloom *et al.* 1997; Gould *et al.* 2007). This is accomplished when coaches are physically and psychologically 'there for their athletes' both on and off the playing field (e.g. Becker 2009; Voight and Carroll 2006). At any given point in time, an athlete may need an extra push, a positive voice, a different perspective, a shoulder to lean on, or a pat on the back. Regardless of whether it is a performance issue or personal problem, great coaches make themselves available when their athletes need them. By showing how much they care, they create an environment in which their athletes are more likely to feel comfortable being themselves and sharing their thoughts and feelings (e.g. Becker 2009). This is important because it presents coaches with an opportunity to build rapport and develop relationships with their athletes that are based on mutual trust and respect, while also providing coaches with information that may help them respond sensitively and appropriately to their athletes' needs (e.g. Dieffenbach *et al.* 1999; Jowett and Cockerill 2003; Stephenson and Jowett 2009; Wang and Goldfine 2007). Taken together, supportive behaviours serve to strengthen athletes' confidence, motivation and satisfaction; thus, playing a significant role in their physical and psychological development.

Throughout the literature, a number of great coaches have stressed the importance of understanding their athletes. This was exemplified by professional soccer coach Steve Harrison, who emphasized how he must know his athletes as individuals and 'view the world from their perspective if he is to get the best out of them' (Jones *et al.* 2003: 226). While it could be assumed that great coaches are better at understanding and empathizing with their athletes, no research has directly compared the empathetic abilities (i.e. awareness and accuracy) of more and less successful coaches. Unfortunately, however, there is evidence to suggest that many coaches are unaware or incapable of detecting and interpreting their athletes' thoughts and emotions (e.g. Lorimer and Jowett 2009). What is even worse is that there are also coaches who consciously disregard this aspect of the coaching process because they do not care how their athletes feel; they just want them to perform well.

Irrespective of the reason, a lack of understanding or empathy on the part of the coach may lead to behaviours that negatively affect athletes' psychological states and performance (e.g. Jowett 2003; Thelwell *et al.* 2008). In an attempt to provide athletes with the support that they need and to reduce the potential ramifications of empathic ignorance, coaches should make an effort to spend time observing, interacting with and getting to know their athletes (e.g. Lorimer and Jowett 2009, 2010). Once a strong relationship is established, however, coaches should also avoid making the mistake of assuming that they know how their athletes are thinking or feeling in any given moment, as this might also lead to behaviours that are inappropriate or psychologically damaging (Lorimer and Jowett 2010).

The final and perhaps most important aspect of supportive coaching behaviours is that they are unconditional. This means that displays of encouragement, caring, understanding and empathy are genuine, and therefore not dependent upon athletes' behaviours or performance outcomes. When athletes receive unconditional support, it is based on who they are as people and not what they do as players. This allows them to perform in the moment, and focus on winning the next point or next play rather than winning their coaches' affection. As a result, their self-worth is contingent upon their own effort rather than outcomes that may or may not be a direct reflection of their effort such as performance results or their coaches' approval (Bartholomew *et al.* 2009). Thus, it appears that unconditional support also allows athletes to focus on aspects of performance that are within rather than outside of their control.

Quality #3: Individualized

While athletes may possess many of the same personality characteristics (e.g. hard work and determination) and athletic abilities (e.g. speed and coordination) that lead to performance success, all individuals have their own life histories, experiences and perspectives that make them unique. As a result, coaches are often faced with the challenge of leading teams made up of several athletes who possess different goals, communication styles, motivational orientations, levels of commitment and more (e.g. Gould *et al.* 2002; Pensgaard and Roberts 2002). They are also likely to interpret and respond to their coaches' behaviours in different ways (e.g. Amorose and Smith 2003; Breakey *et al.* 2009; Kenow and Williams 1999). When participating in practice, for example, one athlete may interpret a coach's yelling as motivational while another athlete may interpret it as demeaning. Thus, it appears that coaching behaviours are more effective when they are directed toward accommodating each athlete's needs, and this is best achieved through individualized treatment (e.g. Côté and Sedgwick 2003; Gould *et al.* 2002; Jones *et al.* 2003; Jowett and Temson-Katchis 2005).

Throughout the literature, coaches and athletes alike have lauded the importance and the positive effects of providing athletes with individualized treatment – particularly when setting goals and expectations, preparing for competition, giving feedback and motivating effort (e.g. Côté and Sedgwick 2003; Pensgaard and Roberts 2002; Vallée and Bloom 2005; Wang and Goldfine 2007). While some athletes may be motivated to please their coach, others may be motivated out of fear. Within a given team, the most effective motivational strategies will vary from one athlete to another, and the same is true for other coaching behaviours. When coaches exhibit behaviours that are individualized, they send the message that they are not only worthy of attention, but also valued as an important member of the team (e.g. Becker and Wrisberg 2008; Voight and Carroll 2006; Wrisberg 1987). By accommodating athletes' individual needs, coaches can more adequately promote the positive psychological states that ultimately facilitate performance.

While some coaches may emphasize the difficulties associated with being able to recognize, understand and accommodate the various needs of all of their athletes (particularly in larger team settings), great coaches do not appear to use this as an excuse or a barrier to achieving success (e.g. Côté and Sedgwick 2003; Gould *et al.* 2007; Dieffenbach *et al.* 1999; Jones *et al.* 2003; Martindale *et al.* 2007). This was reinforced by current American National Football League (NFL) coach, Pete Carroll, who stated, 'I don't treat everyone exactly the same – I treat each player according to what he needs...' (Voight and Carroll 2006: 327). Ultimately, it appears that you are more likely to get what you want as a coach, when you give your athletes what they need.

Quality #4: Fair

Accommodating athletes' individual needs may mean that coaches treat their athletes differently, but it should not mean that coaches treat their athletes unfairly. While most coaches are likely to view themselves as fair, perceptions of favouritism are rampant among sport teams. It is not uncommon for athletes to feel that their head coach 'plays favourites', and unfortunately, there is evidence to suggest that these perceptions are often true (e.g. Solomon *et al.* 1996; Wilson and Stevens 2007). With a strong desire to meet the objective of winning, many coaches exhibit behaviours solely according to their perceptions of athletes' performance capabilities (e.g. Markland and Martinek 1988; Solomon *et al.* 1998; Solomon *et al.* 1996). More specifically, athletes who are perceived to be more talented or have a greater potential for improvement (i.e. high expectancy athletes) are often treated better than those who are considered to be less capable (i.e. low expectancy athletes) (e.g. Markland and Martinek 1988; Solomon *et al.* 1996).

Exhibiting patterns of unfair treatment toward individuals or groups within teams is problematic for two major reasons. First, it hinders the development and performance of those athletes who are perceived to be less talented, and in the process of doing so, it also has a negative effect on their self-perceptions (e.g. Solomon 2001; Wilson and Stevens 2007). When they realize that they are not receiving the same opportunities as some of their teammates, their feelings of self-worth and competence are likely to suffer. The psychological damage that these athletes experience further inhibits their ability to perform well, which consequently strengthens their coaches' initial beliefs about their lack of potential. The indirect reinforcement that coaches receive through their athletes' performance outcomes unfortunately promotes continued patterns of unfair treatment. This is particularly troubling when it occurs in youth sports because the younger athletes within teams are often at a disadvantage due to maturational issues such as being less physically developed, coordinated or emotionally ready for competition (Haubenstricker and Seefeldt 2002). When these types of age-related differences are not acknowledged, younger athletes are likely to be viewed as less capable, and therefore receive fewer opportunities to participate and develop their athletic abilities than their peers.

The second major reason why unfair treatment is problematic is because it can cause disruptions in team cohesion (e.g. Kamphoff *et al.* 2005; Turman 2003). Even though athletes are not responsible for their coaches' behaviours, perceived inequities may cause feelings of jealousy and resentment among team members. When these types of negative emotions surface (even in mild forms), athletes often get distracted, reduce their efforts, or distance themselves from each other (e.g. Kamphoff *et al.* 2005; Turman 2003). The ultimate consequence of social tension or fractured team dynamics is decreased performance. Thus, it is possible that by exhibiting patterns of differential treatment, coaches may unknowingly be undermining or compromising their own objective of winning.

Fortunately, not all coaches allow their performance expectations to influence the way they treat athletes. This was demonstrated in a recent study that examined the practice behaviours of American Hall of Fame collegiate basketball coach, Pat Summitt (Becker and Wrisberg 2008). During the 2004–05 basketball season, Summitt clearly viewed some of her players as being more talented than others; however, she did not display patterns of differential treatment based on those perceptions. In contrast to the predicted hypotheses, the results of this study revealed no significant differences in the quantity or quality of behaviours that Summitt directed toward her players regardless of their athletic talents (Becker and Wrisberg 2008).

Rather than favouring only the best athletes, it appears that great coaches (like Pat Summitt) make a conscious effort to provide fair amounts of treatment to *all* of their athletes (Becker 2009; Gallimore and Tharp 2004; Segrave and Ciancio 1990; Voight and Carroll 2006). Being fair is not about treating athletes equally, but rather investing a comparable amount of time and energy in each and every one of them so that they feel equally valued (Dieffenbach *et al.* 1999).

Quality #5: Appropriate

Great coaches exhibit the right behaviours at the right time. They know when to be compassionate and when to be tough (Côté and Salmela 1996), and when to intervene and when to stand back (Côté *et al.* 1995a). They know *what, when and how* to behave, and this is likely to be due to their awareness and ability to simultaneously process and adjust to information relevant to the characteristics of their athletes (e.g. ability level or emotional state), the situation (e.g. the nature of the task or whether the performance outcome was successful or unsuccessful) and their own knowledge about how their behaviours will be received and interpreted (e.g. Magill 1994; Markland and Martinek 1988; Tzetzis *et al.* 2008; Wang and Goldfine 2007).

After processing all of the relevant information, the appropriateness of any given coaching behaviour may be an issue of the content (i.e. what the coach is doing or saying), delivery (i.e. the method of communication), timing (i.e. when the coach exhibits the behaviour and for how long), or the quantity of information being conveyed. When coaches are incapable of properly aligning any of these behavioural properties to the characteristics of their athletes and the present situation, their behaviours are likely to be more of a distraction than anything. This was particularly evident in a study that examined female ice hockey players' perceptions of their coach's game speeches (Breakey *et al.* 2009). More specifically, the athletes in this study did not like it when their coach held meetings that were too long, spent too much time talking, gave too much or too little information, or behaved in a manner that was unexpected or uncharacteristic of how the coach typically behaved. Furthermore, the athletes also discussed how they got distracted when they did not agree with what their coach was saying (Breakey *et al.* 2009). When athletes disagree with the content of their coach's communication, the coach is not only going to lose their attention, but also his or her own credibility.

While it is clear that inappropriate coaching behaviours may disrupt athletes' attention and mental preparedness, they may also have a negative impact on other psychological states such as increasing athletes' anxiety levels or decreasing their motivation (e.g. Baker *et al.* 2000; Bartholomew *et al.* 2009; Martin *et al.* 2009).

Quality #6: Clear

At the most basic level, all coaching behaviours involve some form of communication. Even when coaches are not actively engaged with their athletes or trying to communicate a specific message, it is common for athletes (who are typically in search of affirmations regarding their own abilities) to pay close attention to their coaches' behaviours and mannerisms. As a result, coaches must be particularly conscious about what they say and do because even something as simple as raising an eyebrow could send a message that is interpreted in several different ways (e.g. Amorose and Smith 2003; Breakey *et al.* 2009). One of the greatest challenges for coaches, then, is to behave in ways such that the *intent* behind their words and expressions is clearly communicated and accurately interpreted by most (if not all) of their athletes. When coaches exhibit behaviours that are clear, athletes are more likely to have a uniform understanding of what their coach is trying to accomplish (i.e. vision, objectives, standards, expectations), as well as what they need to do as athletes to achieve individual and team success.

Although coaches cannot completely control how their behaviours will be received, there are several strategies that they can implement to enhance the clarity and the likelihood that the intent of their messages will be accurately interpreted. First, they should use language that is straightforward and easy to understand. When giving instructions, in particular, coaches should communicate in a manner that is detail oriented, yet specific and concise (e.g. Becker and Wrisberg 2008; Côté and Sedgwick 2003; Jones *et al.* 2003). Furthermore, they should make an effort to simplify information (e.g. Becker 2009; Pain and Harwood 2008). When teaching complex skills or game strategies, it is important to break technical and tactical information down into parts and augment instructions with examples, analogies, visual demonstrations and other techniques to ensure understanding (e.g. Becker 2009).

Second, coaches should provide their athletes with explanations for their behaviours (Becker 2009; Martindale *et al.* 2007). If a coach suddenly removes an athlete from the starting line-up, for example, it is important for that athlete to understand *why* the coach made that decision. If the athlete has played well and does not understand the coach's decision, then the athlete may think that the coach no longer believes in him or her, which could have a negative impact on the athlete's confidence and subsequent performance.

In addition to decreasing the possibility of miscommunications, providing athletes with explanations (such as the purpose for doing a specific drill or implementing a certain play in a pressure situation) may also serve to enhance athletes' understanding of the strategic, technical and tactical aspects of their sport. This leads into the third strategy, which is asking questions. Once a coach has provided information to athletes, the coach should ask questions to make sure that the intent of the message was processed and interpreted as the coach intended. Asking questions provides athletes with an opportunity to engage their mind in the process of their development, which is likely to promote a greater amount of learning than expecting athletes to obediently take orders without understanding *why*.

Finally, coaches should avoid sending mixed messages. If a coach tells an athlete that it is okay to take a risk in a particular situation, then the coach should not act upset or display negative body language if the athlete makes a mistake while taking that risk. Or, if a coach believes that playing time should be based on hard work, then the coach should not start a talented athlete who does not give 100 percent effort. Coaches are less likely to send mixed messages when they exhibit behaviours and mannerisms that match their words and philosophies. Clarity is best achieved when coaches are consistent, which represents the seventh quality of great coaching behaviours.

Quality #7: Consistent

One of the most significant aspects of the coaching process is having the ability or power to influence athletes to think and behave in ways that will hopefully lead to desired performance outcomes (Jones *et al.* 2002). To do this effectively, however, coaches must have credibility with their athletes. According to the literature, credibility is established when coaches are perceived to be believable and trustworthy (e.g. McCann 2007; Voight and Carroll 2006). While this is sometimes automatically granted to coaches who have a track record of success, most coaches achieve their credibility by demonstrating mastery in their sport, behaving in ways that meet the demands of the situation as well as their athletes' expectations and desires and, perhaps most importantly, being consistent in who they are, what they do and how they do things (e.g. Becker 2009; Martindale *et al.* 2007; Jones *et al.* 2002; Voight and Carroll 2006). Taken together, they establish a coaching persona that must be upheld in order to maintain their ability to influence their athletes' thoughts and behaviours (Jones *et al.* 2002). When coaches display inconsistencies or deviate from their established persona, they risk the possibility of losing their credibility and their athletes' trust and belief in them (Gould *et al.* 2002; Jones *et al.* 2002). When this occurs, athletes are less likely to listen and learn from their coaches, and opportunities for individual development and team success eventually diminish.

Imagine a coach who behaves friendly one day and aloof the next, or calm and positive in practice and then loud and negative during games. These types of extreme shifts or inconsistencies in a coach's attitude and behaviours are not only confusing and frustrating to athletes, but may also detract from the athletes' ability to concentrate (Becker 2009). Instead of focusing on what they need to do to perform well, they expend their mental energy thinking about what their coach is doing or might do next. When athletes are uncertain about what behaviours to expect from their coach, they may also be uncertain about how to behave themselves. As a result, they may also spend time monitoring their own behaviours.

Considering that athletes often adopt the attitudes and behaviours of their coaches, one could assume that inconsistencies on the part of coaches would eventually lead to similar patterns of behaviours among their athletes (e.g. Holt and Dunn 2004; Jackson *et al.* 2009). If coaches want their athletes to perform at their best on a consistent basis, then coaches should demonstrate consistent behaviours themselves.

Coaches are more likely to demonstrate consistent behaviours when they have a strong understanding of who they are and what they value, and make a conscious effort to continually illustrate those qualities when interacting with their athletes (Voight and Carroll 2006). Although many coaches develop their craft through personal experiences and interactions with other coaches, great coaching is not about trying to be like someone or something other than oneself (Sullivan and Nashman 1994; Voight and Carroll 2006). Coaches who know themselves well and let themselves be known to their athletes are more likely to display behaviours and emotions that are real and genuine, and this is what athletes prefer and desire (Becker 2009; Breakey *et al.* 2009). It is part of what makes great coaches seem human in the eyes of their athletes (Becker 2009). Thus, it is important for coaches to use their knowledge and experiences to develop their own system of beliefs and philosophies that will serve to guide their decisions and behaviours.

When coaches are firm in their beliefs and philosophies, they are more likely to be consistent in who they are and what they do because their attitudes and behaviours are a reflection of something that is stable (i.e. their belief system) rather than something that is unstable (i.e. situational variables). Coaches who are not firm in their beliefs and philosophies, on the other hand, are more likely to exhibit behaviours that compromise their established persona, rules or standards of conduct. In a study of youth sport coaches, for example, most coaches emphasized the importance of having fun as one of their primary objectives (McCallister *et al.* 2000). However, when confronted with the possibility of winning, these same coaches appeared to adopt a win-at-all cost attitude, and their behaviours no longer reflected their reported philosophies. What was particularly discouraging was that many of the coaches were not even aware of the discrepancy between their words and actions (McCallister *et al.* 2000).

Whether it is for the sake of winning or obtaining some other type of short-term gain, inconsistent behaviours are a distraction. They send mixed messages to athletes and also make coaches more susceptible to losing their credibility (Jones *et al.* 2002; McCann 2007). This reinforces how important it is for coaches to have a strong understanding of who they are and what they believe, and to continually illustrate those qualities in their attitudes, mannerisms and behaviours (Jones *et al.* 2002; Voight and Carroll 2006).

Conclusion

For the purposes of this chapter, a thorough analysis of the coaching literature was conducted to examine the quality versus quantity of coaching behaviours, and seven qualities were discussed that appear to facilitate athletes' development and performance. While there is no specific formula for effective coaching or a profile for success, perhaps it is possible that great coaches exhibit behaviours that consist of some of these same underlying qualities. Based on this extensive review of the literature, it appears that behaviours are more likely to be effective when they are *positive, supportive, individualized, fair, appropriate, clear* and *consistent*. The manner in which coaches integrate these qualities into their behaviours, however, is part of a dynamic process and may depend on a number of factors that are unique to each coach, their athletes and the given context (Côté and Gilbert 2009; Cushion 2010). While this chapter draws attention to an understudied aspect of coaching behaviours, more research is necessary to test the validity of this proposition and to better understand the seven qualities that were highlighted as well as other qualities that may serve to enhance or detract from coaching greatness.

References

Amorose, A.J. and Horn, T.S. (2000) 'Intrinsic motivation: relationships with collegiate athletes' gender, scholarship status, and perceptions of their coaches' behavior', *Journal of Sport and Exercise Psychology*, 22: 63–84.

Amorose, A.J. and Smith, P.J.K. (2003) 'Feedback as a source of physical competence information: effects of age, experience, and type of feedback', *Journal of Sport and Exercise Psychology*, 25: 341–359.

Baker, J., Côté, J. and Hawes, R. (2000) 'The relationship between coaching behaviours and sport anxiety in athletes', *Journal of Science and Medicine in Sport*, 3: 110–119.

Bartholomew, K.J., Ntoumanis, N. and Thøgersen-Ntoumani, C. (2009) 'A review of controlling motivational strategies from a self-determination theory perspective: implications for sports coaches', *International Review of Sport and Exercise Psychology*, 2: 215–233.

Becker, A.J. (2009) 'It's not what they do, it's how they do it: athlete experiences of great coaching', *International Journal of Sports Science and Coaching*, 4: 93–119.

Becker, A.J. and Wrisberg, C.A. (2008) 'Effective coaching in action: observations of legendary collegiate basketball coach Pat Summitt', *The Sport Psychologist*, 22: 197–211.

Bloom, G.A., Schinke, R.J. and Salmela, J.H. (1997) 'The development of communication skills by elite basketball coaches', *Coaching and Sport Science Journal*, 2: 3–10.

Bois, J.E., Sarrazin, P.G., Southon, J. and Boiché, J.C.S. (2009) 'Psychological characteristics and their relation to performance in professional golfers', *The Sport Psychologist*, 23: 252–270.

Breakey, C., Jones, M., Cunningham, C.T. and Holt, N. (2009) 'Female athletes' perceptions of a coach's speeches', *International Journal of Sports Science and Coaching*, 4: 489–504.

Côté, J. and Gilbert, W.D. (2009) 'An integrative definition of coaching effectiveness and expertise', *International Journal of Sports Science and Coaching*, 4: 307–323.

Côté, J. and Salmela, J.H. (1996) 'The organizational tasks of high performance gymnastics coaches', *The Sport Psychologist*, 10: 247–260.

Côté, J. and Sedgwick, W.A. (2003) 'Effective behaviors of expert rowing coaches: a qualitative investigation of Canadian athletes and coaches', *International Sports Journal*, 7: 62–77.

Côté, J., Salmela, J.H. and Russell, S. (1995a) 'The knowledge of high-performance gymnastic coaches: competition and training considerations', *The Sport Psychologist*, 9: 76–95.

Côté, J., Salmela, J.H., Trudel, P., Baria, A. and Russell, S. (1995b) 'A coaching model: a grounded assessment of expert gymnastic coaches' knowledge', *Journal of Sport and Exercise Psychology*, 17: 1–7.

Crust, L. (2007) 'Mental toughness in sport: a review', *International Journal of Sport and Exercise Psychology*, 5: 270–290.

Cushion, C. (2010) 'Coach behavior', in J. Lyle and C. Cushion (eds) *Sports Coaching: Professionalisation and Practice*, London: Elsevier.

Dieffenbach, K., Gould, D. and Moffett, A. (1999) 'The coach's role in developing champions', *Olympic Coach*, 12(2): 2–4.

Gallimore, R. and Tharp, R. (2004) 'What a coach can teach a teacher, 1975–2004: reflections and reanalysis of John Wooden's teaching practices', *The Sport Psychologist*, 18: 119–137.

Gilbert, W.D. and Trudel, P. (2004) 'Analysis of coaching science research published from 1970–2001', *Research Quarterly for Exercise and Sport*, 75: 388–399.

Gould, D., Collins, K., Lauer, L. and Chung, Y. (2007) 'Coaching life skills through football: a study of award winning high school coaches', *Journal of Applied Sport Psychology*, 19: 16–37.

Gould, D., Dieffenbach, K. and Moffett, A. (2002) 'Psychological characteristics and their development in Olympic champions', *Journal of Applied Sport Psychology*, 14: 172–204.

Haubenstricker, J.L. and Seefeldt, V. (2002) 'The concept of readiness applied to the acquisition of motor skills', in F.L. Smoll and R.E. Smith (eds) *Children and Youth in Sport*, Dubuque, IA: Kendall/Hunt.

Holt, N.L. and Dunn, J.G.H. (2004) 'Toward a grounded theory of the psychosocial competencies and environmental conditions associated with soccer success', *Journal of Applied Sport Psychology*, 16: 199–219.

Horn, T.S. (2008) 'Coaching effectiveness in the sport domain', in T.S. Horn (ed.) *Advances in Sport Psychology*, Champaign, IL: Human Kinetics.

Jackson B., Knapp, P. and Beauchamp, M.R. (2009) 'The coach-athlete relationship: a tripartite efficacy perspective', *The Sport Psychologist*, 23: 203–232.

Jones, R.L., Armour, K.M. and Potrac, P. (2002) 'It's all about getting respect: the coaching behaviors of an expert English soccer coach', *Sport, Education, and Society*, 7: 183–202.

Jones, R.L., Armour, K.M. and Potrac, P. (2003) 'Constructing expert knowledge: a case study of a top-level professional soccer coach', *Sport, Education, and Society*, 8: 213–229.

Jowett, S. (2003) 'When the "honeymoon" is over: a case study of the coach–athlete dyad in crisis', *The Sport Psychologist*, 17: 444–460.

Jowett, S. and Cockerill, I.M. (2003) 'Olympic medalists' perspective of the athlete-coach relationship', *Psychology of Sport and Exercise*, 4: 313–331.

Jowett, S. and Temson-Katchis, M. (2005) 'Social networks in sport: the coach–athlete relationship', *The Sport Psychologist*, 19: 267–287.

Kamphoff, C.S., Gill, D.L. and Huddleston, S. (2005) 'Jealousy in sport: exploring jealousy's relationship to cohesion', *Journal of Applied Sport Psychology*, 4: 290–305.

Kenow, L.J. and Williams, J.M. (1999) 'Coach–athlete compatibility and athletes' perceptions of coaching behaviors', *Journal of Sport Behavior*, 22: 251–259.

Lorimer, R. and Jowett, S. (2009) 'Empathetic accuracy, meta–perspective, and satisfaction in the coach–athlete relationship', *Journal of Applied Sport Psychology*, 21: 201–212.

Lorimer, R. and Jowett, S. (2010) 'The influence of role and gender in the empathic accuracy of coaches and athletes', *Psychology of Sport and Exercise*, 11: 206–211.

Magill, R.A. (1994) 'The influence of augmented feedback on skill learning depends on characteristics of the skill and the learner', *Quest*, 46: 314–327.

Markland, R. and Martinek, T.J. (1988) 'Descriptive analysis of coach augmented feedback given to high school varsity female volleyball players', *Journal of Teaching in Physical Education*, 7: 289–301.

Martin, M.M., Rocca, K.A., Cayanus, J.L. and Weber, K. (2009) 'Relationship between coaches' use of behavior alteration techniques and verbal aggression on athletes' motivation and affect', *Journal of Sport Behavior*, 32: 227–241.

Martindale, R.J., Collins, D. and Abraham, A. (2007) 'Effective talent development: the elite coach perspective in UK sport', *Journal of Applied Sport Psychology*, 19: 187–206.

McCallister, S.G., Blinde, E.M. and Weiss, W.M. (2000) 'Teaching values and implementing philosophies: dilemmas of the youth sport coach', *Physical Educator*, 57: 35–45.

McCann, S. (2007) 'The importance of coaching credibility', *Olympic Coach*, 18: 10–11.

Moritz, S.E., Feltz, D.L., Fahrbach, K.R. and Mack, D.E. (2000) 'The relation of self-efficacy measures to sport performance: a meta-analytic review', *Research Quarterly for Exercise and Sport*, 71: 280–294.

Mouratidis, A., Vansteenkiste, M., Lens, W. and Sideridis, G. (2008) 'The motivating role of positive feedback in sport and physical education: evidence for a motivational model', *Journal of Sport and Exercise Psychology*, 30: 240–268.

Pain, M.A. and Harwood, C.G. (2008) 'The performance environment of the England youth soccer teams: a quantitative investigation', *Journal of Sport Sciences*, 26: 1157–1169.

Pensgaard, A.M. and Roberts, G.C. (2002) 'Elite athletes' experiences of the motivational climate: the coach matters', *Scandinavian Journal of Medicine and Science in Sports*, 12: 54–59.

Sagar, S.S. and Stoeber, J. (2009) 'Perfectionism, fear of failure, and affective responses to success and failure: the central role of fear of experiencing shame and embarrassment', *Journal of Sport and Exercise Psychology*, 31: 602–627.

Segrave, J.O. and Ciancio, C.A. (1990) 'An observational study of a successful Pop Warner football coach', *Journal of Teaching in Physical Education*, 9: 294–306.

Smith, S.L., Fry, M.D., Ethington, C.A. and Li, Y. (2005) 'The effect of female athletes' perceptions of their coaches' behaviors on their perceptions of the motivational climate', *Journal of Applied Sport Psychology*, 17: 170–177.

Solomon, G.B. (2001) 'Performance and personality impression cues as predictors of athletic performance: an extension of expectancy theory', *International Journal of Sport Psychology*, 32: 88–100.

Solomon, G.B., DiMarco, A.M., Ohlson, C.J. and Reece, S.D. (1998) 'Expectations and coaching experience: is more better?', *Journal of Sport Behavior*, 21: 444–455.

Solomon, G.B., Striegel, D.A., Eliot, J.F., Heon, S.N., Maas, J.L. and Wayda, V.K. (1996) 'Self-fulfilling prophecy in college basketball: implications for effective coaching', *Journal of Applied Sport Psychology*, 8: 44–59.

Stephenson, B. and Jowett, S. (2009) 'Factors that influence the development of English youth sport coaches', *International Journal of Coaching Science*, 3: 3–16.

Sullivan, P.A. and Nashman, H. (1994) 'Interviews with United States 1992 Olympic team sport coaches: international implications and comparison opportunities', *Journal of the International Council for Health, Physical Education, Recreation, Sport and Dance*, 31: 30–33.

Thelwell, R.C., Lane, A.M., Weston, N.J.V. and Greenlees, I.A. (2008) 'Examining relationships between emotional intelligence and coaching efficacy', *International Journal of Sport and Exercise Psychology*, 6: 224–235.

Turman, P. (2003) 'Coaches and cohesion: the impact of coaching techniques on team cohesion in the small group sport setting', *Journal of Sport Behavior*, 26: 86–104.

Tzetzis, G., Votsis, E. and Kourtessis, T. (2008) 'The effect of different corrective feedback methods on the outcome and self confidence of young athletes', *Journal of Sports Science and Medicine*, 7: 371–378.

Vallée, C.N. and Bloom, G.A. (2005) 'Building a successful university program: key and common elements of expert coaches', *Journal of Applied Sport Psychology*, 17: 179–196.

Voight, M. and Carroll, P. (2006) 'Applying sport psychology philosophies, principles, and practices onto the gridiron: an interview with USC football coach Pete Carroll', *International Journal of Sports Science and Coaching*, 1: 321–331.

Wilson, M.A. and Stevens, D.E. (2007) 'Great expectations: an examination of the differences between high and low expectancy athletes' perception of coach treatment', *Journal of Sport Behavior*, 30: 358–373.

Wang, J. and Goldfine, B. (2007) 'Coaches' winning psychological strategies for champions', *Asian Journal of Exercise and Sports Science*, 4: 1–6.

Wrisberg, C.A. (1987) 'An interview with Pat Head Summitt', *The Sport Psychologist*, 4: 180–191.

16

COACHING ATHLETES WITH A DISABILITY

Brendan Burkett

UNIVERSITY OF THE SUNSHINE COAST, QUEENSLAND, AUSTRALIA

Introduction

To be an effective coach requires the skill of understanding and communicating with a diverse range of people. The experience gained from coaching special populations, or athletes with a disability, will strengthen the pedagogical and psychological theories used by the coach as this population extends and broadens the fundamental coaching skills. Historically, coaching resources have naturally focused on the larger able-bodied population. Due to the relatively small number of participants, and the subsequent uncertainty on how to effectively communicate with an athlete with a disability, coaching resources in this area are scarce (Webborn 1999). In more recent times, however, knowledge about coaching and coaches within this domain has increased (e.g. Banack *et al.* in press; Cregan *et al.* 2007).

In some cases the guidelines for the specific topic are the same regardless of the group of athletes being considered, for example when coaching the tennis serve the objective is the same; toss the ball up to allow an effective serve (Knudson 2007), or in swimming to increase propulsive forces and reduce the drag forces (Formosa *et al.* 2011). When coaching the athlete with a disability a greater understanding of propulsion and drag topic can be required for a swimmer who has a spinal cord injury as the subsequent 'fixed-hip' contractures for these swimmers will naturally create a greater drag force when moving through the water (Burkett 2011; Rice *et al.* 2011). The same fundamental principles of increasing propulsion, reducing drag resistance, or a combination of both, will apply.

The emerging lines of research for effective coaching require the coach to have a clear vision for where the sport is going, and then to lead the direction of their sport via the coach's innovation, intuition and creativity. This innovation can incorporate a more comprehensive assessment of 'what is happening' in the sport, as this way decisions that specifically relate to the topic will be derived (DePauw 1988; Fulton *et al.* 2010). For effective coaching of athletes with a disability the focus needs to shift to *'what can be done'*, rather than a defeatist attitude of *'that can't be done'* (Harris 2010; Jones and Wilson 2009).

The modern-day coach requires a greater breadth of knowledge in a range of disciplines within their sport. This is most effectively achieved with an interdisciplinary team (McKean and Burkett 2010; Psycharakis and Sanders 2010). Knowledge for a coach is derived from the traditional areas of psychology, motor control, exercise physiology, biomechanics and nutrition. Technology now plays an integral role in society, particularly with the current generation; therefore the ability to communicate and assess a sports performance via technology is paramount (Burkett 2010b; Haake 2009). There has been a tendency in the past to focus only on the performance enhancement aspects of the sport, namely how to make the athlete stronger and faster; however, the health of the athlete is just as important. An athlete who is not physically or mentally healthy will not be able to perform to their potential. To address this complex issue requires collaboration from a multidisciplinary team.

In sum, coaching athletes with a disability has been clouded with a lack of knowledge, and therefore coaching within this domain has been well below the potential. The purpose of this chapter is to address this issue by providing some fundamental principles and practical applications for coaching athletes with a disability.

Organizational structures for people with a disability

When coaching any athlete it is useful to understand the organizational structure of the sport as this knowledge can be essential to understand how decisions within the sport are made, the rules that govern the sport and, most importantly, how to create the best opportunities for the athlete you are coaching. From an international structure the highest form of competition for an athlete with a disability is the Paralympic Games (a multi-sport competition) followed by the World Championships (a sport-specific competition).

The summer and winter Paralympic Games are held every four years, as per the Olympic Games. The Paralympic Games are held approximately three weeks following the Olympic Games and utilize the same venue, village and host city. Paralympic athletes compete in 18 summer sports, 14 of which are the same as Olympic sports. The four sports unique to the Paralympics are goalball, boccia, wheelchair rugby and powerlifting (Burkett 2010a). This multi-disciplinary sporting event enables the athlete to not only compete within their chosen sport, but the coach and athlete can also observe and support athletes competing in other sports and disciplines that they may not usually be exposed to.

Classification for athletes with a disability

As there are specific and unique biological requirements associated with particular physical disabilities, an overview of the classification of disability in Paralympic competition will lend clarity to the subsequent discussion (Tweedy and Vanlandewijck 2011). To provide a fair and equal playing field the competition for athletes with a disability incorporates a classification system (Beckman and Tweedy 2009).

The original classification system was based on a medical model and athletes competed within five classes of disability:

- athletes with an amputation, defined as having at least one major joint in a limb missing (i.e. elbow, wrist, knee, ankle);
- athletes with cerebral palsy, defined as having the cerebellar area of the brain affected, which, through palsy, affects the control of movement;
- athletes with a spinal cord injury or other condition that causes at least a 10 percent loss of function in the lower limbs (e.g. traumatic paraplegia or quadriplegia);
- athletes with a visual impairment (i.e. perception of light or hand movement to a visual acuity between 2/60–6/60 and/or a visual field of > 5 degrees and < 20 degrees); and

- athletes with *les autres*, a French phrase meaning 'the others'; this group comprises athletes who do not fit within one of the other disability groups, but nevertheless have a permanent physical disability (e.g. one femur shorter than the other, resulting in a significant difference in leg length).

The following section describes some of the specific requirements for each of these disability groups.

Athletes with an amputation

The athlete with an upper limb amputation tends to have an increased stroke rate and shorter stroke length, when compared to a fully functional upper limb athlete. For example, when swimming, naturally the athlete with an upper limb amputation will rely more on their ability to kick as this will directly translate into their swimming performance (Fulton *et al*. 2009). So this will require some modification from a coaching perspective. Despite the loss of the upper limb, maintaining musculoskeletal symmetry is paramount and the athlete should be encouraged to use an adapted 'stump-connector' to provide necessary resistance to the amputated limb. This load will then facilitate hypertrophy around the remaining musculature and aim toward developing musculoskeletal symmetry for the athlete. Based on the biomechanics of body roll and developing swimming forces, if unsure the swimmer should breathe on their amputated side as this will enable the intact limb to remain longer underwater and therefore generate propulsive force (Lee *et al*. 2007). From sport science observations the majority of swimmers follow this profile; however, if the swimmer feels more comfortable breathing to the other side this should determine the side of breathing. For locomotor or running activities the athlete with an upper limb amputation will also naturally rely more on their lower limbs to run, but will also obtain a more symmetrical lower limb running gait by maintaining an upper-body counterbalance, that is swinging the opposite upper limb forward at the same time as they swing their lower limb forward. As with all coaching the key is to focus on 'what can be done' and making this work as effectively as possible, rather than focusing on what is missing or not operational.

The athlete with a lower limb amputation should be able to maintain a similar stride rate when running (Nolan and Lees 2007), or in the case of swimming a similar stroke rate and stroke length profile as the able-bodied athlete. The timing and type of swimming kick however may vary (Sanders 2007). Swimmers with a lower limb amputation tend to utilize a 'cross-over' kick, that is to kick down on one side in time with the alternate arm stroke, and then to cross-over and kick on the other side to counter that arm stroke. Some swimmers have utilized the typical one-side only kicking, but this tends to inhibit their longitudinal body roll in the water. The kick rate for the lower limb swimmer is naturally slower than for a two-legged swimmer. There is also a higher than normal issue with shoulder injury for the lower limb amputee. This is attributed to the increased load on the shoulder on the opposite side to the leg amputation, as this shoulder needs to 'skull the water' to maintain balance in the water as well as generating underwater force (Lecrivain *et al*. 2010). As with the swimmer with an upper limb amputation, the lower limb amputee should also be encouraged to use a modified fin to provide the required overload for their residual stump and subsequently develop musculoskeletal symmetry.

Athletes with cerebral palsy

The athlete with cerebral palsy generally has two distinct profiles, which relate directly to the level of severity in the disability. For the athlete with mild cerebral palsy their running or swimming stride/stroke rate will initially be very similar to an able-bodied athlete. That is the stride rate, stride length and overall technique will be consistent but, over a short period of time of around 30 seconds, the technique will deteriorate due to their musculoskeletal disability. This phenomena of a decrease in technique is common in athletes, and is often related to the level of fitness, however for the athlete with mild cerebral palsy the level of fitness is not the critical factor in the change of technique, rather it is the consequence of the disability (Barfield *et al.* 2005). From sport science analysis the mechanism to address this issue is to establish a lower intensity race strategy in the earlier stages of the race (be that running, rowing, cycling, swimming etc.) as this will enable the athlete to counter the effects of fatigue in the later stages of the race.

For the athlete with a more severe level of cerebral palsy the ability to control their technique can become a challenge, and therefore a focus on following a traditional sport-specific movement technique should be reduced. Rather the athlete and coach need to identify a movement profile that the athlete can maintain and explore the propulsion and resistance profile for their specific sport further. The neuromuscular impairment that can be associated with cerebral palsy can also influence mechanics of the sport, particularly as these athletes can fatigue earlier than the able-bodied athletes, and this fatigue can exaggerate any asymmetry between left and right sides (Tweedy and Trost 2005). Similarly the loss of abdominal control and core stability can also affect the technique; this will naturally depend on the location of the spinal lesion.

Temperature regulation is a key issue for athletes with cerebral palsy, in particular the extreme hot or cold environments, as these extremes can instigate uncontrollable muscle spasms or tremors. Sport science analysis has found strategies such as increasing the use of the warm-up in the optimum temperature may be required by the coach so that the time spent in the extreme training (or competition) temperatures are reduced. A similar process for a greater dry-land cool down can also be adopted to address this issue. Finally some athletes with cerebral palsy may be more emotional in a stressful situation, such as competing at the World Championships or Paralympic Games. This is a function of the athlete's disability and knowledge of this can alert the coach and support staff prior to this possible issue becoming a problem.

Athletes with a spinal cord injury

Athletes with a spinal cord injury have two key factors to consider, first to avoid overloading the shoulders of the athlete when training or competing in their sport, as the athlete relies on their shoulders to propel their wheelchair; with a possible shoulder injury their daily mobility will subsequently be impaired. This issue can be addressed by careful monitoring of the athlete's range of movement internally and externally using a regular sport science screening measure (Abel *et al.* 2010). This will enable valuable feedback on the intensity levels for each training session and if some form of cross-training or counter movement is required.

Correct sport science assessment can avoid potential shoulder injury issues, unfortunately the second issue can be more challenging to address. As the swimmer spends the majority of their day in a wheelchair, and when coupled with the low stimulation to the lower limbs, the athletes can develop a 'fixed' contracture at the hips. That is their hip joint will maintain the approximate 90 degree sitting flexion position, regardless of if they are sitting upright in a chair or lying prone or supine in the water. For sports where the athlete is based in their chair this will not be a major issue (such as wheelchair basketball, wheelchair tennis etc.), but in sports where the athlete is required to be out of their chair, such as prone shooting, seated volleyball or swimming this fixed contracture can become an issue (de Groot *et al.* 2007).

In the prone freestyle, breaststroke and butterfly strokes this fixed hip contracture will create an excessive frontal drag profile and significantly affect the swimmer. In the supine backstroke position the upright fixed hip position will exaggerate body roll and further challenge the limited (or lack of) abdominal control the swimmer has. Sport science has assisted this issue by having the swimmer utilizing a 'pull-buoy' when swimming in the prone position. The floatation of the buoy in the water actively encourages extension of the hip joint. This alone will not resolve the situation and the athlete in a wheelchair, regardless of which sport they participate in, should daily extend their hip joint to avoid a more permanent fixed contracture.

Athletes with visual impairment or blindness

Broadly speaking there are no physical differences between an Olympic athlete and an athlete with a visual impairment or blindness; however, the lack of vision can affect the opportunities to take part in training and competition, the ability to learn proper technique and the potential to monitor one's race speed patterns via visual feedback. Disabilities, such as visual impairment or blindness have been found to not influence the race strategy in 100 m swimming races when compared to Olympic swimmers (Daly *et al.* 2009). When comparing Olympic swimmers and swimmers with a visual impairment, within the four clean swimming sections of the 100 m event there were no significant differences in stroke rate. This demonstrates the visually impaired swimmers studied did not require the ability to 'see' the opposition swimmer to perform; rather they employed a suitable race strategy.

Athletes with les autres

Athletes with a permanent physical disability but who do not technically meet the criteria of, say, amputation or spinal cord will be classified as part of the *les autres* group. This includes, but is not limited to persons with short stature, congenital limb deficiencies and acquired conditions impacting on muscle strength, joint movement and limb length. Classes are assigned according to the number of limbs affected or the movement or limb affected (Tweedy 2003). The maximum height for athletes with short stature is 145 cm in height. Otherwise, the minimum criterion is a disability equivalent to amputation through the wrist or ankle, or 15–20 points muscle loss as described in spinal cord injury section. Assessment is based on a combination of height, strength and range of movement specific to each sport. The possible variations within this disability group can be large so it is not possible to provide general coaching guidelines other than to emphasize focusing on what is possible from the athlete and what is required for the specific sport.

Research gaps and future directions

People with a disability often depend on some form of equipment to be able to participate in physical exercise – this is fundamentally different when compared to coaching an able-bodied athlete. Past sport science research has identified significant technical developments in wheelchair design and prostheses. In the endeavour to go higher, faster and longer, athletes have found the standard devices which have been designed for activities of daily living, such as walking, do not match the demands of elite sport and therefore can inhibit their sporting performance (Burkett *et al.* 2003). As such the coach and sport scientist need to be open to new ideas, demonstrated by radical equipment designs such as the J-Leg (for transfemoral throwers), seated throwing chairs (for spinal cord throwers) and running arms (for arm amputee runners) that have revolutionized the way of thinking in sports science and the options available to coaches and athletes (Bruggemann *et al.* 2008). This demand has also driven the need for sport science to move from within the controlled laboratory and into the sporting arena, a reported necessary requirement for the current-day high performance sport (Sarro *et al.* 2010).

For the majority of Paralympic sports the coaches, athletes and scientists take the knowledge and experience from Olympic performances and then apply (sometimes with modification) to the Paralympic sport. For example, in designing the training program for a Paralympic runner, the coach and sport scientist would use the Olympic runner's training regime as the start point (Weyand *et al.* 2009). As with any effective coaching program the adaptation process of the athlete must be carefully monitored; this knowledge will enable the strategy for performance enhancement to be developed.

Similarly to the able-bodied sporting model, each sport has their own sport-specific world championships, which allows for another level of competition to be added to the coach's training calendar. For each sport the international governing body has developed the rules and guidelines for that particular sport, for example in athletics this is the International Association of Athletics Federations (IAAF), or for swimming the International Swimming Federation (FINA). These governing bodies have made some essential modifications to the competition rules for athletes with a disability, and coaches need to be aware of any possible modifications. For example, for swimmers who can only extend one hand out in front (either due to amputation or musculoskeletal impairment) for the finishing stroke in breaststroke the swimmer is allowed a one-handed touch. It would seem obvious to make this rule modification, but unfortunately until this was formally made there were officials who followed the previous rules 'to-the-letter' and disqualified athletes (with one hand) for only doing a one-handed finishing touch.

For any of these rule modifications the essence of the sport and activity must be preserved, so taking the swimming example although the swimmer with one functional arm is allowed a one-handed touch, the other aspects such as keeping their shoulder level must be maintained. Other examples include allowing up to two bounces in wheelchair tennis. This modification is required due to the longer time it can take to turn a wheelchair around and propel this toward the ball, but the essence of the game of hitting the ball clear of the net and within the field of play is the same. As there are specific and unique biological requirements associated with particular physical disabilities (Goosey-Tolfrey *et al.* 2006), it is hoped that this overview of the Paralympic classification system lends clarity to the subsequent discussion on the coaching of athletes with a disability.

What we don't know about coaching athletes with a disability

When coaching we rely on the traditional sub-disciplines of exercise physiology, sports biomechanics, metabolism, psychology, and strength and conditioning to provide feedback on the effectiveness of the coaching session as well as to guide future training sessions. When coaching athletes with a disability these fundamentals are necessary, with some specific modifications, as described in the following sub-sections.

Exercise physiology – aerobic capacity and recovery

As with any coaching session, either for an able-bodied athlete, or one with a disability, the training session is built around creating the desired intensity and duration for that particular training objective. The most common measures of intensity are heart rate and blood lactate. The measurement of lactate production after specific training or competition provides feedback on the level of intensity for that exercise.

Established relationships currently exist between heart rate, blood lactate and the training intensity, or training zone. Using this knowledge the coach and athlete have a scientific measure that their training will result in the desired performance outcome. A commonly accepted sport science measure to quantify aerobic capacity is to use an incremental test set on a descending time. This will enable the relationship between lactate, speed and lactate tolerance (ability to remove lactate from the working systems at specific intensities) to be quantified. Of the limited studies that have been conducted on the effect of exercise on a person with a disability there exists a wide range of variability in the suggested recommendations for exercise (Fulton *et al.* 2010). There are also limitations in following the current methods of analysis. For example to determine oxygen uptake (VO_2) with an Olympic athlete the most common method is to measure oxygen uptakes as the subject runs on a treadmill, or cycles on a cycle ergometer (Goosey-Tolfrey *et al.* 2008). A spinal cord injured athlete, or any athlete that does not have the function of their lower limbs (amputee, cerebral palsy, *les autres*) will not be able to pedal the cycle ergometer. Some research studies have then modified the oxygen uptake test and have the athlete use a hand crank (Valent *et al.* 2008). The reliability of this method of assessment needs further investigation. In addition, those confined to a wheelchair will not fit on a conventional treadmill, and will require a specifically built wide treadmill that can safely accommodate the wheelchair.

The appropriate recovery of an athlete is critical to their performance, particularly when the athlete must recover from a morning heat session before the final that night. Furthermore the seven to nine day demands of a World Championship or Paralympic Games will require that the athlete can suitably recover from an event early in the program and avoid any deterioration in performance as the competition goes on. Using the commonly accepted sport science measures of lactate production and rate of perceived effort (RPE) an appropriate recovery strategy can be developed for each individual athlete. For example in swimming sport scientists have found that rather than employing the standard ~1,000 m swimming cool down for each swimmer, alternative modes of recovery are more effective (Burkett and Mellifont 2008). For example, for the swimmer who has an arm disability (arm amputation or loss of function) they rely predominately on their leg kick for swimming performance. Making this swimmer swim after a race has been found to in fact increase blood lactate levels, rather than reducing them. A more effective form of recovery includes a combination of swimming (~300 m) and walking to stimulate recovery. A similar scenario has been found for the swimmer who utilizes a wheelchair. This swimmer is dependent on their shoulders for both swimming and daily mobility, only using swimming as the form of recovery has also elevated lactate levels. The alternative is a combination of swimming (~300 m) and pushing their wheelchair to stimulate recovery. Further research is required to better understand the appropriate recovery strategies for athletes with a disability.

Sports biomechanics

The same biomechanical principles apply to athletes with a disability, that is to increase propulsion, decrease drag, or a combination of both. When analysing the biomechanics for athletes with a disability there may be some variations on how these net forces are generated. For example, athletes with locomotor disabilities, i.e. amputation, cerebral palsy, spinal cord injury may have a different movement pattern due to their disability (Burkett *et al.* 2010). To use a swimming example further, a swimmer who is a single leg amputee will have a modified balance on the blocks prior to entering the pool. This natural compensation of balance on the blocks and subsequent asymmetry in the water can change the swimming mechanics and may also influence the inter-arm stroke coordination (Seifert *et al.* 2010).

Metabolism and thermal adjustment

The net result of energy intake and expenditure, and the development of 'legal' ergogenic nutritional aids are of particular interest to the Paralympic athlete and coach. With the difference between gold and silver, or bronze and fourth, being as small as 0.35 percent, or 0.01 second, anything that can make a difference to the athletic performance is eagerly sought by the Olympic and Paralympic athlete.

Thermal adjustment is also a very important component of exercise, particularly as the chemical reaction of converting energy intake into muscular activity produces a by-product of heat. The preparation and possible adaptation to the hot and humid environments of the past Athens and Beijing Paralympic Games were major issues for Olympic and Paralympic athletes. As with other applications the initial sport science knowledge develops 'generic' guidelines and principles (Buchholz *et al.* 2003). From this starting point the Paralympic coach and sport scientist will either adopt the same guidelines, or modify this approach to address the unique characteristics of the athlete with a disability. With reference to heat adaptation, the able-bodied athlete dissipates their heat through their limbs and available surface area. For example, the athlete with a spinal cord injury tends to have a reduced lower limb surface area due to the associate muscular atrophy, a similar scenario exists for the amputee who has lost part or all of a limb. This different surface area will naturally influence thermal-regulation.

Furthermore, the modified neuromuscular system for some athletes with cerebral palsy has resulted in heightening their sensitivity to hot and cold climates.

Psychology – mood state and visualization

As with Olympic athletes the Paralympian is confronted with the similar issues of the psychological effects of exercise, the problem of exercise adherence, motivation and the anxiety pre-competition as well as in the middle of the major event. The established process of proactively controlling the athlete's mood state, visualization and pre-competition thought process is of particular importance to the outcome of the sporting performance. In most cases, the Paralympic athlete can apply similar visualization processes as the Olympic athlete, but for some disabilities this is not possible (Malone *et al.* 2001). In using visualization techniques, the athlete often will watch a video of a past performance, usually their best performance, so as to 'visualize' the perfect race. For the athlete with a visual impairment or blindness this is not possible so they need to resort to other techniques such as hearing or to rely on their confidence in the predefined race strategy.

For athletes with cerebral palsy, there are a very small number of athletes that may also have an intellectual disability. This could restrict their ability to use the power of the mind to modify the mood state, concentrate or follow the race plan. Likewise, when using muscle relaxation techniques to bring the athlete into the desired mood state, the common procedure of systematically contracting and relaxing muscle groups within the body to create an overall level of relaxation may need to be modified for the athlete with an amputation. In the case of the athlete with a loss of a limb or a spinal cord injury, there may be limited or no ability to systematically contract and relax. The athlete who has an intellectual disability may have a different response mechanism to the 'burnout, or staleness' that is common in athletes following long periods of training and competition.

Compensatory factors

Equipment such as prostheses and wheelchairs are fundamental in allowing some people with disabilities to carry out the tasks of daily living. Lower limb amputees rely on the technical attributes of their prosthetic limbs to ambulate and the specifications of these components have varied considerably in recent years. Of most importance are the 'not-so-obvious' compensatory factors that can detrimentally influence the athlete (Burkett 2010b). At first glance, the impact of a lower limb amputation seems to be confined to the lower limb. However, the skeletal image of an amputee identifies several compensatory factors, as shown in Figure 16.1. The amputation alters the orientation of the pelvis. As the pelvis is connected to the vertebral column, the change in pelvic angle causes a scoliosis of the spine. The altered orientation of the vertebral column in the cervical region then causes the shoulders to change alignment, as well as the orientation of the skull to be altered. Thus the 'compensatory' mechanisms resulting from the amputation can have far-reaching consequences on the functional ability of the athlete, regardless of their chosen sport. This phenomenon highlights the need to address the activities outside of their daily training and competition to provide the most effective opportunities for the athlete.

Periodization and strength and conditioning

Asymmetry is common in the general population and as expected greater in unilateral sports. Studies investigating 'functional asymmetry' in terms of bilateral hand or leg movements have found asymmetric movement patterns can and do exist and these must be addressed by the coach (Lee *et al.* 2010). This asymmetry is higher for the athlete with an amputation – the task for the coach is to modify this asymmetry for the Paralympic athlete. For instance an imbalance in muscular strength, and hence potential force production, may further influence their sporting performance (Burkett *et al.* 2003; Nolan *et al.* 2003).

The same principles of providing a suitable overload stimulus followed by appropriate recovery apply for the adaptive swimmer when designing the periodization and seasonal training design. As with any athlete careful monitoring is required to ensure the athlete has suitable recovery between training bouts as inappropriate loading can be detrimental for performance (Bennett *et al.* 2009). It should be noted that some athletes with a disability could require a longer recovery period due to the complexity of their musculoskeletal system.

Summary and implications for coaching practice

The key message when coaching special populations is to focus on what can be done, rather than what is not possible. By coaching an athlete with a disability the coach will develop a greater understanding of the fundamental features of their sport, as well as new and novel mechanisms to communicate with the athlete (Satkunskiene *et al.* 2005). These new attributes will further the professional development of the coach, and when integrated with current technologies a more fulfilling coaching career will be attained.

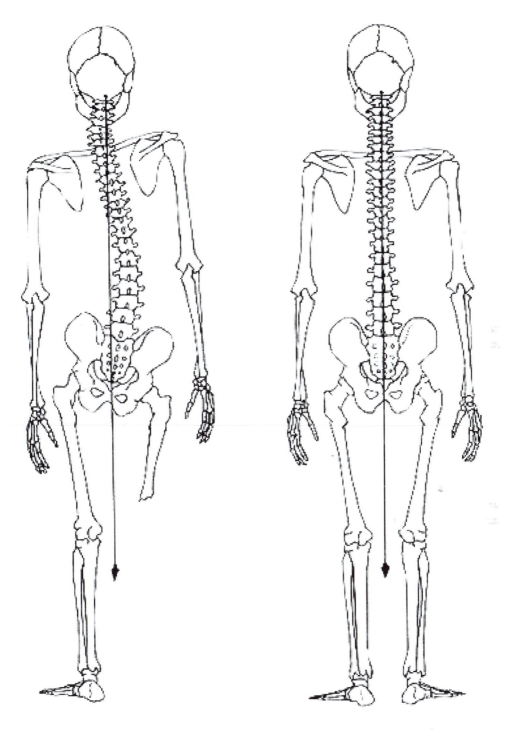

Figure 16.1: Skeletal compensation for athlete with amputation.

An understandable temptation for researchers is to only research 'hot topics' that are more likely to be funded through research grants. As the majority of people with disabilities are aged, research and development has naturally focused on this market. Paralympic athletes have created a new, albeit small market. Not only are these athletes significantly younger than the traditional aged person with a disability, they are also highly active and, as such, place far greater demands on the current established guidelines for coaching. The priority areas for future coaching knowledge are to better understand the adaptation process for people with a disability and to utilize this new knowledge to further enhance sports performance.

In competition athletes may be restricted on the equipment they can use, for example Paralympic swimmers are not allowed to use any equipment other than swimming goggles and cossie, but in their home training environment there is an opportunity for training devices to monitor stroke rates, body roll, or for speed assistance or speed resistance. There are further opportunities to develop disability specific equipment, particularly for the spinal cord athletes and the more severely disabled athletes.

Understanding how and why the human body moves and, importantly, the factors that limit or enhance our capacity to move, are critical to any sporting performance, but especially so for athletes with disabilities. What is also needed is the application of the tremendous technological developments in various spheres of human endeavour (e.g. exploration in space, manufacturing, and medical science) to the challenges faced by Paralympic athletes. The wheel does not need reinventing; rather we need to look at what has been already developed and then determine how to apply this knowledge to the problem at hand. When this lateral thinking approach is applied, the future will really be a better place for Paralympians and all those with disabilities alike.

When considering the market drivers in industries such as the automobile manufacturing industry, most of the technological developments and improvements in design that we all enjoy in the family car have originated in the sport of motor racing. A similar scenario can be applied to the future development of assistive technology, with active Paralympic athletes testing the devices under extreme conditions before mass production for the larger rehabilitation market. This new market demand, in the long term, will result in a better understanding of the relationship between human biology, the biomedical aspects of disability, the activities to be performed and the biomechanics of the assistive devices. However there is still some way to go, as currently the market demand for adaptive technology is overwhelmingly biased towards an aged population.

At both the Olympics and the Paralympics, authorities must fundamentally strive to provide an even playing field, which includes ensuring equity of access to technology. Developed countries have access to both the materials and the knowledge behind the technology and therefore can modify the technology to meet their specific requirements. However, the situation is more problematic for athletes in developing countries. Future technological developments will have far reaching effects on Paralympic athletes: their new assistive anatomy with its higher level of functionality will lead not only to improved efficiency in performing daily tasks, but will also enable more effective performance in the competition arena. If the guidelines on the use of novel technology are too restrictive, this will stifle future progress in technological development; alternatively, in a free-for-all environment, providing an even playing field for all will be a challenge.

One solution could be the development of two 'categories' of competition in those sports that rely on technology. In the first category, the characteristics of the assistive devices in terms of mass, length, etc. would be specified, as in Olympic rowing or cycling, thus providing an even playing field in terms of technology. To facilitate future research, the second category of competition would contain no restrictions or specifications for assistive devices, and would allow the athletes and sport medicine professionals to creatively explore technological options. This scenario may place extra strain on the already crowded competition program at the Paralympics, but is worthy of future consideration.

References

Abel, T., Burkett, B., Schneider, S., Lindschulten, R. and Struder, H.K (2010) 'The exercise profile of an ultra-long handcycling race: the Styrkeproven experience', *Spinal Cord*, 48: 894–898.

Banack, H., Sabiston, C. and Bloom. G. (in press) 'Intrinsic motivation and Paralympic Sport', *Research Quarterly for Exercise and Sport*.

Barfield, J.P., Malone, L.A., Collins, J.M. and Ruble, S.B. (2005) 'Disability type influences heart rate response during power wheelchair sport', *Medicine and Science in Sports and Exercise*, 37: 718–723.

Beckman, E.M. and Tweedy, S.M. (2009) 'Towards evidence-based classification in Paralympic athletics: evaluating the validity of activity limitation tests for use in classification of Paralympic running events', *British Journal of Sports Medicine*, 43: 1067–1072.

Bennett, J., Sayers, M. and Burkett, B. (2009) 'The impact of lower extremity mass and inertia manipulation on sprint kinematics', *Journal of Strength and Conditioning Research*, 23: 2542–2547.

Bruggemann, G., Arampatzis, A., Emrich, F. and Potthast, W. (2008) 'Biomechanics of double transtibial amputee sprinting using dedicated sprinting prostheses', *Sports Technology*, 1: 220–227.

Buchholz, A.C., Mcgillivray, C.F. and Pencharz, P.B. (2003) 'Differences in resting metabolic rate between paraplegic and able-bodied subjects are explained by differences in body composition', *American Journal of Clinical Nutrition*, 77: 371–378.

Burkett, B. (2010a) 'Is daily walking when living in the Paralympic village different to the typical home environment?' *British Journal of Sports Medicine*, 44: 533–536.

Burkett, B. (2010b) 'Technology in Paralympic sport: performance enhancement or essential for performance?', *British Journal of Sports Medicine*, 44: 215–220.

Burkett, B. (2011) 'Contribution of sport science to performance – swimming' in Y. Vanlandewijck and W.R. Thompson (eds) *Handbook of Sports Medicine and Science, The Paralympic Athlete*, Oxford: International Olympic Committee Medical Commission Publication/Wiley-Blackwell Publication.

Burkett, B. and Mellifont, R. (2008) 'Sport science and coaching in Paralympic swimming', *International Journal of Sports Science and Coaching*, 3: 105–112.

Burkett, B., Mellifont, R. and Mason, B. (2010) 'The influence of swimming start components for selected Olympic and Paralympic swimmers', *Journal of Applied Biomechanics*, 26: 134–141.

Burkett, B., Smeathers, J. and Barker, T. (2003) 'Walking and running inter-limb asymmetry for Paralympic trans-femoral amputees, a biomechanical analysis', *Prosthetics and Orthotics International*, 27: 36–47.

Cregan, K., Bloom, G. and Reid, G. (2007) 'Career evolution and knowledge of elite coaches of swimmers with a physical disabilty', *Research Quarterly for Exercise and Sport*, 78: 339–350.

Daly, D., Malone, L., Burkett, B., Gabrys, T. and Satkumskiene, D. (2009) 'Is sight the main deterrent to race peformance in visually impaired competitive swimmers?' *Physical Education and Sport*, 7: 1–15.

de Groot, S., Dallmeijer, A., van Asbeck, F., Post, M., Bussmann, J. and van der Woude, L. (2007) 'Mechanical efficiency and wheelchair performance during and after spinal cord injury rehabilitation', *International Journal of Sports Medicine*, 28: 880–886.

DePauw, K.P. (1988) 'Sport for individuals with disabilities: research opportunities', *Adapted Physical Activity Quarterly*, 5: 80–89.

Formosa, D., Mason, B. and Burkett, B. (2011) 'The force-time profile of elite front crawl swimmers', *Journal of Sports Sciences*, 29: 811–819.

Fulton, S., Pyne, D., Hopkins, W. and Burkett, B. (2010) 'Training characteristics of Paralympic swimmers', *Journal of Strength and Conditioning Research*, 24: 471–478.

Fulton, S.K., Pyne, D.B. and Burkett, B. (2009) 'Quantifying freestyle kick-count and kick-rate patterns in Paralympic swimming', *Journal of Sports Science*, 27: 1455–1461.

Goosey-Tolfrey, V., Alfano, H. and Fowler, N. (2008) 'The influence of crank length and cadence on mechanical efficiency in hand cycling', *European Journal of Applied Physiology*, 102: 189–194.

Goosey-Tolfrey, V.L., Webborn, N. and Castle, P. (2006) 'Aerobic capacity and peak power output of elite quadriplegic games players', *British Journal of Sports Medicine*, 40: 684–687.

Haake, S. (2009) 'The impact of technology on sporting performance in Olympic sports', *Journal of Sport Sciences*, 27: 1421–1431.

Harris, J. (2010) 'The use, role and application of advanced technology in the lives of disabled people in the UK', *Disability and Society*, 25: 427–439.

Jones, C. and Wilson, C. (2009) 'Defining advantage and athletic performance: the case of Oscar Pistorius', *European Journal of Sport Science*, 9: 125–131.

Knudson, D. (2007) 'Qualitative biomechanical principles for application in coaching', *Sports Biomechanics*, 6: 109–118.

Lecrivain, G., Payton, C. J., Slaouti, A. and Kennedy, I. (2010) 'Effect of body roll amplitude and arm rotation speed on propulsion of arm amputee swimmers', *Journal of Biomechanics*, 43: 1111–1117.

Lee, J., Mellifont, R., Winstanley, J. and Burkett, B. (2007) 'Body-roll in simulated freestyle swimming', *International Journal of Sports Medicine*, 29: 569–573.

Lee, J.B., Sutter, K.J., Askew, C.D. and Burkett, B.J. (2010) 'Identifying symmetry in running gait using a single inertial sensor', *Journal of Science and Medicine in Sport*, 13: 559–563.

Malone, L.A., Sanders, R.H., Schiltz, J.H. and Steadward, R.D. (2001) 'Effects of visual impairment on stroke parameters in Paralympic swimmers', *Medicine and Science in Sports and Exercise*, 33: 2098–2103.

McKean, M.R. and Burkett, B. (2010) 'The relationship between joint range of motion, muscular strength, and race time for sub-elite flat water kayakers', *Journal of Science and Medicine in Sport*, 13: 537–542.

Nolan, L. and Lees, A. (2007) 'The influence of lower limb amputation level on the approach in the amputee long jump', *Journal of Sports Sciences*, 25: 393–401.

Nolan, L., Wit, A., Dudzinski, K., Lees, A., Lake, M. and Wychowanski, M. (2003) 'Adjustments in gait symmetry with walking speed in trans-femoral and trans-tibial amputees', *Gait and Posture*, 17: 142–151.

Psycharakis, S.G. and Sanders, R.H. (2010) 'Body roll in swimming: a review', *Journal of Sports Sciences*, 28: 229–236.

Rice, I., Hettinga, F., Laferrier, J., Sporner, M., Heiner, C., Burkett, B. and Cooper, R. (2011) 'Sport biomechanics', in Y. Vanlandewijck and W.R. Thompson (eds) *Handbook of Sports Medicine and Science, The Paralympic Athlete*, Oxford: IOC Medical Commission/Wiley-Blackwell Publication.

Sanders, R.H. (2007) 'Kinematics, coordination, variability, and biological noise in the prone flutter kick at different levels of a "learn-to-swim" programme', *Journal of Sports Sciences*, 25: 213–227.

Sarro, K., Misuta, M., Burkett, B., Malone, L. and Barros, R. (2010) 'Tracking of wheelchair rugby players in the 2008 demolition derby final', *Journal of Sport Sciences*, 28: 193–200.

Satkunskiene, D., Schega, L., Kunze, K., Birzinyte, K. and Daly, D. (2005) 'Coordination in arm movements during crawl stroke in elite swimmers with a loco-motor disability', *Human Movement Science*, 24: 54–65.

Seifert, L., Daly, D., Burkett, B. and Chollet, D. (2010) 'The profile of aquatic motor skills for able-bodied and swimmers with an impairment', in L. Pelligrino (ed.) *Handbook of Motor Skills: Development, Impairment, and Therapy*, New York: Nova Science Publishers.

Tweedy, S.M. (2003) 'Biomechanical consequences of impairment: a taxonomically valid basis for classification in a unified disability athletics system', *Research Quarterly for Exercise and Sport*, 74: 9–16.

Tweedy, S.M. and Trost, S.G. (2005) 'Validity of accelerometry for measurement of activity in people with brain injury', *Medicine and Science in Sports and Exercise*, 37: 1474–1480.

Tweedy, S.M. and Vanlandewijck, Y. (2011) 'International Paralympic Committee position stand – background and scientific rationale for classification in paralympic sport', *British Journal of Sports Medicine*, 45: 259–269.

Valent, L., Dallmeijer, A., Houdijk, H., Slootman, H., Post, M. and Woude, L. (2008) 'Influence of hand cycling on physical capacity in the rehabilitation of persons with a spinal cord injury: a longitudinal cohort study', *Archives of Physical Medicine and Rehabilitation*, 89: 1016–1022.

Webborn, A. (1999) 'Fifty years of competitive sport for athletes with disabilities: 1948–1998', *British Journal of Sports Medicine*, 33: 138.

Weyand, P.G., Bundle, M.W., Mcgowan, C.P., Grabowski, A., Brown, M.B., Kram, R. and Herr, H. (2009) 'The fastest runner on artificial legs: different limbs, similar function?', *Journal of Applied Physiology*, 107: 903–911.

17

BODY POLITICS

Coaching and technology

Ted M. Butryn

SAN JOSÉ STATE UNIVERSITY, CALIFORNIA, USA

Introduction and overview of topic

Coaching in the twenty-first century necessitates some degree of engagement with a whole range of sport technologies. In fact, the image of players gathered around a chalkboard, dust swirling as the coach draws up plays seems almost like something out of a quaint but outdated Norman Rockwell landscape. Indeed, the sidelines of an NFL game resembles some sort of military command centre, with orders relayed via headsets from the booth, to the coach, and directly to the quarterback's helmet. The obviously fake Astroturf of the 1990s has been replaced by artificial turf that looks and feels more like actual grass. Coaches need not rely on stacks of videotapes to scout the tendencies of an upcoming opponent, because they have software that can show them exactly what each player does in a given situation.

That said, even the leaders of the sport technology revolution recognise that some human element is necessary even with the latest high-tech equipment, gadget, or software. For example, a recent issue of *Smith and Street's Sports Business Journal* (September 27–October 3, 2010) devoted a lengthy column to the technology of player evaluation in various sports, most notably baseball, basketball, and football. In the piece, the author quotes Matt Marolda, an executive at a sporting data analysis company, who states that, 'We are qualitative people, but numbers still can't substitute for eyeball stuff' (p. 18). Indeed, this notion of the melding of a humanistic and technological approach to sport is representative of the cyborg era.

In what ways, then, has the coaching profession adapted to the cyborg age, and the new generation of athletes who have grown up not just with computers, but surrounded by and plugged into a thoroughly technologised space? Do coaches still have a space for resistance, or must they either adapt or find another occupation? Further, given the cost of many sport technologies, how can coaches decide which sorts of technologies are best for their sport, their coaching style, and their athletes?

Research gaps

While dozens of studies from several kinesiology sub-disciplines have dealt with various forms of technology, mainly as a means of enhancing performance, very few have focused specifically on coaches' use of technology. Sport studies scholars have examined the role of technology in various sporting contexts, and how 'cyborg sporting bodies' have affected the ways that we view sport and athletes (Cole 1998; Butryn 2003; Miah 2004; Magdalinski 2009). However, little qualitative research has examined how the notion of cyborg sport and how the influx of various types of technology have been incorporated into the coaching profession, and how it has changed the ways coaches do their work. Therefore, throughout this chapter, I draw from interviews with eight Division I college coaches that were conducted as part of a larger qualitative study of coaching and technology. I infuse the voices of these coaches, and their thoughts and perceptions of what technology means to them, how it has affected their coaching, and the types of technology they have used as well as resisted for various reasons.

In the first part of the chapter, I use the data from the coaching interviews to examine the meaning of technology to coaching, and how different coaches may struggle with the place of technology in their profession. In doing so, I draw from Feenberg's (1995, 2002) work on the philosophy of technology in an effort to make sense of how coaches see the various uses of technology in their sport and among their athletes. I discuss the innovations that coaches have used, those they have not used, and attempt to determine how they have affected the coaching process. Finally I discuss a few of the major themes that emerged from the interviews, and discuss the implication of these preliminary findings to the current and future practice of coaching.

In summary, this chapter on coaching in the cyborg era is an initial attempt to examine the challenges and opportunities coaches encounter in their engagements with sport technologies. Understanding how coaches make sense of the cyborgification of sport (Butryn 2003) and the array of technologies available to them and their athletes will contribute to the literature on coaching education, as well as to the existing body of literature on cyborg sport and the philosophy of technology. As Gilbert (2006) noted in his introduction to a special issue of *The Sport Psychologist* on coach education, there has been a lack of research on the 'best practices' in coach education, and the research that does exist on coach education is scattered across an almost absurd amount of publications. Gilbert's comments have relevance to this chapter, because while many of the articles scattered around various publication outlets mention technology, there is no work on how often these technologies are used, how effective they are in teaching athletes, or improving athlete and coaching performance. Indeed, many articles make mention of video analysis software, biomechanical evaluations, sport psychological interventions using biofeedback, and even messages coaches should send about doping technologies. I hope that this chapter stimulates discussion among coaches, coaching education experts, athletes, and even fans not simply about what sorts of technologies are available for coaches to use, or how effective they are, but what effects technology has on coaching, a decidedly humanistic endeavour at its core, in what is an increasingly dehumanised and technocratic sporting environment.

Making sense of technology and sport

The growing interest in technology within philosophical circles has generated numerous theories aimed at explaining the role of technology in modern societies. One of the leading philosophers of technology, Andrew Feenberg (1999, 2002), outlined four theoretical perspectives regarding technology, including the *instrumentalist*, *determinist*, *substantivist*, and *critical* positions. In essence, these positions are like lenses, and depending on which lens we look through, technological advancements in sport and coaching may be viewed positively or negatively. A brief overview of each of these theoretical positions will provide a useful entrée into my subsequent examination of coaches and technology, and hopefully help situate coaches' thoughts regarding various sport technologies within a useful framework.

Instrumentalism proposes that technologies are value-free or neutral tools that humans employ unidirectionally as a means to an end (Borgmann 1984; Feenberg 1995). Feenberg (1995) considers instrumentalism to be a modernist, 'common sense' view of technology which links technological progress with societal progress. While instrumentalism carries with it the possibility that technology can be used for malevolent purposes (e.g. weapons of mass destruction), it has often aligned itself with the idea that technology should be directed at liberating humanity from the burdens and ills of contemporary life, and hence instrumentalists have often maintained a highly optimistic attitude toward new technological developments. Within sport, the instrumentalist perspective would probably view most technologies as tools to be employed in the ongoing quest for improved performance, and also view enhanced performance as the central aim of competitive sport.

This idealized instrumentalist view of technology as the benevolent catalyst of progress has been challenged on several grounds. Feenberg (1999), for example, argues that instrumentalism's attempted neutralisation of technology in the nineteenth century removed it from the realm of political debate, and its supposed generic nature facilitated the formation of a story that portrayed technology's advancement as parallel to that of the human species. This sort of universalism (i.e. 'we' will be better off with more technology) glosses over issues of access to and control of technologies, something that coaches in the study were certainly conscious of.

Theories of technological *determinism* generally share instrumentalism's belief in the neutrality of technology, but question our power to control its development and use (Feenberg 1999). Theorists who espouse this position argue that technologies have their own logic and drive that operate independent of societal constraints (Feenberg 1995, 1999), a notion that led Langdon Winner (1989) to coin the term 'autonomous technology'. According to Winner (1989), technology has become autonomous because modern humans are often incapable of changing the course of technological progress once it is 'unleashed', and because even the most inconspicuous technologies have the potential to reshape society itself. The determinist perspective would consider certain technologies as tools that, once allowed into the athletic sphere, may prompt coaches and athletes to use them whether they wanted to or not. The very presence of these innovations would mean that once one coach or athlete decided to use them, others would feel the pressure to do so as well. Also, if a new technology caused drastic changes or improvements in some aspect of coaching or sport performance, then this one technology could fundamentally alter coaching and sporting practices in unforeseen ways.

One of the assumptions that determinism is grounded in is what Feenberg (1999) calls 'unilinear progress', which refers to the belief that technological progress follows a single course, moving systematically from lesser to greater levels of complexity. While this idea makes intuitive sense when one examines the historical development of virtually any technology, Feenberg (1999) makes an important point in noting that technological progress is, in fact, often not as ordered and sequential as it might at first appear. Within sport, for example, the Professional Golfers Association (PGA) has taken extraordinary measures to prevent the influx of several new types of club designs on the grounds that they essentially de-skill the performance (Tenner 1996). The supposed neutrality of technology espoused by advocates of both instrumentalism and some forms of determinism also contributes to its depoliticisation as well, because once technology becomes viewed as a value-free instrument it is more easily removed from the practice of open democratic debate (Winner 1989, 1995;

Feenberg 1995). Instead, control over the workings of technology is placed in the hands of bureaucratic elites who employ various technological means to retain this control. The system that supports this depoliticisation and de-democratisation of technology has been termed a 'technocracy'.

Among the most vocal sceptics of the increasing technologisation of modern societies have been the technological substantivists. According to those advocating the *substantive* position, society is at the mercy of an autonomous techno-juggernaut that will someday dominate humanity (Feenberg 1995). Substantive theories are thus generally wary, and often openly condemnatory, of technology. Substantivism must therefore also be regarded as an essentialist position, because it precludes any alternative notions of technology other than those that link it to the dehumanisation of the modern world. In many ways, then, substantive theories that frame technology strictly in negative terms run directly counter to instrumentalism's faith in technological progress.

Perhaps the most oft cited proponents of the substantivist position are Martin Heidegger (1977) and Jacques Ellul (1964). Heidegger ranks among the most important twentieth century thinkers on science and technology, and his writings have influenced sport scholars' examinations of technology: it will be beneficial to briefly discuss two specific points he makes that pertain specifically to the human-technology relationship. Heidegger (1977) offers his most concentrated analysis of technology in an essay entitled, 'The Question Concerning Technology'. He argues that humans have yet to fully acknowledge the impact of technology on our lives, and that we remain enslaved by technology as long as we continue to view it as neutral. Perceiving technology as a value-free phenomenon, Heidegger states, ultimately blinds us to what he calls the true 'essence' of technology. Heidegger argues that 'the essence of technology is by no means anything technological' (p. 4) by which he means that technology is not simply the machines and devices that have come to play such a central role in our lives, but rather the way in which technology has enveloped our way of knowing and relating to the world. This epistemological shift has resulted in a revealing of the world as 'standing reserve', or as a set of resources to be maximised and used for instrumental purposes.

Jacques Ellul's (1964) writings echo Heidegger's belief that technology is an all-encompassing force rather than merely a collection of tools and devices (Hoberman 1995). His most important contribution, arguably, has been the notion that technology is intimately tied to an ordering principle that seeks to impose an homogenising efficiency on all it encounters. Ellul's (1964) commentary also includes specific references to sport, and he argues that sport is a total 'extension of the technical spirit' (p. 384), and that the emphasis on quantification and efficiency which manifests itself in the performance ethos of elite sport precludes non-instrumental (e.g. enjoyment, spiritual growth) sporting practices (Hoberman 1995). In the end, technology will drive what sports we play, how we play them, and who is best suited to play.

Finally, Feenberg (2002) calls for a move towards a fourth conceptualisation of technology, which involves a critical stance that asks important questions about power, and the control over the advancement of technology in modern societies. *Critical* theories of technology reassert human agency with respect to technology while rejecting the instrumentalist view that technology is value-free or neutral. Much like substantive theories, then, critical theories of technology accept the notion that technologies are value-laden, and further argue that technology may be the most powerful carrier of political ideology in contemporary post-industrial societies (Pippin 1995; Feenberg 1999, 2002). Critical views of technology recognise that technologies, ultimately, should be controlled by us. A critical theory of technology, like substantivism, sees the politics and values associated with technology. So, critical perspectives of the influx of new tennis racket technologies would call for more open debates on the politics of the technique, and ask questions such as, 'Who will have access to this equipment? Who decides whether they should be legal or restricted on the Pro tour? What will be the long-term effects of new racket technologies on the game?' Where critical theories of technology diverge from substantivism is in their emphasis on the establishment of alternative means–end technological relationships that are within the domain of human control (Feenberg 1995). The democratisation of technology, according to Feenberg, requires that the technological hegemony in place within many Western societies, and that fosters a reliance on 'experts', be acknowledged and contested through increased open debates, as well as counterhegemonic practices that challenge the intended use of various technologies (Ihde 1993; Feenberg 1995; Winner 1989, 1995). It is important to note that none of these theories is completely right or wrong, but they each clearly have different implications for how we evaluate the continued technologisation of sport and the body.

Applying the philosophy of technology to coaches' experiences with technology

In the course of examining the various ways and degrees that contemporary, postmodern coaches and athletes interface with technology, it is necessary to survey the plethora of sport technologies available to them, a task which will be useful in distinguishing between different forms of cyborg coaching identities. As a way of organising coaches' thoughts about various kinds of technologies, this section is loosely organised around Butryn's (2003) typology of sport technologies, with particular attention to how the categories apply to the coaching profession. Using the data gathered from the in-depth interviews, I illustrate how different technologies relate to the experience, practice, profession, and future of coaching. The categories of technologies discussed in this chapter include: (1) self technologies; (2) landscape technologies; (3) implement technologies; and (4) movement technologies. While some of the technologies have more or less relevance depending on the particular sport being discussed, an understanding of the many types of sport technologies may be helpful in obtaining a better perspective on the technocultural realm in which high-level coaches work, and the almost overwhelming amount of decisions they must make regarding which technologies to seek out, use, resist, or discard.

Self technologies have the potential to temporarily or permanently alter an athlete's physical and/or psychological makeup along a continuum from the mundane to the radical. Along with various legal and banned performance–enhancing substances, *self* technologies encompass other kinds of athletic augmentations such as prosthetic limbs and even genetic engineering (Miah 2004). Although all of the coaches I interviewed had a decidedly instrumentalist view of the more common self technologies, it was clear that while some were surprisingly laissez-faire regarding their athletes' use of supplements, in particular, others sought to actively police what their athletes ingested, not because they suspected any intentional wrongdoing, but rather because they had read or heard of other college and pro athletes who had returned positive drug tests due to supposedly contaminated supplements. As Chase, a head swim coach, stated:

> You know in terms of supplements we stay away from that just because there are so many problems with tainted supplements. We talk about some of them, but anything that's got any kind of a purported ergogenic aid, we tell them to stay away from it. If they're having a problem not getting enough protein we'll talk to them

about getting a soy protein or a whey protein, but we want them to get that from a Whole Foods, not from a GNC… Someplace where there is going to be a lot more likelihood of some sort of contamination.

Five of the coaches fundraised for the specific purpose of providing their athletes with the supplements they found most appropriate. For example, Reggie the gymnastics coach talked about the dietary needs of his athletes, and his desire to make supplements available to athletes who wanted them:

> My biggest concern was, especially with athletes and female athletes, the iron deficiencies, anemia, stuff like that. And try to make sure we have kids that are vegetarians, and when you are vegetarian and what not and trying to eat right, and sometimes you lack a lot of the nutrients you use. So it's just a concern, just to make sure that they're getting all of the stuff that they need, that they can take advantage of.

A second type of sport technologies are *landscape* technologies, which refer to those technologies that comprise the sporting environments in which athletes and coaches train and compete. Landscape technologies would therefore include things like the new, multi-purpose sport complexes, complete with their jumbotron screens, retractable domes, and artificial grass surfaces, as well as the practice facilities available to coaches and athletes.

Coaches in the study had much to say about how these types of technologies affected their coaching experiences and practices. For more than half of the coaches, however, it was the *lack* of landscape technologies that stood out most for them. In fact, some of their comments were surprising to hear, given that they were coaching at a Division I institution. For instance, the baseball coach, Timothy, described the stark practice environment he deals with daily:

> We have no running water so there are no bathrooms and we have to cart water out there every day. Yeah, so it's like, 'are you kidding me?' So, that's not fun because that takes time you know, and your trainers got to spend some time … you know trainers are the ones that count on our players! We assign three or four players to help the trainers get the water out there and then they have to come back.

While Timothy was adamant that the facilities, though problematic and far from ideal, were 'functional', the efficiency generally associated with contemporary sporting technocultures was certainly absent.

Other coaches described landscape technologies that were directly related to the performance of their athletes. One of the more interesting examples came from Chase, who described how the technology of the swimming pool could make a big difference in athlete performance, and perhaps how he coached his athletes during competition:

> In terms of the stuff that's going to make the difference on more of a hydrodynamic area, you've got the water depth, and the deeper it is, the less turbulence are bouncing up off the bottom. The fast pools are generally now having the water come out of the pump room and the filter rooms up from the bottom of the pool, so that there's an upward flow.

In contrast, he described pools where the configuration of the pumps and the filters created a circular flow, making it more difficult for athletes in certain lanes. As several scholars have argued, one important aspect of a critical stance towards sport technologies is differential access to technology (Butryn 2002; Feenberg 2002), whether it be between wealthier Western nations and developing nations, or in this case, 'Big-time' college programmes and programmes that struggle for funding.

Implement and equipment technologies include those instruments and pieces of equipment that athletes use in their sport. Thus, implement technologies vary greatly across sports, from different ball, bat, racket, club, and shoe materials to assorted types of protective gear. However, coaching-specific equipment technologies would also include the whole host of communication technologies that coaches now rely on to gather and relay information during practices and games.

The coaches in the study discussed the importance of having the most advanced equipment and implement technologies available for both their players and themselves. Timothy, the baseball coach, relayed an interesting story involving the re-technologisation of the college bat. He described how in previous years, the aluminium bats had a significantly larger 'sweet spot' that favoured batters, and that the ball came off the bats with a much greater velocity than they do off of the new bats. This simple change in equipment prompted a change in coaching. As he stated:

> Of course that's going to change my coaching. We can certainly pitch inside more effectively... just having the sense of being able to tell the pitchers, we can challenge people. You know it's hard to square a baseball up, and if you don't have a larger sweet spot like we've had in the last three to five years where the impact velocity or rebound velocity are so much higher, being able to pitch inside for sure is going to be a bigger aspect [of the game].

While most coaches were at a loss for areas in their sport and coaching that were over-technologised, in terms of equipment, one notable exception involved the relatively recent banning of the ever-evolving swimsuits. Rory described the situation as being almost absurd, with the technology improving at such a rapid rate that any notion of fairness was compromised. The following quote also illustrates one of the few times in the study when coaches approached a substantive view of technology, an inkling that technology did have particular values attached to it, and that it was moving forward without much input from the athletic community:

> Pretty much everybody thinks that that was the best thing in the world when those suits got banned. Because it really had gotten just ridiculous that last summer, where literally there was a new suit coming out every two weeks [...] and if you wanted to be competitive you had to have that suit. It got to the point that everybody was just constantly looking to make sure their competitor didn't have some new suit that no one had heard of.

Movement technologies refer to those devices and procedures that are designed to assess and evaluate athletic performance. The most common of such technologies is the use of videotape analysis, although as the coaches noted, there are an array of more sophisticated instruments that provide detailed digital information on athlete's biomechanics, as well as the almost infinite combinations of outcomes in any given situation in team sports. All but one of the coaches described how they used video extensively as a teaching tool, and all of them viewed the increasing use of video in coaching from an instrumentalist perspective. For the football team, the only team to have its own video coordinator, it was an invaluable tool that the athletes could have access to almost any time. As Rory described in the following exchange:

RORY: The thing the digital video and software has enabled us to do is to watch tape and evaluate the opponent quickly, make faster decisions on how we want to attack them or how we think they are going to attack us, and able to self-evaluate our team also. So those are critical areas that you can do quickly now.

TED: Have you, how have the players responded to that … your use of video?

RORY: Oh, they like it. They like the teaching tools and they understand how to use it and there is another step. We are going to go a step further where we can send it to them on email, and so that's our next step and we just got it the other day. So those are things that we are developing that can help us tremendously with the kids… when they come and we have them here, they have already had some homework so to speak that we have sent them.

Previous research has examined the notion that some athletes view technology as a more reliable indicator of performance than feeling (Butryn 2003). Similarly, several coaches in this study noted that one of the benefits of utilising movement technologies is that they can aid athletes who either are better visual learners, or who are resistant to the coach's verbal feedback, and ultimately help the athlete to see, and to believe, what the coach's feedback itself could not. Chase found this to be the case with his swimmers:

I mean most people are going to learn better visually than by listening and some markedly more so, and there is definitely some of them that I can be telling them over and over and over again and they don't get it. Then, they watch it one time and they completely understand.

Some coaches felt even more strongly about the use of movement technologies, and stated that they were not used simply as tools, but as a form of validation in their efforts to change athletes' movements. Reggie talked about this phenomenon, in the process clearly revealing that the technology does have values attached to it:

This has just allowed a coach to validate everything that they've been saying. And by having a video, it's like… I tell them, 'Video don't lie. That is you. Is that you?' 'Yes, that's me.' 'You're doing that skill?' 'Yes.' 'Your knees are bent?' 'Yes.' So it just validates what you've always been saying and it just kind of helps you in getting kids to believe that they're not doing it the right way you want.

Several coaches viewed movement technologies from a substantivist perspective, especially if they were 'overused'. Indeed, scholars have argued that the move towards 'technosport' (Coakley 1994) would ultimately dehumanise athletes and coaches, thus removing what makes sport a compelling social practice. Although only two of the coaches explicitly tied technology with dehumanisation, most of them talked about the notion that technology has the potential to take some sort of 'human element' out of the practice. The volleyball coach, Oliver, described a time when one of their recently adopted database technologies failed during a match, and how it forced him to confront the extent to which he had become reliant on technology to the extent that his own 'human skills' were no longer as sharp as they had been:

> This year we implemented a program that's been around for a little bit... it's a data systems program. The second match we played that week, our assistant coach who enters the data during games wasn't there, *and* our SID's computer crashed, so we had no in-game stats. It was literally back at your gut feeling, which is very different this year for me, extremely different. I liked it and I didn't like it. I liked it because I identified that we're doing something that is actually very productive for us within the realm of technology, but I also found that you lose the human component and the reason why you play sport in there also. [...] It dehumanises some of what happens and removes a lot of feeling and interpretation to what's going on... which was unnerving and stressful!

Summary and implications for coaching practice

As previously mentioned, we have little academic research on how coaches have interacted with technology, their perspectives of the influx of various technological innovations, and perhaps even times when they have chosen to resist the technologisation of sport. This chapter represents an attempt to answer some of these questions, and to frame coaches' experiences with technology within a philosophical framework of views towards the technologisation of social spheres. Perhaps the most striking thing that came out of the interview sessions was my sense that the coaches were not reeling, but perhaps still a bit unsteady in their footing in the rapidly shifting technological coaching environment. Some of the changes the coaches described had happened very recently, and the fact that most had adapted and moved forward successfully was admirable. That said, it was also clear that as much as technology relieved some of the stress and tedious tasks that they had to cope with previously, it also added a great deal of new stress, particularly where issues of access, funding, and recruiting were concerned. In a Division I college sporting environment where, as Coakley (2009) notes, there is a growing gap between the 'haves and have nots', one area where the discrepancy between big-time programmes and the rest of the institutions is glaring is in the technologies available to them.

With respect to Feenberg's analysis on how we view different sorts of technology, coaches clearly approached most engagements with technology from an instrumentalist perspective. Despite their difficulties procuring the latest innovations or the controversies over certain technologies, they all saw the increased efficiency that the various forms of technology provided as tools of the coaching trade in the twenty-first century. Indeed, in a Division I athletic environment that has been criticised for its 'arms race' nature, coaches felt, for many reasons, that they needed to keep up with the latest technologies or risk losing recruits, or becoming anachronisms in their profession.

However, they did diverge from mere instrumentalism at times, and tread into the realm of technological determinism and substantivism. Coaches clearly saw the introduction of several forms of technology through the lens of determinism, and recognised that technological progress, once initiated, was often difficult to stop. Further, with respect to substantivist views of sport technologies, coaches mentioned a few instances when they considered technology to be a sort of wayward force that threatened the fairness and integrity of competition, and in some cases, threatened to change the nature of the sport.

One notable example where coaches *did* take a critical approach to sport technologies was in swimming, and the coach's recognition that not only did the new swim suits take the sport in a new direction that was difficult to reverse, it changed the nature of the sport itself, and thus the sport's governing bodies and the coaches determined that they needed to de-technologise the swimming attire before competitions became merely performance-based fashion shows. Similarly, as the baseball coach noted, the change in bat construction to a material that actually decreased velocity and power was a conscious decision by coaches and the NCAA. Thus, while Feenberg (2002) makes the argument that, in general, society has fallen under the power of technocultural progress and determinism, within sport it is clear that the coaching community has sometimes, though not often enough, perhaps, taken a stance against the ubiquitous presence of technology in their lives, their athletes' lives, and their sport.

Another clear finding from the interviews in this study is that there can be a technological generation gap between athletes and coaches that directly affects every aspect of the coaching process, from teaching style to communication to athlete management. One of the most striking examples of this gap involved the stories coaches told of athletes relying at least as much on technology for feedback as they did their coaches. Given that youth culture in Western nations has become thoroughly and intimately plugged in, the notion that college athletes would look to technology for the 'objective truth' is certainly not surprising, although it presents some interesting challenges to coaches attempting to preserve the human element of coaching. Some coaches did express very critical views on this aspect of technology in coaching. If the video or biofeedback is perceived as giving more 'correct' information than the coach, and some athletes only respond to coaches if they text message rather than call, as several coaches noted, then coaches will be compelled to either conform to the technological hegemony or become anachronisms.

In short, a great deal of future research is needed on many of the issues raised in this chapter. In particular, further research is needed to gain insight into how cyborg sporting cultures and bodies are negotiated by the coaches. For instance, regarding doping technologies, we have little research on how coaches attempt to manage their athletes and teams and steer them away from illegal performance-enhancing drugs while steering them towards those substances and procedures that, while certainly not natural, are not illegal either. In addition, the tension between a humanistic approach to coaching and the potential dehumanising effects of technology should be researched further. Finally, while Feenberg (2002) has argued for the increased democratisation of technology, the coaches in this study clearly felt as much at the mercy of advancing technologies in coaching and their individual sports as they did in control of their use. Indeed, sometimes they did not see themselves as participants in the process at all, something that should give those fighting for critical views of sport technologies some concern.

References

Borgmann, A. (1984) *Technology and the Character of Contemporary Life*, Chicago, IL: The University of Chicago Press.

Butryn, T.M. (2002) 'Cyborg horizons: sport and the ethics of self-technologisation', in A. Miah and S. Eassom (eds) *Sport Technology: History, Philosophy, and Policy*, Oxford: Elsevier Science.

Butryn, T.M. (2003) 'Posthuman podiums: cyborg narratives of elite track and field athletes', *Sociology of Sport Journal*, 20: 17–39.

Coakley, J.J. (1994) *Sport in Society: Issues and Controversies*, 5th edn, St. Louis, MO: Mosby.

Coakley, J.J. (2009) *Sport in Society: Issues and Controversies*, 10th edn, Boston, MA: McGraw-Hill.

Cole, C.L. (1998) 'Addiction, exercise, and cyborgs: technologies and deviant bodies', in G. Rail (ed.) *Sport and Postmodern Times*, Albany, NY: State University of New York Press.

Ellul, J. (1964) *The Technological Society*, New York: Vintage.

Feenberg, A. (1995) 'Subversive rationalisation: technology, power, and democracy', in A. Feenberg (1999) *Questioning Technology*, New York, NY: Routledge.

Feenberg, A. (2002) *Transforming Technology: A Critical Theory Revisited*, Oxford: Oxford University Press.

Gilbert, W. (2006) 'Introduction to special issue: coach education', *The Sport Psychologist*, 20: 123–125.

Heidegger, M. (1977) *The Question Concerning Technology and Other Essays*, trans. W. Lovitt, New York: Harper & Row.

Hoberman, J. (1995) 'Sport and the technological image of man', in W.J. Morgan and K.V. Meier (eds) *Philosophic Inquiry in Sport* Champaign, IL: Human Kinetics, pp. 202–208.

Ihde, D. (1993) *Philosophy of Technology: An Introduction*, New York: Paragon Press.

Magdalinski, T. (2009) *Sport, Technology and the Body: The Nature of Performance*, Abingdon: Routledge.

Miah, A. (2004) *Genetically Modified Athletes: Biomedical Ethics, Gene Doping, and Sport*, London: Routledge.

Pippin, R.B. (1995) 'On the notion of technology as ideology', in A. Feenberg and A. Hannay (eds) *Technology and the Politics of Knowledge*, Bloomington, IN: Indiana University Press, pp. 43–61.

Smith and Street's Sports Business Journal (September 27–October 3, 2010).

Tenner, E. (1996) *Why Things Bite Back: Technology and the Revenge of Unintended Consequences*, New York: Alfred A. Knopf.

Winner, L. (1989) 'The era of the enhanced athlete', *Technology Review*, 92: 22.

Winner, L. (1995) 'Citizen virtues in a technological order', in A. Feenberg and A. Hannay (eds) *Technology and the Politics of Knowledge*, Bloomington, IN: Indiana University Press, pp. 65–84.

B

Coaching, pedagogy, and communication in sports coaching

18

HUMOUR AND SPORTS COACHING

A laughing matter?

Lars Tore Ronglan

NORWEGIAN SCHOOL OF SPORT SCIENCES, OSLO

Kenneth Aggerholm

AARHUS UNIVERSITY, DENMARK

Introduction

Humour is easily dismissed as frivolous and unworthy of serious consideration. Social inquiry within the field of sport seems to be no exception in this respect. Two decades ago Eldon E. Snyder (1991) published a paper titled 'Sociology of sport and humor'. His conclusion that humour in sport is worthy sociological analysis has, however, hardly yet led to further investigations of the relationship. This lack of attention is a bit surprising, especially because research on organizational humour in general has increased dramatically over the past 15 years (Lang and Lee 2010). After all, humour should be at least as relevant to the sporting context as to the working context. This chapter intends to follow up Snyder's recommendation, related to the specific area of sports coaching. Recently, it was suggested that 'the multi-functional use of humour, its intent, manifestation, and effect within the often emotionally-charged world of coaching, would appear to hold very interesting possibilities' (Jones *et al.* 2011: 185). This formed the point of departure for the work presented in the chapter, aiming to specify approaches, concepts and research questions possible to pursue to increase our understanding of this topic.

Humour is a social phenomenon and a relational concept (Cooper 2008); hence, it can be regarded as a form of communication. Sports coaching, with social interaction as the heart of its process (Jones *et al.* 2004), clearly holds the potential of involving humour in different forms. Coaching includes both speech and bodily actions from the persons involved, which open space for humorous interaction in the form of verbal utterances as well as gestures and face-work. Humorous situations, or strategic uses of humour, may appear both on and off the field, and can be initiated both from athletes and coaches. As such, humour is not something just going on 'beside' the coaching process; rather it should be viewed as embedded in the process itself. Echoing Davies (1979: 109), who postulated that 'sociologists without a sense of humor will never be able to understand the workings of the social world', one could ask if the same is true for coaches. A sense of humour and appropriate uses of it can be seen as part of an overall social competence needed to perform a flexible and adaptable coaching role.

The aim of the chapter is threefold. First, conceptualizations of humour and previous humour research in general is presented and related to sports coaching. Here, four dimensions of humour relevant to coaching are suggested; namely, humour in relation to social identity and belonging, tension regulation, creativity and power relations. Examples of how these dimensions might be further explored within coaching research are given. Second, the literature on leadership and humour from educational and organizational settings is briefly summarized. This leads us to the last part of the chapter, where 'humorous coaching' is focused upon. Inspired by the metaphor of 'coaching as orchestration' (Jones and Wallace 2005), we discuss the potential of a humorous approach in managing the complex and contingent reality of coaching. Our intention is to clarify an argument that to coaches, humour may represent a valuable strategy and communicative resource in productively influencing coaching situations.

What is humorous?

A commonality of all descriptions of humour is that it involves a form of discontinuity or incongruity (Faulkner 1987; Snyder 1991). According to Fine (1983: 160), 'humor reflects a contrast of meaning between two incompatible views of a scene'. Humour results from resolving these two conflicting images in a way that make sense, 'given the distorted logic of humor' (Fine 1983: 160). This logic has been labelled the incongruity theory of humour, and has been recognized for a long time. For example, in the seventeenth century the philosopher Pascal stated that 'nothing produces laughter more than a surprising disproportion between that which one expects and that which one sees' (Morreall 1982: 245). Svebak (1974) has argued that the juxtaposition underlying the incongruity and, particularly, the acceptance of another potential world order that it implies, allows humour to challenge established social meanings.

Although scholars seem to agree on this general logic of humour, it is also recognized that perceptions of incongruity as amusing are personally and socially constructed. What is funny to one person is not necessarily funny to another, and what may be perceived amusing in one cultural context may not be, or even be perceived offensive, in another. For example, recent research has indicated that there are regional differences in humour within the United States (Romero *et al.* 2007). Similarly, cross-national differences in uses of humour in business contexts were described by Mulholland (1997: 103), who stated that 'joking, teasing or leg-pulling between Australians in business interactions can make Asians very uncomfortable'. Rogerson-Revell (2007) concluded that uses and interpretations of organizational humour were clearly 'culture'-bound, but also influenced by other factors such as personality, gender, age, ethnicity, organizational rank and status.

The same diversity can be supposed to exist across the multitude of sporting contexts. Research on sporting 'subcultures' within rugby (Light 2008), rowing (Purdy *et al.* 2008), ice hockey (Bloom and Smith 1986) and windsurfing (Wheaton 2000) give support to the argument that specific sports are marked by cultural characteristics. For example, in heavy contact sports, particular forms of masculinity are expressed (Bloom and Smith 1986; Light 2008). The discourses and language embedded in these fields differ from those found in 'lifestyle' sports like windsurfing (Wheaton 2000) and snowboarding (Thorpe 2006). This illustrates that is it necessary to take into account the particularities of the socio-cultural environment when trying to understand the uses and meanings of humour in different sporting contexts. According to Kahn (1989), humour is often indirect and ambiguous, and contextualized within the tacit knowledge common to the people involved. Therefore, coaches, to be able to adequately interpret their athletes' laughter, or to use humour appropriately as part of their own interactive strategies, need to know both their individual athletes and the social environment in which the interaction takes place.

Social functions of humour

Research suggests that humour can fulfil a wide range of functions in social situations. Here, we will highlight four basic social functions that humour has been shown to perform in organizations and communities of practice. These are humour's role in relation to: (1) social identity and belonging; (2) tension regulation; (3) creativity; and (4) power relations. Rather than being a pure reflection of categories used in the literature, we have chosen to organize the text in line with these dimensions because of their specific relevance to sports coaching.

Social identity and belonging

Frequently, humour's most central role is seen as creating and expressing solidarity (Holmes 2000; Rogerson-Revell 2007), a sense of belonging to a group. 'Sharing a laugh' is signalling common ground, and shared humour is an important in-group versus out-group marker. Within the working context, Romero and Pescosolido (2008: 397) argued that what they called 'positive use of humor' led to improved group cohesion and thereby increased productivity. This might happen through a reduction in social distance between group members (Graham 1995), and higher levels of trust between the members (Hampes 1999). The linkage to trust may further increase our recognition of humour's significance in coaching, because trust is vital in this context (Ronglan and Havang 2011). Trust consists of a cognitive element grounded in rational judgements, and an affective dimension developed in social relationships accompanied by emotive social bonds (Lewis and Weigert 1985). In this regard, humour may contribute to higher levels of mutual trust in a team environment, as it may facilitate both the confidence needed to manage uncertainty (cognitive dimension) and the identification with others in the team (affective dimension).

Reflecting on humour's relation to social identity, it is, however, important to bear in mind that it may be a thin line between 'laughing with' and 'laughing at'. Humour as a means to strengthen internal cohesion implies drawing borders between insiders and outsiders, and can easily be used to create feelings of superiority; we laugh at the expense of someone. In this sense, there is an inevitable trade-off between the affiliative aspect of humour associated with those who 'share the joke' and the distancing aspect associated with being the butt of the joke. Thus, humour may be a 'double-edged sword' (Rogerson-Revell 2007), contributing both to social inclusion and social exclusion. In a study of putdown humour in group dynamics, Terrion and Ashforth (2002) also concluded that shared putdown humour may facilitate solidarity, and they introduced the term 'inclusionary putdowns'. In their study, inclusionary putdowns were typically directed towards people outside the team, but it is easy to imagine that putdowns also can hit own team members, leading to inclusion (of some) and exclusion (of others) rather than reinforcing group solidarity.

Within sport teams, often marked by a tension between collaboration and internal competition (e.g. for playing time or status), more in-depth knowledge is needed on the relationship between humour, group structures and social identities. How is humour used by team members (athletes and/or coaches) to include or exclude others – to develop mutual trust, social bonds or to challenge internal hierarchies? Recognizing and analysing humour as a 'double-edged' sword is a good starting point in producing nuanced portrayals of team dynamics in various coaching contexts. As social identity and belonging is a basic human need, studies of team humour may contribute to our understanding of identity formation through sport participation.

Tension regulation

The stress-relieving function of humour is another dimension emphasized in the literature. It is well known that humour can be used as a coping strategy when facing uncertainty (Grugulis 2002), help to relieve the tension of embarrassment in a social situation (Goffman 1967), while also being able to offer relief from boredom and routines in working life settings (Cooper 2008). In a study of the role of 'the joker' in companies, Plester and Orams (2008) noted that 'jokers' fulfilled a relief function at work by offering a respite from business pressure and stress by creating fun and laughter. Furthermore, Holmes and Meredith (2002) found that workers sometimes used humour as a self-depreciation device, to defuse pressure when they knew they had not acted as they should have. Holmes and Meredith also argued that subordinates used humour to contest their superiors' views or messages, while trying to 'make light' of the erosion of the superior's authority.

In competitive and professional sports, one would suppose that the strain stemming from competitions and rigorous training regimes might be easier to handle within a humorous atmosphere. In contrast to this, Cushion and Jones' (2006) ethnographic study of a professional youth soccer team in England revealed a rather hostile and harsh coaching regime, leaving very little space for shared laughter. The dominant forms of 'humour' being displayed were coaches' ridicule at the expense of certain players. The minimal resistance from the players was discussed in relation to the authoritarian discourse marking the football culture (Cushion and Jones 2006). Case studies from other sporting contexts have however, shown a more lively use of humour (i.e. teasing as part of identity formation in youth baseball teams in the US) (Fine 1984), and locker room humour among French judo elite athletes as a joint protection against unreasonable pressure created by the coaches (d'Arripe-Longueville *et al.* 1998).

We would argue that humour can be used in regulating tension in two directions; to relieve tension or to increase it. The relieving function is far the most described aspect in the literature. However, within coaching increasing tension may also be wanted. For example, the sport philosopher Scott Kretchmar (1975) has argued that 'sweet tension' is an immanent value of sport contesting, to which we could add the dynamic nature of competitive teams. Hence, always striving to relieve stress in competitive situations, hoping to reach a stable state of complete harmony and balance, may not be the best coaching strategy. Using humour to increase tension; to 'provoke' or 'stir up' and thereby stimulate productive interaction, may be fruitful in some situations. Thus, it may be used in flexible ways to balance stability and instability; that is, as a means to *manage* tension. A further exploration of humour's potential as a dual tension regulation resource in sport might contribute to the general research in the area, which to date primarily has focused on humour as a relief strategy.

Creativity

The linkage between humour and creativity refers, among other things, to how humour can 'facilitate the freeing of old mindsets and the seeing of things in a new light' (Lang and Lee

2010: 47). Lang and Lee label this dimension 'liberating humour'. The liberating potential stems from the logic of humour. Creativity, as humour, is about surprising solutions or ideas. Constructing jokes by juxtaposing two different frames of reference provides a glimpse of alternative perceptions of 'reality'. This sensitivity to complexity 'makes humour a particularly appropriate vehicle for conveying ambitions, subversions, triumphs and failures' (Grugulis 2002: 387). In particular, humour has been argued to facilitate organizational creativity, defined as 'the creation of a valuable, useful new product, service, idea, procedure, or process by individuals working together in a complex social system' (Lang and Lee 2010: 47). Usually in organizations and communities of practice established cultural practices are taken as normal and natural. In such environments, humorous exchanges may enable a shift in perspectives such that people can take a fresh look at a phenomenon. By highlighting discrepancies in logic and beliefs, humour can encourage creative and innovative thinking (Duncan 1982).

Within sport, and elite sport in particular, creative and innovative thinking is essential in the quest towards performance enhancement. There is an obvious danger that this kind of thinking may be inhibited in elite sport contexts often marked by strict discipline (Heikkala 1993) and rigorous behaviour control (Denison 2007). It could be alternatively argued that a certain degree of openness and playfulness is needed to facilitate innovations in sport, like Dick Fosbury's 'flop' in high jumping in the 1960s, and Bill Koch's invention of the skating technique in cross-country skiing in the 1970s. This is not to claim that Fosbury and Koch necessarily were particularly funny people, but they definitely were able to think outside the box.

Now, creativity rarely leads to radical innovations in sport; mostly it appears as slightly amended ways of acting and perceiving the world. The main argument we want to make here is that a coaching context marked by a humorous attitude may stimulate the creativity needed to balance continuity and novelty. Indeed, both 'hard work' discipline and creativity are necessary to enhance sporting performances. What potential role can humour play in balancing such dimensions? To what extent are strict training regimes and thorough surveillance suppressing a humorous approach that might be more productive? Are dominant practices leading to docile and hard-working athletes lacking creativity? Linking humour and creativity in coaching studies might shed light on such rather unexplored topics.

Power relations

Humour affects and is affected by power relations. Thus, the relationship between humour and power can be viewed from both an agential and a structural point of view. For example, humour can be used by leaders or subordinates to increase their influence in a social situation. As the sociologist Erving Goffman (1959) has showed us, behaviour and 'face-work' can be seen as performances aimed at leaving the 'right' impression in front of an audience, with the use of humour as a potentially influential part of this 'impression management'. Here, humour functions as a resource available to individual actors aiming to gain control of a situation. Humour can also be affected by established power relations, in the sense that the uses and interpretations of it depend on participants' positions in the social structure. For example, a coach's mocking or teasing of his athletes can be seen (by himself and/or his athletes) as a legitimate strategy to increase effort, while the opposite – athletes' mocking or teasing the coach – can easily threaten his authority as the 'boss'. This illustrates that formal positions in a hierarchical structure influence the meanings of the humour displayed, and to which degree laughter and humorous exchanges fortify, stabilize or challenge existing power relations.

Underlying actors' efficient exercise of power disguised as humour is the basic conception of power as an integral part of the context in which the interaction takes place. Power is not located in one place, institution or person, but is 'everywhere' and always present in our day-to-day interactions (Foucault 1979). Being a relational and omnipresent phenomenon, power resides in discourse and knowledge. Dominant discourses in the social context heavily influence our thinking and behaviour, including our humour and the uses of it. Through contested experiences coaches and athletes adopt situated understandings of when it is appropriate or 'allowable' to laugh, and what kind of joking behaviour is regarded as legitimate in which settings. Thus, culture-bound humour may tell us a lot about the culture in question. Identifying context-specific forms and uses of humour in sport settings may allow admission to basic power relations, values and assumptions characterizing different sports or sporting contexts.

The section above does not imply that humour always contributes to confirm established discourses and social structures. It obviously can be used to contest as well as reproduce power relations. According to Duncan *et al.* (1990), humour may, due to its ambivalent nature, be a particularly suitable strategy to challenge authority. Rather than openly oppose the person in authority, a subordinate might use a joke to 'test the water'; that is, to use humour to communicate messages that are socially risky to the initiator. Related to sport, an interesting research question is to what extent and in what ways athletes make use of humour to challenge coaches' authority or contest established discourses in the field.

Billig (2001), paying attention to the 'darker side' of humour, argued that humour is not only essential to social bonds but also integral to social order. Emphasizing 'the limits of nice-guy theories of social life' (Billig 2001: 23), he particularly discussed the fine line between teasing and ridicule in ensuring compliance with the routine demands of social life. By extension, we would argue that 'sophisticated' use of humour, by balancing laughing *with* and laughing *at* one's co-actors, effective social control may be exercised. As demonstrated in studies examining authoritarian sport cultures, ridicule was one of the strategies applied by coaches as a form of disciplinary power to ensure compliance with the norms (d'Arripe-Longueville *et al.* 1998; Cushion and Jones 2006). Other studies illustrate that such a strategy is not reserved for coaches only. The rowers in the work of Purdy *et al.* (2008) gradually lost respect for their coach due to the latter's actions. Increasing resistance from the athletes was expressed by starting to use a funny nickname and more openly making jokes at the expense of the coach. Eventually, the coach saw no other option than quitting the job. The story illustrates Nyberg's (1981: 53) argument that the ultimate act of confronting power occurs through sarcastic humour, as 'authority fears no threat more than the laughter that comes from scorn'.

We finish the section on humour and power by underlining a central point made by Foucault (1979); namely, that power can be productive as well as repressive. We would argue that the same goes for humour. As a 'double-edged sword' humour has 'bright' as well as 'dark' sides; both possible to apply by social actors aiming to increase their influence on social processes. The 'bright' as well as the 'dark' sides should be highlighted in future coaching research, not at least athletes' use of humour as a potentially efficient means in modifying power relations.

Leadership and humour

Leadership is primarily a communicative activity, and humour provides leaders with a valuable communicative resource (Holmes 2007). While coaches' use of humour has not been subjected to systematic research, humour and leadership has been studied both in pedagogical interactions (teacher–students) and organizational interactions (manager–subordinates). Some of the findings from this literature are briefly summarized below.

Within pedagogical settings there is substantial research indicating a positive relationship between teachers' use of humour and student learning (Wanzer and Frymier 1999). Use of humour in the classroom has been linked to improved perceptions of the teacher (Bryant *et al.* 1980; Gorham and Christophel 1990) and affective learning (Wanzer and Frymier 1999). However, an issue complicating the study of humour in classrooms is the vast array of humour types being performed by teachers. Humour can be represented as jokes, puns, sarcasm, nonverbal behaviours, and the topic of humour can target virtually anything. Wanzer *et al.* (2006) suggested that some forms of teacher humour will violate social classroom norms and be perceived as inappropriate, while other forms will be perceived as appropriate. In line with this, and based on humour as a relational phenomenon, we would argue that it is problematic to determine a fixed positive relationship between instructional humour and student learning in general. Instead, teachers, as well as coaches, may use humour more or less successfully in terms of affecting learning processes (Wanzer *et al.* 2006). Studies focusing on athletes perceptions of coaches' use of humour might produce more in-depth knowledge regarding to what extent and in what ways this actually promotes athletes' learning in specific contexts.

Also within the organizational literature a distinction has been drawn between 'productive' and 'destructive' humour production in managerial relationships (Martin *et al.* 2004). In addition, there is a third aspect often emphasized in this line of research, namely, the expressive dimension of humour, defined as 'the need to tell about oneself or express one's feelings' (Martin *et al.* 2004: 209). Such humorous self-disclosure allows the speaker to impart personal information that may be otherwise socially unacceptable or difficult to communicate. Witty and indirect self-ridiculing humour may increase a speaker's status, allowing one 'to save face while releasing tension and building rapport' (Martin and Gayle 1999: 74). In the coaching literature, there are some examples of coaches' using this strategy. For example, the Australian coach Bob Dwyer described how he deliberately used quirky expressions in his delivery, primarily to lift tension (Jones *et al.* 2004). Another example is the Norwegian coach Øystein Havang, who used humour to make it all less 'serious', and 'to make fun of myself' (Ronglan and Havang 2011: 90). These examples illustrate coaches' deliberate use of humour to de-emphasize power imbalances and to increase the influence of their messages: 'I know they think some of the expressions I use are right funny, but I'm happy about that because they'll remember it' (Jones *et al.* 2004: 127). This shows how humour can be a valuable discursive resource, because it 'makes it possible to accomplish both transactional and relational objectives, often simultaneously' (Holmes 2007: 9).

Another line of leadership research has focused on the use of humour in the construction of workplace culture. To a greater or lesser extent, every organization creates a distinct workplace culture (Holmes and Stubbe 2003), and particular workplace teams often develop as distinctive communities of practice (Wenger 1998). According to Holmes (2007), leaders and their team members collaborate in constructing not only a workplace culture, but also a leadership style appropriate to their particular community of practice. Examining Māori leaders [the indigenous New Zealand population] in New Zealand workplaces, Holmes (2007: 20) found that they faced a conflict between the need to demonstrate leadership by being authoritative on the one hand, and on the other 'the Māori cultural expectation that the individual is appropriately subordinated to the group'. The study showed that humour provided a useful strategy for negotiating ways of doing leadership within this area of potential conflict. Through a fine balance between leaders' self-depreciating humour, which downplayed self-promotion, and subordinates' ambiguous leader parodies indicating respect as well as equality, leadership was a joint construction. Holmes (2007) concluded that humour was a flexible discursive resource in managing the competing demands embedded in the context.

The potential conflict described above is far from unknown to coaches. On the one hand, they are often expected to be strong and charismatic leaders. On the other hand, they are operating in a context characterized by conflicting goals and inherent dilemmas (Jones and Wallace 2005; Saury and Durand 1998), often surrounded by experienced athletes and influential co-actors in the wider environment. Far from being in an omnipotent position, the coach is still held responsible for the athletes' results, preferably without taking too much credit for any achievements made. This requires a finely tuned 'leadership performance'. To explore this further, we conclude the chapter by turning more specifically to humour's potential as an integrated part of coaches' approach in their efforts to make the most out of their limited agency.

The coach as a humorous navigator

Sport coaching implies operating in troubled water. To coaches then, the following question becomes crucial: how to navigate in these waters, combining the handling of complexity and lack of overview with a need to display a sufficient degree of certainty and confidence? Related to this, we will pay attention to two dimensions of 'humorous coaching'. First, we will argue that a humorous *approach* might be a valuable basic attitude for coaches; second, we will suggest some possibilities and limits of a humorous coaching *performance*. As an extension, these concepts may sensitize future investigations of the relationship between humour and coaching.

A humorous approach to contingency

Due to the inherent complexity of the context, Bowes and Jones (2006) argued that coaches work at 'the edge of chaos'. There are simply so many contradictory goals, interests, values, emotions and relationships to be taken into account that it is impossible to pursue them all (Jones *et al.* 2004). Hence, a crucial question is how coaches deal with this complexity. According to the sociologist Niklas Luhmann (1995: 25), complexity, that is, the infinity of possibilities, enforces selectivity, but this has its costs: 'Complexity means being forced to select, being forced to select means contingency; and contingency means risk'. Thus, contingency, the fact that each selection could have been different, results in a basic uncertainty (risk). Every day the coach has to make decisions among a surplus of possibilities; decisions that always could have been different and, therefore, can be questioned. From moment to moment the coach has to 'choose' what to do and say, based on limited information, always knowing that several other ways of acting could have been equally possible (and suitable) in the situation at hand. The coach has to generate sufficient support for his/her selected decisions and behaviours; on the other hand, both the coach and the athletes are aware of the contingent reality that there is always more than one way to skin a cat (and maybe it is not the best idea to skin the cat at all).

We advocate a humorous approach for coaches to be better equipped to handle the immanent contingency. We would claim that a traditional rationalistic view of coaching as a knowable sequence, over which coaches are presumed to have full command, actually is an 'irrational' conception. In contrast, a humoristic stance is not irrational, but provides a reasonable approach more in line with the goal divergence and contingency embedded in the context. A humorous attitude allows the coach an arm's length distance to his own agency as well as to the 'causalities' and 'effects' observed, because of the incongruity and discrepancies characterizing the logic of humorous thinking. Instead of fighting the immanent ambiguity, humour can be part of a strategy of *embracing and coping* with ambiguity, due to its quality of acknowledging and making use of the incongruities.

In their work on 'coaching as orchestration', Jones and Wallace (2005) stressed the fact that coaches, due to the complex environment, always have *limited awareness*. Due to limited information and restricted overview they can never know exactly what is going on in every corner. However, what you can be sure of as a coach is that there is a lot of humour and laughter in the environment. Therefore, humour being a social gesture, it is important to cope with and relate to the (visible and invisible) humour, in order to get situated in the social setting and be able to manage the processes going on. This does not mean that the coach necessarily has to be a 'joker' himself, but he should be able to interpret the humorous glances, quirky remarks and the jargon among the athletes; that is, to display a sufficient *sense* of humour. Taking a too 'serious' approach to the practice, and not noticing the (intended) ambivalence in messages delivered, will probably mean that you will be laughed at when you turn the back to the players.

Finally, we will argue that a coach's humorous attitude holds implications for the coach–athlete relationship, as it will allow athletes a humorous attitude as well. Again, such an attitude is not about telling funny jokes all the time, but appears from balancing commitment with a certain role distance (Goffman 1959), openness and an oblique glance at your own conduct and the interaction going on. This approach to coaching practice is likely to facilitate a more curious and attentive approach to the practice, as demonstrated in the section on humour and creativity. Nurturing a humorous attitude might in a developmental perspective stimulate the overall learning within the community of practice.

A humorous coaching performance

Besides being a basic attitude underlying coaches' general approach, humour can also be used as a communicative resource applied deliberately in specific coaching situations. We call this dimension 'humorous performance', and will elaborate on this as a balancing act. The trick is to use humour as an appropriate and integrated part of coaches' conduct to increase their influence on persons and processes. Below, we will touch upon three aspects of this balancing act; balancing 'authenticity' and 'performance', 'seriousness' and 'fun', and 'authority' and 'equality'.

Erving Goffman (1959) described how, in social encounters, we present an impression of our self that we wish others to receive in an attempt to control how those others see us. However, this performance has to be seen as something else than 'pure acting' if the performance is going to have the intended effect. Successful performances are typically viewed as 'authentic' and well adapted to the situation at hand. The same goes for the use of humour; few things are more embarrassing than a totally inappropriate joke uttered by a person misjudging the situation (Billig 2001), leaving the audience in silence with flickering glances. When coaches themselves note that 'the best coaches would make good actors' (Jones *et al.* 2004: 139), it is worth emphasizing that 'good' acting, for example successful joking behaviour, mirrors the 'true' person in the view of the athletes, as does 'bad' acting. Hence, since joking behaviour does not come as a natural thing for everyone, it might be better to select other ways of behaving from the repertoire we have available. However, if forms of humour are included in coaches' general repertoire it should be no reason to always suppress it in order to present a persistent 'serious' coach front, considering the potential benefits of humorous exchanges discussed previously in the chapter.

Having fun and being serious are not opposites. As a Danish writer, Piet Hein, once stated: 'He who takes jest only as jest, and seriousness only as seriousness, he has actually misunderstood both'. Nevertheless, there is a tension between 'seriousness' and 'fun' in coaching situations. Productive and liberating humour may 'escalate' into nonsense and purposeless fooling around on the training ground, as seriousness may 'degenerate' into mechanical rule following allowing no laughter or degree of freedom. Here too, a balance is needed. To coaches, *timing* is crucial in this balancing effort: when is it productive to deliberately use humour as a strategy to regulate tension, stimulate creativity, or strengthen social bonds? And, when is it more appropriate using other interactional strategies? Furthermore, the *extent* of humour displayed from the coach is another aspect to be considered. It can simply be too much. An inflation of jokes and funny 'face-work' (Goffman 1959) may over time tire out the players leading to growing irritation over the 'desperately' funny coach. Indeed, the significance of the 'clown' as a social figure in communities of practice (Plester and Orams 2008) is relevant also to sport teams, but the coach should probably not be the person playing this role.

This leads us to the balance between authority and equality. As demonstrated in the sections of power and leadership, humour may be used in flexible ways to regulate the status difference between coach and athletes (self irony), as well as to increase the authority and gain control over the situation (impression management). In order to stay in power nothing is more harmful than being laughed at by the athletes. Consequently, a strategy to prevent being laughed at could be to laugh *with* them (Ronglan and Havang 2011). However, to cite the title of a paper examining the behaviours of an expert football coach (Potrac *et al.* 2002) 'It's all about getting respect'; thus, losing respect while laughing with the players would not be very helpful. Respect is something that is given or not by the athletes, based on their holistic judgement of the coach as a professionally and socially competent leader (Potrac *et al.* 2002). Therefore, to gain respect, humour has to be used finely tuned in combination with other competencies and in reasonable accordance with the expectations directed towards the coach role. Such expectations vary across sporting contexts, including to what degree displaying humbleness will strengthen or threaten the coach's authority. Using the 'right' forms of humour in appropriate situations is a vital part of the social competence needed for coaches to appear as trustworthy leaders.

Conclusion

Being a 'double-edged sword', the application of humour is a delicate matter. Shared humour creates feelings of belonging and community, but defining 'insiders' implies at the same time exclusion of 'outsiders'. Moreover, uses of humour can take a number of forms (e.g. witty remarks, puns, jokes, irony, sarcasm, ridicule) and it can be self-directed or other-directed. Generally spoken then, it is possible to use humour to include or exclude, to support or harm, to empower or suppress, and to exert social control or to lose it. Having 'bright' as well as 'dark' sides, humour should be taken seriously by coaches and researchers trying to understand the social nature of sports coaching.

In the chapter, we focused upon four social functions of the phenomenon: shared humour is a social glue, creating and symbolizing belonging (solidarity dimension), it can be used to relieve stress or increase arousal (tension regulation), to stimulate creativity and thinking outside the box (liberating dimension), or to gain control or challenge authority (controlling dimension). As belonging, tension, creativity and power relations are immanent aspects of sports coaching, the chapter has pointed to some potentially fruitful aspects of working deliberately with humour in the coaching practice. Indeed, these dimensions need further exploration, as exemplified throughout the chapter. In this effort, the significance of humour need to be scrutinized both from athletes' and coaches' point of view. We have suggested that a 'humorous approach' and 'humorous performances' might be sensitizing concepts both for coaches and researchers in efforts to deepen our understanding of coaches' challenges and possibilities in managing environmental demands and social relationships.

To establish humour as a part of sports coaching is not to propose a radically new way of coaching. Rather, it is to acknowledge that humour is present in the context anyway, as an inevitable part of the social interaction going on. Hence, the point has not been to 'introduce' humour as the point of departure, but to increase the awareness of the phenomenon and its potential within coaching. Orchestration is the compliance to the limited control experienced by coaches, thus, humour deserves attention and recognition as a valuable tool in orchestrating coaching processes.

References

Billig, M. (2001) 'Humour and embarrassment: Limits of 'nice-guy' theories of social life', *Theory, Culture and Society*, 18(5): 23–43.

Bloom, G.A. and Smith, M.D. (1986) 'Hockey violence: A test of cultural spillover theory', *Sociology of Sport Journal*, 13(1): 65–77.

Bowes, I. and Jones, R.L. (2006) 'Working at the edge of chaos: Understanding coaching as a complex, interpersonal system', *The Sport Psychologist*, 20(2): 235–245.

Bryant, J., Crane, J.S., Cominsky, P.W. and Zillmann, D. (1980) 'Relationship between college teachers' use of humor in the classroom and students' evaluations of their teachers', *Journal of Educational Psychology*, 72(4): 511–519.

Cooper, C. (2008) 'Elucidating the bonds of workplace humour: A relational process model', *Human Relations*, 61(8): 1087–1115.

Cushion, C.J. and Jones, R.L. (2006) 'Power, discourse and symbolic violence in professional youth soccer: The case of Albion FC', *Sociology of Sport Journal*, 23(2): 142–161.

d'Arripe-Longueville, R., Fournier, J.F. and Dubois, A. (1998) 'The perceived effectiveness of interactions between expert French judo coaches and female athletes', *The Sport Psychologist*, 12(3): 317–332.

Davies, M. (1979) 'Sociology through humour', *Symbolic Interaction*, 2(1): 105–110.

Denison, J. (2007) 'Social theory for coaches: A Foucauldian reading of one athlete's poor performance', *International Journal of Sport Science and Coaching*, 2(4): 369–383.

Duncan, W.J. (1982) 'Humour in management: Prospects for administrative practice and research', *Academy of Management Review*, 7(1): 136–142.

Duncan, W.J., Smeltzer, L.R. and Leap, T.L. (1990) 'Humour and work: Applications of joking behaviour to management', *Journal of Management*, 16(2): 255–278.

Faulkner, J. (1987) *Sociology through Humour*, New York: West Publishing Company.

Fine, G. (1983) 'Sociological approaches to the study of humour', in P. McGhee and J. Goldstein (eds) *Handbook of Humour Research*, New York: Springer-Verlag.

Fine, A.G. (1984) *With the Boys: Little League Baseball and Preadolescent Culture*, Chicago, IL: The University of Chicago Press.

Foucault, M. (1979) *Discipline and Punish: The Birth of the Prison*, New York: Vintage.

Goffman, E. (1959) *The Presentation of Self in Everyday Life*, Reading: Penguin Books.

Goffman, E. (1967) *Interaction Ritual*, New York: Pantheon Books.

Gorham, J. and Christophel, D.M. (1990) 'The relationship of teachers' use of humor in the classroom to immediacy and student learning', *Communication Education*, 39(1): 46–62.

Graham, E.E. (1995) 'The involvement of sense of humour in the development of social relationships', *Communication Reports*, 8(2): 158–170.

Grugulis, I. (2002) 'Nothing serious? Candidates' use of humour in management training', *Human Relations*, 55(4): 387–406.

Hampes, W.P. (1999) 'The relationship between humour and trust', *Humor*, 12(3): 253–259.

Heikkala, J. (1993) 'Discipline and excel: Techniques of self and the body and the logic of competing', *Sociology of Sport Journal*, 10(4): 397–412.

Holmes, J. (2000) 'Politeness, power and provocation: How humour functions in the workplace', *Discourse Studies*, 2(2): 159–185.

Holmes, J. (2007) 'Humour and the construction of Māori leadership at work', *Leadership*, 3(1): 5–27.

Holmes, J. and Meredith, M. (2002) 'Having a laugh at work: How humour contributes to workplace culture', *Journal of Pragmatics*, 34(12): 1683–1710.

Holmes, J. and Stubbe, M. (2003) *Power and Politeness in the Workplace: A Sociolinguistic Analysis of Talk at Work*, London: Longman.

Jones, R.L., Armour, K.L. and Potrac, P. (2004) *Sports Coaching Cultures: From Practice to Theory*, London: Routledge.

Jones, R.L. and Wallace, M. (2005) 'Another bad day at the training ground: Coping with ambiguity in the coaching context', *Sport, Education and Society*, 10(1): 119–134.

Jones, R.L., Ronglan, L.T., Potrac, P. and Cushion, C.J. (2011) 'Concluding thoughts and ways forward', in R.L. Jones, P. Potrac, C.J. Cushion and L.T. Ronglan (eds) *The Sociology of Sports Coaching*, Abingdon: Routledge.

Kahn, W.A. (1989) 'Toward a sense of organizational humour: Implications for organizational diagnosis and change', *The Journal of Applied Behavioral Science*, 25(1): 45–63.

Kretchmar, R.S. (1975) 'From test to contest: An analysis of two kinds of counterpoints in sport', *Journal of the Philosophy of Sport*, 2(1): 23–30.

Lang, J.C. and Lee, C.H. (2010) 'Workplace humour and organizational creativity', *The International Journal of Human Resource Management*, 21(1): 46–60.

Lewis, D.J. and Weigert, A. (1985) 'Trust as a social reality', *Social Forces*, 63(4): 967–985.

Light, R. (2008) 'Learning masculinities in a Japanese high school rugby club', *Sport, Education and Society*, 13(2): 163–179.

Luhmann, N. (1995) *Social Systems*, Stanford, CA: Stanford University Press.

Martin, D.M. and Gayle, B.M. (1999) 'It isn't a matter of just being funny: Humour production by organizational leaders', *Communication Research Reports*, 16(1): 72–80.

Martin, D.M., Rich, C.O. and Gaile, B.M. (2004) 'Humour works: Communication style and humor functions in manager/subordinate relationships', *Southern Communication Journal*, 69(3): 206–222.

Morreall, J. (1982) 'A new theory of laughter', *Philosophical Studies*, 42(2): 243–254.

Mulholland, J. (1997) 'The Asian connection: Business requests and acknowledgements', in F. Bargiela-Chiappini and S. Harris (eds) *The Languages of Business*, Edinburgh: Edinburgh University Press.

Nyberg, D. (1981) *Power over Power*, London: Cornell University Press.

Plester, B. and Orams, M. (2008) 'Send in the clowns: The role of the joker in three New Zealand IT companies', *Humor*, 21(3): 253–281.

Potrac, P., Jones, R.L. and Armour, K.M. (2002) 'It's all about getting respect': The coaching behaviors of an expert English soccer coach', *Sport, Education and Society*, 7(2): 183–202.

Purdy, L., Potrac, P. and Jones, R.L. (2008) 'Power, consent and resistance: An autoethnography of competitive rowing', *Sport, Education and Society*, 13(3): 319–336.

Rogerson-Revell, P. (2007) 'Humour in business: A double-edged sword – A study of humour and style shifting in intercultural meetings', *Journal of Pragmatics*, 39(1): 4–28.

Romero, E. and Pescosolido, A. (2008) 'Humor and group effectiveness', *Human Relations*, 61(3): 395–418.

Romero, E.J., Alsua, C., Hinrichs, K. and Pearson, T. (2007) 'Regional humour differences in the United States: Implications for management', *International Journal of Humor Research*, 20(2): 189–201.

Ronglan, L.T. and Havang, Ø. (2011) 'Niklas Luhmann: Coaching as communication', in R.L. Jones, P. Potrac, C.J. Cushion and L.T. Ronglan (eds) *The Sociology of Sports Coaching*, Abingdon: Routledge.

Saury, J. and Durand, M. (1998) 'Practical knowledge in expert coaches: On-site study of coaching in sailing', *Research Quarterly for Exercise and Sport*, 69(3): 254–266.

Snyder, E.E. (1991) 'Sociology of sport and humor', *International Review for the Sociology of Sport*, 26(2): 119–131.

Svebak, S. (1974) 'A theory of sense of humour', *Scandinavian Journal of Psychology*, 15(1): 99–107.

Thorpe, H. (2006) 'Beyond "decorative sociology": Contextualizing female surf, skate, and snow boarding', *Sociology of Sport Journal*, 23(3): 205–228.

Terrion, J.L. and Ashforth, B.E. (2002) 'From "I" to "we": The role of putdown humor and identity in the development of a temporary group', *Human Relations*, 55(1): 55–88.

Wanzer, M.B. and Frymier, A.B. (1999) 'The relationship between student perceptions of instructor humor and students' reports of learning', *Communication Education*, 48(1): 48–62.

Wanzer, M.B., Frymier, A.B., Wojtaszczyk, A.M. and Smith, T. (2006) 'Appropriate and inappropriate uses of humor by teachers', *Communication Education*, 55(2): 178–196.

Wenger, W. (1998) *Communities of Practice. Learning, Meaning, and Identity*, Cambridge: Cambridge University Press.

Wheaton, B. (2000) '"Just do it": Consumption, commitment, and identity in the windsurfing subculture', *Sociology of Sport Journal*, 17(3): 254–274.

19

TOWARDS AN EMOTIONAL UNDERSTANDING OF COACHING PRACTICE

A suggested research agenda

Paul Potrac

UNIVERSITY OF HULL, UK

Robyn L. Jones

CARDIFF METROPOLITAN UNIVERSITY, UK

Laura Purdy

UNIVERSITY OF WORCESTER, UK

Lee Nelson

UNIVERSITY OF HULL, UK

Phil Marshall

UNIVERSITY OF HULL, UK

Introduction

In recent years, scholars have increasingly argued for the need to bring the person back into the study of coaching (e.g. Denison 2007; Jones 2006a, 2009; Jones *et al.* 2004). This has stemmed from a dissatisfaction with the tendency to represent coaching as a clean, sequential, and unproblematic activity underpinned by technical, tactical, and bio-scientific knowledge, methods, and ideas (Jones 2000). Consequently, there is growing evidence to support the contention that coaches must also make connections to people, be they athletes or other stakeholders if they are to successfully implement their coaching programmes (Jones 2006a). In this regard, the literature has provided some valuable initial insights into the strategic actions that coaches use in their attempts to persuade, cajole, and even coerce others to 'buy into' their respective agendas (e.g. Cushion and Jones 2006; Potrac and Jones 2009; Potrac *et al.* 2002). Equally, this work has illustrated how a coach's efforts are surrounded by, and imbued with, considerable ambiguity and pathos (Jones and Wallace 2005). That is, coaches never have complete control over the goals, processes, people and events that comprise their working environments. As such, it could be argued that the coaching role is one characterised by a considerable degree of vulnerability (Jones and Wallace 2005; Kelchtermans 2005).

While such accounts (as cited above) are to be applauded for deepening our understanding of coaching practice, the available literature has so far still failed to pay any concerted attention to the emotional nature of coaching. Indeed, save for a few notable examples (e.g. Jones 2006a, 2009; Jones *et al.* 2005; Purdy *et al.* 2008), existing accounts of coaching have tended to be free of emotionality, with coaches and athletes largely presented as calculated, dispassionate, and rational beings (Fineman 1993; Hargreaves 2005). This neglect has been unfortunate, as no doubt both coaches and athletes experience a variety of strong emotions as they strive to navigate the challenges and opportunities of their dynamic sporting worlds.

The aim of this chapter is to make a case for examining the emotional nature of coaching, and to introduce some theoretical frameworks that could be productively utilised to help our related theorising. Following this brief introduction, the chapter begins by outlining the centrality of emotion in everyday life, and the subsequent need to address the emotional nature of sports coaching. Three frameworks that could be utilised for studying emotion in coaching practice are then presented; that is, those associated with the work of Denzin (1984), Hochschild (2000 [1983]) and Zembylas (2005). Here, the key tenets of these theories and their potential utility for guiding inquiry into the emotional nature of coaching are outlined. It should be noted that, while this chapter is principally framed in relation to the educational literature that has explored the emotional nature of teaching, we certainly do not believe that educational research should be seen as the panacea or 'holy grail' for sports coaching (Jones 2006b). Rather, due to their pedagogical similarities, and to the fact that education continues to be theorised to a much greater extent than coaching, we contend that such an approach offers the potential for coaching to short-circuit some of the growing pains experienced by education (Jones 2006b). Consequently, while we recognise the need for coaching science to develop its own conceptual language, we believe that the theories, concepts, and approaches discussed in this paper can provide scholars with new and sophisticated vantage points from which to view the everyday nature of coaching (Cushion 2007; Jones 2006b).

Why explore emotion in coaching?

In Western thought, emotions have been largely understood as physiological and psychological phenomena with, until relatively recently, little attention paid to them from a socio-political perspective (Turner and Stets 2007). The study of emotions was traditionally seen to lie outside the domain of sociological inquiry (Zembylas 2005). This was because emotions were viewed as the product of the inner working of the individual, directly related to brain functioning and personality. Consequently, the responsibility for their investigation lay with biologists, and cognitive and social psychologists (Turner and Stets 2007; Zembylas 2005).

From the 1970s onwards, however, the invisibility of emotions in sociological and pedagogical research began to be challenged (Turner and Stets 2007; Zembylas 2005). It was initially argued that the production of pedagogies and 'sociologies without emotion' could be attributed to a misinterpretation of 'Weber's idea that the increasing rationalisation of the world means the decreasing significance of emotion in human affairs and conduct' (Barbalet

2001: 13). Within educational and sociological theorising then, reason and emotion came to be regarded as being at the opposite ends of a continuum, with cognition and rationality at one pole and emotions and irrationality at the other (Turner and Stets 2005). Indeed, Zembylas (2005: 4) noted that the study of teacher emotion as a sociological and cultural phenomenon 'was not particularly accepted by educational researchers, who tended to emphasise teaching practice as a primarily cognitive activity'. This sentiment was also expressed by Boler (1999), who suggested that the absence of emotion in science and philosophy was due to the subjective bias being positioned on the 'negative side of a binary division with truth and reason in the academy'. In this regard, Møller (2005: 89) noted how rationality has become 'considered sacred and holy, while emotions [were] perceived as being more or less inappropriate to talk about'.

It has been suggested that educational researchers and sociologists have since made up for lost time, with the study of emotion being at the forefront of micro-sociology in particular (Barbalet 2002; Stets 2003; Turner 2002; Zembylas 2005). In addition, Turner and Stets (2007) have argued that a sociologically orientated approach to the study of emotion can potentially explain the relationship between the physical body, cognitive processes, and cultural constructions. In underlining the potential value of the sociological analysis of emotions, they stated that:

> Emotions are the glue that bind people together and generate commitments to large-scale social and cultural structures; in fact, emotions are what make social structures and systems of cultural symbols viable. Conversely, emotions are also what can drive people apart and push them to tear down social structures and challenge cultural traditions. Thus, experience, behaviour, interaction, and organization are connected to the mobilization and expression of emotions.
>
> *(Turner and Stets 2007: 1)*

In recent years, the centrality of emotion in social relationships has increasingly come to the fore. It has been explored in such topics as 'class and resentment', 'action and confidence', 'conformity and shame', 'rights and vengefulness', and 'fear and change' (see Barbalet 2001 for an overview of this work). For example, with regard to emotion and rationality, Barbalet (2001) argues that reason has its background in emotion, as without the accompanying feelings of calmness, security, and confidence, reason turns to its opposite. Far from arguing against reason, Barbalet (2001: 2) uses this example as a critique of the 'inflation of reason at the expense of emotion'. Similarly, in attempting to understand emotions such as excitement, anger, nervousness, and embarrassment in teaching, Zembylas (2005) suggested that all of these emotions are the consequence of teachers' interactions with significant others within the social milieu of the school; that is, such feelings are produced in a socio-political context. It has also been suggested that emotions are embodied; that they do not exist solely in the mind (Layder 2006). For example, being embarrassed or shy may lead us to blush, shake, or avoid eye contact (May and Powell 2008).

Such work has highlighted how emotion is a central concern for both sociologists (e.g. TenHouten 2007; Lane West-Newman 2007; Williams 2001) and educational researchers (e.g. Day and Lee 2011; Schutz and Pekrun 2007; Schutz and Zembylas 2009). This is because not only is every social action accompanied by an emotional involvement, but also how 'a very large class of emotions result from real, imagined, or anticipated outcomes in social relationships' (Kemper 1978: 43). Indeed, Hargreaves (2000) described how emotions are far from peripheral in people's lives and that they, subsequently, cannot be compartmentalised away from action or from rational reflection on these lives. With specific regard to teaching, he further highlighted the need to better understand the integral connections between emotion, cognition, and action if teacher education provision was to avoid developing overly rationalised models of practice. Given this state of affairs, it is perhaps not surprising that, in the context of educational research, Liston and Garrison argued that:

> For too long we have left emotions in the ontological basement of educational scholarship, to be dragged up and out when a particular topic necessitated it (e.g. classroom management, student motivation, or teacher 'burnout'). That seems ill advised, and it is time to rebuild our academic house. When we teach, we teach with ideas and feelings. When we interact with students, we react and they respond with thoughts and emotions. When we inquire into our natural and social worlds, we do so with desire and yearning.
>
> *(Liston and Garrison 2003: 5)*

We believe that this is an equally valuable lesson for coaching scholars and coach educators to consider in attempts to develop accounts of practice in keeping with the lived experiences of coaches. In their paper addressing ambiguity in coaching, Jones and Wallace criticised the positivistic foundations of existing conceptualisations of coaching for their failure to recognise that coaches face a reality where 'goals are inherently challenging, variables within the process are many and dynamic, and intended outcomes can never be a foregone conclusion' (Jones and Wallace 2005: 119). They suggested that there has been a failure to explore the tensions that may arise for coaches as they strive to fulfil the many and often contradictory goals that form a feature of coaching contexts. Indeed, the challenges, tensions, and dilemmas faced by coaches are not just cognitive or social in nature, but are also emotional phenomena and need to be understood as such; a point highlighted in recent empirical work (e.g. Cushion and Jones 2006; Potrac and Jones 2009; Purdy *et al.* 2008; Jones 2009).

Given the interactive and pedagogical nature of coaching (Jones *et al.* 2004; Jones 2006b), it could be argued that it is impossible for coaches (and athletes) to 'separate feeling from perception' and 'affectivity from judgement' (Nias 1996: 294). This is because coaching involves 'intensive personal interactions' (Nias 1996: 296) and an investment of the self in practice (Jones *et al.* 2004). It has also been argued that emotions are indispensable to rational decision making in pedagogical activities, in terms of narrowing down the range of potential actions into a manageable assortment (Damasio 1994; Hargreaves 2005; Sacks 1995). Here, for example, Hargreaves (2005: 280) stated that 'you can't judge if you can't feel'. While this has certainly been evidenced in the educational literature (e.g. Denzin 1984; Hargreaves 1998, 2000, 2005; Kelchtermans and Ballet 2002a, 2002b; Nias 1996; Zembylas 2005), such realities in coaching, notwithstanding the work of Jones (2006a, 2009) have largely been ignored. Indeed, it could be suggested that emotions within coaching have been treated as little more than another variable that coaches (and athletes) need to manage appropriately so that they can focus on the 'really important' technical and cognitive components of their role (Hargreaves 1998). Despite this 'light investigative touch', some scholars (e.g. Jones *et al.* 2011; Potrac and Marshall 2011) have increasingly suggested that we will not be able to best prepare coaches for the complex realities of their work, until we engage in a substantive exploration of the ambiguities, nuances, and emotional nature of coaching.

Exploring emotions in coaching: selected theoretical frameworks

Within this section of the chapter, we introduce the work carried out on emotions by Denzin (1984), Hochschild (2000 [1983]) and Zembylas (2005), which could help in better recognising and understanding some of the muddled realities of personal feeling in coaching (Jones 2009). By outlining these conceptual frameworks, our intention is to highlight how we may begin to understand emotions, not only as biological phenomena, but also as socio-cultural, political, and institutional forces that continuously shape and reshape the terrain of coaching practice (Hargreaves 1998; Potrac and Marshall 2011). It is a feature of coaching that has remained largely unacknowledged in the muddy waters of practice (Jones 2009; Potrac and Marshall 2011). We are not arguing that these authors' works are the 'best' or 'only' frameworks through which to view emotions. Rather, we simply believe that they can serve as useful starting points for future critical discussion and empirical exploration.

Emotional understanding and misunderstanding

In his seminal text, *On Understanding Emotion*, Denzin (1984) provided a detailed synthesis of classical and contemporary theories of emotion, which he drew upon to develop his own interpretation of emotional experience in everyday life. While it is not possible to engage with all of Denzin's conceptual ideas here, suffice to say that his writing on emotional understanding and misunderstanding has played an important role in the theorisation of emotion in the teaching literature (e.g. Hargreaves 2000). Denzin defined emotional understanding as:

> An intersubjective process requiring that one person enter into the same field of experience of another, and experience for herself the same or similar experiences experienced by another. The subjective interpretation of another's emotional experience from one's own standpoint is central to emotional understanding. Shared and shareable emotionality lie at the core of what it means to understand and meaningfully enter into the emotional experiences of others.
>
> *(Denzin 1984: 137)*

In the context of pedagogical practice then, emotional understanding occurs when teachers and coaches 'reach into the past to interpret and unravel, instantaneously, at a glance the emotional experiences of others' (Hargreaves 2001: 1059). This process entails 'knowing and comprehending through emotional means, including sympathy and imagination, the intentions, feelings, and thoughts expressed by another' (Denzin 1984: 282). Denzin highlighted how an individual's emotional understanding can be developed through a variety of means, which include vicarious emotional reflection (i.e. where we empathise with people's lives or predicaments), sharing emotional experience (i.e. experiences of joy and loss), emotional infection (i.e. spreading optimistic or pessimistic moods to others), and by developing long-standing and close relationships. According to Hargreaves (2001), an emotional understanding of others is important if pedagogues are to successfully engage in constructive and productive working relationships with various contextual stakeholders; a point clearly evidenced in the field of education (see Hargreaves *et al.* 2001).

In the absence of the emotional understanding of others, Hargreaves (2001) highlights how pedagogues may alternatively encounter what Denzin (1984) defined as emotional misunderstanding. This can occur when an individual 'mistakes their feelings for the feelings of others' (Denzin 1984: 84). For example, where close relationships do not exist within the coaching setting, it could be possible for a coach to mistakenly interpret the actions of others. For example, from a coach's perspective, a group of netball players chatting off-task could be seen as behaving inappropriately in terms of the maximisation of their athletic talent. Such behaviour could also be understood by the coach as being somewhat akin to resistance or hostility to his or her methods, and may result in the coach choosing to admonish or punish the players concerned. However, the players could be just airing other concerns and feelings related to individual prestige and standing in the peer group, protecting slight injuries, or discussing home-life issues or petty jealousies; engagements which make their off-task behaviour relevant to them (Jones and Wallace 2005). Hargreaves (2001) argued that such emotional misunderstanding can have a significant impact on the pedagogical process in terms of the learning that takes place and the quality of the relationship that exists. Indeed, when applied to coaching, Hargreaves' (2001) work suggests that coaches need to develop close bonds with athletes and colleagues that make emotional understanding possible if they are to be successful in their pedagogical endeavours.

To date, the coaching literature has paid little attention to the notions of emotional understanding and misunderstanding. Indeed, apart from the recent work of Nelson *et al.* (under review), this aspect of practice has been neglected. Nevertheless, future scholarly inquiry in this area could result in the production of rich in-depth accounts that chart the ways in which coaches develop and utilise their emotional understanding in practice, and how this is subsequently perceived, and responded to, by athletes and other key contextual stakeholders. There is also considerable scope for addressing the specific notion of emotional misunderstanding in coaching and its impact upon athlete learning, as well as on wider coaching relationships in general. Furthermore, Denzin's (1984) notions of 'reflective and unreflective emotional consciousness', 'emotional temporality', and the 'double structure of emotional experience' also appear worthy of further application and deconstruction in relation to coaching.

Emotion management and emotional labour

Hochschild's (1983, 2000) work on emotion management and emotional labour focused on the ways in which individuals manage their emotions 'to create a publicly observable facial and bodily display' (7). In particular, Hochschild was concerned with exploring the relationship between the emotions a person feels, the emotions he or she chooses to display for the benefit of others, and the social context within which these emotions are displayed (Theodosius 2008). In this regard, she described how:

> Acts of emotion management are not simple private acts; they are used in exchanges under the guidance of feeling rules. Feeling rules are the standards used in emotional conversations to determine what is rightly owed in the currency of feeling. Through them, we tell what is 'due' in each relation, each role. We pay tribute to each other in the currency of managing the act. In interaction, we pay, over pay, under pay, play with paying, acknowledge our due, pretend to pay, or acknowledge what is emotionally due to another person.
>
> *(Hochschild 2000 [1983]: 18)*

In building upon the work of Goffman (1959) and Wright Mills (1956), Hochschild illustrated how individuals frequently engage in a certain amount of acting within social encounters that require them to manufacture or mask certain emotional states (Potrac and Marshall 2011). This can include 'surface acting', where we deceive others about what we really feel, but do not deceive ourselves, and 'deep acting', where an individual works on his or her feelings through 'conscious mental work' to the extent that he or she believes in the emotions being expressed (Hochschild 2000 [1983]). In the context of coaching, such acting could include enthusing over athlete performance, showing patience with a frustrating parent or colleague, or remaining calm and controlled in the face of criticism (Potrac and Marshall 2011).

For Hochschild (2000 [1983]), engagement in emotion management and emotional labour could, in some circumstances, have significant psychological costs that may lead to a sense of burnout or the loss of an individual's sense of self. This can be especially so when people feel that they are masking or presenting emotional fronts solely for the benefit of others, or when poor working conditions make it very difficult for them to perform their jobs well (Hargreaves 2000; Stenross and Kleinman 1989). In recent years, critics have also argued that emotion management and emotional labour do not necessarily have to be harmful or detrimental (Isenbarger and Zembylas 2006). In fact, individuals' successful engagement in such acts may also be viewed as an exciting, rewarding, and fun part of their job (Hargreaves 2000). For example, Isenbarger and Zembylas (2006) highlighted how teachers were gratified by the emotional labour demanded in their quest to improve the performances, experiences, and lives of their pupils.

With specific reference to coaching, Hochschild's (1983 [2000]) work on emotion management and emotional labour could be productively considered in order to better understand how coaches and athletes shape and even create emotion (through inducing and exhorting) to achieve desired ends (Potrac and Marshall 2011; Theodosius 2008). Her work provides a useful lens through which we can uncover the emotional experiences of coaches and athletes, and the ways in which they may, at various times, choose to fake, modify, enhance, or suppress their emotions (Potrac and Marshall 2011). Furthermore, Hochschild's (2000 [1983]) conceptual framework also allows us insight into self-alienation in coaching and the related issues of cynicism, burnout, and self-esteem management (Potrac and Marshall 2011). Additionally, her concept of 'feeling rules' can assist in critically considering how coaches' and athletes' socialisation experiences predispose them to think, feel, and act in certain ways. It thus becomes possible to not simply label coaches' emotions and emotional understanding as physiological and psychological attributes, but also to understand them as the products of the socio-political interactions that take place within the coaching context (Potrac and Marshall 2011; Zembylas 2005).

Postmodern accounts of emotion in teaching

In his recent work addressing emotion in teaching, Zembylas (2003, 2005, 2007a, 2007b 2011) utilised a post-structuralist perspective to problematise the dominant discourses addressing how teachers and pupils, should feel, think, and act. A key feature of Zembylas' (2011: 31) work is the attention given to the 'the link between the microscopic perspectives at the level of the teacher self and the macroscopic level of social, cultural, and political structures of schooling'. In this regard, Zembylas (2011) explored how, from a Foucauldian perspective, emotions in teaching relate not only to teachers' psychological and physiological impulses, but are instead constituted through language and refer to wider social life. He provided some fascinating insights into the power relations inherent in the ways in which teachers experienced and talked about emotion, especially in terms of which emotions they felt they were permitted or prohibited from experiencing. Far from being private acts, he believed that classroom emotions occurred in a political space that involved 'a process of determining who must be repressed as illegitimate, who must be foreground as valuable, and the feelings and desires that comes up for them in given contexts and relationships' (Reddy 1997: 335). In this sense then, power is located in expressions of emotion (Campbell 1997). Given this focus, Zembylas' work provides a resource for encouraging coaching scholars to become aware of 'structural rules and processes that determine what can be thought and said about' good coaching and being a proper coach (Kelchtermans 2005: 997).

Interestingly, Zembylas (2011) argued that teachers' emotions are performative in nature, in that teachers experience, understand, and discuss emotion in relation to their sense of identity. Hence, he believed that teacher emotions could be productively studied in classroom settings where pedagogical selves come to be constituted (Zembylas 2011). His ethnographic work highlighted how the dominant discourses surrounding professionalism in teaching often lead teachers to control and manage how they feel inside, as well as the emotions they express publicly. Zembylas' (2007a) fieldwork also revealed how, as a product of surveillance from other teachers and school administrators, as well as themselves, teachers come to increasingly judge themselves against dominant professional norms. For example, he described how a teacher who utilised progressive teaching pedagogies that deviated from the norm of 'teaching to the test' in her school was criticised by colleagues. Their comments regarding 'Why do you want to be so *different?*', 'Why don't you just teach the way science is meant to be taught?' along with her reading of school memos and attendance at meetings, where the importance of state testing outcomes was forcefully stated, acted as warnings to assimilate into the predetermined roles, rules and expectations of the school setting. Consequently, rather than feeling passion and joy towards her chosen classroom pedagogies, she experienced feelings of shame, as she believed her educational aims were not worthy. Indeed, feelings of shame can have many problematic consequences, such as a negative evaluation of one's self, and accompanying feelings of worthlessness, powerlessness, and dismissability (Campbell 1997; Zembylas 2007a).

In the current context, Zembylas' (2007a, 2007b, 2011) work could be fruitfully drawn upon to help understand the politicised nature of coaches' emotions in various situations. His conceptual framework could also help us critically explore the emotional rules that are developed and legitimated in the field of coaching practice, as well as through formal coach education provision. It could be argued that such rules, for better or worse, 'normalise' coaches with all the resultant implications (Zembylas 2007a). While this has been hinted at in recent work addressing coach learning (e.g. Cushion *et al.* 2010; Nelson *et al.* 2006), there remains a paucity of empirical inquiry that seeks to explore the political roots of emotions in coaching. Such research has the potential to historicise emotions in coaching by contextualising them 'in and across specific social and cultural spaces within power, and relations and resistances' (Zembylas 2007b: 303).

Conclusion

The purpose of this chapter was two-fold. First, we wanted to highlight the need to incorporate the emotional experiences of coaching practice into our developing research agendas. In applying the work of Nias (1996), it could be argued that affectivity is of fundamental importance to coaching and coaches (and indeed athletes). No doubt coaches feel emotion in their practice, as one cannot separate cognition from emotion. As such, coaches often have strong feelings about their practices and their engagements with athletes, assistant coaches, administrators, and parents. These emotions cannot be separated from the wider social and cultural forces that shape and inform them. Indeed, we believe that it is important for coaching science to better consider how 'emotion and cognition, self and context, ethical judgement and purposeful action' are 'all intertwined in the complex reality of' coaching than has been achieved to date (Kelchtermans 2005: 996). Developing such a multi-layered understanding of emotion in coaching may help remind those responsible for the education, development, and deployment of coaches that effective coaching has much to do with 'the preparation and continuing support of the head (cognition) and the heart (emotion)' (Day and Gu 2009: 17).

The second purpose was to introduce three conceptual frameworks that could be utilised to explore emotion in coaching practice. These comprised the work of Denzin (1984), Hochschild (2000 [1983]) and Zembylas (2005), which were deemed particularly relevant given our interests in the sociological and pedagogical aspects of coaching. However, it is important to note that we are not dismissing the potentially significant contributions that other theorisations of emotion in the educational (e.g. Hargreaves 2000 among others), sociological (e.g. TenHouten 2007 among others), and psychological (e.g. Lazarus and Lazarus 1994 among others) literature could bring to our scholarly endeavours in coaching science. Indeed, consideration of additional perspectives could no doubt further assist in the quest to 'develop contextualised theoretical, conceptual, and empirical tools that are relevant to the investigation of' coaches' emotions (Zembylas and Schutz 2009: 373). To not do so, would certainly hamper the investigative academic process (Pekrun and Schutz 2007).

Finally, if we are to better prepare and support coaches to meet the demands and challenges of their role, we need to better understand the role of personal feeling in practice. In this regard, Beatty's (2011) innovative pedagogy, which emanated from her work on emotional epistemologies, could provide an initial model for considering how we may fruitfully incorporate emotions into our coaching curricula. She highlighted how the use of individual and shared emotional reflection, collaborative discussion, and action research approaches can contribute to the development of confident, supportive, and facilitative educational leaders, who understand and are responsive to their own emotions and those of the individuals that they interact with. In terms of the preparation and development of coaches, it could be equally argued that coach education may benefit from encouraging practitioners to construct and critically reflect upon their emotional experiences as coaches. Such coverage could include the consideration of the social and political conditions that influence and frame their work as they strive to realise their coaching visions and agendas (Liston and Zeichner 1990; Mayer 2011). Through such work, coaches may establish 'an ethic of collaborative reflection that is grounded in emotional meaning making' (Beatty 2006: 11), which could enable them to recognise, understand, and 'transcend the vulnerability of pedagogical practice' (Nelson *et al.* under review) to the greater benefit of all.

References

Barbalet, J. (2001) *Emotion, Social Theory and Social Structure: A Macro-Sociological Approach*, Cambridge: Cambridge University Press.

Barbalet, J. (2002) *Emotions and Sociology*, London: Wiley.

Beatty, B. (2006) 'Leaning into our fears: A new masters course prepares principals to engage with the emotions of leadership', paper presented at the AARE Annual conference, 26–30 November, Adelaide, Australia.

Beatty, B. (2011) 'Leadership and teacher emotions', in C. Day and J.C.-K. Lee (eds) *New Understandings of Teacher's Work: Emotions and Educational Change*, Basingstoke: Springer.

Boler, M. (1999) *Feeling Power: Emotions and Education*, New York: Routledge.

Campbell, S. (1997) *Interpreting the Personal: Expression and the Formation of Feeling*, Ithaca: Cornell University Press.

Cushion, C.J. (2007) 'Modelling the complexities of the coaching process', *International Journal of Sports Science and Coaching*, 2(4): 395–401.

Cushion, C.J. and Jones, R.L. (2006) 'Power, discourse and symbolic violence in professional youth soccer: The case of Albion FC', *Sociology of Sport Journal*, 23(2): 142–161.

Cushion, C.J., Nelson, L.J., Armour, K.M., Lyle, J., Jones, R.L., Sandford, R. and O'Callaghan, C. (2010) *Coach Learning and Development: A Review of Literature*, Leeds: Sports Coach UK.

Damasio, A. (1994) *Descartes' 'Error': Emotions, Reason and the Human Brain*, New York: Grosset-Putman.

Day, C. and Gu, Q. (2009) 'Teacher emotions: Well-being and effectiveness', in P. Schutz and M. Zembylas (eds) *Advances in Teacher Emotion Research: The Impact on Teachers' Lives*, Dordrecht: Springer

Day, C. and Lee, J.C.-K. (eds) (2011) *New Understandings of Teacher's Work: Emotions and Educational Change*, Basingstoke: Springer.

Denison, J. (2007) 'Social theory for coaches: A Foucauldian reading of one athlete's poor performance', *International Journal of Sports Science and Coaching*, 2(4): 369–383.

Denzin, N.K. (1984) *On Understanding Emotion*, San Francisco: Jossey-Bass.

Fineman, S. (1993) *Emotion in Organizations*, London: Sage.

Goffman, E. (1959) *The Presentation of Self in Everyday Life*, Reading: Penguin.

Hargreaves, A. (1998) 'The emotional practice of teaching', *Teaching and Teacher Education*, 14(8): 835–854.

Hargreaves, A. (2000) 'Mixed emotions: Teacher's perceptions of their interactions with students', *Teaching and Teacher Education*, 16(8): 811–826.

Hargreaves, A. (2001) 'Emotional geographies of teaching', *Teachers College Record*, 103(6): 1056–1080.

Hargreaves, A. (2005) 'The emotions of teaching and educational change', in A. Hargreaves (ed.) *Extending Educational Change: International Handbook of Educational Change*, Dordrecht: Springer.

Hargreaves, A., Moore, E.L. and Manning, S. (2001) *Learning to Change: Teaching Beyond Subjects and Standards*, San Francisco: Jossey-Bass.

Hochschild, A. (2000 [1983]) *The Managed Heart: Commercialization of Human Feeling*, Berkeley: University of California Press.

Isenbarger, L. and Zembylas, M. (2006) 'The emotional labour of caring in teaching', *Teaching and Teacher Education*, 22(1): 120–134.

Jones, R.L. (2000) 'Toward a sociology of coaching', in R.L. Jones and K.M. Armour (eds) *The Sociology of Sport: Theory and Practice*, London: Addison-Wesley Longman.

Jones, R.L. (2006a) 'Dilemmas, maintaining "face" and paranoia: An average coaching life', *Qualitative Inquiry*, 12(5): 1012–1021.

Jones, R.L. (2006b) 'How can educational concepts inform sports coaching?', in R.L. Jones (ed.) *The Sports Coach as Educator: Re-conceptualising Sports Coaching*, London: Routledge.

Jones, R.L. (2009) 'Coaching as caring ("The smiling gallery"): Accessing hidden knowledge', *Physical Education and Sport Pedagogy*, 14(4): 377–390.

Jones, R.L. and Wallace, M. (2005) 'Another bad day at the training ground: Coping with ambiguity in the coaching context', *Sport, Education and Society*, 10(1): 119–134.

Jones, R.L. Armour, K.M. and Potrac, P. (2004) *Sports Coaching Cultures: From Practice to Theory*, London: Routledge.

Jones, R.L., Glintmeyer, N. and McKenzie, A. (2005) 'Slim bodies, eating disorders and the coach–athlete relationship: A tale of identity creation and disruption', *International Review for the Sociology of Sport*, 40(3): 377–391.

Jones, R.L., Potrac, P., Cushion, C.J. and Ronglan, L.T. (2011) *The Sociology of Sports Coaching*, London: Routledge.

Kelchtermans, G. (2005) 'Teachers' emotions in educational reforms: Self-understanding, vulnerable commitment and micro-political literacy', *Teaching and Teacher Education*, 21(8): 995–1006.

Kelchtermans, G. and Ballet, K. (2002a) 'The micro-politics of teacher induction: A narrative-biographical study on teacher socialisation', *Teaching and Teacher Education*, 18(1): 105–120.

Kelchtermans, G. and Ballet, K. (2002b) 'Micro-political literacy: Reconstructing a neglected dimension in teacher development', *International Journal of Educational Research*, 37(8): 755–767.

Kemper, T. (1978) *A Social Interactional Theory of Emotions*, New York: Wiley.

Lane West-Newman, C. (2007) 'Feeling: Emotions', in S. Matthewman, C. Lane West-Newman and B. Curtis (eds) *Being Sociological*, Basingstoke: Palgrave.

Layder, D. (2006) *Understanding Social Theory*, 2nd edn, London: Sage.

Lazarus, R.S. and Lazarus B.N. (1994) *Passion and Reason: Making Sense of Our Emotions*, London: Oxford University Press.

Liston, D. and Garrison, J. (2003) *Teaching, Learning and Loving: Reclaiming Passion in Educational Practice*, New York: RoutledgeFalmer.

Liston, D. and Zeichner, K. (1990) 'Teacher education and the social context of schooling: Issues for curriculum development', *American Educational Research Journal*, 27(4): 610–636.

May, T. and Powell, J. (2008) *Situating Social Theory*, 2nd edn, Maidenhead: McGraw-Hill Education.

Mayer, D. (2011) 'But that's the thing: Who else is going to teach besides the idealist? Learning to teach in emotional contexts', in C. Day and J.C.-K. Lee (eds) *New Understandings of Teacher's Work: Emotions and Educational Change*, London: Springer.

Møller, J. (2005) 'Coping with accountability: A Tension between reason and emotion', in C. Sugrue (ed.) *Passionate Principalship: Learning from the Life Histories of School Leaders*, London: Routledge.

Nelson, L.J., Cushion, C.J. and Potrac, P. (2006) 'Formal, nonformal and informal coach learning: A holistic conceptualisation', *International Journal of Sports Science and Coaching*, 1(3): 247–259.

Nelson, L.J., Potrac, P., Allanson, A., Gale, L. and Marshall, P. (under review) 'Thoughts, feelings, and behaviour in coaching practice: The case of a semi-professional soccer coach'.

Nias, J. (1996) 'Thinking about feeling: The emotions in teaching', *Cambridge Journal of Education*, 26(3): 293–306.

Pekrun, R. and Schutz, P.A. (2007) 'Where do we go from here? Implications and future directions for inquiry on emotions in education', in P.A. Schutz and R. Pekrun (eds) *Emotion in Education*, San Diego: Elsevier Inc.

Potrac, P. and Jones, R.L. (2009) 'Power, conflict and co-operation: Towards a micro-politics of coaching', *Quest*, 61(2): 223–236.

Potrac, P., Jones, R.L. and Armour, K. M. (2002) '"It's all about getting respect": The coaching behaviours of an expert English soccer coach', *Sport, Education and Society*, 7(2): 183–202.

Potrac, P. and Marshall, P. (2011) 'Arlie Russell Hochschild: The managed heart, feeling rules and emotional labour: Coaching as an emotional endeavour', in R.L. Jones, P. Potrac, C.J. Cushion and L.T. Ronglan (eds) *The Sociology of Sports Coaching*, London: Routledge.

Purdy, L., Potrac, P. and Jones, R.L. (2008) 'Power, consent and resistance: An autoethnography of competitive rowing', *Sport Education and Society*, 13(3): 319–336.

Reddy, W.M. (1997) 'Against constructionism: The historical ethnography of emotions', *Current Anthropology*, 38(3): 327–351.

Sacks, O. (1995) *An Anthropologist on Mars*, Toronto: Alfred A. Knopf.

Schutz, P.A. and Pekrun, R. (2007) *Emotion in Education*, San Diego, CA: Academic Press.

Schutz, P.A. and Zembylas, M. (2009) *Advances in Teacher Emotion Research: The Impact on Teachers' Lives*, Dordrecht: Springer

Stets, J. (2003) 'Emotions and sentiments', in J. DeLamater (ed.) *Handbook of Social-Psychology*, New York: Academic Plenum.

Stenross, B. and Kleinman, S. (1989) 'The highs and lows of emotional labour', *Journal of Contemporary Ethnography*, 17(4): 435–452.

TenHouten, W.D. (2007) *A General Theory of Emotions and Social Life*, Abingdon: Routledge.

Theodosius, C. (2008) *Emotional Labour in Health Care: The Unmanaged Heart of Nursing*, Abingdon: Routledge.

Turner, J. (2002) *Face to Face: Toward a Theory of Interpersonal Behaviour*, Stanford: Stanford University Press.

Turner, J. and Stets, J. (2005) *The Sociology of Emotions*, Cambridge: Cambridge University Press.

Turner, J. and Stets, J. (2007) 'Sociological theories of human emotions', in J. Stets and J. Turner (eds) *Handbook of the Sociology of Emotions*, New York: Springer.

Williams, S. (2001) *Emotion and Social Theory: Corporeal Reflections on the (Ir)Rational*, London: Sage.

Wright Mills, C. (1956) *The Sociological Imagination*, Oxford: Oxford University Press.

Zembylas, M. (2003) 'Emotions and teacher identity: A poststructural perspective', *Teachers and Teaching: Theory and Practice*, 9(3): 213–238.

Zembylas, M. (2005) *Teaching with Emotion: A Postmodern Enactment*, Greenwich, CT: Information Age.

Zembylas, M. (2007a) 'Theory and methodology in researching emotions in education', *International Journal of Research and Method in Education*, 30(1): 57–72.

Zembylas, M. (2007b) 'Emotional ecology: The intersection of emotional knowledge and pedagogical content knowledge in teaching', *Teaching and Teacher Education*, 23(4): 355–367.

Zembylas, M. (2011) 'Teaching and teacher emotions: A post-structural perspective', in C. Day and J.C.-K. Lee (eds) *New Understandings of Teacher's Work: Emotions and Educational Change*, London: Springer.

Zembylas, M. and Schutz, P.A. (2009) 'Research on teachers' emotions in education: Findings, practical implications and future agenda', in P.A. Schutz and M. Zembylas (eds) *Advances in Teacher Emotion Research: The Impact on Teachers' Lives*, New York: Springer.

20

EXPECTANCY EFFECTS IN SPORTS COACHING

Gloria B. Solomon

TEXAS CHRISTIAN UNIVERSITY, FORT WORTH, USA

Richard M. Buscombe

UNIVERSITY OF EAST LONDON, UK

Introduction

The concept of *expectancy effects* originated in the field of sociology under the influence of Robert Merton. In his now classic treatise, Merton (1948) postulated that a phenomenon exists whereby expectations of others set up a series of reactions that ultimately affect the outcome of events. Specifically, Merton coined the term, *self-fulfilling prophecy*, to explain societal events such as the dissolution of banks during the Great Depression leading to the worldwide economic depression experienced in the 1930s. In his interpretation, Merton contends that the expectation began with a rumour that the banks were running out of money; this expectation led to behaviours (withdrawing funds) that subsequently made the rumour come true. In this chapter, we will begin by exploring the early origins of the expectancy effects phenomenon. We will then direct your attention to emerging lines of expectancy effects research in competitive sport. Finally, we will discuss gaps in the literature which will then lead to future directions in hopes of lending insight into this compelling topic.

Expectancy theory contends that a stimulus to behaviour causes the behaviour to come true (Merton 1948). This stimulus was further defined contingent upon the context. At the societal level, the stimulus is motivated by events which subsequently influence people's behaviour. At the individual level, the stimulus is commonly a person with significant influence. Thus, a significant other develops expectations for behaviour, based on numerous criteria that serve to influence the interpersonal dyad and subsequently impact individual behavioural responses.

A four-step cycle was created to explain how these expectations influence the dyadic interactions between teachers/coaches and their students/athletes (Horn and Lox 1992; Solomon 2001a). In step one, leaders make initial assessments of ability based on various *impression cues* (personal, performance, psychological). In step two, these assessments influence how the leader treats his/her followers. Rosenthal's (1974) meta-analysis identified four distinct ways in which high versus low expectancy (ability) individuals are treated differently: socioemotional climate, feedback, input and output. In brief, high expectancy individuals are afforded a warmer socioemotional climate (non-verbal behaviours), better quality and quantity of feedback (verbal behaviours), more input opportunities (issued more challenging tasks), and more output opportunities (asked for their opinion). In step three an individual's behaviour conforms to the treatment issued thus impacting performance in a positive or negative direction. Step four completes the cycle as the leader's initial expectation becomes validated reinforcing the perception that s/he is a good judge of ability. Expectancy theory and the four-step cycle which explains the process serve as the framework for much of the literature conducted on expectancy effects in education.

Expectancy effects in education

Psychologist and researcher Robert Rosenthal and his colleagues first began the exploration of expectancy effects as it relates to *experimenter bias* (Rosenthal 1963). This phenomenon refers to the role that experimenters may inadvertently play in influencing the outcome of their research. Rosenthal and Fode (1963) provided early support demonstrating that experimenters communicated their expectations regarding the outcomes of a study to participants through their tone of voice when reading instructions, thus treating participants differently based on group assignment. In animal research, when experimenters believed a selection of rats were bred to be good, or alternatively bad, at a series of maze navigation tasks the rats performed in line with these expectations (Rosenthal and Lawson 1964). Rosenthal (2002) later suggested this outcome might be due to the increased handling that the 'bright' rats received over their 'dull' counterparts. In support, the experimenters responsible for the 'bright' rats reported acting in a more friendly and enthusiastic manner towards their rats. In reflecting on these results, Rosenthal proposed that, 'If rats became brighter when expected to by their experimenters, then it seemed not farfetched to think that children could become brighter when expected to by their teachers' (Rosenthal 1994: 176).

This hypothesis led Rosenthal to the educational setting where he and colleague, Lenore Jacobson, conducted a year-long study on the influence of teacher expectations on student performance (Rosenthal and Jacobson 1968). Employing grades K–6 in a South San Francisco school district, they administered the Harvard Test of Inflected Acquisition, a test of non-verbal intelligence. Based on the pupils' scores from this test the teachers were led to believe 20 per cent of students in each cohort were *late bloomers*, identified by their inflated scores on the Harvard test. In reality, the test merely constituted a measure of intelligence and the supposed bloomers were selected at random from the group. By the end of the academic year, results showed that the bloomers demonstrated significantly higher scores in reasoning and verbal intelligence compared to peers in the control group. Their research provided incontrovertible evidence of the potential impact of teacher expectations on student learning and performance. This classic study, published in 1968 as a book titled *Pygmalion in the Classroom*, prompted hundreds of research investigations on the influence of teacher expectations in the classroom.

While there are several serious critiques of the educational research (cf. Brophy 1983), the results from the vast number of investigations suggest that expectations formed by teachers do have the capacity to influence student development. Further inquiry identified that demographic features of the student population appear to influence this dynamic. Early expectancy effects research found that student race/ethnicity (McCormick and Noriega 1986; Rist 1970; Rubovits and Maehr 1973), gender (Dunbar and O'Sullivan 1986;

Macdonald 1990), and physical attractiveness (Martinek 1981) all served to explain differential treatment in educational settings. Furthermore, results of expectancy effects research outside the classroom mirrored the findings from educational studies among judges (Halverson *et al.* 1997), business leaders (Sutton and Woodman 1989), and military personnel (Dvir *et al.* 1995; Eden 1990).

Published over 30 years ago, Rosenthal and Rubin's (1978) meta-analysis still provides the most comprehensive account of the magnitude of expectancy effects. The review incorporated results from 345 studies conducted across a range of different settings. The results demonstrated that expectancy effects are a real phenomenon and that the magnitude of such effects is of practical importance. This led Rosenthal and Rubin (1978) to conclude that, 'interpersonal expectancy effects are real in the sense of statistical significance and are at least moderate in average magnitude' (p. 381). Similar to the settings of business, school, and the military, the world of competitive sport is also a location where the leader (coach) has the potential to significantly affect the behaviour (performance) of athletes.

Expectancy effects in competitive sport

Interest in expectancy effects in competitive sport garnered the curiosity of sport scholars. The first scientific study utilizing the framework of expectancy theory to study coach–athlete dynamics was conducted with young athletes (Rejeski *et al.* 1979). The early literature in competitive sport focused on step two of the expectancy cycle; comparing feedback patterns of coaches at the youth sport level (Horn 1984; Rejeski *et al.* 1979). Studying feedback issued to high and low expectancy athletes (*feedback patterns*) dominated the coaching literature for the first 20 years. More recently, sport scholars have begun to explore the actual impression cues (*expectancy sources*) utilized by coaches to judge athlete ability (step one of the cycle), to inquire about the stability of initial expectations (*perceptual flexibility*), to identify expectancy sources which predict athlete performance (*performance predictors*), and to understand the role expectations play in shaping coach evaluations of athlete performance (*performance evaluation*). These five distinct lines of research will now be explored.

Feedback patterns

There exists a growing body of information describing patterns of feedback as a function of competitive level. For example, in junior high school softball (ages 11–13) low expectancy athletes were given more feedback (Horn 1984); however, in youth recreational basketball low expectancy athletes were given less feedback (Rejeski *et al.* 1979). In a recent study, coaches offered equitable feedback to all youth basketball players (Solomon 2008a). These findings demonstrate that the expectancy cycle is not uniformly in operation in youth sport. While this warrants further empirical investigation, it is apparent that the youth sport environment differs from higher levels of competition (high school and college) in a number of ways. First, most recreational youth sport programmes in the United States encourage participation among all skill levels. The selection process whereby athletes are required to try out and compete for a place on the team does not become commonplace until the high school years (ages 14–18). Second, many youth sport programmes endorse a philosophy of inclusion which mandates that all players, regardless of ability, are afforded a minimum amount of playing time. One can presume it is in coaches' best interests to prepare all of their athletes to perform, thus delimiting patterns of differential treatment. Third, youth sport is a private entity while high school and college athletics are linked with the educational system.

Therefore, the youth sport experience must be privately funded and parents might expect their child to 'get their money's' worth'. Youth coaches might be sensitive to this personal investment, which may become translated into their feedback patterns.

While expectancy-prone behaviour among coaches may not be as prominent in youth sport, more consistent patterns begin to emerge at the interscholastic level. It is documented that both starters and non-starters receive equal amounts of practice time (Lacy and Martin 1994); however, starters receive significantly more feedback than their teammates on the bench (Markland and Martinek 1988). Evidence verifies that head and assistant high school coaches offer more feedback to their high expectancy players who typically make up the starting line-up (Solomon 2008a; Solomon *et al.* 1998a; Solomon *et al.* 1998b).

This pattern is replicated at the National Collegiate College Association (NCAA) Division I intercollegiate level, but only among head coaches (Solomon 2008a; Solomon *et al.* 1996a; Solomon *et al.* 1996b). Interestingly, assistant coaches appear to offer equitable feedback to athletes. While different roles (head or assistant coach) appear to influence feedback patterns, neither coaching experience (Solomon *et al.* 1998a) nor athlete ethnicity (Solomon *et al.* 1996b) serve to explain differential feedback patterns. Only one study to date, conducted over 20 years ago, has examined expectancy effects via feedback patterns in the elite sport setting (Sinclair and Vealey 1989). Among a national-level field hockey team, researchers found that high expectancy players were afforded more instruction and praise, including more precise performance feedback, than their low expectancy teammates.

This early research on feedback patterns emerged as descriptive inquiry into coach behaviours (Lacy and Darst 1985; Segrave and Ciancio 1990). Later researchers began to ground their work from the perspective of expectancy theory (Solomon 2001a; Solomon and Rhea 2008). As this framework to study coach-athlete dynamics in competitive sport developed, scholars began to dissect the process of the cycle step by step. A common critique of step one was the simplistic categories housing the impression cues. It was theorized that personal (i.e. height, somatotype, age) and performance (past performance, skills tests) impression cues were used to develop expectations of athlete ability (Horn and Lox 1992). One concern was that these two categories ignored psychological cues that coaches might adopt (Solomon 2001a). Another concern was that the discrete factors utilized to inform coach perceptions of athlete ability were still unknown (Solomon and Rhea 2008). Therefore, the next line of inquiry sought to delineate the actual impression cues, termed *expectancy sources*, coaches utilize in step one to develop their expectations of athlete ability.

Expectancy sources

Due to the physical nature of athletic participation, a common assumption is that coaches rely predominantly on performance impression cues to assess athlete ability. The majority of performance-related impression cues, such as strength, speed, and agility, can be objectively measured and evaluated which can offer the coach valuable information about athlete development. However, it is simplistic to assume that tangible, measureable performance criteria are the only sources of information used by coaches. In order to identify these distinct expectancy sources, Solomon and Rhea (2008) queried 18 NCAA Division I head coaches from four different universities. Results showed that coaches use a multitude of expectancy sources to evaluate athlete ability. This four-phase investigation culminated with the creation of the Solomon Expectancy Sources Scale (SESS; Solomon 2008b). The SESS is a 30-item instrument, which is divided into four factors: Coachability (11 items), Team Player (eight items), Physical Ability (six items), and Maturity (five items). This work served to support the position that college coaches are multidimensional in their judgements of athletic ability, relying on both psychological (i.e. concentration, competitiveness, handling pressure) and physical (i.e. strength, speed, agility) qualities.

With the SESS providing an explicit list of expectancy sources used by college coaches, researchers have begun designing studies to identify the influence of expectancy sources on athlete development. Areas of investigation include analysing coaches by level of success, comparing head and assistant coaches, and testing the veracity of this instrument with a cross cultural sample.

In a comparison of more (win percentage >60) and less (win percentage <50) successful coaches, Becker and Solomon (2005) determined that regardless of success, coaches prioritize similar expectancy sources. Items in the Coachability factor (i.e. hard worker, receptivity to coaching, willingness to learn, willingness to listen) were rated highest by all coaches. A key distinction emerged when querying the athletes of these coaches. Athletes who played for successful coaches were aware of the expectancy sources employed by their coaches; athletes on less successful teams were not accurate in identifying the expectancy sources utilized by their coaches. Upon initial inspection, it appears that successful coaches are better at communicating their expectations.

While the roles of head and assistant coach overlap, there are certainly distinct aspects to each position. Regardless of role, there are significantly more assistant coaches than head coaches. However in the coaching literature there is scant research on the role of the assistant coach. A recent study sought to discern expectancy source usage based on coach position (Solomon 2010). A sample of junior college track and field head and assistant coaches (N = 34) reported parallel ratings of the expectancy sources. There were no significant differences in the prioritization of the four SESS factors. Furthermore, all coaches rated Coachability as the most important source and Maturity as least important.

The SESS was created in the United States using four coach samples totalling 292 coaches. A recent interest emerging is the utility of this instrument among coaches outside the US. Are there common expectancy sources used by coaches regardless of nationality or nation where training occurred? In order to explore this question, two coach samples were accessed (Solomon and Lobinger 2011). A comparison of 274 US college coaches and 336 German national level and/or federation coaches found that the US coaches rated all four SESS factors significantly higher than their German counterparts. It becomes apparent that the SESS may not include the most salient expectancy sources for the German coaches. Therefore, the efficacy of this instrument outside of the US is at the current time, questionable. While the creation of the SESS to identify specific expectancy sources has contributed to our understanding of step one of the expectancy cycle, another important area of inquiry is the veracity of these judgements. In order to explore this topic, the concept of perceptual flexibility is introduced.

Perceptual flexibility

While it is known that coaches stratify their athletes based on expectations of ability, it was unclear whether these classifications (i.e. high, medium, low ability) are stable or adapt over time. The term *perceptual flexibility* was coined in order to describe a coach's willingness to adapt expectations over time (Solomon and Kosmitzki 1996). Again, the findings diverge based on level of competition. Specifically at the youth sport level, coach perceptions of athlete ability varied across the season contingent on athlete behaviour, but only for the top and bottom 25 per cent (Horn 1984). However, the majority of research in this limited line of inquiry offers evidence that coach perceptions of athlete ability are stable across time; hence, coaches are perceptually inflexible in their judgements. Researchers explored the perceptual flexibility of high school, college, and elite sport coaches over the course of one competitive season. For both head and assistant coaches, perceptions of athlete ability remained stable from pre- to post-season (Sinclair and Vealey 1989; Solomon et al. 1998b; Solomon and Harrah 2007; Solomon and Kosmitzki 1996). These results demonstrate the magnitude of the coach's first impressions, which become engaged in step one and serve to propel the expectancy cycle. A significant part of the coaching role is talent identification, so it is fair to assume that coaches are commonly accurate in their evaluation of athlete ability. However if those first impressions are inaccurate, or inflexible (even in light of new information such as athlete improvement), this has the potential to undermine athlete development and consequently, performance.

Performance predictors

In the realm of competitive sport, success and winning are synonymous terms. Of vital interest to most involved is the contribution of athlete performance to winning. Yet, the expectancy effects literature is lacking in this area. To date, there are only four studies that explore the link between coach expectations and athlete performance. Among head coaches, it was found that coach perceptions of athlete confidence predicted actual athlete performance (Solomon 2001a, 2002a). However, for assistant coaches perceptions of athlete physical ability predicted actual performance (Solomon 2001b, 2002b). Although this line of research is in its infancy, the initial results appear to demonstrate that assistant coaches might be more focused on concrete performance criteria, while head coaches are comfortable using abstract criteria to judge athlete ability. Therefore, early findings indicate that coaches are relying on different expectancy sources depending on their role, as head or assistant, on the team.

Performance evaluation

It is reliably established that expectations shape coach–athlete interactions and therefore have the power to influence the course of social encounters in sport. Furthermore, research shows that expectations are formed, in part, on the basis of information that is readily observable as soon as a performer is encountered (Solomon and Rhea 2008). As such, at step one of the cycle a coach's expectation of a performer may be established before any direct performance information is observed. If this is the case an early expectation may lead coaches to subsequently see what they expect to see in an athlete's performance, even in situations where the initial expectation of a performer is inaccurate (Fiske et al. 1999). This effect is achieved by perceivers selectively attending to, memorizing, and recalling information that serves to confirm their expectation of another individual. Research suggests that these judgements may occur automatically upon initiation of a social interaction and as such coaches may unavoidably view an athlete's performance level in line with their expectations (Bargh and Chartrand 1999). Given that coaches regularly observe performers for purposes of team selection, awarding scholarships, and providing confirmation of athletes' performance levels to colleagues, it would appear that such judgements may be shaped by the coaches' expectations of these performers. Little is known about the magnitude and frequency with which such effects are witnessed (Brophy 1983; Jussim 1991) and the literature elucidating such effects in sport is scarce (Plessner and Haar 2006). However, it stands to reason that upon viewing a performer for the first time a coach's evaluation of that athlete is likely to be tainted by their expectations of that individual.

Studies employing designs that have considered a judge's or official's rating of an athlete's performance provide some insight into this process. Research incorporating sports such as figure skating (Seltzer and Glass 1991), gymnastics (Ste-Marie and Valiquette 1996), football (Jones *et al.* 2002), boxing (Balmer *et al.* 2005), tennis (Buscombe *et al.* 2006) and Muay Thai (Myers *et al.* 2006) confirms that an observer's characteristics, the conditions under which a judgement is made, and expectations held prior to, or formed early in, an interaction are all factors which influence ratings of an athlete's sporting performance. In an early study investigating expectancy effects in gymnastics, Scheer and Ansorge (1975) demonstrated that when an athlete appeared last in a team order (traditionally the best competitor will perform last on a team) the judges rated the athlete's performance more positively than when the same performance was viewed first in the team sequence. As such, even though the performances being viewed were identical, when the athlete's routine was viewed last in the sequence it was rated higher (more than one-tenth of a point) than in any other position in the team. Researchers subsequently confirmed the veracity of these early findings (e.g. Findlay and Ste-Marie 2004; Jones *et al.* 2002; Plessner 1999; Ste-Marie and Lee 1991; Ste-Marie and Valiquette 1996) thereby establishing the role expectancy effects play in influencing a judge's ratings of an athlete's performance.

Similar results have been observed with athletes reporting judgements of hypothetical opponents. More specifically, Buscombe *et al.* (2006) examined the impact of pre-match body language and clothing on judgements of a tennis player's performance. The study required competitive tennis players to view a period of video footage containing a player completing a pre-determined sequence of warm-up activities and then executing a series of short rallies with an opponent. The target player completed the warm-up displaying one of four combinations of body language and clothing (i.e. good body language with tennis-specific attire, good body language with casual sports attire, bad body language with tennis-specific attire and bad body language with casual sports attire). After the warm-up but before the playing footage commenced, the target performer was seen to move to the back of the court and remove their outer tracksuit. From this point the remaining footage that was viewed was identical across all four video conditions. The results showed that the target's performance was rated more positively when displaying positive body language and wearing tennis-specific clothing. These results provide the first indication in the literature that information displayed by a competitor before they compete may lead to the formation of certain expectancies that in turn influence how positively a perceiver rates the performance of an opponent.

Taken together this body of work serves to confirm that expectations influence judgements in a range of subjective situations that occur in sport. To date, work in this area has focused on an athlete, official's or judge's perception of a sports performance (Plessner and Haar 2006). Given that performers are routinely observed by coaches in a range of contexts it would appear that the field of coaching may not be immune to such effects. Furthermore, following Horn and Lox's (1992) expectancy cycle it would appear that coach expectations may shape perceptions of an athlete's performance (step three) irrespective of whether the athlete's behaviour actually alters at step two. In this way expectations derived from observable pre-performance cues may shape a coach's evaluation of a performer thereafter. These judgements may subsequently serve to confirm the expectation formed at step one and thus complete the cycle.

Strategies for minimizing expectancy effects

Although expectancy effects in coaching may be subtle and often occur unintentionally there are a number of tactics a coach can take in order to minimize the impact that expectations have in shaping a coach's judgements of, and behaviour towards, athletes.

1   Develop an awareness of the existence of expectancy effects to negate the potentially limiting impact that expectations may have on the way one judges and then acts towards athletes.

2   Be mindful of the expectations we hold of athletes and regularly update one's view of the athletes.

3   Set appropriate, realistic performance expectations for athletes based on regular evaluation of improvement.

4   Employ varied coaching patterns within training sessions. For example, rotate players around drill stations on an even basis and make sure all players get an equal opportunity to 'hit with coach'.

5   Vary athletes' training partners during the course of a practice such that the same individuals are not always working together.

6   Always convey high expectations of athletes in relation to court/field discipline and achievement of personal goals.

There is no evidence to suggest that coaches are more susceptible to experiencing expectancy effects than any other group of people who are required to form judgements of others on a regular basis. It is an implicit part of the job description of a coach to evaluate athlete talent. Of concern, is what coaches do with this information. It is hoped that raising awareness of the role expectations play in shaping coaches' judgements and behaviours towards athletes will help promote a climate that ensures all athletes experience an equal opportunity to fulfil their sporting potential.

Future directions

As is true with many topics in the coaching sciences, there are many questions that emerge from the past literature. Here we seek to entertain several pivotal questions that warrant further inquiry. Beginning with the first step of the expectancy cycle, it would be beneficial to identify the primary sources of information coaches of various levels (youth, high school, junior college, college, elite) and various cultures (North American, South American, European, Asian, African) utilize in their evaluation of athlete ability. The Solomon Expectancy Sources Scale (SESS: Solomon 2008b) was created by and for Division I college coaches. It is safe to speculate that youth coaches and Olympic coaches probably differ in their expectancy sources. Recent research demonstrates that the SESS, currently the only measure specifically created to test impression cue usage in step one of the expectancy cycle, is not salient for German national coaches. Clearly further exploration by competitive level and culture is necessary to advance the knowledge base.

The second step of the expectancy cycle is the most researched, yet we do not have a solid understanding of the influence of coach feedback on performance. While we know that differential treatment is exhibited based on coach perceptions of ability, we have no knowledge of the implications of this differential feedback on performance. Horn's (2008) work on coach effectiveness outlines the central role that coach behaviour (of which providing feedback to a performer is a constituent part) plays in influencing an athlete's self-perception, beliefs, attitudes, motivation, and, consequently, performance. Specifically, Horn's Working Model of Coach Effectiveness serves to emphasize the need for unambiguous and effective communication in coach–athlete interactions. This position is supported by Côté and Gilbert (2009) who suggest that through reflecting on the appropriateness of their style of communication, coaches can become more effective practitioners. We challenge future researchers to further this line of inquiry by investigating the influence of specific feedback patterns on athlete cognitions, attitudes, and actual performance. Advances in our understanding of the link between feedback and coach effectiveness would also appear to be a significant contribution to maximizing the coach–athlete relationship.

A third area in need of attention is the conversion of the current knowledge base into practical application. In this chapter we shared six strategies for coaches to maximize positive expectancy effects and minimize negative expectancy effects. The goal of this line of research is ultimately to design coach-training programmes with attention paid toward awareness of the influence of expectations on coach behaviour. As illustrated by Horn (2008), researchers may focus these endeavours on delineating the individual and interactive contribution that sociocultural, organizational, and personal characteristics play in influencing coaches' expectations and beliefs about the performers with whom they interact. First, coaches need to become aware of their expectancy-prone behaviours prior to enacting any change. Research suggests that coaches perceive their communicated behaviours as more positive than reality demonstrates (Solomon *et al.* 1996a; Wandzilak *et al.* 1988). An efficient and effective way to identify feedback patterns for coaches is to videotape several practices and games to note patterns of dyadic feedback. With this information, coaches can then begin to change their communicated behaviours in order to minimize negative expectancy effects. Until we are able to make a direct link to performance outcomes, as suggested by the second recommendation, we cannot expect coaches to jump on our expectancy bandwagon.

Conclusion

In summary, expectancy effects have been witnessed in courtrooms (Halverson *et al.* 1997), the armed forces (Kierein and Gold 2000), classrooms (Rosenthal and Jacobson 1968) and more recently in competitive sport settings (Becker and Solomon 2005; Plessner and Haar 2006). Furthermore, Rosenthal (1995) points to the findings presented in a range of meta-analyses (e.g. Rosenthal 2002; Rosenthal and Rubin 1978; 1994) that consistently support the role that expectations play in shaping social interactions. Over 30 years after Rosenthal and Jacobson's (1968) original study, Mavi and Sharpe (2000) contended that expectancy effects research is still 'an area of academic study that remains rich in productive research and development possibilities' (p. 7). We concur and further conclude that due to the nature of competitive sport, the influence of inaccurate or negative expectations has the capacity to profoundly impact athlete development and consequently, team performance. The goal is for coaches to maximize improvement possibilities and develop realistic and challenging expectations for all athletes.

References

Balmer, N.J., Nevill, A.M. and Lane, A.M. (2005) 'Do judges enhance home advantage in European championship boxing?' *Journal of Sports Sciences*, 23: 409–16.

Bargh, J.A. and Chartrand, T.L. (1999) 'The unbearable automaticity of being', *American Psychologist*, 54: 462–79.

Becker, A.J. and Solomon, G.B. (2005) 'Expectancy information and coach effectiveness in intercollegiate basketball', *The Sport Psychologist*, 19: 251–66.

Brophy, J.R. (1983) 'Research on the self-fulfilling prophecy and teacher expectations', *Journal of Educational Psychology*, 75: 631–61.

Buscombe, R., Greenlees, I., Holder, T., Thelwell, R. and Rimmer, M. (2006) 'Expectancy effects in tennis: the impact of opponents' pre-match non-verbal behaviour on male tennis players', *Journal of Sports Sciences*, 24: 1265–72.

Côté, J. and Gilbert, W.D. (2009) 'An integrative definition of coaching effectiveness and expertise', *International Journal of Sports Science and Coaching*, 4: 307–23.

Dunbar, R.R. and O'Sullivan, M. (1986) 'Effects of intervention on differential treatment of boys and girls in elementary physical education lessons', *Journal of Teaching in Physical Education*, 5: 166–75.

Dvir, T., Eden, D. and Banjo, M.L. (1995) 'Self-fulfilling prophecy and gender: can women be Pygmalion and Galatea?' *Journal of Applied Psychology*, 80: 253–70.

Eden, D. (1990) 'Pygmalion without interpersonal contrast effects: whole groups gain from raising manager expectations', *Journal of Applied Psychology*, 75: 394–98.

Findlay, L.C. and Ste-Marie, D.M. (2004) 'A reputation bias in figure skating judging', *Journal of Sport and Exercise Psychology*, 26: 154–66.

Fiske, S.T., Lin, M. and Neuberg, S.L. (1999) 'The continuum model: ten years later', in S. Chaiken and Y. Trope (eds) *Dual-process Theories in Social Psychology*, New York, London: The Guilford Press.

Halverson, A.M., Hallahan, M., Hart, A.J. and Rosenthal, R. (1997) 'Reducing the biasing effects of judges' non-verbal behavior with simplified jury instruction', *Journal of Applied Psychology*, 82: 590–98.

Horn, T.S. (1984) 'Expectancy effects in the interscholastic athletic setting: methodological considerations', *Journal of Sport Psychology*, 6: 60–76.

Horn, T.S. (2008) 'Coaching effectiveness in the sport domain', in T.S. Horn (ed.) *Advances in Sport Psychology*, Champaign, IL: Human Kinetics.

Horn, T.S. and Lox, C. (1992) 'The self-fulfilling prophecy theory: when coaches' expectations become reality', in J.M. Williams (ed.) *Applied Sport Psychology: Personal Growth To Peak Performance*, Mountain View, CA: Mayfield.

Jones, M.V., Paull, G.C. and Erskine, J. (2002) 'The impact of a team's aggressive reputation on the decisions of association football referees', *Journal of Sports Sciences*, 20: 991–1000.

Jussim, L. (1991) 'Social perception and social reality: a reflection–construction model', *Psychological Review*, 98: 54–73.

Kierein, N.M. and Gold, M.A. (2000) 'Pygmalion in work organizations: a meta-analysis', *Journal of Organizational Behavior*, 21: 913–28.

Lacy, A.C. and Darst, P.W. (1985) 'Systematic observations of winning high school head football coaches', *Journal of Teaching in Physical Education*, 4: 256–70.

Lacy, A.C. and Martin, D.L. (1994) 'Analysis of starter/nonstarter motor-skill engagement and coaching behaviors in collegiate women's volleyball', *Journal of Teaching in Physical Education*, 13: 95–107.

Macdonald, D. (1990) 'The relationship between sex composition of physical education classes and teacher/pupil verbal interactions', *Journal of Teaching in Physical Education*, 9: 152–63.

Markland, R. and Martinek, T.J. (1988) 'Descriptive analysis of coach augmented feedback given to high school varsity female volleyball players', *Journal of Teaching in Physical Education*, 7: 289–301.

Martinek, T.J. (1981) 'Pygmalion in the gym: a model for the communication of teacher expectations in physical education', *Research Quarterly for Exercise and Sport*, 52: 58–67.

Mavi, H.F. and Sharpe, T. (2000) 'Reviewing the literature on teacher and coach expectations with implications for future research and practice', *Physical Educator*, 57: 161–68.

McCormick, T.E. and Noriega, T. (1986) 'Low versus high expectations: a review of teacher expectation effects on minority students', *Journal of Educational Equity*, 52: 224–34.

Merton, R. (1948) 'The self-fulfilling prophecy', *The Antioch Review*, 8: 193–210

Myers, T.D., Balmer, N.J., Nevill, A.M., Lane, A. and Al-Nakeeb, Y. (2006) 'Evidence of nationalistic bias in Muay Thai', *Journal of Sports Science and Medicine*, 5: 21–7.

Plessner, H. (1999) 'Expectation biases in gymnastics judging', *Journal of Sport and Exercise Psychology*, 21: 131–44.

Plessner, H. and Haar, T. (2006) 'Sports performance judgments from a social cognitive perspective', *Psychology of Sport and Exercise*, 7: 555–75.

Rejeski, W., Darracott, C. and Hutslar, S. (1979) 'Pygmalion in youth sport: a field study', *Journal of Sport Psychology*, 1: 311–19.

Rist, R.C. (1970) 'Student social class and teacher expectations: the self-fulfilling prophecy in ghetto education', *Harvard Educational Review*, 40: 411–51.

Rosenthal, R. (1963) 'On the social psychology of the psychological experiment: the experimenter's hypothesis as unintended determinant of experimental studies', *American Scientist*, 50: 268–83.

Rosenthal, R. (1974) *On the Social Psychology of the Self-Fulfilling Prophecy: Further Evidence for Pygmalion Effects and their Mediating Mechanisms*. New York: MSS Modular Publications.

Rosenthal, R. (1994) 'Parametric measures of effect size', in H. Cooper and L.V. Hedges (eds) *The Handbook of Research Synthesis*, New York: Russell Sage Foundation.

Rosenthal, R. (1995) 'Writing meta-analytic reviews', *Psychological Bulletin*, 18: 183–92.

Rosenthal, R. (2002) 'Covert communication in classrooms, clinics, courtrooms, and cubicles', *American Psychologist*, 57: 839–49.

Rosenthal, R. and Fode, K.L. (1963) 'Psychology of the scientist: V. Three experiments in experimenter bias', *Psychological Reports*, 12: 491–511.

Rosenthal, R. and Jacobson, L.F. (1968) *Pygmalion in the Classroom: Teacher Expectations and Student Intellectual Development*. New York: Holt.

Rosenthal, R. and Lawson, R. (1964) 'A longitudinal study of the effects of experimenter bias on the operant learning of laboratory rats', *Journal of Psychiatric Research*, 2: 61–72.

Rosenthal, R. and Rubin, D.B. (1978) 'Interpersonal expectancy effects: the first 345 studies', *Behavioral and Brain Studies*, 3: 377–415.

Rosenthal, R. and Rubin, D.B. (1994) 'The counternull value of an effect size: a new statistic', *Psychological Science*, 5: 329–34.

Rubovits, P.C. and Maehr, M.L. (1973) 'Pygmalion black and white', *Journal of Personality and Social Psychology*, 25: 210–18.

Scheer, J.K. and Ansorge, C.J. (1975) 'Effects of naturally induced judges' expectations on the ratings of physical performances', *The Research Quarterly*, 46: 463–70.

Segrave, J.O. and Ciancio, C.A. (1990) 'An observational study of a successful Pop Warner football coach', *Journal of Teaching in Physical Education*, 9: 294–306.

Seltzer, R. and Glass, W. (1991) 'International politics and judging in Olympic skating events: 1968–1988', *Journal of Sport Behavior*, 14: 189–200.

Sinclair, D.A. and Vealey, R.S. (1989) 'Effects of coaches' expectations and feedback on the self-perceptions of athletes', *Journal of Sport Behavior*, 12: 77–91.

Solomon, G.B. (2001a) 'Performance and personality impression cues as predictors of athletic performance: an extension of expectancy theory', *International Journal of Sport Psychology*, 32: 88–100.

Solomon, G.B. (2001b) 'Performance and personality expectations of assistant coaches: implications for athlete performance', *International Sports Journal*, 5: 10–17.

Solomon, G.B. (2002a) 'Confidence as a source of expectancy information: a follow-up investigation', *International Sports Journal*, 6: 119–27.

Solomon, G.B. (2002b) 'Sources of expectancy information among assistant coaches: the influence of performance and psychological cues', *Journal of Sport Behavior*, 25: 279–86.

Solomon, G.B. (2008a) 'Expectations and perceptions as predictors of coaches' feedback in three competitive contexts', *Journal for the Study of Sports and Athletics in Education*, 2: 161–79.

Solomon, G.B. (2008b) 'The assessment of athletic ability in intercollegiate sport: instrument construction and validation', *International Journal of Sports Science and Coaching*, 3: 509–21.

Solomon, G.B. (2010) 'The assessment of athletic ability at the junior college level', *International Journal of Sports Science and Coaching*, 5: 37–46.

Solomon, G.B. and Harrah, V. (2007) 'Perceptual Flexibility and Expectancy Sources among College Coaches', poster presented at the Association for Applied Sport Psychology (AASP) Conference, Louisville, Kentucky, October.

Solomon, G.B. and Kosmitzki, C. (1996) 'Perceptual flexibility among intercollegiate basketball coaches', *Journal of Sport Behavior*, 19: 163–77.

Solomon, G.B. and Lobinger, B.H. (2011) 'Sources of expectancy information among coaches: a cross cultural investigation', *Theories and Applications: The International Edition*, 1: 46–57.

Solomon, G.B. and Rhea, D.J. (2008) 'Sources of expectancy information among college coaches: a qualitative test of expectancy theory', *International Journal of Sports Science and Coaching*, 3: 251–68.

Solomon, G.B., DiMarco, A.M., Ohlson, C.J. and Reece, S.D. (1998a) 'Expectations and coaching experience: is more better?' *Journal of Sport Behavior*, 21: 444–55.

Solomon, G.B., Golden, A.J., Ciaponni, T.M. and Martin, A.D. (1998b) 'Coach expectations and differential feedback: perceptual flexibility revisited', *Journal of Sport Behavior*, 21: 298–310.

Solomon, G.B., Striegel, D.A., Eliot, J.F., Heon, S.N., Maas, J.L. and Wayda, V.K. (1996a) 'Self-fulfilling prophecy in college basketball: implications for effective coaching', *Journal of Applied Sport Psychology*, 8: 44–59.

Solomon, G.B., Wiegardt, P.A., Yusuf, F.R., Kosmitzki, C., Wayda, V.K., Williams, J. and Stevens, C.E. (1996b) 'Expectancies and ethnicity: the self-fulfilling prophecy in college basketball', *Journal of Sport and Exercise Psychology*, 18: 83–88.

Ste-Marie, D.M. and Lee, T.D. (1991) 'Prior processing effects on gymnastics judging', *Journal of Experimental Psychology: Learning, Memory, and Cognition*, 17: 126–36.

Ste-Marie, D.M. and Valiquette, S.M. (1996) 'Enduring memory-induced biases in gymnastic judging', *Journal of Experimental Psychology: Learning, Memory, and Cognition*, 22: 148–52.

Sutton, C.D. and Woodman, R.W. (1989) 'Pygmalion goes to work: the effects of supervisor expectations in a retail setting', *Journal of Applied Psychology*, 74: 943–50.

Wandzilak, T., Ansorge, C.J. and Potter, G. (1988) 'Comparison between selected practice and game behaviors of youth sport soccer coaches', *Journal of Sport Behavior*, 11: 78–88.

21

COACHING LIFE SKILLS

Daniel Gould

INSTITUTE FOR THE STUDY OF YOUTH SPORTS, MICHIGAN STATE UNIVERSITY, USA

Sarah Carson

DEPARTMENT OF KINESIOLOGY, JAMES MADISON UNIVERSITY, USA

Jed Blanton

INSTITUTE FOR THE STUDY OF YOUTH SPORTS, MICHIGAN STATE UNIVERSITY, USA

Introduction

The word coaching is reported to have its origins in the Hungarian word *koczi*, which described a carriage designed to carry passengers over difficult terrain, protecting them from the elements between their departure and ultimate destination (Hendrickson 1987; as cited in Stern 2004). Thus, it is not surprising that coaching has come to be known as 'the practice of supporting an individual ... through the process of achieving a specific personal or professional result' (Coaching 2011). While a primary role of coaches is to help individuals achieve specific behaviours, in recent years increased attention in both research and professional practice literature has focused on coaching people on secondary 'soft' skills such as communication, leadership, and personal development. One place this type of coaching is often mentioned is the youth sport arena where organizations not only desire to help young people develop physically and learn sport skills and tactics, but want to cultivate social and emotional development as well.

Life skills is the term most often used to define the social and emotional skills and attributes young people can learn through sports participation. Specifically, life skills in the sport context are viewed as 'those internal personal assets, characteristics and skills such as goal setting, emotional control, self-esteem and hard work ethic that can be facilitated or developed in sport and are transferred for use in non-sport settings' (Gould and Carson 2008: 60). In this chapter we focus on what is known about coaching life skills with a particular focus on young athletes and what needs to be known to advance our understanding and related effectiveness.

Understanding how to coach life skills in young athletes is important because of the popularity of sport for children and youth. It is common in countries around the world for at least 50 per cent – and sometimes more than 85 per cent – of youth under the age of 18 to participate in organized sport (Coakley 2009; DeKnop *et al.* 1996; National Center for Culture and Recreation Statistics 2007; Statistics Canada 2005).

With an understanding of these opportunities and the knowledge that participating in sports does not bring about these positive outcomes automatically, youth coaches are now being tasked with having the abilities to instruct the technical and tactical skills of their sport and to structure the learning environment in a way that fosters positive personal growth as well. Recently, Côté and Gilbert (2009) conceptualized the responsibilities of an effective coach as 'the consistent application of integrated professional, interpersonal, and intrapersonal knowledge to improve athletes' competence, confidence, connection and character' (316), further highlighting the importance of positive youth development.

Overview of research on the topic

To date, much of the life skills development work in sport has focused on how relatively small afterschool informal sports programmes or physical education classes, that are specifically designed to teach these skills, can be conducted to achieve their stated missions (Danish 2002; Hellison 2003). Until recently, less attention has been paid to the questions of if and how participation in more traditional sports programmes, like school sponsored sports or Little League Baseball (that have numerous objectives like winning, skill development, and physical fitness), develop life skills in young people. In the remainder of this section, we review some of the key research that has informed our understanding of how life skills are viewed and taught by youth sport stakeholders.

Several investigators have examined coaches' attitudes towards teaching life skills and what life skills they perceive are most needed by young athletes. Gould *et al.* (2006a) surveyed 154 varsity high school coaches representing a number of different sports, and found that coaches ranked psychosocial development and teaching physical skills as most important. In terms of the life skills student-athletes most needed to develop, coaches indicated taking personal responsibility, developing motivation/work ethic, developing better communication and listening skills, dealing with parents, and achieving better grades as the most pressing areas for intervention.

Taking a different approach, Jones and Lavallee (2009) conducted focus groups with adolescent athletes, coaches, and sport psychology professionals to identify how they defined life skills and to determine which life skills should be emphasized in youth sports. Life skills were viewed as a range of transferable skills needed to succeed in life and help individuals thrive. The two broad categories of life skills included: personal skills (e.g. self-organization, goal setting, motivation) and social skills (e.g. respect, leadership, communication, family interaction). Furthermore, social skills were identified as the most important life skills needed.

In another study, Vella *et al.* (2011) conducted interviews with 22 male and female coaches of adolescent Australian sport teams. They assessed coaches' desire to cultivate areas of positive development and their views on what was necessary to bring about these outcomes. Coaches indeed desired and felt responsible for developing athlete competence, confidence, connection, character, life skills (e.g. self-control, goal setting, teamwork), positive climates (e.g. good interpersonal relations), positive affect and psychological capacities (e.g. resilience, forgiveness, optimism). Interestingly, coaches emphasized positive affect as most important outcome for their athletes, but also noted the high degree of interdependence between each of the main categories.

Gould and Carson (2010, 2011) also conducted studies examining the relationship between the development of life skills and youth perceptions of their coaches' actions. Athletes who report higher levels of the coaching behaviours of facilitating competition strategies, goal setting, having coaches who talked about how sport lessons related to life, and building a positive rapport with athletes also report increased opportunities for the development of emotional regulation, cognitive skills, feedback, pro-social norms, and linkages to community in their high school sport experiences. Young athletes who reported greater negative rapport with their coaches and were less likely to perceive their coach as someone who helped them work on mental preparation, goal setting, and competition strategies and were less likely to model good sportsmanship and provide motivation to work hard on one's own were more likely to experience negative sport experiences.

Other research has shown that coaches who create a caring climate and develop positive relationships with young people involved in sport are more likely to facilitate positive youth development (Gano-Overway *et al.* 2009). This finding is consistent with the research of Smith, Smoll and their colleagues (Smoll and Smith 2002), which, through a series of studies over several decades, has shown that youth coaches who are trained to take a more positive approach to coaching (i.e. increased frequency of rewarding and encouraging remarks and decreased criticism and punitive behaviour) enhance player self-esteem and motivation and reduce athlete anxiety and programme attrition. Thus, developing good rapport and a positive caring climate with young athletes seems to be a critical first step in developing life skills through sport.

This literature has been extended in a recent study conducted with underserved high school youth involved in a summer baseball and softball programme (Gould *et al.* 2012). Participants completed the Youth Experiences Scale (YES-2), a self-report instrument that measures the types of developmental experiences youth have in sport and other extracurriculars, the Sport Motivational Climate Scale, the Caring Climate Scale, and assessments of the importance their coaches placed on life skills. The more coaches created caring, mastery-oriented environments, the more likely positive developmental gains resulted. This finding is consistent with previous motivational (Smith *et al.* 2007) and caring climate (Fry and Gano-Overway 2010) research, and further reinforces the idea that coaching actions and climates have an important influence on personal and social development of young people.

Additionally, several studies using qualitative methods have helped better illustrate the process of coaching life skills. Gould *et al.* (2006b, 2007) conducted in-depth interviews with high school football coaches awarded for their effectiveness at developing life skills. They found that these individuals reported using a variety of coaching strategies, both direct (e.g. having former athletes come into practices and talk to current athletes about life skills) and indirect (e.g. creating an environment that emphasizes certain core life skills). More importantly, these coaches had coaching philosophies that placed prime importance on life skills development, fostered strong coach–athlete relationships, utilized specific life skills strategies, and adapted their life skills coaching efforts to the specific context in which their athletes lived. These coaches did not view the teaching of life skills as a separate activity from their other coaching objectives, but integrated life skill strategies with all of their coaching duties.

In an extension of this research, Carson (2010) used a multiple case study design with three experienced coaches to investigate strategies used by high school coaches to facilitate the development and transfer of life skills in their athletes. Additionally, perceived success rates and barriers to this development and transfer were assessed. To corroborate the information gathered from each coach, current athletes from the coaches' programmes participated in focus groups, and one former player and parent of a former player were also interviewed. Three global categories and 17 specific subcategories of life skills coaching strategies were identified. For example, the global category of *Direct Strategies* included themes such as providing clear expectations, collaborating with athletes, and early intervention, while the category of *Indirect Factors* included themes such as establishing a team culture of excellence/class, developing family-like relationships, and being a caring/ dedicated coach. Finally, *Success Rates and Barriers* included themes such as perceptions of mixed success, delayed success, an overemphasis on winning, and athlete distractions. The coaches, therefore, were upholding many of the principles for effective asset/character building strategies that have been established in past literature (e.g. establishing positive relationships, reinforcing life lessons consistently and over time, building a system of development). Furthermore, the resulting discussion indicated several additional guidelines available to practitioners who wish to promote positive youth development through 'naturalistic' sport participation (e.g. integrating lessons into teachable moments and daily drills).

Using a case study design, Holt *et al.* (2008) examined if and how youth learned life skills through soccer participation. One high school soccer team and its coach were studied across a season using both field observations and in-depth interviews. The head coach was found to embrace a philosophy of building relationships with players and involving them in decisions. Respect, teamwork and leadership, and initiative were the life skills identified to be outcomes of soccer participation. Evidence was not found that these young athletes were directly taught these life skills, however. Instead, the coach created opportunities for students to use these life skills and then reinforced proper use or penalized the players for not demonstrating them. Teamwork and leadership were the only life skills athletes felt transferred beyond sport, and it was concluded that the student-athletes were producers of their own learning experiences regarding these two life skills. These findings suggest that current coaching life skills practices may not be as much about direct teaching of skills, but creating conditions where the skills can be self-generated, revealed, and reinforced. It also suggests that young people with certain life skills are drawn to sport where they can further develop their assets, which are then reinforced by their coach's efforts.

Investigators have also begun to examine the specific life skill of leadership and its development in peer leaders (e.g. team captains). For example, Dupuis *et al.* (2006) interviewed six former university male ice hockey captains and found that these individuals cultivated their leadership skills from observing respected sport leaders with whom they had contact starting from an early age. These former captains also expressed the importance of having a strong relationship with their coaches. This rapport helped athletes become effective liaisons between their teammates and the coaching staff. Finally, the types of responsibilities the former captains were given by coaches were perceived to be important leadership developing experiences. These individuals were involved in preseason team planning activities with the coaching staff as well as leading formal and informal meetings with their teammates. In addition to describing ways in which the coach is directly involved in cultivating leadership opportunities for their sport captains, the general nature of the captaincy experience was discussed (e.g. understanding the type and timing of communication and leading by example). The researchers concluded by advocating for coach awareness of these factors.

More recently, Voelker *et al.* (2011) reported results from an exploratory study designed to examine the leadership experiences and development of high school sport captains. Semi-structured interviews were conducted with 13 college freshmen who were high school captains the previous academic year. The majority of captains reported receiving little to no training from coaches for their captaincy role. When captains did receive training, they most often noted that it was indirect or implied rather than formal and deliberate. Similar to the Dupuis *et al.* (2006) study, these captains reported they learned to lead largely from previous life experiences, such as by interacting with and observing significant others and through trial and error. While exploratory, these findings are of concern because while it appears that coaches often talk about the need to develop life skills in their athletes, many may not be taking actions to do so; a finding that has been previously found with youth sports coaches (McCallister *et al.* 2000).

In sum, research on coaching life skills through youth sport has taught us the following:

1   There is clear link between sport participation and life skills development in young people, although we do not know if this link is causal.
2   Coaches feel that it is important to develop life skills, and several key life skills needed by young athletes have been identified (e.g. responsibility, motivation/goal setting, communication).
3   Coaches who appear to be more effective at teaching life skills have philosophies that place prime importance on that objective of sports participation. Life skills are intentionally taught in both direct and indirect manners.
4   The coaches' ability to develop trusting relationships with athletes and create caring climates is critical for developing life skills. The old adage, 'they don't care what you know, until they know you care' certainly seems appropriate when it comes to teaching life skills.
5   The sport context not only provides opportunities to directly teach life skills, but allows young people to test and demonstrate already developing life skills through interactions with their peers and coaches.

Interdisciplinary research considerations

Research on mentoring

Mentoring has been defined as the practice of advising and guiding another, 'providing wisdom and inspiration as a result of the experience' (Miller and Noland 2003: 84). There is a body of research on natural mentors or nonparent adults that influence young people (DuBois *et al.* 2002; Grossman and Rhodes 2002). Given the similarity between natural mentoring and coaching and the fact that both mentoring and coaching life skills can result in positive and negative outcomes, investigators studying the coaching of life skills should look for links and relevant findings from the research on natural mentors and their influence on young people.

Previous research shows that young people who have natural mentors are more likely to experience a number of positive developmental outcomes such as closer ties to school, enhanced self-esteem, and less drug use and delinquent behaviour than peers who do not have these positive adult influences. In fact, using data collected on a large national sample of adolescents, DuBois and Silverthorn (2005) found that youth who had mentoring relationships exhibited more favourable outcomes relating to educational achievement, fewer behaviour problems, and better physical health and psychological well-being. Similarly, Zand *et al.* (2009) used the newly created and validated Mentor-Youth Alliance Scale to assess the relationship between the perceived quality of the mentoring relationship and positive youth developmental outcomes. More specifically, youth who were determined to be more and less 'competent' in the areas of family bonding, relationships with adults, school bonding, and life skills (i.e. peer resistance skills, feelings of self-efficacy, and negative attitudes toward substance use) after eight months of involvement in a mentoring programme were compared. Those who were found to have higher levels in the competency areas were the youth who were female, younger, and who had more positive mentoring relationships. Finally, in a ten-year longitudinal study, Hurd and Zimmerman (2010) found that having a nonparent 'natural' mentor provided a buffering effect, which was related to decreased rates of depressive symptoms and risky sexual behaviour in adolescent African-Americans. However, mentoring effects were not as powerful as exposure to individual and environmental risk factors such as substance abuse or school suspension.

Mentoring has not been shown to be all positive, however, as Burk and Eby (2010) recently examined how negative mentoring (e.g. mismatch within mentor–mentee dyad, lack of mentor experience, mentor misuse of power) predicts intentions to terminate mentoring relationships. Organizations must be aware that not all mentoring will have positive effects and alternate mentors should be available so mentees do not feel entrapped. Mentors should also be evaluated because sometimes mentees may be fearful of mentor retaliation, and strategies should be in place for mentees to exit mentoring relationships in a safe manner.

Research on executive life coaching

An area of scholarship that might be used to help inform the coaching life skills area is the literature on executive business coaching. Specifically, business organizations whose goals are to improve employee performance and effectiveness have used executive coaches to help leaders develop and strengthen skills needed to function more effectively (Jones 2002). Although done with adults, the executive coaching process often focuses on helping leaders develop skills like communication, goal setting, and motivation. Furthermore, because of its shared outcomes with positive youth development, executive coaching may have lessons for coaching these same life skills in youth.

While studies in this area have only developed over the last decade, existing research supports the effectiveness of coaching for increasing executive performance and developmental change (Kampa-Kokesch and Anderson 2007). For example, Kilburg (1996) identified a list of techniques (e.g. role playing, simulations, journaling, reconstructions) used in executive coaching that might be of interest to those developing coaching life skills interventions. More recently, Kombarakaran et al. (2008) conducted a study to assess the effectiveness and influential factors involved in an executive coaching programme. Executives and coaches indicated that the programme significantly impacted executive development in the areas of: (1) people management; (2) relationships with managers; (3) goal setting and prioritization; (4) engagement and productivity; and (5) dialogue and communication. Furthermore, not only were the characteristics of the coach deemed important for successful outcomes, but factors such as organizational support and the commitment of the executives (i.e. mentees) toward their development were essential for success as well.

Major gaps in understanding the coaching of life skills

While the research on coaching life skills is only beginning, a number of questions have emerged as central to advancing the area. Each of these will be briefly addressed below.

Are youth sports too adult-dominated to allow for effective coaching of life skills?

The literature reviewed for this chapter suggests that life skills development is most likely to occur when athletes are given a voice in making decisions in organizations. Noted youth development researcher Reed Larson (2006), for example, suggests that too much structure or direction by adults often leads to a loss of youth ownership in their programmes and subsequently inhibits positive youth development. Similarly, writing about ways to enhance youth leadership through sport and physical education, Martinek and Hellison (2009) suggest that it is essential to gradually shift power to the youth and allow them to have an active voice in decision-making in order for the asset of responsibility to most fully develop. Given the autocratic nature of coaching that sometimes characterizes traditional youth sports programmes, a key question is whether organized youth sports are too adult-dominated to allow youth to take an active role in decision-making and programme direction to reach higher levels of positive life skills development.

To what degree can life skills be effectively taught in large-scale traditional sports programmes with multiple goals and objectives?

Evidence shows that life skills can be developed in programmes that involve small numbers of individuals and/or have the primary aim of psychosocial youth development (e.g. Hellison responsibility model studies). However, most youth sports programmes are conducted at scale, involving numerous teams, multiple coaches, and large groups of young people. The development of life skills is one of a number of equally ranked objectives (e.g. sport skill development, fitness, winning) for most youth sport coaches who participate or complete some type of formal coach training (Trudel and Gilbert 2006). However, there is very little evidence that this training has any durable influence on actual coach behaviours (see review by Trudel *et al.* 2010). As an illustration, a recent study of former high school captains (Voelker *et al.* 2011) showed that coaches were perceived by their athletes as seldom taking actions to intentionally teach life skills. Therefore, the challenge is to identify if, when, how, and under what conditions life skills can be effectively coached. While the evidence from large-scale studies of extracurricular activity participation by Hansen and Larson (2007) and Larson *et al.* (2006) are encouraging in that they show sport participation seems to be correlated with a number of positive life skills (e.g. development of initiative), there is a lack of longitudinal and intervention-based studies that can demonstrate 'true development' and causal relationships. Also, sport has been shown to be an extracurricular activity at times associated with negative experiences (e.g. stress, pressure to do things viewed as morally wrong) (Eccles *et al.* 2003; Hansen *et al.* 2003). So, just because one participates in sport it cannot be assumed he or she will develop life skills!

What are the characteristics of coaches who teach life skills to their athletes?

Another important question in need of additional study is the identification of characteristics of coaches who are more effective at fostering life skills in their players. Why do some coaches place more emphasis on coaching life skills while others do not? Emphasis placed on winning is often identified as a barrier to teaching life skills. This contention seems to be supported by the work of Gould *et al.* (2012), which shows that task-oriented motivational climates created by coaches are correlated with life skills development. On the other hand, in an in-depth study of a youth ice hockey coach's philosophy Wilcox and Trudel (1998) found that a coach can place considerable emphasis on winning while at the same time fostering the development of social skills in players. Flett *et al.* (2010) have also recently reported that university coaches describe intangibles like social character, maturity, resiliency, and work ethic (all potential life skills) as being important factors facilitating athletic performance. The intricacies involved in the emphasis placed on winning by coaches while simultaneously coaching life skills, then, must be further studied.

Other factors to consider might be how a coach's philosophy develops (Collins *et al.* 2009), as well as experiences coaches had in learning life skills as athletes themselves. Lastly, looking at whether coaches are formally trained as teachers (for school sports) and, thus, understand the role of educational athletics might be a factor to contemplate when unravelling this issue.

What coaching strategies are most effective and how can coaches learn these strategies?

Initial evidence shows that coaches who are successful at coaching life skills use both direct and indirect coaching strategies (Carson 2010; Gould *et al.* 2007). Direct strategies involve talking to athletes about the skills they want them to develop and then reinforcing the athletes for carrying out desirable behaviours. Indirect strategies include creating conditions that require athletes to work together and achieve their own goals without direct coach involvement. Causal links between specific coaching strategies and life skills development have not been established, and both intervention and longitudinal studies are certainly needed to resolve the questions in this area.

Recent coach education literature could be particularly helpful in helping coaches learn strategies for teaching life skills. In particular, recent reviews by Trudel *et al.* (2010) and Trudel and Gilbert (2006) show that coaches primarily learn through non-formal and informal experiences as opposed to traditional formal lecture-oriented coach education programmes. They recommend that coaching educators pay more attention to facilitating coach learning through reflection during which the learner must set questions, derive solutions, experiment, evaluate, and discuss their efforts with other coaches who can provide support and feedback. It is further suggested the coaches form communities of practice where they meet regularly with a small group of peers to share ideas and test solutions to context specific coaching issues (Gilbert *et al.* 2009). These findings certainly suggest that if one is interested in educating coaches about teaching life skills that experiential education methods be employed and communities of like-minded coaches meet regularly to discuss life skills coaching efforts. In fact, a model of doing this already exists for physical educators who run afterschool sports clubs (and more recently, competitive athletics) designed to teach personal and social responsibility to young people (www.tpsr-alliance.org).

Do life skills transfer beyond sport and what factors facilitate the development of transfer effects?

A foundational assumption of the life skills development through sports discussion is that the growth that occurs within the sporting context is eventually transferred to and utilized effectively in other life domains. Of course, it makes intuitive sense that if skills such as goal setting, problem solving, effectively processing feedback, demonstration of hard work ethic, and emotional regulation can be applied to the challenges of physical training and competition they should also be available to the individual in other social contexts. However, it is more likely that this transfer of skills happens haphazardly, if at all, because athletes may not be aware that they have acquired skills that may be of use to them outside of sport and/or may not have the requisite knowledge or confidence for carrying out the actual transfer if a later opportunity should arise (Danish *et al.* 1993). Unless initial learning experiences are structured in a way that transfer is addressed and practice of the skills outside of sport is encouraged, the likelihood that sport skills will become life skills is small at best (Danish 2002; Papacharisis *et al.* 2005). More specifically, Petitpas *et al.* (2005) have suggested that for transfer to take place, learning and development must occur in an appropriate context, be carried out by caring adults and within a positive group, and must encompass the skills that are particularly meaningful and important for youth to most effectively meet the challenges of specific environments.

Practical implications: coaching transferable life skills

While research on the transferability of life skills is only now beginning, professional practice literature from other disciplines provides strategies that can be adopted to increase the likelihood of the application of the capabilities acquired through sport participation to life outside of athletics. For example, the conditions outlined by Gass (1985) for the transfer of skills gained through experiential education can be easily modified for use in youth sport settings. A central objective of any programme aimed at promoting positive development should be to structure activities and lessons so that participants are aware from the beginning that the skills they are developing can be utilized in other contexts. Furthermore, the idea of and instructions for skill transfer should be consistently reinforced throughout the duration of their involvement and opportunities for follow-up should be provided. Skill transfer is also more likely to occur if the learning environment and other applicable contexts share similar aspects. In other words, the positive attribute of initiative, if learned in sport, may easily transfer to another activity that requires physical discipline such as participation in physical education classes or doing chores when asked, but may not transfer to a cognitive activity such as doing one's homework on time. Clear similarities between contexts may not always exist or may not be obvious to the young learner, so an important task of a programme leader is to engage youth in discussions during which parallels that exist between contexts are highlighted.

Other suggestions proposed by Gass (1985) to facilitate skill transfer are to provide ample opportunities for individuals to practise adapting skills to different activities and between different contexts. Learners should not be expected to only engage in this practice on their own time, but should be given the opportunity to test out this transfer in situations during which they can receive guidance and feedback. Additionally, the participants should be encouraged to reflect on their practice and experiences of transferring skills so that their awareness is increased and their learning is more thoroughly solidified. Finally, if possible, having new learners interact with peers who have previously practised and implemented the skills in other contexts provides young learners with vicarious experiences of the desired transfer.

When implementing life skills training in their youth developmental programmes, Danish and colleagues adopted several strategies outlined by Gass (1985) (Danish *et al.* 2003). The development and transfer of life skills outside of athletics was facilitated within the physical-skill based lessons by: (1) having discussions with participants about the importance of physical and 'mental skills' (or life skills) to sport performance; (2) providing examples and demonstrations of how these mental skills are practised and cultivated inside and outside of sport; (3) creating opportunities for athletes to practise these skills in sport settings; (4) helping athletes develop and implement a plan to utilize the skills outside of sport; and (5) debriefing with athletes the successes and failures of using the skills in sport and other life contexts. These strategies have been deemed useful in terms of involving life skill lessons within an athletic context, while still distancing the skills enough from the sport environment so that participants can appreciate how the assets are useful beyond their sporting experiences.

Conclusion

When asked if his team had a successful season, the legendary American college football coach Alanzo Stagg indicated that he did not know and would have to wait 30 years to find out, suggesting that the contribution of his players to society as adults was how he judged success. Stagg understood that developing character and life skills in his players was the true measure of coaching success, but took years to really judge the efficacy of doing so. Over the last decade, researchers have begun to uncover how coaches develop life skills in their players. Initial findings show that life skills can be effectively coached and that coaches who do so have strong philosophical bases, know how to develop effective coach–player relationships, have a number of life skills coaching strategies, and consider environmental and contextual factors in their coaching. Several critical questions remain unknown, however, and await further study. These include:

1   Are competitive youth sports too adult-dominated to allow for effective coaching of life skills?
2   Can we identify if, when, how, and under what conditions life skills can be effectively coached in these programmes?
3   What are the characteristics and strategies coaches use to teach life skills to athletes?
4   Can coaches be taught to teach life skills and, if so, what is the best way for doing so? and
5   Do life skills transfer beyond sport and what factors facilitate the development of any transfer effects?

It is hoped that this chapter not only informs coaching education and practice relative to life skills, but also helps stimulate further research in this important area.

References

Burk, H.G. and Eby, L.T. (2010) 'What keeps people in mentoring relationships when bad things happen? A field study from the protégé's perspective', *Journal of Vocational Education*, 77(3): 437–46.

Carson, S.A. (2010) 'Life skills development and transfer through high school sport participation: how life lessons and taught and brought to life', unpublished doctoral dissertation, Michigan State University.

Coaching (n.d.) in Wikipedia, online, available at: http://en.wikipedia.org/wiki/Coaching (accessed May 25, 2011).

Coakley, J. (2009) *Sports in Society: Issues and Controversies*, 10th edn, Boston: McGraw-Hill.

Collins, K., Gould, D., Lauer, L. and Chung, Y. (2009) 'Coaching life skills through football: philosophical beliefs of outstanding high school football coaches', *International Journal of Coaching Science*, 3(1): 1–26.

Côté, J. and Gilbert, W. (2009) 'An integrative definition of coaching effectiveness and expertise', *International Journal of Sports Science and Coaching*, 4(3): 307–23.

Danish, S.J. (2002) SUPER (Sports United to Promote Education and Recreation) *Program Leader Manual*, 3rd edn, Richmond, VA: Life Skills Center, Virginia Commonwealth University.

Danish, S., Petipas, A. and Hale, B. (1993) 'Life development intervention for athletes: life skills through sports', *The Counseling Psychologist*, 21(3): 352–85.

Danish, S.J., Taylor, T.E. and Fazio, R.J. (2003) 'Enhancing adolescent development through sports and leisure', in G.R. Adams and M.D. Berznsley (eds) *Blackwell Handbook of Adolescence*, Malden, MA: Blackwell Publishing.

DeKnop, P., Engström, L., Skirstad, B. and Weiss, M. (1996) *Worldwide Trends in Youth Sport*, Champaign, IL: Human Kinetics.

DuBois, D.L. and Silverthorn, N. (2005) 'Natural mentoring relationships and adolescent health: evidence from a national study', *American Journal of Public Health*, 95(3): 518–24.

DuBois, D.L., Holloway, B.E., Valentine, J.C. and Cooper, H. (2002) 'Effectiveness of mentoring programs for youth: a meta analysis', *American Journal of Community Psychology*, 30(3): 157–97.

Dupuis, M., Bloom, G.A. and Loughead, T.M. (2006) 'Team captains' perceptions of athlete leadership', *Journal of Sport Behavior*, 29(1): 60–78.

Eccles, J.S., Barber, B.L., Stone, M. and Hunt, J. (2003) 'Extracurricular activities and adolescent development', *The Journal of Social Issues*, 59(4): 865–89.

Flett, M.R., Gould, D.R., Paule, A.L. and Schneider, R.P. (2010) 'How and why university coaches define, identify, and recruit "intangibles"', *International Journal of Coaching Science*, 4(2): 15–35.

Fry, M.D. and Gano-Overway, L.A. (2010) 'Exploring the contribution of caring climate to the youth sport experience', *Journal of Applied Sport Psychology*, 22(3): 294–304.

Gano-Overway, L.A., Newton, M., Magyar, T.M., Fry, M.D., Kim, M. and Guivernau, M.R. (2009) 'Influence of caring youth sport contexts on efficacy-related beliefs and social behaviors', *Developmental Psychology*, 45(2): 329–40.

Gass, M. (1985) 'Programming the transfer of learning in adventure education', *Journal of Experiential Education*, 8(3): 18–24.

Gilbert, W., Gallimore, R. and Trudel, P. (2009) 'A learning community approach to coach development in youth sports', *Journal of Coaching Education*, 2(2): 1–21.

Gould, D. and Carson, S. (2008) 'Life skills development through sport: current status and future directions', *International Review of Sport and Exercise Psychology*, 1(1): 58–78.

Gould, D. and Carson, S. (2010) 'The relationship between perceived coaching behaviors and developmental benefits of high school sports participation', *The Hellenic Journal of Psychology*, 7(3): 298–314.

Gould, D. and Carson, S. (2011) 'Young athletes perceptions of the relationship between coaching behaviors and developmental experiences', *International Journal of Coaching Science*, 5(2): 3–29.

Gould, D., Chung, Y., Smith, P. and White, J. (2006a) 'Future directions in coaching life skills: understanding high school coaches' views and needs', *Athletic Insights: The Online Journal of Sports Psychology*, 18(3), online, available at: www.athleticinsight.com/Vol8Iss3/CoachingPDF.pdf.

Gould, D., Collins, K., Lauer, L. and Chung, Y. (2006b) 'Coaching life skills: a working model', *Sport and Exercise Psychology Review*, 2(1): 10–18.

Gould, D., Collins, K., Lauer, L. and Chung, Y. (2007) 'Coaching life skills through football: a study of award winning high school coaches', *Journal of Applied Sport Psychology*, 19(1): 16–37.

Gould, D., Flett, R.M. and Lauer, L. (2012) 'The relationship between psychosocial developmental and the sports climate experienced by underserved youth', *Psychology of Sport and Exercise*, 13(1): 80–87.

Grossman, J.B. and Rhodes, J.E. (2002) 'The test of time: predictors and effects of duration in youth mentoring relationships', *American Journal of Community Psychology*, 30(2): 199–219.

Hansen, D.M. and Larson, R. (2007) 'Amplifiers of developmental and negative experiences in organized activities: dosage, motivation, lead roles, and adult-youth ratios', *Journal of Applied Developmental Psychology*, 28(4): 360–74.

Hansen, D.M., Larson, R.W. and Dworkin, J.B. (2003) 'What adolescents learn in organized youth activities: a survey of self-reported developmental experiences', *Journal of Research on Adolescence*, 13(1): 25–55.

Hellison, D.R. (2003) *Teaching Responsibility through Physical Activity*, 2nd edn, Champaign, IL: Human Kinetics.

Holt, N.L., Tink, L.N., Mandigo, J.L. and Fox, K.R. (2008) 'Do youth learn life skills through their involvement in high school sport?' *Canadian Journal of Education*, 31(2): 281–304.

Hurd, N. and Zimmerman, M. (2010) 'Natural mentors, mental health, and risk behaviors: a longitudinal analysis of African American adolescents transitioning into adulthood', *American Journal of Community Psychology*, 46(1/2): 36–48.

Jones, G. (2002) 'Performance excellence: a personal perspective on the link between sport and business', *Journal of Applied Sport Psychology*, 14(4): 268–81.

Jones, M.I. and Lavallee, D. (2009) 'Exploring the life skill needs of British adolescent athletes', *Psychology of Sport and Exercise*, 10(1): 159–67.

Kampa-Kokesch, S. and Anderson, M.A. (2007) 'Executive coaching: a comprehensive review of the literature', *Consulting Psychology Journal: Practice and Research*, 53(4): 205–28.

Kilburg, R.R. (1996) 'Toward a conceptual understanding and definition of executive coaching', *Consulting Psychology Journal: Practice and Research*, 48(2): 134–44.

Kombarakaran, F.A., Yang, J.A., Baker, M.N. and Fernandes, P.B. (2008) 'Executive coaching: it works!' *Consulting Psychology Journal: Practice and Research*, 60(1): 78–90.

Larson, R. (2006) 'Positive youth development, willful adolescents, and mentoring', *Journal of Community Psychology*, 34(6): 677–689.

Larson, R.W., Hansen, D.M. and Moneta, G. (2006) 'Differing profiles of developmental experiences across types of organised youth activities', *Developmental Psychology*, 42(5): 849–63.

Martinek, T. and Hellison, D. (2009) *Youth Leadership in Sport and Physical Education*, New York: Palgrave.

McCallister, S.G., Blinde, E.M. and Weiss, W.M. (2000) 'Teaching values and implementing philosophies: dilemmas of the youth sport coach', *The Physical Educator*, 57(1): 35–45.

Miller, K. and Noland, M. (2003) 'Unwritten roles for survival and success: senior faculty speak to junior faculty', *American Journal of Health Education*, 31(2): 84–89.

National Center for Culture and Recreation Statistics. (2007) 'Children's participation in organised sport – 2000, 2003, 2006', Report for the Standing Committee on Recreation and Sport. Online, available at: www.ausport.gov.au/__data/assets/pdf_file/0011/276914/ABS_-_Childrens_participation_in_organised_-_2003_-_2006.pdf.

Papacharisis, V., Goudas, M., Danish, S.J. and Theodorakis, Y. (2005) 'The effectiveness of teaching a life skills program in a sport context', *Journal of Applied Sport Psychology*, 17(3): 247–54.

Petitpas, A.J., Cornelius, A.E., Raalte, J.L. and Jones, T. (2005) 'A framework for planning youth sport programs that foster psychological development', *The Sport Psychologist*, 19(1): 63–80.

Smith, R.E., Smoll, F.L. and Cummings, S.P. (2007) 'Effects of a motivational climate intervention for coaches on young athletes' sport performance anxiety', *Journal of Sport and Exercise Psychology*, 29(1): 39–59.

Smoll, F.L. and Smith, R E. (2002) 'Coaching behavior research and intervention in youth sports', in F.L. Smoll and R.E. Smith (eds) *Children and Youth in Sport: A Biopsychosocial Perspective*, 2nd edn, Dubuque, IA: Kendall/Hunt.

Statistics Canada (2005) 'Canadian social trends: kids' sports', online, available at: www.statcan.gc.ca/pub/11-008-x/2008001/article/10573-eng.htm.

Stern, L.R. (2004) 'Executive coaching: a working definition', *Consulting Psychology Journal: Practice and Research*, 56(3): 154–62.

Trudel, P. and Gilbert, W.D. (2006) 'Coaching and coaching education', in D. Kirk, M. O'Sullivan and D. McDonald (eds) *Handbook of Physical Education*, London: Sage.

Trudel, P., Gilbert, W.D. and Werthner, P. (2010) 'Coaching education effectiveness', in J. Lyle and C. Cushion (eds) *Sports Coaching: Professionalisation and Practice*, London: Elsevier.

Vella, S., Oades, L. and Crowe, T. (2011) 'The role of the coach in facilitating positive youth development: moving from theory to practice', *Journal of Applied Sport Psychology*, 23(1): 33–48.

Voelker, D., Gould, D. and Crawford, M. (2011) 'Understanding the experience of high school sport captains', *The Sport Psychologist*, 25(1): 47–66.

Wilcox, S. and Trudel, P. (1998) 'Constructing the coaching principles of a youth ice hockey coach', *Avante*, 4(3): 39–66.

Zand, D.H., Thompson, N., Cervantes, R., Espiritu, R., Klagholz, D., LaBlanc, L. and Taylor, A. (2009) 'The mentor-youth alliance: the role of mentoring relationships in promoting youth competence', *Journal of Adolescence*, 32(1): 1–17.

22

AMBIGUITY, NOTICING AND ORCHESTRATION

Further thoughts on managing the complex coaching context

Robyn L. Jones

CARDIFF SCHOOL OF SPORT, CARDIFF METROPOLITAN UNIVERSITY, UK

Jake Bailey

CARDIFF SCHOOL OF SPORT, CARDIFF METROPOLITAN UNIVERSITY, UK

Andrew Thompson

CARDIFF SCHOOL OF SPORT, INDEPENDENT RESEARCHER, UK

Introduction

The purpose of this chapter is to develop the notion of orchestration as a means to further conceptualise sports coaching. This is done in two principal ways. First, by exploring the latest theoretical writings related to the management of complex change. The work referred to here includes Hoyle and Wallace's (2008) notion of social irony, Keltchermans and Ballet's (2002a, 2002b; Keltchermans 2005) ideas on micro-political literacy and Mason's (2002) discipline of 'noticing'. Second, in an attempt to locate theory in practice, the thoughts of a coach are included about orchestration in terms of its applicability to his professional practice.

In terms of structure, we initially outline how sports coaching has come to be viewed as a complex or even a chaotic endeavour (Bowes and Jones 2006). This is followed by an outline of how the original concept of orchestration, as derived by Wallace (2003), has been used so far to define the role of the sports coach (Jones and Wallace 2005, 2006). A discussion on how to enrich or develop the concept of coach as orchestrator is then provided through recourse to the three aforementioned perspectives (i.e. the work of Wallace and colleagues on pathos and social irony; Ball, Fry, and Keltchermas and Ballet's studies on micro-political literacy; and Mason's work among others on noticing). The chapter progresses to the reflections of Jake Bailey, a coach who used, and continues to use, orchestration in his everyday practice. Finally, a reflective conclusion summarises the main points made, and suggests future research and applied directions.

A look back to where we are

Over the past decade or so, in a conscious movement away from modelling and reductionism, a growing body of work has illustrated the complexity inherent within sports coaching. Seminal papers here include Saury and Durand's (1998) study into the actions of elite sailing coaches, and d'Arippe-Longueville *et al.*'s (1998) research into the behaviours of top-level French judo coaches. Such work, along with that by Cushion and Jones (2006) and Purdy *et al.* (2009), portray coaching as a context bound activity within which coaches, athletes and others collaborate, struggle and negotiate personal directions and meanings. What is advocated here is that the dynamic nature of coaching demands an appreciation of the interaction and interconnectivity of events, and that good practice often emerges from a combination of structure and chaos (Jones *et al.* 2011). It is what Bourdieu termed 'structured improvisation'. Coaching has thus come to be looked upon as being a non-linear, complex activity; one of bounded instability, which exists at the 'edge of chaos'.

This chaotic metaphor for coaching, which was developed by Bowes and Jones (2006) through connecting it to relational schema (the boundaries of the instability), inspired the conceptualisation of coaching as orchestration (Jones and Wallace 2005, 2006). Derived from Wallace's (2001, 2003) and Wallace and Pocklington's (2002) work on managing complex educational change, the concept of orchestration refers to coordinated activity within set parameters expressed by leaders (coaches) 'to instigate, plan, organise, monitor and respond to evolving circumstances in order to bring about improvement in the individual and collective performance of those being coached' (Wallace 2007: 25). Without going over old ground, suffice to say here that orchestration implies steering, as opposed to controlling, a dynamic interactive process involving much 'behind the scenes string pulling' towards desired objectives; of constant analysis, evaluation and scrutiny to keep things going; and of maintaining detailed oversight of the minutiae of each coaching situation (for a fuller account of the orchestration metaphor in sports coaching see Jones and Wallace 2005, 2006).

Such apparent back-stage actions, however, should not be viewed as dark Machiavellian dealings, but as interactive strategies engaged in by actors to make social contexts work (Jones *et al.* 2011). Viewing the sports coach as orchestrator then, marks a move away from the 'coach as exclusive controller' orthodoxy by re-conceptualising coaching as a contested, negotiated activity which practitioners must manage the best they can. Rather than being predominantly charismatic and transformatory, a coach's work is consequently seen as being much more outside the limelight, as unobtrusively arranging, guiding and generally scaffolding the resultant (athletes') public performance. Creating the performance is nevertheless always seen as a pluralistic endeavour, as both coaches and athletes retain enough agency to personally interpret actions and re-actions within given parameters as set by the orchestration (Wallace 2007). It is worth re-emphasising here, however, Wallace's cautionary note about exactly what we are claiming; that is, orchestration is offered as nothing more than a loose metaphor to draw attention to what good coaches do to cope with, and excel within, dynamic complex contexts.

Developing the sports coach as orchestrator

Building on the foundation provided, the next section examines recent writings from a variety of fields which we believe can enrich and develop the orchestration concept in terms of its applicability to coaching. Initially, the discussion will be informed by the work of Wallace and colleagues on managing the processes of complex change in public and educational institutions (Wallace and Schneller 2008; Hoyle and Wallace 2008). Keltchermans and Ballet's (2002a; Keltchermans 2005) and Ball's (1987) work into the micro-political activity evident in pedagogical and management organisations is then drawn upon to illustrate how dynamic change is both initiated and reacted to in the quest to realise desired ends. The final theoretical source to be consulted is that of noticing (Mason 2002); a perspective which perhaps holds the greatest potential for the further development of the orchestration concept within sports coaching.

Further defining coaching as a complex, ironic activity

In a recent paper, Hoyle and Wallace (2008) expanded their work concerning the management of complex change through the notion of social irony. Although they claimed that defining such a slippery term as irony was akin to 'gathering mist', they offered a principled definition in terms of a pathos or gap between the words spoken by an individual and the intended meaning of those words. As opposed to the often-held singularly negative connotations of the term irony, Hoyle and Wallace's definition was expanded to include situations where multiple meanings are compressed in single sentences, where ostensible contraries co-habit, where a gap exists between the policy rhetoric and everyday reality and, often, where unintended consequences result from planned action (Hoyle and Wallace 2008). They argued that irony is endemic in social life, and whilst we have to live with that irony (importantly for the concept of orchestration) there is still room for human agency. This latter phenomenon was termed 'pragmatic irony' which 'refers to the strategies that organisational members use to cope with the ambiguities and dilemmas' of social life (p. 1427). A core claim of this work then, is that 'irony assumes a capacity to live with the dissonance of opposites' (p. 1430); a position which coaches are quite aware of.

Similar to their earlier work, Hoyle and Wallace (2008) consider social (which incorporates organisational) life to be imbued with elements of uncertainty, ambiguity and, irony, which is most often associated with the limits of rationality. From an ironic perspective, such uncertainty cannot be 'solved'; the problem is one of living with it. Here, they borrow from Cohen *et al.*'s (1972) notion of organisational life as 'organised anarchy' and of a 'garbage can' model of decision making. For example, giving athletes greater decision-making opportunities may result in greater commitment to accepting responsibility but weakens managerial or coach control over such decision, for which he or she is held accountable. If players advocate courses of action outside parameters acceptable to coaches (and some other athletes), then pressure mounts to centralise the decision-making process. This, of course, denies some athletes a voice, or the degree of voice they would like, thus increasing pressure for decentralisation again. The point made here by Hoyle and Wallace (2008) is one related to complexity, irony, dilemmas and unintended consequences; that social activities, like coaching, are never straightforward, however much some of us would like them to be.

Irony is also believed to be contingent; that is, it flourishes more under some conditions than others. Within management (and indeed coaching), this can most obviously be seen through the development of a credo of managerialism, incumbent of professionalisation, specific bodies of knowledge, credentialism and the creation of professional organisations. Hoyle and Wallace (2008) term such developments as 'management to excess'. Underlying such a phenomenon is the belief that 'not only *can* everything be managed, but everything *should* be managed' (p. 1435); whilst everything that matters can be measured, and 'what can be measured can be managed' (ibid.). It reflects an obsession with accountability and audit; in sport, perhaps this can most obviously be seen in the voluminous use of statistics to 'measure' and judge athletes' performances. Similarly, the identifying and documenting of coaches' competencies reflect such a manifestation. The irony here is not lost on coaches themselves who were recently found to adopt Goffmanesque tactics as halting practices to demonstrate their mastery of given competencies irrespective of whether athlete improvement was taking place (Chesterfield *et al.* 2010). Such managerialism is also clearly seen in the development of language, with careers being built on its use (a reason offered for its persistence?). It comprises ideas related to 'clean buzz words'; abstract notions that cannot be grounded in the reality of everyday life. So how do coaches get around this problem, or should they just resign themselves to their inability to do so? The core concept of orchestration was an initial suggestion for how managers of others, such as coaches, can survive and indeed thrive within such messy contexts.

Schneller and Wallace (2007) gave an example of orchestration in action from the behaviours of nurses who blocked centralised directives which they considered to be unworkable. The problem here centred on the creation and introduction of 'registered care technicians' (RCTs) to work under the supervision of nurses whilst reporting to physicians; an initiative driven by a nursing shortage, although not arrived at in consultation with the nursing profession. In short, through extensive communication and 'culture building' (centred on a call that the very essence of the profession was being diluted), the nurses' organisation engaged in orchestrating a counter-policy. A principal aspect of this was done through persuading other stakeholders such as key health-care professionals (e.g., hospital managers and medical associations) and the wider public (including patients and their relatives) that any change as suggested would be detrimental to their interests. Activities carried out towards this end included gathering detailed information on the precise nature and scope of the proposals; studying current strategies of nursing care; developing a clear counter proposal; educating all interested parties about the implications of the proposed changes; and creating opportunities and occasions for differing organisations to meet in opposition to the plans. The resulting extensive and focused public relations campaign eventually led to the withdrawal of the centralised proposals; the nurses' organisation had triumphed. The immediate lessons drawn from this case are two-fold. First, as managers, of the need to engage with and never ignore the context-dependent characteristics of social complexity and change; and second, to appreciate the power-full micro-strategies involved in the 'culture building' that went on in reaction to the proposed policy of implementing RCTs. It is to this latter point, in particular, that we now turn.

Coaching as a micro-political landscape

The term micro-politics has been used to describe the political interactions that take place between individuals and groups within organisational settings, such as schools and sports teams (Hoyle 1982; Ball 1987; Blase 1991). Although no specific definition of micro-politics is considered definitive, the most frequently used is that advocated by Blase (1991: 11), as:

> the use of formal and informal power by individuals and groups to achieve their goals. In large part, political actions result from perceived differences between individuals and groups, coupled with the motivation to use power and influence and/or to protect … Both co-operative and conflictive actions and processes are part of the realm of micro-politics [whilst] the macro and the micro frequently interact.

Such a designation builds on Hoyle's (1982) earlier definition of micro-political action as the 'strategies by which individuals and groups in organisational contexts seek to use their resources of power and influence to further their interests' (p. 88). The roots of micro-politics as a theorising framework lie in dissatisfaction with the apolitical model of organisations. Echoing Wallace's initial thoughts on the need for more complex metaphors to describe social action, such organisations were alternatively seen as melting pots for political activities where individuals and groups sought to gain resources and power. Power and politics, however, are often embroiled in negative connotations. Words such as 'manipulation', 'scheming' and 'underhand' frequently lead to them being seen as something bad, as tools to constrain and antagonise rather than being positive phenomena (Hansen and Küpper 2009). Although organisational 'misbehaviour' (Hansen and Küpper 2009) can be interpreted as individuals acting strategically by opposing change to restrict or alter officially planned intentions, power and politics can also be empowering and positive. By positioning and understanding organisations as political entities, studies have revealed how organisations are vulnerable to the regularly conflicting ideologies of the individuals that act within them (Ball 1987; Lindle 1994; Blase and Anderson 1995). Although the field of micro-politics is still in its infancy, it has already provided worthy insights into the often contested and negotiated nature of pedagogical institutions and managerial organisations (Blase and Anderson 1995).

A leading scholar in this regard has been Stephen Ball, much of whose work has examined the 'behind the scenes' nature of life in schools. Ball's (1987) research argues that the different ideologies individuals adopt about the purposes of schools and their formal structures impact upon how people operate within them. In this respect, day-to-day occurrences such as disagreements can trigger the adoption of strategic actions or, as he termed them, political activities as means to gain control over emerging situations and change. Political activity in this context was defined as 'skilled strategic action' engaged in by individuals or groups contesting for control of emerging situations (Ball 1987: 10). Building on this foundation, Fry (1997) utilised a micro-political perspective to examine how one teacher attempted to initiate and deal with applied change in an Australian school. Fry argued that the use of micro-politics as an analytical tool can better reveal the everyday tensions of interpersonal influences within social systems like schools, thus giving a more credible account of how change is instigated and handled on a personal level. By focusing on one individual's attempt to implement change in a deeply entrenched culture, Fry highlighted how personal alliances were forged and re-forged based on developing relationships with contextual stakeholders in an attempt to achieve political goals. In doing so, she contradicted the notion that teachers work is, or should be, non-political, and demonstrated how micro-political activities are entered into outside the classroom to initiate change and achieve personal agendas.

Similar to Fry (1997), Kelchtermans and Ballet (2002a, 2002b; Kelchtermans 2005) examined how beginner teachers come to understand and navigate their way through the political aspects of their work. At the centre of this research was the issue of how new teachers develop 'micro-political literacy'; that is, the process by which new teachers learn to read the micro-political school landscape and write themselves into it (Kelchtermans and Ballet 2002a). Kelchtermans and Ballet's belief in its pervasiveness led them to conclude that any theory on teacher development would be incomplete without appreciation and knowledge of how teachers deal with the inevitable contested character of what they do (Potrac and Jones 2009a). They proposed that micro-political acts are frequently related to the concept of 'working conditions'; that is, how, through micro-political interactions, teachers attempt to create desired working conditions, protect working conditions when they are threatened, and re-establish them if they are removed (Kelchtermans and Ballet 2002a). For example, when their professional identities and self-esteem were threatened by changing working contexts, teachers' self-interests as related to self-affirmation, dealing with vulnerability and striving for visibility in their job, emerged. Here, the teachers under study proactively sought opportunities to demonstrate their competencies in efforts to be redefined as 'proper teachers' by all concerned. Kelchtermans and Ballet (2002a) consequently noted that teachers focused their energies not just on their pupils' immediate learning, but also on strategies to become 'visible as competent, creative, hardworking professionals' to better secure that learning (p. 112).

Whilst the micro-political nature of managerial organisations has been relatively well documented, emerging research has made the case for examining coaching practice through a similar micro-political lens (Potrac and Jones 2009a, 2009b). This developing line of inquiry has begun to question the governing discourse that sporting environments are or should be always characterised by functionality, collaboration and trust (Potrac and Jones 2009a). In building on this rhetorical position, Potrac and Jones (2009b) examined the practice of Gavin, a newly appointed coach at the fictionalised Erewhon City Football Club, and the strategies he employed to first gain acceptance and 'buy in' from the players and, second, to displace a dysfunctional assistant coach who threatened his agenda. Gavin's actions were not only confined to forging and re-forging alliances with contextual stakeholders, but also to extensive 'face-work' (Goffman 1959), where he carefully considered how to behave and manage the impressions of others towards preferred ends (Potrac and Jones 2009b). The case is made that not engaging with the liberating and constraining effects of such tension, action and discord will only result in a distorted Utopian view of a very complex activity (Thompson *et al.* forthcoming).

Noticing, the basis of coaching action: what informs (or should inform) our orchestrated decisions?

The final body of work drawn upon to further develop the embryonic theory of coaching as orchestration is that of 'noticing'; a concept borrowed from the work of John Mason (2002). As stated earlier in the chapter, it is a perspective which perhaps holds the greatest potential for the further enrichment of the orchestration concept within coaching. This is because, if orchestration is built upon micro-realities and management of context, it must be premised on being able to see or notice opportunities to act in the first place.

Mason (2002) begins his book, subtitled *The Discipline of Noticing*, with the premise that noticing is something we do all the time ('at the heart of all practice lies noticing; noticing an opportunity to act appropriately' (p.1)); sometimes, if not most often, unconsciously. The point of his book is to turn such casual noticing into a powerful developmental tool; to enhance and improve the intuitive act of the pedagogue to better effect. Noticing then, is considered an act of attention and is founded on the prior concept of consciousness raising and reflection. What is noticed subsequently becomes intake for learning. Mason goes on to ascertain that, as professionals, we are sensitised or primed to notice certain things. It is argued that this base needs to be widened; and that, although a disturbance or resonance of some kind is needed to notice, this can be as subtle as a ripple on familiar waters as opposed to a 'tidal wave'.

Such a perspective, however, is not totally unique, and echoes the work of critical ethnographers, phenomenologists and micro-sociologists. Here, the emphasis is placed on looking beyond the immediate, to a close analysis of human consciousness and behaviour; to the seemingly ordinary microscopic expression of everyday care and solidarity (Gardiner

2000). Gardiner provides an interesting analogy here when, borrowing from Lefebvre (1991: 87), he asks us to focus not so much on the blooming flowers and trees but on the nourishing earth beneath 'which has a secret life and richness of its own'. This act of observation as linked to recognition also provided a foundation for Niklas Luhmann's (1995) re-conceptualisation of sociology. Inspired by the British mathematician George Spencer-Brown, Luhmann defined observation as a specific operation of creating distinctions. In the words of Spencer-Brown (1969: 1): 'We cannot make an indication without drawing a distinction'. For Luhmann then, by drawing a distinction something comes to the foreground for the observer, against a horizon. In this way, reality is constructed. Such thinking highlights the responsibility of social actors to view, observe and decide upon as rich and relevant a milieu as they can, which allows discrete, nuanced entities to emerge.

Unfortunately, Mason's interpretation of noticing somewhat deviates at times from the work of critical ethnographers and phenomenologists, in that it tends towards a discourse of objectivity as opposed to judicious interpretation. Having said this, the functional advice given within his work in relation to how to stimulate noticing could be useful for better structuring orchestration. For example, labelling salient incidents and alternative acts, thus developing a useful reflective resource. Although being open to criticism on its rather unproblematic tendencies, we nevertheless fully support Mason's (2002) sentiment that pedagogues (read coaches) need to 'increase the range and decrease the grain size' (p. xi) of what they notice as fundamental precursors to developing professional practice. This was a view echoed by Øystein Havang, the current Norwegian men's national handball coach, when he stated:

> The quality of the observations often distinguishes the ordinary coaches from the really good ones. To be respected as a competent coach, I think that you first and foremost have to demonstrate that you are really capable of seeing what is going on both on and off the court.
>
> *(Ronglan and Havang 2011: 92)*

To move this concept of noticing from theory to practice however, the question for coaches remains in terms of what to look for and notice in the first place; that is, what become the triggers for decision making and action (Jones *et al.* 2011). Here, the noticer must decide what is worth noticing, and this is where it becomes a little tricky; because, although noticing advocates a widening of the perceptive lens, it cannot mean that coaches must act on everything they see. We have already hinted that what perhaps should be noticed to a greater extent is the nuance of context. This equates not only to the sport-specific tactical and technical shortcomings and accomplishments of athletes, but also to how they relate to each other and the coaching staff, the dilemmas, joys and paranoias suffered by both parties, the in- and out-groups established, and the conflicting agendas of the various stakeholders. In essence, it is to notice the world of small realities, personal, social and professional, which, as recently highlighted by Jones (2009), can have a lasting impact of performance and achievements. It can thus be argued that noticing is, in many ways, the precursor and sustainer of orchestration.

Orchestration in action: using practice to further the theory

The penultimate section of the chapter contains a critical commentary by Jake Bailey, a trampoline coach, related to his ongoing use of this developed notion of orchestration in practice. Having debated and read about orchestration, Jake consciously tried to implement the perspective's main tenets into his work. His subsequent thoughts address the principal issues of how 'real' was the theory? Why? And how helpful was it in addressing everyday coaching issues?

Before I was introduced to orchestration, I had predominately been exposed to coaching literature, education and discourse that placed the coach as 'controller'. This was further emphasised by my positivistic background as a sports science graduate with an affiliation for biomechanics. Here, my knowledge of the technique of trampoline performance led me to believe that I could control the performance outcomes of the athletes that I coached; I knew how they should perform their skills and routines, and I could make them do it that way. On reflection, this view of coaching and performance was reinforced in and through the culture of the sport, which is ostensibly coach led, towards a performance outcome that is predetermined by a 'code of points' (the competition requirements). Despite this, at some level, I had always been aware that things just weren't that simple. Tacitly, I knew the job was more problematic and uncertain than I had been led (and wanted) to believe. I obviously wasn't in complete control, but continued to try to behave as though I was because I didn't know another way. This created a strange tension, which could be called pathos, that I lived with but couldn't verbalise.

I was in this general state of ignorance when Robyn asked me to read a chapter on coaching as orchestration (Jones and Wallace 2006), and to test out how it might 'fit' my practice. It didn't have an immediate impact; at first I told myself that I already did most of that anyway (something I have heard many others say since). Following that first reading, I have gone back to the work many times, and now I think that the beauty of the orchestration metaphor lies in what initially allowed me to overlook its significance: that it provides a good match to the reality of my everyday experience inside and outside the gym. The subtlety that initially led me to brush over it, is exactly what makes it so useful. By describing the complexity and ambiguity experienced in coaching, it provided me with a language to conceptualise the troubling feeling I had 'that something wasn't quite right' but couldn't previously voice.

The other barrier I experienced was the complexity of the work. There were words I had to look up in the dictionary and concepts that were difficult to grasp which had to be read many times over before they made sense. This wasn't like work I had seen on coaching before. The coaching manuals and textbooks I had previously encountered may not have represented the reality I experienced, but were easily understandable. Unfortunately, they also contributed to my overly simplistic interpretation of coaching. Again, in hindsight, I've come to realise that if you want to explain something that is complex, inevitably you have to write something that embodies the complexity. Whilst that was an initial obstacle, I have grown to see it as a necessary strength of the work. The lack of formulaic 'coach by numbers' prescriptions made me work hard but, having to think incredibly carefully about how I might use the metaphor in concrete and tangible ways, was very powerful.

Importantly, the orchestration metaphor does more than just describe the complexity and ambiguity of coaching; it provides a means to help coaches make sense of and manage it. By helping coaches see their job through a new set of conceptual lenses, it opens up a space for alternative actions (often more creative and strategic). The following section then, includes some thoughts related to my direct implementation of orchestration, particularly in terms of the notions of social irony, noticing and micro-politics.

As I said earlier, I used to think that a coach should be in control, a perception that seems to still be widely held amongst the coaches with whom I talk. The concept of social irony was important in dispelling the echoes of that myth. The ideas that: (1) the words I utter are open to multiple interpretations; (2) that policies are unlikely to be carried out with full effect (reality versus rhetoric); and, (3) that many actions inevitably have unintended consequences, all rang true. However, equally important to an increased sensitisation to these issues was the notion of pragmatic irony. It seemed crucial that I could adopt strategies to cope with (and influence) the ambiguities and dilemmas faced in practice (Hoyle and Wallace 2008). The key questions this raised for me were: What are the limits of my agency? Where can I make the most impact? To what extent can I foresee the unintended consequences of my actions? This links explicitly to the concept of noticing as, to answer these and other questions, I first need to be able to notice what is happening. Without attending to the most important information (how do I know which is the most important?) it is likely that my impact would be decreased and the consequences of my actions less predictable. The difficulty here is that there is so much to which to attend. Broadly speaking, there are the technical, organisational and social aspects of practice, all of which interact in a complex and dynamic environment, of which I can only ever have limited awareness. Here, the tenets of orchestration help broaden my sense-making lens, and, in this regard, I found the concept of micro-politics particularly useful.

When I looked through a micro-political lens I could understand better the organisational (e.g., working with other coaches, administrators and parents) and social issues experienced by myself and the gymnasts. It made it somewhat clear that being a good coach (pedagogy-wise) was not enough; if I could not influence the social and organisational contexts to function adequately, then my technical expertise was obstructed. Noticing that when I grouped them in certain arrangements I 'lost' some gymnasts for the whole session was a real 'eye-opener'. Previously, unquestioned behaviours became fair game for reflection because thoughtless actions meant that relationships with certain gymnasts were negatively affected (and, therefore, my ability to influence them diminished). Of course, I was probably somewhat aware of these things before, but these writings brought them into clearer focus. For instance, shortly after reading about micro-politics, I found out that the international governing body for gymnastics had changed the equipment specification for trampolines. This was a problem, as the new equipment (which would allow the development of more height) was expensive and would require a change of training venue (the ceiling in the previous hall would simply no longer be sufficient). A micro-political reading of the situation led me to consider in detail who I would need to influence, the order in which I would need to speak to them, and the most appropriate manner to approach the interactions. The issue of venue transfer was politically sensitive, as the only suitable alternative was the local athletics centre, where key stakeholders had previously made it clear that they did not think it appropriate for trampolining to take space away from athletes. Earlier attempts to gain access then had not been successful. A powerful framing of the problem ('without this we can no longer compete at a national level'), empathetic listening and compliant disposition toward the operations manager, the director of athletics and the junior academy coordinator (in that order) eventually got us in. I was political, but not in a disingenuous way. I like the people I needed to negotiate with; I just had to help them see how we could all get our needs met. The next micro-political situation was negotiating with the gymnasts which of them were going to be able to train on the new equipment in the new venue!

Closing thoughts

We close with some reflections about how the additional perspectives offered in this chapter, and their tentative engagement with practice, can enrich and make even more relevant the notion of orchestration to sports coaching. By incorporating the recent work of Wallace into social irony (Hoyle and Wallace 2008), we sought to further clarify the complex and ambiguous nature of organisational life, and afforded a brief case study of how it can somewhat be managed (Schneller and Wallace 2007). Although, as previously qualified (Jones and Wallace 2005), we are aware that coaching situations are somewhat removed from those entailed in bringing about system-wide professional change, be it within education or nursing, the idea that coaches orchestrate context towards desired ends has resonated with many. This is because coaches, like other 'social' managers, have to operate in relatively uncontrollable and ambiguous environments. Consequently, we believe that continuing to highlight and better understand the basic irony and uncertainty involved in such contexts has value. This is primarily related to the accompanying exploration of what individuals' coping strategies to deal with social and inter-relational complexities might be, and how far they can be generalised from differing contexts.

We also believe that the orchestration notion is further enhanced by the literature pertaining to micro-politics. Orchestration then, should not just be seen in terms of sport specificity (that is; how well the sport is performed), but in the 'face-work' undertaken by coaches to negotiate contested practice. Consequently, orchestration is also about building alliances with key stakeholders (e.g., players, staff or others) which help coaches secure desired ends, whether those ends refer to professional acceptance or ensuring (as best they can) compliance to a given agenda. In this way, far from ignoring issues of power, orchestration actively engages and privileges it. Such engagement, however, should not be seen as underhand, Machiavellian scheming, but the acting out of considered strategies designed to make social interactions and related contexts work. The link to other social theories here, for example, Erving Goffman's (1959) interaction order and his notions of impression management, is obvious. In this regard, orchestration is a social theory that places emphasis on how we act to get what we want and need from others. In developing orchestrated practice then, we believe that a deeper understanding of the interactions between coach and context will result, whilst providing a more realistic grasp of how coaches initiate and deal with change. In this way, it holds the potential to break the silence that seems to exist regarding issues of conflict and its manipulation in coaching, thus helping us to better recognise and theorise the largely covert aspects of negotiation, compromise and collaboration between coaches and others (Potrac and Jones 2009a, 2009b).

Of course, just accepting the need to engage in such micro-political and pedagogical actions is not enough, as we need to ascertain how and on what evidence we (should) make the decisions to action. This is where noticing (Mason 2002) can help. The close observing advocated by Mason can bring to the fore a heightened sensitivity to what exactly is happening, thus raising the possibility of alternative actions. It marks an effort to see beyond the obvious, to the mundane, to the small things which can have long-lasting impacts. Orchestration then, should rely on such detailed and sensitive noticing, which can inform more considered and appropriate pedagogical practice. So, where to from here? Far from considering the concept of orchestration as being 'solved', there remains much room to further thicken the theoretical soup, with many other theories to draw on. For example, we consider orchestration to be closely aligned with the work of the educational psychologist Lev Vygotsky. In particular, Vygotsky's notions of scaffolding learning within a zone of proximal development (ZPD) hold particular resonance. What Vygotsky (1978) was referring to here was the need to take considerable care in structuring the environment and subsequent opportunities to maximise learners' development. Sometimes, more guidance would be needed, sometimes less, depending on context. It was, according to Vygotsky, in such spaces that optimal learning takes place. Bowes and Jones (2006), whilst borrowing from the tenets of complexity theory, recently echoed such a sentiment in stating that coaching should exist on or near the 'edge of chaos'; a term reflecting the need to ground athletes in a security of structure whilst allowing them the creative agency to explore personal solutions and meanings for themselves. Naturally, we believe that such learning states as the ZPD and 'edge of chaos' are what coaches should orchestrate towards, in order to produce the most favourable and advantageous erudite environments for athletes.

Finally, we believe that orchestration could involve an enhanced appreciation of taking the perspective of others (Mead 1934). This should be done to better anticipate others' responses to our own actions before we carry them out, and to use this anticipation to continually regulate and adjust our own conduct. Such perspective-taking is basic to social competence (for a fuller discussion of such competences, see Jones 2011), and could lead to coaches becoming more aware of how athletes frame various situations, including their motives, their interests, and the way they perceive a coach's conduct. In doing so, coaches could further develop their sensitivity regarding how situations appear to athletes and other co-actors and, thereby, more competently contribute to purposeful interaction. It is a perspective which resonates closely with Armour and Jones's (1998) idea of pedagogical practice as 'chess played fast'. Here, practitioners must constantly engage with 'what if' scenarios, always thinking ahead where current moves or events might lead and how they can be best dealt with. Of course, most of these scenarios do not come to fruition as social life can never be so predictable, but this is the point. To accept the ambiguity of coaching; to be fully capable, sensitised and engaged enough to read the micro-contextual landscape (from political, social and pedagogical standpoints); to constantly remove and reassemble supporting scaffolds depending on what is noticed; all to ensure optimal learning environments for athletes. For orchestration to be accepted and viewed as a mature social theory of coaching then, no doubt more work, both philosophical and empirical, needs to be done. Nevertheless, as highlighted by Jake's considered commentary, we believe that the developed version presented in this chapter goes some way to provide a fuller, more realistic, portrayal of the sports coach as orchestrator.

References

Armour, K.M. and Jones, R.L. (1998) *Physical Education Teachers' Lives and Careers: P.E., Sport and Educational Status*, London: Falmer Press.

Ball, S.J. (1987) *The Micro-Politics of the School: Towards a Theory of School Organisation*, London: Methuen.

Blase, J. (1991) *The Politics of Life in Schools: Power, Conflict and Co-Operation*, Newbury Park, CA: Sage.

Blase, J. and Anderson, G. (1995) *The Micro-Politics of Educational Leadership: From Control to Empowerment*, New York: Teachers College Press.

Bowes, I. and Jones, R.L. (2006) 'Working at the edge of chaos: Understanding coaching as a complex, interpersonal system', *The Sport Psychologist*, 20(2): 235–245.

Chesterfield, G., Potrac, P. and Jones, R.L. (2010) '"Studentship" and "impression management": Coaches' experiences of an advanced soccer coach education award', *Sport, Education and Society*, 15(3): 299–314.

Cohen, M.D., March, J. and Olsen, J.P. (1972) 'A garbage can model of organizational choice', *Administrative Science Quarterly*, 17(1): 1–25.

Cushion, C.J. and Jones, R.L. (2006) 'Power, discourse and symbolic violence in professional youth soccer: The case of Albion FC', *Sociology of Sport Journal*, 23(2): 142–161.

d'Arippe-Longueville, R., Fournier, J.F. and Dubois, A. (1998) 'The perceived effectiveness of interactions between expert French judo coaches and elite female athletes', *The Sport Psychologist*, 12(3): 317–332.

Fry, J.M. (1997) 'Dealing with the powers that be', *Sport Education and Society*, 2(2): 141–162.

Gardiner, M.E. (2000) *Critiques of Everyday Life*, London: Routledge.

Goffman, E. (1959) *The Presentation of Self in Everyday Life*, New York: Doubleday.

Hansen, N.K. and Küpper, W. (2009) 'Power strategies and power sources of management: the micro-politics of strategizing', paper for presentation at the 25th EGOS Colloquium, Barcelona, 2–4 July.

Hoyle, E. (1982) 'Micropolitics of educational organisations', *Educational Management Administration and Leadership*, 10(2): 87–98.

Hoyle, E. and Wallace, M. (2008) 'Two faces of organisational irony: Endemic and pragmatic', *Organisational Studies*, 29(11): 1427–1447.

Jones, R.L. (2009) 'Coaching as caring ("The smiling gallery"): Accessing hidden knowledge', *Physical Education and Sport Pedagogy*, 14(4): 377–390.

Jones, R.L. (2011) 'Introduction', in R.L. Jones, P. Potrac, C. Cushion and L.T. Ronglan (eds) *A Sociology of Sports Coaching*, Abingdon: Routledge.

Jones, R.L. and Wallace, M. (2005) 'Another bad day at the training ground: Coping with ambiguity in the coaching context', *Sport, Education and Society*, 10(1): 119–134.

Jones, R.L. and Wallace, M. (2006) 'The coach as orchestrator', in R.L. Jones (ed.) *The Sports Coach as Educator: Re-conceptualising Sports Coaching*, Abingdon: Routledge, pp. 51–64.

Jones, R.L., Kingston, K. and Stewart, C. (2011) 'Machiavelli in a morality play: Negotiating expectations in football's complex social culture', in D. Gilbourne and M. Andersen (eds) *Critical Essays in Sport Psychology*, London: Human Kinetics, pp. 267–288.

Keltchermans, G. (2005) 'Teachers emotions in educational reforms: Self-understanding, vulnerable commitment and micro-political literacy', *Teacher and Teacher Education*, 21(8): 995–1006.

Kelchtermans, G. and Ballet, K. (2002a) 'The micropolitics of teacher induction: A narrative-biographical study on teacher socialisation', *Teacher and Teacher Education*, 18(1): 105–120.

Kelchtermans, G. and Ballet, K. (2002b) 'Micropolitical literacy: Reconstructing a neglected dimension in teacher development', *International Journal of Educational Research*, 37(8): 755–767.

Lefebvre, H. (1991) *A Critique of Everyday Life Volume 1: Introduction*, J. Moore (trans.), London: Verso.

Lindle, J. (1994) *Surviving School Micro-politics: Strategies for Administrators*, Lancaster, PA: Technomic.

Luhmann, N. (1995) *Social Systems*, Stanford, CA: Stanford University Press.

Mason, J. (2002) *Researching Your Own Practice: The Discipline of Noticing*, New York: Routledge.

Mead, G.H. (1934) *Mind, Self and Societ: From a Standpoint of a Social Behavorist*, Chicago, IL: The University of Chicago Press.

Potrac, P. and Jones, R.L. (2009a) 'Power, conflict and co-operation: Towards a micro-politics of coaching', *Quest*, 61(2): 223–236.

Potrac, P. and Jones, R.L. (2009b) 'Micro-political workings in semi-professional soccer coaching', *Sociology of Sport Journal*, 26(4): 557–577.

Purdy, L., Jones, R.L. and Cassidy, T. (2009) 'Negotiation and capital: Athletes' use of power in an elite men's rowing programme', *Sport, Education and Society*, 14(3): 321–338.

Ronglan, L.T. and Havang, Ø. (2011) 'Niklas Luhmann: Coaching as communication', in R.L. Jones, P. Potrac, C. Cushion and L.T. Ronglan (eds) *A Sociology of Sports Coaching*, Abingdon: Routledge.

Saury, J. and Durand. M. (1998) 'Practical knowledge in expert coaches: On-site study of coaching in sailing', *Research Quarterly for Exercise and Sport*, 69(3): 254–266.

Schneller, E. and Wallace, M. (2007) 'Unsystematic responses to a chaotic service environment: Shaping the division of labour in patient care', in M. Wallace, M. Fertig and E. Schneller (eds) *Managing Change in Public Services*, Oxford: Blackwell, pp.153–172.

Spencer-Brown, G. (1969) *Laws of Form*, New York: Dutton Publishers.

Thompson, A., Potrac, P. and Jones, R.L. (forthcoming) *Micro-political Workings in Professional Football: A Case Study*, manuscript under review.

Vygotsky, L. (1978) *Mind and Society*, Cambridge, MA: MIT Press.

Wallace, M. (2001) 'Sharing leadership of schools through teamwork: A justifiable risk?' *Educational Management and Administration*, 29(2): 153–167.

Wallace, M. (2003) 'Managing the unmanageable? Coping with complex educational change', *Educational Management and Administration*, 31(1): 9–29.

Wallace, M. (2007) 'Coping with complex and programmatic public service change', in M. Wallace, M. Fertig and E. Schneller (eds) (2007) *Managing Change in Public Services*, Oxford: Blackwell, pp.13–35.

Wallace, M. and Pocklington, K. (2002) *Managing Complex Educational Change: Large scale Reorganisation of Schools*, London: Routledge.

Wallace, M. and Schneller, E. (2008) 'Orchestrating emergent change: the "hospitalist movement" in US Healthcare', *Public Administration*, 86(3): 761–778.

23

ATHLETE (NON)LEARNING

Is it time for an interdisciplinary understanding?

Lee Nelson

UNIVERSITY OF HULL, UK

Derek Colquhoun

UNIVERSITY OF TASMANIA, AUSTRALIA

Introduction and overview of the topic

Over the past decade there has been a growing interest in the academic investigation of coaching. The publication of this handbook further evidences that coaching is now recognised as a legitimate area worthy of scientific inquiry. Despite this fact, consideration towards how athletes learn has received relatively little attention within the coaching literature. This would seem somewhat paradoxical as the facilitation of athlete learning is arguably one of those few outcomes that all coaching practitioners desire, irrespective of the context in which they work. Rather, to date, the coaching literature has principally focused on investigating the behaviours of coaching practitioners, coaching knowledge, coach education and coach learning (e.g. Chesterfield *et al.* 2010; Jones *et al.* 2003; Potrac and Jones 2009; Potrac *et al.* 2002, 2007). While such investigations have undoubtedly furthered understanding about the complex nature of this social activity, they have provided little knowledge about how the practices of coaches impact upon the learning of athletes.

A tendency to concentrate on the coach is understandable, especially when recognising that 'the coach occupies a position of centrality and considerable influence in efforts to improve sporting performance' (Cushion 2010: 43). Furthermore, the academic study of coaching remains very much in its infancy; so focusing on the coach would appear a logical starting point. However, there are, as a result, numerous areas within the academic investigation of coaching that have yet to be adequately explored, which includes how interactions between coaches and athletes impact (or not) on athlete learning. The purpose of this chapter, then, is to further discussions about athlete learning. In doing so, this chapter raises some fundamental issues, critical questions, and theoretical and philosophical considerations, that coaching researchers, educators, and practitioners might usefully consider. Therefore, it is hoped that the presented content might help to spark further inquiry and debate into how athletes learn, through which approaches coaching practitioners might best support the development of athlete learning, and ultimately how the field conceptualises the athlete as a learner.

The following chapter opens by providing an account of how mainstream psychological theory has tended to pervade thinking about how athlete learning and coaching practice are conceptualised. This is followed by discussions regarding the purpose and place of sociological and philosophical thinking in this area of coaching inquiry. The chapter then closes by presenting a case for interdisciplinary research. Here we offer the triad of context, meaning, and behaviour as a conceptual framework that we believe might help coaching scholars to advance the study of athlete (non)learning. However, whilst we promote research of an interdisciplinary nature, we conclude, from our earlier analysis, that any attempt to bring together psychological and sociological analysis and theory will inevitably require researchers to engage in philosophical debate.

Athlete learning: built on a foundation of behaviourist psychology

Historically, the field of sports coaching has drawn heavily on, and therefore has been significantly influenced by, the sports psychology literature that considers athlete learning. While it is beyond the scope of the present chapter to explore the findings of this body of research in any detail, an analysis of the concepts and recommendations made within the sport psychology literature serve to demonstrate that this area of research has been heavily influence by behaviourist theories. As such, it will be highlighted that an analysis of behaviourism helps us to understand how athlete learning has historically been defined within the field of coaching.

Burrhus Frederic Skinner (1904–1990) is arguably the most widely acknowledged behavioural psychologist, although Ivan Petrovich Pavlov, Edward Lee Thorndike and John Broadus Watson also significantly contributed to this line of thinking (Hergenhahn 2009). Through his famous work with pigeons and rats, Skinner discovered that reinforcement increases the probability that an operant behaviour will reoccur (Bernstein *et al.* 2008). The work of Skinner and other leading behaviourists has clearly influenced the field of sport psychology and how it conceptualises the enhancement of athletic performance. For example, Smith (2006) provides a useful discussion of how the presentation and removal of positive (i.e. positive reinforcement, extinction, and response cost punishment) and negative (i.e. punishment and negative reinforcement) stimuli effect athletic behaviour through the process of operant conditioning. Discussions about the application of operant conditioning within sport often use terms such as 'influencing', 'controlling', and 'shaping' of 'desired behaviours'. As such, it is perhaps unsurprising to read that when seen through this lens 'virtually everything coaches do can be viewed as attempts to increase certain desired behaviors and to decrease undesirable behaviors' (Smith 2006: 41).

Although behaviourist learning theory remains a prominent feature of psychological thinking, it is perhaps important to acknowledge that behaviourism has been subject to critique. Arguably, one of its fiercest critics was the eminent psychologist Carl Rogers. Indeed, Rogers and Skinner engaged in three public debates about the distinctions between humanistic and behaviourist psychology (Kirschenbaum and Henderson 1989). For example, in their 1962 exchange, Rogers concluded his opening statement by commenting that behaviourism fails to recognise freedom, choice and self-direction. In so doing, it was Rogers's belief that behaviourism seemingly minimises the significance of subjectivity, promoting instead a view of learning that treats persons primarily as malleable objects whose behaviour should be controlled and shaped without his or her choice. While Rogers (1980) did not deny the research findings of behaviourist psychological investigations, his applied experiences and academic work made it impossible for him to deny the reality and significance of human choice. Consequently, Rogers (1980: 57) contended that: 'To me it is not an illusion that man is to some degree the architect of himself'. In light of the findings of behaviourist research, Rogers (1969) considered the humanism–behaviourism debate to be a 'deep and lasting paradox' that we must learn to live with. He later wrote that 'the basic difference between a behavioristic and a humanistic approach to human beings is [resultantly] a *philosophical choice*' (Rogers 1980: 56).

Although there have been some initial discussions about the possible application of humanistic psychology to coaching, they remain limited. While such work should be applauded as a potentially useful starting point for furthering conceptual thought about coaching practice, there is arguably a need for greater theoretical depth of understanding (Nelson *et al.* 2010). For the purpose of this chapter, it seems important to consider what implications humanistic and behaviourist interpretations of learning have for how we conceptualise the athlete and the development of athletes. Indeed, it would appear that behaviourist and humanistic psychologists hold sharply contrasting views about the learner. For example, when viewing athlete learning through a behaviourist lens, little consideration need be given towards an athlete's internal mental state, as learning is identified through observable behaviours. The athlete, then, is like a complex machine, whose behaviour needs to be controlled and shaped by the coach. A humanistic approach, on the other hand, views the athlete as a unique person possessing their own thoughts and feelings. Athletes striving to achieve their potentialities are, according to this way of thinking, considered capable of committing themselves to the process of learning, by engaging in responsible choice and an ongoing process of self-understanding. Whereas a behaviourist approach looks to control the learning of athletes, a humanistic approach strives to facilitate the development of athletes by engaging them in the learning process. Consideration of these differences would seem vitally important. These alternative views not only impact on how we conceptualise athlete learning, but also how we go about researching this topic and the subsequent recommendations that are made to coaching practitioners.

Additionally, there has been increasing discussion of the possible application of constructivist learning theory to coaching. For example, Potrac and Cassidy (2006) drew on the work of Les Vygotsky (1972) when presenting the coach as a 'more capable other'. More specifically, they discussed how coaches might utilise questioning, guided discovery, problem solving and 'game sense' approaches to facilitate the cognitive development of athletes (Cassidy *et al.* 2004; Thorpe 1997). Here, the authors contended that these learner-centred approaches encourage athletes to take responsibility for, and actively engage in, their own learning. Rather than simply telling athletes what to do through instruction, they suggested that

> these pedagogical strategies position the coach as a facilitator of learning who, through the use of questioning, prompts and feedback, leads athletes to gradually discover the solutions to various problems related to the technical and tactical aspects of sporting performance

(Potrac and Cassidy 2006: 44)

Within the coaching literature, then, there would appear to be a growing distinction between coach-directed and athlete-centred practices (Kidman 2005).

Athlete learning: the need for a sociological analysis

The study of behaviour and learning are not restricted to the realm of psychology; these topics are also a concern of sociologists. However, similar to psychology, it would appear that there are a number of theoretical positions within the sociology literature, each of which present different interpretations and understanding about the learning process. For example, functionalist sociological analysis argues that 'a system of goals and rewards is necessary to motivate members of society to want to do what they have to do in order to maintain the system' (Haralambos and Holborn 2004: 937). Fulcher and Scott (2007) explain that functionalists believe that society utilises a normative framework of defined obligations and expectations that shape social relations and govern peoples' actions. Socialisation, according to functionalist theory, is a process that programmes individuals into the values and norms of the social system (Haralambos and Holborn 2004). Here, people are required to engage in social roles which have normative expectations that define appropriate and inappropriate behaviour in particular situations (Fulcher and Scott 2007). When viewed through a functionalist lens human action is 'pictured as an automaton, programmed, directed and controlled by the system' (Haralambos and Holborn 2004: 943–944).

While functionalism was the dominant social theory in American sociology for many years, and has exercised a great influence on the development of sociological understanding, it has steadily dropped from favour (Fulcher and Scott 2007). Haralambos and Holborn (2004) point out that functionalism has been criticised for holding a deterministic view of human action, which portrays human behaviours as being determined by the system. In this respect, they explain that critics have often argued that functionalism depicts 'the individual as having little or no control over his or her own actions' (Haralambos and Holborn 2004: 938). In contrast to functionalism, Anthony Giddens (2001: 5), while recognising that 'we are all influenced by the social contexts in which we find ourselves', points out that 'none of us are simply *determined* in our behaviour by those contexts'. Rather, he contends that as persons we 'possess, and create, our own individuality' (Giddens 2001: 5). For Giddens, human beings do not simply respond passively to events around them, but instead make choices. It is in light of this line of thinking that Giddens (2001: 5, emphasis added) suggests that sociology is ultimately about understanding 'the connections between *what society makes of us* and *what we make of ourselves*'. When viewed through this lens, we can see that there is a degree of agency in the actions of social beings.

At the core of sociological discussion, then, is consideration towards structure and agency. Within the context of coaching, an ethnographic study conducted by Cushion and Jones (2006) served to demonstrate how the behaviours, learning and development of a group of English professional youth soccer players were shaped by an authoritarian discourse that was established, maintained and legitimised by the coaches. Within this environment, it was reported that the coaches continuously berated their athletes' performances and attitudes, while providing them with no right to respond. The players within this investigation were found to have no choice or input into their schedules and training routines. Rather, the context under study was described as being 'coach-led', 'authoritarian', 'aggressive' and 'hierarchal'. In this respect, coaches were found to employ 'abusive language, direct personal castigation, and threats of physical exercise' (Cushion and Jones 2006: 149). Such pedagogical practices seemingly 'held the players within a realm of obedience' (Cushion and Jones 2006: 150). Here, we can see how the structure in which athletes engage can often influence their sporting experiences, views about coaching, and their perceived role within the coaching process. Indeed, it would appear that the dominant discourse within coaching often characterises the coach as the possessor of knowledge, whose role it is to lead from the front, whereas athletes are often viewed as empty vessels, who should subordinate themselves to the coach (Cassidy *et al.* 2009).

While a dominant discourse of authoritarian rule would appear to pervade sports coaching in elite environments, the players in the study by Cushion and Jones (2006) were also found to engage in verbal and physical forms of resistance, which included skipping college classes and secretly conserving effort during training. However, despite these attempts to assert their agency, the authors argued that 'the dominant picture of player participation in the academy was one of compliance to the regime' (Cushion and Jones 2006: 158). Structure would therefore appear to be driving athlete learning within many coaching contexts. While this might be the case, a study by Purdy *et al.* (2008) demonstrated how agency can also significantly influence how athletes' engage within the learning process. In this example, the coach's use of 'curt responses', 'patronising comments' and an increasingly stern, unfriendly and authoritarian approach resulted in a deterioration of the relationship between coach and athletes. This ultimately led the athletes 'to view the coach as a structure to work against' as they 'searched for ways to cope with an oppressive social environment' (Purdy *et al.* 2008: 329). In essence, the athletes had lost respect for the coach and therefore started to actively resist the coach's commands. While some might consider this to be a somewhat negative example of athlete agency, the work of Purdy *et al.* (2008) has nonetheless served to demonstrate that athletes are not necessarily always going to be the 'docile bodies' that the present coaching discourse would seem to desire and expect. On the contrary, it would appear that athletes may have the capacity to resist, and have a desire to engage in the learning process, although often choosing not to exercise their agency, probably in acknowledgment of the consequences that might be enforced in contexts where engagement is not valued or generally permitted (Cassidy *et al.* 2009). Consideration of the structure–agency debate would therefore seem vitally important as it seemingly has considerable implications for how the field goes about conceptualising and researching athlete learning and the pedagogical interactions that occur between coach and athlete more broadly.

Athlete learning: inherently philosophical?

To date, there has been little consideration towards the value of analysing athlete learning through a philosophical lens. While studying athlete learning from both a sociological and psychological perspective is likely to provide richer insights into this complex phenomenon, it would appear incorrect and perhaps slightly naive to assume that philosophy has no application or practical value in the study of this topic. Here, our analysis of the debates that have occurred within the fields of psychology and sociology have led us to appreciate that philosophical considerations are an inherent part of understanding how persons, and for the purpose of this chapter athletes, learn and interact with their environments. Indeed, the behaviourism–humanism and structure–

agency debates within psychology and sociology respectively would appear to have their roots in a topic that has historically been a key consideration of the field of philosophy, namely the determinism–free will debate. As such, it is argued that we might usefully draw on relevant philosophical discussion to further thinking within our own field of inquiry, as such debate might help us to better understand the philosophical assumptions underpinning the different theoretical paradigms within disciplines.

Within philosophy three schools of thought largely dominate, namely: (1) hard determinism; (2) metaphysical libertarianism; and (3) compatibilism. Hard determinism and metaphysical libertarianism comprise incompatibilism, which holds that determinism and free will are in no way compatible. In this respect, hard determinists hold the view that 'freedom is an illusion since behaviour is brought about by environmental and genetic factors' (Audi 1999: 327). On the other hand, metaphysical libertarians assert that 'people are free and responsible and that the past does not determine a unique future' (ibid.). Finally, the third perspective is compatibilism whose advocates are 'unwilling to abandon practical freedom yet unable to understand how a lack of determination could be either necessary or desirable for responsibility' (ibid.). As the name would suggest, those conforming to this perspective believe that free will and determinism are compatible. In addition to this, the utility of chaos theory for philosophising about free will and determinism has also been considered (McFee 2000). Again, thoughts about free will and determinism might influence how the field conceptualises athlete learning, how it is developed, and the approaches it uses to research this area.

Athlete (non)learning: an interdisciplinary agenda

In light of what has been discussed so far, we would like to end by arguing the need for disciplinary and theoretical pluralism if a more in-depth and complete understanding about how athletes learn is to evolve. While others have argued the need of an interdisciplinary understanding of the coaching process and practices within it, research and thinking of this nature remains sparse at present (Jones and Turner 2006). Rather, most investigators have tended to stick to their preferred discipline and argue the value of their relative line of inquiry. Here, the field of coaching might usefully consider and learn from the comments of Pollard (2004: 286), an educational sociologist, who suggests that: 'As our understanding of the social world becomes more sophisticated, it becomes increasingly apparent that the validity of the study of many issues cannot be maximised unless each of the relevant disciplines is drawn on in sustained study'. While Pollard (2004) acknowledges that each discipline has particular strengths for the investigation of certain social phenomena, he also stresses the need for academics to cooperate across disciplinary boundaries. Indeed, Pollard contends that: 'If we are to investigate the issue of learning in valid ways, then our first problem, as social scientists, is really to find ways of bridging the artificial disciplinary boundaries which dissipate our energies' (288).

Like Cassidy *et al.* (2009), we also believe that coaching is a social, cultural and pedagogical practice comprising an interconnection between the coach, athlete, content and context (Lusted 1986). To this end, we would like to suggest that any examination (and development of) athlete learning might wish to consider the relationship between the *context* of that learning (i.e. the physical space and social structure of the pedagogical environment being investigated); the *meaning* behind the learning (i.e. the cognitive and emotional thoughts, feelings and understandings acquired and experienced by the athlete and the coach as a result of their engaging in the context) as well as the *behaviour* being exhibited[1] by the athlete and coach (i.e. how the athlete and coach verbally and nonverbally conduct themselves in the context). What in effect we are suggesting here is that athlete learning can be viewed as socially constructed, imbibed with the social conditions that impact on learning and that learning is replete with individual, cultural and social categories determined through the interactions of athlete and coach. Learning does not exist outside of the athlete, coach or the milieu within which it occurs. As Di Chiro (1997: 454) puts it in relation to the environment, '[learning] should be understood as the conceptual interactions between our physical surroundings and the social, political and economic forces that organize us in the context of these surroundings'.

It is appropriate in any call for inter-disciplinarity that we draw on a broad range of disciplines for our work (see Colquhoun 1997). The triad of context, meaning and behaviour was first introduced as a whole into public health and health promotion by Ilona Kickbusch (1989). She was concerned with simplistic understandings of behaviour which dominated discourses in public health. At that time, individual behaviour was seen by many in public health as the root cause of most of the health problems facing many Western societies. Individual behaviour was the cause of ill health and practitioners focused on changing this damaging behaviour to health enhancing behaviour. Kickbusch (1989) was heavily influenced at the time by environmental psychologists and health promoters such as McLeroy *et al.* (1988), the classic work on the environmental determinants of human behaviour (see Moos 1976), the role of environment in learning (see Vygotsky 1972), as well as unorthodox thinkers who were trying to go outside the traditional way of conceptualising behaviour and even considering learning from the behaviours of other social animals such as dolphins (see Bateson 1972). More recently, Dahlgren and Whitehead (1991) highlighted the need to locate our research within physical and social contexts. Their work on the social determinants of health has been central to interdisciplinary attempts to understand the health of individuals and populations. This broad contextual understanding in health research has often seen calls for ecological approaches to understanding specific health issues such as obesity (see Egger and Swinburne 1997).

Up until this time most research on behaviour was conducted in the sanitised environment of psychology laboratories (Proshansky 1987). However, the appropriateness and validity of much of this laboratory research to enhance our understanding of real life behavioural issues was limited. What was needed was an understanding that the context for behaviour (i.e. the environment, setting or context can be used interchangeably) was actually socially constructed and that there was an inherent dialectical (i.e. two way) relationship between the social (i.e. behaviour) and the physical (i.e. the context), and that neither could be seen in isolation from the other. In addition, the social relationships encountered in any context also impact on the behaviour displayed within that context. So, currently, we understand that in any context we have the social relationships within that context and the physical nature of the context impacting on each other in a dialectical manner. Take for example, a typical lecture theatre in a university. The lecturer stands out at the front as the knower of all knowledge and the students sit behind rows of desks side-by-side listening and taking notes. It is clear that the physical form of the context dictates largely the behaviour of the lecturer and the students and in addition social conventions within universities dictate that students do not talk or interact with each other during a lecture. There is also a dialectical circularity of power happening with any given context, but that is for another chapter. In another context within any university, such as a workshop or even online learning, the social relationships and the physical space are very different, thus determining alternative meanings ascribed to the context and very different behaviours displayed by both lecturer and students, with contrasting power relationships too.

None of this of course denies other approaches to studying athlete learning. Researchers could still profit from examining athlete–coach communication and interactions, the presentation and use of the body, autobiographical research of athlete and coach, pedagogical research and learning per se, the use of video analysis (see Nelson *et al.* in press) from different theoretical perspectives, including examinations of power relationships, inequity, governmentality and so on. What we are arguing for is a greater awareness of athlete learning and coaching within what we have called elsewhere a 'spatial imagination' (Pike and Colquhoun 2009, building on C. W. Mills' 1959 *The Sociological Imagination*). Essentially, this involves a foregrounding or perhaps at least a recognition of the relationship between context, meaning and behaviour in any examination of athlete learning, or to put it bluntly: the relationship between the physical and social environment in athlete learning. This reflects a growing interest in the concepts of place and space (Pike and Colquhoun 2009). Within the coaching and athlete learning context we have recently suggested this from an examination of a single case study of an elite ice hockey player's responses to video feedback sessions (Nelson *et al.* in press) and significantly how the player's learning was influenced by social aspects of the video feedback sessions and specifically the player–coach relationship and the meaning the player ascribed to the video feedback sessions.

Of course, this three-way relationship is apparent in athlete learning and the implications for research are many. Whether it is a one-on-one coaching scenario on the side of an athletic track or a full team pre- or post-match video analysis session, the relationship between context, meaning and behaviour will always be a fruitful source for investigation and understanding for the researcher. In any athletic learning context, social interactions, experiences, relationships and the physical environment are vital to what is learned and how it is learned. Athletes, like all of us, are complex human beings, often with multiple identities (e.g. parent, adolescent, sister, brother, worker, student etc.) and as such come to interactions with coaches with a variety of meanings and thus behaviours. The work of the coach pedagogy researcher is to investigate and elaborate on the social and physical conditions impacting on athlete learning within that particular context in order to enhance that learning.

If we take for example the case of a professional rugby player who fails to turn up for a team photo shoot early one morning during a competitive tournament. The media reports might tell us he 'slept in' after a big night celebrating a victory the day before. However, if we consider what might be the possible different *contexts* of that photo shoot and the different *meanings* involved in the photo shoot (i.e. including the player/s, coaches, sponsors, media, political, economic), and then finally the different *behaviours* involved in the appearance and non-appearance of players at photo shoots, then the possible interpretations are many and probably not as simple as the media would have us believe (i.e. he is a little 'worse for wear').

At this juncture we would like to sound a cautionary note. We would like to stress that we are not advocating that all investigations should demonstrate an interdisciplinary approach, although research of this nature is much needed, in our opinion. A tendency to investigate a topic in light of a preferred discipline is understandable. Education often requires us to specialise within a chosen discipline. Many of us have a preference for the writing and concepts within a certain field. Learning the theories and debates within a given discipline is often very challenging. Having to simultaneously grapple with multiple disciplines can be a daunting prospect. Expecting all researchers to embrace a pluralistic project, then, would seem unreasonable, unrealistic and perhaps unnecessary. Indeed, researching athlete learning from a specified discipline can produce findings that are very insightful and could further understanding with the field of coaching. Nonetheless, it should be recognised that there are inevitable limitations associated with the investigation of athlete learning, and coaching more broadly for that matter, through a singular disciplinary lens. Therefore, researchers are encouraged to consider the potential value of initiating an interdisciplinary project. In instances where there is a genuine desire to conduct interdisciplinary investigations into athlete learning, researchers from alternative disciplinary positions might usefully come together in an attempt to fuse understanding. Likewise, there might be more concerted effort to explore where synergies, as well as differences, exist between disciplines and the findings of studies into athlete learning. However, what should be clear is that coaching scholars need to give careful consideration towards the philosophical underpinnings of certain theoretical positions when determining whether it is possible to align theoretical concepts taken from different disciplines.

Somewhat paradoxically, it would appear that researchers should not only consider how athletes learn from an interdisciplinary perspective, but why athlete learning does not occur in certain instances. The work of Jarvis (2006) and Illeris (2009) have given considerable thought towards non-learning. For example, Illeris distinguishes between non-learning that is caused by psychological defence mechanisms and that caused by resistance. While these might appear conceptually similar, Illeris argues that there is an important psychological difference. He goes on to explain that: 'Whereas the defence mechanisms exist prior to the learning situation and function reactively, resistance is caused by the learning situation as an active response' (Illeris 2009: 16). While the work of theorists such as Illeris (2009) and Jarvis (2006) might help to us to better understand why non-learning occurs in situations where athletes and coaches could potentially learn, a sociological analysis of barriers to learning might also assist with making sense of why some social groups (e.g. females, ethnic groups and lower social classes) have restricted access to participate and learn through sport. For example, in Bruening *et al*.'s 'Women in coaching: the work life interface' (Chapter 33 in this volume), the authors explain how the coaching of female sports tends to be dominated by male coaches who often strive to protect their privileged positions of power by restricting access to females through the hiring of male coaches. They go on to argue that this position serves to limit the aspirations and expectations of female coaches. Additionally, they contend that a lack of female coaches, who could act as mentors to young female coaches, is another deterrent. As such, it would appear that the social landscape of sport significantly contributes towards who does, and does not, have access to athletic, coaching and coach learning opportunities. In this respect, an interdisciplinary understanding of non-learning might be equally as important as the study of learning.

Conclusion

Within this chapter we have stressed the need for greater investigation of athlete (non) learning. Indeed, there remains a paucity of research in this area of academic interest, despite its being a core objective of coaches working across sporting contexts and with athletes of varying levels of ability. While more recent efforts to investigate the everyday realities of coaching from a sociological perspective were identified as being an important development, it was acknowledged that discussions and research into coaching learning have, to date, largely had a psychological focus. Although both psychological and sociological analysis can usefully contribute towards understanding this phenomenon, our reviewing of the historical debates within the fields of psychology and sociology also identified that there are competing positions, often referred to as paradigms, within these disciplines. Alternative paradigms and accompanying theories were found to be underpinned by contrasting philosophical positions. As such, it was argued that any discussion of athlete learning will inevitably involve philosophical discussion.

Having considered how each of the various disciplines have and might continue to independently contribute towards understanding within the field of coaching, we ended the chapter by promoting the need for an interdisciplinary analysis of athlete (non) learning. Here, we contended that the field of coaching might wish to move beyond disciplinary boundaries in an attempt to generate a more complex and nuanced understanding of athlete learning and non-learning. To assist the achievement of this objective, we presented the triad of context, meaning, and behaviour as a conceptual tool that could help to guide future research endeavours. Here, we proposed that this might be achieved through consideration of the relationship between the context, meaning and behaviour triad.

Note

1 It should be noted that while emotions, cognitive thoughts, and behaviours sometimes align, on other occasions it is likely that coaches and athletes (and other key contextual stakeholders) will engage in the management of their emotions and externally observable verbal and nonverbal responses. So a disconnect between meaning and behaviour is not only plausible, but in some situations to be expected. While theoretically interpretable, this feature of coaching practice and athlete learning presents a legitimate issue for coaching scholars to address in their research endeavours.

References

Audi, R. (1999) *The Cambridge Dictionary of Philosophy*, 2nd edn, Cambridge: Cambridge University Press.

Bateson, G. (1972) *Steps to an Ecology of the Mind*, New York: Ballantine Books.

Bernstein, D.A., Penner, L.A., Clarke-Stewart, A. and Roy, E. J. (2008) *Psychology*, 8th edn, New York: Houghton Mifflin.

Cassidy, T., Jones, R.L. and Potrac, P. (2004) *Understanding Sports Coaching: The Social, Cultural and Pedagogical Foundations of Coaching Practice*, London: Routledge.

Cassidy, T., Jones, R.L. and Potrac, P. (2009) *Understanding Sports Coaching: The Social, Cultural and Pedagogical Foundations of Coaching Practice*, 2nd edn, London: Routledge.

Chesterfield, G., Potrac, P. and Jones, R.L. (2010) '"Studentship" and "impression management" in an advanced soccer coach education award', *Sport, Education and Society*, 15(3): 299–314.

Colquhoun, D. (1997) 'Researching with young people on health and environment: The politics of self-esteem and stress', *Health Education Research: Theory and Practice*, 12(4): 101–112.

Cushion, C.J. (2010) 'Coach behaviour', in J. Lyle and C.J. Cushion (eds) *Sports Coaching: Professionalisation and Practice*, London: Elsevier.

Cushion, C.J. and Jones, R.L. (2006) 'Power, discourse, and symbolic violence in professional youth soccer: The case of Albion FC', *Sociology of Sport Journal*, 23: 142–161.

Dahlgren, G. and Whitehead, M. (1991) *Policies and Strategies to Promote Social Equity in Health*, Stockholm: Institute for Futures Studies.

Di Chiro, G. (1997) 'Environmental education and the question of gender: A feminist critique', in I. Robottom (ed.) *Environmental Education: Practice and Possibility*, Geelong: Deakin University Press.

Egger, G. and Swinburne, B. (1997) 'An "ecological" approach to the obesity pandemic', *British Medical Journal*, 315: 477–480.

Fulcher, J. and Scott, J. (2007) *Sociology*, 3rd edn, Oxford: Oxford University Press.

Giddens, A. (2001) *Sociology*, 4th edn, Oxford: Blackwell.

Haralambos, M. and Holborn, M. (2004) *Sociology: Themes and Perspectives*, 6th edn, London: HarperCollins.

Hergenhahn, B.R. (2009) *An Introduction to the History of Psychology*, 6th edn, Belmont, CA: Wadsworth.

Illeris, K. (2009) 'A comprehensive understanding of human learning', in K. Illeris (ed.) *Contemporary Theories of Learning*, London: Routledge.

Jarvis, P. (2006) *Towards a Comprehensive Theory of Human Learning*, London: Routledge.

Jones, R.L. and Turner, P. (2006) 'Teaching coaches to coach holistically: Can problem-based learning (PBL) help?', *Physical Education and Sport Pedagogy*, 11(2): 181–202.

Jones, R.L., Armour, K.M. and Potrac, P. (2003) 'Constructing expert knowledge: A case study of a top-level professional soccer coach', *Sport, Education and Society*, 8(2): 213–229.

Kickbusch, I. (1989) 'Self-care in health promotion', *Social Science and Medicine*, 22(2): 125–130.

Kidman, L. (2005) *Athlete-Centred Coaching: Developing Inspired and Inspiring People*, Christchurch: Innovative Print Communications.

Kirschenbaum, H. and Henderson, V.L. (1989) *Carl Rogers Dialogues*, London: Constable.

Lusted, D. (1986) 'Why pedagogy?' *Screen*, 27(5): 2–14.

McFee, G. (2000) *Free Will*. Teddington, UK: Acumen.

McLeroy, K.R., Bibeau, D., Steckler, A. and Glanz, K. (1988) 'An ecological perspectives on health promotion programs', *Health Education Quarterly*, 15(4): 351–377.

Mills, C.W. (1959) *The Sociological Imagination*, Oxford: Oxford University Press.

Moos, R.H. (1976) *The Human Context: Environmental Determinants of Behaviour*, New York: John Wiley and Sons.

Nelson, L.J., Potrac, P. and Groom, R. (in press) 'Receiving video-based feedback in elite ice-hockey: A player's perspective', *Sport, Education and Society*.

Nelson, L.J., Potrac, P. and Marshall, P. (2010) 'Holism in sports coaching: Beyond humanistic psychology – a commentary', *International Journal of Sport Science and Coaching*, 5(4): 465–468.

Pike, J. and Colquhoun, D. (2009) 'The relationship between policy and place: The role of school meals in addressing health inequalities', *Health Sociology Review*, 18(1): 50–60.

Pollard, A. (2004) 'Towards a sociology of learning in primary schools', in S.J. Ball (ed.) *The RoutledgeFalmer Reader in Sociology of Education*, London: Routledge.

Potrac, P. and Cassidy, T. (2006) 'The coach as a "more capable other"', in R.L. Jones (ed.) *The Sports Coach as Educator: Re-conceptualising Sports Coaching*, London: Routledge.

Potrac, P. and Jones, R.L. (2009) 'Micro-political workings in semi-professional football coaching', *Sociology of Sport Journal*, 26(4): 557–577.

Potrac, P., Jones, R.L. and Armour, K.M. (2002) ' "It's all about getting respect": The coaching behaviours of a top-level English football coach', *Sport, Education and Society*, 7(2): 183–202.

Potrac, P., Jones, R.L. and Cushion, C.J. (2007) 'The coaching behaviours of top-level English soccer coaches: A preliminary investigation', *Soccer in Society*, 8(1): 33–49.

Proshansky, H.M. (1987) 'The field of environmental psychology: Securing its future', in D. Stokols and I. Altman (eds) *Handbook of Environmental Psychology*, New York: John Wiley and Sons.

Purdy, L., Potrac, P. and Jones, R.L. (2008) 'Power, consent and resistance: An autoethnography of competitive rowing', *Sport, Education and Society*, 13(3): 319–336.

Rogers, C.R. (1969) *Freedom to Learn*, Columbus, OH: Merrill Publishing.

Rogers, C.R. (1980) *A Way of Being*, New York: Houghton Mifflin.

Smith, R.E. (2006) 'Positive reinforcement, performance feedback, and performance enhancement', in J.M. Williams (ed.) *Applied Sport Psychology: Personal Growth to Peak Performance*, New York: McGraw-Hill.

Thorpe, R. (1997) *Game Sense: Developing Thinking Players* (video recording), Belconnen, ACT: Australian Sports Commission.

Vygotsky, L.S. (1972) *Thought and Language*, Cambridge, MA: MIT Press.

C

Exploring social relationships in coaching

24

COACH: THE OPEN SYSTEM'S MANAGER

Marvin Washington

UNIVERSITY OF ALBERTA, CANADA

Ian Reade

UNIVERSITY OF ALBERTA, CANADA

Introduction

There is a growing body of literature that makes the case that the job of the coach is complex (Cunningham and Dixon 2003; Dixon and Warner 2009) and as a result coaching has become increasingly stressful (Fletcher and Wagstaff 2009). One of the reasons for this is that the role of the coach has changed over time. Coaches of high-performance athletes are expected to extend their knowledge from technical and tactical areas to know something about aerobic and strength training, nutrition, sport psychology, event scheduling, and many other tasks that enable athletes to perform. As expectations have increased, so has the stress level of coaches. Now, the sport community has realized that it is probably unreasonable to expect coaches to understand or master all these skills and instead coaches at many levels work with a staff of (probably part-time) experts in a variety of functional areas (nutrition, sport psychology, sport therapy, etc.). The coach also acts as the link between the athletes and their own organization, and other organizations with which their organization interacts. As such, the role of the coach has started to resemble that of a manager in an organization (Jones and Wallace 2005). In this chapter, we will elaborate on the implications of these changes as coaches begin to function as managers.

One specific motivation for examining a "coach as manager" perspective is that the increasing complexities of the coaching job have had some negative consequences on coaches. One such consequence is increased stress. In fact, organizational stress has become a topic of recent research (Fletcher and Scott 2010) which has served to highlight the essential and fundamental importance of the consideration of organizational stress for the coach and ultimately the athlete. Specific organizational stressors include athlete selection criteria and processes, financial support for coaches and athletes, work environment issues (Reade and Rodgers 2011) such as contracts and evaluation, competition schedules, travel schedules, and performance expectations as dictated by sport organizations. Another motivation for examining the coach as manager is that conceptualizing the coach as a manager provides a lens for coaches and researchers to address issues of coach education.

Even the need for coaches to remain current in their coaching knowledge can be a source of stress that relates back to the need for management initiatives in dealing with sport science and scientists (Reade and Rodgers 2009).

In addition to a coach's role in leading their athletes or teams, coaches also function as a link between organizations. For example, a club coach is often required to prepare athletes for higher level select teams, or to prepare athletes to navigate their own progress through their sport's system as dictated by the performance of the athlete. Coaches have to coordinate their training schedules within guidelines often "handed down" by provincial or national sport organizations. Coaches also have to negotiate training and competition schedules with another coach, as many youth age athletes might compete in a sport for two different organizations (club system and high school system for example). Furthermore, not only has the coach's role changed in terms of having to interact with more "non-athletes," which has created an additional set of activities associated with an increased stress level, the interactions between the coach and the sport development system in many countries has changed.

There has been renewed emphasis placed upon the need for a variety of sport organizations to better collaborate in an effort to improve a country's national sport delivery system (Green 2004; Green 2005; Sam 2005; Thibault and Babiak 2005; Babiak 2007). Many of these studies have focused on the need for further collaboration and understanding by sport policy makers. Other work has argued that national sport systems need to become more athlete-centered in terms of policies and funding arrangements (Kikulis 2000). What is missing from this line of research is some attention to how the coach fits into this ever-changing system with more national level demands (winning medals) and no additional resources (funding). Thus, we feel that conceptions of the coach not only involves skills and characteristics such as "strong discipline, rigidity of rules, extrinsic motivation, and an impersonal attitude" (Sage 1973: 35), but also involves the "management of microrelations with other stakeholders, be they athletes, other coaches, managers, or owners" (Potrac and Jones 2009: 223). We agree with the more recent research that seeks to build a new grammar of coaching based upon organizational theory concepts (Cassidy *et al.* 2004; Jones and Wallace 2005; Potrac and Jones 2009).

In this chapter, our goal is to locate the coach with respect to their role as a member of the system of inter-related sport organizations. Far from being a dyadic relationship between a coach and an athlete, coaching is always situated within some type of organizational structure. Whether one is a national, regional, school, or club coach, we argue that for a coach to be effective, the coach has to understand how her range of potential actions are influenced by the different organizational and stakeholder demands. Also, current research needs to expand the conceptualization of the challenges of the sport delivery system by understanding how the coach is a key actor in this system, not just an actor that is acted upon by the system. In short, this chapter explores coaching's social "nature" and the construction of the "coach as manager."

Specifically, we think scholars, coaches and sport practitioners can benefit by thinking of coaches as managers from an open system's perspective. We define management as, "the process of working with and through individuals to accomplish organizational goals" (Quarterman *et al.* 2006: 338). By organization we mean, "a tool used by people to coordinate their actions to obtain something they desire or value" (Jones 2004: 2). By open system we mean that in addition to addressing the internal factors associated with production (or the scientific management view), and understanding the issues with a diversity of people with different goals and values (or the human relations view), organizations also are concerned with and are influenced by elements of their environment in terms of obtaining resources

(Pfeffer and Salancik 1977), and legitimacy (Scott 1992; Suchman 1995). Thus, one could define an open system's coach as someone who draws upon and is influenced by key stakeholders in the environment as she tries to manage others in an effort to obtain a goal for their athlete. Note that the management relationships are not just between coach and athlete, but also extend horizontally to include coach and sport psychologist, nutritionist, therapist and also vertically to include coach and national sport organization or other national bodies that the coach needs to work with to reach the goals they have put in place for themselves and their athletes.

In the section that follows, we discuss the consequences of an open systems approach for coaching in terms of their need to understand sport development systems and the skills they need to develop to better coach (or manage) their athletes. Based upon extending the open systems approach to the sport delivery system, we then make an argument for the need to understand the coach, not just as a manager, but as an open system's manager. Specifically, we connect the organizational concept of coach as a manager working within an open system to the current literature on work environment and stress within the coaching profession. We end by providing some advice or tips on how coaches and sport delivery systems can use an open systems perspective to address issues of stress caused by the work environment.

Sport delivery as an open system

The statement that the coach is similar to a manager or a leader is not new (Smoll and Smith 1989; Chelladurai 1990; Potrac and Jones 2009). The coach-as-manager literature has closely followed the mainstream management literature with a focus on both the scientific management aspect of management (Taylor 1911; Sage 1973), and the human relations school of management (Follett 1918; Mayo 1933; Rieke *et al.* 2008). For example, in an early essay, Sage argued that a human relations approach suggests that, "the coach will not assume without question that the total team program takes precedence over the needs and desires of team members" (1973: 39). Rieke *et al.* (2008) examined servant leadership (a style of managing consistent with the human relations movement) in the context of high school basketball teams. They found that basketball players that perceived their coaches as servant leaders were more task oriented, more satisfied with their basketball experience, more mentally tough and performed better than other basketball players.

Just as the human relations perspective of management was an improvement on the scientific management approach, in the 1970s an open-systems approach was introduced as an improvement on the human relationship approach. One of the similarities between the human relationship approach and the scientific management approach was that both approaches directed their attention inside of the organization. One assumption of these two approaches was that improvement of the organization comes from more effective use of the resources inside of the organization. The organization was viewed as a closed system in that the environment did not penetrate the boundaries of the organization. By the 1970s, management scholars began to take seriously that the environment does impact the organization and the boundaries between organization and environment are porous, or more open than previously thought.

Scholars such as Boulding (1956) and Katz and Kahn (1966) were among the first to understand that similar to microorganisms and planets, organizations also could be characterized as open systems. Scholars that examine organizations and managers from an open-system perspective examine how changes in the environment (passage of a new law, or a demographic shift) or changes in other organizations would have implications for the focal manager and the focal organization. An open systems approach has been used to usher in a variety of new organizational theories such as institutional theory (Meyer and Rowan 1977; DiMaggio and Powell 1983), resource dependence theory (Pfeffer and Salancik 1977), and population ecology (Hannan and Freeman 1989). All of these very diverse theories examine how different dimensions of the environment have consequences for the shape, structure, performance, and ultimate survival of organizations.

Research in an open-systems approach to coaching is beginning to emerge. Côté and Salmela (1996) examined the organizational tasks of high-performance gymnastic coaches. Based upon interviews with 17 expert high-performing Canadian gymnastic coaches, they found that five sets of tasks emerged: planning training, working with assistants, working with parents, helping gymnasts with personal concerns, and monitoring weight and esthetics. Planning training and monitoring weight and esthetics could be considered scientific management; helping gymnasts with personal concerns could be considered human relations management, but working with assistants and working with parents would be consistent with an open-systems approach to coaching.

In developing a conceptual definition of coaching, Côté and Gilbert (2009) suggest that one of the components of an integrative definition of coaching effectiveness and expertise is that of the context. Similar to research by Trudel and Gilbert (2006), Côté and Gilbert (2009) suggest that determining the effectiveness of a coach would be different depending upon the context of the coaching. By context, they mean the organization that surrounds the coach and the athlete (recreation, development, or elite level). These organizations would have different goals and expectations, resource allocations, and demands, as well as different stakeholders, and would have a major impact on the work of the coach. One could argue that university, club, or academy contexts might be other contexts that would impact a coaches' ability to coach effectively.

We think there are numerous implications of conceptualizing the coach as a manager in an open system. Once such implication is a better understanding of the work environment, work demands and the organizational stress that is placed upon the coach given the coach is an actor inside of an organization that is itself inside of a wider environment made up of a variety of organizations. Cunningham and Dixon (2003) provide a compelling argument for the consideration of coaches as members of work teams that function across organizational boundaries. They borrow a definition from Cohen and Bailey (1997) that define work teams as:

> a collection of individuals who are interdependent in their tasks, who share responsibilities for outcomes, who see themselves and who are seen by others as an intact social entity embedded in one or more larger social systems (for example, business unit or the corporation), and who manage their relationships across organizational boundaries.
>
> *(Cohen and Bailey 1997: 241).*

Cunningham and Dixon argue that this definition of a team is applicable to coaching staffs because:

> members of these teams (a) are dependent upon one another, (b) share responsibilities for the outcomes produced (e.g. athletic excellence of the athletic team), (c) are seen as a social entity (i.e. the coaching staff), and (d) manage their relationships cross athletic department and university boundaries.
>
> *(Cunningham and Dixon 2003: 182).*

Thus, we agree that coaches function as part of a team, and within an open organizational system that creates a complex work environment. In the next section we connect current research on the work environment of coaches to our conceptualization of coach as manager.

Current thoughts on the work environment of coaches

In other domains that can be argued to function in open-system work environments such as teaching and nursing, researchers have found work environments to be associated with employee job satisfaction, work-related stress, and the retention of employees. After completing a review of the work-stress literature, Sauter *et al.* (1990) proposed six categories of stressors in the work environment:

1   workload;
2   role stressors such as conflict and ambiguity;
3   career concerns, which include factors such as compensation, benefits, contracts, evaluation, and job security;
4   work scheduling;
5   interpersonal relationships (including with supervisors); and
6   job content and control (including interesting and rewarding tasks).

In an open system, we suggest that for coaches, issues with workload, work scheduling, and job content/control are influenced by interactions with parents, facility operators, and competitors as well as relationships with athletes. Issues with role stressor and career concerns could be a function of coaches having more than one job or more than one supervisor, which is also partly due to the open-systems nature of their work. Certainly interpersonal relationships must be dealt with throughout the coaching system. We agree with Bolman and Deal (2008) by suggesting that the goal is to understand that an open systems approach will focus our attention to issues that might have been missed had we worked from the assumption that coaches function within a closed system.

The body of research on work stress has resulted in the development of various models of the work environment that vary in their breadth (Kelloway and Day 2005), but overall it is considered to be a complex construct and the models include various combinations of these six categories proposed by Sauter *et al.* (1990). For example, Karasek (1989) proposed a model that argues for a relationship between workload and control factors such that when employees have more control over their job, the workload is less of an issue. Haas (2006) has argued that work environments that exhibit signs of overload, ambiguity, and politics (defined as the employees manoeuvring for power) have been found to be problematic for employees and are often associated with stress, lack of productivity, and employee turnover. Research on the work environment in service professions such as teaching, nursing, and coaching has employed models that focus on the relationship between work environment as an independent variable and dependent variables such as job satisfaction, employee performance, job stress, turnover, and burnout (Westerman and Simmons 2007) Specifically in the coaching domain, some research has been completed by researchers that includes the work environment (Weiss and Stevens 1993; Woodman and Hardy 2001; Sagas and Cunningham 2005; Fletcher and Wagstaff 2009), and often links variables in the work environment to job satisfaction. As an example, the work of Dixon and Warner (2009) took a qualitative approach to understanding the factors that result in job satisfaction or job dissatisfaction in university-based coaches. Several of the factors identified by Dixon and Warner (which they categorized as job features) are consistent with the six categories of Sauter *et al.* (1990). The job features included flexibility and control, sport policy, quality of supervision, relationships with colleagues, and salary. Their results support the contention that work environment has a tremendous impact on the job satisfaction and effectiveness of a coach. Another example is the work of Allen and Shaw (2009) who studied the work environment of high-performance female coaches from the perspective of the organization's social environment, which included the need for an employee to be connected to others in the organization (relatedness), and to feeling supported by the organization.

Based on the above discussion, there is evidence that mismanaging the work environment and mismanaging within the work environment is a potential source of stress for coaches. Mismanaging within the work environment implies an inability to cope with factors such as workload, work scheduling, and role clarity. Mismanaging the work environment argues for scholars and practitioners to focus efforts on managing relationship with athletes, individuals within the sport delivery system, support staff, and parents. We argue that researchers should focus attention on how environments impact effective performance; specifically whether a coach's inability to understand or manage their environment impacts a coach's stress, burnout, or even their intent to quit. If a satisfied coach is an effective coach, and if the work environment is positively related to a satisfied coach as the research suggests, then coaching development systems should be concerned with understanding more about the work environment for coaches and with ensuring that coaches are adequately prepared for their management challenges. Recent research has begun to provide evidence of the need for management preparation for coaches (Gould *et al.* 2002; Giges *et al.* 2004; Fletcher and Wagstaff 2009). For example, Gould *et al.* (2002) concluded that coaches felt a positive environment was especially important for their effectiveness.

Based on the current literature (Inglis *et al.* 1996; Allen and Shaw 2009; Dixon and Warner 2009), it is apparent that the coaches' work environment has the potential to influence the effectiveness of the coach. What is less clearly understood is the relative impact of the various factors in the work environment that create problems for coaches. For example, would a work environment with excellent compensation offset the absence of a fair evaluation process? Does the provision to a coach of control over their workload offset a workload which is perceived as overly heavy? Do high expectations in terms of winning championships create problems that ultimately lead to coaches making problematic management choices? These are questions which have not yet been answered, but in the next section we discuss some considerations for how coaches could manage their work environments.

Open systems tips for coaches

So far we have conceptualized the coach as an open system's manager. A coach from this perspective has the additional responsibility of understanding influences on their control (from stakeholders and the sport delivery systems) in addition to understanding influences in their control (their athletes). On the surface, this seems to suggest that we have just added to the workload of the coach; a workload that we have already argued is increasingly overburdened. However, we suggest that we are not creating additional stress, but have discussed a way of understanding the current stress on the coach.

Recall that previously we noted six stressors that are important in the work environment:

1   workload;
2   role stressors such as conflict and ambiguity;

3   career concerns, which include factors such as compensation, benefits, contracts, evaluation and job security;
4   work scheduling;
5   interpersonal relationships (including with supervisors); and
6   job content and control (including interesting and rewarding tasks).

The coach benefits from being aware of the impact of the work environment on their daily function, and we have argued that efforts to manage the environment are needed. However, the evidence is very clear that stressors are created by the organizations that coaches must deal with. Fletcher and Scott (2010) used athlete reports to develop a list of "organizational stressors related to the training environment, competition environment, finances, stability, selection, travel, safety, administration, organization, other coaches, athletes, private life, social life, contractual issues, team atmosphere (both athletes and support staff), roles, and communication" (p. 130). It must be noted that in Fletcher and Scott's work, the coach is identified as a source of organizational stress, rather than being identified as buffer for the stressors the athletes feel. However, we believe their study provides empirical evidence that the organization creates stress for the athletes and by extension their coaches must also be affected by the stressors. However, coaches should be aware that they are sometimes seen as sources of stress for their athletes. The ability of the coach to manage within the open system is clearly a challenge to be addressed. As well as athletes, parents have also identified coaches as stressors (Harwood and Knight 2009) which lends further support to the open-system approach to management and to the need for coaches to be trained as managers. We argue that these stressors could be understood as a current inability or unawareness on behalf of coaches to manage their environment. In this section, we offer five different tips, strategies, or opportunity areas that could be utilized to not only help the coach increase their awareness or skill in managing their environment, but to also help the sport delivery system as a key member of the coach's environment reduce some of the stress that is caused by them.

The coaching contract

One artifact that can be used to help assist the coach in managing their environment is a renewed focus and improved use of the coaching contract. First, we advocate that a coach should have a contract. The length of the contract, terms of renewal, financial terms, and benefits should all be articulated in a contractual agreement. It is difficult to understand how a coach would be expected to be in charge of the career of one or more athletes if they do not appreciate the importance of the management of their own career. Coaches that are volunteers, and we know there are many volunteers even at the highest levels of sport, are very likely to function without contracts. When contracts are in place, they are often only for a season, or a year, and do not include benefits. In addition to the basics, the contract should also help both the coach and the sport development system understand their respective roles, responsibilities, and level of authority.

Although a coach's primary job is to train athletes to perform, at any given time the capability of the athletes to produce will vary, so expectations that are set too high will lead to frustration. To protect the athletes, and themselves, coaches need to work toward negotiating reasonable expectations for their programs; managing expectations is a fundamental role. However, we think effort should not only fall on the coach, but also the sport delivery system. Individuals that hire coaches need to make sure that coaches are an active participant in understanding their role, not only in the techniques of coaching the athlete, but also in the organizational and systems issues that could range from meeting with key stakeholders, communicating with the media, to attending national sport organization meetings.

Coach evaluation

If a clear coaching contract helps a coach manage their environment "on the front end" of the process, a clear coach evaluation system will help "on the back end." We argue that an open systems perspective would suggest that the coach as well as the sport delivery system place a high priority on creating an effective evaluation system. The norm for coach evaluation processes include (Barber and Eckrich 1998) athlete evaluations, coach self-reports, and administrator observations, and are also heavily reliant on win/loss records, athlete performance, and success in recruiting. Research suggests that the coach, as manager, should be able to advocate for a multi-faceted evaluation system (Côté and Gilbert 2009) that involves all aspects of the open system within which they operate. Simplistic links between coach behaviors and athlete outcomes should probably be resisted as unrealistic, and unsupported by evidence. Additionally, we advocate for the coach to be involved in the evaluation process of their support staff.

Staff

Given the multiple stakeholders involved in the open system, the management of the work schedule presents a major challenge for coaches. Coaches are under significant pressure to accommodate the schedules of their athletes and parents, to balance the athletes' schedules with facility scheduling, and to meet all of the demands of the competition schedules that are dictated by leagues, and various levels of competition. When schools and clubs are both offering competitive programs in a given sport, work scheduling becomes even more problematic.

One way to help with the multiple stakeholders might be to re-evaluate the set of additional coaches that come with a head coach position. Instead of having one head coach and two assistant coaches that perform the coaching duties, a head coach might lobby for one assistant coach plus a team manager to perform some of the managerial duties.

Education and training

There has been much research on the importance of a coach's interpersonal relationships in their ability to effectively perform their jobs (Côté and Salmela 1996). Certainly, the need for the coach to manage their relationships to their athletes is obvious, but the importance of managing other relationships (parents, assistant coaches, support staff, supervisors) has received less recognition. Recently, Harwood and Knight (2009) have studied relationships with parents from the perspective of athletes, coaches, and parents and have found that each are sources of stress for the other. Allen and Shaw (2009) and Inglis *et al.* (1996) have written about the need for supportive supervisors and the centrality of social support to survival for employees with heavy workloads has been recounted in both the business and sport literatures. We think that more could be done to better prepare coaches to be able to manage individuals in their environment. There is a lot of interpersonal training and development that occurs in traditional management and we would suggest that sport development systems utilize some of this training as a key piece in the education and training of their coaches.

Coping skills

Coping strategies have been studied (Thelwell *et al.* 2008; Olusoga *et al.* 2010), and it would appear that management skill (efficacy and knowledge) would be a natural defence against organizational stress. Olusoga and his colleagues (Olusoga *et al.* 2010) contend that coaches should understand that detailed structuring and advanced planning are essential to effectively coping with stress and effective coaching. They found that structure and planning included four strategies involving planning (e.g. using time productively, allowing enough time so you are not rushing), communication (e.g. identifying roles and responsibilities early, detailed needs analysis with athletes), effective time management (e.g. multi-tasking, dealing with tasks straight away), and taking scheduled time off from coaching (e.g. holidays, taking time off after championships). Within planning, coaches described how they would plan for competitions (pre-game strategies) and for specific situations that might arise. Rather than coping with stress as it occurred, identifying roles and responsibilities early and having clear boundaries and rules were ways in which coaches reduced the potential for stressors to result in strain and negative responses. Thelwell *et al.* (2008) found that stressors such as athlete selection (by the organization) and poor training conditions reflected organizational stressors with specific regard to the work environment, and stressors such as dealing with other coaches reflected organizational stressors with particular regard to the team. They also found that problem-focused coping (e.g. engage in communication), emotion-focused (e.g. use of self-talk), and avoidance coping (e.g. escaping from the situation) strategies similar to those reported by Levy *et al.* (2009) were used to manage organizational stressors.

Conclusion

Research into coaching in all contexts that would describe an open system and explain the impact of the open system on the effectiveness of a coach would contribute to an existing base of literature that has generally recognized the existence of environmental factors, and then ignored the impact. Research has been focused on coach education and preparation, coaching efficacy, and coach behavior as they relate to the effectiveness of coaches. Yet we have argued that a well-educated, experienced, and efficacious coach will have to deal with stressors such as unreasonable workloads, role ambiguity, and politics that could have significantly detrimental effects on the ability of the coach to do their job. Researchers could contribute to our knowledge of the direct effect of these factors on coaching performance and attempt to determine which factors are most problematic, and which are most manageable.

Fletcher and Scott argue that while we have identified sources of stress from organizations, we do not understand much about the stress:

> (i)ncluding the intensity (high vs. low demand), duration (acute vs. chronic), prevalence (frequent vs. infrequent occurrence), quantity (many vs. few demands), and other aspects such as the timing (e.g. competition vs. training settings), specificity (specific vs. global demand), closeness (proximal vs. distal to the individual), and weighting (additive or multiplicative). Finally on this topic, it is likely that managing the interface between performance-related and organizational-related stressors, together with those situated in one's private life, places additional demands on coaches.
>
> *(Fletcher and Scott 2010: 131).*

The recognition of the coach as a manager who functions in a work environment that is part of an open system changes, to an extent, the way we perceive coaching. While it is easy to accept the role of the coach as being responsible for the closed system that incorporates the technical, tactical, psychological, and physical training of athletes, it is also necessary to consider whether a coach can be effective without the knowledge necessary to manage all of the external forces that impinge on the closed system; an undeniably complex open system. In this chapter, we offered some tips and strategies that could be implemented to help coaches better manage their environment. For sport delivery systems we conclude that if coaches are encouraged to view their role as a manager, than the system should view its role as a boss. As such, the system should encourage the use of a more formal contract in the hiring of coaches and for a systemic evaluation system. For coaches, there is a challenge to develop a managerial skill set, but as observers and researchers we can also begin to understand that the link between a coach and their athlete's performance is contingent upon a complex set of factors over which a coach has a questionable degree of control.

References

Allen, J.B. and Shaw, S. (2009) 'Women coaches' perceptions of their sport organizations' social environment: Supporting coaches' psychological needs?' *The Sport Psychologist*, 23(3): 346–366.

Babiak, K. (2007) 'Determinants of interorganizational relationships: The case of a Canadian nonprofit sport organization,' *Journal of Sport Management*, 21(3): 338–376.

Barber, H. and Eckrich, J. (1998) 'Methods and criteria employed in the evaluation of intercollegiate coaches', *Journal of Sport Management*, 12(4): 301–322.

Bolman, L.G. and Deal, T.E. (2008) *Reframing Organizations: Artistry, Choice, and Leadership* (4th edition), San Francisco, CA: Jossey-Bass.

Boulding, K.E. (1956) 'General system theory: The skeleton of science, management,' *Science*, 2(3): 197–208.

Cassidy, T., Jones, R.L. and Potrac, P. (2004) *Understanding Sports Coaching: To Social, Cultural and Pedagogical Foundations of Coaching Practice*, London: Routledge.

Chelladurai, P. (1990) 'Leadership in sports: A review,' *International Journal of Sport Psychology*, 21(4): 328–354.

Cohen, S.G. and Bailey, D.E. (1997) 'What makes teams work: Group effectiveness research from the shop floor to the executive suite,' *Journal of Management*, 23(3): 239–290.

Côté, J. and Gilbert, W. (2009) 'An integrative definition of coaching effectiveness and expertise,' *International Journal of Sports Science and Coaching*, 4(3): 307–322.

Côté, J. and Salmela, J.H. (1996) 'The organizational tasks of high-performance gymnastic coaches,' *The Sport Psychologist*, 10(3): 247–260.

Cunningham, G. and Dixon, M. (2003) 'New perspectives concerning performance appraisals of intercollegiate coaches,' *Quest*, 55(2):177–192.

DiMaggio, P.J. and Powell, W.W. (1983) 'The iron cage revisited: Institutional isomorphism and collective rationality in organizational fields,' *American Sociological Review*, 48: 147–16.

Dixon, M.A. and Warner, S. (2009) 'Employee satisfaction in sport: Development of a multi-dimensional model in coaching,' *Journal of Sport Management*, 24(2): 139–168.

Fletcher, D. and Scott, M. (2010) 'Psychological stress in sports coaches: A review of concepts, research and practice,' *Journal of Sports Sciences*, 28(2): 127–137.

Fletcher, D. and Wagstaff, C.R.D. (2009) 'Organizational psychology in elite sport: Its emergence, application and future,' *Psychology of Sport and Exercise*, 10(4): 427–434.

Follett, M.P. (1918) *The New State: Group Organization and the Solution of Popular Government*, London: Longmans.

Giges, B., Petitpas, A.J. and Vernacchia, R.A. (2004) 'Helping coaches meet their own needs: Challenges for the sport psychology consultant,' *The Sport Psychologist*, 18(4): 430–444.

Gould, D., Greenleaf, C., Guinan, D. and Chung, Y. (2002) 'A survey of U.S. Olympic coaches: Variables perceived to have influenced athlete performances and coach effectiveness,' *The Sport Psychologist*, 16(3): 229–250.

Green, B.C. (2005) 'Building sport programs to optimize athlete recruitment, retention, and transition: Toward a normative theory of sport development,' *Journal of Sport Management*, 19(3): 233–253.

Green, M. (2004) 'Power, policy and political priorities: Elite sport development in Canada and the United Kingdom,' *The Sociology of Sport Journal*, 21(4): 376–396.

Haas, M. (2006) 'Knowledge gathering, team capabilities, and project performance in challenging work environments,' *Management Science*, 52(8): 1170–1184

Hannan, M.T. and Freeman, J. (1989) *Organizational Ecology*, Cambridge, MA: Harvard University Press.

Harwood, C. and Knight. C. (2009) 'Stress in youth sport: A developmental investigation of tennis parents', *Psychology of Sport and Exercise*, 10(4): 447–456.

Inglis, S., Danylchuk, K.E. and Pastore, D. (1996) 'Understanding retention factors in coaching and athletic management positions,' *Journal of Sport Management*, 10(3): 237–249.

Jones, G.R. (2004) *Organizational Theory, Design and Change: Text and Cases*, Upper Saddle River, NJ: Prentice Hall.

Jones, R.L. and Wallace, M. (2005) 'Another bad day at the training ground: Coping with ambiguity in the coaching context,' *Sport, Education, and Society*, 10(1): 119–134.

Karasek, R. (1989) *Control in the Workplace and its Health-related Aspects*, New York: Wiley.

Katz, D. and Kahn, R.L. (1966) *The Social Psychology of Organizations*, New York: Wiley.

Kelloway, E.K. and Day, A.L. (2005) 'Building healthy workplaces: What we know so far,' *Canadian Journal of Behavioural Science*, 37(4): 223–235.

Kikulis, L. (2000) 'Continuity and change in governance and decision-making in national sport organizations: Institutional explanations,' *Journal of Sport Management*, 14(4): 293–320.

Levy, A., Nicholls, A., Marchant, D. and Polman, R. (2009) 'Organisational stressors, coping, and coping effectiveness: A longitudinal study with an elite coach,' *International Journal of Sports Science and Coaching*, 4(1): 31–45.

Mayo, E. (1933) *The Human Problems of an Industrial Civilization*, New York: Macmillan.

Meyer, J.W. and Rowan, B. (1977) 'Institutionalized organizations: Formal structure as myth and ceremony,' *American Journal of Sociology*, 83(2): 340–363.

Olusoga, P., Butt, J. Maynard, I. and Hays, K. (2010) 'Stress and coping: A study of world class coaches', *Journal of Applied Sport Psychology*, 22(3): 274–293.

Pfeffer, J. and Salancik, G.R. (1977) *The External Control of Organizations*, Palo Alto, CA: Stanford University Press.

Potrac, P. and Jones, R.L. (2009) 'Micropolitical workings in semi-professional football', *Sociology of Sport Journal*, 26(4): 557–577.

Quarterman, J., Li, M. and Parks, J.B., (2006) 'Managerial leadership in sport organizations,' in J.B. Parks, J. Quarterman and L. Thibault (eds) *Contemporary Sport Management* (3rd edition), Champaign, IL: Human Kinetics, pp. 335–355.

Reade, I. and Rodgers, W.M. (2009) 'A collaboration model for knowledge transfer from sport science to high performance Canadian interuniversity coaches,' *Journal of Coaching Education*, 2(1): 1–23.

Reade, I. and Rodgers, W.M. (2011) 'The work environments of coaches of high performance athletes: An exploratory study,' unpublished manuscript.

Rieke, M., Hammermeister, J. and Chase, M. (2008) 'Servant leadership in sport: A new paradigm for effective coach behavior,' *International Journal of Sports Science Coaching*, 3(2): 227–239.

Sagas, M. and Cunningham, G. (2005) 'Work-family conflict among college assistant coaches,' *International Journal of Sport Management*, 6: 183–197.

Sage, G. (1973) 'The coach as management: organizational leadership in American sport,' *Quest*, 19 (1): 35–40.

Sam, M. (2005) 'The makers of sport policy: A (task) force to be reckoned with,' *Sociology of Sport Journal*, 21(1): 78–99.

Sauter, S.L., Murphy, L.R. and Hurrell Jr., J.J. (1990) 'Prevention of work-related psychological disorders: A national strategy proposed by the National Institute for Occupational Safety and Health (NIOSH),' *American Psychologist*, 45(10): 1146–1158.

Scott, R.W. (1992) *Organizations: Rational, Natural and Open Systems*, 3rd edition, Prentice Hall: Englewood Cliffs, NJ.

Smoll, F.L. and Smith, R.E. (1989) 'Leadership behaviors in sport: A theoretical model and research paradigm,' *Journal of Applied Social Psychology*, 19(18): 1522–1551.

Suchman, M.C. (1995) 'Managing legitimacy: Strategic and institutional processes,' *Academy of Management Review*, 20(3): 571–610.

Taylor, F.W. (1911) *The Principles of Scientific Management*, Harper: New York.

Thelwell, R.C., Weston, N.J.V., Greenlees, I.A. and Hutchings, N. (2008) 'Stressors in elite sport: A coach perspective,' *Journal of Sports Sciences*, 26(9): 905–918.

Thibault, L. and Babiak, K. (2005) 'Organizational changes in Canada's sport system,' *European Sport Management Quarterly*, 5(2): 105–132.

Trudel, P. and Gilbert, W.D. (2006) 'Coaching and coach education,' in D. Kirk, M. O'Sullivan and D. McDonald (eds) *Handbook of Physical Education*, London: Sage, pp. 516–539.

Weiss, M.R. and Stevens, C. (1993) 'Motivation and attrition of female coaches: An application of social exchange theory,' *The Sport Psychologist*, 7(3): 244–261.

Westerman, J.W. and Simmons, B.L. (2007) 'The effects of work environment on the personality–performance relationship: An exploratory study,' *Journal of Managerial Issues*, 19(2): 288–305.

Woodman, T. and Hardy, L. (2001) 'A case study of organizational stress in elite sport,' *Journal of Applied Sport Psychology*, 13(2): 207–238.

25

EXPLORING TRUST AND DISTRUST IN COACHING

A suggested research agenda

Laura Purdy

UNIVERSITY OF WORCESTER, UK

Paul Potrac

UNIVERSITY OF HULL, UK

Lee Nelson

UNIVERSITY OF HULL, UK

Introduction

In recent years, there has been increasing attention attached to coaches' interactions with athletes and key contextual stakeholders (Cushion and Jones 2006; Jowett and Cockerill 2002, 2003; Poczwardowski *et al.* 2002; Potrac *et al.* 2002; Purdy *et al.* 2008). To date, the theory used to illuminate the social complexity of coaching has been principally informed by theories of power (e.g. French Jr and Raven 1959; Bourdieu 1989; Foucault 1980, 1982, 1991) and interaction (e.g. Goffman 1959). Interestingly, the findings of such studies have hinted at the importance of trust in developing, maintaining and advancing productive and meaningful working relationships. Somewhat surprisingly, however, there has been little consideration and application of the theories of trust and distrust (e.g. Hardin 2002; Hoy and Tschannen-Moran 1999; Luhmann 1979; Mistzal 1996; Sztompka 1999) in the coaching context. Certainly, we argue these existing theorisations have much to offer us in understanding the dynamics of trust between individuals from both an interpersonal and organisational perspective. Given this outlook, we argue that such work could aid our efforts in better understanding the complex interplay between coaches, athletes and other stakeholders within the coaching environment.

Therefore, the aim of this chapter is to introduce a widely utilised theorisation of trust from the social science literature (Sztompka 1999) and to illustrate its potential utility in helping us to understand the dynamic nature of trust within the coaching process. In order to achieve this aim, this chapter will initially define trust and distrust. We then present a short ethnographic fiction, which we seek to understand and explain using some of the key concepts of Piotr Sztompka (1999). Finally we conclude with a summary of the main points raised in this chapter, especially as they relate to future research endeavours on the role of trust and distrust in coaching practice.

What are trust and distrust?

The notions of trust and distrust have been subject to widespread theoretical and empirical scrutiny by scholars in organisational behaviour, management, marketing, political science, philosophy, psychology, social psychology, education and sociology (Lyon *et al.* 2012). Given the variety of perspectives in which trust has been examined, it is unsurprising that there are over 70 definitions regarding what constitutes trust (Lyon *et al.* 2012). Indeed, trust has been defined as a trait (i.e. individual characteristic), state (i.e. cognitive, motivational or affective state) (Marks *et al.* 2001) and a process (i.e. one through which other important behaviour, attitudes and relationships are strengthened or weakened) (Burke *et al.* 2007). In addition to the multiple views on trust, there are various definitions of distrust. Here, distrust can be viewed as a violation of trust (Bies and Tripp 1996), low levels of trust (Dirks and Ferrin 2001), the absence of trust (Gilbert and Tang 1998) and the opposite of trust (Butler and Cantrell 1984).

While it is clear from the literature that there are no uniformly agreed definitions of trust and distrust, we will, for the purpose of this chapter, broadly draw upon a constructivist interpretation of trust and distrust (Weber and Carter 2003; Hoy and Tschannen-Moran 1999; Sztompka 1999). Here, it is suggested that the premise of trust is the belief that an individual will take another's perspective into account when making decisions and will not act in ways to violate the moral standards of the relationship (Weber and Carter 2003). Trust, then, can be considered to be a social product, as it emerges from real or imagined relationships with others (Weber and Carter 2003). As a decidedly social phenomenon, trust develops and maintains itself within the interactions and structures of everyday life (Weber and Carter 2003). In addition, trust can be considered to include elements of risk and vulnerability; if one could be sure of the actions of another person/s there would not be the need for trust (Luhmann 1979). Similarly, distrust will be understood to be the negative expectations that one individual has of other individuals within a particular social setting (Sztompka 1999).

Exploring trust and distrust in coaching: a vignette of practice

The following extracts are fictional accounts that are based upon incidents taken from the second author's (i.e. Paul's) coaching diaries in which he recorded his understandings of different events, dilemmas and experiences that he encountered as a coach. He has utilised these diaries to construct a fictional account of the people, events and issues associated with the selection, development and deployment of a sub-elite male youth football team (players aged between 16 and 18 years) for a national competition. Indeed, rather than being intended to be considered as a 'true' account of Paul's experiences, it is important to recognise that the narrative presented is fictitious in terms of the context, people and the precise nature of the events portrayed. The intention of this story is to highlight how coaching proved, to Paul at least, to be far from the straightforward process that he had initially imagined that it would be. Indeed, the issues that he highlights within the narrative went beyond the technical, tactical and bio-scientific aspects of sport performance, and include a variety of dilemmas and choices related to the individuals with whom he worked with (e.g. players, assistant coaches, administrators). In ruminating on the decisions that Paul has had to make during his time as a coach, it became clear to him that the trust, or indeed the distrust, that he had for individuals became an important dimension in his decision making. From his perspective, the notions of trust and distrust came to lie at the core of his coaching practice. It is perhaps worth noting that the micro-level interactions described in the following vignettes took place in what Paul understood to be a low trust culture; a sporting subculture that, for him, was characterised by degrees of selfishness, back-stabbing and ruthlessness, and where trust between individuals was frequently at a premium. Unfortunately, many of the lessons he learnt in relation to trust and distrust in coaching came through what sometimes proved to be quite painful personal experience and the mutual sharing of stories with other coaches. They were never discussed in any formal coach education provision that he attended, nor did it occupy any curriculum time in his undergraduate studies in sport science and coaching. As such, he firmly believes that if we are to better understand the social complexity of coaching, then our understanding and consideration of the dynamics of trust and distrust warrant further theoretical and practical exploration.

Extract 1: Selecting the squad

The 12-week training programme in the lead up to the tournament is coming to an end. Next week, I have to cut the squad from 25 players and name the 18 players who will travel to the tournament. Telling people they hadn't made the squad wasn't going to be an easy process, it never was. But it was going to be particularly difficult given the intensity and enthusiasm shown by the majority of players in the training sessions. On one level, some players like Warren, Karl and Tim picked themselves. They had the requisite playing attributes that were needed in their positions, they turned up to every training session, they were punctual, listened to the instruction provided and responded in the way that I considered to be necessary. They understood what was required on and off the field. I knew that they'd perform their role within the team framework to the best of their ability. In short, I trusted them. This shouldn't surprise me, as my telephone conversations to their previous coaches had given me a good indication of their attributes and characters.

Some of the other choices are not so easy though. For example, Darren has great pace and the ability to create goal-scoring opportunities for the team. He could be a match winner for us. However, would he contribute to the defensive side of our tactical strategies? Can I rely on him to perform in the way I required? I have my doubts. In training he never appeared to show any appetite for those defensive responsibilities. The competition will be tough at the tournament, with a single goal potentially deciding the outcome of many of the games. I can't afford for our defensive strategy to be let down by an individual not conforming to the team plan. Can I trust him? I want to, but I'm not sure if I can take the risk. I need to think more about Darren. I can see why one of his previous coaches had mentioned this issue to me. It's a real dilemma and one that I hoped I wouldn't have to deal with myself.

Then there's Daniel. I'm not sure if there's a place for him on the squad. He's a good player and applies himself on the pitch, but his temperament gets him into trouble with the referees. I can't afford for anybody to be sent-off in this tournament for losing his temper and reacting to events in an aggressive manner. I'm not sure if he'd adhere to the curfew and the disciplined regime that we will have to implement on and off the field. I hear him talking to the other players about his latest social adventures and mishaps after training sessions. I'm not sure if I can trust him to not get into some kind of trouble off the field when I'm there. I don't want to have to take responsibility for such incidents, especially in front of the national selectors. They'll be making decisions about my coaching qualities and attributes as much as the player performances when I'm there. I want to progress as a coach as much as the players want to be selected for the national team. Can I trust him? I want to but...

On the plus side, there's Chad. He and his family have moved here from the USA. I don't know much about his playing background, but judging him on performances in training and the practice games, he really looks like he could be an important player for the squad. His work ethic is great and, for me, he also has a wonderfully calm and assured temperament on the pitch. He seems like a good kid too. He's punctual, polite, and seems to have mixed well with the players since he's arrived. He has the makings of a future captain from what I have seen so far, so I don't anticipate any behavioural problems when we are away.

Extract 2: **Working with the coaching 'team'**

Seamus, one of the assistant coaches, was late for training again. This is the fourth time in three weeks. He was meant to organise the kit, balls and cones ahead of the training session. Luckily, I got to the training ground earlier than usual as I'd feared that Seamus wouldn't show up on time. I can't keep covering for him like this. I've started to plan for Seamus not being around or on time. I've spoken to him about this, but the situation doesn't seem to be improving. To be honest, I'm rapidly losing faith in him. If he's not late, he's pretty disorganised when it comes to delivering his parts of the training session and his appearance leaves a lot to be desired in my mind. He has turned up in smelly, dirty, training kit, which doesn't create a good impression in the eyes of the players and their parents. I've heard one or two of the players joking about the odour emanating from his training kit. There's also the issue of his curt responses to some of the parents. There have been some complaints that we need to talk about. I think he's a nice guy, but I'm really beginning to wonder if I can trust him to perform his role in the way required. It's not doing any of us any good.

David's, one of the other assistant coaches, actions are making me become increasingly suspicious of his motives for being involved with the team. I overheard him criticising the 4-3-3 formation that we are working on in training to some of the players, parents and committee members. I heard him saying how we should be utilising a 4-4-2 formation. He's never voiced that concern to me directly before. I hope I've been coming across as an approachable person. I've been inviting feedback from the coaching staff. I'm worried about the potential consequences of his actions. Is he trying to make me look bad? Will he use this as a reason if results don't go our way at the tournament? The coaching team needs to present a unified front. Well, at least in public anyway! We can deal with our disagreements behind closed doors. I'm really not comfortable with him involving other people in this way. I know he was disheartened at not getting the role as head coach. Is he trying to manipulate the situation to work towards his best interests? He's made a few strange comments before, but I'd never paid too much attention to them. I've not really had the time to. That said, one of the other coaches in the club had warned me about David's desire to be a head coach and that he has a 'history of trying to rock the boat'. I'll need to keep a closer eye on him. He's a very good coach on the training ground and relates well to the players. It's making me feel uneasy about our working relationship. Are we colleagues or competitors?

Thankfully, I can rely on John (goalkeeping coach). He's been just about everything you'd want from an assistant. He's organised, knowledgeable and good with the players. He's happy to discuss ideas and provide feedback in the sanctuary of the coaches' changing room. I really feel like I'm working with him to develop this team. It's a great feeling.

Extract 3: A parting of company I

Seamus and David have been asked to leave the coaching team. Seamus had turned up to training late and with a strong smell of alcohol on his breath. That was the final straw for me, and our Director of Football, Martin, who was observing our training session tonight. Martin dismissed him from his position on the spot. It wasn't a pleasant experience, but it's done now and we can move on as a group. Part of me is sad to see Seamus go, but how many chances can you give someone?

Extract 4: A parting of company II

Just when I thought I'd seen it all… David has quit his coaching role with the team. I had overheard him criticising the 4-3-3 formation again to the players' parents before this afternoon's practice match. I challenged David about his comments. I asked him why he didn't come to speak to me about his views on our playing formation. He told me in no polite terms where I could 'stick' my 4-3-3 formation. It ended up with David storming off to his car and driving home. I had a phone call this evening from the club to say that he won't be coming back. To be honest, I was relieved when I heard the news. Given David's actions, I didn't really want him in the team environment anymore. On the plus side, I've been told I can appoint a new assistant. This is a great opportunity for me to bring Richard into the coaching team. We've worked together before, we get on well, he's a good coach, and I trust him!

Extract 5: Handshakes, smiles and distrust

'Good luck at the tournament, Paul. We'll be thinking about you and the team from here. I'm sure the team will do well'. Usually, I'd accept these words at face value in terms of their sincerity and genuineness. However, they came from our Club Chairman, who, from my perspective at least, has been difficult to deal with from day one. While I smiled, thanked him for his kind words, and shook his hand before boarding the team coach to travel to the airport, I didn't believe that he meant a single word of what he'd just said. I've heard through the grapevine that he wasn't happy at my appointment as head coach and that, latterly, he was furious at David's dismissal. Apparently, he had a long history and strong connection with David and wanted him to be head coach instead of me. In my more cynical moments, I wonder if that was why we were the last of all the age-group teams to receive the required training kit and equipment, and why we also never seemed to get the best training pitches for our coaching sessions. I've raised these issues with him a couple of times, but nothing ever seems to change. Apparently, my requests are not feasible and that all the age-group teams are being treated equally. His words here seem empty, as I am witnessing first-hand how some of the other teams are allowed some choice and flexibility with their training venues.

This was nothing, however, compared to our encounter of some three weeks ago. We had played a friendly game in preparation for the tournament against our fierce local rivals. The game had finished in a 2–2 draw. The result was fair. We had dominated the first half while our opposition had done the same for the second half. The team shape and pattern of play was coming together nicely for the tournament or so I had thought. Rather than accompany the team into the dressing room straight after the game, as was my usual routine, I had to pop up to the stadium lounge/viewing area to thank the two university students who had volunteered to videotape the game for me to watch and digest during the following days. The last thing I expected to hear and see was the Club Chairman loudly complaining of the 'substandard coaching!', 'all this 4-3-3 stuff is a load of bollocks!' Not only were his comments clearly audible to his colleagues at his table but to just about all the parents and other people in the room. We looked at each other for a few seconds, and then we both continued with our business as though nothing had happened. However, for those few seconds our eyes met, I knew we were confirming what we both felt and knew. We don't like or trust each other. He doesn't trust me as a coach and I don't trust him as the Club Chairman. Rightly or wrongly, I've come to see him as more of a problem than the opposition teams that we will encounter on the pitch. I didn't anticipate any support from him. In fact, I believed he was more likely to sabotage my coaching programme and reputation. Regardless of the results of the team and what I achieve, I came to the conclusion that he is looking forward to ending my tenure as head coach when my contract ends after the tournament. If nothing else, it has made me want to do well with the team. I have to do well to protect my reputation in the football circles, especially when people with his connections in the local football scene are clearly against me. I'm beginning to question why I ever wanted to be a football coach!

An interpretation of Paul's narrative: using Sztompka's analysis of trust

In *Trust: A Sociological Theory*, Sztompka (1999: 21) proposes that trust 'belongs to human and not natural discourse'. Here, his analysis focuses on the fact that humans have to coexist, cooperate and coordinate their actions, which creates uncertainty and uncontrollability as people are required to formulate expectations about the decisions and conduct of others. In this respect, it is Sztompka's belief that our inability to fully predict and control individuals' actions results in our experiencing uncertainty, which necessitates the notion of trust. Ontologically, he suggests that an inability to predict others can be explained by the fact that 'human action is on many occasions significantly undetermined' (Sztompka 1999: 22). Furthermore, epistemologically, Sztompka (ibid.) contests that we often know little in relation to 'the mechanisms of human conduct as well as about other people's motives, intentions, and reasons', which means that we are always missing valuable information when attempting to predict future events. In relation to control, Sztompka (1999) argues that we rarely have full control over others' behaviours and actions. Indeed, he goes on to explain that 'it is only the extremes of physical coercion that fall under this rubric' and that in such instances 'there is no place for trust' (Sztompka 1999: 23). Rather, human consciousness means that people always have some degree of choice (i.e. submit or resist, conform or oppose, obey or evade), which limits our ability to control others.

An inability to predict and control the actions of people, then, leads to our needing to act in spite of uncertainty. In this respect, Sztompka (1999) says that we have to take risks and 'gamble' on the future and free actions of others. In light of this, it is perhaps unsurprising that Sztompka (1999: 25) defines trust as 'a bet about the future contingent actions of others'. For Sztompka, trust is ultimately a strategy for trying to deal with the uncontrollable and uncertain nature of the future actions of individuals. In comparison, Sztompka (1999: 26) treats distrust, like trust, as a bet, but one that 'involves negative expectations about the actions of others'. Distrust is therefore the mirror image of trust in his analysis.

We believe that Sztompka's theorising about trust and distrust could usefully help us to make sense of the dilemmas, thoughts and decisions evident in Paul's narrative. Indeed, Paul's weighing-up of whether or not he could and should trust or distrust the various stakeholders with whom he interacted at the club is a key feature of the stories that he shared. Importantly, implicit within Paul's narrative is the recognition of an inability to retain complete control over the people with whom he worked. Rather, consideration towards who he could and couldn't trust evidences the fact that, at best, Paul could only partially influence the thoughts and behaviours of the key contextual stakeholders with whom he interacted. However, while Paul was only able to exert limited control over his players and coaching staff, Paul's stories clearly demonstrate that the level of trust he afforded these individuals was largely 'measured' in relation to whether or not their actions aligned with his desires and objectives. In this respect, it would appear that Paul placed a lot of importance on what Sztompka (1999: 27) terms anticipatory trust, which he defined as instances 'when I act towards others because I believe that the actions which they carry out will be favourable to my interests, needs, and expectations'.

For example, Paul evidently trusted Warren, Karl and Tim, as they were players that conducted themselves, both on and off the field, in a manner that was consistent with Paul's expectations. While Paul trusted the actions of these individuals, he did not trust those of Darren or Daniel. Paul had concerns about Darren's lack of conformity towards the defensive strategy that Paul had devised for the team and Daniel's temperament during competitive fixtures and inability to follow Paul's instructions off the pitch. Of significance here is how the likely presence of the national selectors at the tournament shaped Paul's deliberations. Paul perceived that the selectors would not only be judging his players' performances, but also his coaching abilities. In this respect, while Paul was of the opinion that they would principally judge how his team performed on the pitch, he was also acutely aware the selectors would also be watching how his team conducted itself throughout the tournament off the pitch. At this time, Paul held strong aspirations to progress as a coach. He therefore wanted to impress the national selectors, as he thought that they might offer access to the next tier of coaching. The desire to impress these individuals seemingly shaped how Paul went about judging what was important and how he would evaluate the trustworthiness of his players and coaching staff.

Paul's narrative might also be further understood in relation to Sztompka's discussion of reflected trustworthiness, which he defines as 'the estimate of trustworthiness of the target on which we are considering whether to confer trust' (Sztompka 1999: 70–71). Sztompka (1999) considers this to be the most common and important foundation for trust. Here, Sztompka contends that there are three bases (i.e. reputation, performance and appearance) on which to determine this primary form of trustworthiness. However, it is important to note that while he separates these concepts for analytical purposes, Sztompka (1999: 83) recognises that, in reality, 'people often take all three, or various combinations of them, into account, sometimes arranging them in a preference order'.

In the present example, his discussion of reputation, performance and appearance could arguably not only help us to make further sense of whether or not Paul trusted his players, but also the coaching staff mentioned in his stories. According to Sztompka (1999: 71), reputation refers to 'the record of past deals'. He goes on to explain that this can include second-hand information (i.e. stories, testimonials) and first-hand experiences about whether or not a person's previous conduct towards others and him/herself was in breach of trust. In the present example, the actions of Darren and Daniel obviously contributed towards Paul's distrusting them. Similarly, Paul's having overheard David's negative critique of his tactical strategising to some of the players, parents and committee members equally caused him to question whether he could trust his assistant coach or not in the future. In both cases, Paul's first-hand experiences were consistent with the information he had acquired from other parties regarding the trustworthiness of these individuals. In this respect, Sztompka (1999) suggested that a crucial metacharacteristic when estimating another person's reputation is the consistency of conduct over time. In the context of Paul's narrative, the information that he had obtained from secondary sources led him to assess whether the conduct that he had witnessed was in line with or out of keeping with their character. Alternatively, the past and present conduct of players such as Warren, Karl and Tim obviously positively contributed towards Paul's deciding to trust them at this important time. Likewise, John's continued exemplary conduct led Paul to trust this member of his coaching team implicitly. This was in keeping with the reputation that John had within the club setting.

Paul's discussion of Chad, the new player from the USA, could be understood in relation to Sztompka's discussion of performance. Sztompka (1999: 77) defined performance, as the 'actual deeds, present conduct, currently obtained results'. Importantly for Sztompka, performance relates to instances when the 'past is suspended, "bracketed", and one focuses on what the potential beneficiary of trust is doing now' (ibid.). Consistent with Sztompka's analysis, Paul's inability to access information relating to Chad's past performances and behaviours as a player led him to make judgements based upon his perceptions of Chad's actions within and around the present coaching setting.

Sztompka's discussion of appearance is particularly useful for making sense of Paul's increasing distrust of Seamus. Sztompka (1999) used the term to capture those instances when cues relating to appearance and demeanour are used to estimate the trustworthiness of others. In this regard, Sztompka suggested that there are three central features to trust that relate to external characteristics. These are personality, identity and status. Paul's narrative illustrated how he had concerns regarding Seamus' bodily discipline and manners. It is apparent that he was continually appraising not only Seamus' coaching practice, but also the way that he presented himself and interacted with others. In this respect, Paul was concerned with Seamus' seeming inability to arrive wearing clean training kit. Indeed, Paul felt that Seamus' attire often looked unprofessional and therefore gave the wrong message to the players and parents. Furthermore, Paul was equally unhappy with Seamus's body language and curt responses to parents, which were not of the standard of coaching behaviour that Paul expected.

Sztompka's (1999) notion of anticipatory trust and discussion of reflected trustworthiness might also assist with making sense of Paul's appraisal of the Club Chairman. In his narrative, Paul clearly distrusted the Club Chairman, a decision that resulted from his having critically considered a number of reports and instances. Paul had learnt through various sources within the game that the Club Chairman was far from happy with Paul's appointment. In addition to this, Paul's dealings with the Club Chairman were difficult from the start of his appointment. Paul started to question whether the Club Chairman's dislike of him explained why his team seemed to be treated differently from the other squads at the club. These concerns were later confirmed when he unintentionally overheard the Club Chairman publically criticising his coaching following what Paul considered to be a promising performance. It is perhaps unsurprising that, following these experiences, Paul somewhat distrusted anything the Club Chairman had to say. This included his 'best wishes' to the team before they travelled to the competition.

In addition to looking at the trust relationships that existed between Paul, the players, coaches and the Club Chairman, we could also consider the trust culture that 'housed' these interactions. The trust culture, or system of rules that relate to the granting, returning and reciprocating of trust and trustworthiness, could be a powerful factor influencing decisions to trust and to reciprocate trust (Sztompka 1999). Consideration of this culture could help us to understand why Paul believed the sporting subculture in which he was operating was 'low trust'.

Sztompka (1999) proposed five macro-societal circumstances that contribute to the emergence of a trust culture: *normative coherence, stability, familiarity, transparency* and *accountability*. While normative coherence, which occurs at the societal level, is less relevant in Paul's narrative, the other circumstances are useful to consider. First, Sztompka (1999) contends that trust cultures develop when people feel a sense of security, support and comfort (i.e. stability) so that meeting obligations and reciprocating trust becomes a habitual response. In contrast, Paul felt that the sporting subculture was characterised by degrees of selfishness and ruthlessness, which rarely contribute to trust. Second, Sztompka (1999) identified familiarity as important in the emergence of a trust culture, as it provides one with feelings of certainty and predictability that breeds trust. However, if the subculture is characterised by feelings of insecurity and uncertainty, as Paul described, trust is unlikely to develop (Sztompka 1999). Furthering this distrust was the lack of transparency within the football club as some coaches were given choice and flexibility in relation to training kit, equipment and venues, while others (i.e. Paul) were not. As Sztompka (1999) attests, transparency encourages trust. The final circumstance that contributes to a trust culture is accountability. This allows people to feel confident that standards will be observed and abuse will be corrected (Sztompka 1999). In addition to providing a sense of confidence, accountability could contribute to the circumstances of stability, familiarity and transparency. An examination of these factors is useful as, we believe, micro-level dealings cannot be understood fully without acknowledging the macro-level factors that create the foundation for such interaction.

Finally, it would seem important to acknowledge that, 'one can never be certain of the outcome that making the bet of trust will bring' (Sztompka 1999: 33). Sztompka (ibid.) points out that, while 'risk is always present', some bets are prudent and others are imprudent. In an attempt to try and make his bets more prudent, Paul ultimately decided to take to the tournament only those players and coaching staff who he believed that he could trust implicitly. While Warren, Karl and Tim 'made the plane', Darren and Daniel did not. Paul was not willing to take the risk of selecting these arguably more gifted, but ultimately less reliable, players. In terms of his coaching staff, John was rewarded for his hard efforts by being asked to attend the competition as Paul's assistant. In contrast, Paul was ultimately happy at the decision to not bring David and Seamus along, as he thought that they might 'show him up' and resultantly cause the national selectors to view him in a less than positive light. A couple of weeks before the tournament, David and Seamus were both relieved of their coaching duties with the team. David confirmed Paul's concerns by publically questioning his chosen formation; Seamus reinforced Paul's judgements by attending a training session while intoxicated with alcohol. At that point, Paul had lost all faith in them. Paul's relationship with the Club Chairman remained the same. Neither of them trusted or respected each other; in spite of this, they continued to work together. In the end, Paul, John and a trusted squad of 18 players attended the tournament. This was Paul's way of managing the situation as best as he could. Ultimately, however, Paul had to trust these individuals. While his past interactions with each of these persons suggested to him that he could and should trust them, ultimately it was a risk and one that had the potential to end positively or negatively in terms of his own personal needs, expectations and interests.

Conclusion

The principal aim of this chapter was to illustrate the potential value of considering the notions of trust and distrust within the coaching literature. Given that 'trust makes social life possible' (Weber and Carter 2003: 1) and is 'the foundation of effective relationships' (Reina and Reina 2006: x), it would seem necessary for future research to illuminate and better understand the dynamics of trust within coaching settings. Indeed, while the issue of trust has been alluded to in recent coaching research (e.g. Jones *et al.* 2005; Potrac and Jones 2009a; Purdy *et al.* 2008; Purdy and Jones 2011), there has been little direct examination of these issues in the coaching literature. Coaching researchers may also wish to develop in-depth and critical understandings of distrust in coaching, as 'the culture of distrust is typically dysfunctional' as it 'prevents co-operation and destroys community' (Sztompka 1999: 112). An examination of this topic would seem warranted, especially when acknowledging that research into the social dynamics of coaching (e.g. Gearity and Murray 2011; Gould *et al.* 1999; Jones *et al.* 2005; Jowett and Cockerill 2002, 2003; Jowett 2005; Potrac and Jones 2009b; Purdy and Jones 2011) have indirectly hinted towards the fact that a culture of distrust can 'limit the pool of potential partners for interaction and discourages the initiation of interactions' (Sztompka 1999: 112) and lead to a social climate that is characterised by 'obsessive paranoiac cynicism' (ibid.).

As trust and distrust are concepts that cannot be easily observed or defined (Lyon *et al.* 2012), qualitative methods might be initially suitable in shedding light on how the two concepts are defined, developed, employed, maintained, damaged and repaired in the coaching process. As such, narrative-biographical interviewing, ethnographic studies and auto-ethnographic work could provide valuable tools to help us explore the trust relationships that exist between coach, player and other key contextual stakeholders. For example, at the micro-level of practice we know very little about the social processes through which coaches and athletes come to trust or distrust each other and the resultant consequences. Equally, little focus has been paid to the involvement and influence of the administrators, directors and parents in the daily work of coaches and athletes, and how trust and distrust between these individuals impacts on working relationships. Indeed, a potentially fruitful line of inquiry is in production of polyvocal accounts (Spindler and Hammond 2006) that consider the role of each of these parties in relation to the development or constraining of a trust culture.

Finally, it is important to note that, while we have paid exclusive attention to the potential utility of Sztompka's (1999) social treatise on trust to start making sense of trust and distrust in coaching, we are by no means advocating his work as the singularly 'best' or, indeed, 'only' way to theoretically explore and understand these notions. His work represents just one of a range of social theories that could be utilised to guide our research efforts in coaching. As such, we would suggest that scholars consider the applicability of alternative frameworks of trust and distrust that have been developed by Hardin (2002), Hoy and Tschannen-Moran (1999), Luhmann (1979) and Mistzal (1996). We believe that an engagement with these existing theories on trust and distrust might allow us, in the long term, to develop our own conceptual and theoretical understandings of these issues in coaching.

References

Bies, R.J. and Tripp, T.M. (1996) 'Beyond distrust: "Getting even" and the need for revenge', in R.M. Kramer and T.R. Tyler (eds) *Trust in Organizations*, Thousand Oaks, CA: Sage.

Bourdieu, P. (1989) 'Social space and symbolic power', *Sociological Theory*, 7(1): 14–25.

Burke, C.S., Sims, D.E., Lazzara, E.H. and Salas, E. (2007) 'Trust in leadership: A multi-level review and integration', *Leadership Quarterly*, 18(6): 606–632.

Butler Jr, J.K. and Cantrell, R.S. (1984) 'A behavioral decision theory approach to modeling dyadic trust in superiors and subordinates', *Psychological Reports*, 55(1): 19–28.

Cushion, C.J. and Jones, R.L. (2006) 'Power, discourse and symbolic violence in professional youth soccer: The case of Albion F.C.', *Sociology of Sport Journal*, 23(2): 142–161.

Dirks, K.T. and Ferrin, D.L. (2001) 'The role of trust in organizational settings', *Organisation Science*, 12(4): 450–467.

Foucault, M. (1980) *Power/Knowledge: Selected Interviews and Other Writings*, New York: Pantheon.

Foucault, M. (1982) 'Afterword: The subject and power', in H.L. Dreyfus and P. Rabinow (eds) *Michel Foucault: Beyond Structuralism and Hermeneutics*, Chicago, IL: University of Chicago Press.

Foucault, M. (1991) *Discipline and Punish: The Birth of the Prison*, London: Penguin.

French Jr, J.R.P. and Raven, B. (1959) 'The basis of social power', in D. Cartwright (ed.) *Studies in Social Power*, Ann Arbor, MI: University of Michigan Press.

Gearity, B.T. and Murray, M.A. (2011) 'Athletes' experiences of the psychological effects of poor coaching', *Psychology of Sport and Exercise*, 12(3): 213–221.

Gilbert, J.A. and Tang, L.-P.T. (1998) 'An examination of organizational trust antecedents', *Public Personnel Management*, 27(3): 321–338.

Goffman, E. (1959) *The Presentation of Self in Everyday Life*, Garden City, NY: Doubleday.

Gould, D., Guinan, D., Greenleaf, C., Medberry, R. and Peterson, K. (1999) 'Factors affecting Olympic performance: Perceptions of athletes and coaches from more and less successful teams', *The Sport Psychologist*, 13(4): 371–394.

Hardin, R. (2002) *Trust and Trustworthiness*, New York: Russell Sage Foundation.

Hoy, W.K. and Tschannen-Moran, M. (1999) 'The five faces of trust: An empirical confirmation in urban elementary schools', *Journal of School Leadership*, 9(3): 184–208.

Jones, R.L., Glintmeyer, N. and McKenzie, A. (2005) 'Slim bodies, eating disorders and the coach-athlete relationship: A tale of identity creation and disruption', *International Review for the Sociology of Sport*, 40(3): 377–391.

Jowett, S. (2005) 'On repairing and enhancing the coach–athlete relationship', in S. Jowett and M. Jones (eds) *The Psychology of Sport Coaching*, Leicester: The British Psychological Society Sport and Exercise Psychology Division.

Jowett, S. and Cockerill, I.M. (2002) 'Incompatibility in the coach–athlete relationship', in I.M. Cockerill (ed.) *Solutions in Sport Psychology*, London: Thomson Learning.

Jowett, S. and Cockerill, I.M. (2003) 'Olympic Medallists' perspective of the athlete–coach relationship', *Psychology of Sport and Exercise*, 4: 313–331.

Luhmann, N. (1979) *Trust and Power*, London: Wiley.

Lyon, F., Möllering, G. and Saunders, M.N.K. (2012) *Handbook of Research Methods on Trust*, Cheltenham: Edward Elgar.

Marks, M.A., Mathieu, J.E. and Zaccaro, S.J. (2001) 'A temporally based framework and taxonomy of team processes', *Academy of Management*, 26(3): 356–376.

Mistzal, B. (1996) *Trust in Modern Societies: The Search for the Bases of Social Order*, Cambridge: Polity Press.

Poczwardowski, A., Barott, J.E. and Henschen, K.P. (2002) 'The athlete and coach: Their relationship and its meaning – results of an interpretive study', *International Journal of Sport Psychology*, 33(1): 116–140.

Potrac, P. and Jones, R.L. (2009a) 'Power, conflict and co-operation: Towards a micro-politics of coaching', *Quest*, 61(2): 223–236.

Potrac, P. and Jones, R. (2009b) 'Micro-political workings in semi-professional football coaching', *Sociology of Sport Journal*, 26(4): 557–577.

Potrac, P., Jones, R.L. and Armour, K.M. (2002) ' "It's all about getting respect": The coaching behaviours of an expert English soccer coach', *Sport, Education and Society*, 7(2): 183–202.

Purdy, L., Potrac, P. and Jones, R.L. (2008) 'Power, consent and resistance: An autoethnography of competitive rowing', *Sport Education and Society*, 13(3): 319–336.

Purdy, L. and Jones, R.L. (2011) 'Choppy waters: Elite rowers' perceptions of coaching', *Sociology of Sport Journal*, 28(3): 329–346.

Reina, D.S. and Reina, M.L. (2006) *Trust and Betrayal in the Workplace*, San Francisco, CA: Barrett-Koehler.

Spindler, G. and Hammond, L. (2006) *Innovations in Educational Ethnography: Theory, Methods, and Results*, London: Routledge.

Sztompka, P. (1999) *Trust: A Sociological Theory*, Cambridge: Cambridge University Press.

Weber, L.R. and Carter, A.I. (2003) *The Social Construction of Trust*, New York: Kluwer.

26

EMPATHIC UNDERSTANDING AND ACCURACY IN THE COACH–ATHLETE RELATIONSHIP

Ross Lorimer

UNIVERSITY OF ABERTAY DUNDEE, UK

Sophia Jowett

LOUGHBOROUGH UNIVERSITY, UK

Introduction

In recent years, there has been an increasing appreciation of the coaching process as a complex social cognitive system. Although it can be argued that coaching practice is primarily concerned with teaching the skills, techniques, strategies, and tactics of the sport, it can also be argued that successful teaching depends on considering the ever-changing needs of athletes (Jones *et al.* 2010). Coaching is often defined by the nature and quality of interaction that occurs between coaches and athletes (Lyle 2002). Subsequently, considering the manner to which coaches interact with their athletes is vital in unravelling the complex social cognitive process of coaching.

An essential quality for effective interaction between coaches and athletes is the coach's ability to understand each athlete in their team or squad (Jones *et al.* 2004). It has been noted that the ability of coaches to understand each athlete allows them to be responsive to their athletes' specific needs (e.g. Jones and Cassidy 2004; Lyle 2002). For example, Lynch (2001: 35) refers to a coach's ability to 'ask yourself, what is this athlete feeling right now? [to] Try to understand and empathize with her position' as essential to successful coaching. Moreover, researchers have reported coaches' understanding as a central aspect of coaching philosophy and practice. In an analysis of forty interviews, Lyle (1999) reported that coaches highlighted mutual understanding as being one of the most important elements of their own coaching philosophies. In another study, where Jones *et al.* (2004) interviewed elite coaches, understanding emerged as a common theme and one elite football coach described his coaching practice as 'recognising the people and responding to the people you are working with' (18).

The notion of understanding within the coaching context would appear to be consistent with what is known as 'athlete-centred coaching' (Kidman 2005) and 'personal side of coaching' (Jowett 2005). On one hand, a key feature of the athlete-centred coaching is for coaches to understand their athletes in order to promote in them such capacities as self-awareness and regulation (e.g. taking ownership, becoming accountable). On the other hand, a key feature of the personal side of coaching is for coaches to appreciate the strengths and weaknesses of their athletes in order to prepare the ground for their self-actualisation (i.e. reaching their potential). Subsequently, both coaching approaches are underpinned by coaches' understanding with the specific aim to facilitate athletes' growth as self-reliant, disciplined, and successful individuals. While understanding may be viewed as a characteristic of the coach, understanding may be equally viewed as a characteristic of the relationship. Galipeau and Trudel (2006) have emphasised its importance in promoting the coordination of both the coach and the athlete's efforts and goals. Subsequently, shared understanding within the relationship may be as equally important as the coach's ability to understand the athlete.

The concept of understanding as an important dimension of effective and successful coaching has been the topic of much discussion over the years. Yet while there is consensus that understanding is beneficial for coaching and performance, there has been an observable gap in conceptualising, operationalising, and measuring this concept. The following discussion aims to clarify the terminology that describes this phenomenon and present recent conceptual and methodological issues associated with understanding within the coach–athlete dyad.

What is shared understanding?

An essential element of the coach–athlete partnership is the capacity of its members to interact effectively and successfully (Jowett and Poczwardowski 2007). It can be argued that the level of shared understanding between the coach and the athlete can play a vital role in their interactions. *Shared understanding* can be defined as coaches and athletes' capacity of accurately perceiving each others' feelings, thoughts, and behaviours. Shared understanding originates from acknowledging another's actions and reactions and recognising in as precise a way as possible the meanings they attach to them. Ultimately, shared understanding becomes a resource of information and knowledge that coaches and athletes can use to better manage their interactions and relationships.

The topic of shared understanding has both theoretical and practical significance. From a practical point of view, it is likely to help coaches and athletes 'be on the same page' and 'take the other's perspective'. Subsequently, a level of shared understanding within the coach–athlete partnership that concerns performance and relationship issues will improve their interactions, prevent conflict, and develop effective and successful partnerships/teams. From a theoretical point of view, the concept of shared understanding could further expand conceptual models including coach–athlete relationship and coach leadership models and thus contribute to the knowledge of social relationships and interactions. It is therefore important that researchers and practitioners have the tools (e.g. conceptual frameworks and measures) to examine shared understanding. Acknowledging the importance of the concept of shared understanding within the coaching context, two approaches have recently been put forward known as empathic understanding and empathic accuracy.

Empathic understanding within the 3+1Cs model

The 3+1 Cs conceptual model (Jowett 2007) was introduced to capture the quality of the coach–athlete relationship. This model defines the coach–athlete relationship as a situation in which the coach and athlete's feelings, thoughts, and behaviours are interdependent. The constructs of Closeness, Commitment and Complementarity form the first part of the model (i.e. 3Cs). Closeness reflects affective ties such as mutual trust, respect, appreciation, and liking. Commitment reflects their cognitive bond and dedication. Complementarity reflects co-operation and is characterised by mutual responses such as readiness, easiness, and friendliness. The construct of Co-orientation forms the second part of the model (i.e. +1C). Co-orientation attempts to unravel the nature of the interdependence within the relationship. It is within this part of the model that the concept of understanding, namely empathic understanding, resides.

Co-orientation incorporates the different interpersonal perspectives coaches and athletes are likely to take in perceiving the quality of the athletic relationship. Additionally, Co-orientation considers the interplay of these interpersonal perspectives. Overall, Co-orientation defines the degree to which coaches and athletes are co-oriented in the ways they view and understand the quality of their relationship (Jowett and Poczwardowski 2007).

The term Co-orientation was coined by Newcomb (1953), however, others (e.g. Acitelli *et al.* 2001; Laing *et al.* 1966) have referred to this notion using the terms such as common ground, mutual frame of reference, and agreement. Laing and colleagues (1966) explained that those involved in relationships can view their experiences from multiple perspectives and that a comparison of these perspectives can reveal how individuals perceive and understand each other. Guided by the method proposed by Laing *et al.* (1966), Jowett (2007) proposed that the quality of the coach–athlete relationship is shaped by two perspectives, the *direct-perspective* and the *meta-perspective*. The *direct-perspective* refers to coaches' and athletes' own perceptions about the quality of the relationship. For example, the direct-perspective is reflected in the following statements made by the coach and athlete respectively, 'I am committed to my athlete' and 'I am committed to my coach'. Conversely, the *meta-perspective* refers to coaches' and athletes' perceptions of their partners' views of the quality of the relationship. The meta-perspective is a form of perspective taking where the individual considers – based on past experiences – how the other feels, thinks, and behaves. For example, meta-perspective is reflected in the following statements made by the coach and the athlete respectively, 'My athlete is committed to me' and 'My coach is committed to me'.

The comparison of these two perspectives allows for the assessment of three dimensions of Co-orientation: (1) actual similarity (one's own direct-perception compared to other's direct-perception); (2) assumed similarity (one's own direct-perception compared to one's own meta-perception); and (3) empathic understanding (one's own meta-perception compared to other's direct-perception). Essentially each dimension of Co-orientation represents the congruence of the two perspectives being compared. Of the three dimensions, *empathic understanding* reflects the ability of coaches and athletes to accurately infer their partners' thoughts, feelings, and behaviours toward himself or herself. Thus, empathic understanding can be said to be an assessment of the degree to which the coach and athlete understand each other.

The construct of Co-orientation has been explored in a series of qualitative studies by Jowett and colleagues (Jowett 2003; Jowett and Cockerill 2003; Jowett and Frost 2007; Jowett and Meek 2000; Jowett and Timson-Katchis 2005). Findings suggested that both coaches and athletes viewed Co-orientation positively (e.g. 'One of her qualities was that she made us feel she understood us' extract from Jowett and Cockerill 2003) while viewing a lack of understanding negatively (e.g. '[the coach] did not understand how I felt and he pushed me, something I could not tolerate at the time' extract from Jowett 2003), while those coaches and athletes failing to grasp each other's purpose or meaning were more likely to experience interpersonal conflict, power struggles, and a sense of incompatibility (Jowett 2003; Jowett and Cockerill 2003; Jowett and Frost 2007). Furthermore, these studies show that coaches and athletes' knowledge of each other allowed them to more easily 'read' as well as more appropriately act and react to each other.

The construct of Co-orientation within the 3+1Cs conceptual model of the coach–athlete relationship has also been studied and measured quantitatively via self-report measures. These self-report measures assess the quality of the coach–athlete relationship as operationalised by the 3Cs from both a direct- (Jowett and Ntoumanis 2004) and a meta-perspective (Jowett 2009). Thus, all three dimensions of Co-orientation including empathic understanding can be assessed. A number of studies have been conducted to investigate the direct- and the meta-perspectives of the 3Cs. However, the majority of these studies have focused on investigating a single perspective rather than their possible combinations. For example, in Adie and Jowett (2010), athletes' meta-perspective (i.e. thoughts about their coaches' respect and trust as well as commitment and responsiveness and support toward them) predicted the adoption of a mastery approach goal (i.e. task or self-referenced performance goals) which in turn promoted athletes' intrinsic motivation. In addition, it has been found that both direct- and meta-perspectives independently link to the coach-created motivational climate (Olympiou *et al.* 2005), harmonious passion for sport (Lafrenière *et al.* 2008), and athletes' level of satisfaction (Jowett and Don Carolis 2003). Overall, this research has indicated that positive direct- and meta-perspectives are associated with a range of benefits. However, to investigate the construct of Co-orientation and more specifically empathic understanding, research designs must allow for comparisons between coaches' *and* athletes' direct- *and* meta-perspectives.

In their study, Jowett and Clark-Carter (2006) focused on examining the proportion of empathic understanding of coach–athlete dyads. They collected data from 121 coach–athlete dyads who participated in individual sports. Athletes and coaches recorded their direct- and meta-perspectives of Closeness, Commitment, and Complementarity. The results indicated that the dyads had a level of understanding about one another's points of view as these pertain to the quality of the relationship. There were no observed differences in the abilities of the coach and athlete to accurately understand each other's commitment and complementarity, yet athletes seemed more capable of accurately understanding the closeness of their coach. Furthermore, athletes in moderately developed relationships (six months to two years) were more capable of understanding the content of their coaches' commitment and complementarity than athletes in more established relationships. This suggests that coaches and athletes who had worked together longer seemed to understand each other less well, perhaps because they made more habitual inferences or made assumptions about their partner based on out-dated knowledge of them.

Co-orientation and the concept of empathic understanding are extremely important for the exploration of the coach–athlete relationship. It provides an intuitive conceptualisation of 'understanding' and situates this construct within a model of the coach–athlete relationship. The self-report measures developed to assess the direct and meta-perspective of both coaches' and athletes' 3Cs (Jowett and Ntoumanis 2004; Jowett 2009) on one hand enables researchers to assess among others the dimension of empathic understanding relative to important outcomes and on the other hand enables practitioners to diagnose areas of understanding and misunderstanding. Co-orientation and its dimension of empathic understanding is a potential key factor in the success and effectiveness of the coach–athlete relationship.

Empathic accuracy within the dyadic interaction paradigm

The most important forum for the coach–athlete relationship to develop and flourish is arguably the training environment; it is during periods of practice that coaches and athletes primarily interact. The ability of coaches and athletes to interact successfully in these sessions is likely to directly impact upon the effectiveness of the athletes' training and their ongoing development. However, while the measurement of empathic understanding as conceptualised within the 3+1 Cs model provides an insight into the understanding between coaches and athletes' perspectives of each other regarding the quality of their relationship it does not allow for the assessment of how coaches and athletes understand each other moment-to-moment during training. This capacity to perceive, from one moment to the next, the thoughts, feelings, and intentions of another is known as *empathic accuracy* and is thought of as a vital element in successful social interaction (Ickes *et al.* 1990). This section aims to discuss this different approach to the study of shared understanding in coach–athlete dyads.

Ickes (1993), a social psychologist, has argued the importance of shared understanding in two-person relationships and has developed assessments that capture the degree to which moment-to-moment understanding is accurate. Empathic accuracy is described as the accuracy of ongoing moment-to-moment inferences regarding the psychological state of another individual. To assess empathic accuracy Ickes *et al.* (1990) proposed a procedure known as 'the dyadic interaction paradigm'. In this procedure, two individuals are unobtrusively filmed while interacting in a social setting. Afterwards, both individuals are asked to independently review the recording of their interaction. They are asked to stop the video whenever they remember specific thoughts or feelings they were having during that interaction, and to record both these and the time at which they occurred. In this way they build up a chronological record of their thoughts and feelings during the recorded interaction. Subsequently, the individuals are asked to watch the recording again. This time the video is stopped for them at the time points where their partner had indicated remembering a specific thought or feeling. The individual's task is then to make an empathic inference, and to write down what they believe their partner reported thinking and feeling at that point. Empathic accuracy is then determined by comparing each individual's self-reported thoughts and feelings with their partner's empathic inference and scoring them based upon their congruence; a team of independent raters assess the similarity of each pairing of inferences and self-reports and an average score for each individual is calculated.

Recently Lorimer and Jowett (2009a) have applied 'the dyadic interaction paradigm' to the context of coach–athlete interaction. They moved the video recording out of the laboratory and into real life events, in this case the training environment. During filming coaches wore a small lapel microphone that allowed coach–athlete conversations to be remotely recorded onto the videotape while the actual video footage was recorded from an unobtrusive position. As training sessions varied in length and were often far longer than the brief discussions used in previous empathic accuracy research each video recording was uploaded to a computer and reviewed and a representative sample of discrete coach–athlete interactions were randomly selected as follows: 20 per cent of the sample was selected from the first third of the footage (usually the warm up), 50 per cent from the middle (main training session), and 30 per cent from the final section (usually the cool down and conclusion). As proposed by Ickes *et al.* (1990), these interactions were then viewed by the participants who reported what they remembered thinking and feeling at each point and then were asked to make inferences about what their partners had thought and felt at each point. Accuracy was then calculated by comparing the similarity of participants' self-reports and inferences. To date, Lorimer and Jowett have applied this procedure in four studies (2009a, 2009b, 2010a, 2011) investigating empathic accuracy in sports coaching.

Lorimer and Jowett (2009a) found that the empathic accuracy of coaches and athletes is influenced by a variety of situational characteristics such as the size of the group of athletes a coach works with, the type of sport, and the length of training sessions. Their results indicated that accuracy for coaches was lower when working with larger groups of athletes and that coaches working in individual sports displayed greater accuracy than coaches in team sports. They also found that while the differences in group size did not explain the differences observed between individual and team sports that the shared cognitive focus of coaches and athletes (the similarity of their thoughts and feelings during each interaction) was lower in team sports relative to individual sports, and that this fully mediated the effect of sport-type on coach empathic accuracy. This suggests that the interaction between coaches and athletes in individual sports is different compared to team sports; with coaches in individual sports working individually with athletes in each group while coaches in team sports generally address the group as a whole. Additionally, Lorimer and Jowett (2009a) found that coaches whose training sessions were longer demonstrated increased empathic accuracy.

Further correlates of empathic accuracy were examined by Lorimer and Jowett (2009b) who measured how positively coaches and athletes believed their partner perceived them and their relationship using the meta version of the CART-Q and also assessed their satisfaction with their training and personal treatment by their partner. Results showed that empathic accuracy was significantly associated with the positive perceptions coaches and athletes hold about their relationship and with the satisfaction they had with the training being provided. This would seem to indicate that increased empathic accuracy does lead to positive relationship outcomes and therefore a more successful and effective coach–athlete relationship.

Lorimer and Jowett (2010a) investigated the influence of the coaches and athletes' roles and gender on empathic accuracy. They found that female coaches were more accurate than male coaches. Additionally, for athletes, the highest accuracy scores were displayed by female athletes working with male coaches, and the least by female athletes working with female coaches. It is a popular stereotype that women possess a greater insight and sensitivity into the feelings of others than men (Ickes *et al.* 2000). However it has been suggested that the traditional subordinate status of women in society, that placed them under the authority of others, may have led them to exhibit greater empathic accuracy which has in turn led to this stereotype; suggesting any differences in gender are primarily one of perceived authority (Snodgrass 1985). A female athlete with a male coach is not only in a position of subordination as an athlete but as a female resulting in increased motivation to make accurate empathic inferences about her coach.

Finally, Lorimer and Jowett (2011), using the interpersonal perception model proposed by Kenny and Acitelli (2001), examined empathic accuracy, shared cognitive focus, and assumed similarity (the congruence of a participant's own self-reported thoughts and feelings and their inference about their partner's thoughts and feelings). The results indicated a significant association between shared cognitive focus and empathic accuracy for both coaches and athletes. This relationship was significantly mediated by assumed similarity suggesting that a shared cognitive focus increases empathic accuracy and that this association is at least in part due to coaches and athletes recognising this similarity exists.

An adapted procedure known as 'standard stimulus' has also been proposed and applied in counselling to examine the empathic accuracy of counsellors (Marangoni *et al.* 1995). This adapted procedure is identical in that it involves the filming of naturalistic interactions between individuals who are then asked to watch the video and report the specific thoughts and feelings they remember having. However, following this the video recording and self-reported thoughts and feelings are then used as the stimulus materials for other observers. The video can be shown to multiple observers who were not involved in the interaction, and the criterion for accuracy is the self-reported thoughts and feelings of those actually depicted in the recordings. This alternate procedure additionally allows the comparison of participants to be made and is therefore more suited to exploring the individual factors of both observers and targets that affect accuracy.

To date only a single study has applied this 'standard stimulus' design in a sport setting. Lorimer and Jowett (2010b) investigated changes in the empathic accuracy of badminton coaches over the duration of watching a video of an athlete's technical training session with her coach. Additionally, they split the coaches into two groups with one set of coaches being given corrective feedback on the athlete's thoughts and feelings following each inference they made. They found that the empathic accuracy of both groups of coaches improved over the course of watching the video but that the group receiving feedback improved significantly more than the group that received none. This would seem to indicate the empathic accuracy of coaches significantly improves as the amount of information on which to base an inference increases, either in response to ongoing observation or feedback.

Empathic understanding and empathic accuracy approaches

This chapter presents two possible approaches for the investigation of shared understanding in coach–athlete dyads in the context of sports; empathic understanding and empathic accuracy. The 'empathic understanding' approach allows for the measurement of coaches and athletes' understanding of how they generally feel, think, and act towards each other and is an indicator of the quality of their relationship. The 'empathic accuracy' approach allows for the measurement of coaches and athletes' understanding of how they think and feel moment-to-moment and is an indicator of the quality of their moment-to-moment interactions. Both approaches underline the role and significance of shared understanding within the context of sport coaching. While they take different approaches they are not mutually exclusive concepts and are likely in fact to be interdependent; an increase in moment-to-moment understanding in individual training sessions (empathic accuracy) may improve coaches and athletes' understanding of each other and their relationship (empathic understanding) and vice versa.

Jowett (2007) has highlighted the nature of coaching as a partnership that is reflected in the coach–athlete relationship, a relationship in which its members are mutually and causally interdependent. Therefore any investigation into the coaching process must acknowledge the dyadic nature of that process and consider both the interdependent contributions of the coach and the athlete. The approaches proposed in this chapter for the investigation of shared understanding in the coach–athlete relationship highlight the benefits of assessing both the coaches' and athletes' perspectives and so underlines that future researchers would benefit from utilising similar dyadic analytical methods.

Each approach has its own benefits and limitations; the empathic accuracy approach has several advantages, being both temporally extended and allowing participants to form complex and detailed inferences of their own as opposed to selecting responses from a limited list. However, despite being a powerful tool, it is time and labour intensive in comparison to the relatively straight forward methodology for assessing empathic understanding proposed by Jowett and colleagues. Empathic accuracy allows the interdependence of participants' inferences to be more fully explored; the perceiver is actually involved in the interaction, and individuals can react to each other and play an active role. While empathic understanding has the benefit of allowing researchers to investigate coaches and athletes' long-term perspectives regarding their athletic partnership, providing insight into how they perceive their relationship with each other beyond just individual training sessions which may provide a prejudiced view depending on specific circumstances.

Each of these two approaches therefore provides an additional method for the continued exploration of a variety of vital components of successful and effective coach–athlete interaction and relationships. Each offers its own benefits and limitations that need to be considered in light of the nature of the investigation being carried out. Hence, any future investigations must carefully consider the aims and objectives of that research before deciding on what approach to take.

Future research

While the findings presented above show how knowledge of the coach–athlete relationship is continuously advancing, it is evident that there is much more work that remains to be done. There are several key questions that need to be addressed and there are various lines of enquiry open to future researchers.

There already exists an expansive body of work that has explored coach behaviours employing coach leadership models (Smith and Smoll 2007). Establishing how empathic understanding and empathic accuracy independently and together affect how these behaviours are manifested, and hence the effectiveness of the work carried out in training sessions by coaches and athletes, is a future priority as this will have a direct impact on athletes' development and performance.

Another important direction/area for future research is establishing links between empathic understanding and empathic accuracy and the desired outcomes of the coach and athlete. While the outcome generally of most interest to coaches, athletes, and others in sport is performance, establishing the link between these approaches and performance is not an easy task. Performance itself is very difficult to measure directly and objectively, especially in mixed sport samples. Researchers may find it easier then to establish links between shared understanding, empathic understanding and/or empathic accuracy and other factors potentially associated with performance. These include intrapersonal factors like self-efficacy (Moritz *et al.* 2000) and anxiety (Kleine 1990), and interpersonal factors such as collective efficacy (Shearer *et al.* 2009) and team cohesion (Mullen and Copper 1994).

The empathic understanding approach has the advantage of allowing researchers to assess the quality of the coach–athlete relationship. It may be advantageous then to look at how empathic understanding changes over time using a longitudinal design. This has the benefit of allowing researchers to investigate links between empathic understanding and long-term goals such as improvements in performance, sport commitment, or changes over time in such factors as coaching efficacy and team cohesion. While cross-sectional designs have shown differences between new and established coach–athlete dyads in levels of both empathic understanding (Jowett and Clark-Carter 2006) and empathic accuracy (Lorimer and Jowett 2009a) longitudinal designs would allow researchers to establish how and when these changes occur as well as exploring possible interventions and training methods.

The empathic accuracy approach allows for the investigation of actual moment-to-moment interaction and allows researchers to look at individual training sessions in more depth. Previous findings have shown that dyads who have longer training sessions display higher levels of empathic accuracy (Lorimer and Jowett 2009a). Yet it is not known whether such factors as who initiated the interaction and what type of exchange (e.g. social, instruction, encouragement, punitive), affect coaches' and athletes' empathic accuracy. Particularly important may be exploring individual factors that could potentially influence these moment-to-moment interactions such as coaching style, personal expectations, and motivations.

While a relatively new area of investigation in coaching and the coach–athlete relationship, the concepts of empathic understanding and empathic accuracy have a long history of investigation in the field of social psychology. However, many unanswered questions remain. Hence, not only does the exploration of empathic understanding and empathic accuracy offer a potentially important insight into coaching, the exploration of those processes within that relationship will also increase researchers' understanding of empathy as a whole.

Practical applications

Based on theory and research, it can be suggested that in order for coaches and athletes to increase their shared understanding they should be encouraged to actively attempt to understand each other. Perhaps the easiest way to facilitate this is by looking for ways by which they can improve their communication. Communication is an essential interpersonal skill and fundamental in the forming and maintenance of any relationship. It is the process by which coaches and athletes actively exchange information (LaVoi 2007).

Rhind and Jowett (2010) have shown that the type (e.g. dialogue, monologue), volume (e.g. how much), and frequency (e.g. how often) of communication is linked to the quality of the coach–athlete relationship as defined by the 3+1Cs model. Additionally, Lorimer and Jowett (2010b) have shown that the empathic accuracy of coaches significantly improves as the amount of information on which to base an inference also increases. Communication also allows coaches and athletes to maintain a degree of congruence in their perspectives. Lorimer and Jowett (2009a; 2011) have shown that a similarity in thoughts and feelings increases empathic accuracy, while Jowett (2007) suggests that a similarity in coaches and athletes' views of their relationship is an indicator of relationship quality.

It can be argued that communication underpins empathic understanding and empathic accuracy, in turn leading to a more effective coach–athlete relationship. This exchange of information via communication helps coaches and athletes establish common ground, mutual goals, and objectives, and hence leads to increased empathic understanding and empathic accuracy, furthering the development of a shared understanding (LaVoi 2007; Lorimer and Jowett 2010b).

Rhind and Jowett (2010) have proposed the COMPASS model as a way of helping coaches and athletes develop and maintain their relationship. Standing for Conflict management, Openness, Motivation, Preventative, Assurance, Support, and Social networks, COMPASS is a series of guidelines and strategies that can be implemented by coaches and athletes. Underpinning these guidelines is a strong need for communication.

Rhind and Jowett (2010) suggest that coaches and athletes need to be open about their feelings and opinions and foster a social element to their relationship that allows them to interact beyond just technical instruction, taking the time to develop the relationship in a way that allows them to work more effectively together. They suggest that not only does this allow for an increased shared understanding but this in turn acts as a preventative method of addressing potential conflict. Therefore opportunities should be provided to enhance communication by altering the dynamics of the training session, such as encouraging more feedback, asking more questions, and engaging in dialogue during training sessions. This may also mean taking time outside training sessions, lengthening those sessions, or attempting to do less in the session to allow for conversation and interaction within the allotted time.

Coaches and athletes should also be encouraged to give time over to actively considering themselves and each other, both during and outside of training sessions. This can potentially improve their self-awareness and lead to improvements in their understanding of themselves and each other, and hence an increase in their empathic understanding and empathic accuracy. For example coaches could make a point to ask for feedback at regular intervals: not only would this make more information on athletes' thoughts and feelings available to the coach, but it may help the coach and the athlete focus on the topic at hand, increasing their congruence as well as allowing coaches to check their own understanding of their athletes.

Coaches should also be attentive to the verbal and non-verbal cues given by their athletes. They must not assume that because an athlete, situation or context is similar to one previously encountered, that athletes will react in the same or similar fashion as before. This does not mean that experience and prior knowledge are not useful to a coach in aiding their understanding of an athlete. However, coaches must be aware of the limitations of such knowledge and that similar situations are not necessarily the same. Hence, an open communication between coaches and athletes is crucial.

Concluding remarks

Empathic understanding and empathic accuracy are still relatively new fields of investigation in sports coaching. While established in social psychology they are an innovative approach to the growing field of study investigating coach–athlete interactions. Although only a handful of studies have currently employed these paradigms in sport, they have shown that understanding as conceptualised as empathic understanding and empathic accuracy can be assessed in the coach–athlete relationship and in actual coach–athlete training sessions. Additionally, these paradigms offer an interesting possibility for coach development and self-reflection. These paradigms then offer a solution to the confusion surrounding the concept of 'understanding' between coaches and athletes in the coaching process; providing both a coherent conceptualisation and also appropriate tools of measurement that allow them to be assessed and investigated. As such these paradigms will be employed in future investigations to generate valuable insights to further expand our knowledge and understanding in this complex yet exciting area of research.

References

Acitelli, L.K., Kenny, D.A. and Weiner, D. (2001) 'The importance of similarity of partners' marital ideal to relationship satisfaction', *Personal Relationships*, 8: 167–185.

Adie, J.W. and Jowett, S. (2010) 'Meta-perceptions of the coach-athlete relationship, achievement goals and intrinsic motivation among sport participants', *Journal of Applied Social Psychology*, 40: 2750–2773.

Galipeau, J. and Trudel, P. (2006) 'Athlete learning in a community of practice', in R.L. Jones (ed.) *The Sports Coach as Educator: Re-conceptualising Sports Coaching*, Abingdon: Routledge.

Ickes, W. (1993) 'Empathic accuracy', *Journal of Personality*, 61: 587–610.

Ickes, W., Gesn, P.R. and Graham, T. (2000) 'Gender differences in empathic accuracy: differential ability or differential motivation?' *Personal Relationships*, 7: 95–109.

Ickes, W., Stinson, L., Bissonnette, V. and Garcia, S. (1990) 'Naturalistic social cognition: empathic accuracy in mixed-sex dyads', *Journal of Personality and Social Psychology*, 59: 730–742.

Jones, R., Armour, K. and Potrac, P. (2004) *Sports Coaching Cultures*, London: Routledge.

Jones, R., Bowes, M. and Kingston, K. (2010) 'Complex practice in coaching: studying the chaotic nature of coach–athlete interactions', in J. Lyle and C. Cushion (eds) *Sports Coaching: Professionalisation and Practice*, London: Churchill Livingstone/Elsevier.

Jones, R. and Cassidy, T. (2004) *Understanding Sports Coaching: The Social, Cultural and Pedagogical Foundations of Coaching Practice*, London: Routledge.

Jowett, S. (2003) 'When the honeymoon is over: a case study of a coach-athlete relationship in crisis', *The Sport Psychologist*, 17: 444–460.

Jowett, S. (2005) 'On repairing and enhancing the coach–athlete relationship', in S. Jowett and M. Jones (eds) *The Psychology of Coaching*, Sport and Exercise Psychology Division, Leicester: The British Psychological Society, pp. 14–26).

Jowett, S. (2007) 'Interdependence analysis and the 3+1Cs in the coach-athlete relationship', in S. Jowett and D. Lavallee (eds) *Social Psychology in Sport*, Champaign, IL: Human Kinetics.

Jowett, S. (2009) 'Validating coach–athlete relationship measures with the nomological network', *Measurement in Physical Education and Exercise Science*, 13: 34–51.

Jowett, S. and Clark-Carter, D. (2006) 'Perceptions of empathic accuracy and assumed similarity in the coach–athlete relationship', *British Journal of Social Psychology*, 45: 617–637.

Jowett, S. and Cockerill, I.M. (2003) 'Olympic Medallists' perspective of the athlete-coach relationship', *Psychology of Sport and Exercise*, 4: 313–331.

Jowett, S. and Don Carolis, G. (2003) 'The coach-athlete relationship and perceived satisfaction in team sports', in R. Stelter (ed.) *XIth European Congress of Sport Psychology Proceedings*, Copenhagen: Det Samfundsvidenskabelige Fakultets.

Jowett, S. and Frost, T.C. (2007) 'Race/ethnicity in the all-male coach-athlete relationship: black footballers' narratives', *International Journal of Sport and Exercise Psychology*, 3: 255–269

Jowett, S. and Meek, G.A. (2000) 'The coach-athlete relationship in married couples: an exploratory content analysis', *The Sport Psychologist*, 14: 157–175.

Jowett, S. and Ntoumanis, N. (2004) 'The Coach-Athlete Relationship Questionnaire (CART-Q): development and initial validation', *Scandinavian Journal of Medicine and Science in Sports*, 14: 245–257.

Jowett, S. and Poczwardowski, A. (2007) 'Understanding the coach-athlete relationship', in S. Jowett and D. Lavallee (eds) *Social Psychology in Sport*, Champaign, IL: Human Kinetics.

Jowett, S. and Timson-Katchis, M. (2005) 'Social networks in the sport context: the influence of parents on the coach-athlete relationship', *The Sport Psychologist*, 19: 267–287.

Kenny, D.A. and Acitelli, L.K. (2001) 'Accuracy and bias in the perception of the partner in a close relationship', *Journal of Personality and Social Psychology*, 80: 439–448.

Kidman, L. (2005) *Athlete-centred Coaching: Developing Inspired and Inspiring People*, Christchurch: Innovative.

Kleine, D. (1990) 'Anxiety and sport performance: a meta-analysis', *Anxiety, Stress and Coping*, 2: 113–131.

Lafrenière, M.K., Jowett, S., Vallerand, R.J., Donahue, E.G. and Lorimer, R. (2008) 'Passion in sport: on the quality of the coach-athlete relationship', *Journal of Sport and Exercise Psychology*, 30: 541–560.

Laing, R.D., Phillipson, H. and Lee, A.R. (1966) *Interpersonal Perception: A Theory and a Method of Research*, New York: Harper & Row.

LaVoi, N.M. (2007) 'Interpersonal communication and conflict in the coach-athlete relationship', in S. Jowett and D. Lavallee (eds) *Social Psychology in Sport*, Champaign, IL: Human Kinetics.

Lorimer, R. and Jowett, S. (2009a) 'Empathic accuracy in coach-athlete dyads who participate in team and individual sports', *Psychology of Sport and Exercise*, 10: 152–158.

Lorimer, R. and Jowett, S. (2009b), 'Empathic accuracy, meta-perspective, and satisfaction in the coach-athlete relationship', *Journal of Applied Sport Psychology*, 21: 1–12.

Lorimer, R. and Jowett, S. (2010a) 'The influence of role and gender in the empathic accuracy of coaches and athletes', *Psychology of Sport and Exercise*, 11: 206–211.

Lorimer, R. and Jowett, S. (2010b) 'Feedback of information in the empathic accuracy of sport coaches', *Psychology of Sport and Exercise*, 11: 12–17.

Lorimer, R. and Jowett, S. (2011) 'Empathic accuracy, shared cognitive focus, and the assumptions of similarity made by coaches and athletes', *International Journal of Sport Psychology*, 42: 40–54.

Lyle, J. (1999) 'Coaching philosophy and coaching behaviour', in N. Cross and J. Lyle (eds) *The Coaching Process: Principles and Practice for Sport*, Oxford: Butterworth-Heinemann.

Lyle, J. (2002) *Sports Coaching Concepts*, London: Routledge.

Lynch, J. (2001) *Creative Coaching*, Champaign, IL: Human Kinetics.

Marangoni, C., Garcia, S., Ickes, W. and Teng, G. (1995) 'Empathic accuracy in a clinically relevant setting', *Journal of Personality and Social Psychology*, 68: 854–869.

Moritz, S.E., Feltz, D.L., Fahrbach, K.R. and Mack, D.E. (2000) 'The relation of self-efficacy measures to sport performance: a meta-analytic review', *Research Quarterly for Exercise and Sport*, 71: 280–294.

Mullen, B. and Copper, C. (1994) 'The relation between group cohesiveness and performance: an integration', *Psychological Bulletin*, 115: 210–227.

Newcomb, T.M. (1953) 'An approach to the study of communicative acts', *Psychological Review*, 60: 393–404.

Olympiou, A., Jowett, S. and Duda, J.L. (2005) *Coach-athlete Relationship and Optimal Functioning in a Team Sport Context*, paper presented at the 11th World Congress of Sport Psychology, Sydney, Australia.

Rhind, D.J.A. and Jowett, S. (2010) 'Relationship maintenance strategies in the coach-athlete relationship: the development of the COMPASS model', *Journal of Applied Sport Psychology*, 22: 106–121.

Shearer, D., Holmes, P. and Mellalieu, S.D. (2009) 'Collective efficacy in sport: the future from a social neuroscience perspective', *International Review of Sport and Exercise Psychology*, 2: 38–53.

Smith, R.E. and Smoll, F.L. (2007) 'Social-cognitive approach to coaching behaviours', in S. Jowett and D. Lavallee (eds) *Social Psychology in Sport*, Champaign, IL: Human Kinetics.

Snodgrass, S.E. (1985) 'Women's intuition: The effect of subordinate role on interpersonal sensitivity', *Journal of Personality and Social Psychology*, 49, 146–155.

27

DANGEROUS LIAISONS

Harassment and abuse in coaching

Kari Fasting

NORWEGIAN SCHOOL OF SPORT SCIENCES, OSLO, NORWAY

Introduction

Most people will agree that participation in sport is a very positive activity, that the sporting field is a safe arena, and that the role of the coach is very important in securing a safe environment for the athletes. According to Raakman *et al.* (2010) there is evidence that suggests that the coach is the most influential person in the youth sport environment.

Sport is an important socialisation arena for children and young people, and we know that through sport children can learn social and physical skills, tolerance, discipline and respect for others (Elkind 2007). We also know that teenage female athletes start being sexually active later than their non–athlete counterparts (Sabo *et al.* 1998), and we have some evidence that sport can help to build resilience against sexual exploitation (Fasting *et al.* 2008) and against delinquent behaviours more generally (Nichols 2007) – so being active in sport helps tackle more than just the obesity crisis. But research over the last 20 years has also shown that problems related to abuse and harassment seem to occur in sport. An example of abuse is former San Jose swim coach Andrew King who was sentenced to 40 years for having molested 20 children (Ktvu.com 2010). An example of sexual harassment is Peter Mueller's behaviour towards the Norwegian female athlete Maren Haugli. Mueller, the coach for the Norwegian national speed skating team, admitted saying to her at a dinner after an international competition in Berlin: 'I heard you are good at sucking cock? So are you?' (*Agderposten* 2009). The victim complained to the board of the Norwegian Skating Association about this event, subsequently Mueller was fired.

In both of these cases the role of the perpetrator was that he was a coach. The coach–athlete relationship can therefore be a dangerous liaison. In this chapter what is known from research on sexual harassment and abuse in sport will be presented, with a focus on the coach. It is divided into: prevalence, impacts, coaching styles and behaviours, and prevention strategies.

What is meant by sexual harassment and sexual abuse?

Central in the definitions of these concepts is that the behaviour experienced is unwanted or threatening, troublesome, insulting or offensive. It is also common to separate gender harassment, sexual harassment and sexual abuse. In the Norwegian Gender Equality Act 'gender harassment' is defined as follows: 'The term gender-based harassment shall mean unwelcome conduct that is related to a person's gender and that has the effect or purpose of offending another person's dignity' (Government.no 2011). Sporting environments that allow insulting and degrading remarks about one's gender contribute to a culture that can have very negative effect on the people in that particular sport, whether they are athletes, coaches or employees.

Sexual harassment is defined as: 'unwanted sexual attention that is offensive to the object of such attention' (Government.no 2011). Unwanted sexual attention refers to a wide range of verbal and non-verbal behaviours that are offensive, unwanted and unreciprocated. Sexual harassment may therefore be verbal, non-verbal and/or physical. Verbal sexual harassment may be: unwanted intimate questions relating to one's body, clothes or private life; 'jokes' with a sexual innuendo; and proposals or demands for sexual services or sexual relationships. Non-verbal sexual harassment might be staring or showing pictures of objects with sexual allusions. Physical sexual harassment is unwanted or unnecessary physical contact of a sexual nature, such as 'pinching', pressing oneself onto the body of others or attempting to kiss or caress another person.

Common for definitions of sexual abuse include that it is non-consensual sexual contact and that it is forced or coerced. Attempted rape or rape are examples of sexual abuse. The National Society for the Prevention of Cruelty to Children (NSPCC) in England defines sexual abuse as follows:

> Sexual abuse involves forcing or enticing a child or young person to take part in sexual activities, including prostitution, whether or not the child is aware of what is happening. The activities may involve physical contact, including penetrative (e.g. rape, buggery or oral sex) or non-penetrative acts. They may include non-contact activities, such as involving children in looking at, or in the production of, sexual online images, watching sexual activities, or encouraging children to behave in sexually inappropriate ways.
>
> *(NSPCC 2011)*

The NSPCC also mentions coaching when it defines what sexual abuse is: 'In sport, coaching techniques which involve physical contact with children could potentially create situations where sexual abuse may go unnoticed.'

Behaviours that are characterised as sexual harassment may include abuse depending on the age of the victim. Behaviours mentioned under physical sexual harassment that are experienced by children may be an example. There is both a grey zone and a continuum from sex discrimination to sexual harassment to sexual abuse (Brackenridge 1997). The distinction between harassment and abuse may, however, be useful in trying to understand what sometimes goes on between coaches and young athletes. The process of grooming can be said to be the tool the abuser may employ to gain a position from which to carry out the abuse. This may continue for years, without the person who is object of the attention being aware that an ever-stronger bond is being tied between her/him and the 'abuser', until she/he is caught in a kind of net and unable to withstand the abuser's sexual wishes. The process of grooming and/or coercing someone for sexual abuse means that one slowly gains the trust of a person before systematically breaking down interpersonal barriers. It can begin very innocently such as when the coach offers rides home or other special privileges. The young athletes can become trapped, because his or her compliance is assured by using threats such as being cut from the team and/or giving or withholding privileges (Bringer *et al.* 2002).

According to the United Nations, 90 states have some form of legislative provision against sexual harassment (United Nations 2006). In relation to sport, we find that sport organisations may or may not be covered by these various laws. The protections that athletes and coaches have in relation to legislation differ widely when viewed from an international perspective. In legal terms, USA operates with two kinds of sexual harassment: *Quid Pro Quo* and Hostile Environment. *Quid Pro Quo* is a Latin legal term which, when applied to sport, exists when benefits are granted or withheld as a result of an athlete's willingness or refusal to submit to the sexual demands of a person in authority. A coach, for example, might cut an athlete from the team because she refused sexual advances. A hostile environment exists when a person's conduct is pervasive or severe enough to disturb an athlete and interfere with his or her ability to perform. A hostile environment can affect more than the targeted person. For example a team member, who witnesses repeated incidents, even if they are not directed at her or him, may also be considered a victim of sexual harassment (WSF 1994).

What do we know from research on sexual harassment and abuse in sport?

Given the relatively recent history of research in this area, it is not surprising that there is a marked variety of approaches to the subject, both theoretical and methodological. In addition to quantitative prevalence studies, qualitative studies have been used to gather descriptions of harassment and abuse experiences and their consequences (Fasting *et al.* 2002). From these, risk factors have been described, and theoretical models and propositions grounded in athletes' experiences have been generated (Cense and Brackenridge 2001). These studies have primarily concerned former athletes who have been abused by their coaches, often when they were relatively young, i.e. near puberty.

The main sources of sexual harassment and abuse in sport seem to be coaches and athlete peers. Most of the published work on sexual harassment in sport has focused on male harassment of females which seems to be the most prevalent form, particularly male coach–female athlete, but some research has shown female–female harassment (Fasting *et al.* 2000; Fasting and Knorre 2005; Shire *et al.* 2000). Accordingly there is a huge gap in the knowledge about male–male harassment and female–male harassment. Hartill (2005) focuses on this when he writes that 'sport researchers, to date have been driven by the "male perpetrator–female victim"' paradigm, and that 'this focus has influenced the type of research that has been conducted and has inadvertently contributed to the further silencing of the sexually abused male' (p. 287).

Prevalence of sexual harassment and abuse in sport

It is important to have in mind that the various approaches mentioned above lead to the fact that it is difficult to compare figures from different studies. This is due to differences in sampling procedures, methodological approaches, vocabulary and connotative meanings of questionnaire items, anonymity and confidentiality of disclosures, statistical analyses employed etc. (Timmermann 2005). The chances of underreporting are also large, due to the sensitivity of the topic. The studies available present prevalence percentages of experienced sexual harassment and abuse in sport between 19 and 57 per cent. Many of these studies are about sexual harassment, but some also include experience of sexual abusive behaviours. Information about sexual abuse only however is more rare. We do not have prevalence data on sexual abuse, but we have some information from surveys, from media, from interviews with former athletes and from criminal court cases. A study among female sport students in the USA found that 19 per cent of the female students had experienced sexual harassment (Volkwein *et al.* 1997), in UK 21 per cent of female club athletes had experienced sexual harassment (Tomlinson and Yorganci 1997) and a Canadian study by Holman (1995) revealed that 57 per cent of male and female students had experienced sexual harassment. In a study from Turkey 200 sportswomen out of 356 revealed that they had been sexually harassed in sport. The most frequent time of harassment was found to be after games or training, and the most frequently occurring location of harassment was the sports centre (Gündüz *et al.* 2007). A Danish study of sport science students by Toftegaard Nielsen (2001) found that 25 per cent either knew about or had themselves experienced situations where a sport participant under the age of 18 years had been sexually harassed by the coach. Four of these reported having been sexually abused. In a later study (2004) Toftegaard Nielsen analysed 160 court cases about sport and sexual abuse in Denmark. Among these cases that had been taken to criminal court, 65 per cent of the victims were boys. All perpetrators were men, even though 37 per cent of all coaches in sport in Denmark are women.

In the first ever national-level survey of sexual harassment and abuse in sport, a questionnaire was administered to 1,200 of Canada's high performance and recently retired Olympic athletes by Kirby and Greaves (1996). 22 per cent of the 266 respondents replied that they had had sexual intercourse with persons in positions of authority in sport. Nine per cent reported they had experienced *forced* sexual intercourse, or rape, with such persons. Using a screening questionnaire of 2,118 Australian athletes Leahy *et al.* (2002) found that 31 per cent of the female and 21 per cent of male athletes reported experiencing sexual abuse at some time in their lives. Of these 41 per cent of females and 29 per cent of males had been sexually abused within the sports environment. Both the Kirby and Greaves (1996) survey and the Leahy *et al.* (2002) survey suffered from low response rates (22 and 19 per cent respectively). This raises questions about underreporting and bias in the data.

A survey among all female elite-level athletes in Norway found that 28 per cent had experienced sexual harassment in a sport setting, and that sexual harassment seems to occur in all sports (Fasting *et al.* 2000, 2004). A follow-up study revealed that most of these experiences were from male coaches. The most common forms of sexually harassing behaviours were gender harassment (ridicule) followed by unwanted physical contact. The following example of unwanted physical contact from a male coach was told by Mari. The incident took place when the athlete was 14–15 years of age:

> 'when we didn't perform well, then the punishment was that we should sit on his lap. I remember I thought it was disgusting. He touched us and was really very disgusting. I don't understand today that we accepted it at all. We had a drill where we had to sprint, and the one who came last had to sit on his lap, so everyone was running like hell'
>
> *(Fasting et al. 2002: 42)*

A study among female athletes in the Czech Republic found that 45 per cent of the participants had experienced sexual harassment in a sport setting. This study also found that the chances to be harassed from someone inside sport increased with performance level, from 33 per cent among the exercisers to 55 per cent among the elite-level athletes (Fasting *et al.* 2010). In this study 27 per cent had experienced sexual harassment from a coach, 9 per cent from a manager and 30 per cent from a peer athlete. The type of harassing behaviour that the athletes had experienced the most was 'Repeated unwanted sexually suggestive glances, comments, teasing and jokes, about your body, your clothes, your private life etc.' This was illustrated by Martina when she told about a coach she had when she was 14–15 years of age: 'During games and practice he was provoking me by pinching and verbal remarks. And it went too far, it got unpleasant. For example, he ridiculed my name and started to use quite rude language in the end' (Fasting and Knorre 2005: 43).

A study among female sport students in three different European countries found that 6 per cent had experienced sexual harassment from female coaches. As shown in other studies the percentages from men were much higher, 20 per cent (Sand *et al.* 2011).

Consequences of sexual harassment and abuse

Studies from the workplace and educational institutions show that the impact of sexual harassment, both lighter and more severe forms, can be very serious. Victims of sexual harassment and abuse experience a variety of symptoms, including anxiety, feelings of humiliation and alienation, anger, fear, guilt, a sense of vulnerability and helplessness, decreased self-esteem, self-confidence and life satisfaction, fear of rape and an increased fear of crime in general. Sexual harassment and abuse may also be regarded by the victim as a shameful experience, which may lead to social isolation.

Other negative health consequences which have been reported are physical complaints such as headaches, sleep disturbance, weight loss or gain, gastrointestinal disturbances and nausea, fatigue, neck and back pain (Kilpatrick and Dansky 1997).

What, then, is the impact of experiences of sexual harassment in a sport setting? If we apply the above results to sport, one should expect as a consequence of sexual harassment that the following could occur: a decline in practice and in performance, decreased satisfaction with one's own performance, decreased self-confidence in relation to one's sport's skills, decreased motivation for participating, a negative effect on the relationship to teammates and the partial or total withdrawal from sports. It is understandable that some of these impacts will occur particularly if the harasser is the coach of the athlete. One might also suspect that if a club had a high-profile coach known in the sporting milieu for his harassing behaviour that it could have a negative effect on the recruitment to that club. Concerning economic consequences one might assume that a sport might have problems with getting sponsors if they had had a high-profile harassment case in the media.

In their book *The Dome of Silence: Sexual Harassment and Abuse in Sport* Kirby *et al.* (2000) wrote, based on their study among Canadian male and female athletes, that the outcomes for the athletes who were victimised by sexual assault or attempted sexual assault were serious in both the short and the long term:

> For many, it changed how they behaved in sport and in their day-to-day lives. Athletes found ways to take care of themselves by not associating with the perpetrators, by changing the training routine, by changing personal behavior to become more professional, or by changing the situation or location so they would be less at risk. Several athletes continue to have long-term personal problems.
>
> *(Kirby et al. 2000: 96)*

The Norwegian study mentioned earlier gives a few examples of the impact of sexual harassment and abuse, that corresponds with the studies outside sport just mentioned (Fasting *et al.* 2002), for example increased fear of crime in general, as Ingrid said: 'I became afraid of going out alone … I started to have a knife in my pocket when I was going out … I also started practicing karate at that time' (p. 43).

Many athletes also felt that the sexual harassment episodes had damaged the coach–athlete relationship, and had led to changes in their own behaviour towards the coach. 'I try to have as little to do with him as possible … and avoid being alone with him. If we must look at a video for example, I always bring someone along…' (Mette in Fasting *et al.* 2002: 43). The athletes' experiences of sexual harassment had affected both their self-esteem and their body image. As Hanne said: 'He [the coach] destroyed much of my self-esteem … and I left Norwegian sport because of that episode.' (ibid.: 44).

It is a problem that athletes very often do not report incidents of sexual harassment and abuse. This was also the fact among the athletes in the Norwegian study mentioned above. In a study from Canada of 537 athletes and 72 coaches, the reasons mentioned that people were reluctant to report harassment were: fear of being cut from the team and fear of not being believed; being ashamed/embarrassed; loyalty to the coach/team; and do not know who to talk to (Fairholm 1998). It is important for coaches to understand the severe impacts of sexually harassing behaviour. Consequently it is also very important that coaches report harassment or abusive behaviour made by others if they see it. In the above-mentioned study from Canada the athletes answered that it was not only the coach who had initiated the harassment they had experienced. Others included teammates, officials, spectators and parents. This shows that there are many other potential harassers in an athlete's environment than just the coach. The coach therefore can and should play an important role also in preventing sexual harassment and abuse from other athletes. A sporting environment that permits gender and sexual harassment from peers will, for many athletes of both genders, be experienced as offensive, which again can have a negative effect on the performance of the athletes.

Coaching style and coaching behaviours

We have little direct knowledge about the abusive and/or harassing coach. The information about the abusive and harassing coach stems from media reports, court reports and interviews with athletes. Brackenridge *et al.* (2008) conducted an analysis of 159 cases of criminally defined sexual abuse in sport, reported in the print media over a period of 15 years. In almost all cases the perpetrator was a male coach. The main aim of the study was to identify the nature of sex offending in sport, focusing on the methods and locations of offences. The findings indicated that there are specific themes that can be identified within the perpetrator's strategies that include 'intimate', 'aggressive', and 'dominant' modes of interaction, which are consistent with themes that emerge from studies outside sport. Theorisations outside sport often characterise paedophile sexual abuse as a response to one's lack of success, feelings of resentment and intimacy deficits (Hudson and Ward 1997). But many of the accounts of sexual exploitation in sport indicate that perpetrators' feelings of power and control arise from confidence and feelings of superiority (Cense and Brackenridge 2001). According to these studies, sexually abusing coaches have good social skills, high visibility, popularity and a high level of sexual confidence. Popular media presentations of harassing coaches also suggest that not only do they have a reputation of being successful coaches but they are often regarded as 'very nice' people (Brackenridge 2001).

Kjølberg (2009) analysed Norwegian court reports in which the perpetrators had been sentenced for sexual abuse in sport. He was interested in finding out if he could determine some common characteristics of the perpetrators who had been sentenced for sexual abuse in sport. Altogether 15 cases were analysed, and in 11 of these the perpetrators had been the coaches of the victims. All perpetrators were men, the youngest 19 years old and the oldest 58 years. The civil status of the perpetrators varied, and none were full-time coaches. The author concluded that no clear profile of a perpetrator emerged.

Most perpetrators of sexual abuse and sexual harassment in sport never reach the criminal justice system because of victim's fears of reprisals, de-selection or not being taken seriously. We may however learn more about these perpetrators by listening to the voices of those whom they have abused or harassed.

An interview study of female elite-level athletes who had been sexually harassed by their coaches produced a sport typology that consists of three main types: (1) The Flirting-Charming Coach; (2) The Seductive Coach; and (3) The Authoritarian Coach (Fasting and Brackenridge 2009). The 'Flirting-Charming Coach' was characterised by always flirting, joking, trying to touch and so on. The 'Seductive Coach' went further and was characterised by trying to 'hit on everyone'. The 'Authoritarian Coach' was in addition to being powerful and using his power, also characterised by having psychological/psychic problems and often had a degrading, almost negative view of women in general. This study however concluded that rather than being one type only, sexually harassing coaches select from a repertoire that may include several different harassment scripts that vary according to situational conditions.

The European study mentioned earlier took place in the Czech Republic, Greece and Norway, and found that the prevalence of sexual harassment was significantly higher among female athletes who had experienced authoritarian coaching behaviours from their coaches compared with those athletes who did not have such experience. This was the fact whether the coach was a male or female (Sand *et al.* 2011). Authoritarian coaching behaviour is characterised by negative feedback, directive communication, coach-led decision making, task-centred role orientation and goal-oriented performance (Lyle 2002). That coaches sometimes express such behaviours was also shown in a study among ten elite-level female athletes in the Czech Republic (Thoresen *et al.* 2007). The results showed that male coaches tended to scream more, use direct communication and seemed to use body language more often than female coaches did. Male coaches are also described as using tougher language, compared to female coaches. Some athletes also expressed fear of their coaches and felt threatened by their choices of communication. The fear was more often experienced from male than from female coaches. Very often male coaches used rude language and body language or body contact (i.e. sexually harassing behaviour), and they also took advantage of a congratulatory hug and sometimes brought it too far by touching different body parts of the athletes. Verbal messages actually more often included comments on their bodies or the way they looked, compared to their sport results. Silje says:

> 'When I was not getting the good results we both would like, I would hear comments like I can't run, or that I'm clumsy. Also I heard from him that I should take off some weight and what I should eat or shouldn't eat. And then of course he tried to seduce me as he tried to seduce many other women.'
>
> *(Thoresen et al. 2007: 4)*

Autocratic communication styles were commonly practised by coaches in this study. The athletes seldom experienced communication as a dialogue between themselves and their coaches, although sometimes younger male coaches and female coaches tend to involve more personally in the communication process with their athletes. The most common choices of communication were the use of non-verbal communication or use of body language to communicate with the female athletes. Mette expressed this in the following way; 'my coach pinched me and a lot of girls on our teams, many times' (Thoresen *et al.* 2007: 3). In addition to pinching, slapping and kicking are often used as physical choices of communication with the girls. Almost all athletes had experienced these kinds of methods from their coaches.

Coaches should be aware that there is a power difference between them and his or her athletes, because the athletes are dependent on these experts and usually have complete trust in them. If misunderstood, this power difference can lead to exploitative sexual relationships with athletes. The same argument is mentioned in a study by Stirling and Kerr (2009) which found that 'coaches' power is a contributor to an athlete's risk of abuse' (p. 237). The examples given above indicate that it may be difficult to create a safe and trustworthy environment when the communication between the coach and his or her athletes are not characterised by a mutual dialogue. This increases the risk of misunderstandings, unclear communication, etc. and the athletes may perceive actions or behaviours from the coach as offensive and unwelcome (i.e. harassment), even if this is not the intention of the coach. An authoritarian coaching style therefore seems to increase the chance of being harassed and/or abused, because there is a risk of overlooking and intruding on the needs and will of the athlete. The alternative is a more holistic coaching style, where the coach will be more focused on the athlete's individual differences and needs and have a better understanding of what kind of behaviours are perceived as unwelcome or offensive.

Prevention of sexual harassment and abuse in sport

An open, sound and safe sporting environment will in itself serve as a protection against harassment and abuse, and also against false accusations. A condition for maintaining and strengthening a sound sporting environment is that the management of a sport agrees on what constitutes a sound environment. This concerns questions on how to interact with one another, which expectations and requirements one places on parents, coaches and managers, how the club should be managed etc. Some sports clubs and many international and national sport associations and federations have ethical guidelines, written or unwritten, but these are often linked to alcohol, when to go to bed on trips etc. There are however a number of awareness-raising measures that may also have a preventative effect on sexual harassment and abuse. These relate to bullying, racism, fair play and language use. All sports should have some kind of ethical guidelines, and the boundaries for acceptable behaviour should be apparent from these. The role of the coach is very important here because she or he is often the person who spends the most time among the athletes at the same time that she or he acts as a role model for them. Ethical guidelines should therefore be referred to in the employment contract for coaches. It may also be important to procure a police certificate of good conduct before coaches are hired.

The Norwegian Olympic, Paralympic and Confederation of Sports (NIF) has recently developed guidelines to prevent sexual harassment and abuse in sports. These shall apply to all Norwegian sports (NIF 2011):

1 Treat everyone with respect, and refrain from all forms of communication, action or behaviour that may be perceived as offensive.
2 Avoid body contact that may be perceived as unwanted.
3 Avoid all types of verbal intimacy that may be perceived as sexually charged.
4 Avoid expressions, jokes and opinions that relate to the athlete's gender or sexual orientation in a negative way.

5   Seek to have both sexes represented in the support network.
6   Avoid contact with the athletes in private spaces unless there are several persons present or in agreement with parents/guardians or the sports management.
7   Show respect for the athletes', coaches' and leaders' private life.
8   Avoid dual relationships. If a reciprocal relationship is established, the situation should be raised and clarified openly in the milieu.
9   Do not offer any form of reward with the purpose of demanding or anticipating sexual services in return.
10   Take action and give notice if a breach of these rules is experienced.

It is well known that many female athletes have married their male coaches. One question that often is discussed concerns sexual relationships between coaches and athletes, this is also referred to in point 8 above. The US Women's Sports Foundation (WSF) is one of those organisations that have adopted a position statement on this particular issue. They focus upon the fact that consensual sexual relationships between coaches and athletes compromise the professional integrity of the coach, and are wrong when the coach has professional responsibility for the athletes. Further that such situations increase the opportunities for a coach to abuse his or her power and/or sexually exploit the athletes, and that voluntary consent by the athlete in such a relationship is suspect, given the fundamentally unequal nature of the relationship, which also can cause a conflict of interest (WSF 2011).

The importance of coach education

The data presented in this chapter strongly indicate that education is very important. Unfortunately sexual harassment training for sport coaches is often either missing from coach education programmes altogether or subsumed within broader themes such as (gender) equity or diversity management. It seems however to be crucial to educate coaches about good communication skills, about appropriate behaviours and about the consequences that their behaviours may have for their athletes. This ought to be implemented at all levels of coaching education. By doing this, coaches will develop a better understanding and enhance their awareness of their athletes' needs and feelings. Consequently, the risk of unintentional actions from the coach that can be experienced as unwanted and unwelcome by the athlete may be reduced.

During the last 15 years, countries such as USA, Canada, New Zealand, Australia, UK, Norway and the Netherlands to mention a few, have developed policies and codes of practice for preventing sexual harassment and abuse from occurring in sport. But in a worldwide perspective sexual harassment and abuse in sport is in many countries an ignored issue. However since 2006 this issue has been a concern for the International Olympic Committee (IOC). As a consequence they adopted in 2007 a consensus statement on sexual harassment and abuse (IOC 2007). The statement ends with the following recommendations:

All sport organisations should:

1   develop policies and procedures for the prevention of sexual harassment and abuse;
2   monitor the implementation of these policies and procedures;
3   evaluate the impact of these policies in identifying and reducing sexual harassment and abuse;

4 develop an education and training program on sexual harassment and abuse in their sport(s);

5 promote and exemplify equitable, respectful and ethical leadership;

6 foster strong partnerships with parents/carers in the prevention of sexual harassment and abuse; and

7 promote and support scientific research on these issues.

The question is whether and how the IOC itself will effectively communicate this ideal to the different national Olympic committees and the international sport federations, and whether these organisations are willing to follow up these recommendations in practice? The IOC itself however is following up this with two projects, one is *The Development of an Athlete Protection Model of Best Practice* and another one is an educational programme on *Athlete's Right to Safe Sport* via an interactive online programme.

Schwartz Tangri and Hayes (1997) point out however that although models may help us understand the causes of sexual harassment, one should not forget that the two most opportune points of interventions are in the policies, procedures, and commitment to change in organisations and in the educational system. Applied to sport it means that all sport bodies should have a policy and that sexual harassment should be a theme in all education of managers, coaches and athletes. If this happens parallel with a change in the masculine dominance of sport and society then future sport may also become a more positive environment for women.

References

Agderposten (2009) Innrømmer seksuell trakassering, 28 November, *Agderposten*: 44.

Brackenridge, C. (1997) '"He owned me basically": women's experiences of sexual abuse in sport', *International Review for the Sociology of Sport*, 32: 115–130.

Brackenridge, C. (2001) *Spoilsports: Understanding and Preventing Sexual Exploitation in Sport*, London: Routledge.

Brackenridge, C.H., Bishop, D., Moussalli, S. and Tapp, J. (2008) 'The characteristics of sexual abuse in sport: a multidimensional scaling analysis of events described in media reports', *International Journal of Sport and Exercise Psychology*, 6: 385–406.

Bringer, J.D., Brackenridge, C.H. and Johnston, L.H. (2002) 'Defining appropriateness in coach-athlete sexual relationships: the voice of coaches', *The Journal of Sexual Aggression*, 2: 83–98.

Cense, M. and Brackenridge, C. (2001) 'Temporal and developmental risk factors for sexual harassment and abuse in sport', *European Physical Education Review*, 7: 61–79.

Elkind, D. (2007) *The Power of Play: How Spontaneous, Imaginative Activities Lead to Happier, Healthier Children*, Cambridge, MA: Da Capo Lifelong.

Fairholm, J. (1998) *Speak Out! – Act Now! A Guide to Preventing and Responding to Abuse and Harassment for Sport Clubs and Associations*, Ottawa: Canadian Hockey Association.

Fasting, K. and Brackenridge, C. (2009) 'Coaches, sexual harassment and education', *Sport, Education and Society*, 14: 21–35.

Fasting, K. and Knorre, N. (2005) *Women in Sport in the Czech Republic: The Experiences of Female Athletes*, Oslo/Prague: Norwegian School of Sport Sciences/Czech Olympic Committee.

Fasting, K., Brackenridge, C. and Knorre, N. (2010) 'Performance level and sexual harassment prevalence among female athletes in the Czech Republic', *Women in Sport and Physical Activity Journal*, 19: 26–32.

Fasting, K., Brackenridge, C.H., Miller, K.E. and Sabo, D. (2008) 'Participation in college sports and protection from sexual victimisation', *International Journal of Sport and Exercise Psychology*, 6: 427–441.

Fasting, K., Brackenridge, C. and Sundgot-Borgen, J. (2000) *The Norwegian Women Project. Females, Elite Sports and Sexual Harassment*, Oslo: The Norwegian Olympic Committee and Confederation of Sport.

Fasting, K., Brackenridge, C. and Sundgot-Borgen, J. (2004) 'Prevalence of sexual harassment among Norwegian female elite athletes in relation to sport type', *International Review for the Sociology of Sport*, 39: 373–386.

Fasting, K., Brackenridge, C. and Walseth, K. (2002) 'Consequences of sexual harassment in sport for female athletes', in C. Brackenridge (ed.) *Sexual Harassment and Abuse in Sport: International Research and Policy Perspectives*, London: Whiting and Birch.

Government.no (2011) *The Act relating to Gender Equality*, Norwegian Ministry of children and equality, online, available at: www.regjeringen.no/en/doc/Laws/Acts/The-Act-relating-to-Gender-Equality-the-.html?id=454568 (accessed 17 February 2011).

Gündüz, N., Sunay, H. and Koz, M. (2007) 'Incidents of sexual harassment in Turkey on elite sportswomen', *The Sport Journal*, 10(2), online, available at: www.thesportjournal.org/article/incidents-sexual-harassment-turkey-elite-sportswomen (accessed 15 February 2011).

Hartill, M. (2005) 'Sport and the sexually abused male child', *Sport, Education and Society*, 10: 287–304.

Holman M.J. (1995) 'Female and male athletes, accounts and meanings of sexual harassment in Canadian interuniversity athletes', PhD thesis, University of Windsor.

Hudson S.M. and Ward T. (1997) 'Rape: Psychopathology and Theory', in W. O'Donohue (ed.) *Sexual Deviance: Theory, Assessment, and Treatment* (1st edition), New York: Guilford Press.

IOC (International Olympic Committee) (2007) *IOC Adopts Consensus statement on Sexual Harassment and Abuse in Sport*, 8 February, online, available at: www.olympic.org/Assets/ImportedNews/Documents/en_report_1125.pdf (accessed 17 February 2011).

Kilpatrick, D.G. and Dansky, B.S. (1997) 'Effects of sexual harassment', in W. O'Donohue (ed.) *Sexual Harassment: Theory, Research, and Treatment*, Boston, MA: Allyn and Bacon.

Kirby, S. and Greaves, L. (1996) 'Foul play: sexual abuse and harassment in sport', paper presented at the Pre-Olympic Scientific Congress, Dallas, July.

Kirby, S., Greaves, L. and Hankivsky, O. (2000) *The Dome of Silence: Sexual Harassment and Abuse in Sport*, Halifax, NS: Fernwood Publishing.

Kjølberg, G. (2009) *Seksuelle overgrep i idrett: en dokumentanalyse av domfelte saker i Lagmannsretten*, Master thesis, Oslo: Norwegian School of Sport Sciences.

Ktvu.com (2010) *Former Swim Coach Given 40 Years In Prison*, 29 January, online, available at: www.ktvu.com/news/22384970/detail.html (accessed 18 February 2011).

Leahy, T., Pretty, G. and Tenenbaum, G. (2002) 'Prevalence of sexual abuse in organised competitive sport in Australia', *The Journal of Sexual Aggression*, 2: 16–36.

Lyle, J. (2002) *Sports Coaching Concepts: A Framework for Coaches' Behaviour*, London: Routledge.

Nichols, G. (2007) *Sport and Crime Prevention: The Role of Sport in Tackling Youth Crime*, Abingdon: Routledge.

NIF (Norwegian Olympic and Paralympic Committee and Confederation of Sports) (2011) *Guidelines to Prevent Sexual Harassment and Abuse in Sports*, online, available at: www.idrett.no/tema/lover/retningslinjer/Documents/BROSJYRE_seksuell%20trakassering_ENGELSK_WEB.pdf (accessed 17 February 2011).

NSPCC (National Society for the Prevention of Cruelty to Children) (2011) *Defining Child Abuse*, online, available at: www.nspcc.org.uk/Inform/cpsu/helpandadvice/organisations/defining/definingchildabuse_wda60692.html (accessed 18 February 2011).

Raakman, E., Dorsch, K. and Rhind, D. (2010) 'The development of a typology of abusive coaching behaviours within youth sport', *International Journal of Sports Science and Coaching*, 5: 503–515.

Sabo, D., Miller, K., Farrell, M., Barnes, G. and Melnick, M. (1998) 'The Women's Sports Foundation report: sport and teen pregnancy', *Volleyball USA*, 26: 20–23.

Sand, T.S., Fasting, K., Chroni, S. and Knorre, N. (2011) 'Coaching behaviour: any consequences for the prevalence of sexual harassment'? *International Journal of Sport Science and Coaching*, 6: 229–242.

Shire, J., Brackenridge, C. and Fuller, M. (2000) 'Changing positions: the sexual politics of a women's field hockey team 1986–1996'. *Women in Sport and Physical Activity Journal*, 9: 35–64.

Stirling, A.E. and Kerr, G.A. (2009) 'Abused athletes' perceptions of the coach-athlete relationship', *Sport in Society*, 12: 227–239.

Schwartz Tangri, S. and Hayes, S.M. (1997) 'Theories of sexual harassment', in W. O'Donahue (ed.) *Sexual Harassment: Theory, Research, and Treatment*, Boston, MA: Allyn and Bacon.

Thoresen, T., Fasting, K. and Knorre, N. (2007) 'Consequences of coach communication', paper presented at the International Sociology Association Congress, Copenhagen, 31 July–5 August.

Timmermann, G. (2005) 'The impact of male domination on the prevalence of sexual harassment: An analysis of European Union surveys', in J.E. Gruber and P. Morgan (eds) *In the Company of Men: Male Dominance and Sexual Harassment*, Boston, MA: Northeastern University Press.

Toftegaard Nielsen, J. (2001) 'The forbidden zone: intimacy, sexual relations and misconduct in the relationship between coaches and athletes', PhD thesis, *International Review for the Sociology of Sport*, 36: 165–182.

Toftegaard Nielsen, J. (2004) *Idrættens illusoriske intimitet*, Copenhagen: Københavns Universitet, Institut for idræt.

Tomlinson, A. and Yorganci, I. (1997) 'Male coach/female athlete relations: gender and power relations in competitive sport', *Journal of Sport and Social Issues*, 21: 134–155.

United Nations (2006) *Ending Violence Against Women: From Words to Action*, New York: United Nations.

Volkwein, K.A.E., Schnell, F.I., Sherwood, D. and Livezey, A. (1997) 'Sexual harassment in sport: perceptions and experiences of American female student-athletes', *International Review for the Sociology of Sport*, 32: 283–297.

WSF (Women's Sports Foundation) (1994) *Policy Statement on Sexual Relationships Between Coaches and Athletes*, n.p.: WSF Board of Trustees.

WSF (Women's Sports Foundation) (2011) *Sexual Harassment - Sexual Harassment and Sexual Relationships Between Coaches, Other Athletic Personnel and Athletes: The Foundation Position*, online, available at: www.womenssportsfoundation.org/home/advocate/title-ix-and-issues/title-ix-positions/sexual_harassment (accessed 18 February 2011).

28

TEAM COHESION IN SPORT

Critical overview and implications
for team building

Todd M. Loughead

UNIVERSITY OF WINDSOR, CANADA

Gordon A. Bloom

MCGILL UNIVERSITY, CANADA

Introduction

Team unity or cohesion is one of the cornerstones for helping a group of athletes achieve a common goal (e.g. Pain and Harwood 2009; Yukelson 1997). In fact, empirical research has indicated that coaches feel that team cohesion is directly linked to improvements in team performance and success (Bloom *et al.* 2003; Carron *et al.* 2002a). One of the most effective ways for coaches to improve team cohesion is through the implementation of team building activities (Bloom *et al.* 2003). According to Woodcock and Francis (1994) an effective team building program can lead to the following six outcomes: (1) team leadership being coherent, visionary, and acceptable; (2) team members understanding and accepting their responsibilities and roles; (3) team members dedicating their efforts to the team's goals and objectives; (4) a positive, empowering climate surrounding the team; (5) team members making better use of their time and resources during meetings; and (6) team members being able to identify and correct team weaknesses.

Consequently, the purpose of this chapter is to critically review the area of team cohesion and team building in sport. This chapter will provide readers with an overview of cohesion research as applied to sport coaching by examining how cohesion has been conceptualized and measured, and its relationship to performance in sport. Further, this chapter will also provide a critical overview of team building research in sport and implications for team building research by examining Carron and Spink's (1993) team building model and approaches to team building. The chapter will conclude by highlighting potential future directions in the area of team building.

Critical overview of team cohesion research

Cohesion has been viewed historically as the most important small group variable (Golembiewski 1962; Lott and Lott 1965). As a result, researchers have attempted to define and operationalize the construct of cohesion. One of the first definitions of cohesion was advanced by Festinger *et al.* (1950) in their research examining group dynamics in a student housing community at the Massachusetts Institute of Technology. These researchers suggested that cohesion be viewed as 'the total field of forces that act on members to remain in the group' (164). Gross and Martin (1952) argued that the Festinger *et al.* definition emphasized individual perceptions and failed to consider the importance of the group as a totality. As a result, Gross and Martin (1952) defined cohesion as 'the resistance of a group to disruptive forces' (553). However, Mudrack (1989) noted that both the Festinger *et al.* and the Gross and Martin definitions were virtually impossible to operationalize leading to numerous inconsistencies in research findings. Another limitation of these two definitions was that they viewed cohesion as a unidimensional construct, focusing on either the individual or group orientation of cohesion (Carron *et al.* 1998). Furthermore, these unidimensional definitions of cohesion failed to distinguish between the task and social concerns of groups and their members. Given these shortcomings in trying to explain cohesion, Carron (1982) argued that a multidimensional definition of cohesion was needed that incorporated both the group/individual and task/social orientations. Consequently, Carron (1982) defined cohesion as 'a dynamic process which is reflected in the tendency for a group to stick together and remain united in the pursuit of its goals and objectives' (259). This definition was later revised by Carron *et al.* (1998) to include an affective dimension and was defined as 'a dynamic process that is reflected in the tendency for a group to stick together and remain united in the pursuit of its instrumental objectives and/or for the satisfaction of member affective needs' (213). The Carron *et al.* definition is the most widely used and accepted definition of cohesion (Loughead and Hardy 2006).

Conceptual model of cohesion

Based on Carron's (1982) definition of cohesion, Carron *et al.* (1985) proposed a conceptual model of cohesion based on three fundamental assumptions from group dynamics theory. The first assumption was cohesion can be assessed through the perceptions of individual team members. That is, teammates interact with one another and experience various social situations together, leading individual team members to develop certain beliefs about their team.

The second assumption focused on the need to distinguish between the team and the individual. Thus, the cognitions that each individual team member holds about the cohesiveness of the team are related to the team as a whole, and to the degree the team satisfies personal needs and objectives. These cognitions were labelled *group integration* and *individual attractions to the group*. In particular, *group integration* reflects an individual's perceptions about the closeness, similarity, and bonding within the group as a whole, and the degree of unification of the group. In contrast, *individual attractions to the group* reflects an individual's perceptions about personal motivations acting to retain the individual in the group, and the individual's personal feelings about the group.

The third assumption distinguished between task- and social-oriented concerns of the group and its members. The *task orientation* represents a general orientation or motivation towards achieving the team's goals. Conversely, the *social orientation* represented a general orientation or motivation toward developing and maintaining social relationships and activities within the team.

Based on these three assumptions, the Carron *et al.* (1985) conceptual model of cohesion is a combination of the individual/group and task/social orientations that resulted in a four factor conceptual model. This multidimensional model of cohesion is represented by the following four factors:

- *individual attractions to the group-task* (ATG-T)
- *individual attractions to the group-social* (ATG-S)
- *group integration-task* (GI-T)
- *group integration-social* (GI-S).

The cohesion factor of ATG-T is defined as the attractiveness of the team's task, productivity, and goals for the individual personally. The cohesion factor of ATG-S is viewed as each group member's feelings about his or her personal acceptance, and social interaction with the team. The cohesion factor of GI-T represents an individual's perceptions of the similarity, closeness, and bonding within the team as a whole around the team's task. Finally, the cohesion factor of GI-S refers to an individual's perceptions about the similarity, closeness, and bonding within the entire group as a social unit.

Measurement of cohesion: the Group Environment Questionnaire

Using the conceptual model of cohesion as a basis, Carron *et al.* (1985) then developed a measure of cohesion that incorporated these four factors (i.e. ATG-T, ATG-S, GI-T, GI-S). The result was the development of the *Group Environment Questionnaire* (GEQ), an 18-item inventory that assesses the four dimensions of cohesion. Specifically, the ATG-T scale consists of four items and an example item is: 'I am unhappy with my team's level of desire to win'. The ATG-S scale consists of five items and an example item is: 'Some of my best friends are on this team'. The GI-T scale comprises five items and an example item is: 'Our team is united in trying to reach its goals for performance'. Lastly, the GI-S scale comprises four items and an example item is: 'Members of our team would rather go out on their own than get together as a team'. All items are measured on a nine-point Likert scale anchored at the extremes of 1 (*strongly disagree*) to 9 (*strongly agree*). The GEQ is the most widely used inventory to assess cohesion in sport and has been used in many team-building studies (Prapavessis *et al.* 1996; Senécal *et al.* 2008; Stevens and Bloom 2003). One reason for its widespread use is related to the fact that this inventory has demonstrated to be a valid and reliable measure of cohesion (Carron *et al.* 1998).

Cohesion and performance

One question often asked by coaches is whether developing cohesion via team building is related to performance. Research findings have been equivocal, finding either a positive (e.g. Carron *et al.* 2002a; Tziner *et al.* 2003; Williams and Widmeyer 1991), a negative (e.g. Landers and Lueschen 1974), or no relationship (Davids and Nutter 1988) between cohesion and performance in sport. Given these mixed findings, a more systematic and objective method to summarize research in this area is by examining the results of two comprehensive meta-analyses on the cohesion–performance relationship.

The first meta-analysis was conducted by Mullen and Copper (1994) using 49 studies from a variety of sub-disciplines that included business, the military, and sport. Overall, the results revealed a small effect in that cohesion was positively related to performance. A second meta-analysis was carried out by Carron *et al.* (2002b), partly because they felt the results from Mullen and Copper were limiting given the number of sports studies sampled was quite low (only eight of their 49 studies were in sport). Thus, Carron *et al.*'s (2002b) meta-analysis only included research examining the cohesion-performance relationship in sport. A total of 46 studies were obtained for analysis that contained data on 9,988 athletes from 1,044 sport teams. The overall result revealed a significant moderate to large ($ES = 0.66$) positive relationship between cohesion and performance, indicating that higher cohesion in teams was related to better performance. Equally important, this meta-analysis also examined the influence of several variables on the cohesion–performance relationship. In particular, the authors examined how the type of cohesion, sport type, athlete gender, and competition level influenced the cohesion–performance relationship.

When examining whether the type of cohesion (ATG-T, GI-T, ATG-S, GI-S) moderated the cohesion-performance relationship, Carron *et al.* (2002b) found that both task (ATG-T, GI-T) and social (ATG-S, GI-S) cohesion were equally related to successful performance in team sports. Thus, both task and social cohesion are important for enhancing performance. In terms of sport type, the results indicated that regardless of the team sport, from interdependent (e.g. basketball, baseball) to coactive (e.g. wrestling, track and field), having strong team cohesion is positively related to performance. When gender was examined, the findings indicated that both male and female athletes benefited from being on a cohesive team since it led to better performance. However, female athletes benefited to a greater extent than male athletes. Finally, when the authors examined the level of competition, the results showed that professional, intercollegiate, high school, and recreational athletes benefited equally from being on a cohesive team. In other words, regardless of the level of competition being on a cohesive team is associated with teams that perform better.

In sum, the meta-analysis by Carron *et al.* (2002b) showed a positive relationship between being on a cohesive team and performance in sport. This relationship transcends the gender of the athlete, the type of team sport being played, is present regardless of the level of competition, and affects all types of cohesion. Given that cohesion is universally beneficial for sport performance, it is not surprising that attempts have been made to enhance cohesion and ultimately performance through team building.

Critical overview of team building in sport research

Although it might be relatively easy to argue that team building is important to develop in sport teams, translating its importance into an operational definition has been a challenge for this field. Consequently, researchers have defined team building from several different perspectives (Hardy and Crace 1997). One approach defines team building as a method to help a group achieve four objectives: (1) satisfy the needs of team members; (2) increase team effectiveness; (3) improve working conditions; and (4) enhance team cohesion (Brawley and Paskevich 1997). Another approach views team building as a method of assisting a team to promote an increased sense of unity and cohesiveness and enable the team to function more smoothly and effectively (Newman 1984). A third perspective from Widmeyer and DuCharme (1997) describes team building as the process of attempting to enhance a team's locomotion as well as its maintenance. Locomotion is related to productivity or performance whereas maintenance is reflective of a team's ability to stay together or be cohesive. A final definition that has been forwarded for physical education teachers may also be applicable for coaches. According to the authors (e.g. Glover and Midura 1992; Midura and Glover 2005), team building involves intellectual, physical, and emotional problem-solving tasks and challenges, while emphasizing elements of fun, cooperation, communication, and adventure.

In sum, whatever definition is used, one thing that remains clear is the emphasis placed on enhancing a team's cohesiveness.

Given that there is no one accepted definition of team building, it is perhaps not surprising that research from this body of knowledge has yielded equivocal results. Some studies have found a positive team building-cohesion relationship (e.g. Senécal *et al.* 2008; Stevens and Bloom 2003; Voight and Callaghan 2001) while others have found no changes in perceptions of cohesion (e.g. Bloom and Stevens 2002; Prapavessis *et al.* 1996) following a team building intervention program. On the one hand, Voight and Callaghan examined the effects of a team building intervention program with elite soccer teams. The results demonstrated that the team building interventions enhanced individual and team performance, and improved team unity. Similar findings were noted by Stevens and Bloom in their investigation of the effectiveness of a multidimensional team-building intervention program (consisting of role behaviour, social support, team leadership, social interaction, and clarification of team goals) with elite softball teams. Results indicated the team-building group reported significantly higher perceptions of both task and social cohesion following the intervention compared to the control group.

On the other hand, Prapavessis *et al.* (1996) conducted a team-building intervention study with coaches who were randomly assigned to a team-building, an attention-placebo, or a control condition. Coaches in the team-building condition attended a workshop and developed team-building strategies related to the clarification of roles, leadership, team norms, and team goals that were implemented with their teams. Coaches in the attention-placebo condition were provided with information on topics such as nutrition. Perceptions of cohesion were assessed at three different times throughout the season, but no differences were found across the three conditions. Bloom and Stevens (2002) carried out an intervention study on one university equestrian team to examine whether the implementation of a team building program consisting of various topics (e.g. development of leadership, norms, and communication) would enhance perceptions of cohesion. Results revealed no significant differences in perceptions of cohesion between pre- and post-intervention.

Because empirical sport research on team building in sport is still in its infancy, a lot of information can be gleaned from examining the studies on team building in sport and particularly looking at some of the factors that may have contributed to their findings. For example, the *research design* has not always involved a control group. One study that did use a control group was Senécal and colleagues (2008) whose season-long team-building intervention program used team goal-setting with female high school basketball teams. The authors randomly assigned teams to either a team goal-setting condition or a control condition. Results revealed that levels of cohesion for athletes in the team goal-setting condition remained stable while athletes' perceptions of cohesion in the control condition decreased over the season. Without the use of a control group, these authors would have concluded that the team-building intervention had no influence on cohesion, when in fact the opposite was true. Related to that point, some studies have been limited by only using quantitative measurements. For example, while the quantitative measurement used in the Bloom and Stevens (2002) equestrian study did not find any significant differences, the qualitative portion of their study revealed improved team harmony and closeness, and improved coach–athlete and athlete–athlete relationships.

Another explanation influencing the results of previous team-building research is the *individual in charge* of implementing the team-building program. For example, Eitington (1989) noted not all coaches will be successful as the agent of change in a team-building intervention. More specifically, coaches may lack motivation, patience, commitment, and the know-how to successfully introduce and facilitate the team building intervention (Brawley and Paskevich 1997). Moreover, the interventions may not be able to overcome the possibilities that differences may result from coaching style, performance records, and team atmosphere (Bloom and Stevens 2002).

An additional reason is the *duration* of the interventions. Several studies have assessed the effects of team building on perceptions of cohesion over a relatively short-term period, usually less than eight weeks. It has been noted that the assessment of any team-building intervention in sport should require a minimum of one full season for any meaningful, enduring changes to be validly assessed (Brawley and Paskevich 1997). In fact, Martin *et al.* (2009) found that team-building interventions lasting 20 weeks or more were the most beneficial for teams at enhancing cohesion and performance; while interventions lasting two weeks or less had no impact on the team environment.

One final explanation influencing the results of the team-building interventions has been the use of *multiple team building strategies*. While several researchers have implemented multiple intervention strategies concurrently, some researchers have implemented only one team-building intervention and assessed its influence on cohesion. In their evaluation of intervention types, Martin *et al.* (2009) found that the most effective team-building interventions focused on only one type of intervention compared to interventions that implemented multiple strategies.

Implications for coaching practice

A model of team building in sport

As noted earlier in the chapter, one of the main goals of team building is to enhance team cohesion. Carron and Spink (1993) created a team-building model that focuses on the development of cohesion by manipulating the team's environment, the team's structure, and its processes (see Figure 28.1). Although there is no one formula or strategy to improve cohesion using this team building model, what follows is the rationale for having each factor in the model and examples of how coaches can impact those factors.

In terms of the team's *environment*, Carron and Spink (1993) noted that when features related to the team's immediate physical environment and/or the appearance of the actual team members are distinctive, athletes develop a stronger sense of 'we', distinguishing themselves from non-team members (i.e. 'they') more often, and ultimately developing stronger perceptions of cohesion. For example, coaches can implement strategies that involve making the team feel distinctive by using team slogans and having team apparel.

As for the team's *structure*, it is comprised of role understanding, team leadership, and team norms. Carron and Spink (1993) noted that when team members understand and accept their role within the team, team cohesiveness is enhanced. One strategy to help foster the team's structure is to clarify player roles. To achieve this, athletes say what they perceive to be their responsibilities to their teammates and the coaching staff. Following this, the coaching staff and teammates discuss the responsibilities listed by each player. The use of this strategy should be avoided if the team is not comprised of mature athletes offering a supportive environment. This approach helps clarify each player's role in front of the coaches and their teammates. A second method to enhance the team's structure is to include team leaders in team decision-making. It is hypothesized that cohesion is influenced when coaches allow for a participative style of decision-making. One example is to establish a team council allowing team leaders to bring issues forward to the coaching staff for discussion. A third method of

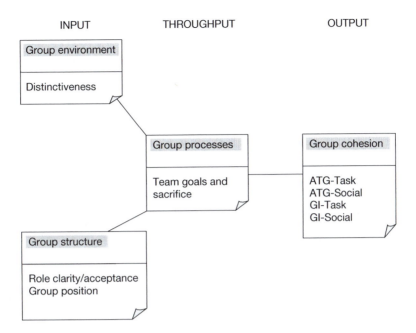

Figure 28.1: Model for team building (adapted from Carron *et al.* 1997).

impacting the team's structure is to develop team norms. Athletes who conform to the expectations of the team contribute to enhancing a team's cohesiveness. To accomplish this objective, coaches and team leaders work together to establish a behavioural code of conduct on matters that are important to team functioning. For example, team members are asked to generate a profile of how an ideal teammate would react to particular game or practice situations. The team is divided into small working groups having the same list of hypothetical but realistic situations for which they generate ideas on how the ideal teammate would react. The team then discusses and reaches a consensus as to what is acceptable and unacceptable behaviour for the situations. Upon consensus, it is agreed that this is the standard by which teammates should judge one another.

A final factor in this model is team *processes*. This involves individual sacrifices, team goals, and team cooperation. When high-status team members (e.g. team leaders) make sacrifices for the good of the team, team cohesion is enhanced. For instance, when a coach asks a team captain to 'take a player under his/her wing' whereby the team captain is responsible for integrating the new member into the team's fabric it represents a sacrifice by the team captain that is being made for the good of the team. As for team goals, involving all team members in establishing a team's collective objective will improve perceptions of team cohesion. One strategy coaches can implement is regularly scheduled team meetings to develop various team goals and objectives. For team cooperation, it is assumed that athletes displaying cooperative behaviours are superior to improving both individual and team performance, which in turn enhances team cohesion. For instance, when a coach encourages his/her veteran athletes to provide individual athletes with instruction on the skills and strategies that are beneficial for team functioning.

Approaches to team building

Within the team-building literature, two general approaches have been advanced by researchers and sport psychology consultants. The first approach involves the sport psychology consultant working directly with the coaching staff. Thus, the implementation of ideas and strategies for developing a more cohesive team becomes the direct responsibility of the coaching staff in consultation with the sport psychology consultant. In essence, the sport psychology consultant works via the coach to influence team cohesiveness. Consequently, this has been termed the *indirect* approach to team building (Carron *et al.* 1997).

Carron and Spink (1993) developed a protocol for implementing an indirect approach to team building for the exercise domain, which has since been adapted for the sport environment (see Carron *et al.* 1997; Prapavessis *et al.* 1996). Their indirect approach to team building consists of four stages. The sport psychology consultant typically covers the first three stages in a workshop with the coaches. First, the *introductory stage* presents the rationale for the team-building program, and the benefits of having high team cohesion are highlighted (e.g. improved team cohesion, better team communication, enhanced role clarity). Once the benefits have been outlined, the second step presented is the *conceptual stage* where the coaches are presented with an overview of Carron and Spink's (1993) team-building protocol (see above for a complete description of the model). The goal in presenting the team building is linked to the idea that coaches will gain a greater understanding of the elements or factors that go into building a highly cohesive team. The third step is labelled the *practical stage*, which allows the coaches to brainstorm with the sport psychology consultant to identify strategies that will impact on the factors included in the team-building model. That is, specific and concrete team-building strategies are developed that focus on enhancing aspects of the team structure, team environment, and team processes. Based on the strategies developed in the previous step, the fourth and final step labelled the *intervention stage* has the coaches returning to their respective teams in order to implement the team-building strategies previously developed. Advantages to utilizing an indirect approach to team building include reduced time commitment for the sport psychology consultant as well as the application of the program when there is a geographical barrier between sport psychology consultant and the coaching staff.

The second approach to team building involves the sport psychology consultant working closely with the team and its players in a hands-on fashion. That is, athletes, coaches, and the sport psychology consultant form a partnership, working together to build a more cohesive team. This has been labelled the *direct* approach to team building where the sport psychology consultant is a direct participant in the team-building process (Carron *et al.* 1997). In addition to the consultant working directly with the team members, another difference between the two approaches is that the direct method actively includes athletes in the team-building process, thus empowering them, which in turn fosters a sense of ownership in the team-building program. Yukelson (1997) advocated this approach and reported his experiences working with sport teams at Penn State University in the United States. Yukelson's direct approach to team building consists of four stages. First, the *assessment stage* allows the consultant to gain an understanding of the existing team dynamics. Observation and discussion with team members, coaches, and support staff helps to achieve this end. Second, the *education stage* presents an overview of the nature of groups. This could include discussion of Tuckman's (1965) model of group development (i.e. forming, storming, norming, and performing). Third, the *brainstorming stage* involves the identification of areas for improvement. And fourth, the *implementation stage* consists of applying tailored team-building strategies that were generated in the previous stage. Advantages of the direct approach to team building include the active attempt to empower team members throughout the process, the ability to purposely shape the team-building program to the needs of the team as well as allowing the sport psychology consultant to lead team sessions.

This begs the question as to which team-building approach, indirect or direct, is best for enhancing team cohesion. Based on results of a recent meta-analysis examining team building in sport (Martin *et al.* 2009), the answer is both are equally effective in enhancing team cohesion. In fact, Loughead and Hardy (2006) suggested that a mixed-method approach containing elements from both the indirect and direct approaches to team building may be useful to coaches and sport psychology consultants. While there is no simple and easy recipe to improving team cohesion (Yukelson 1997), incorporating elements from both approaches may be beneficial in terms of filling in the gaps that exist in both approaches; thus making for a more complete and comprehensive method of team building. For instance, Prapavessis *et al.* (1996) noted the absence of an assessment stage in the indirect team building method is a limitation. However, Yukelson stressed its importance in his approach to team building, suggesting that assessing the situation is a critical component of any good team-building intervention program. Consequently, it would be best practice for either the coaches or sport psychology consultant to assess the team's dynamics paying particular attention to the components contained in Carron and Spink's (1993) team-building model. A result of using this combined approach has the advantage of applying sound theory, in the case of Carron and Spink's team-building model, along with the thorough assessment of actual team dynamics as suggested by Yukelson. Assessing the team's dynamics prior to implementing a team-building program allows the coaches and/or sport psychology consultant to pinpoint areas for improvement specific to the team's needs. As a result, more efficient use of team-building strategies is achieved.

Future research directions

Despite the benefits of team building, much research is still required in this area. Future research should address best practices from a coach's perspective, including how coaches identify strategies that should be used to enhance the cohesiveness of their teams. In addition, research would benefit from knowing how coaches at different skill levels (youth sport, intercollegiate, professional) develop and implement team-building strategies. Moreover, empirical research supporting the benefits of team building in sport is restricted to able-bodied athletes. This is unfortunate because team building may be particularly important for those athletes with a physical disability who are at greater risk than those without a disability (Campbell and Jones 2002; Giacobbi Jr *et al.* 2008). For example, Campbell and Jones found that wheelchair athletes identified poor group interaction and ineffective communication about team and individual performances as sources of stress.

Another avenue for future research is to examine the effectiveness of incorporating interventions from the physical education setting into sport. One such program is the Team Building through Physical Challenges (TBPC) program which is implemented by physical education specialists for their students (Glover and Midura 1992; Midura and Glover 2005). This program involves intellectual, physical, and emotional problem-solving tasks and challenges, while emphasizing elements of fun and adventure. Gibbons and Black (1997) tested the effectiveness of a TBPC program on the self-concepts of seventh and eighth grade physical education classes. Activities included tasks focused on teamwork, organization, communication, and cooperation. Results revealed participants in the team building intervention experienced increased self-perceptions of athletic competence, social acceptance, scholastic competence, and global self-worth compared to the control group. Similar results were found by Ebbeck and Gibbons (1998) in their investigation of the effectiveness of a TBPC program on the self-conceptions of sixth and seventh grade students. Their post-intervention results revealed both male and female students in the team-building group were significantly higher on perceptions of global self-worth, athletic competence, physical appearance, and social acceptance than the control group.

Drawing on the principles of the TBPC program, Newin *et al.* (2008) created and implemented a season-long team building intervention program for youth hockey teams. Coaches attended an introductory workshop at the beginning of the season where the rationale for the team-building program was explained, where they were given a description of the team-building activities, and where they had their roles and responsibilities explained to them. Each coach then proceeded to implement five team-building activities over the course of the season using the TBPC principles. The results of this study provided initial evidence that the TBPC principles could be applied to the youth sport setting. In particular, coaches believed athletes enjoyed the team-building program and developed a variety of important life skills and abilities (e.g. listening, teamwork) due to their participation. Likewise, coaches felt their own communication and motivational skills improved as a result of their involvement in the team-building program. Coaches also felt athletes bonded during activities and improved their abilities to work together as a team. Finally, and perhaps most importantly, coaches endorsed the program for athletes of all ages and ability levels, and said they would continue conducting the team-building sessions even if this program were no longer available. While these results were positive from this one study, more research is required to determine if this program is suitable for other age groups and skill levels.

Although it is evident that team-building programs whose duration is greater than 20 weeks produces the best results (Martin *et al.* 2009), future research should examine the impact of team building over longer periods of time. For instance, coaches who implement team-building protocols with their teams over several seasons should be monitored to determine the impact this has on the team's structure, environment, and processes. It would be hypothesized that coaches who adopt a long-term approach to team building would not only have teams that are more cohesive but also would have developed a team climate or culture that fosters a positive approach to athlete growth and development.

As explained earlier in the chapter, Carron and Spink (1993) proposed a theoretical model of team building to enhance perceptions of cohesion. Despite being used in applied studies (e.g. Newin *et al.* 2008; Senécal *et al.* 2008), very little research has tested which components (e.g. group environment, group structure, group processes) of the model have the greatest impact on perceptions of cohesion. While it could be argued that all of the components are important to team building, it would be interesting to determine which components of the model are effective under different conditions (e.g. soccer vs. swimming).

Another area for future investigation is to compare approaches to team building. As noted earlier in the chapter, Martin *et al.* (2009) found that both the direct and indirect approaches to team building were equally effective. However, Loughead and Hardy (2006) proposed that a mixed-method approach that combined both elements of direct and indirect may be the most beneficial. Despite this claim, no research has directly examined if the mixed-method approach is viable and its effectiveness in relation to either the direct or indirect approaches.

The general focus of this chapter has been to outline recent literature in the area of team building with a focus on enhancing perceptions of team cohesion. In comparison to other areas in sport psychology (e.g. leadership, imagery), team-building research is in its infancy. However, the influence of team building on enhancing perceptions of cohesion cannot be overstated. Any attempt by coaches to improve the cohesiveness of their teams is welcomed. It is evident that the development of cohesion is one effective way of building a sense of team.

References

Bloom, G.A. and Stevens, D.E. (2002) 'A team-building mental skills training program with an intercollegiate equestrian team', *Athletic Insight*, 14(1), online, available at: www.athleticinsight.com/Vol4Iss1/Applied_Issue.htm (accessed 14 January 2003).

Bloom, G.A., Stevens, D.E. and Wickwire, T.L. (2003) 'Expert coaches' perceptions of team building', *Journal of Applied Sport Psychology*, 15: 129–143.

Brawley, L.R. and Paskevich, D.M. (1997) 'Conducting team building research in the context of sport and exercise', *Journal of Applied Sport Psychology*, 9: 11–40.

Campbell, E. and Jones, G. (2002) 'Cognitive appraisal and sources of stress experienced by elite male wheelchair rugby players', *Adapted Physical Activity Quarterly*, 19: 100–108.

Carron, A.V. (1982) 'Cohesiveness in sport groups: interpretations and considerations', *Journal of Sport Psychology*, 4: 123–138.

Carron, A.V. and Spink, K.S. (1993) 'Team building in an exercise setting', *The Sport Psychologist*, 7: 8–18.

Carron, A.V., Brawley, L.R. and Widmeyer, W.N. (1998) 'Measurement of cohesion in sport and exercise', in J.L. Duda (ed.) *Advances in Sport and Exercise Psychology Measurement*, Morgantown, WV: Fitness Information Technology.

Carron, A.V., Bray, S.R. and Eys, M.A. (2002a) 'Team cohesion and team success in sport', *Journal of Sport Sciences*, 20: 119–126.

Carron, A.V., Colman, M.M., Wheeler, J. and Stevens, D. (2002b) 'Cohesion and performance in sport: a meta analysis', *Journal of Sport and Exercise Psychology*, 24: 168–188.

Carron, A.V., Spink, K.S. and Prapavessis, H. (1997) 'Team building and cohesiveness in the sport and exercise setting: use of indirect interventions', *Journal of Applied Sport Psychology*, 9: 61–72.

Carron, A.V., Widmeyer, W.N. and Brawley, L.R. (1985) 'The development of an instrument to assess cohesion in sport teams: the Group Environment Questionnaire', *Journal of Sport Psychology*, 7: 244–266.

Davids, K. and Nutter, A. (1988) 'The cohesion-performance relationship of English national league volleyball teams', *Journal of Human Movement Studies*, 15: 205–213.

Ebbeck, V. and Gibbons, S.L. (1998) 'The effect of a team building program on the self-conceptions of grade 6 and 7 physical education students', *Journal of Sport and Exercise Psychology*, 20: 300–310.

Eitington, J.E. (1989) *The Winning Trainer*, 2nd edn, Houston, TX: Gulf Publishing.

Festinger, L., Schachter, S. and Back, K. (1950) *Social Pressure in Informal Groups*, New York: Harper & Row.

Giacobbi Jr, P.R., Stancil, M., Hardin, B. and Bryant, L. (2008) 'Physical activity and quality of life experienced by highly active individuals with physical disabilities', *Adapted Physical Activity Quarterly*, 25: 189–207.

Gibbons, S.L. and Black, K.M. (1997) 'Effect of participation in team building activities on the self-concepts of middle school physical education students', *Avante*, 3: 46–60.

Glover, D.R. and Midura, D.W. (1992) *Team Building through Physical Challenges*, Champaign, IL: Human Kinetics.

Golembiewski, R. (1962) *The Small Group*, Chicago, IL: University of Chicago Press.

Gross, N. and Martin, W.E. (1952) 'On group cohesiveness', *American Journal of Sociology*, 52: 546–554.

Hardy, C.J. and Crace, R.K. (1997) 'Foundations of team building: introduction to the team building primer', *Journal of Applied Sport Psychology*, 9: 1–10.

Landers, D.M. and Lueschen, G. (1974) 'Team performance outcome and cohesiveness of competitive co-acting groups', *International Review of Sport Sociology*, 9: 57–69.

Lott, A.J. and Lott, B.E. (1965) 'Group cohesiveness as interpersonal attraction: a review of relationships with antecedent and consequent variables', *Psychological Bulletin*, 64: 259–309.

Loughead, T.M. and Hardy, J. (2006) 'Team cohesion: from theory to research to team building', in S. Hanton and S. Mellalieu (eds) *Literature Reviews in Sport Psychology*, Hauppauge, NY: Nova Science Publishers.

Martin, L.J., Carron, A.V. and Burke, S.M. (2009) 'Team building interventions in sport: a meta-analysis', *Sport and Exercise Psychology Review*, 5: 3–18.

Midura, D.W. and Glover, D.R. (2005) *Essentials of Team Building: Principles and Practices*, Champaign, IL: Human Kinetics.

Mudrack, P.E. (1989) 'Defining group cohesiveness: a legacy of confusion?' *Small Group Behavior*, 20: 37–49.

Mullen, B. and Copper, C. (1994) 'The relation between group cohesiveness and performance: an integration', *Psychological Bulletin*, 115: 210–227.

Newin, J., Bloom, G.A. and Loughead, T.M. (2008) 'Youth ice hockey coaches' perceptions of a team-building intervention program', *The Sport Psychologist*, 22: 54–72.

Newman, B. (1984) 'Expediency as benefactor: how team building saves time and gets the job done', *Training and Development Journal*, 38: 26–30.

Pain, M. and Harwood, C. (2009) 'Team building through mutual sharing and open discussion of team functioning', *The Sport Psychologist*, 23: 523–542.

Prapavessis, H., Carron, A.V. and Spink, K.S. (1996) 'Team building in sport', *International Journal of Sport Psychology*, 27: 269–285.

Senécal, J., Loughead, T.M. and Bloom, G.A. (2008) 'A season-long team-building intervention program: examining the effect of team goal setting on cohesion', *Journal of Sport and Exercise Psychology*, 30: 186–199.

Stevens, D.E. and Bloom, G.A. (2003) 'The effects of team building on cohesion', *Avante*, 9: 43–54.

Tuckman, B.W. (1965) 'Development sequences in small groups', *Psychological Bulletin*, 63: 384–399.

Tziner, A., Nicola, N. and Rizac, A. (2003) 'Relation between social cohesion and team performance in soccer teams', *Perceptual and Motor Skills*, 96: 145–148.

Voight, M. and Callaghan, J. (2001) 'A team building intervention program: application and evaluation with two university soccer teams', *Journal of Sport Behavior*, 24: 420–431.

Widmeyer, W.N. and DuCharme, K. (1997) 'Team building through team goal setting', *Journal of Applied Sport Psychology*, 9: 97–113.

Williams, J.M. and Widmeyer, W.N. (1991) 'The cohesion-performance relationship in a coacting sport', *Journal of Sport and Exercise Psychology*, 13: 364–371.

Woodcock, M. and Francis, D. (1994) *Teambuilding Strategy*, Aldershot: Gower Publishing.

Yukelson, D. (1997) 'Principles of effective team building interventions in sport: a direct services approach at Penn State University', *Journal of Applied Sport Psychology*, 9: 73–96.

PART III

Influences on becoming a sports coach

What do we know about the processes of becoming, and developing as, a sports coach?

A

Critical perspectives on becoming a sports coach

29

COACH EDUCATION AND LEARNING

Developing the field

Christopher Cushion

UNIVERSITY OF LOUGHBOROUGH, UK

Lee Nelson

UNIVERSITY OF HULL, UK

Introduction

A problem in considering coach learning is an apparent lack of definitional clarity, well illustrated by the wide range of terminology employed, at times uncritically, to describe coach development (Cushion *et al.* 2010). For example, coach learning, coach education, coach training, coach development, continuing professional development, plus coaching and sport instructor certification are terms used interchangeably and inconsistently. Coach learning has only recently been presented as a term bringing together research into, and understanding about, the broader learning of coaches (Cushion 2011a; Cushion *et al.* 2010; Nelson *et al.* 2006). The recognition of coach learning enables a view that 'extends far beyond any formal training program' (Côté 2006: 221). Yet, within the literature there remains a 'lack of concern about how coaches learn' (Nelson and Cushion 2006: 174). Indeed, Lyle (2007) has argued that coach educators are often unaware of frameworks that could guide and underpin practice.

Learning is an important term as it places the emphasis on the person in whom change is expected (Jarvis 2006). Learning can happen through a number of means; for example, through experience, reflection, study or instruction and can embrace all of the mechanisms through which coaches acquire the knowledge that informs their practice (Nelson *et al.* 2006; Cushion 2011a). Jarvis (2004: 43) supports this stating that 'many different learning processes occur during the human lifespan, but not all of them may be considered educational'. Coach learning therefore not only occurs inside, but outside of educational settings (Nelson *et al.* 2006; Cushion *et al.* 2003). Consequently, while the coach learner is the essential element in the learning process, the coach educator is not. Nevertheless, the coach educator still plays a central role in coach learning, contributing to efforts to raise coaching standards and develop coaching as a profession.

This chapter addresses the central issue of coach learning, and aims to draw conclusions from the existing literature to suggest how coach learning across development structures and interventions can be developed. While there are numerous prescriptions *for* coach learning, the evidence *of* coach learning is limited. Therefore, the chapter argues for a more comprehensive understanding of coach learning and its development supported by empirical research. Suggestions are provided that offer a research agenda to plug obvious gaps and push the field toward a more in-depth and complete understanding of how coaches learn, and how the learning of coaches might be better supported.

The purpose of coach learning

Certification demonstrates that coaches have satisfied sports governing bodies' criteria by acquiring and displaying a minimum level of competency (Nelson *et al.* 2006). Thus, an assumption is made that coaches will leave a given learning episode having the requisite knowledge, and a battery of strategies, to work effectively as coaches at the level for which they have been prepared (Cushion *et al.* 2010). This process suggests an emphasis on learning in 'formal' situations that fulfil purely instrumental means. However, the complex nature of coaching, replete with its many subtleties and nuances, seriously calls into question the legitimacy and value of an overly instrumental approach to coach learning and its provision (Cushion 2011a, 2011b). In an attempt to move beyond this instrumental perspective, there have been calls for coach learning to develop what have been termed 'imaginative, dynamic, and thoughtful coaches' (Cushion *et al.* 2003: 216). Indeed, it has been suggested that coach education should encourage practitioners to think creatively about alternative ways of coaching, thus better preparing coaches to deal with the associated realities of their professional work (Cassidy *et al.* 2009).

In the broader learning literature there remains considerable debate about understanding learning (Hodkinson *et al.* 2008). This body of work argues the respective merits of cognitive as opposed to situational theories of learning (e.g. Anderson *et al.* 1996; Greeno 1997). Similarly, writers such as Sfard (1998) and Säljö (2003) approach the issue from the root metaphors of acquisition (cognitive) and participation (situated) to conceptualise and debate learning (Mason 2007). Indeed, Trudel and Gilbert (2006) have used Sfard's (1998) metaphors as a useful tool to examine the coach education literature. Understanding these broader differences in conceptualising learning matter, however, the epistemological dualisms that these differences produce create a fundamental meta-theoretical dilemma. It is not the purpose here to attempt to resolve the tension between these conceptualisations of learning, if indeed they could be solved (Cushion *et al.* 2010). Instead, the chapter is structured to illustrate and discuss research examining avenues through which coaches learn. To achieve this, the chapter is structured around the formal, nonformal, and informal learning distinction broadly accepted and used within the adult learning literature (Coombs and Ahmed 1974; Merriam and Caffarella 1999; Tuijnman and Boström 2002). However, in applying this conceptual framework, we agree with Jarvis (2006: 195) who contends that 'the terms formal, nonformal and informal learning have crept into the educational vocabulary when we have actually meant *learning in* formal, nonformal and informal situations'. There are debates and complexities around the use of these terms. However, in this case they have enabled an organisation of the research, a platform to structure the discussion surrounding coach learning, and provided a framework to integrate research from relevant domains. The chapter, therefore, presents an overview of research conducted in coach learning (specifically informal and formal) and where relevant integrates and considers research from related learning domains. A word of caution is required here.

For the purpose of clarity, the categories are discussed separately, but they should be understood as interconnected modes of a complex learning process rather than discrete entities (Cushion *et al.* 2010). In reality, they may exist simultaneously in concert or conflict. Indeed, we recognise that learning acquired in one situation will inevitably influence a coach's learning engagement in other situations (Nelson *et al.* 2006).

Overview of informal and formal coach learning

Coaches' learning: informal situations

Learning takes place in a wide variety of contexts, the majority of which occur in informal settings beyond dedicated formal learning environments (Brookfield 1986; Merriam and Caffarella 1999). Research into coach learning has consistently demonstrated that practitioners learn through a variety of learning sources identified as between three and seventeen learning categories (see Table 29.1). Learning through practical coaching, observation and discussion with 'others' is a recurring theme that has been reported consistently in the literature (e.g. Bloom *et al.* 1995; Cushion *et al.* 2003; Irwin *et al.* 2004; Reade *et al.* 2008; Schempp *et al.* 1998; Wright *et al.* 2007). It is clear that learning in informal situations is a well-established learning pathway for coaches, with its implications for knowledge development and professional socialisation being recognised in the coaching literature (e.g. Cassidy *et al.* 2009; Cushion *et al.* 2003).

Self-directed learning is a term used interchangeably with informal learning (Merriam and Caffarella 1999), although the former implies an instrumental sense of purpose that may not apply to some 'experiential' learning (Cushion 2011a). There has been significant interest in developing informal learning. However, this is as much a commentary on the efficacy of other learning provision than on the effectiveness of learning in informal situations (Cushion *et al.* 2010). Indeed, the dominance of informal and self-directed learning is due largely to the limitations and low impact of current formal provision (Cushion *et al.* 2003, 2010). Moreover, coach education has lacked any coherent or overarching structure meaning that coaches have been left to 'go it alone', resulting in often ad hoc, negotiated and individual learning curriculum (Cushion *et al.* 2010; Cushion 2011a, 2011b; Nelson *et al.* 2006). Therefore, learning in informal situations often occurs without a prescribed curriculum, facilitated by an 'other'. This can ignore power relations where the 'other' dominates the learning process and where particular ideological interpretations of high-status knowledge are enforced (Cushion *et al.* 2010). Coaches actually learn and prefer to learn from a range of sources, and, coaches may desire greater opportunities to learn in more formal situations, thus presenting a more balanced approach (Erickson *et al.* 2008; Cushion *et al.* 2010).

Learning from experience or experiential learning is considered in the wider learning literature in many different ways with different processes involved (e.g. Moon 2004; Jarvis *et al.* 2003; Jarvis 2004). In terms of the coaching literature, experiential learning has not been treated with the same clarity, with research often using the terms interchangeably and without definition (e.g. Cushion *et al.* 2003, 2006; Jones *et al.* 2004). While it seems that there is no single all-encompassing definition of experiential learning, there are many ways in which the term can be used (Moon 2004). Some clarity around the distinctive features of this learning process would seem useful to help understand coach learning, particularly as it is cited consistently as a key mechanism in coach development.

Table 29.1 Overview of research and learning sources

Study	Participants	Method(s)	Data Analysis	Learning Categories
Abraham *et al.* (2006)	16 expert coaches from 13 sports	In–depth interviews	Inductive/ deductive analysis	Courses, experience, other coaches and serendipitous (i.e. reading books, encounters with sport scientists, and experiences outside of sport).
Erickson *et al.* (2008)	44 voluntary coaches, mixed sports on Canadian NCCP level 2 or 3	Interviews	Qualitative and quantitative	Experience, other coaches/peers, formal courses, mentor, observing others, clinics, print/ electronic material.
Fleurance and Cotteaux (1999)	10 expert coaches	In–depth interviews	Inductive analysis	Formal education, interaction with high-level athletes, ongoing education, mentors, personal commitment to coaching, playing experience and professional experience.
Irwin *et al.* (2004)	16 elite gymnastics coaches	In–depth interviews	Inductive analysis	Coaching courses, coaching manuals, foreign coach and travel, mentor coaches, past experiences as a performer, squad sessions, trial and error and video and observations.
Jones *et al.* (2003)	1 elite soccer coach	Field notes and five interviews	Life-story narrative	Coach certification, learning from others and learning from the self (i.e. experiential learning and past playing experiences).
Jones *et al.* (2004)	8 elite coaches, from 5 individual and team sports	In–depth interviews	Life-story narrative	Athletes, athletic experience, coach certification, coaching experience, conferences, mentors, other coaches, previous jobs, teacher training, seminars/ workshops, and reading.
Lemyre *et al.* (2007)	36 voluntary coaches from 3 team sports	In–depth interviews	Deductive analysis	Interactions, Internet, resource materials and training courses.

There is a distinction between mediated and unmediated (Moon 2004) or primary and secondary (Jarvis 2004) experiences. Jarvis (2004) describes a primary experience as where a person enters a situation and experiences it subjectively. The secondary experience is mediated and is not always interactive (from other's primary experiences) (Jarvis 2004). Newman (1999) suggests that this experience is constructed, or engineered in some way. Often learning experiences are presented as a sequence (e.g. Kolb's cycle) with the assumption that learning results from the experience if it is simply organised correctly (Moon 2001). However, Moon (2004: 8) suggests a need to recognise experience as more 'slippery', and cites Eraut (2000: 28) stating that, 'tidy images of learning are usually deceptive'. Indeed, the evidence suggests that learning experiences are of a complex constructed nature (Fraser 1995). Experiential learning is more than just doing. Coaches must become competent at setting problems and then developing and evaluating their strategies for solving the problems they have identified (Trudel and Gilbert 2006). Without a form of reflective process, coaches uncritically accrue experience without it meaningfully impacting on their practice (Cushion *et al.* 2010; Gilbert and Trudel 2001). Instead, coaches are more likely to 'non-reflectively' accept, and be socialised into, the knowledge, values, beliefs and expectations of the sporting culture (Jarvis 2006).

Reflection

Ideas about reflection have spread across a range of domains (e.g. nursing, Burns and Bulman 2000; healthcare, Taylor and White 2000; teaching, McAlpine and Weston 2002; Moon 2004). In this literature, there remain concerns about the relationship between reflection and effective behaviour (e.g. Ferry and Ross-Gordon 1998; McAlpine and Weston 2002; Moon 2004). However, reflection appears to offer a great deal for understanding coaches' experiential learning (e.g. Cushion *et al.* 2003; Cushion 2006; Cassidy *et al.* 2009), but these arguments tend not to be supported empirically. Arguably, the best theoretically framed explanation for how coaches learn experientially, through the process of reflection, has come from Gilbert and Trudel's (2001) experiential learning model. The authors' demonstrated how coaches learned by engaging in three forms of reflective practice: (1) reflection-in-action (i.e. during the action present); (2) reflection-on-action (i.e. within the action present but not in the midst of activity); and (3) retrospective reflection-on-action (i.e. outside of the action present). Gilbert and Trudel (2001, 2004, 2005) presented evidence that Schön's (1983) theory of reflective practice provides an effective framework for analysing and explaining how coaches frame their knowledge and learn from practical coaching experiences.

While Gilbert and Trudel have provided insight into how coaches engage in the process of reflection, there remain concerns about the relationship between reflection and effective coaching behaviour and practice (Cushion *et al.* 2010). Related to this is what Moon (2004) describes as an increasing awareness of a 'depth dimension' to reflection and a recognition that superficial refection may not be effective as a means of learning (Cushion 2011a). Often it is difficult to get learners to engage with reflection and actually reflect, but this can be overcome. However, reflection can be undertaken in a superficial way, which in fact might be little different from recounting events in a form of descriptive writing (Cushion *et al.* 2010). Several authors have commented on the inadequacy of much activity performed as reflection because it is in fact non-critical and non-reflective (e.g. Kim 1999; Moon 2004). Reflection has a range of application with a continuum from shallow description at one end to deep critical reflection at the other (Cushion *et al.* 2010; Cushion 2011a). The key to this process is learning the skill of reflection and allowing enough time for it to be developed and supported. Indeed, Knowles *et al.* (2001: 204) suggested that, the 'development of reflective skills is not a simplistic process even with structured support. Coach educators cannot therefore assume that development of reflective skills will be a naturally occurring phenomena that runs parallel to increasing coaching experience'. Reflective strategies can be used in coach learning, but these approaches require time, commitment and programmatic effort (Gilbert and Trudel 2006). The question therefore remains, how much might learning to reflect on a course be used in actual coaching practice? A similar issue can be found in education where 'educators seem to assume that reflective thinking learned via reflective practice would be retained, generalised and or transferred to ordinary settings. No evidence exists to support this assumption' (Tsangaridou and Siedentop 1995: 228).

Mentoring

Mentoring has been identified as offering both structured and unstructured support for coach learning (Cushion *et al.* 2010; Cushion 2011a), and several authors have outlined the pervasiveness and impact of mentoring in coaching (e.g. Bloom *et al.* 1998; Cushion *et al.* 2003). Mentoring is the most visible example of a practice where formal and informal learning meet (Colley *et al.* 2003). Indeed, influencing the experiences and interactions of coaches is suggested by a number of authors (e.g. Cushion *et al.* 2003; Werthner and Trudel 2006; Trudel and Gilbert 2006), where mentoring is conceived as bringing an increasing formalisation to inherently informal practice (Colley *et al.* 2003).

Colley *et al.* (2003) strike a cautionary note concerning formalising mentoring as 'fervour without infrastructure' (Freedman 1999: 2). They argue that the perception of mentoring as inherently informal means minimal training and support for mentors. Formal mentoring can expose the frailty of dyadic models of mentoring relationships and introduces the triadic element of external interests pursued by dominant groupings (Colley *et al.* 2003; Jones *et al.* 2009). The findings from reviews and research into mentoring suggest that there can be unthinking assumptions that such transference is straightforward (Cushion *et al.* 2010). In fact, the mentoring process changes as it becomes applied through planned programmes in formalised situations. The success of learning will be dependent upon the quality of the relationship between mentor and protégé (Dymock 1999; Cushion 2006). Indeed, there are common issues identified that negatively impact mentoring including: lack of time and training, personal or professional compatibility, undesirable attitudes or behaviours, and unnoticed workloads (Cushion *et al.* 2010; Cushion 2011a). Mentees were concerned with a lack of mentor interest and training and problematic behaviours (overly critical, defensive, controlling) (Cushion *et al.* 2010). In addition, Jones *et al.* (2009) highlight the possibilities of 'toxic mentoring' with asymmetric power relationships shaping both the mentoring experience and the learning that takes place. Ehrich *et al.* (2004: 533) state 'mentoring is a highly complex dynamic and interpersonal relationship that requires at the very least, time interest and commitment of mentors and mentees and strong support from educational or organisational leaders responsible for overseeing programmes'. Like much of the wider mentoring literature, Cushion (2006) offers theories and ideas *for* mentoring, rather than evidence *of* mentoring. This is a perspective reiterated by Jones *et al.* (2009), who suggest that many of the claims about mentoring are largely unfounded. These authors cite Colley *et al.* (2003: 1) who conclude that 'existing research evidence scarcely justifies [mentoring's] use on such a massive scale, [while] the movement has not yet developed a sound theoretical base to underpin policy or practice'.

Situated learning

Situated learning theory has been offered as having utility to explain and frame learning within the coaching domain (e.g. Cushion 2006; Cassidy *et al.* 2009). Lave and Wenger (1991) were unhappy with overly simplistic views of learning 'by doing' (Fuller *et al.* 2005), arguing instead for learning to be conceived as a complex, relational and situated endeavour. This required a conceptual shift from the traditional view of 'the individual as learner to learning as participation in the social world, and from the concept of cognitive process to the more-encompassing view of social practice' (Lave and Wenger 1991: 43). Lave and Wenger (1991) argue that social practice is the primary, generative phenomenon, and learning is one of its characteristics, and as such should be analysed as an integral part of social practice. This view seems to be analogous with the evidence from coaching on how knowledge evolves from practice (Cushion *et al.* 2010).

Learners progress from less important tasks toward crucial 'core' tasks, thus moving from peripheral to full or central participation, with understanding unfolding as the learner develops a view of what the activity entails (Cushion 2011a). This process ensures that learning itself is an improvised practice where the 'curriculum' unfolds in opportunities for engaging in practice (Fuller *et al.* 2005). The individual is located within the community of practice and facilitates learning through mutual engagement in an activity that is defined by negotiations of meaning both inside and outside the community (Fuller *et al.* 2005). As communities are social structures they involve power relations, and the way power is exercised can make legitimate peripheral participation empowering or disempowering (Lave and Wenger 1991; Fuller *et al.* 2005). Examples from coaching are presented by Culver and Trudel (2006), Lemyre *et al.* (2007) and Culver *et al.* (2009), who drew on the work of Wenger (1998) to cultivate coaching communities of practice (CCoPs). The results of these studies suggested that a facilitator played an important role in the group learning process, adding a certain amount of structure to the learning (Culver and Trudel 2008). However, it is the processes, relationships and experiences that constitute the participants' sense of belonging that underpin the character and extent of subsequent learning (Fuller *et al.* 2005). Therefore, it could be argued that the nature of 'manufactured' or 'facilitated' CCoPs do not engage the coaches' sense of belonging, existing only in a superficial sense and thus inhibiting any meaningful learning (Cushion 2008, 2011b).

Informal learning situations: implications

Learning for coaches most frequently occurs outside educational settings, and often in environments where the primary purpose is not learning (Cushion *et al.* 2010). This has been due to the limitations of current formal provision, the lack of an overarching structure and issues around volunteerism, which combine to allow a negotiated and individual learning curriculum. However, this curriculum is not unproblematic; it can ignore underlying power relations and can promote and reinforce certain ideological interpretations of knowledge and practice. Trudel and Gilbert (2006) suggest: experience and interaction with others are inevitable phenomena in coaching; this type of learning deals with knowing not knowledge (Sfard 1998); and control of the learning content is therefore impossible. To develop coach learning and ensure an even developmental experience for coaches, coach education must find ways to control and facilitate these experiences (Cushion *et al.* 2003; Cushion 2006; Werthner and Trudel 2006).

Reflection appears particularly important in framing coaches' learning from experience. In reality coaches may reflect in a superficial and descriptive way, which is inadequate because it lacks critical thinking and, indeed, actual reflection. There is a depth dimension to reflection and the evidence demonstrates that coaches need to be supported and allowed time to move toward deep critical reflection and away from shallow and meaningless description. Support is highlighted in developing reflection, and this support is an important determinate of experiential and informal learning more broadly. Situated, collaborative reflection within a mentoring relationship has potential to develop practice (Cushion *et al.* 2010). However, the research in coaching supporting these approaches is limited, presenting an argument *for* their use, rather than evidence *of* their use. Therefore, the following issues need to be addressed:

1   Evidence linking mentoring, reflection and situated learning to changes in coaching practice and athlete outcomes.
2   Evidence to see if the model of reflection applies to coaches working in diverse contexts and levels beyond youth domains.
3   Many coaches are non-reflective and simply accrue experience without it impacting their practice. The reasons behind this and 'descriptive' or weak reflection require further elucidation.
4   Reflection and situated learning, while not issue free, can structure learning, but they require time and effort to develop and become embedded into coach learning. How might this be achieved?
5   Mentoring plays a key role in informal and formal learning, can be experienced both positively and negatively, but needs more evidence to identify its impact on practice.
6   The role of mentor's content knowledge on the process and impact of mentoring requires investigation.

Coaches' learning: formal situations

So far the chapter has considered learning occurring outside of educational settings and often in environments where the primary purpose is not learning. Now the chapter turns to learning that occurs in formal situations. Activities conforming to this definition of coach learning include large-scale coach certification programmes developed by the national governing bodies of sport and higher education courses relating to coaching and the sport sciences (Nelson *et al.* 2006). Formal coach education has understandably attracted considerable attention with numerous scholars having researched (e.g. Cassidy *et al.* 2006; Culver and Trudel 2006; Demers *et al.* 2006; Gilbert and Trudel 1999; Hammond and Perry 2005; Jones and Turner 2006; Knowles *et al.* 2005; McCullick *et al.* 2005; Nelson and Cushion 2006; Vargas-Tonsing 2007; Wiersma and Sherman 2005) and specifically written about this topic (e.g. Cassidy *et al.* 2004; Cushion *et al.* 2003; Lyle 2002, 2007; Trudel and Gilbert 2006). Despite a seemingly large body of work, closer inspection reveals that, to date, there have been few studies that have attempted to directly investigate and evaluate coach education programmes (Cushion *et al.* 2010; McCullick *et al.* 2009). As a result, there remains no evidence to link coach education certification with coaching competency or developments in practice, despite many courses being competency-based (Cushion *et al.* 2010). In other words, it cannot be said that the competency achieved has been as a result of the programme.

Coaches have tended to attach much less importance to formal coach education for acquiring knowledge (Gould *et al.* 1990; Irwin *et al.* 2004; Schempp *et al.* 1998). When asked to comment on their experiences, coaches have suggested that: (1) courses often give little more than a basic understanding but offer a starting point (e.g. Abraham *et al.* 2006); (2) they often arrive already knowing about, and putting into practice, much of what is covered, meaning that little new knowledge is gained (Gilbert and Trudel 1999; Irwin *et al.* 2004); (3) some of the theoretical material covered is considered too abstract from everyday practice to be considered worthwhile (Lemyre *et al.* 2007); (4) courses try to cram too much information into a relatively short period of time (Lemyre *et al.* 2007); and (5) they have come to question much of the information acquired during courses later in their careers (Irwin *et al.* 2004). As a result, some coaches have even admitted to attending later awards because of their being a compulsory requirement (Wright *et al.* 2007). The element of compulsion and the need for certification means that coaches are unlikely to directly contest the programme or coach educator (Cushion *et al.* 2003; Chesterfield *et al.* 2010). Indeed, Chesterfield *et al.* (2010) found that coaches purposely gave an outward appearance of acceptance, while harbouring and restricting their disagreement with, and rejection of, the official coaching orientation.

We have recently questioned the 'education' within coach education and whether it is appropriate that provision of this nature is conceived of as an educational endeavour (e.g. Nelson *et al.* 2006; Cushion 2011a; Cushion *et al.* 2010). 'Coach education' is the terminology most frequently employed to describe formalised provision. Despite this, developmental courses could, perhaps even should, be more appropriately labelled coach training or even indoctrination in some cases. According to Buckley and Caple (2000), education and training have a number of conceptual differences. Training is more job-orientated, focusing on the acquisition of knowledge, behaviours and skills specific to a profession. Training 'tends to be a more mechanistic process which emphasises uniform and predictable responses to standard guidance and instruction reinforced by practice and repetition' (Buckley and Caple 2000: 2). Education, on the other hand, is more person-orientated, focusing on providing 'more theoretical and conceptual frameworks designed to stimulate an individual's analytical and critical abilities' (ibid.). While training promotes uniformity of knowledge and practices, education attempts to increase variability, by emphasising and explicating individual differences (Nelson *et al.* 2006; Cushion 2011a).

As we have argued elsewhere (e.g. Nelson *et al.* 2006; Cushion *et al.* 2010; Cushion 2011a, 2011b), the research critiquing formal provision seems to locate it as training rather than education. In this respect, the literature suggests that coaches are frequently subjected to a standardised curriculum privileging a technocratic rationality through a 'tool box' of professional knowledge and a 'gold standard' of coaching (e.g. Abraham and Collins 1998; Cushion *et al.* 2003; Cushion *et al.* 2010; Cushion 2011a, 2011b). This is aimed at developing coaches with standardised knowledge to overcome perceived typical coaching dilemmas in their domain, suggesting that much of coach education provision could in fact be labelled as coach training (Nelson *et al.* 2006; Cushion *et al.* 2010; Cushion 2011a, 2011b). Viewed in this way, coach training is arguably effective in achieving its desired learning objectives, with the gaining of certification providing evidence that many practitioners have satisfied the governing bodies' criteria for minimum levels of coaching competency (Nelson *et al.* 2006; Cushion *et al.* 2010; Cushion 2011a, 2011b).

Some provision in formal situations could even be described as indoctrination, 'activities that set out to convince us that there is a "right" way of thinking and feeling and behaving' (Rogers 2002: 53) Indeed, Chesterfield *et al.* (2010) provided evidence supporting the claim that coach education can be appropriately considered indoctrination in certain instances. In this respect, indoctrination denies the learner choice, instead exposing them to a single set of expected values and attitudes. This might include indoctrinating a prescribed method of delivery, feedback sequence, coaching philosophy, or tactical and technical approach (Jones *et al.* 2003; Nelson *et al.* 2006; Cushion *et al.* 2010; Cushion 2011a, 2011b). Currently, coach learning in formal situations defines what knowledge is necessary for coaches to practice and how that knowledge can 'best' be transmitted, and certification requires coaches to structure sessions, deliver information to athletes and provide feedback in a prescribed manner to be deemed competent (Nelson *et al.* 2006; Cushion *et al.* 2010; Cushion 2011a, 2011b). With this in mind, coach education that delivers a bio-scientific discourse, within a techno-rational approach to coaching, might be appropriately described as training or even indoctrination in certain instances (Cushion *et al.* 2010).

Responding to criticisms of formal learning and drawing on principles from adult learning, alternative approaches such as problem-based learning (PBL) (Jones and Turner 2006) have been proposed. As part of a wider drive to adopt principles of 'adult learning', a problem-based approach has been suggested as an effective instructional method (Trudel and Gilbert 2006). Although new to coach learning, the approach has been used in other domains (e.g. medicine and education) (Trudel and Gilbert 2006; Collier and O'Sullivan 1997). In a problem-based approach, delivery starts with role-related problems rather than with the presentation of disciplinary knowledge. As such, 'the key to PBL is using material through which students engage with problems in situations as near as possible to real life' (Jarvis *et al.* 2003: 117).

While PBL can be viewed as participation learning (Sfard 1998), Trudel and Gilbert (2006) point out that the participation metaphor involves the focus on the actual practice of coaching. In actual coaching practice: (1) problems are not presented, they have to be recognised and defined; (2) problems have their origins in events that happen weeks, months or even years before (Gilbert and Trudel 2001); (3) the process of creating solutions includes interactions with other participants in the sports environment (Gilbert and Trudel 2001); and (4) there is no appointed facilitator to stimulate the reflective process (Trudel and Gilbert 2006). In light of this, Trudel and Gilbert (2006) argue that coach education should instead use an issue-based approach that is based around actual practice in an attempt to assist and promote the development of reflective skills in coaching practitioners (Cushion *et al.* 2010).

Formal learning situations: implications

Formal mediated modes of learning are crucial to developing coach learning and coaching. However, the evidence concerning formal coach learning is largely critical, and to date only one study has considered the impact of formal learning on developing coaches' knowledge and understanding, impacting coaches' practice, or if the programme matched the expectations of the learner (Gilbert and Trudel 1999). Clearly evidence of formal learning's impact is urgently required and those developing coach education should also incorporate more rigorous monitoring and evaluation into programmes.

Numerous prescriptions *for* formal coach learning exist drawing on approaches from adult learning. However, few studies have assessed the basic tenets of adult learning principles, and the theories underlying these principles are not rigorously derived from scientific theory, that, in turn, has been shown to be evidence based (Cushion *et al.* 2010). With changes to provision and alternative approaches, there is currently no evidence that evaluates the impact of these or that show if one method will be more or less effective than another. Moreover, a key issue that limits the potential of any new approach is that coaching courses tend to be condensed (Trudel and Gilbert 2006). For example, a PBL approach requires time to develop and if participants are encouraged to work in small groups this requires time to develop trust and rapport (Trudel and Gilbert 2006). The limited time that coaches have to invest in their preparation has been noted (Abraham and Collins 1998), and to facilitate coach learning and development based on experience the appropriateness of 'weekend education programmes' is questionable (Trudel and Gilbert 2006). These reservations notwithstanding, any learning method needs clear tutor/facilitator training and support, and needs a well-planned curriculum with clear learning objectives (Cushion *et al.* 2010). Therefore, it would appear that the following need to be addressed:

1   Issues already identified from existing research of current formal provision.
2   Evidence how existing formal learning impacts coaches' knowledge, practice, and athlete learning.
3   Comparisons between different approaches to coach learning and their impact on coaches' knowledge, practice, and athlete learning.

Coach learning: methodological and theoretical issues

For coach learning to develop it needs to ensure that it is meeting the needs of coaches and athletes. Linked to this is understanding how coach educators can ensure that coach learning leads to enhanced coach and athlete development. Any current prescriptions for coach learning are 'substantively and strategically' incomplete because they are missing data and evidence (McLaughlin and Zarrow 2001; Armour 2010). As a result, it seems crucial that research is undertaken to determine the complex ways coaches learn and, in turn, how coach and athlete learning are linked. However, learning is complex, not linear, and as a result is difficult to quantify. There are a myriad of variables that impact learning that can make 'measuring' in experimental or causal studies problematic. However, coach learning needs to be evaluated beyond cross-sectional, self-report or 'opinionaire' type studies. There has been scant systematic research on the effects of coach learning on improvements in coaching practice or on athlete outcomes. Coach learning needs effective longitudinal evaluation without which it is impossible to determine what works, why and for whom. Indeed, the existing limited research evidence gives us little appreciation of the teaching and learning preferences, and needs, of coaches across coaching domains and within the developmental spectrum.

Here, we contend that coach learning scholars need to more critically engage with learning theory and consider what implications the underpinning tenets of each theory has for how the field goes about conceptualising the coach learner and the development of learning. Indeed, Rink (2001: 112) argues that all pedagogy has its 'roots in particular learning theory'. For example, theories such as behaviourism reduce learning to a simple linear process, while cognitive approaches take an impersonal view of learning as knowledge acquisition. The discourse of behavioural and cognitive approaches can be seen to dominate current coach education (Cassidy *et al.* 2009; Cushion *et al.* 2010). More constructivist approaches are reflected in recent research; however, the research area, while still emerging, has largely developed serendipitously and is driven by individual research interests, and such work often cites 'in-vogue' theories or has a particular theoretical agenda (Cushion *et al.* 2010).

In responding to issues raised in coach learning, it is perhaps tempting to bring 'new' theories to coaching that are, in fact, recycled learning approaches and theories from other domains. Coaching needs to critically engage with the central tenets behind the theories and alternative approaches to learning to specifically develop 'coach learning' theory. Currently there is a tendency to look at 'second order' research that has taken ideas from 'first order research' (Cushion *et al.* 2010). Uncritically recycling theory and learning approaches into coaching therefore runs the risk of compounding limited thinking (Cushion *et al.* 2010). Indeed, while there is considerable support from the literature for a range of learning theories, the transfer of theory directly to coaching is neither neat nor unproblematic. The research to date has been unable to link any of these to effective practice across domains, not just in coaching, and this needs to be addressed.

Theoretical perspective and perceptions of coaching will also impact approaches to researching it. Research methodology will probably be different if one assumes that coaching is stable, consistent and identical across and between contexts, and the aim of research is to generate best practice models. In contrast, those who believe that coaching is individual, has its own contextual make-up, is in constant flux, and that the aim of research is to understand these inherent complexities and diversities, and assist coaches in becoming capable of adapting to contextual demands, may adopt an alternative methodological stance. Recent research in education (e.g. Day *et al.* 2008) has utilised integrated qualitative and quantitative methodology to research the broad and diverse factors contributing to teacher effectiveness. Indeed, Gilbert and Trudel's (1999) proposed coach education evaluation methodology calls for a mixed methods approach to investigate coaches' experiences, knowledge development and changes in coaching practice.

Currently, the coach learning literature, as well as learning literature from other domains suffers from being of mixed quality. A number of issues need to be addressed by future research to improve the quality and impact to the field:

1. A developed theoretical position.
2. Make explicit the underlying assumptions about coaching and learning and set conceptual boundaries for coaching or the domain under study (i.e. performance coaching versus participation coaching).
3. Use coaches and coaching as the focus of the research rather than in education with students.
4. Avoid cross-sectional perception/satisfaction studies.
5. Avoid stretching findings of context specific studies to try and fit all coaches and all coaching domains.

Conclusion

Here and elsewhere we have contended that coaches learn through engaging with a wide range of sources in various learning situations (e.g. Cushion *et al.* 2010; Nelson *et al.* 2006). While much material exists about informal and formal learning, it is difficult, if not impossible, to be prescriptive about a specific, optimal mix. However, an important observation is that coach learning should be a mix, the research is consistent in suggesting learning is optimised with both informal and formal learning situations and an interaction of the two (Cushion *et al.* 2010; Cushion 2011a). Indeed, Colley *et al.* (2003) point out it is often the blending of learning types that is significant, not their separation. Indeed, it would be unrealistic to think that coaches would, could or should switch off their ability to learn when operating in a given situation be it formal, nonformal, or informal. Rather, it seems important that the field assists coaches with developing the necessary abilities to fully engage within all situations so that they can maximise their ongoing learning and development.

This chapter has served to demonstrate that our understanding of how coaches learn remains partial and largely superficial at best. As such, we have argued that further research is required if a more detailed and comprehensive understanding of coach learning is to be established. Indeed, it is our contention that the field of coaching needs to move beyond the simple identification of coach learning sources and situations by considering the complexities, intricacies, and nuances that are an inherent part of the learning process. Evaluation of all approaches and methods is essential, and understanding how these link to changes in practice and learning is needed. Lastly, while the coaching environment is a place of learning for both coach and athlete, coach educators must also be recognised along with their developmental and learning needs.

Acknowledgments

Material for this chapter was taken from research funded by Sports Coach UK.

References

Abraham, A. and Collins, D. (1998) 'Examining and extending research in coach development', *Quest*, 50(1): 59–79.

Abraham, A., Collins, D. and Martindale, R. (2006) 'The coaching schematic: Validation through expert coach consensus', *Journal of Sports Sciences*, 24(6): 549–564.

Anderson, J.R., Reder, L.M. and Simon, H.A. (1996) 'Situated learning and education', *Educational Researcher*, 25(4): 5–11.

Armour, K.M. (2010) 'The learning coach, the learning approach: Professional development for sports coach professionals', in J. Lyle and C.J. Cushion (eds) *Sports Coaching: Professionalisation and Practice*, London: Elsevier.

Bloom, G.A., Durand-Bush, N., Schinke, R.J. and Salmela, J.H. (1998) 'The importance of mentoring in the development of coaches and athletes', *International Journal of Sport Psychology*, 29(3): 267–281.

Bloom, G.A., Salmela, J.H. and Schinke, R.J. (1995) 'Expert coaches' views on the training of developing coaches', in R. Vanfraechem-Raway and Y. Vanden Auweele (eds) *Proceedings of the Ninth European Congress on Sport Psychology*, Brussels: Free University of Brussels.

Brookfield, S.D. (1986) *Understanding and Facilitating Adult Learning*, Milton Keynes: Open University Press.

Buckley, R. and Caple, J. (2000) *The Theory and Practice of Training*, 4th edn, London: Kogan Page.

Burns, S. and Bulman, C. (2000) *Reflective Practice in Nursing*, Oxford: Blackwell Science.

Cassidy, T., Jones, R.L. and Potrac, P. (2004) *Understanding Sports Coaching: The Social, Cultural and Pedagogical Foundations of Coaching Practice*, London: Routledge.

Cassidy, T., Jones, R.L. and Potrac, P. (2009) *Understanding Sports Coaching: The Social, Cultural and Pedagogical Foundations of Coaching Practice*, 2nd edn, Abingdon: Routledge.

Cassidy, T., Potrac, P. and McKenzie, A. (2006) 'Evaluating and reflecting upon a coach education initiative: The CoDe of rugby', *The Sport Psychologist*, 20(2): 145–161.

Chesterfield, G., Potrac, P. and Jones, R.L. (2010) '"Studentship" and "impression management": Coaches' experiences of an advanced soccer coach education award', *Sport, Education and Society*, 15(3): 299–314.

Colley, H., Hodkinson, P. and Malcolm, J. (2003) *Informality and Formality in Learning: A Report for the Learning Skills Research Centre*, London: Learning and Skills Research Centre.

Collier, C.S. and O'Sullivan, M. (1997) 'Case method in physical education higher education: A pedagogy of change?' *Quest*, 49(2): 198–213.

Coombs, P.H. and Ahmed, M. (1974) *Attacking Rural Poverty: How Non-Formal Education Can Help*, Baltimore, MD: Johns Hopkins University Press.

Côté, J. (2006) 'The development of coaching knowledge', *International Journal of Sports Science and Coaching*, 1(3): 217–222.

Culver, D. and Trudel, P. (2006) 'Cultivating coaches' communities of practice', in R. L. Jones (ed.) *The Sports Coach as Educator: Re-conceptualising Sports Coaching*, London: Routledge.

Culver, D. and Trudel, P. (2008) 'Clarifying the concept of communities of practice in sport', *International Journal of Sports Science and Coaching*, 3(1): 1–10.

Culver, D.M., Trudel, P. and Werthner, P. (2009) 'A sport leader's attempt to foster a coaches' community of practice', *International Journal of Sport Science and Coaching*, 4(3): 365–383.

Cushion, C.J. (2006) 'Mentoring: Harnessing the power of experience', in R.L. Jones (ed.) *The Sports Coach as Educator: Re-conceptualising Sports Coaching*, London: Routledge.

Cushion, C.J. (2008) 'Clarifying the concept of communities of practice in sport', *International Journal of Sport Science and Coaching*, 2(4): 15–17.

Cushion, C.J. (2011a) 'Coaches' learning and development', in R. Bailey and I. Stafford (eds) *Coaching Children in Sport*, Abingdon: Routledge.

Cushion, C.J. (2011b) 'Coach and athlete learning: A social approach', in R.L. Jones, P. Potrac, C.J. Cushion and L.T. Ronglan (eds) *The Sociology of Sports Coaching*, Abingdon: Routledge.

Cushion, C.J., Armour, K.M. and Jones, R.L. (2003) 'Coach education and continuing professional development: Experience and learning to coach', *Quest*, 55(3): 215–230.

Cushion, C.J., Armour, K.M. and Jones, R.L. (2006) 'Locating the coaching process in practice: Models "for" and "of" coaching', *Physical Education and Sport Pedagogy*, 11(1): 83–99.

Cushion, C.J., Nelson, L.J., Armour, K.M., Lyle J., Jones R.L., Sandford, R. and O'Callaghan, C. (2010) *Coach Learning and Development: A Review of Literature*. Leeds: Sports Coach UK.

Day, C., Sammons, P. and Gu, Q. (2008) 'Combining qualitative and quantitative methodologies in research on teachers' lives, work, and effectiveness', *From Integration to Synergy Educational Researcher*, 37(6): 330–333.

Demers, G., Woodburn, A.J. and Savard, C. (2006) 'The development of an undergraduate competency-based coach education program', *The Sport Psychologist*, 20(2): 162–173.

Dymock, D. (1999) 'Blind date: A case study of mentoring as workplace learning', *The Journal of Workplace Learning*, 11(8): 312–317.

Ehrich, L., Hansford, B. and Tennent, L. (2004) 'Formal mentoring programs in education and other professions: A review of the literature', *Educational Administration Quarterly*, 40(4): 518–540.

Eraut, M. (2000) 'Non-formal learning, implicit learning and tacit knowledge', in F. Coffield (ed.) *The Necessity of Informal Learning*, Bristol: The Policy Press, pp. 12–31.

Erickson, K., Bruner, M., MacDonald, D. and Côté, J. (2008) 'Gaining insight into actual and preferred sources of coaching knowledge', *International Journal of Sport Science and Coaching*, 3(4): 527–538.

Ferry, N.M. and Ross-Gordon, J.M. (1998) 'An inquiry into Schön's epistemology of practice: Exploring links between experience and reflective practice', *Adult Education Quarterly*, 48(2): 98–112.

Fleurance, P. and Cotteaux, V. (1999) 'Construction de l'expertise chez les etraîneurs sportifs d'athlètes de haut-niveau Français', *Avante*, 5(2): 54–68, cited in: Wright, T., Trudel, P. and Culver, D. (2007) 'Learning how to coach: the different learning situations reported by youth ice hockey coaches', *Physical Education and Sport Pedagogy*, 12(2): 127–144.

Fraser, W. (1995) *Learning from Experience*, Leicester: NIACE.

Freedman, M. (1999) *The Kindness of Strangers: Adult Mentors, Urban Youth and the New Voluntarism*, Cambridge: Cambridge University Press.

Fuller, A., Hodkinson, H., Hodkinson, P. and Unwin, L. (2005) 'Learning as peripheral participation in communities of practice: A reassessment of key concepts in workplace learning', *British Educational Research Journal*, 31(1): 49–68.

Gilbert, W. and Trudel, P. (2006) 'The coach as a reflective practitioner', in: R.L. Jones (ed.) *The Sports Coach as Educator: Re-conceptualising Sports Coaching*, London: Routledge, pp. 114–127.

Gilbert, W.D. and Trudel, P. (1999) 'An evaluation strategy for coach education programs', *Journal of Sport Behavior*, 22(2): 234–250.

Gilbert, W.D. and Trudel, P. (2001) 'Learning to coach through experience: Reflection in model youth sport coaches', *Journal of Teaching in Physical Education*, 21(1): 16–34.

Gilbert, W.D. and Trudel, P. (2004) 'Role of the coach: How model youth team sport coaches frame their roles', *The Sport Psychologist*, 18(1): 21–43.

Gilbert, W.D. and Trudel, P. (2005) 'Learning to coach through experience: Conditions that influence reflection', *Physical Educator*, 61(1): 32–45.

Gould, D., Gianinni, J., Krane, V. and Hodge, K. (1990) 'Educational needs of elite U.S. national Pan American and Olympic coaches', *Journal Teaching in Physical Education*, 9(4): 332–344.

Greeno, J.G. (1997) 'On claims that answer the wrong questions', *Educational Researcher*, 26(1): 5–17.

Hammond, J. and Perry, J. (2005) 'A multi-dimensional assessment of soccer coaching course effectiveness', *Ergonomics*, 48(11/14): 1698–1710.

Hodkinson, P., Biesta, G. and James, D. (2008) 'Understanding learning culturally: Overcoming the dualism between social and individual views of learning', *Vocations and Learning*, 1(1): 27–47.

Irwin, G., Hanton, S. and Kerwin, D.G. (2004) 'Reflective practice and the origins of elite coaching knowledge', *Reflective Practice*, 5(3): 425–442.

Jarvis, P. (2004) *Adult Education and Lifelong Learning: Theory and Practice*, 3rd edn, London: Routledge.

Jarvis, P. (2006) *Towards a Comprehensive Theory of Human Learning*, London, Routledge.

Jarvis, P., Holford, J. and Griffin, C. (2003) *The Theory and Practice of Learning*, 2nd edn, London: Kogan Page.

Jones, R.L. and Turner, P. (2006) 'Teaching coaches to coach holistically: can problem-based learning (PBL) help?' *Physical Education and Sport Pedagogy*, 11(2): 181–202.

Jones, R.L., Armour, K.M. and Potrac, P. (2003) 'Constructing expert knowledge: A case study of a top-level professional soccer coach, *Sport, Education and Society*, 8(2): 213–229.

Jones, R.L., Armour, K.M. and Potrac, P. (2004) *Sports Coaching Cultures: From Practice to Theory*, London: Routledge.

Jones, R.L., Harris, R.A. and Miles, A. (2009) 'Mentoring in sports coaching: A review of the literature', *Physical Education and Sport Pedagogy*, 14(3): 267–284.

Kim, H.S. (1999) 'Critical reflective inquiry for knowledge development in nursing practice', *Journal of Advanced Nursing*, 29(5): 1205–1212.

Knowles, Z., Borrie, A. and Telfer, H. (2005) 'Toward the reflective sports coach: Issues of context, education and application', *Ergonomics*, 48: 1711–1720.

Knowles, Z., Gilbourne, D., Borrie, A. and Nevill, A. (2001) 'Developing the reflective sports coach: A study exploring the processes of reflective practice within a higher education coaching programme', *Reflective Practice*, 2(2): 185–207.

Lave, J. and Wenger, E. (1991) *Situated Learning: Legitimate Peripheral Participation*, Cambridge: Cambridge University Press.

Lemyre, F., Trudel, P. and Durand-Bush, N. (2007) 'How youth-sport coaches learn to coach', *The Sport Psychologist*, 21(2): 191–209.

Lyle, J. (2002) *Sports Coaching Concepts: A Framework for Coaches' Behaviour*, London: Routledge.

Lyle, J. (2007) 'A review of the research evidence for the impact of coach education', *International Journal of Coaching Science*, 1(1): 17–34.

Mason, L. (2007) 'Bridging the cognitive and sociocultural approaches in research on conceptual change: Is it feasible?' *Educational Psychologist*, 42(1): 1–7.

McAlpine, L. and Weston, C. (2002) 'Reflection: Issues related to improving professors' teaching and students' learning', in N. Hativa and P. Goodyear (eds) *Teacher Thinking: Beliefs and Knowledge in Higher Education*, Dordrecht: Kluwer.

McCullick, B.A., Belcher, D. and Schempp, P. (2005) 'What works in coaching and sport instructor programs? The participants' view', *Physical Education and Sport Pedagogy*, 10(2): 121–137.

McCullick, B., Schempp, P., Mason, I., Foo, C., Vickers, B. and Connolly, G. (2009) 'A scrutiny of the coaching education program scholarship since 1995', *Quest*, 61(3): 322–335.

McLaughlin, M.W. and Zarrow, J. (2001) 'Teachers engaged in evidence based reform: Trajectories of teacher's inquiry, analysis and action.', in L. Leiberman and L. Miller (eds) *Teachers Caught in the Action: Professional Development that Matters*, New York: Teacher's College.

Merriam, S.B. and Caffarella, R.S. (1999) *Learning in Adulthood*, 2nd edn, San Francisco, CA: Jossey-Bass.

Moon, J. (2001) *Short Courses and Workshops: Improving the Impact of Learning and Professional Development*, London: Kogan Page.

Moon, J.A. (2004) *A Handbook of Reflection and Experiential Learning: Theory and Practice*, London: Kogan Page.

Nelson, L.J. and Cushion, C.J. (2006) 'Reflection in coach education: The case of the national governing body coaching certificate', *The Sport Psychologist*, 20(2): 174–183.

Nelson, L.J., Cushion, C.J. and Potrac, P. (2006) 'Formal, nonformal and informal coach learning: A holistic conceptualisation', *International Journal of Sport Science and Coaching*, 1(3): 247–259.

Newman, M. (1999) *Maeler's Regard*, Sydney: Stewart Victor Publishing.

Reade, I., Rodgers, W. and Hall, N. (2008) 'Knowledge transfer: How do high performance coaches access the knowledge of sport scientists?' *International Journal of Sport Science and Coaching*, 3(3): 319–334.

Rink, J. (2001) 'Investigating the assumptions of pedagogy', *Journal of Teaching in Physical Education*, 20(2): 112–128.

Rogers, A. (2002) *Teaching Adults*, 3rd edn, Buckingham: Open University Press.

Säljö, R. (2003) 'From transfer to boundary-crossing', in T. Tuomi-Gröhn and Y. Engeström (eds) *Between School and Work: New Perspectives on Transfer and Boundary-Crossing*, Amsterdam: Elsevier.

Schempp, P.G., Templeton, C.L. and Clark, B. (1998) 'The knowledge acquisition of expert golf instructors', in M. Farrally and A.J. Cochran (eds) *Science and Golf III: Proceedings of the World Scientific Congress of Golf*, Champaign, IL: Human Kinetics.

Schön, D.A. (1983) *The Reflective Practitioner: How Professionals Think in Action*, New York: Basic Books.

Sfard, A. (1998) 'On two metaphors for learning and the dangers of choosing just one', *Educational Researcher*, 27(2): 4–13.

Taylor, C. and White, S. (2000) *Practicing Reflexivity in Health and Welfare*, Buckingham/Philadelphia, PA: Open University Press.

Trudel, P. and Gilbert, W. (2006) 'Coaching and coach education', in D. Kirk, D. Macdonald and M. O'Sullivan (eds) *The Handbook of Physical Education*, London: Sage.

Tsangaridou, N. and Siedentop, D. (1995) 'Reflective teaching: A literature review', *Quest*, 47(2): 212–237.

Tuijnman, A. and Boström, A.K. (2002) 'Changing notions of lifelong education and lifelong learning', *International Review of Education*, 48: 93–100.

Vargas-Tonsing, T.M. (2007) 'Coaches' preferences for continuing coaching education', *International Journal of Sport Science and Coaching*, 29(1): 25–35.

Wenger, E. (1998) *Communities of Practice: Learning, Meaning and Identity*, Cambridge: Cambridge University Press.

Werthner, P. and Trudel, P. (2006) 'A new theoretical perspective for understanding how coaches learn to coach', *The Sport Psychologist*, 20(2): 198–212.

Wiersma, L.D. and Sherman, C.P. (2005) 'Volunteer youth sport coaches' perspectives of coaching education/certification and parental codes of conduct', *Research Quarterly for Exercise and Sport*, 76(3): 324–338.

Wright, T., Trudel, P. and Culver, D. (2007) 'Learning how to coach: The different learning situations reported by youth ice hockey coaches', *Physical Education and Sport Pedagogy*, 12(2): 127–144.

30

LOOKING AT COACH DEVELOPMENT FROM THE COACH-LEARNER'S PERSPECTIVE

Considerations for coach development administrators

Pierre Trudel

UNIVERSITY OF OTTAWA, CANADA

Diane Culver

UNIVERSITY OF OTTAWA, CANADA

Penny Werthner

UNIVERSITY OF OTTAWA, CANADA

Introduction

Recently, a number of researchers have indicated that sport coaching is very complex and context dependent (e.g. Côté and Gilbert 2009; Cushion and Lyle 2010). It has also been suggested that completing a formal coach education program, often offered over a short period of time (Vargas-Tonsing 2007), is not sufficient to adequately prepare coaches (Côté and Gilbert 2009), even though completing such programs is generally the only way to become certified (Nelson *et al.* 2006; Rynne *et al.* 2006). Moreover, we are now living in a 'knowledge society' influenced by globalization and technology, and are constantly being exposed to new learning opportunities (Jarvis 2006). Therefore, various researchers in the coaching science field (e.g. Mallett 2010; Nelson *et al.* 2006) suggest that coaches should involve themselves in as many learning opportunities as possible – formal, nonformal, informal. The danger with this suggestion is that of falling into the 'more is better' syndrome where coaches might feel pressured to devote more time than they realistically have to learning activities that do not necessarily correspond to their needs. Ironically, we know very little about coaches' capacities/readiness to participate in different learning opportunities. Are all coaches eager to know more about coaching? Why is the same learning opportunity meaningful for one coach and not for another? To what extent is coach development idiosyncratic? Finally, what role should coach development administrators (CDAs) play in this new knowledge world without borders? To adequately answer these types of questions we need to look at coach development from a coach-learner's perspective. The purpose of this chapter is to expand on our recent efforts (Werthner and Trudel 2006, 2009) and our work with colleagues (Mallett *et al.* 2009; Lyle *et al.* 2009; Trudel *et al.* 2010) in an attempt to illustrate how, using a constructivist informed approach, CDAs can design and nurture three types of learning situations for coaches. We believe this chapter is timely, as Armour (2010) recently suggested that constructivist theories are appropriate for studying coaching and coach development; and doing so is a refreshing way of looking at the teaching and learning process (Merriam *et al.* 2007). This chapter is divided into three sections. First, we present some key elements of a constructivist view of learning using the works of two authors: Peter Jarvis and Jennifer Moon. In the second section, we revisit a model, derived from Moon's works that we published (Werthner and Trudel 2006, 2009) and for each of the three learning situations in the model (mediated, unmediated, and internal) we discuss what might be the role of CDAs to help coaches maximize their learning. Finally, we conclude by discussing the contribution of this chapter to coaching science and more specially coach development.

Key elements of a constructivist view of learning

Books (e.g. Gagnon and Collay 2006) and articles (e.g. Donnelly 2010; Hodkinson and Macleod 2010) discussing the constructivist view of learning are numerous in the education field and this perspective has, for some years, been used in the physical education context (e.g. Butler 2005; Kirk and Macdonald 1998; Rovegno 1998). In the sport field, some researchers have suggested using this approach to teach sport teams (e.g. Gréhaigne *et al.* 2010) and individual sport (e.g. Light and Wallian 2008) but very few have used it to investigate coach development (e.g. Ollis and Sproule 2007). Considering the space limit that we have to work with, a decision has been made to present the constructivist view of learning by focusing on some key elements highlighted in the work of Peter Jarvis and Jennifer Moon.

Through his work, Jarvis (2006: 6) reminds us that:

> At the heart of all learning is not merely what is learned, but what the learner is becoming (learning) as a result of doing and thinking – and feeling... Indeed, the demands of our life-world also determine to a great extent the opportunities that we have to learn.

Because learning is a process of becoming, the elements of time and space must be considered, especially now when globalization and technology influence the quantity and quality of learning opportunities. Thus, in this rapidly changing world, we are more likely to experience intellectual disharmony or what Jarvis (2006: 16) calls *disjuncture*: 'Disjuncture occurs when our biographical repertoire is no longer sufficient to cope automatically with our situation, so that our unthinking harmony with our world is disturbed and we feel unease'. Jarvis stresses the fact that it is not because a person is faced with or provided with learning opportunities that there will be learning. A person's *biography*, which can be defined as the sum of previous experiences from which one has learned (e.g. new knowledge, skills, emotions), plays a key role in the decision to take or not take advantage of learning opportunities. Disjuncture and biography are regrouped in the definition of *lifelong learning*, the central concept of Jarvis' books (2006, 2007, 2008, 2009):

> The combination of processes throughout a lifetime whereby the whole person – body (genetic, physical, and biological) and mind (knowledge, skills, attitudes, values, emotions, meaning, beliefs, and senses) – experiences social situations, the content of which is then transformed cognitively, emotively or practically (or through any combination) and integrated into the individual person's biography resulting in a continually changing (or more experienced) person.
>
> *(Jarvis 2009: 25)*

Without using the same terminology, Moon's generic view of learning matches Jarvis' explanation in many aspects. For example, instead of using the term disjuncture, Moon (2004: 19) uses *cognitive dissonance* to 'describe the – often uncomfortable situations – in which new material of learning is in conflict with the learner's cognitive structure'. Also, Jarvis' definition of biography can be applied to the term *cognitive structure*: 'The network of concepts, emotion, knowledge, experiences and beliefs that guides a person's functioning at a particular time' (Moon 2004: 231). For Moon:

> In the constructivist view of learning, the learner constructs their own knowledge and the knowledge is conceived to be organized more as a network … What is already known is employed in guiding the new learning in organizing the process of assimilation (taking in the material of learning). In meaningful learning, where the learner intends to understand the material of learning instead of just memorizing it, the learner accommodates or adapts an area of the network in response of the new learning.
>
> *(Moon 1999: 106)*

The terms assimilation and accommodation are important in Moon's (2004) conceptualization of learning and she provides these definitions:

> *Assimilation*: The processing of new material of learning such that learning occurs. The process of assimilation is guided by the current internal experience (prior experiences in current state of cognitive structure) of the object of learning, and any given current purposes for the learning. In meaningful learning, assimilation is accompanied by the process of accommodation.
>
> *Accommodation*: The process of modification of new material of learning or current cognitive structure in a learning process that results in change of conceptions (i.e. understanding or state of knowledge). Accommodation follows the process of assimilation.
>
> *Moon (2004: 231)*

Moon (1999, 2001) has developed a 'map of learning and the representation of learning' to illustrate the links between many key elements of her constructivist view of learning. In Table 30.1, we present Moon's five stages of learning regrouped under two broad categories of learning approaches: Surface learning and deep learning.

Table 30.1: Stages of learning

Surface learning		
1	Noticing : Looking at the information and trying to memorize it	Assimilation
2	Making sense: Slotting ideas together on the basis of relatively superficial similarity	

Deep learning		
3	Making meaning: Seeking meaning and understanding that relates new learning to current knowledge and understanding in the cognitive structure	Accommodation
4	Working with meaning: The learning material is now modified as part of the cognitive structure	
5	Transformative learning: More comprehensive stage of accommodation of the cognitive structure; ability to step outside his/her own and others' processes of reasoning in order to evaluate the frames of references that he/she or they are using	

Source: Adapted from Moon 2001: 69–76.

A surface learning approach will be privileged when learners think, for example, that they already know the content (new material of learning), or the content appears useless, or they are under time pressure. We can assume that through the stages of 'noticing' and 'making sense' the learner assimilates the content to a certain extent, but there is no accommodation process. 'Making meaning' is the first stage of learning that can be considered 'deep learning' because the learner's interest is in understanding and not just knowing. Learners will use that new material of learning to change their biography/cognitive structure, through the process of accommodation. At the 'working with meaning' stage, the learner is at a stage of greater accommodation – or re-accommodation – of the cognitive structure. In this stage, learners are not directly using new material of learning coming from what teachers are saying or from reading books, for example. Instead, they work with and reflect on what they already have 'inside their head'. The final stage, 'transformative learning', involves learners taking a critical overview of their own biography/cognitive structure and learning process.

A model for understanding how coaches learn to coach

In the literature on coach development, researchers often use the expressions formal learning, nonformal learning, and informal learning, which can result in confusion (Mallett *et al.* 2009). As indicated by Jarvis (2006), learning processes tend to be similar to all learners but the settings in which we learn are different and therefore it is more appropriate to talk of learning in formal, nonformal, or informal *situations*. Moon (2001) however, goes one step further and suggests a distinction between learning context and learning situation. The *learning context* is the 'setting in which learning occurs – the course, the instructor, relevant organizations, and so on – and the *learning situation*, is the learner's perception of the context and unique to the learner' (Moon 2001: 48). The distinction between learning context and learning situation is important because it will allow us to discuss learning from both the coach-learner's perspective (learning situation) and from the coach development administrators' (CDAs) perspective – the individuals in charge of providing adequate learning contexts to coaches.

We present, in Figure 30.1, an adapted version of a visual representation of Moon's generic view of learning that we have previously published (Werthner and Trudel 2006). At the centre of the model is the coach's cognitive structure/biography. If we apply the concept of lifelong learning, the cognitive structure cannot be limited to coaching knowledge (being declarative or procedural). The cognitive structure should also include early socialization at home and at school (Callary *et al.* 2011; Jarvis 2006); experiences in different settings (education, work, family, athletic/coaching experiences) (Trudel *et al.* 2010); as well as the learner's conception of knowledge and approaches to learning, emotional states, future perspectives; and what Moon (2004) calls *internal experience*: What the coach already knows about the specific topic. It is with his/her unique cognitive structure that a coach will experience learning opportunities. Using Moon's (2004) terminology, we can categorize these learning opportunities into three learning situations. It is worth reiterating the importance of keeping in mind that the three learning situations (mediated, unmediated, and internal) are not different ways of learning but different learning situations from the coach-learner's perspective.

Lyle (2010) stresses that the role of coach development is to accelerate the learning process which implies that CDAs have a key role. If such an endeavour is to be accomplished using a constructivist approach, it is essential to differentiate teaching from learning, and not work under the incorrect common assumption 'that what is taught [the material of teaching] is

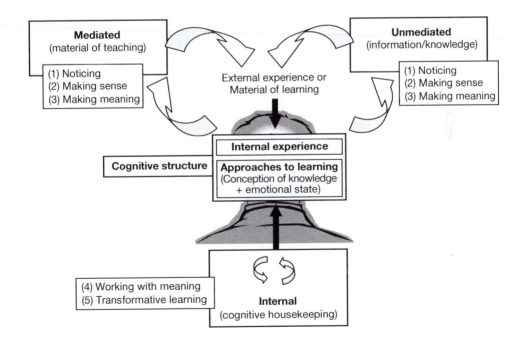

Figure 30.1: Representation of Moon's conceptual framework (learning situations and stages of learning).

learnt [the material of learning] or that the subject matter of training is learnt without modification by the learner other than the erosion or distortion of memory' (Moon 2004: 13). This means that CDAs should try to offer (design and nurture) the best learning contexts for coaches. However, ultimately it is the individual coach who will determine the usefulness of the learning context. In other words, a group of coaches attending a course (mediated) will be exposed to the same material of teaching (mediated) but the material of learning will be specific to each coach. Likewise, even if information/knowledge contained in websites (unmediated) is available to all coaches, what is learned by each coach will vary depending on their unique previous experiences, approaches to the learning situations, and the assimilation and accommodation processes.

As one can imagine, taking a constructivist approach when discussing coach development has an impact on CDAs' role. If CDAs want to use such an approach in their efforts to design and nurture learning contexts, they will have to include the following key elements: 'the person, as learner; the social situation within which the learning occurs; the experience that the learner has of that situation; and the process of transforming it and storing it within the learner's mind/biography' (Jarvis 2006: 198). In an attempt to help CDAs in their work, we will discuss each learning situation and highlight elements that CDAs should take into consideration to facilitate learning, and more specifically the progression through the five learning stages (see Figure 30.1).

Mediated learning situations

A mediated learning situation is defined as an episodic learning experience where the learner does not select the material to be taught. In other words, the learning context is controlled by other individuals; an expert or group of experts chooses the material of teaching, the delivery format, and when and where the learning activity takes place. CDAs are the orchestrators of these learning contexts and the typical learning contexts are the large-scale coach education programs often delivered over a few weekends, and other shorter workshops or seminars. Coaches either participate in these learning opportunities because of their own interest or because they are obliged to attend for certification. The so-called formal learning and nonformal learning contexts fall into this category. For coaches, such learning contexts can be a learning situation where they will learn about a coaching topic in a time efficient manner without, as the expert(s) did, spending a lot of time searching out and reflecting on the appropriate information. Unfortunately, even a great summary can be useless if coaches do not find the coaching topic pertinent to them. Trudel *et al.* (2010) have argued that in most coach education courses, the different coaches' biographies make it difficult to provide a course that will please all attending coaches. Studies showing that coaches diverge in their opinion on the usefulness of their formal coach education programs support this affirmation (Jones *et al.* 2004; Irwin *et al.* 2004; Wright *et al.* 2007). For Moon (2001: 7),

> a short course needs to be underpinned by considerations that are both precise and clear about direction and the outcomes to be achieved, but are deployed within the context of continuous awareness of the state of learners and their learning.

Below are five points that CDAs should consider when designing and leading formal and nonformal learning contexts.

Selecting the quantity of the material of teaching and the assessment format

Because short courses are what they are, short, the expectations should be modest in terms of the quantity of material to be presented to the coaches. By trying to cover too much material, the focus becomes the material of teaching instead of the learning. Being exposed to a large amount of new material, coaches will likely adopt a surface approach to learning since there is no time for linking the new material to previous experience (making meaning). When CDAs present a wide variety of material to a large number of coaches, the assessment format will often be a test composed of many multiple choice questions. This type of assessment requires the learner to memorize; taking a surface approach.

Selecting the appropriate 'messengers'

In large-scale coach education programs, the delivery of the content is usually given to a person who has not been involved in the design of the program and therefore, it is important to differentiate between the 'messenger' and the 'message' (Moon 2001: 88). If the program is designed and delivered following a constructivist approach, then the messenger will usually be called a 'facilitator' instead of an 'instructor/teacher' because his/her task is to guide the learners and not to teach them. Thus, facilitator selection has to be judicious and cannot be based purely on sport experiences. As well as the coach's cognitive structure influencing how the coach will participate in a learning context, the facilitator's own biography (e.g. sport experiences as athlete and/or coach, beliefs of what is the best way to learn) will influence how he/she will interact with the coaches.

A facilitator who rushes through the material without providing the coaches with the time to link the content with their previous experiences will leave most of the coaches unable to reach the 'making meaning' stage of learning. To make it more complicated for the facilitator, in this type of learning context, there will be a variety of coaches. Some coaches will arrive expecting that an instructor will teach them new tricks to make their work easier; waiting to be informed about the 'right' way to coach. These coaches do not have a constructivist approach to learning. Contrastingly, some coaches will want to pursue deep learning and may ask a lot of questions and perhaps challenge the content and/or the facilitator. This requires the facilitator to be an expert on the material being taught.

Providing adequate information to situate the material of teaching

Because time and money are factors that influence coaches' participation in coach education programs/workshops (Wiersma and Sherman 2005), CDAs need to condense the teaching material into a few hours or days. Indeed, there is no time to waste, and the facilitators should consider beginning their intervention by discussing how the material of teaching can be useful to the coaches. These first few minutes seem to be crucial because 'the learner constructs her new understandings and conceptions according to the manner in which she perceives the material to be' (Moon 2001: 6). If coaches have difficulties seeing the links between what will be presented to them and their coaching practice (their experience) they are less likely to adopt a deep approach to learning.

Regrouping coaches with similar cognitive structures/biographies

For Trudel and Gilbert (2006), the criticisms regarding the low ecological validity attributed to coach education programs have contributed to the emergence of programs designed for specific coaching contexts. For example, in Canada, sport federations are encouraged to develop, within certain parameters, courses with specific teaching material for coaches working within community sport, competitive, or instructional coaching contexts. These courses are more likely to be perceived as useful mediated learning situations by novice coaches who tend to prefer attending courses with other coaches of the same sport, which is contrary to elite coaches for whom discussing with coaches from other sports seems more appreciated. While there are some advantages to regrouping coaches by sport and/or coaching context (meaning that they will have somewhat similar biographies and learning needs) organizational and financial factors often make this problematic. In communities outside of large cities, the number of coaches might be too low making it almost impossible to have enough coaches to offer context specific courses (Roy *et al.* 2010).

Offering online coach education programs

Coaches seem to be open to training through less formal approaches including online support (Vargas-Tonsing 2007; Wiersma and Sherman 2005), and technology now makes it easier to offer online coach education programs. A quick search on the Internet shows many online training programs for coaches (e.g. Babe Ruth League Coaching Education Center (n.d.); Baseball Canada (n.d.)). However, we do not know the effectiveness of these learning contexts. The number of coaches who have registered and had access to the material is often presented as a success criterion but there are no clear indications that online education programs help coaches adopt a deep approach to their learning. Therefore, Cohen's (1992: 25) comment might apply even more for online coach education programs: 'There are governing bodies that certify coaches based on the successful completion of our program, but we don't certify competency of coaches'.

There are still many aspects related to mediated learning situations that need better understanding. For example, considering the interdependence of all the actors involved we need longitudinal studies that will start with the program designers, and then move to the facilitators/instructors/teachers, to the coaches attending the courses, and finally that will look at coaches performing at competitions and training sessions. We also need more studies about online coach education programs. What are their limits and their advantages? Our suggestion to researchers would be to avoid comparing these programs with more traditional coach education training programs because each type of program will be favoured by some coaches, and not by others, based on the differences in their biographies.

Unmediated learning situations

In unmediated learning situations coaches decide by themselves what information they need and different sources can be consulted. Trudel and Gilbert (2006) defined two categories of unmediated learning situations. The first category regroups situations where coaches learn the sub-culture of a sport. This learning is mostly unconscious and we have to look deep into the individual's biography to find its origin (e.g. parents, family, athletic career). The second category refers to the conscious effort made by coaches to find the appropriate information to solve coaching issues or investigate a new area. We will address the latter of these two categories, and more specifically, interactions with 'others'.

Studies have shown that coaches highly value their interactions with 'others' as a way to learn how to coach (Erickson *et al.* 2008) and, based on a constructivist approach to learning, this should not be a surprise. Gilbert and Trudel (2001, 2006) highlighted the importance of 'others' when coaches want to find solutions to their coaching issues. Because the information that coaches are looking for is closely related to their practice, they will likely be at the 'making meaning' learning stage. Considering the learning potential of unmediated learning situations, it has been suggested that 'any attempts to facilitate coaches' learning through social networks should be encouraged' (Mallett 2010: 131). The question then becomes: 'To what extent should CDAs be involved?' If CDAs get too involved the potential benefits of the unmediated learning situations will be lost because they will quickly become mediated learning situations. We suggest that CDAs' implications could be understood on two levels. First, CDAs should recognize that coaches' interactions with others are a form of learning and it is important to encourage/help coaches to develop their own networks. Material related to 'how to develop a personal network' should be presented to coaches during training programs or workshops. Second, CDAs' actions could serve to identify important limitations of networking as highlighted by Teigland (2003). Because 'individuals normally have the discretion to interact with a range of people when they are performing their work tasks, they form relationships based on biases and preferences for others as opposed to what the formal organization dictates' (Teigland 2003: 2). Also, since knowledge is situated in a local practice, boundaries are often created around this practice and therefore 'sharing the group's knowledge with others outside the group presents difficulties even if there is a willingness to share due to the embeddedness of the knowledge' (Teigland 2003: 2). Coaches' tendency to share their knowledge with a limited number of coaches has been documented (Lemyre *et al.* 2007; Trudel and Gilbert 2004). We argue that CDAs can positively influence coaches' learning through unmediated learning situations by nurturing learning contexts where coaches have the possibility to expand their network. For example, when coaches travel abroad, their trip could be extended by a day or two to allow more time for meeting coaches from other countries. Similarly, when national/international competitions are organized, coaches of all levels from the host region should be invited to attend the competitions and to participate in group discussions with invited coaches who are there for the competitions. Here, CDAs could provide access to sport specialists: a group of 'others' who the coaches have yet to discover (Reade *et al.* 2008; Williams and Kendall 2007). Finally, online chat groups are another possible venue in which CDAs could aid coach interactions, although coaches have indicated some trepidation concerning such groups because, without adequate facilitation, they can turn into a venue for complaints (Wright *et al.* 2007).

To further our understanding of the development of coaches in unmediated learning situations, researchers could follow at least two avenues. First, they can investigate coaches' motivations to look for new information and also the accessibility of sources of information. Second, researchers can take advantage of the work done on community-based learning research in teacher development to then propose strategies to foster coaches' communities of practice (Gilbert *et al.* 2009).

Internal learning situations

Internal learning situations are situations where there is no new material of learning coming from either a mediated or unmediated learning situation. Instead learners reorganize what they already know or, to use Moon's (2006: 27) expression, they perform 'cognitive housekeeping'. In this instance, we are clearly at the stages of 'working with meaning' or 'transformative learning'. Considering the nature of internal learning situations, the role played by CDAs will be to encourage coaches to systematically include in their busy schedule a time period reserved for such learning. For Moon, keeping a learning journal can be an effective strategy because journaling requires people to stop and think, providing opportunities to engage in this 'cognitive housekeeping'. She explains that:

> The learners are forced to be self-sufficient because there is no specific answer to any question that they might ask about 'what shall I write', though there may be structures or questions that will prompt their writing. To the degree that journal-writing is independent, it is also 'owned' by the writer.
>
> *(Moon 2006: 27)*

However, to what degree are coaches willing to engage in such a learning activity? Werthner and Trudel's (2009) study highlighted that, while coaches at the elite level contend that they are thinking about coaching all the time, very few of them seem to use a learning journal. Similar results were found in studies by Knowles and colleagues (2001, 2005, 2006). Such inquiry has concluded that coach education programs rarely 'provide clear structures for the development of reflective skills alongside the delivery of sport specific technical knowledge' (Knowles *et al.* 2006: 171). Furthermore, this work has shown that although coaches 'acknowledged that written reflection was an important component in the reflective process' (Knowles *et al.* 2006: 174), few coaches are willing to commit to this exercise, most claiming a lack of time. Considering that reflecting on one's practice is not easy (Cassidy *et al.* 2009) and keeping a learning journal seems to be perceived by coaches as a daunting task, CDAs should develop ways to introduce coaches to this learning situation.

Among the three types of learning situations, the internal learning situation is the one with few empirical studies, although the potential for learning is evident. A possibility would be for researchers to study a group of coaches who seem to be exemplary in terms of learning from internal learning situations, to discover the ways in which they make such learning happen. Following from this study, an action research project could be initiated with the objective of accompanying individual coaches in the development of habits that are conducive to learning from internal learning situations.

To facilitate the presentation of the model (see Figure 30.1), we have described each learning situation isolated from the other two, but in some circumstances it might be difficult to tell when one situation ends and another starts. For example, when interviewed about the learning experience during their participation in seminar/coach education courses (mediated) some coaches stress the importance of discussion time with other coaches during the breaks and lunch; an opportunity for learning new things and developing a network (unmediated) (Lemyre *et al.* 2007). The process of mentoring is another example. In a structure where coaches are paired with a mentor whose mandate is to cover specific content when working with a protégé, this situation should be considered a mediated learning situation. Yet, at the opposite end of the continuum coaches often make their own contact with a trusted colleague to discuss coaching (unmediated), and if that mentor acts mainly as a 'sounding-board', then the coach will have the opportunity to reflect on his/her knowledge and his/her practice (internal learning situation). A coach's level of independence and autonomy can also be placed on a continuum, and as a result, it could be difficult to identify specific types of learning situations. Readers interested in learning more about mentoring processes and their application to sport coaching are referred to Jones *et al.*'s (2009) article and Bloom's chapter (Chapter 38) in this volume.

Conclusions

As we were writing this chapter, we realized that the content presented could complement the recent work of Côté and Gilbert (2009). These authors proposed an integrative definition of coaching effectiveness composed of three elements: coaches' knowledge, athletes' outcomes, and coaching contexts. The coaches' knowledge was divided into three types: professional, interpersonal, and intrapersonal. Because professional knowledge is composed of sport-specific knowledge, pedagogical knowledge, and sport science knowledge, coaches will often be exposed to this information through mediated learning contexts. The interpersonal knowledge refers to the capacity to interact with others (e.g. athletes, parents, assistant coaches, sport scientists, administrators, friends), and the contexts to develop this type of knowledge will generally be applicable to the unmediated learning category. The intrapersonal knowledge 'refers to the understanding of oneself and the ability for introspection and reflection' (Côté and Gilbert 2009: 311). To develop this type of knowledge coaches will have to create their own internal learning situations and learning journals will be an important tool.

Finally, it is our hope that this chapter will contribute to the literature on coaching science and more specifically coach development. There are many theories about how people learn and each of them 'adds a little bit more to our understanding of human life and learning, but we do not and cannot know everything about it' (Jarvis 2006: 199). It seems to us that the following quote by Knowles *et al.* (2005: 1713) reflects a consensus among those interested in coach development and it can be applied to all levels of coaches: 'It appears that coaching expertise cannot be created within formal educational courses alone but requires coaches to engage mentally with their own practice to learn and develop'. So far, the criticisms received by CDAs regarding the limits of their coach education programs were rarely accompanied with concrete suggestions on what they can do to impact positively the learning of the coaches in the different learning contexts. By presenting a model based on a constructivist approach and providing examples of concrete actions CDAs could take, we have attempted to bridge that gap. If CDAs agree with the suggestions, the expression 'coach education' to describe what they want to impact is too restrictive. The expression 'coach development' would be more appropriate as it includes mediated, unmediated, and internal learning situations (Trudel *et al.* 2010). It is also important to recognize that for a constructivist approach to coach development to be successful, all the various agents involved – the organization, the designers, the facilitators, the assessors, the mentors, and the coaches – need to understand and subscribe to its principles.

References

Armour, K.M. (2010) 'The learning coach … the learning approach: Professional development for sports coach professionals', in J. Lyle and C.J. Cushion (eds) *Sports Coaching: Professionalisation and Practice*, London: Elsevier.

Babe Ruth League Coaching Education Center (n.d.) www.baberuthcoaching.org (accessed 21 January 2011).

Baseball Canada (n.d.) http://nccp.baseball.ca (accessed 21 January 2011).

Butler, J.I. (2005) 'TGfU pet-agogy: Old dogs, new tricks and puppy school', *Physical Education and Sport Pedagogy*, 10(3): 225–240.

Callary, B., Werthner, P. and Trudel, P. (2011) 'Shaping the way five women coaches develop: Their primary and secondary socialization', *Journal of Coaching Education*, 4(3): 76–96.

Cassidy, T., Jones, R.L. and Potrac, P. (2009) *Understanding Sports Coaching: The Social, Cultural and Pedagogical Foundations of Coaching Practice*, 2nd edn, London: Routledge.

Cohen, A. (1992) 'Standard time', *Athletic Business*, December: 23–28.

Côté, J. and Gilbert, W.D. (2009) 'An integrative definition of coaching effectiveness and expertise', *International Journal of Sport Science and Coaching*, 4(3): 307–323.

Cushion, C.J. and Lyle, J. (2010) 'Conceptual development in sports coaching', in J. Lyle and C.J. Cushion (eds) *Sports Coaching: Professionalisation and Practice*, London: Elsevier.

Donnelly, R. (2010) 'Interaction analysis in a "Learning by Doing" problem-based professional development context', *Computers and Education*, 55(3): 1357–1366.

Erickson, K., Bruner, M.W., MacDonald, D.J. and Côté, J. (2008) 'Gaining insight into actual and preferred sources of coaching knowledge', *International Journal of Sport Science and Coaching*, 3(4): 527–538.

Gagnon, G.W. and Collay, M. (2006) *Constructivist Learning Design: Key Questions for Teaching to Standards*, Thousand Oaks, CA: Corwin Press.

Gilbert, W.D. and Trudel, P. (2001) 'Learning to coach through experience: Reflection in model youth sport coaches', *Journal of Teaching in Physical Education*, 21(1): 16–34.

Gilbert, W.D. and Trudel, P. (2006) 'The coach as a reflective practitioner', in R.L. Jones (ed.) *The Sports Coach as Educator: Re-conceptualising Sports Coaching*, London: Routledge.

Gilbert, W.D., Gallimore, R. and Trudel, P. (2009) 'A learning community approach to coach development in youth sport', *Journal of Coaching Education*, 2(2): 1–21.

Gréhaigne, J.-F., Caty, D. and Godbout, P. (2010) 'Modelling ball circulation in invasion team sports: A way to promote learning games through understanding', *Physical Education and Sport Pedagogy*, 15(3): 257–270.

Hodkinson, P. and Macleod, F. (2010) 'Contrasting concepts of learning and contrasting research methodologies: Affinities and bias', *British Educational Research Journal*, 36(2): 173–189.

Irwin, G., Hanton, S. and Kerwin, D. (2004) 'Reflective practice and the origins of elite coaching knowledge', *Reflective Practice*, 5(3): 425–442.

Jarvis, P. (2006) *Towards a Comprehensive Theory of Learning*, London: Routledge.

Jarvis, P. (2007) *Globalization, Lifelong Learning and the Learning Society: Sociological Perspectives*, Abingdon: Routledge.

Jarvis, P. (2008) *Democracy, Lifelong Learning and the Learning Society: Active Citizenship in a Late Modern Age*, Abingdon: Routledge.

Jarvis, P. (2009) *Learning to be a Person in Society*, Abingdon: Routledge.

Jones, R., Armour, K. and Potrac, P. (2004) *Sports Coaching Cultures: From Practice to Theory*, London: Routledge.

Jones, R.L., Harris, R. and Miles, A. (2009) 'Mentoring in sports coaching: A review of the literature', *Physical Education and Sport Pedagogy*, 14(3): 267–284.

Kirk, D. and Macdonald, D. (1998) 'Situated learning in physical education', *Journal of Teaching in Physical Education*, 17(3): 376–387.

Knowles, Z., Borrie, A. and Telfer, H. (2005) 'Towards the reflective sport coach: Issues of context, education and application', *Ergonomics*, 48(11/14): 1711–1720.

Knowles, Z., Gilbourne, D., Borrie, A. and Nevill, A. (2001) 'Developing the reflective sports coach: A study exploring the processes of reflective practice within a higher education coaching programme', *Reflective Practice*, 2(2): 185–207.

Knowles, Z., Tyler, G., Gilbourne. D. and Eubank, M. (2006) 'Reflecting on reflection: Exploring the practice of sports coaching graduates', *Reflective Practice*, 7(2): 163–179.

Lemyre, F., Trudel, P. and Durand-Bush, N. (2007) 'How youth-sport coaches learn to coach', *The Sport Psychologist*, 21(2): 191–209.

Light, R. and Wallian, N. (2008) 'A constructivist-informed approach to teaching swimming', *Quest*, 60(3): 387–404.

Lyle, J. (2010) 'Coaches' decision making: A naturalistic decision making analysis', in J. Lyle and C.J. Cushion (eds) *Sports Coaching: Professionalisation and Practice*, London: Elsevier.

Lyle, J., Mallett, C.J., Trudel, P. and Rynne, S.B. (2009) 'From sterile debate to rich discussion: Responding to commentaries on formal vs. informal coach education', *International Journal of Sport Science and Coaching*, 4(3): 359–364.

Mallett, C.J. (2010) 'Becoming a high-performance coach: Pathways and communities' in J. Lyle and C.J. Cushion (eds) *Sports Coaching: Professionalisation and Practice*, London: Elsevier.

Mallett, C.J., Trudel, P., Lyle, J. and Rynne, S.B. (2009) 'Formal vs. informal coach education', *International Journal of Sport Science and Coaching*, 4(3): 325–334.

Merriam, S.B., Caffarella, R.S. and Baumgartner, L.M. (2007) *Learning in Adulthood: A Comprehensive Guide*, 3rd edn, San Francisco, CA: Jossey-Bass.

Moon, J.A. (1999) *Reflection in Learning and Professional Development: Theory and Practice*, London: Kogan Page.

Moon, J.A. (2001) *Short Courses and Workshops: Improving the Impact of Learning, Training and Professional Development*, London: Kogan Page.

Moon, J.A. (2004) *A Handbook of Reflective and Experiential Learning: Theory and Practice*, London: Routledge.

Moon, J.A. (2006) *Learning Journals: A Handbook for Reflective Practice and Professional development*, 2nd edn, London: Routledge.

Nelson, L.J., Cushion, C.J. and Potrac, P. (2006) 'Formal, nonformal and informal coach learning: A holistic conceptualisation', *International Journal of Sport Science and Coaching*, 1(3): 247–259.

Ollis, S. and Sproule, J. (2007) 'Constructivist coaching and expertise development as action research', *International Journal of Sport Science and Coaching*, 2(1): 1–14.

Reade, I., Rodgers, W. and Hall, N. (2008) 'Knowledge transfer: How do high performance coaches access the knowledge of sport scientists?' *International Journal of Sport Science and Coaching*, 3(3): 319–334.

Rovegno, I. (1998) 'The development of in-service teachers' knowledge of a constructivist approach to physical education: Teaching beyond activities', *Research Quarterly for Exercise and Sport*, 69(2): 147–162.

Roy, M., Beaudoin, S. and Spallanzani, C. (2010) 'Analyse des connaissances des entraîneurs inscrits à une formation: Introduction à la compétition – Partie B' en matière de planification d'entraînement' ['Analysis of the knowledge of coaches in a training module: Competition-introduction (Part B, planning for training)'], report submitted to the Coaching Association of Canada, online, available at: www.crifpe.ca/publications/liste/pubcat:9.

Rynne, S.B., Mallett, C.J. and Tinning, R. (2006) 'High performance sport coaching: Institutes of sport as sites for learning', *International Journal of Sport Science and Coaching*, 1(3): 223–234.

Teigland, R. (2003) 'Knowledge networking: Structure and performance in networks of practice', unpublished doctoral thesis, Stockholm University, Sweden.

Trudel, P. and Gilbert, W.D. (2004) 'Communities of practice as an approach to foster ice hockey coach development', in D.J. Pearsall and A.B. Ashare (eds) *Safety in Hockey*, Philadelphia, PA: ASTM.

Trudel, P. and Gilbert, W.D. (2006) 'Coaching and coach education', in D. Kirk, M. O'Sullivan and D. McDonald (eds) *Handbook of Physical Education*, London: Sage.

Trudel, P., Gilbert, W.D. and Werthner, P. (2010) 'Coach education effectiveness', in J. Lyle and C.J. Cushion (eds) *Sports Coaching: Professionalisation and Practice*, London: Elsevier.

Vargas-Tonsing, T.M. (2007) 'Coaches' preferences for continuing coaching education', *International Journal of Sport Science and Coaching*, 2(1): 25–35.

Werthner, P. and Trudel, P. (2006) 'A new theoretical perspective for understanding how coaches learn to coach', *The Sport Psychologist*, 20(2): 198–212.

Werthner, P. and Trudel, P. (2009) 'Investigating the idiosyncratic learning paths of elite Canadian coaches', *International Journal of Sport Science and Coaching*, 4(3): 433–449.

Wiersma, L.D. and Sherman, C.P. (2005) 'Volunteer youth sport coaches' perspectives of coaching education/certification and parental codes of conduct', *Research Quarterly for Exercise and Sport*, 76(3): 324–338.

Williams, S.J. and Kendall, L. (2007) 'Perceptions of elite coaches and sport scientists of the research needs for elite coaching practice', *Journal of Sport Sciences*, 25(14): 1577–1586.

Wright, T., Trudel, P. and Culver, D. (2007) 'Learning how to coach: The different learning situations reported by youth ice hockey coaches', *Physical Education and Sport Pedagogy*, 12(2): 127–144.

31

EFFECTIVE COACHING AS A MODERNIST FORMATION

A Foucauldian critique

Jim Denison

UNIVERSITY OF ALBERTA, CANADA

Joseph Mills

UNIVERSITY OF ALBERTA, CANADA

Luke Jones

UNIVERSITY OF ALBERTA, CANADA

Introduction

Over the course of its history and development, sport has been viewed as a social and cultural activity intended to achieve ends far beyond the 'playing of games'. Themes related to order, discipline, obedience, health, production, education, personal development, social change, efficiency, and rationality have pervaded every conception of sport at every level. Burstyn (1999), for example, argued that the athleticization of the nineteenth century belonged to a much larger movement of material secularization where science and medicine began to displace theology as the most authoritative account of nature; sport reflected the change to a man-made, knowable (read scientific) world. Moreover, to manage the challenges of rapid industrialization, urbanization, nation–building and imperialism sport began to colonize a myriad of institutions – public education, recreation, military training, church sociability, the workplace (Horne *et al.* 1999; Hughson 2009). In this way, sport became respectable and productive, appropriated as a means to an end rather than holding any intrinsic value. Participation in sport was also seen as an imperative for developing virtues congruent with a capitalist society – 'character', loyalty, teamwork, self-sufficiency, courage, cooperation, fairness, and obedience (Mangan 1981) – to make young men into competent leaders (Coakley 2009) and to reform troubled youths (Cunningham 1980; Holt 1989).

The development of the major sciences – biomechanics, exercise physiology, motor learning – that first constituted the sport sciences also illustrated processes of control and rationalization. Biomechanics used engineering principles to analyze biological systems, structures, and functions, leading to the production of textbooks that explained human movement as a series of levers and pulleys. Exercise physiology emerged from the new anatomists who explained movement by dissecting static cadavers. Mathematical law was also applied to the body to provide accurate measurements – anthropometry – that would better calculate and predict its performative capabilities. Likewise, motor learning, initially a science for selecting suitably skilled pilots, conceptualized the brain as a kind of computer that processed select inputs to produce specific outputs.

Out of these cultural developments modern physical education also emerged (Kirk 2002), leading to early forms of rational gymnastics and team games taught by male teachers who promoted the scientific acquisition of skills over other movement qualities (Vertinsky 2007). Maximizing human performance in the early twentieth century, thus, became a process to manage – the correct selection of methods, means, and personnel. As a result, understandings began to form concerning the knowledge and skills required to be an effective coach – scientific, rational, decisive, masculine. Thus was born the modern coach.

In this chapter we would like to discuss how this history and the subsequent formation of modern understandings of effective coaching has influenced coaches' development today. More specifically, we will refer to coaches involved in athletics (track and field). To make our argument we will draw on the work of Michel Foucault (1995) and discuss how his analysis of disciplinary techniques, as part of his larger project concerning technologies of dominance, points to a number of limitations concerning contemporary planning practices used by athletics coaches. For us these limitations suggest that athletics coaches need to view planning not as a technical process alone – the 'what to do' and 'when' of training theory – but as an interactional process formed through a range of complex power relations that make understanding how to implement one's plan just as important.

Effective coaching

According to Côté and Gilbert (2009) research examining effective coaching – what it is and how to develop it – has dominated the last forty years of the coaching science literature. Despite all this attention ambiguity still exists around the qualities and characteristics that make a coach effective. This should not come as a surprise considering that coaching's complexities go well beyond the application of an autonomous body of facts (Jones *et al.* 2002; Cassidy *et al.* 2004). Moreover, reaching a general understanding of effective coaching – the necessary behaviours, dispositions, education, and experiences – will always prove difficult because of the particulars of every sporting culture. As just one example, what is effective coaching for a team sport will unlikely account for what is effective coaching for an individual sport. However, efforts to account for effective coaching still persist, as they must given how important coaches are to the development of athletes. The question must therefore become, how should we proceed to understand the qualities that comprise effective coaching?

As we referred to in our introduction, we believe it is vital to consider sport's history as a modern technique for changing society in order to understand what is meant by effective coaching. For example, through modern sport and coaching practices the body has come to be viewed as an object and target of power that can be analyzed and manipulated for greater ends. This has without a doubt influenced contemporary understandings of effective coaching as well as what needs to be done to develop effective coaches. The history of sport as a modern technique for disciplining subjects makes it very difficult to imagine effective coaches as anything more than technicians focused on the efficient organization and development of productive sporting bodies (Heikkala 1993; Chapman 1997; Shogan 1999;

Johns and Johns 2000; Phillips and Hicks 2000; Halas and Hanson 2001; Denison 2007; Barker-Ruchti and Tinning 2010; Denison 2010). As a result, many coach educators, sports scientists, and sports administrators charged with developing effective coaches have created programs that are highly technocratic and rigid in their intent and design (Lacy and Darst 1985; Claxton 1988; Douge and Hastie 1993; Salmela *et al.* 1994; Salmela 1995; Schinke *et al.* 1995; Gilbert *et al.* 2006; Erickson *et al.* 2007).

However, recent work by a number of sociologically informed coach educators has led to 'the coach' being seen as a social agent whose actions, opinions, and beliefs are 'inextricably linked to both the constraints and opportunities of human interaction' (Potrac *et al.* 2002: 184). To be an effective coach it is no longer good enough to rely on knowledge from the traditional sports sciences alone or to assume a functional or mechanistic understanding of the body and human performance (Howe 2004, 2006; Hockey and Allen Collinson 2007). It is now recognized that how a coach implements his or her training plan is essentially about power and 'who can speak where, when and with what authority' (Ball 1990: 17). But few coaches think about how they coach being a 'political process intimately linked with power, control, and what counts as legitimate knowledge' (Tinning 1997: 108). However, as a number of sports scholars have shown, such a non-contextual or rational understanding of coaching and the body, where athletes are treated in objective or instrumental ways, can result in athletes experiencing a number of performance-related problems (e.g. Chapman 1997; Markula and Martin 2007; McMahon *et al.* 2011).

In order for coaching to advance as a field, coaches need to become more sceptical of the nature of their subject-matter knowledge and continually ask, on whose authority have certain coaching practices become privileged over others (Bell 1997; Tinning 2002; Jones 2006)? This should begin to reveal to coaches that there is no such thing as permanent coaching knowledge, but rather multiple truth claims produced by a range of discourses that prescribe how coaches should relate to everything from problem solving, the application of science, their relationships with their athletes, and their interpretation of their coaching experiences (Denison 2010). Armed with this scepticism, Tinning (2002) stated, should enable coaches to experiment and to adapt their practices beyond the received traditions of their sport knowing that the coaching process cannot be completely controlled or that one's approach to coaching must be based on some objective value system. For as Cushion (2006) explained, a coach's knowledge and action is always tied to a specific cultural understanding of how one should behave as a coach. Along these lines, we have found Foucault's (1995) analysis of techniques of discipline that he used to examine the development of modern society particularly useful to critique and rethink what is effective coaching in athletics.

Modern coaching

As Foucault (1995) discussed, disciplinary techniques that were deployed over the last two centuries to modernize society were so widespread and encompassing that even today we are bound by this history in terms of how we understand contemporary operations on the body. So ubiquitous were these disciplinary processes that Foucault utilized a huge number of terms to convey the completeness of their hold. According to Foucault these disciplinary techniques were a 'general formula for domination', a 'new scale of control', a 'subtle coercion', an 'infinitesimal power over the active body', an 'uninterrupted, constant coercion', a 'policy of coercions', a 'calculated manipulation', a 'machinery of power', a 'mechanics of power', a 'multiplicity of often minor processes, of different or in and scattered location', the 'blueprint of a general method', a 'new micro-physics of power', 'small acts of cunning', 'subtle arrangements, apparently innocent but profoundly suspicious'. Disciplinary techniques made 'the meticulous control of the operations of the body' possible and assured the 'constant subjection of its forces'.

Not surprisingly, critical analyses of effective coaching as a process that disciplines subjects have been few given the taken-for-granted nature of coaching as a disciplinary practice (Shogan 1999). Such a critique is particularly relevant in athletics because of the extreme emphasis coaches place on designing training programs – the what to do and when of coaching. For Foucault (1995) such techniques, no matter how small or minor, were important to analyze because of the disciplinary control they can exert over the body. The analysis of discipline, he argued, should begin from such small details; it is the foundation, without which it would be impossible to understand anything. In what follows we discuss the disciplinary details typically found within modern athletics coaches' training programs by closely following Foucault's (1995) analysis of discipline outlined in his book, *Discipline and Punish*. Through this exercise we intend to illustrate the limitations these details present and the need to problematize them as natural in order to develop new approaches and understandings of planning that are less restrictive and hopefully serve to expand how athletics coaches are educated and developed.

The art of distributions

One detail that is almost always referred to when describing an effective athletics coach is his or her ability to design training programs that clearly identify and select specific places where specific things are to happen. Foucault (1995) termed this technique, enclosure, 'the protected place of disciplinary monotony' (p. 141). For Foucault, enclosure enabled production to become more concentrated, to 'derive the maximum advantages and … neutralize the inconveniences' … such that labour forces became 'mastered' (p. 142). Determining a suitable training space to carry out a particular workout or block of training, however, is not enough for an athletics coach to be effective as he or she also needs that space to be somewhat flexible to be able to partition athletes so that each athlete has a specific place within the greater space. In this way, 'useful communication' could be established and each individual could be judged and therefore supervised – 'a procedure aimed at knowing, mastering and using' (p. 143) that also served to make coaches into experts.

Effective or expert coaches, therefore, with their knowledge of bodies and training systems that enable them to judge their athletes' progress and development, regularly turn training spaces into functional 'useful' spaces by how they classify or rank athletes according to their abilities. In this way, confusion is minimized, efficiency is maximized and the judgement of ability is made simpler. Think here of an athletics coach with athletes in various event groups organized around the track all of whom are fixed into their very specific positions and relations – long jump pit, shot put circle, starting blocks. Is this totally bad or wrong? No. Could it be problematic? Yes, and that is our point: training programs can, if the coach is not careful how he or she implements them, place athletes in positions, or lead to the formation of relations, that stifle their autonomy and control and limit their development (Denison 2007). A truly effective coach, we would argue, would consider the possibility of these effects and think as carefully about *how* his or her training plan organizes athletes as he or she does about what workouts comprise that plan. Otherwise, a training program can become like a machine that 'supervises, hierarchises and rewards' only specific behaviours that maximize economy of time and individual obedience. A more effective coach would design a training program that is fluid in its intentions and design with the aim of developing individuals' unique capacities for performance. In this way, how a coach designates the use and function of space can, if the coach is not careful, turn a training program into a technique of power and a procedure of knowledge … that has the function of characterizing (and consequently reducing individual singularities) and constituting classes (Foucault 1995: 149). Therefore, by virtue of its spatial distribution, Foucault (1995) called discipline *cellular*.

The control of activity

According to Foucault (1995), having set the controls for the way a space organizes production, the next disciplinary task or detail was to timetable it – and what athletics coach could ever be considered effective who did not implement a training plan that 'established rhythms, imposed particular occupations and regulated the cycles of repetition' (p. 149)? Through temporal organization, Foucault argued, the quality of time could be assured, 'totally useful time … in which the body is constantly applied to its exercise' (p. 151).

Importantly, we are not saying that an athletics coach should devise a training system where monitoring and recording results is ignored. These are useful practices to help a coach determine what to do to maximize an athlete's development. A training plan should have a temporal logic: what activities to prioritize and when. However, to be effective coaches must also recognize the demands that various temporal techniques place on athletes' bodies. For example, a 'collective and obligatory rhythm' can be constraining and penetrate the body such that every movement must be the most precise and efficient – the 'best relation'. How a coach uses a stopwatch could obscure his or her attention from other factors that contribute to an athlete's performance such as effort, foot contact, body position, expression, and enjoyment, and as a result make decisions about an athlete's progress with inadequate information (Denison 2010).

For Foucault (1995) the precise use of time also included the efficient manipulation of whatever object the body was using, a 'body–object articulation'. In athletics a myriad of objects hold the body together while it performs, such as straps, braces, or orthotics; or think of the javelin, discus, shot put, hammer, hurdle, pole vault, cross bar, baton, or takeoff board. An effective coach needs to have a detailed understanding of the technical deployment of these objects measured and controlled by rhythm, speed, and coordination. But for Foucault this also had the effect of producing a 'body-weapon, body-tool, body-machine complex' (p. 153). Is such an effect considered when teaching coaches what to do to progress athletes' skills? Likely not. Instead, as Foucault discussed, time is typically thought of as an objective element to be exhausted never wasted, 'from time, ever more available moments and, from each moment, ever more useful forces' (p. 154). As a result, the body can easily become objectified, a mechanical body, subjected to new forms of power, and consequently knowledge. The body is inserted into the 'natural machinery' of the institutions (sport and coaching) where all activities are subject to disciplinary control; the body 'manipulated by authority … of useful training' (p. 155) is 'required to be docile in its minutest operations' (p. 156), and so is subject to 'a number of natural requirements and functional constraints' (p. 155). In this way, the organized requirements of the machine-like (disciplinary) institutions become naturalized. And because these requirements are considered basic elements of human life, disciplinary power is 'not only analytical and "cellular", but also assumed to be natural and "*organic*" ' (p. 156, emphasis added). Accordingly, effective coaching is defined in line with these principles of discipline and docility that ironically can run counter to athlete development as the individual attainment of an 'exquisite performance' (Shogan 1999).

The organization of genesis

Evidence of the pervasiveness around the disciplined organization of space and time as taken-for-granted activities was what Foucault (1995) argued follows next in the examination of disciplinary techniques' hold on bodies: the development of successive or parallel segments of time, organized and structured within an allotted time frame to form an analytical plan, 'a succession of elements of increasing complexity.' This process became what Foucault called an 'analytical pedagogy … meticulous in its detail' (p. 159).

For athletics coaches the training plan is the 'blueprint' for how to progress and develop athletic performance. However, as Foucault (1995) argued, the division of activities defined by a plan enabled each stage, e.g. general preparation, specific preparation, general competition, specific competition, recovery, to be subject to meticulous control and intervention, 'a whole investment of duration by power.' In other words, the plan produces a linear timeframe where all progress orients to a fixed, stable point. Progress is understood as a general concept easily measured and widely accepted. As a result, what Foucault called the *genesis* (evolution) of individuals and the progress of societies combine to form a new power of domination. A series of workouts – a training plan – 'make possible a perpetual characterization of the individual either in relation to this term, in relation to other individuals, or in relation to a type of itinerary' (p. 161). Accordingly, graduated exercises – athletic, military, didactic, punitive – that are repetitive can become constraining.

Again our question is, are coaches taught to consider the constraining nature of a series of workouts when they are taught how to implement their training plans? Together, we can testify to having attended hundreds of hours of planning workshops, conferences, and clinics led by expert coaches and not once have we ever heard one of these coaches raise the issue of constraint when outlining how he or she implements his or her training system. Rather, exactly as Foucault (1995) discussed, coaches are taught to tinker endlessly with the details – the 'series upon series' of exercises, the 'disciplinary polyphony' of exercises, the what to do and when of coaching that defines each individual athlete's level or rank and so maximizes time and efficiency. As a result, the knowledge needed to become something or someone useful (with utility) as a graduated exercise begins to govern behaviour.

> The striving of the whole community (a group of athletes under a coach) towards salvation became the collective, permanent competition of individuals being classified in relation to one another … a collectively useful aptitude … that served to economize the time of life … a subjection that never reaches its limit. *(Foucault 1995: 162)*

Composition of forces

The disciplining techniques we have been discussing that were required for modern society to function efficiently also meant that large numbers of people were no longer required to maximize a group's effectiveness. Better organized, smaller units – a 'whole calculated practice of individual and collective dispositions, movement of groups or isolated elements' (Foucault 1995: 163) – constituted a new productive machinery. The effects of this machine, therefore, needed to be optimized. Accordingly, discipline was not just about an increasing distribution and effective organization of individuals but of combining these forces in order to develop an efficient machine. This occurred in a number of ways.

An individual body was but one *element* in this machine. Its placement was therefore more important than any of its individual qualities. The performance of each individual must be held in perfect *time* with the performance of others to ensure the maximum force of all parts of what was now, a multi-segmentary machine. Foucault (1995) elaborated that the architects of this design aimed to ensure that there was not one moment in life in which one could not extract forces, because it was now clear how to differentiate and combine force with others. In order to achieve this combination of force the component parts of the machine needed to respond to *precise commands* that were clear, concise, and did not need elaboration. Pre-arranged commands needed to be perceived and responded to immediately. Foucault thus called the final aspect of the disciplines *combinatory*, because of the composition of all the forces which then result in effective tactics.

Interestingly, athletics is generally considered an individual sport where success is determined solely by the individual. Distance runners, for example, are habitually required to reach deep inside themselves to find reserves of ever decreasing energy with which to drive themselves forward. However, most distance runners train as part of a group that operates under the precise commands, rituals, and customs of the coach. In this group, or pack, every athlete knows his or her place as well as the accompanying array of habits, behaviours, and idiosyncrasies that determine what he or she should be doing. The space runners occupy in a group at the start of each repetition, and the speed at which it is appropriate to run, are drilled into runners by their coaches so no one interferes with anyone else. In particular, lesser runners need to be kept out of the way of the better runners. Runners also come to know when they are likely to be asked to join with others in the group, or to form smaller mini-groups or to do different workouts entirely. They know when they should force the pace of the group and when they should back off. As a result of all of this, each individual's tailor-made training plan is actually a broken-down version of the master plan the coach uses for everyone – his or her own general blueprint for success. Thus coaching runners is not necessarily individual in nature, even if a coach is working with one athlete, but part of the 'multi-segmentary machine' organized by the coach where the training of one member of the group is virtually identical to every other group member. For example, when runner x reaches runner y's level, he or she will start program y. Each individual program is therefore actually no more than a different 'stage' of progress pre-determined and controlled by the coach.

To summarize, Foucault (1995) was able to define discipline as being cellular, organic, genetic, and combinatory. The move to a modern society, which sport helped to facilitate, necessitated a 'military dream' as a 'general blueprint' for society. To ensure the efficient and maximal organization of large numbers of people that would result in perfect tactics, it had to include knowledge of the things that made up its various parts. The main focus of society became the 'meticulously subordinated cogs of a machine … permanent coercions … to indefinitely progressive forms of training … to automatic docility' (p. 169). Having outlined some of the essential disciplinary techniques that most easily spread from one to another, Foucault stated that the main aim of this power was to 'train' the mass of confusion into a 'multiplicity of individual elements'. 'Discipline "makes" individuals; it is the specific technique of a power that regards individuals both as objects and as an instrument of its exercise' (p. 170). And it has been our argument up to this point that this process, which has greatly influenced how we understand and develop effective athletics coaches, can limit coaches' effectiveness. However, our argument thus far has been largely descriptive, outlining the disciplinary details typically found within athletics coaches' training plans and what can happen when disciplinary techniques go unchecked and what coaches can begin to do to avoid these problems. Therefore, in the next section of this chapter we would like to discuss why this happens, which according to Foucault (1995) meant discussing the manner in which power was derived from various disciplinary techniques and how discipline's mechanisms worked to produce specific effects on bodies.

Coaching's effects

As we have illustrated through numerous examples presented above, the disciplinary details typically present in athletics coaches' training plans are clearly visible in that they are always something done on bodies – what coaches have athletes do. Foucault (1995) argued that this was essential for discipline to be effective as power emanates from action and 'exact observation'. In particular, when the rewards of production dramatically rose, as they did in the early nineteenth century, effective supervision became crucial as even the slightest incompetence could be extremely costly. In the same way, it can be said that productive athletic bodies are rewarded more and more today. In Olympic sports such as athletics, where medals are extremely difficult to come by, supervision (coaching) has become an increasingly important role. Mistakes such as injury, burnout, or poor planning can seriously damage a national sport organization's viability. Therefore, leaving athletes unsupervised to make mistakes in their training is not an option if athletes are to be managed effectively.

However, as Foucault (1995) said, to be truly disciplinary this supervision or observation needs to be discreet so that it does not suffocate those being viewed – an intense, continuous supervision that becomes a 'decisive economic operator'. So great the rewards, so intense and discreet the surveillance – 'a multiple, automatic and anonymous power ... its functioning is that of a network of relations from top to bottom, but also to a certain extent from bottom to top and laterally ... supervisors perpetually supervised' (p. 177). Thus it is that observation, and consequently power, is always everywhere.

On the track or on the field this would mean athletes continually subjecting themselves to someone else's idea of 'normal'. And such power, because it functions 'largely in silence', does not need coercion or force to fulfil its needs of surveillance and control and the making of docility. Does this mean observation should be eliminated? Of course not. What it does mean is that effective coaches need to understand that increasing control may make peak performance less, not more, likely because it is more apt to lead to athlete docility.

Related to observation as a characteristic of effective coaching is the important role coaches have to play in correcting mistakes or errors by their athletes to reduce the gaps between deficiencies and preferred behaviours. This not only includes correcting technical and tactical errors but ways of being, thinking, and acting. In other words, non-conformity of any kind becomes a potentially punishable offence.

Planning is largely about reducing non-conformity and locating athletes, in all senses of their being, within a particular bandwidth of development and progression. This is not to say that a technical model for an event such as the long jump is irrelevant as clearly there are certain biomechanical positions an athlete must be able to put her or himself into to jump world-class distances. However, from a Foucauldian perspective we are interested in how coaching techniques surrounding any kind of binary of 'permitted and forbidden' leads to individuals being judged according to a fixed set of truths. If a coach is not careful, this judgement can begin to make all individuals feel that they need to be like one another by instilling a constant pressure to conform. So it is that punishment (correction) 'compares', establishes 'rules' and 'standards', 'measures', 'hierarchises' and lastly 'excludes'. But discipline also rewards, providing awards for attaining higher ranks and places – another form of punishment that operates in reverse. In short, this entire process of judgement normalizes all behaviours and can make athletes docile.

Combining both observation and normalization, Foucault (1995) argued that the process of examination established a continual 'visibility' that enabled individuals to be judged. At the same time individuals would be subject to a new invisible power that objectified them, so that a mass of writing 'captures and fixes them'. For example, planning documents can enable the effective monitoring of anything into categories, averages, and distributions where norms become fixed. In this way, individuals become describable and therefore analyzable objects. They are 'under the gaze of a permanent corpus of knowledge' (p. 190); each individual becomes a 'case' – an object of knowledge and a hold of power. Through the examination individuals can be described, judged, measured, and compared but also have to be trained, corrected, normalized, and excluded: 'a procedure of objectification and subjection'.

Such procedures are clearly evident surrounding the development of effective coaches in athletics where case after case is discussed in terms of what the coach had the athlete do, when, and to what effect. These cases are scrutinized in books, websites, and conferences as a way of educating coaches. Are these discussions bad? Of course not, as the case-study method is a powerful way to learn. The issue becomes how the examination, 'by combining hierarchical surveillance and normalising judgement, assures great disciplinary functions of distribution and classification, maximum extraction of forces and time, continuous genetic accumulation, optimum combination of aptitudes and thereby, the fabrication of cellar, organic, genetic and combinatory individuality' (p. 1). In short, the disciplines, operating through these instruments, produce reality – 'the domains of objects and rituals of truth' (p. 194). Given all of this, what Foucault did next was consider the techniques that facilitated these effects and for this he used the concept of the panopticon.

The panopticon was a model that could effectively instil a state of consciousness and permanent visibility in all individuals, and so defined everyday power relations. In this way, Foucault (1995) was clear that whenever a particular form of behaviour needed to be imposed on any group or institution, the panoptic mechanism should be used. It was 'a way of making power relations function in a function, and of making a function function through these power relations' (p. 207). It became the general principle of the new 'political anatomy' that ensured disciplining relations, and that crucially Foucault stated, spread through the entire social body. Through the design of the panopticon, power spreads to the minds of individuals – as one is continually aware of being visible but is also never able to verify it. Consequently, it does not matter who the supervisor is, anyone can exercise power – or operate the machine. The transparency of the panoptic scheme meant that power was more efficient because it increased the number of people who could be controlled and decreased the number of people who were needed to operate it. The panoptic mechanism spreads throughout the entire social body and we can now talk about the formation of a disciplinary society – a whole 'disciplinary generalization'.

This discipline becomes a type of power that operates a whole set of procedures which may be taken over by any institution, where the aim is maximum efficiency in every aspect of an ever-growing, modern, capitalist society – the 'maximum intensity' for the 'lowest cost'. 'In short, to increase both the docility and the utility of all the elements in the system' (Foucault 1995: 218). Panopticism, therefore, is the technique that explains how and why widespread coercion occurs. Further, it is a machinery that is 'immense and minute', that affords 'panopticisms' every day, and that is given a 'respectable face' by science – a 'set of physio-political techniques'. Planning as a process, therefore, becomes political as it becomes a science – a disciplinary politics of control and management where individuals can be placed under constant observation in their quest for reaching the standards imposed by 'experts in normality'.

Conclusion

In an effort to bring Foucault's (1995) analysis of discipline and its effects to the study of sporting bodies, and more specifically to the development of a new understanding of effective coaching in athletics, we have tried to illustrate that how athletics coaches set targets and sequence workouts largely derives from a particular nineteenth century understanding of how to organize space, time, and movement. As a result, planning athletes' training has for the most part become a technical process made up of a number of objective variables that observe, normalize, and judge athletes' actions and behaviours. It has been our argument that this needs to be challenged if as coach educators we hope to develop coaches who do more than create docile athletes.

It is in this way, we believe, that effective planning in athletics requires constant and continuous thought, an ongoing commitment to lifelong learning and a willingness to change and listen to others (Denison 2007; Denison and Avner 2011). Moreover, planning cannot be conceptualized as a 'divided process' made up of physical and technical (read scientific) aspects and non-physical or non-technical (read unscientific) aspects. Such a split is not conducive to producing maximal performances as athletes' bodies move holistically (Howe 2004). Moreover, delineating physical or technical aspects from non-physical or non-technical aspects is nearly impossible. Is an athlete's 'psyching-out' a result of anxiety or poor physical preparation? How are the two related? Further, when a coach's knowledge is situated in the context within which it was created, we know that he or she will be much more likely to develop lasting critical thinking skills that can equip him or her to be a more effective learner and ultimately practitioner (Cushion 2006).

Accordingly, to prevent the further production of uncritical coaches in athletics, or as Foucault (1995) would say, docile coaches who do not ask themselves why they do what they do, one of our primary aims as coach educators should be to teach coaches how to navigate the complexities of training theory – the critical evaluation and application of concepts and theories (Cushion 2006; Nash and Collins 2006) – to enable them to do more than simply organize a training system founded on the rational production of disciplined, docile athletes but to help them bring each athlete they coach to his or her own level of brilliance by carefully considering how to implement the training program they design.

References

Ball, S.J. (1990) *Politics and Policy-Making in Education: Explorations in Policy Sociology*, London: Routledge.

Barker-Ruchti, N. and Tinning, R. (2010) 'Foucault in leotards: Corporeal discipline in women's artistic gymnastics', *Sociology of Sport Journal*, 27: 229–250.

Bell, M. (1997) 'The development of expertise', *Journal of Physical Education, Recreation and Dance*, 68: 34–38.

Burstyn, V. (1999) *The Rites of Men Manhood, Politics, and the Culture of Sport*, Toronto, ON: University of Toronto Press.

Cassidy, T., Jones, R.L. and Potrac, P. (2004) *Understanding Sports Coaching: The Social, Cultural and Pedagogical Foundations of Coaching Practice*, London: Routledge.

Chapman, G. (1997) 'Making weight: Lightweight rowing, technologies of power, and technologies of the self', *Sociology of Sport Journal*, 14: 205–223.

Claxton, D.B. (1988) 'A systematic observation of successful and less successful high school tennis coaches', *Journal of Teaching in Physical Education*, 7: 302–310.

Coakley, J. (2009) *Sports in Society Issues and Controversies* (10th ed.), New York, NY: McGraw-Hill.

Côté, J. and Gilbert, W. (2009) 'An integrative definition of coaching effectiveness and expertise', *International Journal of Sports Science and Coaching*, 4: 307–323.

Cunningham, H. (1980) *Leisure in the Industrial Revolution c. 1780–c. 1880*, London: Croom Helm.

Cushion, C. (2006) 'Mentoring: Harnessing the power of experience', in R.L. Jones (ed.) *The Sports Coach as Educator: Re-Conceptualising Sports Coaching*, London: Routledge, pp. 128–144.

Denison, J. (2007) 'Social theory for coaches: A Foucauldian reading of one athlete's poor performance', *International Journal of Sports Science and Coaching*, 2: 369–383.

Denison, J. (2010) 'Planning, practice and performance: the discursive construction of coaches' knowledge', *Sport, Education and Society*, 15: 461–478.

Denison, J. and Avner, Z. (2011) 'Positive Coaching: Ethical Practices for Athlete Development', *Quest*, 2: 209–228.

Douge, B. and Hastie, P. (1993) 'Coach effectiveness', *Sport Science Review*, 2: 14–29.

Erickson, K., Côté, J. and Fraser-Thomas, J. (2007) 'Sport experiences, milestones and educational activities associated with high-performance coaches' development', *The Sport Psychologist*, 21: 302–316.

Foucault, M. (1995) *Discipline and Punish*, New York, NY: Vintage.

Gilbert, W., Côté, J. and Mallet, C. (2006) 'Developmental paths and activities of successful sport coaches', *International Journal of Sports Science and Coaching*, 1: 69–76.

Halas, J. and Hanson, L.L. (2001) 'Pathologizing Billy: Enabling and constraining the body of the condemned', *Sociology of Sport Journal*, 18: 115–126.

Heikkala, J. (1993) 'Discipline and excel: Techniques of the self and body and the logic of competing', *Sociology of Sport Journal*, 10: 397–412.

Hockey, J. and Allen Collinson, J. (2007) 'Grasping the phenomenology of sporting bodies', *International Review for the Sociology of Sport*, 42: 115–131.

Holt, R. (1989) *Sport and the British – A Modern History*, Oxford: Oxford University Press.

Horne, J., Tomlinson, A. and Whannel, G. (1999) *Understanding Sport: An Introduction to the Sociological and Cultural Analysis of Sport*, London: E. and F.N. Spon.

Howe, P.D. (2004) *Sport, Professionalism and Pain: Ethnographies of Injury and Risk*, London: Routledge.

Howe, P.D. (2006) 'Habitus, barriers and the [ab]use of the science of interval training in the 1950s', *Sport in History*, 26: 325–344.

Hughson, J. (2009) *The Making of Modern Sporting Cultures*, London: Routledge.

Johns, D.P. and Johns, J. (2000) 'Surveillance, subjectivism and technologies of power: An analysis of the discursive practice of high-performance sport', *International Review for the Sociology of Sport*, 35: 219–234.

Jones, R.L. (2006) 'Dilemmas, maintaining "face," and paranoia: An average coaching life', *Qualitative Inquiry*, 12: 1012–1021.

Jones, R.L., Armour, K.M. and Potrac, P. (2002) 'Understanding the coaching process: A framework for social analysis', *Quest*, 54: 34–48.

Kirk, D. (2002) 'The social construction of the body in physical education and sport', in A. Laker (ed.) *The Sociology of Sport and Physical Education: An Introductory Reader*, London: Routledge, pp. 79–91.

Lacy, A.C. and Darst, P.W. (1985) 'Systematic observation of behaviors of winning high school head football coaches', *Journal of Teaching in Physical Education*, 4: 256–270.

Mangan, J.A. (1981) *Athleticism in the Victorian and Edwardian Public School: The Emergence and Consolidation of an Educational Ideology*, Cambridge: Cambridge University Press.

Markula, P. and Martin, M. (2007) 'Ethical coaching: Gaining respect in the field', in J. Denison (ed.) *Coaching Knowledges: Understanding the Dynamics of Sport Performance*, Oxford: A.C. Black, pp. 51–82.

McMahon, J., Penny, D. and Dinan-Thompson, M. (2011) 'Body practices – exposure and effect of a sporting culture?' Stories from three Australian swimmers', *Sport, Education and Society*, 17: 1–26.

Nash, C. and Collins, D. (2006) 'Tacit knowledge in expert coaching: Science or art?' *Quest*, 58: 465–477.

Phillips, M. and Hicks, F. (2000) 'Conflict, tensions and complexities: Athletic training in Australia in the 1950s', *International Journal of the History of Sport*, 17: 206–224.

Potrac, P., Jones, R.L. and Armour, K.M. (2002) '"It's all about getting respect": The coaching behaviors of an expert English coach', *Sport, Education and Society*, 7: 183–202.

Salmela, J.H. (1995) 'Learning from the development of expert coaches', *Coaching and Sport Science Journal*, 2: 3–13.

Salmela, J.H., Draper, S.P. and Desjardins, G. (1994) 'Transitional phases of expert ice and field hockey coaches' careers', *Access to Active Living*, Victoria, BC: University of Victoria Press.

Schinke, R.J., Bloom, G.A. and Salmela, J.H. (1995) 'The career stages of elite Canadian basketball coaches', *Avante*, 1: 48–62.

Shogan, D. (1999) *The Making of High-Performance Athletes: Discipline, Diversity, and Ethics*, Toronto, ON: University of Toronto Press.

Tinning, R. (1997) 'Performance and participation discourses in human movement: Toward a socially critical physical education', in J.-M. Fernandez-Balboa (ed.) *Critical Postmodernism in Human Movement, Physical Education, and Sport*, Albany, NY: SUNY Press, pp. 99–119.

Tinning, R. (2002) 'Engaging Siedentopian perspectives on content knowledge for physical education', *Quest*, 21: 378–391.

Vertinsky, P.A. (2007) 'Movement practices and fascist infections: From dance under the swastika to movement education in the British primary School', in P.A. Vertinsky and J. Hargreaves (eds) *Physical Culture, Power and the Body*, London: Psychology Press, pp. 25–52.

32

WHAT A FOUCAULDIAN APPROACH MIGHT DO FOR THE LOSS OF THE FEMALE COACH

Jane M. Stangl

SMITH COLLEGE, USA

Introduction

The past few years, at least from 2006 to 2010, the state of women in intercollegiate coaching ranks in the U.S. had stabilized. Meaning, the continual decline of women as coaches – once set at a remarkable 90 percent of all coaches of women's teams prior to 1972 – held constant at approximately 42 percent of coaching opportunities. However, stability is a misleading notion when looking at the long-term data which notes more accurately that, "even though the number of women's teams is near an all time high, the representation of females among the coaching ranks of women's intercollegiate athletics is near its all time low" (Acosta and Carpenter 2010). In sum, the female as coach continues to reflect a marginalized proportion of the coaching labor force.

The work on the decline of women as coaches has now spanned over three decades, and while approaches to understanding this demise have varied, analysis lies largely within the sociocultural realm of sport studies. In her recent work, *Gender Games: Why Women Coaches are Losing the Field* (2009), Christina Cruz melds the sociocultural research with a psychological bend moving more toward a subjective sense of self. She engages this process first by enhancing a liberal feminist sensibility, and second, by working through a qualitative turn, advocating self-reflexivity and more broadly psychologies of the self. In this piece I intend to pick up on Cruz's contributions by advancing notions of the coaching self as subject, yet enriching the sense of the subjective self through the lens of Foucault. By concentrating more specifically on his work with sexuality, and the technologies of self, that is, governing the self as subject, I argue that a Foucauldian approach toward the *practice of coaching* may render our persistent efforts to make others aware of the dire state of women coaches as outmoded. Alternately, I am also suggesting that the structural and everyday experiences of women as coaches may benefit from Foucault's ideas. Foucault was as interested in historical documents as he was the individual's everyday experience, and though his work is widely critiqued, the evolution of his theories around relations of power make attention to the intersection of the decline of females in coaching, labor practices within the field, and the rationale as to why women leave (or perhaps never consider the profession) – appealing, as well as applicable. As Cruz's subtitle suggests, women coaches are losing in the field, and I would argue, have actually lost that game. In this post-Title IX era, it is doubtful that the percentage of women coaches will ever return to the previous AIAW state, where women – almost exclusively – coached girls and women.[1]

To begin this chapter, I share a piece of myself that has been experienced, felt, and presented at a Title IX conference some years ago when my own awareness of Foucault's theoretical influence was admittedly amateurish; at that time, I wrote:

> I ended each and every season of the last five years of a fifteen year coaching career slumped over my kitchen table in tears; drained and exhausted, my well run-dry. Even more apparent than those waning days of a career going south, was the overwhelming sense that I was choking, literally and figuratively. My throat was constantly clenched; the "knot" seemed permanent. Yet the knot "spoke" clearly to my dissatisfaction, I had come to a junction in my life in which I knew I could simply go no further, my methods of self-assurance, self-sufficiency, self-stability and self-ease were crumbling. These methods seemed intimately tied to my work, my sense of self as a coach. In short, I felt I was "losing it." I quit coaching.
>
> In a world where the notion of "quitting" is shunned, I did it – I simply quit.
>
> *(Stangl 2005)*

Upon reading this vignette one might reasonably ask, "who cares?" especially given that tales of personal transitions are rarely honored as impetus for social change much less social justice. Sadly, narratives of self, such as the reflection above are often treated as stories of victimization, even though by sharing my stream of consciousness my intention was more toward offering a direct link between everyday working experiences, and the need for institutional change. I present it in this context, however, as an example of a relatively common narrative of the female as coach that has social and political consequences. Indeed, Cruz's work offers a number of similar reflections. Still, at least within the literature of the female coaches' demise, it is the evidence-based research that has held sway over subjective reflections due in great part to the tireless efforts of Vivian Acosta and Linda Carpenter, Title IX advocates who have perennially tracked this data over the span of thirty-plus years. While their data set has been formidable in demonstrating a consistent decline in women's presence in the coaching ranks, the rationale as to why this has occurred is varied and often times questioned. Yet, the Acosta and Carpenter data – instrumental as it is to the ranks of women as coaches, offers little hope of altering the hegemonic male-stream of sports inequities as an institutionalized practice. What it does tell us is that the problem is historical, empirically evident, and continuous. Additionally, the data makes apparent that Title IX, a benefit for girls in competitive sport, has been detrimental to women coaches.

This work intends to offer an alternative lens to this social fact by attempting to tease out an explanation via two major threads, initially, by questioning the application and use of R.W. Connell's notion of hegemonic masculinity as a central explanation for the decline; and second, by considering how a Foucauldian approach may help empower the female coach at least in terms of addressing her role within the decline literature. My goal is to advance an alternative approach to the practice of coaching that can offer the disconcerted female coach some peace of mind about her markedly insecure profession.

Overstating the masculine

First, let us visit Connell's (1995) concept of masculine hegemony. As this concept applies to women coaches many researchers have employed the notion of hegemonic masculinity in their rationale toward understanding the decline, at least to some extent. Overall, the reasons for the demise have varied considerably, from burnout, to lack of support, to hiring practices, to monetary compensation, to name just a few. Notable critical sociologists of sport, such as Coakley (2008), Messner (2002) and Kane (1995) have all employed Connell's approach as well, especially as it relates to gender performance noting that gender regimes constrain yet also enable women's sporting opportunities. They also make note of how gendered identities are constructed within the sporting context. As stated, hegemonic masculinity – meaning literally a hegemony that is potentially supported by force, but largely by way of an "ascendancy achieved through culture, institution and persuasion" (Connell and Messerschmidt 2005: 832), has been set up as an underlying explanatory thread throughout the demise literature making its way into the discourse of rationale. Consider this from Cruz (2009): "[m]en remain the dominant group in athletics, and hegemonic masculinity (male dominance) remains the preferred gender role for those in power" (p. 13).

Indeed, the early research on women and coaching, led in part by Annelies Knoppers (1987, 1989) found a pertinent vein of explanation through the notion of power. This explanatory paradigm has withstood the test of time and remains rooted in our collective understanding of the demise literature, although Connell's notion of masculine hegemony became the more convincing catchall summation. Knoppers' early work around power and Rosemary Kanter's seminal book, *Men and Women of the Corporation* (1977) prompted the claim of Stangl and Kane's (1991) work on coaches as products of homologous reproduction, that is, those in positions of power (largely white, male, and heterosexual) hired those more closely resembling themselves. This evidence was confirmed even when women, regardless of race/ethnicity or sexuality, were found to be more educated and more qualified (see Hasbrook 1988). Central to the idea of replicating institutionalized patterns then, hegemonic masculinity still remained central to the interpretation and explanation. Whisenant (2008) reified this position despite his counter claims about the value of the homologous reproduction rationale, stating, "with sport being so dominated by men, hegemonic masculinity has become the prevailing model sustaining a male dominated organizational structure, [at least] in high school athletics" (p. 769). Yet, by employing hegemonic masculinity as the underlying reason for women's demise, we are beholden to the rationale of ascendancy, that is, examining who rises to the top within hierarchical infrastructures, and especially sex-segregated workspaces, and as in the case of women's coaching. This structural position can also be argued from the perspective of labor practices. In *The Body in Late-Capitalist USA*, (1995) Donald Lowe[2] wrote,

> the labor process is a contested terrain between management and labor. The contest is carried out beyond the bargaining table, occurring daily on the shop floor. Social and ideological conflicts outside of the workplace are also reflected in the day-to-day politics of production

(p. 36)

Arguably the politics of coaching is equally as contested, driven not only by management (athletic directors, booster clubs, alumni and college and university presidents), but a cultural win–at–all–costs ethos. Instead of playing itself out on a shop floor the contest is held on playing fields and courts worldwide. In the case of women's coaching in the U.S., looking at the decline literature from the top down does little to empower those subjected to such a pecking order.

Recently, Connell and Messerschmidt (2005) reassessed their own position toward the catchall category of hegemonic masculinity and asserted that it served as support "for much of the developing research ... on men and masculinity, replacing sex-role theory and categorical models of patriarchy," and as such, they contend that the concept was more of a "framework" and less an explanation for such findings (p. 834). Yet, if a simple Google search on "female coaches" offers as the opening citation a 2007 piece in *TIME* magazine addressing the very question, "Where are the women coaches?," scholars must continue to ask questions that move the conversation further along; away from where the female coaches have gone, and toward a deeper understanding of why the demise continues, despite the recent "stabilization." Cruz's work offers a new twist on an old story by extending an effort toward asking female coaches directly why their job is taxing and prompts their leaving the profession. This approach to assessing the demise literature moves the female coach relationally from one of objecthood, to subjecthood.

In brief, a partial goal of this chapter is to advance this trajectory and consider how research on the demise of women's coaches might shift away from the neo-liberal framework of seeking equity, toward a more sensitized approach that accents the individual's possibility for freedom by enhancing the awareness of the (female) coach as subject, rather than object position. In other words, how can the practice of coaching – as a female aware of her subject position – become more informed and hence utilize what Foucault calls, and we will discuss later, technologies of self in order to achieve greater satisfaction in her work. Here Cruz's work (2009) has helped set us on a clearer path by starting with the voice of women coaches themselves and getting them to articulate the challenges of their position, or in her own words, "how the male dominated culture may influence female coaches thinking," or "how the gendered world of athletics influences women sense of self as coach" (p. 23). My point is that by problematizing the notion of hegemonic masculinity and unpacking its constitutive rationale for explaining the demise, we may come to an alternative understanding of *coaching* as a subjective practice (a verb), rather than assuming the problem as wholly laden in the female *coach*, (a noun) as a particular type of role within the labor force.

Not only Connell's critique of hegemonic masculinity, but other assessments as well speak to the fact that the demise has been dependent upon the categorical model of the gender-sex dichotomy – which inevitably assumes an underlying essentialism, leaving little or no room for a multiplicity of social practices. As sport is coded as a masculinist practice, for women coaches this entails making room for masculiniti*es* enacted by people in female bodies (see Halberstam 1998). Not only does a dichotomous approach deny the intersectional subjectivities of any individual, and in this case a coach, it also falls short of taking into account gender*s* as configurations of practice or performative expressions (see Butler 1990), that, "can differ according to the gender relations of a particular social setting" (Connell and Messerschmidt 2005, p. 836). Coud makes this point distinctively clear in his work, *Metrosexual* (2008), "gender is a doing, not a state of inner being" (p. 29). Those of us who work in what are considered everyday sex-segregated work environments – education, medicine, policing – understand this point well.

Cruz's work attends to this notion by identifying female coaches who describe themselves as engaging in masculine practices; however, she also constructs these actions or performances as distinctive gendered practices of particular female coaches. However, Cruz also situates the female coach into yet another potentially dichotomous relationship, that is, the coach as either coach or colleague, arguing that it is in her capacity as colleague that the coach engages in more metaphorical turf battles, which she labels micro-competitions. As such, Cruz's thesis rests on the notion that it is the micro-competitions most often with male colleagues that prompts the female coach to leave to the profession. The role of the coach as colleague then, arguably sets up the working relationship as both a site and a subject of a discursive struggle, while the practice of coaching – the engagement of sport with the student-athlete especially – affirms that many women enjoy their work (Cruz 2009).

Extending on the problem of utilizing hegemonic masculinity as the catchall of explaining where the female coach has gone, is the dichotomous set up of the research itself where the system serves to maintain boundaries of the binary sex-gender codes rendering the coaching subject as either male or female, and as an unwitting consequence, masculine or feminine. Note also that this pairing privileges the male by its primary placement within the binary. More unsettling in this approach is that static typologies of the binary sex/gender classification system render homosexuals especially suspect. When translated through sport, this has largely meant questioning lesbian and gay athletes with paltry attention toward bisexual, intersexual, or transgendered participants. Historically however, lesbian coaches have borne the brunt of this inquisition, and though the rationale of homophobia enters the demise literature (Lenskyj 1991) and is especially relevant to lesbian coaches, crying or decrying homophobia has not significantly altered the landscape of women's coaching either (Griffin 1998). Indeed this lens may be contributing to upping the policing of heterosexuality, still prevalent in many institutional settings (see Connell and Messerschmidt 2005: 837).

The separate spheres of influence argument then – a research approach frequently used to assess women in sport, and in the relatively recent past, taken up by men's studies as well – has not shifted the balance of female coaches either. To that end, men and masculinities are as relevant to coaching females as are women and femininities, but so are white feminine gay men and brown masculine straight women, as well as lesbian mothers and straight fathers. Yet as dichotomous and distinctive as these taxonomies seem, they do reveal how unstable our platform of analysis is, even though it is worth recalling that the dominant scientific research frame (often read as "truth") concludes repeatedly that differences within groups can yield more interesting and significant results than differences between groups.

In short, hegemonic masculinity is not a conclusive rationale at every level precisely because it expects notions of consent and participation – a sense of complicity – by the group outside of the power relations. That said, and as Connell and Messerschmidt (2005) remind, "the concept of hegemony was never intended to be a catchall or a prime cause – it is a means of grasping a certain dynamic within the social process" (p. 841). So if the concept of masculine hegemony cannot satisfy the character structure of female coaches as a group then we must ask, who or what is the woman coach as a subject position?

The female coach, or for that matter, any coach can subscribe to multiple subject positions and multiple sexualities. In as much as coaches can be successful coaches, autocratic coaches, or depressed coaches, they can also be sexual, pansexual, or asexual coaches for that matter. Whatever subject position to which we subscribe, coaches are a product of this genealogy as well, and in the demise literature, the salient subject remains that of a female coach – but arguably one who is less subject, and more numerical object, and it is at this juncture that I turn to the lens of Foucault.

Thus far, I am suggesting that hegemony is not the fail-safe answer, and that the derivative frames of the binary classification system have rendered the decline literature conclusive evidence. A Foucauldian perspective however, reflects on and deems "the cultural constructions and ideological fictions on gender and sexuality as developed over time … shaping the experiences of *being* human" (Valocchi 2005, p. 753). Gender then, like sexuality is not a "natural feature or fact of human life but a constructed category of experience which has historical, social and cultural, rather than biological origins" (see Spargo cited in Markula and

Pringle 2006, p. 100). Many Foucauldian frames have at their center the role of sexuality, yet this particularity is only one of the many variables we can use to understand the politics of who gets to coach female athletes. As Pirkko Markula (2004) implied in her work titled, "Tuning into one self," individuals alone cannot ignore nor change the ideal of who is validated.

With the help of other scholars I now turn to three other prevailing frames of Foucault's that are most pertinent to the work and practice of coaching; they include the coach as docile body (and I add, the seed of power), the coach and technologies of self, and coaching and points of resistance. It is my hope that these particular frames find their way into the explanatory paradigms lost on past research efforts.

Foucauldian approaches to women's labor as coach

Flanking the research and writings on the decline of the female coach has been a thread of sport scholarship that has taken on Foucauldian approaches, not only in philosophical and theoretical arguments (see Andrews 1993; Rail and Harvey 1995; Hall 1996; McDonald and Birrell 1999; Smith Maguire 2002; Markula 2003) but as an applied practice as well (see Duncan 1994; Markula 1995, 2001, 2004; Schultz 2004; Chase 2008). Here, it is worth noting that some feminist scholarship has been ahead of the curve on Foucault's thinking (see Dworkin and Wachs 1998), and though this is hardly an exhaustive exhumation of all Foucauldian sport scholarship, the body of work clearly runs parallel with the scholarship on the decline of the female coach, even though never on a merging track.

Regarding coaches however, few scholars address the usefulness of Foucauldian thought to coaching as a practice. A noteworthy exception is the work of Jim Denison (2006, 2010) where he links Foucault with coaching pedagogies particularly. In a discussion that calls to question (over)-training practices, Denison (2010) noted, "when a coach relies on 'hard' evidence to make training decisions, a great deal of relevant information can go unexamined: mood, context, relationships" (p. 150). His piece, "Social theory for coaches" (2007) offers coaching scholars a refreshing respite from the research paradigm driven by exercise science where Denison advocates for "an analytical approach … that would augment [the coaches'] existing applied sport science knowledge by enabling them to consider how traditional coaching practices … might … produce some other effect" (2007: 377). In brief, Denison (2010), along with a few others[3] are attempting to "demonstrate how the construction of knowledge within coaching can be understood to be the result of a range of discursive processes that constitute some types of evidence as [more] legitimate [than others]" (p. 152).

Arguably any theoretical vein that is connected with the soft (read social) sciences that calls to question the traditional standards and practices of coaching is often deemed as less foundationally important. Additionally, our cultural attachment to the idea of winning does little to advance a reflective agenda much less offer coaches a voice through which their queries may be heard. That said, it is readily understood that shedding light on the practice of coaching through a Foucauldian lens is hardly an easy sell – and not only because reading Foucault can be difficult. But through this lens a rationale of hope and an affirmation of the self as subject, now more conscientious of their complicity in the process, offers possibilities for keeping those passionate about their work – and in this case female coaches –in their work.

The coach as docile body and seed of power

The docile body to Foucault did not simply mean the body was an instrument of passivity. Arguably, the female coach as a body – a site of both struggle and resistance, is also a referent that represents social relationships. As this pertains to the practice of coaching, Acosta and Carpenter (2010) contend that female coaches can impart a richer, fuller athletic experience – one that encourages self-esteem and also encourages women to become strong leaders not just in athletics but also in society at large. As a coach of five different sports at every level from fifth grade through graduate students over the course of thirty-plus years, standing in agreement with Acosta and Carpenter is easy. Their wish and affirmation for women as coaches is quite possible, albeit in their assertion, organically grown. I would add however, that advancing that possibility through Foucault's frames further enhances such possibilities for women.

To dismiss the role of the coach as it plays into the effects of sport and its construction of gendered and sexed identities is naïve, yet the variability that a coach allows for self-expression may be multifarious. However, it still holds that under the will of the coach, activities are created that an athlete is expected to perform. This includes structuring workouts, organizing space, and maximizing time. Most obvious however, is the fact that the coach evaluates the efficiency expressed by the athletes under the coaches' control, often under the auspices of "maximizing player potential." More pointedly, coaches rank and file athletes based on performance outcomes – as a Foucauldian reminder, and Markula and Pringle (2006) re-affirm, "discipline is the art of rank."

As the seed of power then, the coach serves as the mouthpiece for the discursive devices of bio-power. Today, such devices are linked largely to sport science – for example, maximizing an athlete's VO2 capacity, engaging in strengthening the core with plyometric exercises, HIIT (high intensity interval training), periodization; the list is endless. Rather than incorporating social theory and taking into account the sociocultural and historical construction of coaching practices, the coach becomes the "doctor," delivering exercise prescription orders depending upon the particularities of the sport. Here, the docile body of the coach creates the docile body of the athlete accordingly. The coach, emboldened with the power to judge, re-enacts a hierarchy of relationships, whereby the athlete is disciplined to the point of not only self-surveillance, but through the necessity of sports' execution via repetition – think Coach Brooks in the film *Miracle* (2004), mandating that the athletes skate sprints, "again, and again, and again."

In a Foucauldian sense, it is not possible to conceptualize oneself outside of relations of power (Markula and Pringle 2006). Hence, the subjugated coach re-enacts through the subjected athlete, further relational practices. This power/knowledge nexus becomes in the eyes of the coach and as a consequence of the athlete's acceptance, normalized. Furthermore, through this structured way of working, coaching productivity and proclivities become routinized, not just masculinized. How then, does a coach shift away from the normalized discourses of their role and move toward engaging the technologies of self in an agreeable manner?

Technologies of self: coaching or coach as subject(s)

Foucault argued that power is relational, and individuals are caught in a historical web of relations whereby they may act on others – even if they are subject to being acted upon themselves. Like the self that I shared at the beginning of this piece, each female coach that Cruz interviewed felt at some level that the role of colleague had impinged her role of coach enough for her to consider leaving the profession. A snippet of transcribed interpretations between one of her subjects – Terri, and an athletic trainer illustrates this point.[4]

So, I went to bring that up in a meeting and I was immediately shot down by saying, "well, that's why we need to measure percentage body fat." And I was like, "no it's not, you guys don't understand." And here is, it's our [sports medicine] trainer, our men's [lacrosse] coach and another male coach who think that that's the way it's going to work for women.

(Cruz 2009, p. 91)

What has become consistently prevalent is the social fact that coaching as male-identified is a naturalized and rationalized position. Accepting this position is less about acquiescing to it than it is about enhancing an awareness that can help the subject – in this case, the female coach – refine or re-examine the choice of what type of coach they can be (Denison 2006). Here is where a Foucauldian bent would suggest employing technologies of the self; that is engaging through one's own means, what he termed "operations" on one's own being to "include thoughts, conducts, ways of being" to transform oneself in an effort to attain a state of satisfaction "happiness, purity, wisdom, perfection or immortality" (Martin, *et al.* 1988, p. 18). Markula and Pringle (2006), speak of this transformation as "problematiz[ing] the limits of [one's] identity." To do so, it becomes necessary to build a more aesthetic self, where ethical self-care becomes primary. This process is actively chosen and intentionally engaged in, necessitating a critical awareness of the disciplinary discourses that impact ones identity (p. 153). To this end, the coach as subject promotes ethical practices that do use power, but with a minimal intent to dominate.

Coaching and points of resistance

Narratives of resistances have helped frame a number of ways in which athletes have acted against the prevailing norms to recuperate what have been normalized as losses (see Iannotta and Kane 2002; Chase 2008). From the lens of Foucault, and "in as far as an individual is part of the power relations, there is a possibility for freedom." To do so as a coaching subject however means that the subject must engage in practices that are liberating for the self. Markula and Pringle (2006) advocate this position by reiterating Foucault's point that freedom be practiced ethically, "it is the power over self, which will regulate power over others" (p. 147). To challenge the system is not necessarily a liberating practice, but cooperating with the powers to be as a coach, is not necessarily oppressive either. To move in this direction active problematizing is necessary. Consider an example as simple yet fraught with an unfortunate label as the "suicide drill" – a sprint training mechanism used for anaerobic conditioning. On my basketball teams we called them "quarter-courts" to draw attention to the intent of the drill rather than the implications of pain that arise from doing the drill. A "man-to-man" defense became a "player" defense. In soccer – a game laden with male specific metaphors, "man on," became "woman on." Though much to the chagrin of the athletes I worked with at the time, in their correspondence back to me over the years they acknowledge that my reasons for doing such things were indeed less superfluous than they had originally thought.

If a coach does not have the freedom to recreate the way in which they go about the practice of coaching, they will find little freedom in coaching as a profession. This approach calls to question one of sports contemporary slogans – "refuse to lose." By employing more Foucauldian frames to the practice of coaching, the coach can upend that refusal by giving over to the subject athlete a critical sensibility that allows the athlete the possibility of finding particular practices problematic/hurtful or unhealthy. What the demise approach to women's losses in coaching need is for more of us on the losing end of the game to give over to ourselves a self-care that incorporates the knowledge we have acquired over time and inform those who wield dominant power practices over us as subjects – that we will no longer stand for it. Like the women in Cruz's study who actively sought ways to maintain their desire to continue in the profession, wittingly or not, they were arguably engaging in Foucauldian-like response to a politics of refusal and, as well, a politics of practice.

Coaches who seek ways to navigate the course of a biased profession do not necessarily need to read and abide by Foucault. Advanced work in critical pedagogies and alternative practices may draw similar conclusions (see McDonald and Birrell 1999; Giardina 2005). However, I would argue that it remains questionable whether or not pursuing women's place in the coaching ranks via the repeated question "where have all the coaches gone?", is worth the energy. It is my contention that the energy of the female coach, even the most essentialist among them, be put into practice through a reflective and reflexive sense of self with self-care as a first priority, which makes caring for others not just easier, but more ethical and responsible. In sum, my hope is that the explanations around the loss of women as coaches prompted by the decline research continue its trajectory away from the female coach as object, and move more towards utilizing practices informed by their own subjectivities, enriched with critical pedagogies, and enlightened by theoretical and philosophical bends that challenge notions of the self as coach – and practices that in the long run, just might consider Foucault in the process.

Notes

1 Here I am alluding to the era after the mandated legislative enactment of Title IX as federal law, i.e. after 1972. The Association of Intercollegiate Athletics for Women (AIAW) was the governing body equivalent to the NCAA for men, from 1971 to 1980.
2 Cites the work of Michael Burawoy, a researcher who studied assembly line manufacturing and criticized the labor process as structure.
3 See R. Jones *et al. Sports Coaching Cultures* (2004).
4 Worth noting is that the background topic of this tension/micro-competition was built around female athletes with eating disorders, and the differences in philosophies between she and the (male) athletic trainer.

References

Acosta, V. and Carpenter, L. (2010) 'Women in intercollegiate sport: a longitudinal national study thirty three year update, 1977–2010,' online, available at: http://webpages.charter.net/womeninsport [accessed 22 October 2010].

Andrews, M. (1993) 'Desperately seeking Michel: Foucault's genealogy, the body and critical sport sociology,' *Sociology of Sport Journal*, 10(2): 48–167.

Butler, J. (1990) *Gender Trouble: Feminism and the Subversion of Identity*. New York: Routledge.

Chase, L. (2008) 'Running big: Clydesdale runners and technologies of the body,' *Sociology of Sport Journal*, 25(1): 130–147.

Coakley, J.J. (2008) *Sports in Society: Issues and Controversies*, 10th ed., New York: McGraw-Hill.

Connell, R.W. (1995) *Masculinities*, Cambridge: Polity.

Connell, R.W. and Messerschmidt, J.W. (2005) 'Hegemonic masculinity: Rethinking the concept,' *Gender and Society*, 19(6): 829–859.

Coud, D. (2008) *The Metrosexual: Gender, Sexuality and Sport*, Albany, NY: SUNY Press.

Cruz, C. (2009) *Gender Games: Why Women Coaches are Losing the Field*, Saarbrucken, Germany: VDM Verlag Dr. Muller Aktiengesellschaft & Co. KG.

Denison, J. (2006) 'The way we ran: Reimagining research and the self,' *Journal of Sport and Social Issues*, 30(4): 333–339.

Denison, J. (2007) 'Social theory for coaches: A Foucauldian reading of one athlete's poor performance,' *International Journal of Sports Science and Coaching*, 2(4): 369–383.

Denison, J. (2010) '"Messy texts," or the unexplainable performance: Reading bodies' evidence,' *International Review of Qualitative Research*, 3(1): 149–160.

Dworkin, S.L. and Wachs, F.L. (1998) 'Disciplining the body: HIV-positive male athletes, media surveillance, and the policing of sexuality,' *Sociology of Sport Journal*, 15(1): 1–20.

Duncan, M.C. (1994) 'The politics of women's body images and practices: Foucault, the panopticon and *Shape* magazine,' *Journal of Sport and Social Issues*, 18(1): 48–65.

Giardina, M. (2005) *Sporting Pedagogies: Performing Culture and Identity in the Global Arena*, New York: Peter Lang.

Griffin, P. (1998) *Strong Women, Deep Closets: Lesbians and Homophobia in Sport*, Champaign, IL: Human Kinetics.

Halberstam, J. (1998) *Female Masculinity*, Durham, NC: Duke University Press.

Hall, M.A. (1996) *Feminism and Sporting Bodies*, Champaign, IL: Human Kinetics.

Hasbrook, C.A. (1988) 'Female coaches: Why the declining numbers and percentages?' *Journal of Physical Education, Recreation and Dance*, 59(6): 59–63.

Iannotta, J.G. and Kane, M.J. (2002) 'Sexual stories as resistance narratives in women's sports: Reconceptualizing identity performance,' *Sociology of Sport Journal*, 19(4): 347–369.

Jones, R., Armour, K. and Potrac, P. (eds) (2004) *Sports Coaching Cultures: From Practice to Theory*, London: Routledge.

Kane, M.J. (1995) 'Resistance/transformation of the oppositional binary: Exposing sport as a continuum,' *Journal of Sport and Social Issues*, 19(1): 191–218.

Kanter, R.M. (1977) *Men and Women of the Corporation*. New York: Basic Books.

Knoppers, A. (1987) 'Gender and the coaching profession,' *Quest*, 39(1): 3–22.

Knoppers, A. (1989) 'Coaching: An equal opportunity occupation?' *Journal of Physical Education, Recreation and Dance*, 60(3): 38–43.

Lenskyj, H. (1991) 'Combating homophobia in sport and physical education,' *Sociology of Sport Journal*, 8(1): 61–69.

Lowe, D. (1995) *The Body in Late-Capitalist USA*, Durham, NC: Duke University Press.

Markula, P. (1995) 'Firm but shapely, fit but sexy, strong but thin: The postmodern aerobicizing female bodies,' *Sociology of Sport Journal*, 12(4): 424–453.

Markula, P. (2001) 'Beyond the perfect body: Women's body image distortion in fitness magazine discourse,' *Journal of Sport and Social Issues*, 25(2): 158–179.

Markula, P. (2003) 'The technologies of the self: Sport, feminism and Foucault,' *Sociology of Sport Journal*, 20(2): 87–107.

Markula, P. (2004) '"Tuning into one self:" Foucault's technologies of the self and mindful fitness,' *Sociology of Sport Journal*, 21(3): 302–321.

Markula, P. and Pringle, R. (2006) *Foucault, Sport and Exercise: Power, Knowledge and Transforming the Self*, New York: Routledge.

Martin, L.H., Gutman H. and Hutton, P.H. (eds) (1988) *Technologies of the Self: A Seminar with Michel Foucault*, Amherst, MA: University of Massachusetts Press.

McDonald, M.G. and Birrell, S. (1999) 'Reading sport critically: A methodology for interrogating power,' *Sociology of Sport Journal*, 16(4): 283–300.

Messner, M. (2002) *Taking the Field: Women, Men and Sports*, Minneapolis, MN: University of Minnesota Press.

Rail, G. and Harvey, J. (1995) 'Body at work: Michel Foucault and the sociology of sport,' *Sociology of Sport Journal*, 12(2): 164–179.

Schultz, J. (2004) 'Discipline and push-up: Female bodies, femininity, and sexuality in popular representations of sports bras,' *Sociology of Sport Journal*, 21(2): 185–205.

Smith Maguire, J. (2002) 'Michael Foucault: Sport, power, technologies and governmentality,' in J. Maguire and J. Young (eds) *Theory, Sport and Society*, Boston, MA: JAI.

Stangl, J.M. (2005) 'On the cusp or at the center: Pre-suppositions and post-consequences of *Being* in Title IX,' paper presented at Women and Sport: Before, During and After Title IX Conference, BGSU, Bowling Green, Ohio, February 2.

Stangl, J.M. and Kane, M.J. (1991) 'Structural variables that offer explanatory power for the underrepresentation of women coaches since Title IX: The case of homologous reproduction,' *Sociology of Sport Journal*, 8(1): 47–60.

Valocchi, S. (2005) 'Not yet queer enough: The lessons of queer theory for the sociology of gender and sexuality,' *Gender and Society*, 19(6): 750–770.

Whisenant, W.A. (2008) 'Sustaining male dominance in interscholastic athletics: A case of homologous reproduction … or not?' *Sex Roles*, 58(11/12): 768–775.

33

WOMEN IN COACHING

The work–life interface

Jennifer Bruening

UNIVERSITY OF CONNECTICUT, USA

Marlene Dixon

UNIVERSITY OF TEXAS, USA

Laura Burton

UNIVERSITY OF CONNECTICUT, USA

Rachel Madsen

NIAGARA UNIVERSITY, USA

Introduction

Acosta and Carpenter (2009) reported that the number of female coaches of women's teams in interscholastic and intercollegiate sports in the United States of America (USA) is at the second lowest point in history. Despite the number of women participants being at its highest point ever, these women, or the natural pool of applicants for coaching positions, are not pursuing coaching as a career. Scholars outside the United States have also investigated the athletic environment for women as well (Hoeber 2007; Palmer and Leberman 2009; Shaw and Allen 2009; Shaw and Hoeber 2003). What research has argued is that women face unique and inevitable challenges as coaches, including the male-dominated nature of the field, a lack of social networks and role models, and reported conflicting interests between the work and non-work realms (e.g. Inglis *et al.* 2000; Kelley 1994; Knoppers 1992; Weiss and Stevens 1993). Whether women choose not to enter into the field or decide to leave after some time as a coach, these barriers impact their decisions (Bruening and Dixon 2007; Cunningham and Sagas 2005; Dixon and Bruening 2007; Sagas *et al.* 2006).

In the current chapter, we will address the history of women in coaching and the role of mentoring in this history. We will also highlight emerging lines of research focused on women in coaching, including that which investigates organizational cultures that promote balance between work and life, as well as policies and practices allowing for positive non-work time for their employees. A section is devoted to work–life balance research, as this line of inquiry has begun to expand to coaching. Then, interdisciplinary research considerations will be explored. In the final portion of the chapter, we devote time to examining the gaps that still exist in the research concerning work-life supports and barriers for women coaches – organizational level investigations and research on the socio-cultural views of gender as manifested in both work in general and work in sport.

Recruitment and retention

Historically, the attractiveness of coaching as a career for women has become weaker and weaker since the passage of Title IX, a federal statute in the United States mandating equitable opportunities for women in federally funded educational institutions. In 1970, more than 90 percent of women's teams had a woman head coach. Now, less than half of these teams do (Acosta and Carpenter 2009). Men fill most of coaching roles, so women athletes' expectations and aspirations are often limited. And, pairing gender-role norms of women as caregivers and the perception of coaching as a work first, life second type of career, women who are and want to become parents find they have a difficult road to travel (Gregory 2007).

Sagas *et al.* (2006) examined homologous reproduction as a significant factor in women viewing coaching as a viable career, or for not progressing up the ranks once they became coaches. The basic premise is that those in power (i.e. male head coaches and athletic directors) strive to protect their power and privilege by 'systematically reproducing themselves' (Sagas *et al.* 2006: 503) in the coaches they hire. What these scholars found was that women were more likely to hire women than men were to hire men. At least two issues were presented in this research. First, that male head coaches already felt secure with their surroundings as they had other male head coaches and most likely a male athletic director. Women, on the other hand, participated in more than homologous reproduction as there was intent behind their hiring female assistant coaches. These women were well aware of the statistics concerning women in coaching and took the opportunity to increase those numbers. Not only could that change the demographic landscape of coaching, but this hiring pattern was one of the only ways a female head coach could change her departmental landscape as well. For women who choose to enter coaching, retention has been an issue. Understanding the factors considered important for retaining coaches has potential significance for reversing the decline of the number of individuals, in particular, women, from these positions, and for increasing the attractiveness of such career pathways (i.e. recruiting) (Inglis *et al.* 1996).

As research in recruitment and retention of coaches has progressed, these areas are still viewed as among the most important aspects of personnel management. Research in recruitment (Sagas *et al.* 2006, 2004) and retention has grown to include a more comprehensive retention framework and instrument, to examine which retention factors are most important and which retention factors are being fulfilled, and to develop management strategies for sport managers to provide leadership. It has been shown that the influence of family and friends impacts the coaching aspirations of both men and women similarly, however, work–family conflict impacts women significantly more than men and serves as a barrier to women considering entering or already pursuing coaching careers (Sagas *et al.* 2006).

Mentoring is defined as 'a process in which a more experienced person (mentor) serves as a role model, provides guidance and support to a developing novice (protégé), and sponsors that individual's career progress (Weaver and Chelladurai 1999: 25). Individuals who are not able to form effective mentoring relationships are thought to be at a disadvantage because a strong mentoring relationship provides protégés with a network of information and experience that can result in the protégés being promoted more often and receiving a higher salary. Mentored individuals also report being more satisfied with work than their non-mentored counterparts (Weaver and Chelladurai 2002).

One possible explanation for the low numbers of women in coaching is the lack of same-sex mentoring opportunities that exist for women in most athletic environments. In coaching, a mentor is someone who helps younger or less experienced coaches learn the ropes and navigate the athletic landscape (Wickman and Sjodin 1997), and is typically in a position of organizational power with significant career knowledge and experience. However, there are very few women in these positions of power in US athletic organizations, making the pool of female mentors quite small. The Tucker Center at the University of Minnesota (www.cehd.umn.edu/tuckercenter), which examines the effects of sport on women and girls, found that women in leadership positions are important in order to 'provide evidence that women can be successful at the highest levels, and challenge outdated stereotypes about gender and power' (Tucker Center 2009: 3).

An annual study that tracks the numbers of women who work in intercollegiate sport in the USA reports that only 20 percent of collegiate head coaches are women (Acosta and Carpenter 2010). Female athletic administrators could also serve as mentors for young coaches, but the gender situation among administrators is very similar with only 21.3 percent of athletic directors being women (Acosta and Carpenter 2010). Female high school coaches seem to be even rarer than at the college level and they make up about 17 percent of head coaches in the USA (Tucker Center 2009). Even at the youth level, women constitute approximately 14 percent of coaches (Messner 2009). At the professional level, the Women's National Basketball Association is the only league that has any female coaches at all (50 percent in 2010). In an attempt to remedy the lack of female leadership at the Olympic level, the International Olympic Committee has mandated that at least 20 percent of all decision-making positions (including coaches) at national levels need to be filled by women (Tucker Center 2009). The need for women to serve as mentors for other women is important because research shows that mentoring relationships composed of people with similar demographics often result in more information and social support being provided to the protégé (James 2000). When women in sport have male mentors, they may be better off than those who have no mentor at all, but recent inquiry has suggested that cross-gender mentoring relationships are less likely to exist than same-sex mentoring (Avery *et al.* 2008).

In most athletic situations, mentoring is an informal process rather than a structured program. This means that either the mentor or the protégé needs to actively seek out a willing partner and often 'natural mentoring' will take place. However, 'natural mentoring' tends to occur among people who are comfortable with each other, which often requires some similarity. Because males make up the bulk of the workplace, women are less likely to be in situations where natural mentoring takes place (Feist-Price 1994). This state of affairs leads to an abundance of same-sex mentoring opportunities for young men but the lack of women in athletic leadership provides fewer opportunities for mentoring for young women. Such a situation provides an example of an 'old boys' network' in operation and is what a majority of female administrators agree has been a barrier to women reaching administrative positions in athletics.

Some of the most successful women who do work in sport leadership place high value on the mentoring they received and they believe that an increase in formal mentoring for females in sport would help increase the numbers of women in the field (Massengale 2009). Overall it has been found that the vast majority of the current highly successful female coaches have had other female coaches in the past that have served as mentors and many credit them for their positions today (Fazioli 2004; Gogol 2002). For example, Beverly Kearney (seven-time national champion track and field coach, University of Texas) affirms that a main reason for her rapid advancement through the college coaching ranks was because of the female mentors she had and the networks she was able to become a part of during her times as an assistant coach.

Not only does the lack of female mentors make it difficult for female coaches to progress through the ranks, it may also serve as a deterrent for the younger generation to enter coaching. Research shows that female athletes with female head coaches are more interested in the field of coaching than those who have male head coaches (Gogol 2002). Women who have had female coaches are specifically more likely to pursue head coaching jobs, while others female athletes tend to be split between being a head coach and an assistant coach (Lirgg *et al.* 1994). The low numbers of women in athletic leadership then becomes a cyclical issue because the vast numbers of girls who currently participate in sport are missing out on a same-sex role model, which in itself may reduce their chances of a successful career in sport.

The need for having a mentor is magnified when we consider that much of the hiring in US athletic organizations is done through an informal process where new employees are recommended and hired based on the social network they belong to (Young 1990). The benefit of having a powerful mentor is evident when we consider the coaching trees associated with legendary US men's college basketball coaches such as: Dean Smith, Tom Izzo and Mike Krzyzeski. In each of these examples, being associated with a successful coach greatly assisted in many players and assistant coaches going on to hold powerful careers in sporting organizations. The fact that women are lacking similar opportunities for mentoring places them at a disadvantage.

While ongoing, informal mentoring is difficult to find for women in athletics, there are, however, several structured mentoring programs in the US that could greatly assist young women to network and learn the skills necessary to advance in a sport career. Some examples include:

1   'So You Want to be a Coach,' sponsored by the Women's Basketball Coaches Association (WBCA): www.wbca.org/education/wbca-events/so-you-want-to-be-a-coach-program.
2   Institute for Administrative Advancement, sponsored by the National Association of Collegiate Women Athletic Administrators (NACWAA): www.nacwaa.org/?page_id=480.
3   Women's Leadership Symposium, sponsored by the National Collegiate Athletic Association (NCAA): www.wlsathletics.com.

Emerging lines of research

The work-family interface in coaching

The study of the work-family interface in the coaching realm began in earnest with some of Chalip's (1978) work in role conflict within the coaching profession. It has advanced much since then, especially in terms of empirical and theoretical development and the application of both quantitative and qualitative approaches. As an organizing framework to explore this topic, it is helpful to adopt Dixon and Bruening's (2005) multi-level theory of work-family conflict in sport. These authors argued that the work–family interface has antecedents and outcomes at the individual, structural, and socio-cultural levels (see Knoppers 1992 for a similar model of male dominance in coaching). That is, socio-cultural, structural, and individual factors can all influence the amount and level of work–family conflict or balance in the coaching profession. Similarly, the effects of the conflict and/or balance can also be manifested at any or all of the three levels. The following review and discussion is organized using this framework.

The individual approach

The individual approach to work-family issues is a product of the rational choices model (Allison 1971). In essence, it suggests that work–family outcomes are the result of rational choices made by individuals in the face of various rewards or contingencies. In this model, the influence of gender, personality, work-life values, family structure, and coping mechanisms may be seen in the work–family interface. For example, studies regarding gender suggest that female coaches experience higher levels of work–family conflict than males. Empirically, a number of scholars have found that indeed work–family conflict among female coaches is quite high (e.g. Bruening and Dixon 2007; Dixon and Bruening 2007; Palmer and Leberman 2009; Pastore *et al.* 1996). However, few studies have actually included both males and females, and the ones that have included both did not find gender significantly related to work–family conflict (Dixon and Sagas 2007). Regarding personality, the coaching mothers in both Dixon and Bruening's (2007) and Palmer and Leberman's (2009) work self-identified as 'Type A' personalities, and reported that their personalities drove some work–family conflict in that they pressured themselves to perform well in all areas of their lives. Thus, there seems to be a potential connection between personality and work–family conflict that deserves further consideration.

A work–life values approach suggests that one can value only work or family, but not both, and that the strain from these competing values causes work–family conflict. Chalip's (1978) study of swimming coaches in New Zealand found that coaches experienced high levels of role conflict, and that it impacted their performance and retention in the field. Dixon and Bruening (2007), Knoppers (1992) and Theberge (1992) also argued that the coaching profession is embedded in a culture that promotes sacrifice of anything that hinders winning – which further exacerbates the experience of competing values among coaches. Family structure and coping are related to how well individuals deal with the work–family conflict both practically (juggling childcare) and emotionally. Dixon and Bruening (2007) and Palmer and Leberman (2009) found that both of these factors were strong influences on felt work–family conflict. As women had better support systems and coping mechanisms, they experienced less work–family conflict. Conversly, Knoppers (1992), Theberge (1992) and McKay *et al.* (2000), in particular, argued that male coaches may be buffered from this conflict, as their spouses or partners tend to not only care for all domestic duties, but also contribute to their spouse's or partner's coaching job as well.

Organizational approach

While individual approaches recognize differences between genders and individual people in their management of potential work–family conflict, this can often ignore the environment in which these 'rational choices' are made. Thus, an organizational level approach has added much value to the exploration of work–family conflict in coaching. This approach suggests that the structure and culture of organizations in which coaches work impacts their work–family conflict and/or balance.

Development of a more supportive organizational culture for coaches within an athletic department can help to address retention factors, reduce burnout, and improve job and life satisfaction. The most widely held definition of organizational culture as developed by Schein describes culture as:

> Patterns of basic assumptions – invented, discovered or developed by a given group as it learns to cope with its problems of external adaptation and internal integration – that has worked well enough to be considered valid and, therefore, to be taught to new members as the correct way to perceive, think, and feel in relation to those problems.
>
> *(Schein 1988: 9)*

The culture of an organization has a significant impact on the individuals working within the organization. As noted by Cunningham, organizations that adopt a culture that values diversity and inclusion are more likely to have:

> Diversity enmeshed into all organizational activities, create mentoring activities that better enable persons of color to move up the organizational hierarchy, have bold top management leadership, and be proactive in their recruitment and hiring of persons from historically under-represented groups.
>
> *(Cunningham 2010: 403)*

The culture established by an organization can influence who remains within that organization, and who withdraws from it. Therefore, when changes are made at the structure level of the organization (i.e. the athletic department) there can be significant impacts on individual level outcomes (i.e. coaches within the athletic department) (Cunningham 2010). Dixon and Bruening (2005) suggest the current organizational culture in coaching is one that values 'face time' in the office, long work hours as an indication of success, and the necessity of extensive travel to identify and recruit suitable talented athletes. As a result, those who work long hours, particularly those that provide 'face time' (i.e. are visible to supervisors and co-workers) and travel constantly for competition and recruiting have been viewed as ideal workers. These work patterns have come to be seen as 'normal' and expected in order to be successful in coaching. This culture, however, results in significant negative impacts at the individual level, including work–family conflict, family–work conflict, and low job and life satisfaction leading to high levels of coach turnover (Bruening and Dixon 2007; Dixon and Bruening 2007; Dixon and Sagas 2007; Ryan and Sagas 2009).

Examining work–family culture within an athletic department can help address issues around work–family and family–work conflict experienced by women in coaching. The concept of work–family organizational culture is described as the beliefs, values, and shared assumptions, regarding the extent to which an organization supports and values the integration of employees' work and family lives (Thompson *et al.* 1999). Work–family culture captures two important concepts of organizational culture. These are the positive influences of culture, specifically managerial support of family, and the negative influences of culture, including organizational time demands and negative career consequences. Managerial support of family is the extent to which employers are perceived as supporting and sensitive to employees' family needs. Family needs include care for children, care for aging relatives, and single person households; therefore, 'regardless of family structure, many workers have home care responsibilities and can be assumed to make tradeoffs between work and leisure time' (Premeaux *et al.* 2007: 706). The concept of negative career consequences, as addressed by work–family culture, result from the perception that there will be negative career development implications as a consequence of using family-friendly work benefits or spending time in family related activities. Finally, organizational time demands, as addressed by work–family culture, include the expectations and socialized norms that employees should prioritize work over family (Mauno 2010).

The direct supervision and flexibility of work hours and expectations has been shown to have the strongest effect on work–family outcomes in coaching (Bruening and Dixon 2007; Dixon and Bruening 2007; Dixon and Sagas 2007; Inglis *et al.* 2000; Kelley 1994; McKay *et al.* 2000; Pastore *et al.* 1996; Theberge 1992). As female coaches, in particular, have more flexibility and control over their own schedules as well as a timetable for success, work–family conflict decreases (Dixon and Bruening 2007; Inglis *et al.* 2000). Supportive supervisors (typically athletic directors) also strongly influence a coach's experience of work–family conflict (Dixon and Sagas 2007; Inglis *et al.* 2000; Mauno 2010; Premeaux *et al.* 2007). Employees who perceive managerial support for family within their organizations report significantly less work–family conflict.

Indeed, inflexible structures combined with a strong organizational culture can have a powerful impact on work–family conflict. So much so, that a number of scholars suggest that a focus on structure and culture area, rather than individual level solutions, is the key to reducing work–family conflict among female coaches in particular, and thereby increasing female coaching presence in the field (Carlisle 2002; Coakley 2004; Dixon and Bruening 2007; Dixon and Sagas 2007; Inglis *et al.* 2000; Knoppers 1992; McKay *et al.* 2000; Palmer and Leberman 2009; Theberge 1992).

Socio-cultural approach

Finally, a socio-cultural approach examines the meanings, values, and norms associated with family and work as social institutions. In many ways, it seeks to understand how organizational and/or occupational cultures are formed, how gender norms are formed and impact lives, and how work, family, and work–family are understood and interpreted within the context of the larger society. Probably the strongest cultural influence in relation to the work–family interface in coaching is a traditional gender ideology where masculinity is associated with being the breadwinner and femininity is associated with childcare and domestic tasks (Williams 1995). These notions create barriers for females to enter male-dominated careers and make them feel that they must work harder and longer to prove themselves, which can create enormous tension between work and family (Bruening and Dixon 2007; Dixon and Bruening 2007; Everhart and Chelladurai 1998; Fox 1999; Inglis *et al.* 2000; Hart *et al.* 1986; McKay 1997; Palmer and Leberman 2009; Pastore *et al.* 1996). In cultures where it is assumed that males work and females care for children, organizational structures often reflect that assumption – where work demands assume the employed person is free from personal 'distractions' and/or where the organization is not expected to provide support for non-work endeavors such as family life. For example, it is well established that family-friendly policies are less prevalent in male-dominated professions such as coaching (Dodds 2003; Goodstein 1995; Inglis *et al.* 2000; McKay *et al.* 2000; Theberge 1992).

Sport organizations are heavily gendered and dominated by men and, as a result, women continue to encounter organizational practices that discriminate and perpetuate male dominance (Cunningham and Sagas 2008; Sibson 2010). The male-dominated sport environment, despite gains made by women in gender equity, still does not value or reflect a

417

deep concern for gender equity (Hoeber and Frisby 2001; Shaw and Frisby 2006). As such, intercollegiate athletics continues to be male dominated, with men representing the majority of athletic directors (80.7 percent) and head coaching positions (57.4 percent) across all three divisions (Acosta and Carpenter 2010). Men hold the most influential positions within intercollegiate athletics (Whisenant *et al.* 2002), and there continues to be an assumption that men are most likely to lead athletic departments (Burton *et al.* 2011). Overall, women are underrepresented in intercollegiate athletics, marginalized to particular roles, and paid less for their work (Cunningham and Sagas 2008).

Role congruity theory contends that the underrepresentation of women in leadership positions may be the result of gender-role stereotyping of leadership positions (Eagly and Karau 2002). As a result of prejudice against female leaders and resistance when women occupy leadership roles, women may suffer a disadvantage in leadership (Eagly 2007). Social role theory preceded role congruity theory and helps explain gender-role stereotyping in the evaluation of leaders. Essentially, there are qualities and behavioral tendencies believed to be desirable for each gender, as well as expectations as to which roles women and men should occupy (Eagly and Karau 2002). Women should display more communal characteristics, for instance, and be affectionate, helpful, kind, sympathetic, interpersonally sensitive, nurturing, and gentle (Eagly 1987; Eagly *et al.* 2000). On the other hand, men are expected to show more agentic characteristics, such as aggressiveness dominance, forcefulness, self-confidence and self-sufficiency (Eagly 1987; Eagly *et al.* 2000). Prescriptive gender-role stereotypes, then, suggest that women should display more communal characteristics and roles, while men should exhibit more agentic qualities (Eagly and Karau 2002). Following social role theory, role congruity theory, then, posits that a prejudice exists against female leaders because leadership ability is more generally ascribed to men who exhibit agentic qualities, than to women who display more communal characteristics (Eagly and Karau 2002). Hence, women may be disadvantaged in obtaining leadership positions because of the perception that they do not possess the requisite skill set to lead effectively. Additionally, even if women are in leadership positions, they may not be evaluated as favorably as men if they are perceived as violating gender norms attributed to women (Eagly and Karau 2002).

Major gaps in understanding of work–life interface

Although most developmental and occupational issues with women coaches have manifested themselves at the individual level, there are consequences at the organizational level, as well. For example, potential long-term effects of a lack of recruitment and/or turnover could impact organizations with narrowing of labor force and lack of female role models in coaching (Gregory 2007). Research has shown that women are choosing not to enter or to enter and prematurely exit the coaching profession (Bruening *et al.* 2008; Tiell *et al.* 2008). It does not appear that the women have become less competitive or that they have not attempted to build support networks for themselves in order to stay in coaching. Instead, the structure and culture of coaching create a situation that is extremely difficult for women, in particular, to survive. For sport, this type of culture functions to assure that only the most 'dedicated' coaches last, serving to narrow the coaching ranks. This begs the question of the ultimate impact on both the quality of life and job satisfaction in a work climate that constantly presses for more and longer hours at the perpetual expense of quality of life outside of work (Hewlett and Luce 2005; Hochschild 1997; Rapoport *et al.* 2002).

By incorporating a multi-level approach (i.e. organizational, socio-cultural, and individual), we have also highlighted the need to examine coaching as an occupation in which socio-cultural views of gender play themselves out. More investigations on how people view gender, sport, and work will help in filling in gaps in understanding the work experiences of women in coaching. Dixon and Bruening (2005, 2007) have focused their examinations of work–family conflict and balance on American collegiate female head coaches who have remained in the profession. Following this work, more research is needed on women who have had long, successful coaching careers. Attention needs to be paid to what factors led to them enduring in athletics.

Second, we recommend future investigations focus on the policies and culture in athletic departments to expand the understanding of the nature of structural/organizational practices related to work and gender (Sagas *et al.* 2006). This longitudinal investigation would serve the line of research well by identifying more impacts at the organizational level, what is working at individual institutions, and areas to target for change. In particular, case studies of athletic departments who implement best practices in terms of flexibility and autonomy, both with time and place, are recommended. Of interest would be employee satisfaction and retention in these athletic departments, as well as the level of competitiveness of the teams. Another form of analysis could also be employed to investigate the impact of positive work–family cultures in departments identified to have best practices. Survey-based inquiry of coach perceptions of the work–family culture in their departments is also crucial in identifying the influence of a positive work–family culture on job embeddedness, commitment to the organization, intent to turnover. Analysis of differences between genders, ages, and tenure could also occur through this method.

Recent findings strongly support that work–family conflict significantly influences both job and life satisfaction among both male and female coaches (Dixon and Sagas 2007). Therefore, a need remains for the continuation of exploring ways to help coaches achieve better work–family balance and mitigate the negative effects of role conflict. Future research should continue to explore both work–family conflict and work–family balance, as they may not be opposites on a continuum – that is, lack of work–family conflict may not mean that the two roles are balanced (Schenewark and Dixon 2012). Future research must also explore this relationship in multiple contexts, as most studies, to date, have been conducted in a college coaching setting. It may be that other settings provide different contingencies that influence the work–family interface, particularly with reference to organizational structures, cultural expectations, and family–work supports. Work in this area must also continue to probe the experiences of both coaching mothers and fathers, preferably within the same study, such that the potential gender similarities and differences are not overlooked. For instance, a large-scale survey-based investigation of athletic administrators would be able to ascertain if coaching fathers are given more leeway than coaching mothers – both from their families and in the workplace. Can one gender or the other take time away to be a parent without being questioned about their dedication to work? In addition, what factors related to work–family conflict and balance are highlighted when a coach is successful? When a coach is unsuccessful?

Finally, while much of the research on women in coaching focuses on reasons why women they leave the field early or fail to progress at the same rate as men, little attention has been paid to the female athletes who never pursue an athletic career at all. Because so few women pursue athletic careers, it is certain that a large number of talented women are missing from the coaching ranks (Drago *et al.* 2005). This systematic loss of talent reduces the overall quality of coaching and athletics in the USA. Although it cannot be assumed that all female athletes will or should pursue athletic careers, the most likely applicant pool for coaches comes from those who have competed in the sport. Therefore, we would suggest that female athletes are undoubtedly among the most qualified women for these careers.

There are several reasons that female athletes may not choose to pursue careers in sport, one being that US societal values lead many to see sport as male domain which makes it very difficult for women to be serious about sport (Madsen 2010). As a result, women may not develop the same confidence in sport as male athletes do. Furthermore, women do not receive much encouragement to become coaches but are instead socialized to develop career interests that value nurturing skills and accommodate childcare. In fact, many female college athletes report that they consider work schedules when deciding on a career and are less likely to choose coaching because it does not align well with childcare.

An additional factor that may deter women from pursuing coaching positions is related to the fact that there are very few viable professional sport careers available to women. Women see very few opportunities to continue as an athlete after college and thus plan for different careers (Madsen 2010). Future investigations around gender and coaching should consider how traditional gender-role assumptions impact female athletes choosing/not choosing to pursue athletic careers. Questions to ask include: Why do we not allow girls/women to play certain contact sports? Why do we change the rules to feminize games? What is the impact of feminizing girls sport on the participants and the spectators? What types of reinforcement do young female and male athletes receive from the influential adults in their lives in regards to the importance of sport? Among college athletes, do males and females receive the same encouragement to go into coaching?

Summary

Women are participating in sport in record numbers, but their representation in the coaching ranks does not reflect the same growth. Women are recruited and retained as coaches to a lesser degree than their male counterparts. Developing women coaches through mentoring, retaining them through positive organizational culture with continued mentoring, and assisting them throughout their careers to be both productive and satisfied in their positions are the keys to the representation of women in coaching changing for the better.

References

Acosta, V. and Carpenter, L. (2009) 'Thirty-seven years later, Title IX hasn't fixed it all,' *Academe*, 95(4): 22–24.

Acosta, R. and Carpenter, L. (2010) *Women in Intercollegiate Sport, A Longitudinal, National Study: Thirty Three Year Update 1977–2010*, West Brookfield, MA: The project on women and social change of Smith College and Brooklyn College of the City University of New York.

Allison, G. (1971) *Essence of Decision: Explaining the Cuban Missile Crisis*, Boston, MA: Little Brown.

Avery, D., Tonidandel, S. and Phillips, M. (2008) 'Similarity on sports sidelines: How mentor-protégé similarity affects mentoring,' *Sex Roles*, 58(1/2): 72–80.

Bruening, J. and Dixon, M. (2007) 'Work-family conflict in coaching II: Managing role conflict,' *Journal of Sport Management*, 21(4): 471–496.

Bruening, J., Dixon, M., Tiell, B., Osborne, B., Lough, N. and Sweeney, K. (2008) 'The role of the supervisor in the work-life culture in college athletics,' *International Journal for Sport Management*, 9(3): 250–272.

Burton L., Grappendorf, H. and Henderson, A. (2011) 'Perceptions of gender in athletic administration: Utilizing role congruity to examine (potential) prejudice against women,' *Journal of Sport Management*, 25(1): 36–45.

Carlisle, U. (2002) 'Female coaches: Why are there so few at the top level?' *Swimming in Australia*, 18: 1–2.

Chalip, L. (1978) 'Role conflicts in a coaching subculture,' in J. Hinchcliff (ed.) *The Nature and Meaning of Sport in New Zealand*, Auckland, NZ: University of Auckland Press.

Coakley, J. (2004) *Sport in Society: Issues and Controversies*, 8th edn, Boston, MA: McGraw-Hill.

Cunningham, G. (2010) 'Understanding the under-representation of African American coaches: A multilevel perspective,' *Sport Management Review*, 13(4): 395–406.

Cunningham, G. and Sagas, M. (2005) 'Access discrimination in intercollegiate athletics,' *Journal of Sport and Social Issues*, 29(2): 148–163.

Cunningham, G. and Sagas, M. (2008) 'Gender and diversity in sport organizations: Introduction to a special issue,' *Sex Roles*, 58(1/2): 3–9.

Dixon, M. and Bruening, J. (2005) 'Perspectives on work-family in sport: An Integrated approach,' *Sport Management Review*, 8(3): 227–254.

Dixon, M. and Bruening, J. (2007) 'Work-family conflict in coaching I: A top-down perspective,' *Journal of Sport Management*, 21(3): 377–406.

Dixon, M. and Sagas, M. (2007) 'The relationship between organizational support, work–family conflict, and the job-life satisfaction of university coaches,' *Research Quarterly for Exercise and Sport*, 78(3): 236–247.

Dodds, P. (2003) 'Coaching: A significant career step for women entering the professoriate,' *Research Quarterly for Exercise and Sport*, 74(1): 42–44.

Drago, R., Hennighausen, L., Rogers, J., Vescio, T. and Stauffer, K. (2005) 'The Coaching and Gender Equity Report,' final report for the NCAA, NACWAA and Penn State (August).

Eagly, A. (1987) *Sex Differences in Social Behavior: A Social-Role Interpretation*, Hillsdale, NJ: Erlbaum.

Eagly, A. (2007) 'Female leadership advantage and disadvantage: Resolving the contradictions,' *Psychology of Women Quarterly*, 31(1): 1–12.

Eagly, A. and Karau, S. (2002) 'Role congruity theory of prejudice toward female leaders,' *Psychological Review*, 109(3): 573–598.

Eagly, A., Wood, W. and Diekman, A. (2000) 'Social role theory of sex differences and similarities: A current appraisal,' in T. Eckes and H.M. Trautner (eds) *The Developmental Social Psychology of Gender*, Mahwah: NJ: Lawerence Erlbaum Associates.

Everhart, B. and Chelladurai, P. (1998) 'Gender differences in preferences for coaching as an occupation: The role of self-efficacy, valence, and perceived barriers,' *Research Quarterly for Exercise and Sport*, 69(2): 188–201.

Fazioli, F. (2004) *The Advancement of Female Coaches in Intercollegiate Athletics: Background Paper for the Coaching and Gender Equity Project*, University Park, PA: The Pennsylvania State University.

Feist-Price, S. (1994) 'Cross-gender mentoring relationships: Critical issues,' *Journal of Rehabilitation*, 60(2): 13–17.

Fox, C. (1999) 'Women's perceived access to elite coaching positions in Australian sport,' *Sport Educator*, 11(2): 25–27.

Gogol, S. (2002) *Hard Fought Victories: Women Coaches Making a Difference*, Terre Haute, IN: Wish Publishing.

Goodstein, J. (1995) 'Employer involvement in eldercare: An organizational adaptation perspective,' *Academy of Management Journal*, 38(6): 1657–1671.

Gregory, S. (2007) 'Where are the women coaches?' *TIME*, August 16.

Hart, B., Hasbrook, C. and Mathes, S. (1986) 'An examination of the reduction in the number of female interscholastic coaches,' *Research Quarterly for Exercise and Sport*, 57(1): 68–77.

Hewlett, S. and Luce, C. (2005) 'Off-ramps and on-ramps: Keeping talented women on the road to success,' *Harvard Business Review*, 83(3): 43–53.

Hochschild, A.R. (1997) *The Time Bind: When Work Becomes Home and Home Becomes Work*, New York: Metropolitan Books.

Hoeber, L. (2007) 'Exploring the gaps between meanings and practices of gender equity in a sport organization,' *Gender, Work and Organization*, 14(3): 259–280.

Hoeber, L. and Frisby, W. (2001) 'Gender equity for athletes: Rewriting the narrative for this organizational value,' *European Sport Management Quarterly*, 1(3): 179–209.

Inglis, S., Danylchuk, K. and Pastore, D. (1996) 'Understanding retention factors in coaching and athletic management positions.' *Journal of Sport Management*, 10(3): 237–249.

Inglis, S., Danylchuk, K. and Pastore, D. (2000) 'Multiple realities of women's work experiences in coaching and athletic management,' *Women in Sport and Physical Activity Journal*, 9(2): 1–26.

James, E. (2000) 'Race-related differences in promotions and support: Underlying effects of human and social capital,' *Organization Science*, 11(5): 493–508.

Kelley, B. (1994) 'A model of stress and burnout in collegiate coaches: Effects of gender and time of season,' *Research Quarterly for Exercise and Sport*, 65(1): 48–59.

Knoppers, A. (1992) 'Explaining male dominance and sex segregation in coaching: Three approaches,' *Quest*, 44(22): 210–227.

Lirgg, C., Dibrezzo, R. and Smith, A. (1994) 'Influence of gender of coach on perceptions of basketball and coaching self-efficacy and aspirations of high school female basketball players,' *Women in Sport and Physical Activity Journal*, 3(1): 1–15.

Madsen, R. (2010) 'Female student-athletes intentions to pursue careers in college athletics leadership,' unpublished doctoral thesis, University of Connecticut, USA.

Massengale, D. (2009) 'The underrepresentation of women in interscholastic sport leadership: A qualitative study on the effects of role incongruity,' unpublished doctoral thesis, University of Nevada, USA.

Mauno, S. (2010) 'Effects of work–family culture on employee well-being: Exploring moderator effects in a longitudinal sample,' *European Journal of Work and Organizational Psychology*, 19(6): 675–695.

McKay, J. (1997) *Managing Gender: Affirmative Action and Organizational Power in Australian, Canadian, and New Zealand Sport*, Albany, NY: SUNY Press.

McKay, J., Messner, M. and Sabo, D. (2000) 'Studying sport, men, and masculinities from feminist standpoints,' in J. McKay (ed.) *Masculinities, Gender Relations, and Sport*, Thousand Oaks, CA: Sage.

Messner, M. (2009) *It's All for the Kids: Gender, Families and Youth Sports*, Berkeley, CA: University of California Press.

Palmer, F. and Leberman, S. (2009) 'Elite athletes as mothers: Managing multiple identities,' *Sport Management Review*, 12(4): 241–254.

Pastore, D., Inglis, S. and Danylchuk, K. (1996) 'Retention factors in coaching and athletic management: Differences by gender, position, and geographic location,' *Journal of Sport and Social Issues*, 20(4): 427–441.

Premeaux, S., Adkins, C. and Mossholder, K. (2007) 'Balancing work and family: A field study of multi-dimensional, multi-role work-family conflict,' *Journal of Organizational Behavior*, 28(6): 705–727.

Rapoport, R., Fletcher, L. and Pruitt, B. (2002) *Beyond Work-Family Balance*, San Francisco, CA: Jossey-Bass.

Ryan, T.D. and Sagas, M. (2009) 'Relationships between pay satisfaction, work–family conflict, and coaching turnover intentions,' *Team Performance Management*, 15(3/4): 128–140.

Sagas, M., Cunningham, G. and Pastore, D. (2006) 'Predicting head coaching intentions of male and female assistant coaches: An application of the theory of planned behavior,' *Sex Roles*, 54(9): 695–705.

Sagas, M., Cunningham, G., Pastore, D. and Waltemyer, S. (2004) 'Understanding head coaching behavior among female NCAA assistant coaches,' *Research Quarterly for Exercise and Sport*, 75(1): 93–94.

Schein, E.H. (1988) *Organizational Psychology*, 3rd edition, Englewood Cliffs, NJ: Prentice Hall.

Schenewark, J. and Dixon, M. (2012) 'A dual model of work–family conflict and enrichment in collegiate coaches,' *Journal of Issues in Intercollegiate Athletics*, 5: 15–39.

Shaw, S. and Allen, J. (2009) 'The experiences of high performance women coaches: A case study of two Regional Sport Organisations', *Sport Management Review*, 12(4): 217–228.

Shaw, S. and Frisby, W. (2006) 'Can gender equity be more equitable? Promoting an alternative frame for sport management research, education, and practice,' *Journal of Sport Management*, 20(4): 483–509.

Shaw, S. and Hoeber, L. (2003) '"A strong man is direct and a direct woman is a bitch": Gendered discourses and their influence on employment roles in sports organizations,' *Journal of Sport Management*, 17(4): 347–376.

Sibson, R. (2010) 'I was banging my head against a brick wall: Exclusionary power at the gendering of sport organizations,' *Journal of Sport Management*, 24(4): 379–399.

Theberge, N. (1992) 'Managing domestic work and careers: The experiences of women in coaching,' *Atlantis: A Women's Studies Journal*, 17(2): 11–21.

Thompson, C., Beauvais, L. and Lyness, K. (1999) 'When work-family benefits are not enough: The influence of work-family culture on benefit utilization, organizational attachment, and work-family conflict,' *Journal of Vocational Behavior*, 54(3): 392–415.

Tiell, B., Sweeney, K., Lough, N., Dixon, M., Osborne, B. and Bruening, J. (2008) 'The work/life interface in intercollegiate athletics: An examination of policies, programs and institutional climate,' *Journal for the Study of Sports and Athletes in Education*, 2(3): 137–159.

Tucker Center (2009) 'Research on girls and women in sport,' online, available at: www.cehd.umn.edu/tuckercenter/newsletter/2009-spring/TCN-2009-Spring.pdf (accessed February 13, 2011).

Weaver, M. and Chelladurai, P. (1999) 'A mentoring model for management in sport and physical education,' *Quest*, 51(1): 24–38.

Weaver, M. and Chelladurai, P. (2002) 'Mentoring in intercollegiate athletic administration,' *Journal of Sport Management*, 16(2): 96–116.

Weiss, M. and Stevens, C. (1993) 'Motivation and attrition of female coaches: An application of social exchange theory,' *The Sport Psychologist*, 7(3): 244–261.

Whisenant, W., Pedersen, P. and Obenour, B. (2002) 'Success and gender: Determining the rate of advancement for intercollegiate athletic directors,' *Sex Roles*, 47(9/10): 485–491.

Wickman, F. and Sjodin, T. (1997) *Mentoring*, New York: McGraw-Hill.

Williams, C. (1995) *Still a Man's World*, Berkeley, CA: University of California Press.

Young, D. (1990) 'Mentoring and networking: Perceptions by athletic administrators,' *Journal of Sport Management*, 4(1): 71–79.

34

COACH BURNOUT

Thomas D. Raedeke

EAST CAROLINA UNIVERSITY, USA

Göran Kenttä

SWEDISH SCHOOL OF SPORT AND HEALTH SCIENCES, STOCKHOLM

Introduction

The burnout concept gained notoriety in the mid-1970s based on Freudenberger's and Maslach's efforts to describe an exhausted state accompanied by an erosion of motivation, idealism, and passion for one's job as well as a variety of other mental and physical symptoms (see Maslach *et al.* 2001). A majority of the early burnout descriptions and research occurred in human service and health care settings where the norm was to be selfless, work long hours, do whatever it took to help a patient/client and in some cases with minimal compensation. Soon thereafter, burnout began to draw attention in the sport community. Although coaching has the potential to be a rewarding experience due to the joys of working with athletes in the pursuit of excellence, sport scientists noted the coaching profession was replete with qualities similar to human service and health care settings that might make coaches vulnerable to burnout.

Although some of the early research evaluating burnout in sport settings focused on coaches (e.g. Caccese and Mayerberg 1984; Capel *et al.* 1987; Dale and Weinberg 1989), in recent years athlete burnout has garnered greater attention. In a review, Goodger *et al.* (2007) report that 27 studies have examined athlete burnout and 23 have assessed coach burnout. Since then, there have been more than 30 studies on athlete burnout with approximately seven studies focused on coach burnout (e.g. Hjälm *et al.* 2007; Karabatsos *et al.* 2006; Koustelios 2010; Malinauskas *et al.* 2010; Ryska 2009; Tashman *et al.* 2010). Given the paucity of coach burnout studies in recent years, this chapter is intended to stimulate future empirical inquiry. To accomplish this, we overview the research on this issue, identify gaps in the knowledge base and provide future research directions, describe our contribution in designing an intervention to prevent burnout, and provide a summary and implications for coaching practice.

Overview of coach burnout research

A variety of reviews (e.g. Dale and Weinberg 1990; Fender 1989; Goodger *et al.* 2007; Smith 1986) have discussed burnout in sport settings. These papers have focused primarily on athletes with a secondary, if any, discussion of coach burnout. Across reviews, several issues emerged that will serve as the foundation for this section including: (1) definitional issues; (2) assessing coach burnout; (3) developing and testing conceptual frameworks to guide research on this issue; and (4) developing intervention strategies to prevent and treat burnout. We will evaluate the current state of knowledge on coach burnout in light of these issues.

Defining burnout

Compared to the early reviews there is now greater consensus within the sport community on definitional issues surrounding coach burnout. Within the coaching literature, most researchers have adapted Maslach *et al.*'s (1996) description of burnout as a psychological syndrome. Here, burnout is described in terms of three primary defining features including emotional exhaustion; cynicism and detachment from one's job; and a reduced personal accomplishment characterized by a feeling of professional inefficacy and incompetence (Maslach *et al.* 1996). Of these three dimensions, exhaustion is considered the central feature of burnout. The nature of cynicism and its manifestation is dependent on the exact occupational context. In general work settings, this burnout dimension is described as developing a detached, indifferent, and cynical attitude toward the job and is often accompanied by a lack of idealism. In people-oriented occupations, where the provider–client relationship is central, cynicism is manifested in depersonalization characterized by a negative, callous, detached attitude toward the recipients of one's care. Applied to sport, coaches experiencing burnout may be physically and mentally exhausted from the demands of coaching. They may also begin to doubt their ability to succeed as a coach and develop a negative attitude toward the athletes and psychologically distance themselves from them.

Once experienced, burnout is thought to be a relatively enduring state. For example, in the organizational psychology literature, researchers report that burnout scores exhibit a moderate degree of stability when across time with test/retest correlations typically falling in the 0.60 range (e.g. Maslach *et al.* 1996; McManus *et al.* 2002). Raedeke (2004) found similar results in a sample of coaches with the correlation of burnout measured on two occasions 12 months apart being $r = 0.66$.

Assessing burnout

Along with casting burnout as a syndrome, Maslach and Jackson's (1981) scale development efforts provided an impetus for empirical inquiry on burnout research. Today Maslach's Burnout Inventory (MBI) (Maslach *et al.* 1996) is the primary assessment tool to measure burnout across occupational settings. Originally, the MBI was designed to assess burnout in human service occupations (MBI–Human Services Survey) but was followed shortly by the development of the MBI for use in educational settings (MBI–Educators Survey). Thereafter, a general version of the MBI was developed given a growing interest in burnout in occupational settings that are not necessarily people-oriented. This version of the MBI assesses the three same dimensions as the original MBI but in slightly broader terms than the original scale by defining the dimensions and item content with respect to the job rather than relationships central to people-oriented occupations. At this point, the MBI and its variants are considered the standard tool for research on burnout, both within the United States and internationally (Maslach and Goldberg 1998). However, the nature of burnout, along with assessment strategies, continues to be discussed (for reviews see special issues of *Work and Stress*, 2005; Schaufeli *et al.* 2009).

Conceptual frameworks

In terms of conceptual frameworks used to understand coach burnout, research has progressed from atheoeretical and descriptive studies to research couched in stress and motivational frameworks. Much of the early research focused in part on demographic (e.g. age, gender, marital status, coaching experience) factors that may relate to burnout with an emphasis on gender differences (e.g. Caccese and Mayerberg 1984; Pastore and Judd 1993). Although this work revealed some significant differences across comparison groups, the amount of explained variance was small and findings inconsistent across studies. Research outside the coaching domain has also found that demographic factors are not very predictive of burnout (Maslach *et al.* 2001). More predictive than demographic factors, some of the early research did establish an association between stress-related factors and burnout such as coping, role-related appraisals (e.g. conflict and overload), and a leadership style that may predispose coaches to experiencing higher stress levels (Capel *et al.* 1987; Dale and Weinberg 1989; Kosa 1990).

It is widely accepted that burnout is a reaction to chronic stress and occurs when workplace demands exceed or tax an individual's resources over an extended period. Not only is burnout linked to an imbalance between work demands and the resources, Maslach and Goldberg (1998) note that burnout is also rooted in conflict (e.g. interpersonal conflicts, conflicting job demands, or conflict between job and personal values). As such, burnout is theoretically linked to a variety of work-related stressors (e.g. high workload, time pressure, lack of control, inadequate rewards, role conflict, and role ambiguity).

However, not all individuals who work in demanding settings experience burnout, personal resources (e.g. social support, feedback, autonomy, decision making involvement) also play a role in the burnout process with social support being the resource most extensively examined (Maslach *et al.* 2001). Finally, a variety of intrapersonal characteristics that make a person more likely to perceive high stress (e.g. perfectionism, trait anxiety, Type A behavior pattern, neuroticism) theoretically increase the risk whereas other personality qualities (e.g. hardiness) decrease the risk of burnout.

Within the coaching literature, researchers have examined burnout from a stress perspective (e.g. Kelley 1994; Kelley *et al.* 1999; Tashman *et al.* 2010; Vealey *et al.* 1992). Overall, Kelley and colleagues have supported the contention that burnout is related to perceived stress and also associated with factors such as role conflict, satisfaction with support, hardiness, leadership style, and a variety of other coaching issues. Also based on a stress perspective, Vealey *et al.* (1992) found that overall, trait anxiety was the strongest predictor of burnout, followed by various cognitive appraisals, including perceived rewards, value of coaching, excitement, overload, support, control, success, and meaningful accomplishments. Demographic variables and actual workload (e.g. athletes under direct care and contact hours) were not meaningful predictors of burnout. Tashman *et al.* (2010) report that maladaptive forms of perfectionism (i.e. self-evaluative perfectionism) are associated with stress and burnout whereas more adaptive forms of perfectionism (i.e. conscientious perfectionism) were not. However, it is still currently debated as to whether perfectionism can ever be adaptive and thus whether subscales labeled adaptive perfectionism truly reflect perfectionism.

At this point, it is widely recognized that burnout, especially exhaustion, is a stress-related strain. However, burnout is a complex and multifaceted process involving an erosion of motivation as well as a process of disillusionment. For example, Pines (1993: 38) states 'while everyone can experience stress, burnout can only be experienced by people who entered their careers with high expectations, goals, and motivation – people who expected to derive a sense of significance from their work.' Similarly Freudenberger and Richelson (1980: 13) mention that burnout is a 'state of fatigue or frustration brought about by devotion to a cause or way of life that failed to produce expected reward.'

Given the apparent link between commitment and burnout, researchers (e.g. Raedeke 1997; Raedeke *et al.* 2002; Raedeke 2004; Schmidt and Stein 1991) have developed a commitment perspective on burnout drawing from the organizational psychology and relationship literatures. Although a variety of factors influence commitment, commitment can be influenced by positive pulls (e.g. passion, attraction, enjoyment, satisfaction) and non-positive pushes (e.g. too much invested to quit, lack of attractive alternatives). In other words individuals can be committed for a combination of reasons related to *wanting to be* involved and feeling they *have to be* involved.

Individuals committed to coaching because they find it satisfying, coupled with high benefits and low costs, are theoretically less likely to burnout. Because of their favorable outlook, these individuals are hypothesized to invest a great deal of time and energy into coaching and perceive that it is more attractive than alternative options. In contrast, entrapment occurs when individuals have decreasing attraction to coaching (i.e. fewer positive pulls) but maintain their involvement because they feel they have to continue (i.e. increasing non-positive pushes). This is evident by decreasing satisfaction coupled with decreasing benefits and increasing costs. Despite declining coaching attraction, these individuals maintain involvement because they feel locked into the role of coaching. They may feel they have too much invested to quit, perceive few attractive career opportunities, and/or perceive that other people expect them to maintain their involvement (i.e. non-positive pushes).

Raedeke and colleagues (Raedeke *et al.* 2002; Raedeke 2004) provided some support for a commitment perspective on coach burnout using both cross-sectional and longitudinal research designs. Most notably, coaches who reported the highest burnout scores noted decreasing satisfaction and increasing costs. Despite their decreasing coaching attraction, they reported investing increased time and energy into coaching. However, contrary to predictions, these coaches did not highlight decreased alternative option attractiveness or increasing social constraints. Rather than reflecting entrapment, the rise in costs and investments could alternatively mean that coaches found their jobs increasingly stressful and time/energy demanding from a stress perspective. Research comparing and/or integrating theoretical perspectives is needed.

Designing interventions to prevent burnout

Few studies, if any, have been conducted within the sport domain evaluating intervention strategies to prevent or treat burnout. As stated in the adage 'an ounce of prevention is worth a pound of cure,' interventions designed to prevent burnout are likely more effective than treating burnout once it occurs. Drawing from public health frameworks, Maslach and Goldberg (1998) note that primary prevention strategies involve changing the work environment to eliminate or modify worksite stressors with the intent of reducing the incidence of new cases of stress. In contrast, interventions designed to help individuals manage or cope with worksite stressors are secondary prevention as the goal is to reduce stress, whereas interventions designed to help people already suffering from burnout are tertiary prevention. Thus, potential interventions range from those focused on altering the work environment to those aimed at helping individuals cope more effectively with occupational stressors.

Historically, most discussion of burnout interventions have focused primarily on individual-centered approaches where the goal is to help individuals cope more effectively with high job demands through stress management strategies. These involve helping individuals learn to change their work habits such by reducing hours worked, taking breaks, finding a balance between work/personal life, and learning time-management strategies. The person-centered intervention strategies might also involve stress inoculation training, relaxation/mediation, assertiveness training, interpersonal and social skill training. In addition, lifestyle management (e.g. fitness, relaxed lifestyle, health enhancement), social support, and team building might also be the target of the intervention. These strategies primarily target the exhaustion burnout dimension with a lesser focus on the other burnout components. Although people can learn to cope with stress, it is less clear whether these strategies can be applied effectively at work to reduce work-related stress. In fact, Maslach *et al.* (2001) note that these approaches have not been very effective in reducing burnout. Compared to person-centered approaches, less research has evaluated the impact of organizational changes on burnout. Maslach and Goldberg (1998) suggest this is somewhat paradoxical given that situational and organizational factors have been more strongly associated with burnout than individual characteristics throughout the history of burnout research (Maslach and Schaufeli 1993). Thus, interventions that target the organization and work environment are likely more efficacious than those that target the individual and focus on helping the person more effectively manage stress. Moreover, interventions that reside early in the stress process and focus on removing salient stressors will likely have a greater influence on preventing burnout than those that simply help individuals learn to cope with stressful work environments.

Research gaps: Where to from here?

Although Schaufeli *et al.* (2009) note that over 6000 books, chapters, dissertations, and journal articles have been published on burnout in human service and organizational settings, research on coach burnout is minimal in comparison. Thus, gaps in our understanding are numerous and large. The available literature tends to be limited to part-time or recreational coaches. Few studies have used longitudinal designs (e.g. Drake and Hebert 2002; Kelley 1994; Raedeke 2004) or sampled elite sport coaches (e.g. Hjälm *et al.* 2007). Furthermore, little work has evaluated the potential negative consequences associated with burnout (e.g. health, motivation, performance) and no research has examined the extent to which burnout is linked to a complete withdrawal from coaching. Consequently, even basic issues surrounding coach burnout such as the epidemiological significance of studying burnout is not well established.

To stimulate empirical investigation of this issue, research is needed that justifies the importance of studying coach burnout. This can be addressed by examining its prevalence and its impact on coach well-being, retention, and performance. In addition, the impact of this issue on the athletes under coaches' care could be examined as coach burnout may influence player development, satisfaction/enjoyment, and performance. Finally, research shedding insights on why coaches may, or may not, experience burnout is needed to establish the foundation for developing and testing interventions to prevent it.

Establishing the importance of investigating coach burnout

One common theme of the early coach burnout research, which continues today, has been to compare the level of coach burnout to norms or the mean scores based on responses to the MBI outside of coaching. In comparison to MBI norms, some studies report that coach burnout levels are low to moderate in magnitude (Capel *et al.* 1987; Karabatsos *et al.* 2006; Koustelios 2010; Ryska 2009) whereas others report that a substantial number of coaches who score in the moderate to high range on burnout (e.g. Kelley and Gill 1993; Vealey *et al.* 1992).

It is important to note that the MBI norms cannot directly establish the prevalence of coach burnout. It is not a diagnostic assessment tool. The MBI was designed to examine the relationship between burnout and potential antecedents/consequences and not intended to diagnose burnout. In developing normative data, Maslach *et al.* (1996) view burnout in multidimensional terms and conceptualize it as being continuous (i.e. low to high), rather than dichotomous (i.e. present or absent). Consequently, normative data was developed by dividing the distribution derived from large samples into thirds with scores in the upper third defined as high burnout, those in the middle third as average burnout, and those in the bottom third reflecting low burnout. Based on a normative distribution, by definition, 33 percent of the population falls into each of the low, average, and high categories. Thus, there is no diagnostic threshold for MBI scores that is indicative of the dichotomous conceptualization of burnout (i.e. burned out versus not burned out) as the norms for the MBI are not linked to clinically derived cut-off points or diagnostic criteria. However, some researchers outside the sport setting have made preliminary progress in using external criteria to develop clinically derived cut-off points to assess the clinical significance of burnout (e.g. Schaufeli *et al.* 2009).

Related to that, a valuable direction for future research would be to link coach burnout scores with negative work- and health-related consequences to help establish the significance of studying coach burnout. Burnout is thought to be associated with a variety of negative occupational outcomes such as turnover, decreased job performance, and increased mental and physical health problems (Maslach *et al.* 2001). However, it is not known whether higher burnout scores on the MBI are associated with job performance and health-related consequences in the coaching realm as most studies have examined potential antecedents, not consequences of burnout.

Even if coach burnout scores are not excessively high, one could argue that burnout is nonetheless a significant issue given the profound impact it could have on the individuals suffering from it. Burnout not only has a detrimental impact on coaches themselves, but also potentially a negative impact on the athletes playing for those coaches (Vealey *et al.* 1998; Price and Weiss 2000). The potential for burnout to effect both the coach and athletes under their care might be perhaps the strongest reason to justify research on coach burnout.

Toward a greater understanding of the burnout process

Although burnout is a multidimensional construct, most of the coaching research has not adequately treated burnout in multidimensional terms. Theoretically, each burnout dimension reflects a different aspect of the experiential process with potentially unique antecedents and consequences, along with requiring unique intervention strategies. Although researchers have treated burnout multidimensionally in evaluating associations between burnout and theoretically related constructs, the conceptual models have treated burnout unidimensionally in nature and have focused on identifying associations between a variety of variables and burnout without specific predictions as to what variables should associate with which specific burnout dimensions.

A majority of coach burnout studies have been descriptive and cross-sectional in nature. Although these studies have been useful in identify potential burnout correlates, research is needed that develops a richer conceptual understanding of the underlying burnout process. For example, although Raedeke (2004) showed that changes in satisfaction were related to changes in burnout measured two times across a 12-month period, those results do not clarify the nature of the burnout process. One explanation could be that changes in satisfaction resulted in changes in burnout or alternatively that changes in burnout resulted in changes in satisfaction, or that changes in both constructs were caused by others factors such as a poor work and team atmosphere. Both qualitative and quantitative approaches using a time–series approach could shed insights on the burnout process.

In terms of understanding the burnout process from a stress perspective, applying process-oriented research designs from contemporary stress perspectives is warranted. Researchers evaluating coach burnout have not yet fully evaluated burnout from a transactional stress perspective. For example, scholars have not adopted a process-oriented view of stress and its measurement in evaluating the relationship of stress with burnout. Although sport science researchers have assessed variables related to demands, social support, and personality characteristics, other components of the stress process have received less attention such as coping skills, strategies, and resources. Lack of recovery has recently been acknowledged as a contributor to stress-related strain and burnout (Kellmann 2002; Sonnentag *et al.* 2010). Although recovery processes are important, research in general has generated far more knowledge relevant to understanding stress and exhaustion compared to recovery.

Given the extensive literature on negative stress-related reactions outside sport, several parsimonious conceptual stress–strain models may proffer a greater understanding of coach burnout. For example, although results have not been entirely consistent (Demerouti *et al.* 2001), Karasek and Theorell's (1990) demand–control model suggests that individuals in occupations characterized by high demands and low control (and low work-related social support) are most susceptible to negative stress–related health outcomes. More recently, another significant framework for examining negative consequences associated with stress stems from the reward–investment model. According to this model, negative work- and health-related outcomes, including burnout, are theorized to be associated with an imbalance between occupational rewards (e.g. money, esteem, job security/career opportunities) and effort (e.g. job demands and obligations) (Siegrist *et al.* 2004; Tsutsumi and Kawakami 2004; van Vegchel *et al.* 2005). Furthermore, overcommitted individuals who have an inability to withdraw from work are theorized to be at risk of experiencing stress-related strain. However, the overcommitment construct has been less consistently examined compared to reward–effort imbalance and its association with negative health-related outcomes has been somewhat inconsistent.

Although stress–strain models are certainly applicable to understanding burnout, Raedeke (1997) noted that although burnout is stress related, not everyone who experiences high demands burnouts in response. The reasons why this is the case are not well understood. Burnout is a complex and multifaceted process. As such, alternative perspectives including motivation-related theories may help develop a greater understanding of this phenomenon as burnout is linked to a process of disillusionment and an erosion of motivation. One illustrative theory (amongst several others including achievement motivation theory) that provides a promising theoretical lens for developing a better understanding of the burnout process is self-determination theory (SDT).

According to SDT, the fulfillment of basic psychological needs including perceived competence, autonomy, and relatedness along with more self-determined or autonomous types of motivation are associated with higher levels of well-being. In contrast, need thwarting is associated with amotivation and nonself-determined or controlled types of extrinsic motivation and markers of ill-being such as burnout. Although SDT has not been applied to coaching burnout, Van den Broeck *et al.* (2008) found that basic needs partially mediated the relationship between job demands and resources on exhaustion/vigor in a worksite sample. Researchers have also used SDT to examine athlete burnout. While very few studies have included a complete assessment of SDT constructs within a single study, researchers have supported that basic needs and behavioral regulations are related to burnout (e.g. Lonsdale and Hodge 2011; Lonsdale *et al.* 2009; Perreault *et al.* 2007). Conceptually, it appears that the burnout dimensions map onto different levels of SDT. Specifically, amotivation (behavioral regulation) is conceptually similar to cynicism or devaluation whereas competence (basic need) holds conceptual similarity to a reduced sense of accomplishment creating some conceptual ambiguity.

Advancing the knowledge base on preventing burnout

Two advances within the organizational psychology literature have potential for advancing our understanding of coach burnout as well as strategies to prevent it. These include framing burnout in terms of a person–job mismatch along with a focus on engagement, the conceptual antithesis of burnout. Maslach and Leiter (1997) initiated the development of a model that frames burnout in terms of job–person interaction rather than focusing on either the individual or the work environment. In doing so, they specifically highlighted six areas where a misfit between the person and the organizational climate. These include:

1   Work overload: This is characterized by high job demands, long hours, and too few resources.
2   Lack of control: This mismatch happens when individuals have little control over the work they do and perceive a diminished sense of autonomy.
3   Insufficient reward: This occurs when individuals perceive inadequate external rewards such as compensation and recognition for their work as well as internal rewards such as pride in doing something meaningful.
4   Community in the work group: This area can lead to mismatch and stress when there is a perceived lack of trust, communication, support, and collaboration.
5   Absence of fairness: This occurs when individuals feel they are not treated fairly compared to others such as in terms of workload, pay, promotion opportunities, and recognition for their efforts.
6   Value conflict: This occurs when there is a misfit between job requirements and individuals' personal values and principles.

Accordingly, the greater the misfit between the person and the job, the greater the likelihood of burnout. It is also plausible that a person may not be negatively impacted by a mismatch in one area if other areas provide a strong person–job fit. It is also possible that the importance of each of these areas varies across individuals. This approach has potential to offer greater insights on the causes of coach burnout and strategies to prevent it as it focuses attention on the interaction of the person and job rather than either the person or the job environment in isolation of the other. It also offers a greater range of potential intervention strategies compared to past efforts (Maslach and Goldberg 1998). Few sport science researchers have evaluated coach burnout from a person-organization match perspective (e.g. Ryska 2009), and none have examined whether the specific areas of potential mismatch identified by Maslach and Leiter (1997) are salient features of the coaching experience.

Within the organizational psychology literature, research has begun to examine the engagement construct in line with tenets of positive psychology. Although the exact dimensions underlying engagement are still debated, the overall construct is argued to be the antithesis of burnout. For example, Maslach and Leiter (1997) suggest that burnout is the erosion of engagement and highlight that engagement is characterized by energy (opposite of exhaustion), involvement (opposite of cynicism), and efficacy (opposite of ineffectiveness). Maslach *et al.* (2001) contend that engagement can be assessed by the opposite pattern of scores on the MBI. In contrast, Schaufeli *et al.* (2002a, 2002b) developed an alternative conceptualization and define engagement as a persistent, positive, affective-motivational state of fulfillment characterized by vigor (high energy levels), dedication (strong work-related involvement and feeling enthusiastic and significant), and absorption (total immersion into work and inability to detach oneself from the job). Regardless of the engagement conceptualization, Maslach *et al.* (2001) note that burnout is more strongly associated with work demands whereas engagement is more associated with job resources.

Although sport science researchers interested in coaching issues have not yet examined engagement, they have initiated research on athlete engagement (Hodge *et al.* 2009). Developing an understanding of the nature of engagement itself and the processes underlying it might provide the underpinnings for developing effective intervention strategies for increasing coach engagement and thereby preventing burnout.

Our contribution

To date, there are minimal, if any, published empirical studies evaluating strategies for preventing coach burnout. While recognizing the importance of framing burnout as a person–job mismatch, a current approach used with ten Olympic coaches in Sweden focuses on preventing burnout and simultaneously promoting well-being and coach retention based on a stress perspective with a focus on recovery processes.

At the onset of the program, stress and recovery issues experienced in the context of elite coaching are discussed from theoretical and experiential perspectives. Moreover, burnout is discussed with an emphasis on symptoms, potential contributing factors, and consequences (e.g. health and performance). Finally, recovery as process of minimizing fatigue and maximizing vitality is promoted as a key strategy to maintain well-being and performance (Lundqvist and Kenttä 2010). Following, coaches are taught to monitor their perceived coaching demands/stress load and recovery to heighten self-awareness. During critical periods, they are encouraged to complete a daily self-monitoring form on stressful situations and recovery actions. They also complete stress and recovery questionnaires bi-monthly (e.g. perceived stress, emotional recovery, sleep, overcommitment).

Along with self-monitoring to increase awareness, potential recovery methods are taught to coaches including strategies to promote healthy sleeping behavior and to mentally detach from sport. Mindfulness exercises are included as well as ways to incorporate energizers into one's lifestyle as a central aim of facilitating recovery in order to promote a well-balanced life. Unfortunately, stressful periods with difficult demands usually result in down-regulation of recovery activities (e.g. poorer sleep quality/quantity, nutrition, habits, lifestyle management, along with less time with family and friends and decreased physical activity). Becoming aware of recovery needs, learning effective recovery strategies, and increasing the perceived value of devoting time to recovery activities is a critical element of the prevention program to maintain coaching vitality and well-being.

Although the program is still in progress and under evaluation, coaches have reported an enhanced ability to monitor stress load and recovery, and have self-reported more frequently engaging in strategies to enhance recovery. In addition, coaches reported more regularly paying attention to body signals related to stress and recovery.

Summary and implications for coaching

On the surface, burnout is simple – it is a reaction to chronic stress characterized by high demands and low resources. Although it is undoubtedly stress related, it is also embedded within motivational processes. Burnout involves a process of disillusionment marked by value conflict and an erosion of motivation. Underlying that, burnout is a complex issue that is influenced by a variety of factors ranging from individual characteristics, interpersonal factors, to organizational issues. As such, developing a comprehensive and integrated understanding of coach burnout is indeed a challenging undertaking that can be approached from a variety of theoretical perspectives. Although common theoretical approaches used within the sport psychology literature provide a strong starting point for generating a more in-depth understanding of coach burnout, the organizational psychology literature provides insights that can be used to further the understanding of coach burnout.

Given that coach burnout studies to date are descriptive and correlational in nature, inferences about potentially effective intervention strategies can only be stated in tentative terms. Having said that, the most effective interventions are likely multimodal in nature due to the wide variety of interacting factors associated with burnout. At this point of knowledge development, one potential avenue for designing interventions to prevent burnout will be to target theory-based variables associated with burnout in the intervention design. These can range from individual characteristics associated with stress-related process (e.g. perfectionism) to organizational stressors that create a person–job mismatch. Targeting the individual and teaching individuals how to cope with organizational stressors might ultimately be less effective than targeting the organizational structure or the person and job mismatch creating the stress-strain. Although general stress management interventions have been used in occupational settings outside of coaching, these interventions will not likely be effective unless they target specific factors contributing to burnout.

References

Caccese, T.M. and Mayerberg, C.K. (1984) 'Gender differences in perceived burnout of college coaches,' *Journal of Sport and Exercise Psychology*, 6: 279–288.

Capel, S.A., Sisley, B.L. and Desertrain, G.S. (1987) 'The relationship between role conflict and role ambiguity to burnout in high school basketball coaches,' *Journal of Sport Psychology*, 9: 106–117.

Dale, J. and Weinberg, R. (1990) 'Burnout in sport: A review and critique,' *Journal of Applied Sport Psychology*, 2: 67–83.

Dale, J. and Weinberg, R.S. (1989) 'The relationship between coaches' leadership style and burnout,' *The Sport Psychologist*, 3: 1–13.

Demerouti, E., Bakker, A., de Jonge, J., Janssen, P. and Schaufeli, W.B. (2001) 'Burnout and engagement at work as a function of demands and control,' *Scandinavian Journal of Work and Environmental Health*, 27: 279–286.

Drake, D. and Hebert, E.P. (2002) 'Perceptions of occupational stress and strategies for avoiding burnout: Case studies of two female teacher coaches,' *The Physical Educator*, 59: 170–183.

Fender, L.K. (1989) 'Athlete burnout: Potential for research and intervention strategies,' *The Sport Psychologist*, 3: 63–71.

Freudenberger, H.J. and Richelson, G. (1980) *Burnout: The High Cost of High Achievement*, Garden City, NY: Anchor.

Goodger, K., Gorely, T., Lavallee, D. and Harwood, C. (2007) 'Burnout in sport: A systematic review,' *The Sport Psychologist*, 21: 27–151.

Hjälm, S., Kenttä, G., Hassmén, P. and Gustafsson, H. (2007) 'Burnout among elite soccer coaches,' *Journal of Sport Behavior*, 4: 415–427.

Hodge, K., Lonsdale, C. and Jackson, S.A. (2009) 'Athlete engagement in elite sport: An exploratory investigation of antecedents and consequences,' *The Sport Psychologist*, 23: 186–202.

Karabatsos, G., Malousaris, G. and Apostolidis, N. (2006) 'Evaluation and comparison of burnout levels in basketball, volleyball, and track and field coaches,' *Studies in Physical Culture and Tourism*, 13: 79–83.

Karasek, R.A. and Theorell, T. (1990) *Healthy Work: Stress, Productivity, and the Reconstruction of Working Life*, New York: Basic Books.

Kelley, B.C. (1994) 'A model of stress and burnout in collegiate coaches: Effects of gender and time of season,' *Research Quarterly for Exercise and Sport*, 65: 48–58.

Kelley, B.C. and Gill, D.L. (1993) 'An examination of personal/situational variables, stress appraisal, and burnout in collegiate teacher-coaches,' *Research Quarterly for Exercise and Sport*, 64: 94–102.

Kelley, B.C., Eklund, R.C. and Ritter-Taylor, M. (1999) 'Stress and burnout among collegiate tennis coaches,' *Journal of Sport and Exercise Psychology*, 21: 113–130.

Kellmann, M. (2002) *Enhancing Recovery: Preventing Underperformance in Athletes*, Champaign, IL: Human Kinetics.

Kosa, B. (1990) 'Teacher-coach burnout and coping strategies,' *The Physical Educator*, 47: 153–158.

Koustelios, A. (2010) 'Burnout among football coaches in Greece,' *Biology of Exercise*, 6: 5–12.

Lonsdale, C. and Hodge, K. (2011) 'Temporal ordering of motivational quality and athlete burnout in elite sport,' *Medicine and Science in Sport and Exercise*, 43: 913–921.

Lonsdale, C., Hodge, K. and Rose, E. (2009) 'Athlete burnout in elite sport: A self-determination perspective,' *Journal of Sport Sciences*, 27: 785–795.

Lundqvist, C. and Kenttä, G. (2010) 'Positive emotions are not simply the absence of the negative ones: Development and validation of the Emotional Recovery Questionnaire (EmRecQ),' *The Sport Psychologist*, 24: 468–488.

Malinauskas R., Malinauskiene, V. and Dumciene, A. (2010) 'Burnout and perceived stress among university coaches in Lithuania,' *Journal of Occupational Health*, 52: 302–307.

Maslach, C. and Goldberg, J. (1998) 'Prevention of burnout: New perspectives,' *Applied and Preventive Psychology*, 7: 63–74.

Maslach, C. and Jackson, S.E. (1981) 'The measurement of experienced burnout,' *Journal of Occupational Behavior*, 2: 99–113.

Maslach, C. and Leiter, M.P. (1997) *The Truth About Burnout*, San Francisco, CA: Jossey-Bass.

Maslach, C. and Schaufeli, W.B. (1993) 'Historical and conceptual development of burnout,' in W.B. Schaufeli, C. Maslach and T. Marek (eds) *Professional Burnout: Recent Developments in Theory and Research*, Washington, DC: Taylor and Francis.

Maslach, C., Jackson, S.E. and Leiter, M.P. (1996) *Maslach Burnout Inventory Manual*, 3rd edn, Palo Alto, CA: Consulting Psychologists Press.

Maslach, C., Schaufeli, W.B. and Leiter, M.P. (2001) 'Job burnout,' *Annual Review of Psychology*, 52: 397–422.

McManus, I.C., Winder, B.C. and Gordon, D. (2002) 'The causal links between stress and burnout in a longitudinal study of UK doctors,' *Lancet*, 359: 2089–2090.

Pastore, D.L. and Judd, M.R. (1993) 'Burnout and gender differences in two year college coaches of women's athletic teams,' *Sociology of Sport Journal*, 10: 205–212.

Perreault, S., Gaudreau, P., Lapointe, M.C. and Lacroix, C. (2007) 'Does it take three to tango? Psychological need satisfaction and athlete burnout,' *International Journal of Sport Psychology*, 38: 437–450.

Pines, A.M. (1993) 'Burnout: An existential perspective,' in W.B. Schaufeli, C. Maslach and T. Marek (eds) *Professional Burnout: Recent Developments in Theory and Research*, Washington, DC: Taylor and Francis.

Price, M.S. and Weiss, M.R. (2000) 'Relationships among coach burnout, coach behaviors, and athletes' psychological responses,' *The Sport Psychologist*, 14: 391–409.

Raedeke, T.D. (1997) 'Is athlete burnout more than just stress? A sport commitment perspective,' *Journal of Sport and Exercise Psychology*, 19: 396–417.

Raedeke, T.D. (2004) 'Coach commitment and burnout: A one year follow-up,' *Journal of Applied Sport Psychology*, 16: 333–349.

Raedeke, T.D., Warren, A.H. and Granzyk, T.L. (2002) 'Coaching commitment and turnover: A comparison of former and current coaches,' *Research Quarterly for Exercise and Sport*, 73: 73–86.

Ryska, T.A. (2009) 'Multivariate analysis of program goals, leadership style, and occupational burnout among intercollegiate coaches,' *Journal of Sport Behavior*, 32: 476–488.

Schaufeli, W.B., Leiter, M.P. and Maslach, C.M. (2009) 'Burnout: 35 years of research and practice,' *Career Development International*, 14: 204–220.

Schaufeli, W.B., Martinez, I.M., Marques-Pinto, A., Salanova, M. and Bakker, A.B. (2002a) 'Burnout and engagement in university students,' *Journal of Cross-Cultural Psychology*, 33: 461–481.

Schaufeli, W.B., Salanova, M., Gonzalez-Roma, V. and Bakker, A.B. (2002b) 'The measurement of engagement and burnout: A two sample confirmatory factor analytic approach,' *Journal of Happiness Studies*, 3: 71–92.

Schmidt, G.W. and Stein, G.L. (1991) 'Sport commitment: A model integrating enjoyment, dropout, and burnout,' *Journal of Sport and Exercise Psychology*, 13: 254–265.

Siegrist, J., Starke, D., Chandola, T., Godin, I., Marmot, M., Niedhammer, I. and Peter, R. (2004) 'The measurement of effort-reward imbalance at work: European Comparisons,' *Social Science and Medicine*, 58: 1483–1499.

Smith, R.E. (1986) 'Toward a cognitive-affective model of athletic burnout,' *Journal of Sport Psychology*, 8: 36–50.

Sonnentag, S., Kuttler, I. and Fritz, C. (2010) 'Job stressors, emotional exhaustion, and need for recovery: A multi-source study on the benefits of psychological detachment,' *Journal of Vocational Behavior*, 76: 355–365.

Tashman, L., Tenenbaum, G. and Eklund, R. (2010) 'The effect of perceived stress on the relationship between perfectionism and burnout in coaches,' *Anxiety, Stress and Coping*, 23: 195–212.

Tsutsumi, A. and Kawakami, N. (2004) 'A review of empirical studies on the model of effort-reward imbalance at work: Reducing occupational stress by implementing a new theory,' *Social Science and Medicine*, 59: 2335–2359.

Van den Broeck, A., Vansteenkiste, M., De Witte, H. and Lens, W. (2008) 'Explaining the relationship between job characteristics, burnout, and engagement: The role of basic psychological need satisfaction,' *Work and Stress*, 22: 277–294.

van Vegchel, N., de Jonge, J., Bosma, H. and Schaufeli, W. (2005) 'Reviewing the effort-reward imbalance model: Drawing up the balance of 45 empirical studies,' *Social Science and Medicine*, 60: 1117–1131.

Vealey, R.S., Armstrong, L., Comar, W. and Greenleaf, C.A. (1998) 'Influence of perceived coaching behaviors on burnout and competitive anxiety in female college athletes,' *Journal of Applied Sport Psychology*, 10: 297–318.

Vealey, R.S., Udry, E.M., Zimmerman, V. and Soliday, J. (1992) 'Intrapersonal and situational predictors of coaching burnout,' *Journal of Sport and Exercise Psychology*, 14: 40–58.

B

Developing competency in sports coaching

35

COACHING EXPERTISE AND THE QUANTITATIVE EXAMINATION OF DEVELOPMENTAL EXPERIENCES

Bradley W. Young

UNIVERSITY OF OTTAWA, CANADA

Introduction

This chapter reviews research pertaining to the long-term development of skilled coaches in the elite context of competitive sport. In particular, it appraises emerging quantitative research that has examined the types of activities and experiences that aspiring coaches should accrue in order to progressively learn and become increasingly more competent. While pointing out the many merits of extant studies, the chapter also attempts to address limitations and to outline possibilities for improved rigour in future research. The chapter advances eight themes for consideration in future work, and finishes by considering how findings from quantitative coach development research might inform aspiring individuals as well as strategies for broader coach development schemes.

Efforts to enumerate the developmental path towards coaching expertise have been influenced by the deliberate practice (DP) framework (Ericsson 2003) and social-ecological perspectives on human development (Bronfenbrenner 2005). DP is a metric for quantitatively understanding expert development, especially in fields that have strong cognitive underpinnings like coaching. Research has yet to specifically ask what constitutes DP for coaches, however, literature that identifies activities/venues in which rigorous opportunities for coach learning occur allow us to infer DP coaching opportunities (Trudel and Gilbert 2006). In a socio-ecological model, a coach's development of knowledge, competencies, and behavioural tendencies is a product of the social domains where they invest their time and the network of coaches, mentors, communities of practice, and athletes within which they often function and have exchange opportunities (Côté 2006).

Coaching studies using the structured retrospective protocol

The DP framework requires researchers to quantify coaches' learning histories, and the socio-ecological perspective encourages enumerating the time that developing individuals spend in coaching domains interacting with others. Borrowing protocol for collecting data relating to phenomena in athletes' past, Gilbert *et al.* (2006) refined the structured retrospective interview method for research on coach development. The survey asks participants to report information about (1) demography, education, and accreditation; (2) engagement in various coaching contexts and roles; (3) coach learning opportunities; and (4) former athletic experiences. Data are analyzed for particular developmental periods, or cumulatively across a career, and are instrumental for deriving milestones when coaches begin certain activities.

The procedure is reliable and valid when objective, quantifiable, potentially verifiable data involving simple units (e.g. discrete activities) are collected. Although work is needed to validate coach-reported data using external sources, test-retest analyses on various development measures (taken 16 months apart) showed strong reliability for the past ten years of recall, with intra-class coefficients (ICC) exceeding 0.79 (Brophy and Young 2009). Coaches reliably recalled time spent interacting with athletes in months (ICC = 0.81), and weekly hours in-season (0.69), on a year by year basis, as distant as 14 years ago. Coaches reliably recalled data from 10–19 years ago for number of collegiate coaching courses, and symposia attended, former athletes now coaching, and former assistant coaches (all ICCs >0.76). Young *et al.* (2009) reported reliable coefficients for career-long total years of coaching (0.99) and years as a primary coach (0.98), and accumulated hours working with athletes in each sport year (0.74). Initial work indicates that recall of total years in a secondary/assistant coach role and total number of mentors across a career is challenging for coaches whose careers extend beyond ten years.

At least five studies have employed the structured retrospective method to examine coaches who are engaged in an elite context of competitive sport, and who work with athletes in the investment years of athletic participation (see Côté *et al.* 2007 for defining criteria for this context). First, Gilbert *et al.* (2006) found that successful American collegiate football and volleyball coaches spent very little time in formal coach education activities. Before coaching, these coaches spent at least 13 years playing the game at a reasonably competent level but not necessarily as a designated team leader. They specialized in a few sports during their younger playing days. Investigators determined that coaching success was related to accumulations of total coaching activity, however, they could not answer how much non-formal (e.g. organized learning opportunities outside the education system, such as clinics and workshops) and informal (e.g. learning via activities of daily coaching, interaction with peer coaches, self-directed learning) activity was critically related to development. Second, Lynch and Mallett (2006) found that Australian high-performance coaches (n = 5) spent most of their time directly interacting with athletes in preparation for, or at competitions, averaging over 20,000 hours in active coaching across their careers in contrast to 900 hours invested in formal coach education. Additionally, they typically spent about 14,000 hours in administrative and planning duties. Of the four coaches who acknowledged having important mentors, they each reported at least two mentors across a career. All coaches reported formerly competing in athletics themselves, for an average of 11 years, and most coaches were modestly high-level performers, though not outstanding.

Erickson *et al.* (2007) examined the past activities of Canadian university coaches in relation to 18 development experiences. Results demonstrated that several experiences were necessary at minimum to achieve university status: (1) having five (for individual sport coaches) or eight seasons (team sport coaches) of former experience playing the sport that one now coaches; (2) having one (for team sport coaches) or two mentors (individual sport coaches) when starting out as a coach between 24–29 years of age; (3) either coaching for three seasons in the developmental context (i.e. school-based, less competitive) early in one's career, or being an assistant coach for one season in the elite context before age 29. Furthermore, career development as a high-performance coach focused on a primary sport and not on the same variety of sports played when they had been athletes. Although necessary, time spent in formal coaching education activities was diminutive. Team sport coaches adopted leadership positions and had general experience in multiple team sports during their playing days. Investigators discounted having been an exceptionally elite athlete, and past coaching in the recreational context (i.e. participatory, novice instructional), as necessary for becoming a high-performance coach. Interestingly, due to wide variability on many developmental measures, investigators emphasized that *minimal threshold experience* (MTE) values could better inform coach development practices. MTEs were determined for those developmental activities for which more than 75 percent of high-performance coaches had reported values. On a within-participant basis, the additive scores for quantities reported in just these MTEs amounted to 64 percent of the total quantity of developmental experience that elite coaches reported overall across their career for *all* possible learning activities. The remaining time spent in developmental activities not accounted for by MTEs likely represented the highly diversified and individualized learning paths upon which elite coaches embark.

Young *et al.* (2009) compared skilled Canadian athletics coaching groups (ranging from local up to national level) on 14 learning activity measures. Investigators used tests of significance in analyses of variance, post hoc tests, and effect sizes, to draw conclusions about group differences. The most-skilled group accumulated more years of coaching experience in either a head or assisting capacity, than less-skilled groups. More skilled groups invested more time interacting directly with athletes, and with assisting coaches, at any point in a career. National-level coaches took more post-secondary coaching courses than lesser-skilled counterparts. Former experience as a track and field athlete was necessary to coach beyond the local club level, however, no differences were found between senior club, provincial, and national-level coaches for former athletic prowess (i.e. all were moderately high-level performers), length of one's former athletic career, number of years that they self-coached, or the number of personal coaches they had as athletes. Finally, Koh *et al.* (2011) discovered that national basketball coaches in Singapore had typically been above-average elite basketball players, had coached for at least ten years before reaching the elite level, with most of those years in the developmental context. These coaches averaged only 110 hours in formal coach accreditation sessions across their careers, which ranged in duration from 3–23 years. Perhaps reflecting cultural nuances, mentorship activities were absent and entry ages for various coaching experiences were delayed compared to prior works.

In sum, a few common trends appear across these five quantitative studies. First, the studies highlight the diverse number of activities that can be measured and, on a within-variable basis, data demonstrate substantial variance with standard deviations often exceeding group mean values. Second, skilled high-performance coaches report little time in formal coach education activities, amounting to less than 5 percent of coaching-affiliated time annually (Gilbert *et al.* 2006), or less than 3 percent of time spent relative to other coaching roles across a career (Lynch and Mallett 2006). Regardless, it is still notable that national coaches complete significantly more coaching workshops than all lesser-skilled groups at any point within a career (Young *et al.* 2009). Third, coaches accumulate vast amounts of coaching experience before becoming a head coach in the elite context. These amounts derive from head or assisting coaching experience in the elite context, and possibly experiences in the developmental context, although experiences in the recreational context appear unimportant. Fourth, mentorship 'received' and 'given' both appear critical to becoming a highly skilled coach, with the former being most important before age 30. Fifth, former athletic experience is a prerequisite, and should have been in the elite context of the sport one now coaches, and at least at a moderately competent performance level for five years. Uniquely for team sport coaches, former playing experiences should have been in several team sports besides the one that they now coach, and included multiple leadership roles.

Appraisal of extant research: finding a path forward

This section attempts to recognize the merits of recent studies as well as possible limitations in relation to eight identified themes. These themes are advanced for possible consideration with respect to future research. Where possible, specific recommendations and refined research questions are presented, which are informed by coaching science literature, but also by empirical works from broader literature on expertise.

1 Future research should focus on group discriminability rather than description

Most studies have recruited a sample of successful coaches, numerically described their past experiences in various learning activities, and then compared these data to data for coach samples *in other studies* (which are often from different sports). If researchers wish to explain the activities that lend themselves to long-term development, then between-group analyses within the same sport and within the same study are instrumental. For example, pertinent research on long-term athlete development allows that quantities for developmental activities (i.e. DP) be submitted to inter-group analyses to explain differences in performance status – cumulative DP consistently distinguishes between elite and less-elite athletic groups on a within-study basis, with elite groups amassing the greatest practice overall (e.g. Ward *et al.* 2004) or more practice in critical activities (e.g. Young and Salmela 2010). Similar use of inferential statistics will allow coaching researchers to reliably judge the contribution of certain learning activities to development. When employing these analytic strategies, confidence in between-group findings is heightened when results show significant differences across multiple groups that represent incremental levels of coaching competency in the same sport (see Figure 35.1).

2 Researchers should employ similar metrics for quantifying coach learning to be able to compare results across studies

In an effort to find consensus, this section catalogues learning 'metrics' that have been employed as measures in prior quantitative research, and which consistently are identified as critical learning opportunities driving development (Côté 2006; Erickson *et al.* 2007; Lynch and Mallett 2006; Mallett *et al.* 2009; Nelson *et al.* 2006; Werthner and Trudel 2006; Young *et al.* 2009). Future researchers might consider several possible metrics for quantifying activities, which fall into four broad categories of learning: (1) coach education activities; (2) mentoring; (3) experiential learning activities; and (4) former athletic experience (see Table 35.1).

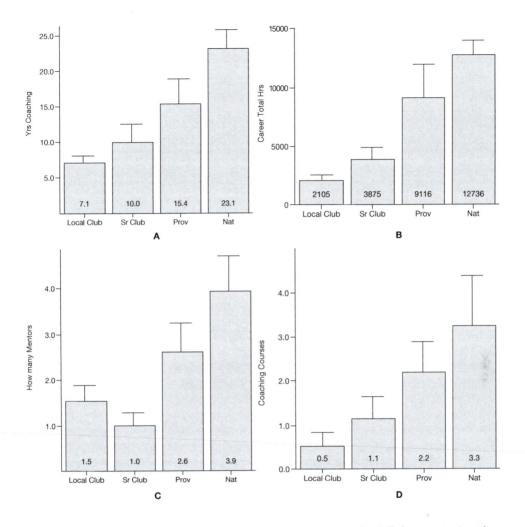

Figure 35.1: Data for select learning activities across four incrementally skilled groups in Canadian athletics coaching – local club, senior club, provincial level, and national level. Between-group trends are displayed for total years of coaching (A), cumulative hours interacting with athletes across a career (B), total number of mentors (C), and number of post-secondary coaching courses (D), as a function of skill group (Young *et al.* 2007).

'Coach education activities' include college and university-level courses, accreditation-based sessions affiliated with a formal coach-education program, which all conform to 'mediated' (Werthner and Trudel 2006) learning opportunities. This category also includes other mediated but non-formal experiences such as clinics/symposia/workshops. 'Mentoring' comprises unmediated learning opportunities in that one watches other coaches and has somewhat informal interactions with a coaching peer. Apprenticeships with a coach mentor have been measured by the discrete number of relationships that a person reports in the past. Due to reciprocal learning benefits for both mentor and apprentice (Bloom *et al.* 1998), future work might continue to assess the discrete number of apprentices that coaches have in turn mentored.

Table 35.1: *Metrics for assessing relevant activities and experiences according to category of learning*

Category	Activity or Experience	Suggested Metrics
Coach education activities	• institutional-affiliated, post-secondary coaching courses	number
	• coach accreditation-based courses, sessions	
	• clinics, symposia, workshops attended	
Mentoring	• relationships as a coach apprentice	number
	• relationships as a mentor, assisting coaches	
Experiential learning	• interaction with athletes in training	for each calendar year: • months per year • hours per week, for an average week during the in-season
	• interaction with athletes in competition	
	• investment in administration, planning, organization	
	• reflective investments	
Former athletic experiences	• career duration in sport now coaching (at elite level)	number of seasons played
	• performance indices in elite context	recall of verifiable statistics (times/scores), performance bests, roster selections, starts in line-up
	• coaches while an athlete (at elite level) in sport now coaching	number
	• team sports played while an athlete (including sports besides one now coaching)★	number
	• leadership positions on teams (all sports) as an athlete★	percentage of all seasons/years in which one was designated captain or assistant captain

★ These transferable experiences should be assessed uniquely for team sport coaches.

Coaching involves constant behavioural interactions between training, competition, and organizational venues (Côté *et al.* 1995), thus, researchers should refrain from narrow conceptualizations of the informal/incidental learning that occurs through active coaching experience. For example, Young *et al.* (2009) assessed only coaching interactions in training and competitive venues. Assessing time invested in training, competitive, and organizational capacities using three separate metrics (e.g. Gilbert *et al.* 2006) is preferred. Finally, studies have yet to enumerate an integral process of daily experiential coach learning, which is coaches' deliberate reflection on their experiences (e.g. Irwin *et al.* 2004). Both 'reflection on action' after games/practices, and 'retrospective reflection' at season's end, afford opportunities for coaches to refine/gain knowledge (Gilbert and Trudel 2001). In sum, future researchers might consider employing reliable and valid metrics for each of training interactions, competitive interactions, organizational investments, and reflective investments, under a broad category entitled 'experiential learning'.

'Former athletic experiences' in the sport one now coaches appear important for the assimilation of knowledge which one may later apply when reaching the coaching ranks (Côté 2006; Lynch and Mallett 2006), and because prior athletic experience is a major source of coaching efficacy (see Chase and Martin, Chapter 6 in this volume). However, the common practice of self-reporting former athletic ability is possibly fraught with difficulties due to memory distortion and self-presentation. Future researchers should verify the reliability of estimates using archived statistics for playing performance and roster selections in team sports, and former performance indices can be normalized across standardized events to give reliable performance estimates in individual sports like track and field (Young *et al.* 2009). Quantifying the portion of one's athletic experiences in leadership roles (e.g. Erickson *et al.* 2007) will continue to be important with respect to coach development in team sports. Finally, it might be fruitful to survey the number of different coaches that they had as a former athlete in elite sport, because elite players who later progress to coaching may assimilate strategies from the very coaches for whom they played (Cushion *et al.* 2003; Salmela 1995). As informal coach learning opportunities, former athletic experiences are assessed for the sport one now coaches, but may also be considered with respect to alternative sports one may have 'sampled' previously from which critical learnings may have transferred to the sport one now coaches (Erickson *et al.* 2007).

3 Researchers should examine how transferable (non-specific) experiences are associated with skilled coaching status

In particular, (1) former athletic experiences in sports besides the one now coaching, and (2) coach learning experiences in the developmental sport context may provide breadth which may become particularly formative in terms of coaching knowledge and leadership competencies later in the elite context (e.g. Erickson *et al.* 2007). At least among team sport coaches, Table 35.1 recommends assessing the number of team sports formerly played (besides the team sport one now coaches), and percentage of experiences in which one adopted leadership (assistant captain/captain) positions on teams from all sports. To measure accumulations of experiential learning in the developmental context, future survey instructions should have face validity to carefully direct participants about how to respond in relation to defining criteria for this context (see Côté *et al.* 2007). Moreover, researchers may submit these data to analyses that consider how non-specific activities (i.e. not related to one specific sport context) during an early developmental stage can influence requisite amounts of investment in specific activities at a later developmental stage on the road to skilled coaching in the elite context. In the domain of long-term athlete development, for example, Baker *et al.* (2003) performed such analyses to illustrate how non-specific activities (e.g. sampling and deliberate play) in the early playing years resulted in transferable skills that subsequently reduced the number of hours that players later required in sport-specific activities before making elite national teams.

4 The linearity of stage models may be problematic and proper analyses are required to determine their suitability

Quantitative research evolved from qualitative work with elite coaches, which was important for articulating stage-based models of development (e.g. Schinke *et al.* 1995). Recent quantitative studies have advanced similar models that are 'linear' in nature, meaning that individuals who aspire to be elite coaches should necessarily pass through one stage before progressing to the following stage, with certain developmental roles and activities being unique to some stages and less represented during others (Erickson *et al.* 2007; Koh *et al.* 2011). However, the linearity of the developmental path may be problematic (Trudel and Gilbert 2006) in that many individuals who reach elite coaching levels are able to bypass certain stages en route, and considering that possibly 'no common pathways lead to national elite coaching positions' (Schinke *et al.* 1995: 58). Assuming that the value of any developmental framework is judged by whether it captures the experience of nearly all aspiring competitive coaches, then linear models may be challenged to accommodate diverse experiences that accumulate with differential pacing across coaches. If one considers recent works underscoring the highly personalized preferences associated with coach learning activities (Erickson *et al.* 2008), and the idiosyncrasies of elite coaches' developmental paths (Werthner and Trudel 2009), then the advancement of stage models is possibly premature. Still, if the articulation of stage models using quantitative data is preferred, then sufficiently large samples involving multiple coach skill groups should be recruited in order to conduct mixed-model analyses of variance (ANOVAs) or repeated measures ANOVAs. The interpretation of group (e.g. skilled versus less-skilled) by time interactions for various learning metrics would be helpful in determining which developmental activities are critical at different points (e.g. after one year of coaching, after three years, five years, etc.) in the progression. Results from such analyses would move researchers beyond the specification of role types (e.g. player in sport now coaching, assistant/head coach) and determination of milestone ages for each stage; instead, results would allow investigators to determine the critical amounts in accumulated learning metrics that significantly distinguish skilled and less-skilled coaching groups at designated points during career-long learning, irrespective of starting age.

Although the recruitment of multiple skill groups for between-group analyses might necessarily be incremental (e.g. a ladder of skill groups), the path by which individuals accumulate learning activities and develop their coaching skills is not necessarily linear. In fact, future research that analyzes cumulative measures for various learning metrics across the long-term may instead determine that coach learning proceeds in a non-linear or quadratically accelerated pattern as is the case in other fields of expertise. According to the DP framework and trends observed for elite wrestlers (Hodges and Starkes 1996), team ball sport players (Baker *et al.* 2003), and musicians (Ericsson *et al.* 1993), a 'monotonic benefits assumption' establishes how aspiring individuals on the road to expertise accrue greater time in learning activities at each subsequently observed time point in the developmental path, and that the trend for accumulating practice activities inflects upwards as time passes. This trend assumes continually increasing personal investment in learning activities (and concurrent benefits) over time, which may be a more flexible perspective to the linear assumption that one 'needs to do this, or have this experience, by this age, before passing to the next stage'.

5 It is important to control for career length when comparing differently skilled coaching groups on accumulated learning metrics

This could be accomplished by conducting group (i.e. those who become highly skilled coaches versus those who do not) by time analyses with all groups anchored at the same starting point and comparing measures after start age, after three years, after five years, and onwards. This approach challenges investigators to find sufficient sample sizes for lesser-skilled comparison groups at progressive periods in a career, because their career length may not be sufficiently lengthy, or there may be problems with intermittent participation. Alternatively, one could conduct analyses of co-variance on cumulative career totals while controlling for 'slow-moving' career duration variables (e.g. years or seasons of coaching) for all participants (e.g. Young *et al.* 2009). This is important because the most successful coaches in the elite context commonly report earlier entry ages into coaching, and have more years of experience that will typically bias the cumulative measures in their favour. A pressing question is whether coaches who eventually become highly skilled invest more in certain developmental activities *at any point within their career*, which is determined after controlling for career length and possibly coach starting age. This would help determine whether the achievement of most-skilled coaching status results from relatively greater investments in coach learning opportunities, rather than being a by-product of a lengthy career.

6 It may be important to employ statistical approaches that use the full intra-individual variability of data for learning metrics and that acknowledge our limits in explaining variance in skilled coach development

In studies of MTEs, investigators have condensed the repertoire of dependent measures based on whether all, or 75 percent, of elite coaches report pertinent experiences, and have converted the values of certain measures to become a percentage of the maximal value reported by an elite coach (e.g. Erickson *et al.* 2007). The former step reduces the number of developmental variables considered, and the second step reduces the range of variability in the distributions of developmental variables under examination, which may preclude researchers from observing interesting findings. Instead, researchers might consider examining data from all coaches including lower values in the distributions. To this end, if researchers were to adopt ANOVAs, then within-group variance would be fully considered when testing for group differences without unnecessary transformations or manipulations by the researchers. By the nature of these analyses, the likelihood of finding significant group differences between successful and less-successful coaches is greater if there are veridical differences in the mean levels between the groups, but also if the intact and unmanipulated variability around each group mean happens to be minimal.

Future research should investigate how individual differences on various learning metrics predict skill group assignment, perhaps using a discriminant function analysis (e.g. Helsen and Starkes 1999). For example, results might tell us that 68 percent of membership in either a skilled or a less-skilled coaching group is explained by a host of independent variables representing coach learning metrics. Results might also compel us to admit that we cannot confidently explain 32 percent of variance in skill group assignment, thereby challenging us to improve the validity and reliability of our quantitative designs. Moreover, this approach could afford qualitative researchers a mandate for complementary or mixed-methods research that addresses the quantitatively 'unexplained', particularly researchers who are interested in detailing coach learning biographies and describing personalized idiosyncrasies in the pursuit of learning.

7 Future research should explore affordances and ensure that all sampled coaches have similar aspirations

Expert coaches likely seek out many resources in the form of people, organizations, funding, and programs to support their learning. However, experts may also be *afforded* resources in their environments to engage in critical learning opportunities. Affordances are inherently differential, meaning that they predispose certain individuals to benefit from their surroundings irrespective of personal decisions or actions, while others are disadvantaged or face barriers by not having similar affordances. For example, long-term athletic development is influenced by inequitable affordances related to where an athlete grew up and when they were born (Côté *et al.* 2006), and whether they had access to a master coach in the developing years (Kalinowski 1985). Inequities in coach development may similarly arise from a number of factors whereby some coaches benefit from 'being in the right place at the right time' (Schinke *et al.* 1995: 57), including the differential availability of coach education activities, mentor programs, vacancy of coaching jobs, and inequitable access due to geography (e.g. remote locales) amongst others, and which possibly interact with demographic factors such as gender and ethnicity. More research needs to establish the priority of affordances facilitating learning opportunities for many coaches, and commensurate non-affordances which act as barriers to learning. One approach might involve surveys of barrier items with coaches being asked to report the frequency and limiting degree for each item with respect to the learning process. An understanding of affordances might encourage us to adopt non-linear functions for portraying the coach development path, by recognizing that the pace of individuals' investment in learning activities might be somewhat inconstant and becomes instantly accelerated following a specific affordance (e.g. an opportunity such as the sudden posting of a graduate assistantship coaching position). It behoves researchers to determine exactly what these affordances are and how they might influence the pattern of aspiring coaches' investments in learning metrics over time.

Although coach development surveys appear to have implicitly assumed that all coaches are equally motivated to ascertain higher skill levels, motivational factors likely mediate the degree of coaches' investment in developmental activities. For example, a senior club coach might be motivated to engage in developmental activities that they deem sufficient for the level at which they are presently, and do not aspire to more skilled roles which may demand greater investment. In future, therefore, researchers should ensure that coaches have similar motivational orientations towards coaching as a vocation requiring expertise, and similar perceptions towards the value of coach developmental activities, ensuring that these are inclusion criteria for the purposeful sampling of participants.

8 Future researchers should validate skill indices that distinguish between expert and less-expert coaches, and regress skill indices on data for developmental learning activities

It is critical that coaching groups be discriminated based on outcome indices that validly reflect gradients in competency. To date, studies have validated the most-skilled coaches using one or more criteria, including win–loss records, numbers of teams/athletes coached to championship finals, recognition from peers, an MTE related to five years of coaching, and accreditation levels (e.g. Gilbert *et al.* 2006; Lynch and Mallett 2006). Only Young *et al.* (2009) showed how incrementally higher skilled coaching groups also exhibited correspondingly higher values for these outcomes as well as for the quality of the athletes they had coached. Two important points can be made about these outcome indices: first, although potentially verifiable, their validity has never been confirmed using external archives of information; second, these were outcomes reflecting coaching 'success' and not coaching skill. Indices of *success* and indices of *skill* are not necessarily related. For example, a highly skilled coach may fall short on success indices, and a less-skilled coach may have great success, because success outcomes depend highly on athletes' performances in competition. Mallett and Côté (2006) cautioned that athletes' performances are very unstable factors and accomplishment outcomes for athletes or teams are therefore indirect and unreliable measures of coaching effectiveness.

Coaching effectiveness should instead be judged according to more stable indices, called 'skills', which underlie superior performance in the domain (see Ericsson 2003). Ford *et al.* (2009) advised coaching researchers who might use this approach to first identify representative tasks that capture the essence of expertise in coaching. If expert groups repeatedly perform better on these representative skill tasks than less-expert groups in a controlled empirical setting, results would enable investigators to identify the *skill mechanisms* that mediate expert coaches' performance. Although this approach has yet to be popularly received in coaching, representative skill tests can be modified from pedagogy (Berliner 2001) and physical education (Dodds 1994) domains. Examples of pertinent tasks include: (1) procedural tests for coach-athlete exchanges (Erickson and Côté, Chapter 9 in this volume) and interactive decision-making (Jones *et al.* 1997); (2) visual recognition tasks (Imwold and Hoffman 1983), think-aloud protocol (Rutt Leas and Chi 1993), or eye movement registrations (Petrakis 1987); (3) tests of pedagogical content knowledge (Block and Beckett 1990) (see also work by Schempp and colleagues, e.g. Schempp *et al.* 2004).

Finally, an expertise approach dictates that researchers trace the amount of learning activity associated with the acquisition of these coaching skills, to identify when and how these skills were acquired (Ford *et al.* 2009). This brings us 'full circle', in a sense, as each of the existing quantitative studies (using the retrospective guide) has profiled practice histories and enumerated developmental activities (or metrics) that are likely associated with crucial coaching skills. Future researchers will need to *integrate* the quantitative data for the various learning metrics in which coaches have invested their time across their career with measures for stable coaching skills which validly discriminate experts and less-experts. Such analyses would tell us which coaching skills (deemed valid requisites for expertise) are amenable to change (learning) and which cumulative developmental activities are most critical in facilitating their acquisition.

Summary and implications for coaching practice

In sum, the enumeration of learning activities and subsequent submission of these data to between-group analyses are necessary if researchers are to articulate the path to coaching expertise. It is important for researchers to focus less on chronological stages through which coaches might pass in their development, and instead focus on cumulative measures relating to the learning metrics that are accepted with consensus amongst researchers. Attempts to discriminate multiple skill groups should consider controlling for confounding variables relating to career length, levels of individual aspiration, and should consider moderating variables (i.e. affordances, barriers) that establish inequitable conditions for long-term development.

Quantitative coach development research cannot be a simple exercise in 'bean counting' – results must inform the long-term process of coaching skill acquisition. Emergent research possibly has implications for coach development schemes and coach education programs. Findings might determine which learning metrics best predict coaching expertise, and whether there needs to be a significant investment in each learning metric and particular sub-activities within each metric. For example, if experiential learning metrics are most important, coach education systems might afford more credit to coaches' interactions in this domain, publish guidelines that dictate how much direct coaching is required, and introduce policies to effectively account for such experience before bestowing accreditation. If mentoring proves critical in discriminating skill groups, then steps can be taken to better entrench mentoring experiences in coach education schemes, and to tailor programs wherein mentors and apprentices are properly matched. If former athletic experiences are salient, strategies might be invoked to expose late-adolescent and early-adult elite athletes to coaching roles. Whereas early coaching recruitment might focus on playing ranks, later coach curricula might ask young coaches to reflect on prior scenarios when they themselves had been players, getting them to draw lessons from their former coaches' tactics. If transferable experiences are important, coach development systems may be able to sequence early coaching activities within the developmental sport context into graduated roles in the elite competitive coaching context. Using valid success outcome indices and/or representative skill tests, future quantitative research will be instrumental in determining how quantities in each learning metric contribute to expert versus less-expert group differences. The relative predictive weight for each metric could dictate the prescription for how much time and how many resources should be invested to support learning in the experiential, mentoring, former athletic, and formal coach education domains. Though any recommendations would depend on replicable results in future work, these prescriptions as well as information about critical affordances have implications for coach education programs deciding where to best allocate scarce organizational resources to support the development of a great number of coaches. Finally, prescriptions for where to invest time, energy and personal resources will be instrumental for aspiring individuals seeking a long-term developmental route to coaching expertise. Knowing the most important learning domains in which one should invest, when to invest during certain periods in the developmental progression, and knowing which specific environmental affordances to pursue – these are all aspects that developing coaches can take under advisement when charting their course.

References

Baker, J., Côté, J. and Abernethy, B. (2003) 'Sport-specific training, deliberate practice and the development of expertise in team ball sports', *Journal of Applied Sport Psychology*, 15: 12–25.

Berliner, D.C. (2001) 'Learning about and learning from expert teachers', *International Journal of Educational Research*, 35: 463–482.

Block, K.K. and Beckett, K.D. (1990) 'Verbal descriptions of skill by specialists and nonspecialists', *Journal of Teaching in Physical Education*, 10: 21–37.

Bloom, G., Durand-Bush, N., Schinke, R.J. and Salmela, J.H. (1998) 'The importance of mentoring in the development of coaches and athletes', *International Journal of Sport Psychology*, 29: 267–281.

Bronfenbrenner, U. (2005) *Making Human Beings Human: Bioecological Perspectives on Human Development*, Thousand Oaks, CA: Sage.

Brophy, K. and Young, B.W. (2009)'Test-retest reliability of long-term retrospective recall methodologies', presented at the Eastern Canadian Symposium for Sport and Exercise Psychology, Toronto, ON, March.

Côté, J. (2006) 'The development of coaching knowledge', *International Journal of Sports Science and Coaching*, 1: 217–222.

Côté, J., MacDonald, D., Baker, J. and Abernethy, B. (2006) 'When "where" is more important than "when": birthplace and birthdate effects on the achievement of sporting expertise', *Journal of Sport Sciences*, 24: 1065–1073.

Côté, J., Salmela, J.H., Trudel, P., Baria, A. and Russell, S. (1995) 'The coaching model: A grounded assessment of expert gymnastic coaches' knowledge', *Journal of Sport and Exercise Psychology*, 17: 1–17.

Côté, J., Young, B., North, J. and Duffy, P. (2007) 'Towards a definition of excellence in sport coaching', *International Journal of Coaching Science*, 1: 3–18.

Cushion, C.J., Armour, K.M. and Jones, R.L. (2003) 'Coach education and continuing professional development: Experience and learning to coach', *Quest*, 55: 215–230.

Dodds, P. (1994) 'Cognitive and behavioral components of expertise in teaching physical Education', *Quest*, 46: 153–163.

Erickson, E., Bruner, M.W., MacDonald, D.J. and Côté, J. (2008) 'Gaining insights into actual and preferred sources of coaching knowledge', *International Journal of Sports Science and Coaching*, 3: 527–538.

Erickson, K., Côté, J. and Fraser-Thomas, J. (2007) 'Sport activities, milestones, and educational experiences associated with high-performance coaches' development', *The Sport Psychologist*, 21: 302–316.

Ericsson, K.A. (2003) 'Development of elite performance and deliberate practice: an update from the perspective of the expert performance approach', in J.L. Starkes and K.A. Ericsson (eds) *Expert Performance in Sport: Recent Advances in Research on Sport Expertise*, Champaign, IL: Human Kinetics.

Ericsson, K.A., Krampe, R.Th. and Tesch-Römer, C. (1993) 'The role of deliberate practice in the acquisition of expert performance', *Psychological Review*, 100: 363–406.

Ford, P., Coughlan, E. and Williams, M. (2009) 'The expert-performance approach as a framework for understanding and enhancing coaching performance, expertise and learning', *International Journal of Sports Science and Coaching*, 4: 451–463.

Gilbert, W.D. and Trudel, P. (2001) 'Learning to coach through experience: Reflection in model youth sport coaches', *Journal of Teaching in Physical Education*, 21: 16–34.

Gilbert, W.D., Côté, J. and Mallett, C. (2006) 'Development paths and activities of successful sport coaches', *International Journal of Sports Science and Coaching*, 1: 69–75.

Helsen, W. and Starkes, J.L. (1999) 'A multidimensional approach to skilled perception and performance in sport', *Applied Cognitive Psychology*, 13: 1–27.

Hodges, N.J. and Starkes, J.L. (1996) 'Wrestling with the nature of expertise: A sport specific test of Ericsson, Krampe and Tesch-Römer's theory of deliberate practice', *International Journal of Sport Psychology*, 27: 400–424.

Imwold, C.H. and Hoffman, S.J. (1983) 'Visual recognition of a gymnastics skill by experienced and inexperienced instructors', *Research Quarterly for Exercise and Sport*, 54: 149–155.

Irwin, G., Hanton, S. and Kerwin, D.G. (2004) 'Reflective practice and the origins of the elite coaching knowledge', *Reflective Practice*, 5: 425–442.

Jones, D.F., Housner, L.D. and Kornspan, A.S. (1997) 'Interactive decision making and behaviour of experienced and inexperienced basketball coaches during practice', *Journal of Teaching in Physical Education*, 16: 454–468.

Kalinowski, A.G. (1985) 'The development of Olympic swimmers', in B.S. Bloom (ed.) *Developing Talent in Young People*, New York: Ballantine.

Koh, K.T., Mallett, C.J. and Wang, C.K.J. (2011) 'Developmental pathways of Singapore's high performance basketball coaches', *International Journal of Sport and Exercise Psychology*, 9: 338–353.

Lynch, M. and Mallett, C. (2006) 'Becoming a successful high performance track and field coach', *Modern Athlete and Coach*, 44: 15–20.

Mallett, C. and Côté, J. (2006) 'Beyond winning and losing: Guidelines for evaluating high performance coaches', *The Sport Psychologist*, 20: 213–218.

Mallett, C.J., Trudel, P., Lyle, J. and Rynne, S.B. (2009) 'Formal vs informal coach education', *International Journal of Sports Science and Coaching*, 4: 325–341.

Nelson, L.J., Cushion, C.J. and Potrac, P. (2006) 'Formal, nonformal and informal coach learning: A holistic conceptualisation', *International Journal of Sports Science and Coaching*, 1: 247–259.

Petrakis, E. (1987) 'Analysis of visual search patterns of dance teachers', *Journal of Teaching in Physical Education*, 6: 149–156.

Rutt Leas, R. and Chi, M.T.H. (1993) 'Analyzing diagnostic expertise of competitive swimming coaches', in J.L. Starkes and F. Allard (eds) *Cognitive Issues in Motor Expertise*, Amsterdam: Elsevier.

Salmela, J.H. (1995) 'Learning from the development of expert coaches', *Coaching and Sport Science Journal*, 1: 3–13.

Schempp, P.G., McCullick, B., St. Pierre, P., Woorons, S., You, J. and Clark, B. (2004) 'Expert golf instructors' student-teacher interaction patterns', *Research Quarterly for Exercise and Sport*, 75: 60–70.

Schinke, R.J., Bloom, G. and Salmela, J.H. (1995) 'The career stages of elite Canadian basketball coaches', *Avante*, 1: 48–62.

Trudel, P. and Gilbert, W. (2006) 'Coaching and coach education', in D. Kirk, D. Macdonald and M. O'Sullivan (eds) *The Handbook of Physical Education*, London: Sage.

Ward, P., Hodges, N.J., Williams, A.M. and Starkes, J.L. (2004) 'Deliberate practice and expert performance: defining the path to excellence', in A.M. Williams and N.J. Hodges (eds) *Skill Acquisition in Sport: Research, Theory and Practice*, New York: Routledge.

Werthner, P. and Trudel, P. (2006) 'A new theoretical perspective for understanding how coaches learn to coach', *The Sport Psychologist*, 20: 198–212.

Werthner, P. and Trudel, P. (2009) 'Investigating the idiosyncratic learning paths of elite Canadian coaches', *International Journal of Sports Science and Coaching*, 4: 433–449.

Young, B.W. and Salmela, J.H. (2010) 'Examination of practice activities related to the acquisition of elite performance in Canadian middle distance running', *International Journal of Sport Psychology*, 41: 73–90.

Young, B.W., Jemczyk, K., Brophy, K. and Côté, J. (2009) 'Discriminating skilled coaching groups: quantitative examination of developmental experiences and activities', *International Journal of Sports Science and Coaching*, 4: 397–414.

Young, B.W., Jemczyk, K. and Washington, M. (2007) 'Quantifying the activities associated with the incremental development of coaches in Canadian track and field', report presented to the Coaching Association of Canada and Athletics Canada, April.

36

PSYCHOSOCIAL TRAINING INTERVENTIONS TO PREPARE YOUTH SPORT COACHES

Larry Lauer

MICHIGAN STATE UNIVERSITY, USA

Kristen Dieffenbach

WEST VIRGINIA UNIVERSITY, USA

Introduction

Youth sport coaches are entrusted with a great responsibility to adequately supervise, teach, and lead youth. Indeed, the need for youth sport coaches to be competent is as great as it has ever been. The National Council of Youth Sports (2008) estimates that 44 million youth participate in sport in the United States (US) alone. Are youth sport coaches prepared for these responsibilities? How should we prepare them? These are questions without simple answers since coaches' experiences vary in range from novice to professional teacher (Hammermeister 2009; Hedstrom and Gould 2004) and it is difficult to meet coaches' training needs in a large-scale format and educate enough coaches in a customized approach. Adding to the difficulty is that many coaches in North America are 'walk-ons' and have no training beyond their playing days (Clark 2000; Hedstrom and Gould 2004).

What harm can a volunteer youth sport coach with little training do? Unfortunately, stories of coaches ranting and raving on the sidelines at officials, cheating to win, being critical and mean towards youth athletes, and in some of the worst cases getting in fights and being abusive are all too familiar. Sadly, Engh (2002) noted a large drop-off of youth participation occurs when athletes reach 13 years old, implicating, in part, the contribution of the negative youth sport coaching practices and culture that currently exists. Gould (2009) and Coakley (2008) have argued that youth and high school sport have adopted a professional model of sport/performance ethic where winning and performance are more important than the traditional goals of youth sport: fun, personal, and athletic development.

For every tragic headline of a youth sport coach behaving poorly there are many untold stories of coaches changing the lives of young people. Many athletes talk about how their coach was the most important person in their lives. In fact, a recent survey conducted by the United States Anti-Doping Agency revealed that youth athletes often rank coaches as the number one positive adult influence in their lives (USADA 2011). Youth sport coaches can make a tremendous difference in the lives of youth, teaching life skills and supporting them in their development (Gould *et al.* 2007). The issue at hand – is it mere chance or fortune that a young athlete receives quality coaching in sport? Or can adults be trained to provide coaching that develops great athletes and great people of character?

The purpose of this chapter is to examine the status and impact of research on youth sport coaching education. A review of program intervention research efforts is presented and emerging lines of research and practice are outlined that can positively impact coaches during educational efforts. Ultimately, we challenge the readers to consider that youth sport coaches should be subject to realistic professional training/education expectations.

Youth sport coach-education program evaluations and significant lines of coach intervention research

While the importance of training youth sport coaches is evident, what is not clear is the impact of the efforts being made worldwide. In the United States alone four programs with national footholds in the youth sport coaching domain (American Sport Education Program, National Alliance for Youth Sports, National Federation of High Schools, and Positive Coaching Alliance) have had no published evaluations of program effectiveness. In fact, there has not been research examining the effectiveness of large-scale coaching education programs (Lyle 2007; Smoll and Smith 2002) and very few research interventions. Coaching science has instead been in a formative stage for many years with few researchers developing a line of research. Indeed, 98 percent of coaching research can be labeled as 'one-off' studies (Gilbert and Trudel 2004; Trudel and Gilbert 2006).

Research on large-scale youth sport coach-education programs

Coaching education programs have not been evaluated systematically and published in a refereed journal forum. However, Feltz and colleagues have conducted a line of research evaluating the impact of the Program for Athletic Coaches' Education (PACE) on coach efficacy demonstrating that coaches experience a sense of enhanced efficacy following education (Campbell and Sullivan 2005; Feltz *et al.* 1999; Malete and Feltz 2000). Coaching efficacy is defined as the coach's belief in the ability to affect the learning and performance of his or her athletes (Feltz *et al.* 1999). The coaching efficacy model forwards four dimensions of efficacy: (1) game strategy; (2) motivation; (3) technique; and (4) character building. In turn, coach efficacy in these dimensions is purported to enhance athlete and team outcomes of satisfaction, performance, and efficacy. Research has exhibited that coach efficacy is related to coaching behavior (more praise and instruction than an untrained control group), player satisfaction, current success; and team efficacy (Feltz *et al.* 1999; Myers *et al.* 2005; Vargas-Tonsing *et al.* 2003).

A limitation of the previous research was that it was mostly conducted with paid high school and college coaches. Responding to this, Feltz *et al.* (2009) tested the coaching efficacy scale with 492 volunteer youth sport coaches. The authors found an acceptable fit for using the coaching efficacy scale with a youth sport coach population. Further, the results revealed that coaches with more athletic and coaching experience were more confident. However, this study did not measure coach perceptions post-training.

In summary, coaching efficacy is an active line of research revealing that coaches do benefit from participation in formal coach education. It is inferred that a more efficacious coach will be a more effective coach. However, this link has not been confirmed (Trudel and

Gilbert 2006). Moreover, an increase in self-efficacy post-education may be short lived. Maintenance studies have not been conducted to show if coaches maintain a higher level of efficacy over time nor how it impacts those being coached (Trudel *et al.* 2010).

Coaching interventions

While coaches may gain confidence from attending a large-scale coaching program, the actual effect of the training on coach behavior has been less studied. Coach interventions have been undertaken that are not part of larger programs. Cassidy *et al.* (2006) evaluated the theory-based coach program CoDe using a community of practice approach with developmental coaches. The coaches found value in the CoDe; specifically, they appreciated the opportunity to communicate with other coaches in a forum-type situation, learn different ways to accommodate for athlete learning styles, and examine the complexities of coaching beyond technical and tactical aspects. In a second coach intervention, Weiss *et al.* (1991) evaluated the Oregon Women in Coaching workshop and coaching internship. The coaches generally felt it was a worthwhile experience. Therefore, coaches are finding benefit from training, if only feeling more confident, but these studies are the exception and not the norm.

The most extensive line of coaching behavior research comes from the Coaching Effectiveness Training (CET) program. A series of studies has exhibited that psychosocial interventions with coaches can have positive effects not only on the coach, but the youth that they lead. The creators of the program attribute success to the fact that CET is easy to learn and has a strong impact (Smoll and Smith 2002).

Smith *et al.* (1979) exhibited the effectiveness of training youth baseball coaches in positive coaching methods of information-modeling, behavioral feedback, and self-monitoring. The trained coaches differed from the control group. Specifically, the trained coaches provided more reinforcement for good performance and effort, responded with more mistake-contingent reinforcement and technical instruction, and fewer punitive responses than the control group coaches. Players liked the trained group coaches more and rated them as better teachers. Interestingly, the athletes with trained coaches also liked each other and enjoyed their sport experience more. Why? The coaches created a socially supportive climate. The benefits do not end there, however. Players with trained coaches had an increase in general self-esteem, while players in the control coach group did not. A limitation of this study was that it did not directly measure sport climate. Nonetheless, it exhibited how coach training could not only influence the coach, but the athlete as well.

These promising results were replicated in a study involving three Little League baseball leagues, 18 coaches, and 152 children (typically ages 9–12). It was also revealed that athletes in the experimental group (i.e. CET) experienced a decrease in performance anxiety, whereas the control group athletes did not (Smoll and Smith 2002). The benefits of CET and a positive, supportive, mastery climate in enhancing self-esteem for those children low in self-esteem were replicated in several additional studies (Coatesworth and Conroy 2006; Smith and Smoll 1990; Smoll *et al.* 1993).

Barnett *et al.* (1992) studied retention rates for these youth the following season. The control group athletes had a dropout rate of 26 percent, while those on trained coach teams had only a 5 percent dropout despite the fact there was no difference in win-loss record between the groups. Thus, children on teams with a positive mastery climate were more likely to return.

Self-efficacy research purports that coaches feel more efficacious about their duties after receiving training. However, the literature lacks interventions designed to enhance coach efficacy (or evaluations of those that exist). Harwood (2008) conducted an intervention that could serve as a template for developing self-efficacy in youth sport coaches. Six coaches working in a professional soccer academy were trained with the goal of enhancing their efficacy to deliver the '5 Cs' to their teams (i.e. commitment, communication, concentration, control, and confidence). While the results were mixed, two coaches did not complete the workshops and those that did were not always willing to implement the advanced skills being taught (e.g. set piece routines, imagery), three of the four coaches experienced meaningful increases in domains that they were less confident about at baseline. The most telling development may have been that in the sessions where coaches focused on creating mastery, socially supportive climates, the athletes were perceived to have elevations in concentration, self-control, and self-confidence. In using this cooperative approach where interpersonal skills were valued and practiced the coaches felt most efficacious when reflecting on their coaching.

In summary, there are very few lines of consistent coach intervention research, and evaluations of existing coaching education programs do not exist in the literature. Those studies that have been conducted suggest that psychosocial interventions with coaches may be successful. However, the magnitude of change in the coach has been questioned, as has the generalizability of the results (Trudel *et al.* 2010). Another limitation is the lack of maintenance studies to show coaches have changed from the educational experience. Finally, it has been argued that previous research has been too focused on behavioral indices of coach effectiveness (Lyle 2002).

Enhancing the field of youth sport coaching science

Despite the paucity of coaching intervention studies there are emerging lines of coaching research that will inform future educational efforts such as research on creating caring team climates (Fry 2010), developing effective leadership styles such as transformational (Callow *et al.* 2009), and effective decision-making (Lyle 2010). First, however, there is a need for coaching effectiveness models to inform coaching education efforts and integrate new areas of coaching science research and application. This includes accounting for the coaching of life skills.

Models of coaching effectiveness

Theoretical models have been designed to provide a comprehensive overview of coaching effectiveness. Horn (2008) presented a comprehensive and general model of coaching effectiveness that is excellent for coaching scientists. It accounts for the complexity of coaching in a socio-cultural, organizational context that also considers coach and athlete characteristics, perceptions, and behaviors. However, in practice, it does not provide coaches the 'how to' coach or enough specifics to necessarily guide coaching education or the coaching process. Hence, it is useful to researchers but maybe not as much for practitioners. Lyle (2002) made an impressive effort to provide a comprehensive coaching process model that covers the complexity of coaching. The issue is that it is so complex and has so many working parts, thus being ecologically valid, but hard to use in practice. Côté and Gilbert (2009) also provide a more coaching specific model to both understand and potentially develop coaching effectiveness and expertise. Basically, the coaching process was organized into three elements related to coach effectiveness: (1) coaching knowledge; (2) athlete outcomes; and (3) coaching contexts. Coaching knowledge consists of professional knowledge, interpersonal knowledge; and self- or intrapersonal knowledge. Competence, confidence, connection; and character define athlete outcomes. And, coaching contexts consists of two areas – participation and performance based coaching contexts. The authors offer the framework both as a potential template for developing coaching education programs as well as for conducting more meaningful and specific research to evaluate the impact of current coaching education models.

Coaching life skills

As models of coaching effectiveness evolve there has been more attention on holistic athlete development. This is important as personal and athletic development should not be considered separate. Moreover, society expects that involvement in youth sports provides life skills and develops desirable adult qualities such as determination, focus, and positive social skills. However, we know that sport participation alone does not provide these growth opportunities; it is only through a thoughtful environment created by the coach (Conroy 2006; Smith *et al.* 2007). As such, many programs seek to provide this training. Unfortunately, no peer reviewed research focuses on the effectiveness of such training.

Perhaps because too much emphasis is placed on performance coaching and not enough on the role that a coach has in positively developing youth, the potentially positive things that coaches are doing have been overlooked and under studied. Relatively few studies have examined the behaviors and philosophies of youth sport coaches who are having positive community impact. Preliminary evidence reveals that coaches who are purposefully attempting to teach life skills have success. For instance, Gould *et al.* (2007) demonstrated, via interviews with football coaches known for developing youth, that these coaches used multiple strategies for teaching life skills including making this strategy a priority and developing good relationships with their athletes. A model for coaching life skills was forwarded that accounted not only for the coach and the coach's philosophy, but also the athlete and the team environment. Recently, Gould and Carson (2010) exhibited a correlation between coaching actions and positive youth development. Therefore, it seems that coaches can directly and indirectly develop youth. However, we need to know more about how they do it, and then implement a model of coaching life skills like the one forwarded by Gould *et al.* (2006) to train coaches to teach life skills and character.

Practical models of coaching to enhance coaching education efforts

While the psychosocial and pedagogical models of coaching provide a framework for preparing young athletes, modern coaching is also supported by the numerous developing sport science fields such as sports nutrition, sport psychology, exercise physiology, and motor learning. Ultimately, quality coaching is much more than just coaching style or delivery and must be based on science (Lyle 1999, 2002). However, to date, performance-related science, while useful, is inexact and many coaches are unclear on where to gain this knowledge (Reade *et al.* 2008). Further, Stone *et al.* (2004) have lamented the lack of science to 'application' in the American coaching model and in the systematic preparation and evaluation of sport training plans. A potential solution may be to frame the coach's role within long-term athlete development models (e.g. Balyi *et al.* 2005; Bloom 1985; Côté *et al.* 2007). Talent development models focus on athlete growth for lifetime physical literacy and performance, and can provide potential practical and applied guidelines for coaching education programs. These models would help coaches see how their development and knowledge of the sport sciences would benefit not only the athletes they lead, but also their respective sports.

Even at the youngest ages, routine practice is viewed as a central part of sport. Practices are designed with an emphasis on fitness and skills. Given the common player to coach model of entry into coaching (Cushion *et al.* 2003), youth practices often inappropriately emulate higher level sport practices likely because coaches coach as they have been coached. Age-appropriate talent and performance development requires level-appropriate development planning, evaluation, and adjustment. Many coaches, particularly youth sport coaches, are under equipped and poorly prepared to develop season and daily training plans that are developmentally appropriate. Models such as Bloom's (1985) phases of talent development and more complex conceptualizations such as Côté *et al.* (2007) Developmental Model of Sports Participation (DMSP) and the Long Term Athlete Development Model (LTAD) (Balyi *et al.* 2005) provide possible frameworks for examining the age-appropriate skills and coaching behaviors required to facilitate true physical as well as psychosocial growth and development. Research (e.g. Durand-Bush and Salmela 2002; Gould *et al.* 2002) has used Bloom's (1985) framework of introductory years, middle learning years and elite high-performing years to examine athlete talent development have suggested coaches play a specific role in each stage. Empirical studies have not yet been conducted to examine coach contribution and effectiveness within other talent development models.

Barriers to successful coach education

So, why has formal coaching education had minimal impact? Currently, large gaps exist between the needs and preferences of the coaches, the needs and wants of the associations in charge of educating coaches, and the current standards of coach training (NASPE 2006). Educational efforts may not be focused on what coaches want because they do not necessarily view sport sciences training as relevant to their personal development. While coach preferences are important to consider, so too is the youth sport context. The recognition of the key educational and teaching roles of the coach (Wikeley and Bullock 2006) should inform the discussion and examination of how best to coach the coaches. Recently, Jones (2006) has suggested that coaching education benefits from understanding and incorporation of the concepts and theories of education and pedagogy. For example, the struggles and efforts of related professions, such as the issue of subjective warrants (i.e. teaching informed by the current climate not by philosophy or training) in physical education teacher education (Lawson 1983), could be examined to better understand how to structure coaching education to address preconceived ideas and frameworks of pre-trained coaches.

To facilitate coach development researchers must understand the context within which coaches operate, how coaches learn, and how best to deliver the most important information in a way they will open up to learning and transfer it into practice. Current programs need to be evaluated for effectiveness and recommendations made for enhancing coach development in training interventions based on emerging coaching science research and theory. At the same time, youth sport coaches must value the process of becoming an educated coach and how they belong to a profession that comes with continuing education.

Social learning perspectives

Framing coach education in a social learning perspective has emerged as a common theme in recent coach education literature (Barnson 2010; Bertram and Gilbert 2011; Culver and

Trudel 2006, 2008a, 2008b; Gilbert *et al.* 2009; Nelson *et al.* 2006; Trudel *et al.* 2010). At least three different types of social learning networks have been described in the coach education literature: Networks of Practice, Information Knowledge Networks, and Communities of Practice. Networks of Practice are people whom coaches infrequently interact with and do not know well (e.g. acquaintances at large-scale coach education program). Information Knowledge Networks are individuals that know each other and trust each other to share, but do not work together (e.g. mentor coaches from another school). Finally, Community of Practice indicates individuals that share a common interest or passion on a topic and regularly interact with one another (e.g. athletic department).

Ongoing professional development is certainly worthy of development and evaluation. Routinely coaches report appreciating the opportunity to communicate with other coaches about sport issues (Cassidy *et al.* 2006). If coaches feel more involved in their development, instead of being forced to go to a weekend clinic, the potential for enhancing the professionalism and training of youth sport coaches would exist. In what was considered a pilot community of practice approach, Cassidy *et al.* (2006) evaluated the theory-based coach program CoDe with eight rugby developmental coaches. While classroom based, the coaches perceived benefits from viewing the athlete as a learner, engaging in a reflective process which enhanced their confidence, and enjoyed talking with other coaches. This study provides preliminary evidence that a community of practice approach can be successful. Still, there is a need to implement and conduct a process and product evaluation of Gilbert *et al.*'s (2009) assertions that there are five key elements for creating an effective community of practice in youth sport: (1) stable settings dedicated to instruction and learning; (2) job-alike teams; (3) published protocols that guide but do not prescribe; (4) trained peer facilitators; and (5) working on athlete learning goals until there are tangible gains in athlete development. Bertram and Gilbert (2011) attempted to implement communities of practice in three different sport settings with limited success but were unable to evaluate it fully. The community of practice model has potential but has to be implemented in multiple settings and evaluated.

How best to educate youth sport coaches

Communities of practice have the potential to provide the continued education needed by coaches, however, some adjustments may be needed to make it easier to establish at scale. To educate coaches we must meet where they are convening, teach in a way that they learn, and set up environments that make education accessible, engaging, and relevant. Coach education should move from instructor-centered approaches to student-centered; basing the content and the delivery on coach needs (and the needs of the athletes they coach) and how best to engage them. These are the best recommendations we have read to meet the aims of making youth sport coaching a profession and creating the interest in coaches to develop their expertise because they are realistic and supplement large-scale coaching education.

To develop continuing education as a valued and integral part of youth sport coaching Gilbert *et al.* (2009) recommend first to conduct continuing education at stable settings of games, practices, and league meetings because of a concern of asking too much of these volunteer coaches. These conversations could be peer lead in groups based on age, skill level, and of course, sport, which would meet the conditions of job-alike teams and being coach-led. Questions could be posed by coaches and discussed thus creating relevancy because learning would happen in setting. The value of sport sciences and formal education could be identified by coaches in their search for answers. League administrators could make available resources and educational trainings could help resolve the dilemmas that the 'coach team' is discussing.

In communities of practice coaches are empowered to take control of the learning process thus enhancing their motivation for continued education. Empowerment comes from creating flexible guidelines that give the coaches enough structure to engage in the process of learning from their experiences, but yet keeps the coach in control of the learning experience. Instead of being a 'top-down' model where league directors or an educator directs the coaches on what they should do, the student-centered approach would allow coaches to select a facilitator from their group to move them towards their educational goals. The coaching director, league administrator, or supervisor could train the coach facilitator to lead the group towards reaching their goals.

The community of practice approach is intriguing but may be too radical for some and still asking too much in terms of commitment from others. Furthermore, it assumes coaches will want to talk about issues and collaborate with other coaches which may fly in the face of the competitive environment of many organizations. An intermediate approach would include training the administrator to provide continuing education as a supplement to formal coaching workshops and as facilitators of continuing professional development. Training of coaches is thought of in a systemic fashion. Administrators recruit coaches who fit the philosophy of the program and are willing to learn. One or more workshops are held that are coach-centered and engage the coaches in dialogue with other coaches about problems and solutions (i.e. using the community of practice guidelines). In these sessions, coaches could be introduced to a coaching model as well as LTAD to create a structure in which to elicit questions and ideas. Coaches are then asked to assess themselves, create personal action plans, and report to the administrator on the action strategies and progress. Administrators would observe coaches and provide feedback based on the action plan. Concurrently, the administrator would send reminders and new resources to coaches like the 'tip of the week' with the rationale of following up on the workshop and looking for change in the coach's practices. While this approach is more administrator-facilitated, it treats coaching as a system that involves the administrator in evaluation of coaching development versus relying on the commitment of volunteers or coaches that are paid little for coaching.

It is important to have administrators create communities of practice continually emphasizing the importance of the professional coach role, with standards and responsibilities that include continual education. As we have recommended here, helping coaches see their role in terms of the development of athletes over time (i.e. LTAD) can potentially incite them to strive for more education.

Future directions in the evaluation of youth sport coaching education programs

Evaluation of innovative efforts to train coaches, such as Gilbert *et al.*'s (2009) community of practice approach, must occur to identify if education is making a difference. At this time little research has been conducted to evaluate programs, let alone evaluate components of these programs. Professional frameworks, such as described by Côté and Gilbert (2009) and Gilbert and Trudel's (1999) coach education evaluation case study can be used as a template for evaluation. The recent trend of studying coaching in context and in its complexity is promising and makes us believe that many breakthroughs will occur in the next decade. To hopefully guide future research here is a listing of the nine most pertinent issues that we believed should be addressed.

1   Does large-scale formal coaching education influence attitudinal and behavioral change in coaches; and does it then impact the athlete? Can researchers link education to coach learning to coach practice to athlete outcomes?

2   Models of coaching effectiveness need to be tested, refined, and then used as ways to conceptualize the coaching process and how to help coaches understand the complexity of their role. Valid models should be used in the development and refinement of coaching programs.

3   Do more effective approaches that can be taken to scale exist? Do large-scale programs inherently suffer from being competency-based and not necessarily meet the needs of the individual coach? How effective is online coaching education as well as hybrid programs (i.e. face-to-face mixed with online education) in an effort to educate the masses? Are current training methods worth the cost?

4   How can educators persuade youth sport coaches of the value of coaching education, particularly training that includes psychosocial development, as a lifelong continual undertaking? In what ways do coaches best learn and then transfer learning to practice? How can we teach programs in ways that coaches enjoy and are motivated to attend in the future? Researchers should study the community of practice intervention and the alternative approach suggested in this chapter. Ultimately we need to know if these models enhance the motivation of coaches to be continual learners.

5   If coach efficacy and CET training are expected to create positive outcomes interventions to enhance coaches' efficacy in using positive communication styles should be implemented and outcomes for athletes measured as well. For example, is it more likely that a confident coach creates a positive motivational climate? Harwood's (2008) intervention with academy coaches suggests that this could happen.

6   A need exists to evaluate current programs and make recommendations for improvement. Full-scale process and product evaluations of current programs from recruitment to athlete learning and satisfaction are needed. Researchers should heed Coatesworth and Conroy's (2006) recommendation to conduct randomized, controlled studies of coach education while also using qualitative methods to understand the complexity and richness of the coaching process.

7   There is a need to conduct studies that link coaching practices to positive youth development outcomes such as leadership, work ethic, responsibility, and initiative (Horn 2008).

8   Horn (2008) also recommends studying other dimensions of coaching behavior including nonverbal behavior, communication and coordination capabilities, coach–athlete interactions and relationships, coaches' cognitions, perceptions, and decision-making processes, and coaches' ability to clarify team roles. Research in these areas and others (such as best ways to conduct tryouts or communicating with parents) may provide the relevant information that would attract coaches to coaching education.

9   Coaching educators need to reach across disciplines to learn from related fields such as physical education and pedagogy to ensure the teaching aspects of coaching are taught and reinforced. Coaching education research would be strengthened by related research to examine how these constructs work in the coaching education environment.

Conclusion

Currently, the education and preparation of youth sport coaches is undervalued, underserved, and poorly understood. Youth sport coaching interventions and evaluations of coaching programs are seriously lacking. At this time educators do not know if coaching education initiatives actually change coaches' behaviors, attitudes, and cognitions, and most certainly are unclear if educational efforts influence the athlete.

Sport administrators and coaches need to view coaching as a profession that has continued education as a fundamental part of the process. Youth sport coaching is more than *x*'s and *o*'s and more than a hobby. Youth deserve educated coaches that create positive, mastery climates and can develop athletic skills and character. Education for youth sport administrators and coaches regarding the elements and benefits of healthy talent development, and the critical roles and responsibilities of coaches within this model, are necessary to facilitate a change in the current outcome-focused climate. Youth sport coaching should be treated as a profession – one deserving training programs backed by science that supports its current practices and values coach engagement. Understanding the multidisciplinary needs of coaching and how a multidisciplinary profession is best taught should inform future education. Coaching education programmers, administrators, and coaching directors must strive to develop coaches to be experts. It does not happen on one Saturday or over five clinics in a year. It is an interactive process where a coach learns from reading, watching video, going to camps and clinics, and then goes back and experiments, and reflects upon, his or her practice. While the worldwide passion for sport and the opportunities for youth sport participation continue to grow, a research-based understanding of best practices both for coaching practices and for the education of coaches lags far behind. Much remains to be explored and both the profession of coaching and ultimately, the youth sport athletes themselves, stand to benefit from continued development of holistic and cross-discipline-based coaching education programs.

References

Balyi, I., Way, R., Norris, S., Cardinal, C. and Higgs, C. (2005) *Canadian Sport for Life: Long-Term Athlete Development Resource Paper*, Vancouver, BC: Canadian Sport Centres.

Barnett, N.P., Smoll, F.L. and Smith, R.E. (1992) 'Effects of enhancing coach–athlete relationship on youth sport attrition,' *The Sport Psychologist*, 6(2): 111–127.

Barnson, S.C. (2010) 'Communities of coaches: The missing link,' *Journal of Physical Education, Recreation and Dance*, 81(7): 25–29, 37.

Bertram, R. and Gilbert, W. (2011) 'Learning communities as continuing professional development for sport coaches,' *Journal of Coaching Education*, 4: 40–61.

Bloom, B.S. (1985) *Developing Talent in Young People*, New York: Ballantine.

Callow, N., Smith, M.J., Hardy, L., Arthur, C.A. and Hardy, J. (2009) 'Measurement of transformational leadership and its relationship with team cohesion and performance level,' *Journal of Applied Sport Psychology*, 21(4): 395–412.

Campbell, T. and Sullivan, P. (2005) 'The effect of standardized coaching education program on the efficacy of novice coaches,' *Avante*, 11(1): 38–45.

Cassidy, T., Potrac, P. and McKenzie, A. (2006) 'Evaluating and reflecting upon a coach education initiative: The CoDe of rugby,' *The Sport Psychologist*, 20(2): 145–161.

Clark, M.A. (2000) 'Who's coaching the coaches?' in J.R. Gerdy (ed.) *Sports in Schools: The Future of an Institution*, New York: Teacher's College Press.

Coakley, J. (2008) *Sport in Society: Issues and controversies*, 10th edn, New York: McGraw-Hill.

Coatesworth, J.D. and Conroy, D.E. (2006) 'Enhancing the self-esteem of youth swimmers through coach training: Gender and age effects,' *Psychology of Sport and Exercise*, 7(2): 173–192.

Conroy, D.E. (2006) 'Enhancing motivation in sport,' *Psychological Science Agenda*, 20(2), online, available at: www.apa.org/science/about/psa/2006/02/conroy.aspx.

Côté, J. and Gilbert, W. (2009) 'An integrative definition of coaching effectiveness and expertise,' *International Journal of Sport Science and Coaching*, 4(3): 307–314.

Côté, J., Young, B., North, J. and Duffy, P. (2007) 'Towards a definition of excellence in coaching,' *International Journal of Coaching Science*, 1(1): 3–16.

Culver, D. and Trudel, P. (2006) 'Cultivating coaches' communities of practice: Developing the potential for learning through interactions,' in R.L. Jones (ed.) *The Sports Coach as Educator: Re-conceptualising Sports Coaching*, London: Routledge.

Culver, D. and Trudel, P. (2008a) 'Clarifying the concept of communities of practice in sport,' *International Journal of Sport Science and Coaching*, 3(1): 1–10.

Culver, D. and Trudel, P. (2008b) 'Clarifying the concept of communities of practice in sport: A response to commentaries,' *International Journal of Sport Science and Coaching*, 3(1): 29–32.

Cushion, C.J., Armour, K.M. and Jones, R.L. (2003) 'Coach education and continuing professional development: Experience and learning to coach,' *Quest*, 55(3): 215–230.

Durand-Bush, N. and Salmela, J.H. (2002) 'The development and maintenance of expert athletic performance: Perceptions of World and Olympic champions,' *Journal of Applied Sport Psychology*, 14(3): 154–171.

Engh, F. (2002) *Why Johnny Hates Sports*, Garden City Park, NY: Square One Publishers.

Feltz, D.L., Chase, M.A., Moritz, S.E. and Sullivan P.J. (1999) 'Conceptual model of coaching efficacy: Preliminary investigations and instrument development,' *Journal of Educational Psychology*, 91(4): 765–776.

Feltz, D.L., Hepler, T.J., Roman, N. and Paiement, C. (2009) 'Coaching efficacy and volunteer youth sport coaches,' *The Sport Psychologist*, 23: 24–41.

Fry, M.D. (2010) 'Creating a positive climate for young athletes from Day 1,' *Journal of Sport Psychology in Action*, 1(1): 33–41.

Gilbert, W. and Trudel, P. (1999) 'An evaluation strategy for coach education programs,' *Journal of Sport Behavior*, 2(2): 234–250.

Gilbert, W. and Trudel, P. (2004) 'Analysis of coaching science research published from 1970–2001,' *Research Quarterly for Exercise and Sport*, 75(4): 388–399.

Gilbert, W., Gallimore, R. and Trudel, P. (2009) 'A learning community to approach to coach development in youth sport,' *Journal of Coaching Education*, 2(2): 1–21.

Gould, D. (2009) 'The professionalisation of youth sports: It's time to act!' *Clinical Journal of Sport Medicine*, 19(2): 81–2.

Gould, D. and Carson, S. (2010) 'The relationship between perceived coaching behaviors and developmental benefits of high school sports participation,' *The Hellenic Journal of Psychology*, 7(3): 298–314.

Gould, D., Collins, K., Lauer, L. and Chung, Y. (2006) 'Coaching life skills: A working model,' *Sport and Exercise Psychology Review*, 2(1): 4–12.

Gould, D., Collins, K., Lauer, L. and Chung, Y. (2007) 'Coaching life skills through football: A study of award winning high school coaches,' *Journal of Applied Sport Psychology*, 19(1): 16–38.

Gould, D., Dieffenbach, K. and Moffett, A. (2002) 'Psychological characteristics and their development in Olympic champions,' *Journal of Applied Sport Psychology*, 14(3): 172–204.

Hammermeister, J. (2009) *Cornerstones of Coaching: The Building Blocks of Success for Sport Coaches and Teams*, Traverse City, MI: Cooper Publishing.

Harwood, C. (2008) 'Developmental consulting in a professional football academy: The 5Cs Coaching Efficacy Program,' *The Sport Psychologist*, 22(1): 109–33.

Hedstrom, R. and Gould, D. (2004) 'Research in youth sports: Critical issues status,' online, available at: www.educ.msu.edu/ysi/past_projects.htm (accessed December 24 2010).

Horn, T. (2008) 'Coaching effectiveness in the sport domain,' in T. Horn (ed.) *Advances in Sport Psychology*, 3rd edn, Champaign, IL: Human Kinetics.

Jones, R.L. (2006) 'How can educational concepts inform sports coaching?' in R.L. Jones (ed.) *The Sports Coach as Educator: Re-conceptualising Sports Coaching*, London: Routledge.

Lawson, H.A. (1983) 'Toward a model of teacher socialization in physical education: The subjective warrant, recruitment, and teacher education,' *Journal of Teaching in Physical Education*, 2(3): 3–17.

Lyle, J. (1999) 'The coaching process: An overview,' in N. Cross and J. Lyle (eds) *The Coaching Process: Principles and Practice for Sport*, Oxford: Butterworth-Heinemann.

Lyle, J. (2002) *Sports Coaching Concepts: A Framework for Coaches' Behavior*, London: Routledge.

Lyle, J. (2007) 'A review of the research evidence for the impact of coach education,' *International Journal of Coaching Science*, 1(1): 19–36.

Lyle, J. (2010) 'Coaches' decision making: A naturalistic decision making analysis,' in J. Lyle and C. Cushion (eds) *Sports Coaching: Professionalisation and Practice*, London: Elsevier.

Malete, L. and Feltz, D.L. (2000) 'The effect of a coaching education program on coaching efficacy,' *The Sports Psychologist*, 14(4): 410–417.

Myers, N.D., Vargas-Tonsing, T.M. and Feltz, D.L. (2005) 'Coaching efficacy in intercollegiate coaches: Sources, coaching behavior, and team variables,' *Psychology of Sport and Exercise*, 6(1): 129–143.

NASPE (National Association for Sport and Physical Education) (2006) *Quality Coaches, Quality Sports: National Standards for Sport Coaches*, 2nd edn, Reston, VA: AAHPERD.

National Council of Youth Sports (2008) 'Report on trends and participation in organized youth sports,' online, available at: www.ncys.org/publications/2008-sports-participation-study.php.

Nelson, L.J., Cushion, C.J. and Potrac, P. (2006) 'Formal, nonformal and informal coach learning: A holistic conceptualisation,' *International Journal of Sports Science and Coaching*, 1(3): 247–259.

Reade, I., Rodgers, W. and Spriggs, K. (2008) 'New ideas for high performance coaches: A case study of knowledge transfer in sport science,' *International Journal of Sport Science and Coaching*, 3(3): 335–55.

Smith, R.E. and Smoll, F.L. (1990) 'Self-esteem and children's reactions to youth sport coaching: A field study of self enhancement processes,' *Developmental Psychology*, 26(6): 987–993.

Smith, R.E., Smoll, F.L. and Cumming, S.P. (2007) 'Effects of motivational climate intervention for coaches on young athletes' sport performance anxiety,' *Journal of Sport and Exercise Psychology*, 29(1): 39–59.

Smith, R.E., Smoll, F.L. and Curtis, B. (1979) 'Coach effectiveness training: A cognitive-behavioral approach to enhancing relationship skills in youth sport coaches,' *Journal of Sport Psychology*, 1(1): 59–75.

Smoll, F.L. and Smith, R.E. (2002) *Children in Youth Sport: A Biopsychosocial Perspective*, Boston, MA: McGraw-Hill.

Smoll, F.L., Smith, R.E., Barnett, N.P. and Everett, J.J. (1993) 'Enhancement of children's self-esteem through social support training for youth sport coaches,' *Journal of Applied Psychology*, 78(4): 602–610.

Stone, M.H, Sands, W.A. and Stone, M.E. (2004) 'The downfall of sports science in the United States,' *Strength and Conditioning Journal*, 26(2): 72–75.

Trudel, P. and Gilbert, W. (2006) 'Coaching and coach education,' in D. Kirk, D. McDonald and M. O'Sullivan (eds) *Handbook of Physical Education*, London: Sage.

Trudel, P., Gilbert, W. and Werthner, P. (2010) 'Coach education effectiveness,' in J. Lyle and C. Cushion (eds) *Sport Coaching: Professionalisation and Practice*, London: Elsevier.

Vargas-Tonsing, T.M., Warners, A.L. and Feltz, D.L. (2003) 'The predictability of coaching efficacy on team efficacy and player efficacy in volleyball,' *Journal of Sport Behavior*, 26(4): 396–407.

USADA (United States Anti-Doping Agency) (2011) 'What sport means in America: A study of sport's role in society,' *Journal of Coaching Education*, 4(1): 2–44.

Weiss, M.R., Barber, H., Sisely, B.L. and Ebbeck, V. (1991) 'Developing competence and confidence in novice female coaches: II. Perceptions of ability and affective experiences following a season-long coaching internship,' *Journal of Sport and Exercise Psychology*, 13(4): 336–363.

Wikeley, F. and Bullock, K. (2006) 'Coaching as an educational relationship,' in R.L. Jones (ed.) *The Sports Coach as Educator: Re-conceptualising Sports Coaching*, London: Routledge.

37

DEVELOPING HIGH PERFORMANCE COACHING CRAFT THROUGH WORK AND STUDY

Clifford J. Mallett

UNIVERSITY OF QUEENSLAND, AUSTRALIA

Steven B. Rynne

UNIVERSITY OF QUEENSLAND, AUSTRALIA

Sue Dickens

UNIVERSITY OF QUEENSLAND, AUSTRALIA

Introduction: background and aims

The ongoing quest for elite athletes to produce world best performances at major international competitions, such as the Olympics, has generally required talented athletes to be better prepared (e.g. physically, mentally, tactically) than their opponents. This desire for success in the sporting arena has become increasingly international and a key driver in the pursuit for excellence. High performance coaches are considered central to the development of successful elite athletes (Lyle 2002). These coaches are usually purported to lead and manage the coaching process in facilitating athletes' (and nations') goals for international glory. Key questions include: (1) How might coaches guide the development of athletes in the pursuit of excellence? and (2) How do high performance coaches learn their craft? For the purposes of this chapter, we are more interested in the second question. The development of coaches is key to improving the quality of high performance sports coaching (Mallett *et al.* 2009) and in turn, how athletes experience that coaching (Armour 2010; Mallett 2011). Hence, the development of high performance coaches is central to optimising the coach–athlete–performance relationship (Mallett 2010). Findings from research examining how high performance coaches learn can guide future development opportunities. Specifically, an appropriate mix of formal (e.g. university or higher education), nonformal (e.g. conferences, workshops) and informal (e.g. coaches' work, social networks) modes of learning (Coombs and Ahmed 1974; Mallett *et al.* 2009; Nelson *et al.* 2006) can meaningfully contribute to coaches' continuing professional development.

In this chapter, we consider the development of high performance coaches. Specifically, our discussion will revolve around two key 'spaces' where development is said to occur – coaching workplaces, which are highly contested, complex environments; and more recently, through engagement in university (tertiary or higher education) programs of study on sports coaching. In the first section, an examination of what coaches do will underscore the multifaceted nature of this work. In the second section, a review of the literature on high performance coaches' sources of development will emphasise two key sources of learning – in the workplace (informal) and through university education (formal). This discussion will highlight what we know and what are some of the limitations of our current knowledge and understanding. In the third section, we present some thoughts on future lines of enquiry, including theories and concepts that might inform such work and methodologies to explore and promote understanding. Moreover, a consideration of the translation of research and theory to practice will provide some practical benefits to those responsible for high performance coach development. Finally, some concluding comments on the development of high performance coaches will highlight some key insights and understandings.

High performance coaching work

As previously alluded to, research has shown that coaches have the powerful and unique potential to influence athlete development (Côté *et al.* 2010). Associated with this influence is the notion that high performance coach development is central to the enhancement of the coach–athlete–performance relationship (Lyle 2002). Given the perceived importance of coaches to athlete performance, it is not surprising that there has been an historical interest in sports coaches. Indeed, the great majority of empirical literature on coaching has pertained to what coaches do (that is, their coaching behaviours), with this type of research comprising up to 75 percent of the total coaching literature from 1970–2001 (Gilbert 2002). While this information certainly provides some basic understanding about the behaviours of coaches, it is reductionistic and heavily informed by the behaviourist tradition. This recipe of appropriate behaviours has the potential to oversimplify the work of the coach and reduce their role to that of 'technician'. Furthermore, this perspective also fails to recognise that there are 'other ways of doing things' and indeed, there is much variation in what constitutes modern high performance coaching work (Mallett 2010).

It is clear then that high performance coaching work is not simple. It is a dynamic process involving the interaction of a multitude of variables leading authors to describe high performance coaching work as 'structured improvisation' (Cushion *et al.* 2006) and to highlight its 'chaotic' nature (Bowes and Jones 2006). Much of the acknowledgement of the complexity and dynamism inherent in coaching has been as a result of researcher engagement with qualitative methodologies (e.g. ethnographies). Such work and the resultant theorisations have led to more textured accounts of what constitutes coaching. As a result of these more thorough depictions of coaching it has become possible to make distinctions between types of coaching. In this chapter, we focus on 'high performance sports coaching' which, in contrast to other forms of coaching, involves the highest levels of athlete and coach commitment, public performance objectives, intensive commitment to the development and implementation of programs, highly structured and formalised competitions, typically full-time work, heavy emphasis on decision-making and data management, extensive interpersonal contact, and very demanding and restrictive athlete selection criteria (Lyle 2002; Trudel and Gilbert 2006).

In this section, we propose a model to discuss what encompasses high performance coaching work. Despite the limitations inherent in describing coaches' work in this way (e.g. reductionistic), we felt that if we were to continue to advance the case for 'learning in and through work and study' that it was important to at least attempt to provide some sound reference points regarding what entails coaching work based on empirical research. The categorisations remain sufficiently broad so as to accommodate some of the 'muddiness' of coaching work, but this complexity tends to be obscured by the seemingly neat representations found in Figure 37.1. Similarly, the utility of the model is further limited by representing the model as two-dimensional. In trying to clarify what coaching work entails, a number of researchers have sought to categorise coaching work. We have drawn upon the work of Lyle (2002) and MacLean and Chelladurai (1995) in the design of Figure 37.1 and have incorporated data collected from more than 40 Australian Institute and Academy of Sport (AIA) Coaches over more than five years (Rynne and Mallett in press).

The category of direct task behaviours as described by MacLean and Chelladurai (1995: 199) refers to the 'application of interpersonal skills and appropriate strategies and tactics used to enhance the performance of individual athletes and the team as a whole'. In this way, it is somewhat similar to Lyle's (2002) direct intervention coaching role descriptor. The notable difference is the inclusion of planning and programming in the former whereas Lyle's (2002) conceptualisation includes planning activities in a separate categorisation (intervention support). We advocate including programming in a separate category because although it is acutely related to the performance of the athletes, it is generally performed at a time and place removed from the direct coaching context. We would consider adaptations to programs 'in situ' as being part of hands on coaching craft.

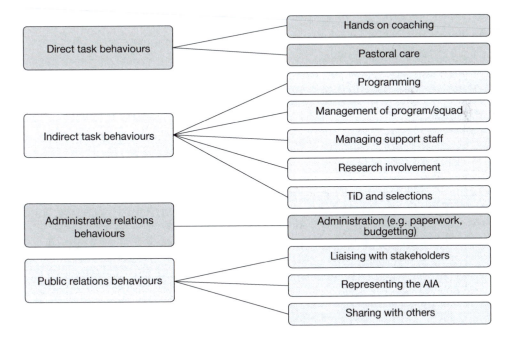

Figure 37.1: Representation of the categories of high performance coaching work.

MacLean and Chelladurai (1995) quite narrowly define indirect task behaviours. We propose a wider conceptualisation, and given the edict of activities that 'contribute indirectly to the success of the program' (MacLean and Chelladurai 1995: 199) it seems appropriate to include the pre-existing talent identification element but also broaden the focus to include management of the program and support staff, research involvement, and programming.

Administrative maintenance behaviours refer to coaches' 'adherence to policies, procedures, and budget guidelines, and interpersonal relations with supervisors and peers that strengthen the administration of the whole enterprise' (MacLean and Chelladurai 1995: 199). Given the governmental and subsequently bureaucratic nature of some AIA operations, this dimension is a particular strength of this model as other models often marginalise or ignore this aspect of coaching work.

The description of public relations behaviours by MacLean and Chelladurai (1995: 199) makes reference to 'liaison activities between one's program and relevant community and peer groups'. We have attempted to apply the perceived intention of those items to the AIA setting. In doing this, we have included a number of the inductive categories including liaising with stakeholders, representing the AIA, and sharing with others.

The interaction of all of these elements of coaching work (as crudely indicated by the interconnections at the far right of Figure 37.1), means that AIA coaches function in a turbulent social world that will affect how they interact, what they attend to, what tasks they engage with, and therefore what and how they learn.

High performance coach sources of development

At international level, the established importance of high performance coaches to the success of national sporting systems (see Rynne *et al.* 2006 for an Australian example) means that there is a pressing need to support the development of high performance coaches. Nonetheless, how coaches develop the skills and capacities to carry out this complex work has not historically gained much attention.

Formal coach accreditation (certification) courses comprise the largest form of coach education present in many Western countries. Reviews and research within the field of high performance sports coaching have acknowledged that these education courses are inadequate for learning what high performance sports coaches need to know (e.g. Dickson 2001; Lynch and Mallett 2006). To date, despite some positive achievements of national coach accreditation systems, it is clear that high performance coaches have developed, and will continue to develop their practice, largely through other means.

As high performance coaching has gradually gained increasing acceptance as a legitimate vocation, there have been associated advancements in education and training (Bales 2006). Nevertheless, it should also be considered that coaching as a vocation is in a period of relative infancy. For this reason, there is a limited foundation of empirical research specifically focussed on high performance coaching. Coaches (as a vocational grouping) appear to develop their craft in idiosyncratic ways (Mallett *et al.* 2007). This serendipitous approach to developing high performance coaching craft might be attributed to the modest contribution of coach education/accreditation programs (Dickson 2001; Trudel and Gilbert 2006), a lack of employment opportunities, limited sharing of information between coaches (Mallett *et al.* 2007), and few established pathways for development and career advancement (Gilbert and Trudel 1999). Moreover, the lack of agreement regarding the most appropriate ways for coaches to develop has arguably contributed to coaches taking personal responsibility to develop their craft. Of interest to coaching science scholars and those responsible for coach education and accreditation (certification) is: how coaches learn their craft in lieu of well-established pathways typical of other vocations and how that knowledge might inform the coach development process in more systemic ways.

Several recent projects have considered the kinds of learning experiences reported by 'successful' or 'high performance' coaches in developing their coaching craft (e.g. Abraham *et al.* 2006; Gilbert *et al.* 2006; Irwin *et al.* 2004; Lynch and Mallett 2006). The analyses and discussions in some of these cited studies (Gilbert *et al.* 2006; Lynch and Mallett 2006) have generally been associated with developing an understanding of 'pathways' that current high performance coaches have taken. While these retrospective accounts are certainly valuable, they are not necessarily accounts of 'best practice' or 'optimal pathways'; they are simply descriptions of what has gone before. Similarly, while they inform the field regarding patterns of *experience* in relation to quantities (e.g. number of hours invested by coaches), there has been limited discussion of the patterns of *learning* experiences that might be considered in relation to the development of effective coaching practices. There is a need to move beyond discussions of quantities of experience to consider the quality of those experiences, whether they were formal, nonformal or informal (Mallett *et al.* 2011). When considering high performance coach development in this vein, it is not enough that coaches engage in coaching work – other conditions are necessary if development is to occur (or at least be more likely to occur).

Learning in and through coaching work: the individual (coach) and the social (workplace)

Current literature suggests that learning in and through coaching work remains the dominant source of coach learning (see Cushion *et al.* 2003; Erickson *et al.* 2008; Irwin *et al.* 2004; Rynne *et al.* 2010). In considering this learning, workplace theorists such as Billett (2004) propose that learning should be viewed as a consequence of everyday thinking and acting, and it is about making sense of the things we encounter throughout our lives. Moreover, a key aspect of workplace learning theory is that neither social suggestion nor individuals' agency alone is sufficient to promote learning and the remaking of the cultural practices that constitute work (Billett *et al.* 2005).

Conceptualising places where high performance coaches work as 'workplaces', coaches learn (or at least have the potential to learn) through interactions with others (e.g. athletes) and non-human artefacts (e.g. budget documents and annual reports). At a basic level, the kinds of work tasks that high performance coaches are responsible for, and have access to, influence what is and is not possible to learn. Those with access to novel and varied tasks will have opportunities to develop in ways that are not possible for those with more restricted responsibilities, that is, those engaged in only routine tasks. Regarding AIA coaches' development through interactions with others, administrative and managerial staff, paraprofessionals, current and former athletes, and coaches within and outside of their sports were all reported to be of value (e.g. Mallett *et al.* 2010; Rynne *et al.* 2010). The AIA coaches engaged with these 'people of influence' in a variety of ways. These mostly shallow professional relationships were dynamic in terms of membership, which tended to be more representative of Dynamic Social Networks (see Mallett 2010; Mallett *et al.* 2007; Occhino *et al.* in press) as opposed to Communities of Practice or other networks (see Allee 2000; Culver and Trudel 2006; Lave and Wenger 1991; Nichani and Hung 2002). It should be considered, however, that not all coaches are afforded equal access to people and resources.

It is acknowledged that situational factors alone are insufficient to understand workplaces as learning environments (Billett 2004). Perceptions of a workplace's value reside with the individual. Often, AIA coach development was contingent upon the strength of personal agency in overcoming a number of potential barriers. The fundamentally competitive elite sport context means that sources that are highly valued by these coaches (e.g. learning from other coaches) are often extremely difficult to access. Interactions are typically guarded and the kinds of generative relationships that coaches require at the high performance level can take years to establish (Mallett *et al.* 2007). For this reason, it is up to the particular coach regarding how persistent and open they will be in fostering these interactions. As a general rule, the more secure and comfortable the coaches felt in their coaching and employment status, the stronger their personal agency appeared to be. Given that we have previously established that the individual's perceptions of the workplace are critical to learning, it is perhaps unsurprising that coaches are most reluctant to engage during periods of threat or insecurity (e.g. team or program performing poorly). This might be viewed as highly problematic given that coaches may require the greatest learning assistance when in positions where they feel threatened or insecure.

University-based coach education programs: a vision for the future

In addition to learning in and through coaching work, the development of coaches through formal tertiary study has been proposed as a way of both conceptualising and advancing the discussion of how coaches develop their capacities (Cassidy 2008; Demers *et al.* 2006; Mallett and Dickens 2009; Rynne *et al.* 2006; Mallett *et al.* 2010). While the majority of high performance coaches have at least an undergraduate degree (Trudel and Gilbert 2006), coaching-specific university programs and qualifications have been less common. However, university education has become a growing field of coach learning with increases in the number of programs (predominately undergraduate), especially in the UK (Cushion *et al.* 2010; Jones 2006; Lyle 2002). With the growth of tertiary qualifications as a possible means of promoting career advancement, it is imperative that these programs are well designed to contribute to coach development. Findings from research conducted with high performance coaches in Australia (Mallett *et al.* 2010; Rynne 2008) highlight that participation in higher education courses allow coaches to leverage more from their regular interactions with paraprofessionals (through greater confidence and competence) and reportedly improved their critical thinking skills through engagement with university study. These and other outcomes were contingent, however, on the pedagogy underpinning quality program design. University courses in high performance sports coaching should consider the incorporation of authentic tasks, provision of opportunities for collaboration, offer a learner-centred approach and provide authentic and integrated assessment tasks able to be applied to coaching contexts.

The increase in university programs could be considered as a response to the emergence of sports coaching as a vocational grouping. Jones (2006) suggested that the provision of higher education for sports coaching has probably resulted from an increasing perception and acceptance of coaching as an intellectual endeavour. The quality of high performance coaching is somewhat contingent upon the coach possessing a bank of knowledge from a range of disciplines (Abraham and Collins 1998) to inform their practice. Universities are considered responsible for producing graduates with extensive content knowledge as well as critical and independent thinking skills (among other attributes). These skills or abilities, which are argued as requisite for quality coaching, assist coaches to develop a 'quality of mind' (Jones and Turner 2006: 185) in responding to the challenges of the highly contested (Rynne *et al.* 2010), complex, unpredictable and uncertain context of elite sport (Cushion 2007; Lyle 2007).

There have been few studies that examined the development of key abilities (e.g. reflection) in university-based coach education programs but, unfortunately, there has been little evidence supporting the efficacy of these programs (e.g. Knowles *et al.* 2001, 2006; Nash 2003). Moreover, such work has also tended not to examine the impact of these interventions on coaching practice (Cushion *et al.* 2010). Several studies have highlighted the importance of reflective practice in the generation of coaching knowledge to recognise and solve problems (e.g. Cushion *et al.* 2003; Gilbert and Trudel 2001); that is, reflective practice is linked inextricably to knowledge generation and learning with the intention to enhance coaching. Some interesting work has examined the effectiveness of university-based programs in facilitating the development of reflection, with the view of influencing coaching practice (Knowles *et al.* 2001, 2006; Nash 2003). These investigations of undergraduate coaching students showed that developing reflective skills was challenging (Knowles *et al.* 2001), and the level of reflection was superficial (technical reflection) (Knowles *et al.* 2006). Two other studies of undergraduate coaching students used a problem-based (and competency-based) learning approach (Jones and Turner 2006; Demers *et al.* 2006) to engage students in a 'learner-centred' approach to problem solving an issue in coaching in which they work collaboratively to solve. Problem-based learning (PBL) is grounded in social constructivist theories of learning and considered more 'authentic' than the traditional didactic approach to learning. A key aim of both investigations was the development of reflective practitioners and, while both studies found that a problem-based or a competency-based approach to learning had potential, the approach was deemed to be challenging and required significant preparatory work. Moreover, there was no evidence that it impacted on coaching practice. Collectively, these aforementioned studies showed modest improvements in reflective practice and to date there is no evidence on its impact upon coaching practice.

Trudel and Gilbert (2006) have conceptualised coaches' learning using Sfard's (1998) two metaphors – acquisition and participation. Importantly, consistent with Sfard's view on learning, they argue for consideration of both metaphors in the development of coaches. Specifically, they promote large-scale coach education programs to shift the current emphasis on acquisition towards a stronger emphasis on the participation metaphor. This movement towards increased engagement on the learning process is consistent with the aforementioned work on PBL and reflection with undergraduate students. Although the authors of this work (e.g. Knowles *et al.* 2006) proposed ways forward in future endeavours to promote reflection, there is much to be done to develop approaches that embrace Sfard's (1998) participation metaphor in facilitating coaches' learning. Arguably, this line of inquiry was conducted with undergraduate students, who were most likely younger adults and studying for the purpose of future employment as a coach. Furthermore, perhaps most of the education was aimed at community coaches. It is probably difficult to expect young adults to embrace problem-based approaches to learning for a vocation that they have both a limited understanding of due to a relative lack of experience in the field. Undergraduate sports coaching programs have the disadvantage of preparing aspiring coaches for a career in contrast to those programs that are designed for practising coaches with sufficient work experience (i.e. continuing professional development [CPD]).

Learner-centred approaches are likely to be most beneficial to those students who are already engaged in coaching and some experiences upon which to reflect. To reflect upon current practice (and not that which is under the supervision of a mentor coach as may be the case with undergraduate students undertaking practicum) allows the student-coach to reflect upon their current work in unison with what they are learning at university. University-based sports coaching programs that provide a form of CPD for practising coaches enable university coach educators to embrace pedagogies that integrate both the acquisition and participation metaphors.

An example of this integration of acquisition and participation metaphors for the development of coaches is the postgraduate sports coaching program at The University of Queensland (UQ) (Mallett and Dickens 2009). Preparing coaches for the highly contested and multi-layered, unpredictable and chaotic world of high performance coaching is unsurprisingly a complex challenge. The experiences of student-coaches at UQ have shown the potential of programs to connect study meaningfully with coaching work – this authentic approach to development facilitates legitimate links between the acquisition of knowledge and coaching practice (praxis). Although research on these programs has not been published in academic journals, we can give an account of independent reports (see Mallett and Dickens 2009) as well as some unsolicited feedback from student-coaches and graduates on their experiences with integrating study with coaching work. Overall, our evidence to date has shown that these adult learners (coaches) have reported increased coaching self-efficacy, developed their critical thinking skills, learned through more functional relationships with paraprofessionals (e.g. sports medicine), and importantly perceived they have improved their coaching practice. Of course, systematic and rigorous research is needed to substantiate some of these claims. Nevertheless, we provide some evidence of university-based coach education for practising (adult) coaches.

If a key aim of university-based sports coaching programs is to develop innovative and 'thinking' coaches who critically examine their coaching practices then the ability to provide learning opportunities to connect information with practice is fundamental:

> The course has improved my coaching by giving me the ability to understand the principles behind many 'accepted' coaching practices. More than that, I now understand why these may not always work and now have the ability to devise an alternative exercise.
>
> *(Rebecca, student, 2009)*

> I really enjoyed the subject matter in this course and it has given me a lot of ideas for the future about how to do things differently.
>
> *(Bill, student, 2009)*

Although it is important to critically reflect upon current and future coaching, it is proposed that a central aim of university-based coach education is to enhance coaching practice:

> I also wanted to take the opportunity to say thank you for this unit this semester as well as your support with my challenging role. As an ex-psych, I have found the information very useful on multiple levels and now as a coach have implemented a few strategies that I picked up in this unit on my [rowing] crew that competed this week and managed to snare [World Championship] gold medal so again, thanks!
>
> *(Joe, student, 2009)*

Our contention is that university-based sports coaching programs can facilitate coach development that reflects in their improved practice. Despite some positive feedback about the integration of study with coaching work, there have been some barriers to completion of the various academic awards, including: (1) prioritising time for study (some prioritise the practice of coaching over their studies); (2) competing demands (coaches lead busy lives); and (3) some have a stated preference for learning face-to-face rather than exclusively online as is the case with the UQ program.

There is potential for 'authentic' university-based programs to meaningfully facilitate coach development (Mallett and Dickens 2009). Connecting study with coaching work has potential to facilitate both understanding and the subsequent re-shaping of practice for coaches. Systematic research is foundational to guiding the structure of these programs, the pedagogies, and importantly the impact on coach practice. It is proposed that future research into various models of learning that integrate Sfard's (1998) two metaphors will not only help in understanding coach development but guide those responsible for coach development.

Progressing understanding of high performance coaches' work and development

Progressing the development of high performance coaches is central to enhancing the coach–athlete–performance relationship as well as the professionalisation of coaches. As stated earlier in the chapter, high performance coaching is a relatively young vocation and, unsurprisingly, there has been limited empirical investigation to date. It is expected that the vocation will receive increasing attention in due course. Nevertheless, some suggestions to the nature and purpose of future research on high performance coach development are proposed.

The work of high performance coaches is complex and multifaceted (Cushion 2007; Lyle 2002; Mallett 2010); it is also highly contested and has elements of unpredictability and excitement that makes this form of coaching interesting for researchers to examine. Furthermore, high performance coaches' work continues to evolve into a more demanding and complex occupation with significant advances in technology (e.g. GPS tracking systems; movement analysis software), creation of specialist disciplines and associated personnel (e.g. strength and conditioning, performance analysts), and the subsequent requirement to lead and manage an increasing workforce, to name a few. Hence, the challenge of exploring how these coaches develop their craft and operate in that complex and chaotic environment is likely to have a fascination for some coaching science scholars, but more importantly, such research is important to inform the development of high performance coaches, which to date has been serendipitous at best. Specifically, how individual coaches negotiate (and do not negotiate) learning for and during high performance coaching work is worthy of investigation.

The complexity of high performance coaching practice is captured in many studies (e.g. Bowes and Jones 2006; Irwin *et al.* 2004; Rynne *et al.* 2010); however, further studies are necessary to continue to examine this complexity and dynamism. How coaches negotiate with the 'culture' of the sport and the associated traditional coaching practices in both reproducing and producing cultural practices is important for advancing coach development. This examination of how the individual negotiates with the social in developing their craft is important for understanding some of the challenges for high performance coaches in being perceived as competent and knowing but at the same time innovative and progressive. Examination of the interdependent relationship between the coach and the culture and its impact on coach development will typically require some interpretivist research methodologies that are prospective and retrospective and therefore longitudinal in design.

There are many unanswered questions in understanding high performance coaching work and how individuals develop their knowledge, skills, abilities and capacities, and subsequent practice. Some key questions in understanding how high performance coaches learn their craft include:

1 How do coaches learn (and potentially learn) through paraprofessionals, such as sports physiotherapists?
2 How do coaches (and how might they) lead and manage increasing numbers of personnel within teams or squads?
3 How do coaches and those responsible for coach development prepare coaches for an unknown future? This question is particularly pertinent when one considers the evolving nature of their work and subsequent shifts in requisite knowledge, skills and abilities.
4 How do (and should) athletes experience high performance coaching? Moreover, how do other actors within the specific high performance coaching context learn for and during work?

All engaged actors in each high performance sporting context (e.g. team) have the potential for learning. An examination of the subjective experience and its (facilitative and thwarting) influence on learning for all actors in the high performance context will provide a more holistic understanding of the context. It is therefore recommended that the use of multiple voices from the same context is necessary to more fully appreciate the interdependent relationship between each actor and the specific high performance coaching context. To examine the self-reports of coaches with the voices of the athletes and other actors would make for a more comprehensive understanding of the complexity of the high performance environment and the subsequent influence on coach development.

Perhaps a focal point in the examination of all actors and their development in high performance contexts might be investigations of the central role of identity. Many high performance coaches were previously elite athletes and some understanding of the transitions and associated challenges in shifting from an athlete identity to a coach identity might inform coach development for those coaches who come from an elite playing background. Furthermore, to examine the identities of high performance coaches who were not elite athletes and how alternative life histories have influenced their learning and practice is a pathway that warrants investigation to guide coach development for those on that journey. Moreover, characteristic of high performance coaching work seems to be an understanding of the interacting forces of order and predictability with disorder and unpredictability associated with complex and dynamic human systems. Therefore, complexity theory might be a suitable alternative lens for examining coaches' learning in and through work.

The emergence of university-based coach education programs (Jones 2006) has provided some opportunities for those in the dual roles of educator and researcher to examine some alternative approaches to coach education. These have included problem-based (and competency-based) learning (Jones and Turner 2006; Demers *et al.* 2006), reflection (Knowles *et al.* 2001, 2006) and communities of practice (Cassidy *et al.* 2006; Culver and Trudel 2006; Occhino *et al.* in press). University-based coach education programs have the potential to investigate the complex, dynamic, uncertain and highly contextualised practice of high performance coaching (Lyle 2007). Nevertheless, as Lyle (2007: 29) argued, there is need for research that provides 'evidence of' rather than proposing 'arguments for'.

University-based coach education programs were likely developed to facilitate coach development, and research to date is scarce in demonstrating that expected key outcome. What is needed is evidence of university-based coaching programs impacting upon coach behaviour change, especially in the long term. Moreover, future research might examine how higher order thinking skills that are supposedly developed through university education impact on coaching practice. Finally, much of the research on high performance coaching and university sports coaching programs has emerged from the United States and the United Kingdom. It is imperative in progressing the field that university-based programs in other cultures are examined to contribute to a better understanding of their work and development as well the professionalisation of high performance coaches. We encourage researchers in other continents to contribute to the knowledge base.

Summary

Coaches are considered the architects of the coach–athlete–performance relationship and their ongoing professional development is central to improving and sustaining high quality coaching practice. High performance coaching practice is complex and composed of various interdependent components. In performing this work, typically high performance coaches develop their craft in rather idiosyncratic ways. Nevertheless, this serendipitous approach to developing high performance coaching craft is inconsistent with the professionalisation of coaching. A more systematic and evidence-based approach to CPD of high performance coaches is essential to the professionalisation of the vocation. Such evidence requires complementary research approaches to better understand the development of high performance coaches' craft.

Learning through work and study are two ways that have traditionally been undertheorised but are potentially generative ways of understanding high performance coach development. Neither avenue for development (work and university study) is the panacea but both represent ways whereby meaningful development can occur.

In the case of workplace learning, those responsible for the environment (i.e. high performance managers, coaches and administrators) need to consider how potentially generative the learning context is for their high performance coaches. It is necessary for such people to ask the question: do our high performance coaches have sufficient time and resources allocated with the intended outcome of development? But it is not enough to have a potentially rich learning environment, it is the coach's perception of the environment that is of greatest importance. The individual must be considered to be central to what is and is not possible with regard to learning and development.

With regard to university-based study, while there may have been an increase in the number of coach-focussed tertiary education courses, there is need to undertake a program of empirical examination of these learning opportunities for better understanding of high performance coaching work, development of key abilities (e.g. specific interventions to develop reflective practice) and its impact on practice. Those designing and considering enrolling in coach-specific tertiary education study should consider the authenticity of programs, the relationship with coach accreditation programs, and of course the content of programs (i.e. does it match with the demands of high performance coaching work?). For the field more generally, there is a need to further establish a research base on coaching (rather than continued 'borrowing' of theoretical frameworks from other fields). Similarly, institutions should develop concerted research agendas in high performance coaching rather than ad hoc, opportunistic projects.

References

Abraham, A. and Collins, D. (1998) 'Examining and extending research in coach development', *Quest*, 50(1): 59–79.

Abraham, A., Collins, D. and Martindale, R. (2006) 'The coaching schematic: Validation through expert coach consensus', *Journal of Sport Sciences*, 24(6): 549–564.

Allee, V. (2000) 'Knowledge networks and communities of practice', *OD Practitioner*, 2(4): 4–13.

Armour, K.M. (2010) 'The learning coach ... the learning approach: Professional development for sports coach professionals', in J. Lyle and C.J. Cushion (eds) *Sports Coaching: Professionalisation and Practice*, London: Elsevier.

Bales, J. (2006) 'Introduction: Coach education', *The Sport Psychologist*, 20(2): 126–127.

Billett, S. (2004) 'Workplace participatory practices: Conceptualising workplaces as learning environments', *Journal of Workplace Learning*, 16(6): 312–324.

Billett, S., Smith, R. and Barker, M. (2005) 'Understanding work, learning and the remaking of cultural practices', *Studies in Continuing Education*, 27(3): 219–237.

Bowes, I. and Jones, R.L. (2006) 'Working at the edge of chaos: Understanding coaching as a complex, interpersonal system', *The Sport Psychologist*, 20(2): 235–245.

Cassidy, T. (2008) 'Coach education or coach development: A paradigm shift or more of the same?' paper presented to the International Council for Coach Education (ICCE) Asian Regional Coach conference, 7–9 November, Seoul, South Korea.

Cassidy, T., Potrac, P. and McKenzie, A. (2006) 'Evaluating and reflecting upon a coach education initiative: The CoDe of rugby', *The Sport Psychologist*, 20(2): 145–161.

Coombs, P.H. and Ahmed, M. (1974) *Attacking Rural Poverty: How Non-Formal Education Can Help*, Baltimore, MD: Johns Hopkins University Press.

Côté, J., Bruner, M., Erickson, K., Strachan, L. and Fraser-Thomas, J. (2010) 'Athlete development and coaching', in J. Lyle and C.J. Cushion (eds) *Sports Coaching: Professionalisation and Practice*, London: Elsevier.

Culver, D.M. and Trudel, P. (2006) 'Cultivating coaches' communities of practice: Developing the potential for learning through interactions', in R.L. Jones (ed.) *The Sports Coach as Educator: Re-conceptualising Sports Coaching*, London: Routledge.

Cushion, C.J. (2007) 'Modelling the complexity of the coaching process', *International Journal of Sport Science and Coaching*, 2(4): 395–401.

Cushion, C.J., Armour, K.M. and Jones, R.L. (2003) 'Coach education and continuing professional development: Experience and learning to coach', *Quest*, 55(3): 215–230.

Cushion, C.J., Armour, K.M. and Jones, R.L. (2006) 'Locating the coaching process in practice: Models "for" and "of" coaching', *Physical Education and Sport Pedagogy*, 11(1): 83–99.

Cushion, C.J., Nelson, L.J., Armour, K.M., Lyle, J., Jones, R.L., Sandford, R. and O'Callaghan, C. (2010) *Coach Learning and Development: A Review of Literature*, Leeds: Sports Coach UK.

Demers, G., Woodburn, A.J. and Savard, C. (2006) 'The development of an undergraduate competency-based coach education program', *The Sport Psychologist*, 20(2): 162–173.

Dickson, S. (2001) *A Preliminary Investigation into the Effectiveness of the National Coach Accreditation Scheme*, New South Wales: Australian Sports Commission.

Erickson, K., Bruner, M.W., MacDonald, D.J. and Côté, J. (2008) 'Gaining insight into actual and preferred sources of coaching knowledge', *International Journal of Sport Science and Coaching*, 3(4): 527–538.

Gilbert, W.D. (2002) 'An annotated bibliography and analysis of coaching science', unpublished report sponsored by the Research Consortium of the American Alliance for Health, Physical Education, Recreation and Dance.

Gilbert, W.D. and Trudel, P. (1999) 'An evaluation strategy for coach education programs', *Journal of Sport Behaviour*, 22(2): 234–250.

Gilbert, W.D. and Trudel, P. (2001) 'Learning to coach through experience: Reflection in model youth coaches', *Journal of Teaching in Physical Education*, 21(1): 16–34.

Gilbert, W.D., Côté, J. and Mallett, C. (2006) 'The talented coach: Developmental paths and activities of successful sport coaches', *International Journal of Sport Science and Coaching*, 1(1): 69–76.

Irwin, G., Hanton, S. and Kerwin, D.G. (2004) 'Reflective practice and the origins of elite coaching knowledge', *Reflective Practice*, 5(3): 425–442.

Jones, R.L. (2006) 'How can educaitonal concepts inform sports coaching?' in R.L. Jones (ed.) *The Sports Coach as Educator: Re-conceptualising Sports Coaching*, London: Routledge.

Jones, R.L. and Turner, P. (2006) 'Teaching coaches to coach holistically: Can problem-based learning (PBL) help?' *Physical Education and Sport Pedagogy*, 11(2): 181–202.

Knowles, Z., Gilbourne, D., Borrie, A. and Neville, A. (2001) 'Developing the reflective sports coach: A study exploring the processes of reflective practice within a higher education coaching programme', *Reflective Practice*, 2(2): 185–207.

Knowles, Z., Tyler, G., Gilbourne, D. and Eubank, M. (2006) 'Reflecting on reflection: Exploring the practice of sports coaching graduates', *Reflective Practice*, 7(2): 163–179.

Lave, J. and Wenger, E. (1991) *Situated Learning: Legitimate Peripheral Participation*, Cambridge: Cambridge University Press.

Lyle, J. (2002) *Sports Coaching Concepts: A Framework for Coaches' Behaviour*, London: Routledge.

Lyle, J. (2007) 'A review of the research evidence for the impact of coach education', *International Journal of Coaching Science*, 1(1): 17–34.

Lynch, M. and Mallett, C. (2006) 'Becoming a successful high performance track and field coach', *Modern Athlete and Coach*, 22(2): 15–20.

MacLean, J.C. and Chelladurai, P. (1995) 'Dimensions of coaching performance: Development of a scale', *Journal of Sport Management*, 9(2): 194–207.

Mallett, C.J. (2010) 'High performance coaches' careers and communities', in J. Lyle and C.J. Cushion (eds) *Sports Coaching: Professionalism and Practice*, London: Elsevier.

Mallett, C.J. (2011) 'Quality coaching, learning and coach development', *Japanese Journal of Sport Education Studies*, 30(2): 51–62.

Mallett, C.J. and Dickens, S. (2009) 'Authenticity in formal coach education: Online postgraduate studies in sports coaching at The University of Queensland', *International Journal of Coaching Science*, 3(2): 79–90.

Mallett, C.J., Rossi, T. and Tinning, R. (2007) *Coaching Knowledge, Learning and Mentoring in the AFL*, Brisbane: University of Queensland.

Mallett, C.J., Rynne, S.B., Billett, S., Tinning, R. and Rossi, A. (2010) *Learning and Mentoring in High Performance Sports Coaching*, Brisbane: Australian Sports Commission.

Mallett, C.J., Rynne, S.B. and Billett, S. (2011) 'High performance coach development: Valued learning sources over coaches' careers', paper presented to the International Council for Coach Education (ICCE) Global Coach conference, 25 August, Paris, France.

Mallett, C.J., Trudel, P., Lyle, J. and Rynne, S.B. (2009) 'Formal vs. informal coach education', *International Journal of Sport Science and Coaching*, 4(3): 325–334.

Nash, C. (2003) 'Development of a mentoring system within coaching practice', *Journal of Hospitality, Leisure, Sport and Tourism Education*, 2(2): 39–47.

Nelson, L.J., Cushion, C.J. and Potrac, P. (2006) 'Formal, nonformal and informal coach learning: A holisitc conceptualisation', *International Journal of Sport Science and Coaching*, 1(3): 247–259.

Nichani, M. and Hung, D. (2002) 'Can a community of practice exist online?' *Educational Technology*, 42(4): 49–54.

Occhino, J, Mallett, C.J. and Rynne, S. (in press) 'Dynamic social networks in high performance football coaching', *Physical Education and Sport Pedagogy*, DOI: 10.1080/17408989.2011.631003.

Rynne, S.B. (2008) 'Opportunities and engagement: Coach learning at the Queensland academy of sport', unpublished doctoral thesis, University of Queensland, Australia.

Rynne, S.B. and Mallett, C.J. (in press) 'Understanding the work and learning of high performance coaches', *Physical Educaiton and Sport Pedagogy*, DOI: 10.1080/17408989.2011.621119.

Rynne, S.B., Mallett, C. and Tinning, R. (2006) 'High performance sport coaching: Institutes of sport as sites for learning', *International Journal of Sport Science and Coaching*, 1(3): 223–233.

Rynne, S.B., Mallett, C.J. and Tinning, R. (2010) 'Workplace learning of high performance sports coaches', *Sport, Education and Society*, 15(3): 315–330.

Sfard, A. (1998) 'On two metaphors for learning and the dangers of choosing just one', *Educational Researcher*, 27(2): 4–13.

Trudel, P. and Gilbert, W.D. (2006) 'Coaching and coach education', in D. Kirk, D. Macdonald and M. O'Sullivan (eds) *The Handbook of Physical Education*, London: Sage.

38

MENTORING FOR SPORT COACHES

Gordon A. Bloom

MCGILL UNIVERSITY, CANADA

Introduction

There is little doubt that sport coaches spend a great deal of their effort mentoring their young athletes. For example, Walton's (1992) book on the lives and philosophies of six expert coaches found that these coaches were more than just teachers of sport skills. They taught athletes life skills that remained ingrained throughout the lives of their protégés. One coach was the legendary American swim tutor, James 'Doc' Counsilman. Walton outlined how Counsilman mentored his swimmers using an adapted version of Maslow's hierarchy of human needs. The following is an example of how he mentored them: 'He took a deep personal interest in them [his swimmers]. He knew their studies and pinned to memory their grade point averages, best swimming times, and best workouts; he knew their goals and aspirations, their girlfriends and their problems' (Walton 1992: 84). There is likely to be little debate that coaches spend a great deal of their career mentoring their athletes. However, the topic of coaches being mentored is not as clear and straightforward.

Despite the efforts of the International Council for Coach Education (ICCE) and various coach education programs in different countries, there has historically been a lack of scientific research on optimal ways of developing coaches. The majority of work that exists has focused on the impact of factors such as past athletic experiences, coach education, and informally observing and interacting with other coaches (Bloom *et al.* 1998; Jimenez *et al.* 2009; Schinke *et al.* 1995). Intuitively, one might have expected mentoring to be at the top of that list. To date, literature on mentoring in coaching is limited, although research from around the world has identified the positive elements of coach mentoring. For example, work from Canada (Bloom *et al.* 1998), the United States (Gould *et al.* 1990), Spain (Jimenez *et al.* 2009), Ireland (Bertz and Purdy 2011), Australia (Dickson 2001), and the United Kingdom (Cushion 2006; Jones *et al.* 2003) has professed the value of mentoring for sport coaches. Moreover, these studies have all called for the development of structured mentoring programs in their countries. Despite this, there does not seem to be the same level of support and urgency that appears to exist in other professions. For example, pilots, doctors, and police officers were known to spend years refining their skills under the guidance and supervision of experienced and knowledgeable colleagues who ensured they were allowed to grow and develop in an environment designed to minimize errors and build knowledge and confidence. Due to the many positive benefits and intuitive appeal that have been attributed to mentoring both inside and outside of sport, it is important to explore this topic in the context of coach development, including best practices.

The purpose of this chapter is to explain the often ill-clarified concept of mentoring in sport coaching. The key mentoring issues for sport coaches are who to receive it from and how to get it. This chapter will attempt to answer these questions by defining mentoring and explaining how it can lead to positive coach development and performance if correctly implemented. This will be achieved by looking at research both inside and outside of sport. Finally, some of the shortcomings of mentoring research in sport will be addressed, as well as areas for future inquiry into mentoring in sports coaching.

What is mentoring?

Although mentoring is a phenomenon that is centuries old, there is currently a lack of clarity in its definition. Examples of famous mentoring relationships include Socrates and Plato, Freud and Jung, Lorenze de Medici and Michelangelo, and Haydn and Beethoven. The term originated from Greek mythology, where Mentor was a wise and trusted advisor to the young Telemachus (Merriam 1983). The term mentor has been used in many domains and its definition is slightly varied in each case, often depending upon the scope of the research. Most experts would agree that mentoring involves a non-familial and non-romantic relationship between an experienced person and a less experienced person in their field, where the former has more influence and is conscious of it. It involves a relationship between a mentor and his/her protégé where the former has a direct influence in the development of the latter and personally commits his/her time for the other's personal growth and development. The pillars of the relationship are trust and respect.

The outcomes of mentoring could broadly be categorized into two areas: career support and psychosocial (Gibson 2004; Kram 1985, 1988). Career support involves increased job satisfaction, enhanced career mobility, higher promotion rate, exposure and visibility, higher income levels, increased commitment, and decreased work alienation. Psychosocial aspects include the protégé's sense of professional competence, confidence, and identity. According to Kram (1983), there are four traditional phases of the mentoring relationship: initiation; cultivation; separation; and redefinition. In the initiation phase the mentor and protégé admire, respect, and trust each other. During the second phase, cultivation, the mentee develops competence as well as confidence from the career and psychosocial support the mentor has provided. Separation refers to the time when the relationship between the mentor and mentee changes, the mentee may become more independent and empowered potentially leading to a non-positive affective experience. Lastly, redefinition is the time where the mentor–mentee relationship is restructured to meet more collegial needs.

Interdisciplinary mentoring research

Business

The process of mentoring has been well documented in business, where mentorships have played a major role in the professional progression and development of individuals (Borman and Colson 1984; Hunt and Michael 1983; Kram 1983). A review of literature by Hunt and Michael (1983) found that a mentoring system was used by businesses to develop the organization's managerial talent. These relationships assisted young professionals in 'learning the organizational ropes, developing a sense of competence and effectiveness, and learning how to behave at successive management levels' (Hunt and Michael 1983: 478). Mentors benefited from these relationships as well by redirecting their energies into the career development of a young professional. Mentors felt rejuvenated by passing on the knowledge and experience that they had gained throughout their careers.

As in sport, mentoring in organizations occurs through formal or informal relationships (Friday *et al.* 2004). Informal relationships are more prevalent in business and occur when the mentor and protégé realize they have common interests, admiration, and commitment allowing a more personal relationship to develop (Friday *et al.* 2004). Formal mentoring programs began to surface in the 1980s and typically have a set duration with specific objectives (Parise and Forret 2008). Although organizations are beginning to use formal mentoring programs, there appear to be few companies integrating the programs into a long-term plan or the strategic positioning of their organization (Jones *et al.* 2009).

Recently, there has been a shift from the traditional dyadic model involving a mentor and a mentee to a triadic model incorporating a third element; an organization. Dyadic relationships allow mentees to obtain information from one source which may limit the number of dyadic relationships that may form due to a limited number of senior members in an organization. Incorporating the organization can contribute to the success of the mentoring relationship by providing networking possibilities for the mentee, as well as other forms of mutual support from a variety and number of sources (Walker *et al.* 2009). Some have suggested that this triadic relationship yields benefits for the mentor, the mentee, and the organization (Marks and Goldstein 2005).

Education

A large body of research on mentoring can be found in the educational field. Stroble and Cooper (1988) noted that teacher mentoring programs only began to emerge in the early 1980s. Since then, researchers have been examining the different mentoring programs created for young teachers, as well as the mentors who assisted and evaluated them (Carter 1988; Stroble and Cooper 1988). Mentor teachers, teacher consultants, school-based teacher educators, or peer teachers are individuals who have been assigned roles to assist beginning educators. One of the most frequently studied areas of mentoring in education has focused on the experiences of novice teachers. Bowers and Eberhart (1988) stated that collaboration and assistance from colleagues was an essential part of a young teacher's development. In fact, these researchers also noted that mentoring made the school 'a learning place for both the novice and master teacher, thereby enhancing the school as a learning place for students' (Bowers and Eberhart 1988: 229–230).

Models of 'partnership' have been developed in a number of schools in order to train student teachers (Maynard 1997). Formalized programs in teaching have been created to eliminate some of the difficulties that beginning teachers faced in their first year (Stroble and Cooper 1988). School-based initial teacher training (ITT) courses were organized between schools and higher education institutions in order to allow beginning educators the opportunity to gain teaching experience under the supervision of a master teacher (Maynard 1997; Tomlinson 1995). Both teacher educators and master teachers saw ITT courses as an opportunity to improve teacher preparation and make it more relevant and effective (Tomlinson 1995).

Following these earlier studies, research on teacher mentoring programs began to implement qualitative research methods to interview student teachers and their mentors

(Abell *et al.* 1995; McNamara 1995). Abell *et al.* (1995) found that beginner teachers involved in these programs improved their self-confidence, classroom management, lesson planning, discipline, voice inflection, eye contact, and review techniques. They also found that the mentors involved in these programs believed it was important to work with beginning teachers as it helped them refine the young teachers' style. Other significant findings were that mentors assumed a helping role as opposed to an evaluative one, and that respect and trust between the two individuals was crucial for the program to work effectively. Of interest, many of these studies identified the need for a more standardized program for training and supervising teachers (Stroble and Cooper 1988), and the need for numerous funding changes in order for mentoring programs to be successful (Carter 1988).

Although the large majority of literature on mentoring in education has highlighted the positive aspects of it, there is also some research that identified the drawbacks involved in this process. These concerns range from the merit, skills, and knowledge of the mentors, to tensions between the master teachers and their mentees that ranged from manipulative behaviour to personality mismatches (Ballantyne *et al.* 1995; Freiberg *et al.* 1994; Graham 1997). As well, some studies mentioned the lack of time involved to properly carry out the mentoring process (Ackley and Gall 1992; Robinson 1993). Finally, it is difficult to conduct a meta-analysis on the value of mentoring programs since there are few statistical results provided in the empirical literature and there has been a growing trend toward the use of qualitative methods in the mentoring literature.

Medical field

Doctors

In a recent survey of Canadian medical program directors, 65 percent of those who responded confirmed the presence of a mentorship program (Donovan and Donovan 2009). This survey also revealed that mentoring programs were more present in larger programs, internal-medicine-based training programs, as well as in programs where the directors themselves had been part of a mentoring program or felt a mentoring program had an important role in their professional development. In the United States, Castiglioni *et al.* (2004) surveyed internal medicine program directors and found that 60 percent favoured mentoring programs with 49 percent of residency programs fostering formal mentoring. In another American study conducted at the Medical College of Wisconsin, all faculty members who reported having a mentor (N = 25) believed this arrangement aided them in career advancement (Kirsling and Kochar 1990). It seems that the mentors provided advice beyond career-centered situations including how to adapt to the work environment, organize their time, and maintain a productive network of colleagues.

In 2000, a formalized mentoring program was created in the department of medicine at Brigham and Women's Faulkner Hospital in Boston, Massachusetts (Levy *et al.* 2004). The program consisted of more than 80 faculty members who were assigned one to three mentees and who met two or three times per year. Several documents were provided to help the mentor with his/her responsibilities. Quarterly emails from the Medical Education Office reminded the mentors to meet with the mentees, they provided up-to-date information on changes in residency programs, invitations to house staff events, as well as a stipend to cover the cost of meeting with mentees. A few years after the mentoring program was initiated, a survey was conducted with the participants and revealed that over 90 percent of the respondents believed that it was important and beneficial for the department to assign a senior faculty member to a resident (Levy *et al.* 2004). However, the respondents also reported the difficulty experienced arranging times to meet, mostly because of scheduling conflicts (Levy *et al.* 2004).

Nurses

According to the Canadian Nurses Association, there has been a growing emphasis on the importance of mentoring in nursing in the last 30 years. In today's society, nurses are required to generate outcomes which are measurable and cost effective. This could be achieved more effectively if mentoring were implemented in a formal manner. This may be difficult since numerous mentoring models have been put forth in this field, yet none have been universally accepted. Moreover, the mentoring models have varied widely from one-on-one relationships, to team mentoring, to e-mentoring (Byrne and Keefe 2002).

According to Andrews and Wallis (1999), mentees participating in a nursing mentoring program preferred a mentor who was a newer practitioner and who was able to more easily recall their personal student experiences. Successful mentoring largely depended on the characteristics of the mentor, such as approachability, effective interpersonal and teaching skills, all of which led to a caring and nurturing environment for the mentee. There are several Canadian nursing mentoring programs that are organized by the health services division of the federal government. In most cases, a recent graduate was paired with an experienced registered nurse who acted as mentor in their area of specialization. In these cases, mentoring has led to a number of benefits for the mentor, such as enhanced self-fulfillment, and, for the mentee, increased confidence. Ultimately, the institution was considered to benefit from an improved quality of care.

Sport coach mentoring research

One of the most direct empirical studies of coach mentoring in sport was conducted by Bloom *et al.* (1998). Using an interview technique to acquire data from current and former Canadian Olympic team sport coaches, the researchers looked at various facets of mentoring beginning with their athletic careers and continuing throughout their coaching careers. Their results found that mentoring was an ongoing process in sport. Mentoring began during their athletic careers and continued through the early and middle stages of their coaching careers. Trusting relationships were established between their own coaches and their mentor coaches that enhanced athletic development and career progression. The mentors benefited from being challenged to refine their coaching or teaching methods. The knowledge and experience they acquired from their expert coaches went beyond technical, tactical, and physical knowledge, and involved the acquisition of knowledge that helped them shape their eventual coaching style and philosophy. Because of the positive experiences they received, these coaches also discussed the significance of being perceived as a potential mentor. Some were honoured and willing to serve as mentors for aspiring coaches due to the positive experiences they went through during earlier stages of their careers. Although these experts were often demanding as mentors, they still provided young assistant coaches with opportunities to access valuable sources of information and make other important personal contacts. Unfortunately, there was no set path for acquiring a mentor coach. According to these coaches, it was simply a case of being in the right place at the right time. Perhaps this explains why many of these expert coaches were calling for the introduction of a more formalized mentoring program.

There is currently a lack of direct empirical research on coaches being formally mentored in sport. However, widening the definition of the term mentor to include instances where coaches have been informally helped/assisted by a more experienced coach will be included. Gould *et al.* (1990) studied the educational needs of 130 expert American coaches from a variety of sports. One of their findings was that coaching textbooks and seminars were the least important sources of coaching information. The elite coaches felt the two most important knowledge sources that helped them develop their coaching styles were coaching experience and observing other successful coaches. The coaches also believed there were no definite sets of concepts or principles to follow in their profession.

Communities of practice (CoP) (Culver and Trudel 2008; Gilbert *et al.* 2009) are an informal type of coach learning that contains elements of mentoring and has the potential to positively impact coach learning and development. A CoP includes the roles that peers play in the learning process and has been defined as a 'group of people who share a concern, a set of problems, or a passion about a topic, and who deepen their knowledge and expertise in this area by interacting on an ongoing basis' (Wenger *et al.* 2002: 4). Although they range in size, CoPs involve an active learning process that is sustained in a systematic manner by a competent and dedicated facilitator. Although not formally labeled as mentors in the coach education literature, these peer facilitators appear to share some of the qualities and characteristics of mentors. For example, they are trained, they hold regular 'formal' learning meetings with colleagues, and they aim to create long-term substantial learning relationships with their peers (Gilbert *et al.* 2009). It will be interesting to see if this line of enquiry develops further and even more so if the facilitators assume a life-long mentoring relationship with the younger coaches.

Research from the UK has also examined mentoring in sport (e.g. Cushion *et al.* 2003; Jones *et al.* 2003, 2004, 2009). Consistent with Gould *et al.*'s (1990) findings, the studies in the UK found that informal bases of knowledge, such as ongoing interactions with peers and observing coaches during practices, were deemed to be the most important facets of knowledge acquisition. Perhaps unsurprisingly then, these authors have also called for more formalized and structured mentoring programs to be included in coach education.

Salmela and Moraes (2003) have discussed mentoring for coaches in the unique context of developing countries, where formalized coach education opportunities are typically not as available as they are in developing countries like Canada, the UK, or Australia. As such, they believe that structured mentoring programs are even more important for coaches in their countries compared to coaches in developing countries. Moreover, this lack of structure in coach education may have led to a culture of not sharing knowledge or 'trade secrets' in some countries, thus greatly inhibiting the development of coaches mentoring up-and-coming coaches. It certainly appears that studying mentoring practices in countries with and without formalized coach education training seems warranted.

Models of sport coach mentoring

Formalized and structured coach mentoring programs have been developed in countries like Canada and Australia, and are beginning to gather momentum in the UK (Cushion 2006). In Canada, coach education and development is governed by the Coaching Association of Canada (CAC),[1] which was created in 1970. The mission of the CAC is to provide the foundation of skills, knowledge, and attitudes needed to ensure effective coaching leadership for Canadian athletes. In 1974, the CAC created the National Coaching Certification Program (NCCP) to meet the needs of all coaches, from the beginner to the most experienced practitioners. Most sources have credited Canada's NCCP as being the first widely adopted national coach education program in the world.

Canada presently has seven National Coaching Institutes (NCIs)[2] located across the country whose mission is to enhance the training environment for high performance coaches (and athletes) through a variety of services. The directors of each center meet twice a year and have conference calls on four or five other occasions to develop consistency in the services they offer to coaches and athletes. All of the high performance coaches learn at the NCIs which involves a combination of classroom study with a coaching apprenticeship under the guidance of a highly qualified master coach. The mentoring program consists of four themes, which are broken down into units and lessons. Between their courses, the mentees meet with their master coach on their own, by phone, email, or on-site during training sessions.

Although the mentoring program in Canada appears to be more advanced than other countries, there are some challenges with this current system. First, there is no definitive schedule: the mentoring is done on the coaches' time and at the coaches' availability. Second, the mentoring does not always occur face-to-face, and can involve phone calls, emails, or conversations on Skype. Third, due to the lack of professionalization of coaching (compared to education and the medical field), it can be difficult to find, hire, and train people to perform these duties. Typically, they are retired individuals who do not have to rely on a steady income of mentoring. One could argue that it would be more effective to have current elite coaches working in a mentoring capacity. Fourth, some of the smaller sports in Canada have to integrate mentor coaches from other sports due to a lack of qualified and available mentors. Finally, there is a lack of resources to ensure that the mentoring is successful.

Similar in many ways to Canada, both Australia and the UK have coach education systems that are fewer than 35 years old and were developed in part with government participation and assistance. Created around the same time as Canada's program, Australia's program[3] ensures that its accredited coaches have received training in coaching principles. The National Coaching Accreditation Scheme (NCAS) is an initiative of the Australian Sports Commission (ASC) and is a progressive coach education program offering courses at various levels. The ASC has developed an initiative to encourage inexperienced coaches to enter their program and has launched the Beginning Coaching General Principles (BCGP), a free basic skills course to assist beginner coaches in Australia.

The BCGP course consists of five modules that address a variety of topics such as the roles and responsibilities of a coach, planning, and dealing with parents, for example. For those who progress to the intermediate level (club or regional level coaches), there are more advanced forms of knowledge that are delivered in 13 modules that range from sports safety to sport psychology. The program is available through the departments of sport and recreation of states and territories with some offering the modules in person while others are delivered via distance learning.

To assist in the development of individuals who have been identified as potential high performance coaches or to further develop existing high performance coaches, the ASC created the National Coaching Scholarship Program (NCSP) (Mallett *et al.* 2010). The ideal duration of the scholarship is two years and the program consists of three pillars; placement with a mentor coach, a program of tertiary study at the University of Queensland in a post-graduate coaching course, as well as involvement in Sport Coach and Official Section's (SCO) professional development blocks (Mallett *et al.* 2010). Since 1993, under the NCSP, over 220 coaches have completed the coaching scholarship (Mallett *et al.* 2010). The outcomes of the Australian coach mentoring system seem to mirror Canada's in many ways.

While the coaches and the mentors see the value in the system, there are difficulties in creating a formalized mentoring system that chooses and trains the mentor and is adaptable and flexible to the time constraints that exist in this demanding profession.

Future research directions

This chapter has focused on the often misunderstood topic of mentoring. Although few people question the value and importance of mentoring for coaches, particularly since the role of the coach often involves mentoring athletes, it is surprising there is a lack of research on this topic combined with a lack of formalized structured mentoring programs for coaches around the world. Despite the development of coach education in countries like Canada, Australia, and the UK, and their efforts to integrate mentoring into the training and development of their coaches, there is still a long way to go before mentoring becomes integrated for coaches in the same manner that it does for teachers, doctors, and many other professionals. Moreover, making this program geared for coaches at all levels, (i.e. youth sport, amateur, and elite) also seems far away.

There are currently many limitations/struggles related to mentoring that have likely contributed to the lack of research into, and development of, formalized coach mentoring programs. First, funding is required to help professionalize the process. Funds are needed to hire coordinators to oversee the mentoring program, to train the mentors, and to pay the mentors for their time and expenses (travel, food, etc.). Second, there is a lack of consistency regarding types of mentoring, whether it is done face-to-face, through electronic means, one-on-one, or in a group setting. Third, the lack of a recognized definition and theoretical framework has undoubtedly limited research in this area. For example, sport psychology topics like cohesion and leadership have definitions and conceptual models that have traditionally framed the research in these domains for the past 30–40 years. The same cannot be said for mentoring. Fourth, coaching is a profession that includes individuals with different traits and leadership styles. Care and effort needs to be given to matching the mentors and mentees as far as their thoughts and styles related to communication, discipline, or feedback styles or their personal make-up. Fifth, lack of time is problematic, especially in a profession like coaching that is not a nine-to-five job. Finally, there are currently no clear indicators to define the effectiveness of formalized coach mentoring programs.

Despite the difficulties and challenges that are present with the creation of formalized coach mentoring programs, it is undoubtedly something that is worth pursuing. A good starting point would be empirical research on coach mentoring. Perhaps the ideal framework would be having academics working in partnership with sport governing bodies in various countries to design, implement, and evaluate coach mentoring programs. The combination of sport governing bodies working with academics would help provoke reflective and reflexive thinking and would lead to a greater likelihood that the results would be transferred into coach mentoring practices around the world.

In sum, the recent creation of mentoring programs in Canada and Australia are a good first step in moving coach mentoring programs forward. As with other fields, having a mentor can improve protégés' confidence and competence, can provide them with a positive role model, and can promote them and introduce them to others who might be able to help with their career progression. The key is identifying and then training the right people to act as mentors. Some of the variables that have been identified as important include approachable, respectful, knowledgeable, up-to-date with current information, organized (time management skills), and trustworthy. If these factors are considered and mentoring programs are implemented, then one could argue that the mentoring process would benefit the coaching mentees, the mentors, and the organizations who train them. This would undoubtedly lead to a more fulfilling sport experience for the many athletes who work with these coaches.

Notes

1 www.coach.ca.
2 www.coach.ca/national-coaching-institutes-p137482.
3 www.ausport.gov.au/participating/coaches.

References

Abell, S.K., Dillon, D.R., Hopkins, C.J., McInerney, W.D. and O'Brien, D.G. (1995) 'Somebody to count on: Mentor/intern relationships in a beginning teacher internship program', *Teaching and Teacher Education*, 11: 173–188.

Ackley, B. and Gall, M.D. (1992) 'Skills, strategies and outcomes of successful mentor teachers', paper presented at the annual meeting of the American Educational Research Association, 28 April, San Francisco, USA.

Andrews, M. and Wallis, M. (1999) 'Mentorship in nursing: A literature review', *Journal of Advanced Nursing*, 29: 201–207.

Ballantyne, R., Hansford, B. and Packer, J. (1995) 'Mentoring beginning teachers: A qualitative analysis of process and outcomes', *Educational Review*, 47: 297–307.

Bertz, S. and Purdy, L. (2011) 'Coach education in Ireland: Observations and considerations for high performance', *Journal of Coaching Education*, 4: 29–43.

Bloom, G.A., Durand-Bush, N., Schinke, R.J. and Salmela, J. H. (1998) 'The importance of mentoring in the development of coaches and athletes', *International Journal of Sport Psychology*, 29: 267–281.

Borman, C. and Colson, S. (1984) 'Mentoring: An effective career guidance technique', *The Vocational Guidance Quarterly*, 3: 192–197.

Bowers, G.R. and Eberhart, N.A. (1988) 'Mentors and the entry year program', *Theory into Practice*, 27: 226–230.

Byrne, M.W. and Keefe, M.R. (2002) 'Building research competence in nursing through mentoring', *Journal of Nursing Competence*, 34: 391–396.

Carter, K. (1988) 'Using cases to frame mentor-novice conversations about teaching', *Theory into Practice*, 27: 214–222.

Castiglioni, A., Bellini, L.M. and Shea, J.A. (2004) 'Program directors' views of the importance and prevalence of mentoring in internal medicine residencies', *Journal of General Internal Medicine*, 19: 779–782.

Culver, D. and Trudel, P. (2008) 'Clarifying the concept of communities of practice in sport', *International Journal of Sports Science & Coaching*, 3: 1–9.

Cushion, C.J. (2006) 'Mentoring: Harnessing the power of experience', in R.L. Jones (ed.) *The Sports Coach as Educator: Re-conceptualising Sports Coaching*, London: Routledge.

Cushion, C.J., Armour, K.M. and Jones, R.L. (2003) 'Coach education and continuing professional development: Experience and learning to coach', *Quest*, 55: 215–230.

Dickson, S. (2001) *A Preliminary Investigation into the Effectiveness of the National Coach Accreditation Scheme*, Armidale, New South Wales: Australian Sports Commission.

Donovan, A. and Donovan, J. (2009) 'Mentorship in postgraduate training programmes: Views of Canadian programme directors', *Medical Education*, 43: 155–158.

Freiberg, M.R., Zbikowski, J.M. and Ganser, T. (1994) 'The anatomy of a mentoring program for beginning urban teachers', paper presented at the annual meeting of the Mid-Western Educational Research Association, 12–15 October, Chicago, USA.

Friday, E., Friday, S.S. and Green, A.L. (2004) 'A reconceptualization of mentoring and sponsoring', *Management Decision*, 42: 628–644.

Gibson, S.K. (2004) 'Mentoring in business and industry: The need for a phenomenological perspective', *Mentoring and Tutoring*, 12: 259–275.

Gilbert, W., Gallimore, R. and Trudel, P. (2009) 'A learning community approach to coach development in youth sport', *Journal of Coaching Education*, 2: 1–21.

Gould, D., Giannini, J., Krane, V. and Hodge, K. (1990) 'Educational needs of elite U.S. National Team, Pan American and Olympic coaches', *Journal of Teaching in Physical Education*, 9: 332–344.

Graham, P. (1997) 'Tensions in the mentor teacher-student teacher relationship: Creating productive sites for learning within a high school English teacher education program', *Teaching and Teacher Education*, 13: 513–527.

Hunt, D.M. and Michael, C. (1983) 'Mentorship: A career training and development tool', *Academy of Management Review*, 8: 475–485.

Jimenez, S., Lorenzo, A. and Ibanez, S. (2009) 'Development of expertise in Spanish elite basketball coaches', *International Journal of Sport Science*, 17: 19–32.

Jones, R.L., Armour, K.M. and Potrac, P. (2003) 'Constructing expert knowledge: A case study of a top-level professional soccer coach', *Sport, Education and Society*, 8: 213–229.

Jones, R.L., Armour, K.M. and Potrac, P. (2004) *Sports Coaching Cultures: From Practice to Theory*, London: Routledge.

Jones, R.L., Harris, R. and Miles, A. (2009) 'Mentoring in sports coaching: A review of literature', *Physical Education and Sport Pedagogy*, 14: 267–284.

Kirsling, R.A. and Kochar, M.S. (1990) 'Mentors in graduate medical education at the Medical College of Wisconsin', *Academic Medicine*, 65: 272–274.

Kram, K.E. (1983) 'Phases of the mentor relationship', *Academy of Management Journal*, 26: 608–625.

Kram, K.E. (1985) *Mentoring at Work*, Glenview, IL: Foresman.

Kram, K.E. (1988) *Mentoring at Work: Developmental Relationships in Organizational Life*, New York: University Press.

Levy, B.D., Katz, J.T., Wolf, M.A., Sillman, J.S., Handin, R.I. and Dzau, V.J. (2004) 'An initiative in mentoring to promote residents' and faculty members' careers', *Academic Medicine*, 79: 845–850.

Mallett, C., Billet, S., Tinning, R., Rossi, T. and Rynne, S. (2010) *Learning and Mentoring in High Performance Sports Coaching*, St Lucia: The University of Queensland.

Marks, M.B. and Goldstein, R. (2005) 'The mentoring triad: Mentee, mentor, and environment', *The Journal of Rheumatology*, 32: 216–218.

Maynard, T. (1997) *An Introduction to Primary Mentoring*, London: Wellington.

McNamara, D. (1995) 'The influence of student teachers' tutors and mentors upon their classroom practice: An exploratory study', *Teaching and Teacher Education*, 11: 51–61.

Merriam, S. (1983) 'Mentors and protégés: A critical review of the literature', *Adult Education Quarterly*, 33: 161–173.

Parise, M.R. and Forret, M.L. (2008) 'Formal mentoring programs: The relationship of program design and support to mentors' perceptions of benefits and costs', *Journal of Vocational Behavior*, 72: 225–240.

Robinson, M. (1993) 'Warwick University PGCE Mentoring Scheme', *Mentoring*, 1: 23–30.

Salmela, J.H. and Moraes, L.C. (2003) 'Developing expertise: The role of coaching, families, and cultural context', in J.L. Starkes and K.A. Ericsson (eds) *Expert Performance in Sports: Advances in Research in Sport Expertise*, Champaign, IL: Human Kinetics.

Schinke, R.J., Bloom, G.A. and Salmela, J.H. (1995) 'The career stages of elite Canadian basketball coaches', *Avante*, 1: 48–62.

Stroble, E. and Cooper, J.M. (1988) 'Mentor teacher: Coaches or referees?' *Theory into Practice*, 27: 231–236.

Tomlinson, P. (1995) *Understanding Mentoring: Reflective Strategies for School-Based Teacher Preparation*, Buckingham: Open University Press.

Walker, W., Kelly, P. and Hume, R. (2009) 'Mentoring for the new millennium', *Medical Education Online*, 7(15), available at: http://med-ed-online.org (accessed 21 August).

Walton, G.M. (1992) *Beyond Winning: The Timeless Wisdom of Great Philosopher Coaches*, Champaign, IL: Human Kinetics.

Wenger, E., McDermott, R. and Snyder, W.M. (2002) *Cultivating Communities of Practice*, Boston, MA: Harvard Business School Press.

39

INNOVATIVE APPROACHES IN COACH EDUCATION PEDAGOGY

Kevin Morgan

CARDIFF METROPOLITAN UNIVERSITY, UK

Robyn L. Jones

CARDIFF METROPOLITAN UNIVERSITY, UK

David Gilbourne

UNIVERSITY OF HULL, UK

David Llewellyn

LIVERPOOL JOHN MOORES UNIVERSITY, UK

Introduction

Thanks to a surge of research in the past decade, it has come to be generally acknowledged that the dynamic and intricate nature of coaching precludes any 'paint by number' plans that practitioners can easily follow (Gilbert and Trudel 2004; Jones and Wallace 2005). Despite such recognition, however, coach education programmes continue to be criticised for their largely didactic methods of delivery and rather superficial engagement with the complex reality of practice (Chesterfield *et al.*; 2010; Jones and Turner 2006). The effect has been a very limited impact on coaches' actions and behaviours, as such explicit knowledge is deemed far from the everyday reality of what coaches do. Clearly then, means must be found whereby coaches are allowed to better engage with both 'cutting-edge' content inclusive of the nuance and complexity of context and the learning process in general. Following from the above, the aims of this chapter are three-fold. First, to discuss recent developments in coach education pedagogy that we, as authors, have been variously engaged in and their relative merits in developing deeper coach learning. These include problem-based learning (PBL) (Jones and Turner 2006), action research (Jones *et al.* 2012) and ethnodrama (Morgan *et al.* in press). Second, to outline a research agenda to help us better understand the impact of such pedagogies on coach education and coach learning; and, third, to signal possible future methods which we believe hold considerable potential to better prepare coaches for the complexity of their everyday practice.

What's already out there: a problem-based learning approach

In moving somewhat away from the competencies-based approach, it has been increasingly argued that the aim of coach education should be to develop in practitioners a 'quality of mind' so that they are better equipped to deal with the problematic and dynamic nature of their work (Jones 2000; Cassidy *et al.* 2009). In an effort to do this, some years ago Jones and Turner (2006) experimented with a problem-based learning (PBL) approach to educate a class of final year undergraduate coaching students. PBL is an approach to teaching and learning that uses realistic, problematic scenarios and facilitative tutor questioning, to challenge and instil in students critical ways of thinking (Jones and Turner 2006). In PBL, students work in groups and use 'triggers' from the scenarios to define their own learning objectives, and subsequently carry out independent, self-directed research before returning to the group to discuss and refine their acquired knowledge. Thus, PBL is not just about problem solving; rather it uses problems to increase knowledge and understanding, and to facilitate learning.

PBL is based on the pragmatic philosophy of John Dewey, and aims to develop competencies such as a critical logic, an analytical approach to problems, decision making and self-evaluation (Engel 1999). It is, therefore, a way of learning about how to be a capable professional (Engel 1991). By promoting professional growth through 'reflective conversations' triggered by practice dilemmas (Schön 1987), the approach takes into consideration the constructivist nature of practitioner learning. Specific benefits claimed for PBL include: (1) improved abilities to make decisions and solve problems; (2) a raised awareness of the complexity of real world issues; (3) exposure to several bodies of knowledge; (4) increased abilities to extend learning beyond the presented problems and to think holistically across disciplines; (5) a heightened awareness of the integration of theory and practice; resulting in (6) individuals who are better able to learn effectively throughout their professional lives (Boud and Feletti 1991; Drinan 1991).

Such claims prompted Jones and Turner (2006) to research PBL in a sports coaching context. In their study, PBL was presented as a way through which the goal of coaching holistically could be better aspired to. They defined holistic coaching, not as multidisciplinary, comprising unconnected strands of differing content knowledges, but as interdisciplinary, where such knowledges meet, interconnect and dissect (Jones and Turner 2006). The aim of the PBL module, therefore, was to develop an ability in students to employ a flexible and holistic approach to coaching. The specific content to be discussed was structured around problematic scenarios which reflected the complex and integrated nature of coaching knowledge in real-life situations. The emphasis was student-centred, which brought an expectation that students would take an active part in planning, organising and conducting their own learning within a group framework. To engage with the problem-based group work, the students also had to review their collective knowledge, identify the information they needed to solve a particular problem, research and learn that knowledge, and relate it to the problem. The problems, therefore, were designed to be challenging, complex, controversial and not least, interesting for the students (Allen *et al.* 1996). In addition, the problems had to be reasonably open-ended in nature, so that students considered them in an integrated cross-discipline way with no single 'right answer', thus allowing them to explore their own and others' points of view. The structure of the module involved groups of students working on a specific scenario over a six-week period. Here, the students organised themselves into groups; and decided how to identify and research the main issues evident within their scenario. Over the subsequent weeks they were also subject to some interruptions, which they had to address (see Jones and Turner (2006) for a detailed account of procedures here). They eventually shared their 'solutions' to the problematic scenarios with the class in the form of short group presentations.

Following some initial insecurities and anxieties, the students reported that they enjoyed the PBL approach as it provided them with an explicit opportunity to use theoretical knowledge in a practical situation for the first time. In relation to the learning outcomes of the module the students reported that it had 'opened their eyes to something new'. There was also some evidence that the student coaches had started to think differently about their practice as a result of the PBL and had developed a better appreciation of the inherent complexities of coaching and the interdisciplinary knowledge needed. Furthermore, there was a greater appreciation and recognition of the structural constraints upon coaches' role fulfilment and the limits of their agency. Consequently, although mindful of what can be claimed from a small scale study with one group of students, the authors concluded that the approach holds the potential to help coaches towards the goals of transferable knowledge, and critical reflection among others.

Although encouraged by such early findings, we remain acutely aware that many and various other strands of research need to be engaged with to buttress our claims for the value of PBL to teach coaching. An example of this could be to explore the transformative claims of PBL; that is, the transformation by learners of the knowledge found or presented to them. According to Entwistle (2000), this knowledge transformation depends, in part, on students' understanding of the concepts used within the teaching, which have to resonate with everyday experience and be couched in accessible language, preferably with metaphorical associations. In this respect, to provoke critical reflection on practice, the teaching approach should possess a (high) degree of pedagogical fertility (Entwistle 1995). It is an aspiration, which reflects Schön's (1987: 25) belief that simply learning a theory (and even applying it to practice) is insufficient. Rather, what is required is for a quality of reflection and interpretation which enables practitioners to construct 'an integrated knowledge-in-action'. Through researching PBL's transformative claims a little more then, we could develop a better understanding of exactly what and how students learn what they learn through the approach. This could be particularly in terms of developing coaches' decision making and problem-solving abilities, and to think holistically across disciplines (Boud and Feletti 1991; Drinan 1991).

Recent developments: using action research within a 'communities' framework

In further searching for innovative and creative pedagogies through which to teach sports coaching, Jones *et al.* (2012) utilised an action-research based approach. Action research is a methodology which pursues outcomes of both action (change) and research (understanding). It involves cycles of reconnaissance, planning, action, reflection and interpretation (including the integration of theory), leading to improved understanding and learning (Tsai *et al.* 2004). Borrowing from Lewin (1946), action research was initially defined as 'a method that enabled theories produced by the social sciences to be applied in practice and tested on the basis of their practical effectiveness' (Carr 2006: 423). Drawing on Lewin's vision, Dick (1997) suggested that the purpose of action research, through critical and considered reflection, was to allow both tacit and explicit knowledge to inform each other in order to recognise thorny practical issues as they arise and to devise pragmatic responses. Action research, therefore, allows us to cope with the kind of organised complexity facing our everyday lives in the 'real' world (Allen 2001), and is often viewed in collaborative terms (Carr and Kemmis

1986).This is somewhat consistent with Wenger's (1998) notion of a community of practice, which has been defined as 'a group of people who share a common concern, set of problems, or a passion about a topic, and who deepen their knowledge and expertise in this area by interacting on an ongoing basis' (Wenger *et al.* 2002: 4). According to Wenger (1998), learning is essentially a social phenomenon, and in order to best support it he advocates bringing people together in common activities to discuss and deconstruct what they learn through their mutual engagement in those activities.

Consequently, a key characteristic of both action research and communities of practice relate to the quality of the collaboration between participants, a process which enables the development and acceleration of mutual understanding particularly in relation to developing action (Oja and Smulyan 1989). Both methods, therefore, can be seen as cogenerating knowledge through collaborative communication, where the diversity of experiences within a group is viewed as a catalyst for enrichment (Greenwood and Levin 2003). Both also recognise that people learn through the active adaptation of their existing knowledge in response to their contextual experiences, and the subsequent sharing of that knowledge. Such experiences may be through shared discussion with others or engagement with new explicit knowledge through theory. For most people, this experiential learning process is a natural one, but a structured pedagogy (e.g. action research) can help in providing a framework for formalising and making this process more effective (Jones *et al.* 2012). The collaborative aspect also provides the support required to make fundamental changes in individuals' practice which often endure beyond the life of any research project (Oja and Smulyan 1989). This point is particularly salient to the current debate about the change process in coaching (Cassidy 2010).

As stated at the beginning of this section, we recently applied an action-research approach to a postgraduate coach education unit in order to address the practice–theory gap (Jones *et al.* 2012). In principally drawing on elements from action research and student 'communities of practice' (Wenger 1998), the curriculum was established around a set of theoretically driven practical experiences and discussion groups. The basic intent was to develop in students an integrated, realistic knowledge base of how theory can and should be reflected in practice. The unit involved students being introduced to a particular theoretical position with the expectation that they would integrate that theory into their practice in the upcoming week. The students then shared their experiences in structured discussion groups during the following class. It was considered that such an innovative pedagogy would allow students an opportunity to better engage in the process of their own learning, thus increasing the relevancy of the experience inclusive of an explicit nexus between theory and practice (Jones and Turner 2006). The eight theoretical perspectives given to the students included: social orchestration which refers to how individuals manage others in a dynamic, fluid world (Jones and Wallace 2005, 2006); social role and impression management (Goffman 1959); virtue theory, which is tied to notions of both moral (i.e. patience, courage and generosity) and intellectual (i.e. practical skill, intuition and resourcefulness) virtue (MacIntyre 1985); teaching styles as related to Mosston and Ashworth's (2002) spectrum; shared leadership or athlete empowerment (Jones and Standage 2006); developing a favourable motivational climate for learning (Ames 1992); followership (Russell 2003); and social exchange (Blau 1986). In many ways, such a structure was inspired by Sfard's (1998) dual metaphors of learning by acquisition and participation, and the dangers of choosing only one. The students were stimulated by, and positive about, the approach in terms of it better ordering the knowledge they had and in developing new insights about coaching practice. Similar to Cassidy *et al.*'s (2006) work, through progressive engagement with new theoretical concepts and each other's experiences, the student coaches within our project came to increasingly recognise the specificity and limitations of their own knowledge. According to Wenger (1998: 5), when new 'light is shed on our world' in this way, our intuitions are pushed, deepening our understanding of familiar phenomena. This seemed to happen to our students, as they came to better problematise, deconstruct and subsequently order what they recognised as known practice, resulting in a sharpening of perceptions in relation to existing experiences (Wenger 1998). The broad action research structure of the unit forced critical reflection on practice, giving credence to the students' existing coaching knowledge with the subsequent impact being an improved ability to conceptualise that knowledge (Elbaz 1983). This raised awareness of practice also helped the students to clarify personal philosophies by providing them with a means of reflecting methodically upon familiar experience and the previously vague notions about what they considered their individual philosophies to be. The students' critical reflection on their actions in light of previously unconsidered theoretical frameworks also provided them with new insights and a renewed sense of responsibility over their coaching delivery through the process of self-monitoring. The approach, therefore, gave the students a greater sense of empowerment encouraging them to inquire and self-regulate their own development (Ollis and Sproule 2007); a central tenet of 'first person' action research (Reason and Bradbury 2001).

The students' experience on this unit also gave support to Wenger's (1998) belief that engagement in social practice is the fundamental process by which we learn. In Wenger's (1998) terminology then, the students colluded, collided, conspired and conformed in 'making sense of situations, sharing new tricks and ideas' (Wenger 1998: 47). This was reinforced through the action research approach which allowed progressive structured discussion on practiced concepts, and is consistent with the work of Cassidy *et al.* (2006) where coaches considered conversations grounded in everyday issues with peers and colleagues as being vital for their professional development.

Although this pedagogical approach was considered critical and enjoyable by the students, their evaluations were not universally positive (Jones *et al.* 2012). For example, more time to engage with the theories given would have been beneficial, allowing further exploration and subsequent reflection upon the nuances of each position. Additionally, there was some tension between the needs of the individual and the dominant voices of the group. Such issues, however, were focused on structure, content and practical delivery as opposed to the unit's philosophy, or the realisation of the learning outcomes. The result here then, was a seeming convergence of practice and theory, which has obvious implications for coach development. These findings again echo Schön's (1987: 25) work and his call to develop 'an integrated knowledge-in-action approach', much of which can be spontaneous, reflecting a 'professional artistry' in practice (Schön 1983). The findings also give weight to Ollis and Sproule's (2007) belief in the importance of challenge in development, although care has to be taken in relation to how that challenge is framed, and the support given to learners in dealing with it.

Similar to the use of PBL already mentioned, more work is needed on an action-research (and/or a communities of practice) approach to teaching coaching before too much can be claimed on its behalf. A particular avenue here could relate to problematising the notion of learning through reflection; in that far from being an individual activity, reflective learning is communal in nature as it is 'embedded in the institutionally structured context shared by a community of practitioners' (Schön 1987: 33). A particular issue to explore here then, could relate to the role of personal reflection both within and without a group structure in developing coaches' knowledge. This could be in relation to how coaches' exclusive reflections impact on learning developed both within a shared community and through individual coaching practice; an agenda which recognises both the structural or social and agential aspects of coach development (Jones *et al.* 2004). A further worthy issue to possibly investigate allied to this approach could include those of exposure, collaboration and/or power involved in establishing an effective 'community', where coaches are open (or not) to sharing their ideas and practices with others.

A future agenda? Using ethnodrama to teach coaching

Building on the aforementioned critical pedagogies, we have also experimented with ethnodrama as a potential means to better engage and educate sports coaches (Morgan *et al.* in press). Ethnodrama has been promoted as a means of communicating the emotional and contextual complexities of lived experiences (Gilbourne 2007). It has also been described as 'a new form of theatre', that seeks to translate research into reflexive, reflective performances to effect meaningful change (Mienczakowski and Morgan 2001). The aim is to promote empathetic understanding and learning by providing circumstances where individuals recognise themselves in the scenarios, and are confronted by the multiple interpretations and ramifications of those representations (Mienczakowski and Morgan 2001). The theoretical focus of ethnodrama is based on nascency; embryonic moments of insight or enlightenment (Saldaña 2005). The power of this form of theatre, therefore, lies in its presentation of the detail and depth of human experience including the sub-texts of thought and emotion through vocal and physical pretence (Llewellyn *et al.* 2011). It is a form of theatre that has the responsibility to create entertainingly informative experiences that are emotionally evocative, aesthetically sound and intellectually rich (Saldaña 2005). The performance allows text to 'come alive' through voice, gesture and posture, making what might be challenging in written form even more powerful via the skills of actors and the prompting of the director. Consequently, using the foundational work of Gilbourne, Llewellyn and others (i.e. Gilbourne and Triggs: 2006; Gilbourne 2007; Gilbourne and Llewellyn 2008), we tried to utilise ethnodrama as a pedagogical strategy to stimulate learning around real-life issues encountered by sports coaches. The specific aims of the project were related to facilitating the learning and challenge the perspectives of sports coaching students by exploring the multilayered coaching context through live visual ethnodrama scenarios.

The first stage of the process involved writing the sports coaching scenarios. These were based on ethnographic research and 'lived' and 'learned' coaching experiences. The essential element here was to ensure the reality of the coaching scenes in order to engage the students in post-performance interactions which informed, contested and promoted change in their perceptions and behaviours (Mienczakowski and Morgan 2001). In the words of Denzin and Lincoln, (2005: xi), we wanted to privilege 'the primacy of experience' and to turn 'enquiry into spaces where democratic public discourse can take place.' The authenticity of the scenarios was, therefore, of paramount importance. The writing process is central to this. Here, as authors of the scenarios, we decided to seek each other's advice and comments on various writing drafts. Whilst other writers may wish to work in isolation, we considered that collaboration could only assist in the development of authentic, detailed work; a process we found to be collectively enlightening.

The second step of the research project involved a theatre director and actors rehearsing the written scenarios in collaboration with one of the teaching team. This was followed by live performances of the scenes and their subsequent deconstruction by the coaching students. The discussion was facilitated by questions such as:

- What did you see in the scene(s)?
- What are the issues here?
- What has the coach got to deal with?
- Have you altered your perceptions? On the basis of what?
- What are your 'solutions'? Why?
- What informs your thinking?
- What could further inform your thinking?

In subsequently evaluating the experience, the student coaches universally agreed that the ethnodrama scenes were successful in depicting the multifaceted complex nature of coaching. In the words of one:

> they certainly illustrated the holistic side of things. So much of coaching is about the interactions between people at a particular time, the behavioural issues that go on, the roles people play and the power struggles. In my experience, it happens all the time with parents, with players. You can't get the sense of that in written words, the visual is much more realistic. The presentation is still very strong in my mind, I can picture exactly what went on. It's the impact of interaction and body language that makes it real to me.

The students then were supportive of the emotional engagement and the educational experience they had encountered, along with the approach's potential to effect meaningful change (Mienczakowski and Morgan 2001). The characters, the situations and the action, combined with the intellectual stimulus of the live drama, led to significant post-production analysis and debate. The students appeared to recognise the pedagogical efficacy of the enthodrama and readily engaged in interaction with each other through further sharing of related and relevant incidents from their own practice. Although, again, we would not wish to over-claim a totally functional experience here, we nevertheless believe that as with the other approaches already mentioned, the student evaluations were generally very positive and provided a catalyst for thinking about how we could develop the approach in future.

For example, a possible future direction for the use of ethnodrama in coach education could be based around both the coaches' involvement in the script writing and the performances, and in their interactions with the actors. Mienczakowski and Morgan (2001) identify an informant-led ethnodrama process in their work with health professionals, involving the gathering of ethnographic accounts, participant observation and a grounded theory approach to dramatic performances. As an innovative future research project, a similar critical process could be adopted in sports coaching using coaches, performers, parents and support staff to inform the development of problematic scenarios. This could produce an insightful opportunity for 'cutting-edge' coach education that deals with the 'messy realities' of the job whilst giving all informants 'a voice in the explanation of their lived realities' (Mienczakowski and Morgan 2001: 220). That said, such a project would require a significant amount of time and resources, as well as close collaboration with a professional theatre company or such like in order to be successful.

In proposing such a research agenda, we are not claiming significant originality as such work builds on that of Telesco (2006) who used sociodrama in the training of police officers in the US. Here, the central situational scenes were based on actual incidents and set the context for the trainee audience to interact with the actors, who remained in character. The role of the facilitator/educator was to 'freeze' the scenes from time to time in order to guide discussion between the audience and the actors. Questions asked of both actors and audience, included; 'How are you feeling right now?' and 'What do you think would make your situation better'? In order to answer these questions, the actors need to be fully immersed in the character's motivation and background, as well as the subculture of the context. The process also provided opportunities for members of the audience to step into the scenes, taking on the roles of the central characters and revealing what they would do. Again, such an approach is not without its shortcomings, not least of which include the training of the actors and the make up and dynamics of the groups which inevitably dictate the success, or otherwise, of such an educational experience.

The production of a DVD-based resource of ethnodrama scenes is a further future development that could be used for distance or e-learning packages for coach education forums. Such a resource would open up further teaching and learning opportunities to enable online synchronous learning. Potential also exists to create international coach education forums using such a resource, which would be an exciting development for coach learning in perhaps generating a physically disparate, yet culturally rich, coaches' community of practice.

Future developments and concluding thoughts

As touched upon earlier, the skills of coach educators in facilitating the learning of student coaches are crucial to the effectiveness of the pedagogies discussed in this chapter. Indeed, the success of PBL is generally considered to be dependent on the ability and willingness of the tutors to adopt the facilitative guiding role necessary (Savin-Baden 2003). Savin-Baden highlights the fact that a change away from long-practiced reproductive pedagogies, which have deep roots, is not always easy and can result in frustration and dissonance. Resistance from tutors to such changes, particularly if they are imposed, is not uncommon, with many wanting to give more structure to the learning environment and to demonstrate their content expertise (Dornan *et al.* 2005). Coach educators, therefore, must be committed to the approaches outlined in this chapter and to invest the time and work necessary to learning new skills if they are to be successfully implemented (Savin-Baden 2003). Such skills reflect the tutors' role as facilitators of learning, rather than transmitters of knowledge (Dornan *et al.* 2005) whilst demonstrating a commitment to modelling the principles of experiential learning (Jones and Turner 2006). We found that teaching in this way resulted in a raised degree of responsibility on behalf of the tutors, not so much in relation to their content delivery, but for the subsequent student interaction and learning (Jones *et al.* 2012). In this sense tutors took greater care to listen and react to group interactions, recognising that their (non)interventions at (in)appropriate times could genuinely affect and frame ensuing students' discussions and perceptions (Jones *et al.* 2012). A further area of research, therefore, could be to explore the issues surrounding the training and support of coach educators in implementing such constructivist pedagogical approaches to coach education.

What we are, of course, alluding to here is that the person of the coach educator, as opposed to merely what he says or does, plays an important role in the development and facilitation of coaching knowledge. This was an issue recently highlighted by Jones (and Santos) (2011), although in a more direct coaching context, in stating that to have influence over others, both credibility and the presentation of an authentic self are crucial. Here, he borrowed from both Agne's (1999) work in stating that students learn by absorbing 'who you are, not what you say', and Hamacheck (1999) who linked 'effectiveness' in terms of influencing others, into being fair, open and empathetic. Exactly how these and other attributes can and should be developed in coach educators (and coaches themselves) remains very much open to investigation.

Finally, all of the pedagogies discussed within this chapter have emerged from usage outside the realm of sports coaching; such as education, the medical profession, organisational management, community development, agriculture and theatre. Nevertheless, we believe that the pedagogies promoted are means by which the goal of coaching holistically can be more realistically aspired to. They provide examples of innovative student-centred, constructivist learning opportunities that enhance the nexus between theory and practice (Lave and Wenger 1991). It is considered that such cutting-edge pedagogies allow coaches opportunities to better engage in the process of their own learning and with the dynamic intricacy of their subject matter, thus increasing the relevancy of their experience and possibly promoting change in their own practice. Much work, however, remains to be done to develop the full potential of the approaches discussed. The research questions dotted throughout this chapter mark possible ways forward for those with the interest and inclination to do so. We certainly think it is an area worth engaging with.

References

Agne, K.J. (1999) 'Caring: The way of the master teacher', in R.P Lipka and T.M. Brinthaupt (eds) *The Role of Self in Teacher Development*, Albany, NY: State University of New York, pp. 165–188.

Allen, D., Duch, D. and Groh, S. (1996) 'The power of problem-based learning in teaching introductory science courses', in L. Wilkerson and W. Gijselaers (eds) *Bringing Problem-Based Learning to Higher Education: Theory and Practice*, San Francisco, CA, Jossey-Bass, pp. 43–52.

Allen, W.J. (2001) 'Working together for environmental management: The role of information sharing and collaborative learning', unpublished PhD thesis, Massey University, New Zealand.

Ames, C. (1992) 'Achievement goals, motivational climate, and motivational processes', in G.C. Roberts (ed.) *Motivation in Sport and Exercise*, Champaign, IL: Human Kinetics, pp. 161–176.

Blau, P. (1986) *Exchange and Power in Social Life*, Edison NJ: Transaction Publishers.

Boud, D. and Feletti, G. (eds) (1991) *The Challenge of Problem-Based Learning*, London: Kogan Page.

Carr, W. (2006) 'Philosophy, methodology and action research', *Journal of Philosophy of Education*, 40(4): 421–435.

Carr, W. and Kemmis, S. (1986) *Becoming Critical: Education, Knowledge and Action Research*, Lewes: Falmer.

Cassidy, T. (2010) 'Understanding the change process: Valuing what it is that coaches do', *International Journal of Sport Science and Coaching*, 5(2): 143–147.

Cassidy, T., Jones, R.L. and Potrac, P. (2009) *Understanding Sports Coaching: The Social, Cultural and Pedagogical Foundations of Coaching Practice*, 2nd edition, London: Routledge.

Cassidy, T., Potrac, P. and McKenzie, A. (2006) 'Evaluating and reflecting upon a coach education initiative: The CoDe of rugby', *The Sport Psychologist*, 20(2): 145–161.

Chesterfield, G., Jones, R.L. and Potrac, P. (2010) ' "Studentship" and "impression management": Coaches' experiences of an advanced soccer coach education award', *Sport, Education and Society*, 15(3): 299–314.

Denzin, K. and Lincoln, S. (2005) 'Foreword', in J. Saldaña (ed.) *Ethnodrama: An Anthology of Reality Theatre*, Lanham, MD: AltaMira, p. viii.

Dick, B. (1997) 'What *is* "action research"?' Occasional pieces in action research methodology, Piece 2, online, available at: http://www.aral.com.au/arm/op002.html. Accessed 1st September 2010.

Dornan, T., Scherpbier, A., King, N. and Boshuizen, H. (2005) 'Clinical teachers and problem-based learning: A phenomenological study', *Medical Education*, 39(2): 163–170.

Drinan, J. (1991) 'The limits of problem-based learning', in D. Boud and G. Felletti (eds) *The Challenge of Problem-Based Learning*, London: Kogan Page, pp, 315–321.

Elbaz, F. (1983) *Teacher Thinking: A Study of Practical Knowledge*, London: Croom Helm.

Engel, C. (1991) 'Not just a method of teaching but a way of learning', in D. Boud and G. Feletti (eds) *The Challenge of Problem-Based Learning*, London: Kogan Page, pp. 23–33.

Engel, C. (1999) 'Problem-based learning in medical education', in J. Leach and B. Moon (eds) *Learners and Pedagogy*, London: Paul Chapman/Sage, pp. 202–209.

Entwistle, N. (1995) 'The use of research on student learning in quality assessment', in G. Gibbs (ed.) *Improving Student Learning: Through Assessment and Evaluation*, Oxford: Oxford Centre for Staff Development. AQ13.

Entwistle, N. (2000) 'Promoting deep learning through teaching and assessment: Conceptual frameworks and educational contexts', paper presented at TLRP conference, Leicester, November.

Gilbert, W. and Trudel, P. (2004) 'Role of the coach: how model youth team sports coaches frame their roles', *The Sport Psychologist*, 18(1): 21–43.

Gilbourne, D. (2007) Symposium: 'Narrative and its potential contribution to sport and health psychology', Chair: Brett Smith. Invited presentation 'Self narrative: Illustrations of different genre and explorations of the underlying rationale for writing', FEPSAC Greece, performed with David Llewellyn, Jamie Wells and Angela Simms: Liverpool John Moores University Drama.

Gilbourne, D. and Llewellyn, D. (2008) 'Fate Mates and Moments', performance of 'Informed Fiction' in D. Gilbourne (Organiser/Chair) Story Analysts and Story Tellers Conference: Wales Millennium Centre, Cardiff.

Gilbourne, D. and Triggs, C. (2006) *Your Breath in the Air*, directed by Ros Merkin, Unity Theatre Liverpool, 2nd International Qualitative Research Conference, Liverpool.

Goffman, E. (1959) *The Presentation of Self in Everyday Life*, Reading: Penguin Books.

Greenwood, D. and Levin, M. (2003) 'Reconstructing the relationship between universities and society through action research', in N. Denzin and Y. Lincoln (eds) *The Landscape of Qualitative Research: Theories and Issues*, 2nd edition, Thousand Oaks: Sage, pp. 131–166.

Hamachek, D. (1999) 'Effective teachers: What they do, how they do it, and the importance of self-knowledge', in R.P. Lipka and T.M. Brinthaupt (eds) *The Role of Self in Teacher Development*, Albany, NY: State University of New York Press, pp. 189–224.

Jones, R.L. (2000) 'Towards a sociology of coaching', in R.L. Jones and K.M. Armour (eds) *The Sociology of Sport: Theory and Practice*, London: Addison Wesley Longman.

Jones, R.L. (and Santos, S.) (2011) 'Who is coaching? Understanding the person of the coach', keynote lecture given at the 'Sports and Coaching; Pasts and Futures' Conference, Manchester Metropolitan University, 25–26 June.

Jones, R.L. and Standage, M. (2006) 'First Among Equals: Shared leadership in the coaching context', in R.L. Jones (ed.) *The Sports Coach as Educator: Re-conceptualising Sports Coaching*, London: Routledge, pp. 65–76.

Jones, R.L. and Turner, P. (2006) 'Teaching coaches to coach holistically: The case for a Problem-Based Learning (PBL) approach', *Physical Education and Sport Pedagogy*, 11(2): 181–202.

Jones, R.L. and Wallace, M. (2005) 'Another bad day at the training ground: Coping with ambiguity in the coaching context', *Sport, Education and Society*, 10(1): 119–134.

Jones, R.L. and Wallace, M. (2006) 'The coach as orchestrator', in R.L. Jones (ed.) *The Sports Coach as Educator: Re-conceptualising Sports Coaching*, London: Routledge, pp. 51–64.

Jones, R.L., Armour, K.M. and Potrac, P. (2004) *Sports Coaching Cultures: From Practice to Theory*, London: Routledge.

Jones, R.L., Morgan K. and Harris, K., (2012) 'Developing coaching pedagogy: seeking a better integration of theory and practice', *Sport, Education and Society*, 17(3): 313–329.

Lave, J. and Wenger, E. (1991) *Situated Learning: Legitimate Peripheral Participation*, Cambridge: Cambridge University Press.

Lewin, K. (1946) 'Action research and minority problems', *Journal of Social Issues*, 2(4): 33–46.

Llewellyn, D., Gilbourne, D. and Triggs, C. (2011) 'Representing applied research experiences through performance: Extending beyond text', in D. Gilbourne and M.B. Andersen (eds) *Critical Essays in Sport Psychology*, Champaign, IL: Human Kinetics.

MacIntyre, A. (1985) *After Virtue*, London: Duckworth.

Mienczakowski, J. and Morgan, S. (2001) 'Constructing participatory experiential and compelling action research: Participative inquiry and practice', in P. Reason and H. Bradbury (eds) *Handbook of Action Research: Participatory Inquiry and Practice*, London: Sage, pp. 219–227.

Morgan, K., Jones, R.L., Gilbourne, D. and Llewellyn, D. (in press) 'Changing the face of coach education: Using ethno-drama to depict lived realities', *Physical Education and Sport Pedagogy*, DOI: 10.1080/17408989.2012.690863.

Mosston, M. and Ashworth, S. (2002) *Teaching Physical Education*, 5th edition, Columbus, OH: Merrill.

Oja, S.N. and Smulyan, L. (1989) *Collaborative Action Research: A Developmental Approach*, London: The Falmer Press.

Ollis, S. and Sproule, J. (2007) 'Constructivist coaching and expertise development as action research', *International Journal of Sport Science and Coaching*, 2(1): 1–14.

Reason, P. and Bradbury, H. (2001) *Handbook of Action Research*, London: Sage.

Russell, M. (2003) 'Leadership and followership as a relational process', *Educational Management and Administration*, 31(2): 145–157.

Saldaña J. (ed.) (2005) *Ethnodrama: An Anthology of Reality Theatre*, Lanham, MD: AltaMira.

Savin-Baden, M. (2003) *Facilitating Problem-Based Learning*, Maidenhead: SRHE and Open University Press.

Schön, D. (1983) *The Reflective Practitioner: How Professionals Think in Action*, New York: Basic Books.

Schön, D. (1987) *Educating the Reflective Practitioner*, San Francisco, CA: Jossey-Bass.

Sfard, A. (1998) 'On two metaphors for learning and the dangers of choosing just one', *Educational Researcher*, 27(2): 4–13.

Telesco, G. (2006) 'Using sociodrama for radical pedagogy: Methodology for education and change', *Radical Pedagogy*, 8(2): 1–11.

Tsai, S.D., Pan, C.-Y. and Chiang, H.-Q. (2004) 'Shifting the mental model and emerging innovative behaviour: Action research as a quality management system', *E:CO*, 6(4): 28–39.

Wenger, E. (1998) *Communities of Practice: Learning, Meaning and Identity*, Cambridge: Cambridge University Press.

Wenger, E., McDermott, A.A. and Snyder, W. (2002) *Cultivating Communities of Practice: A Guide to Managing Knowledge*, Harvard, MA: Harvard Business School Press.

INDEX

References to tables are shown in **bold** and figures are in *italics*.